www.wadsworth.com

www.wadsworth.com is the World Wide Web site for Wadsworth and is your direct source to dozens of online resources.

At *www.wadsworth.com* you can find out about supplements, demonstration software, and student resources. You can also send email to many of our authors and preview new publications and exciting new technologies.

www.wadsworth.com
Changing the way the world learns®

Modern East Asia

A Brief History

Conrad Schirokauer
Senior Scholar, Columbia University
Professor Emeritus, City University of New York

Donald N. Clark
Professor of History, Trinity University

THOMSON ™

WADSWORTH

Australia • Canada • Mexico • Singapore • Spain
United Kingdom • United States

Publisher: *Clark Baxter*
Assistant Editor: *Julie Yardley*
Editorial Assistant: *Eno Sarris*
Technology Project Manager: *Jennifer Ellis*
Marketing Manager: *Caroline Croley*
Marketing Assistant: *Mary Ho*
Advertising Project Manager: *Tami Strang*
Project Manager, Editorial Production: *Paula Berman*
Print/Media Buyer: *Jessica Reed*
Permissions Editor: *Kiely Sexton*

Production Service and Compositor: *Scratchgravel Publishing Services*
Text Designer: *Andrew Ogus*
Copy Editor: *Abbie Stryker*
Illustrator: *Greg Draus*
Cover Designer: *Preston Thomas*
Cover and Interior Origami and Kirigami Art: *Lore Schirokauer*
Text and Cover Printer: *Webcom*

Printed in Canada

4   5   6   7   07   06

For more information about our products, contact us at:

Thomson Learning Academic Resource Center
1-800-423-0563

For permission to use material from this text, contact us by:

Phone: 1-800-730-2214
Fax: 1-800-730-2215
Web: http://www.thomsonrights.com

Library of Congress Control Number: 2003101775

Student Edition with InfoTrac College Edition: ISBN 0-15-506847-4

Wadsworth/Thomson Learning
10 Davis Drive
Belmont, CA 94002-3098
USA

Asia
Thomson Learning
5 Shenton Way #01-01
UIC Building
Singapore 068808

Australia
Nelson Thomson Learning
102 Dodds Street
South Melbourne, Victoria 3205
Australia

Canada
Nelson Thomson Learning
1120 Birchmount Road
Toronto, Ontario M1K 5G4
Canada

Europe/Middle East/Africa
Thomson Learning
High Holborn House
50/51 Bedford Row
London WC1R 4LR
United Kingdom

Latin America
Thomson Learning
Seneca, 53
Colonia Polanco
11560 Mexico D.F.
Mexico

Spain/Portugal
Paraninfo
Calle/Magallanes, 25
28015 Madrid, Spain

Contents

Preface

Our decision to expand an earlier brief history of modern China and Japan to include all of East Asia is based on our belief in the intellectual value of regional approaches and the growing importance of East Asia as a major part of our world. We hope to introduce students to the region in a way that will help them make comparisons and go on to explore in greater depth some of the topics and areas we discuss.

Following our initial decision, we had to decide on the geographic and temporal parameters of our project. The vast land mass of Eurasia does not consist of clearly demarcated zones any more than time comes neatly packaged into periods. Our choices in this respect, as in others, result from our understanding of current scholarship as well as the experiences and approaches that we have found useful in our own teaching.

To the best of our knowledge, everyone considers China, Japan, and Korea as belonging to East Asia, and we give these countries primary emphasis in our book. We also discuss Vietnam, although in somewhat less detail. Vietnam is often treated as belonging to Southeast Asia, and we acknowledge its position as being roughly on the boundary of the two regions. Vietnam exemplifies how East and Southeast Asia are not entirely exclusive of each other. However, we put it in a special category and exclude the rest of Southeast Asia for two basic reasons.

First, Vietnam shares the commonalities we discuss in Chapter 1, and its differences from the rest of East Asia are probably no greater than those of, say, Japan. In none of the four countries under consideration are the commonalities the whole or "essential" story, but at the same time, in none can they be ignored. And they are by no means confined to the past, as is clear from the continuing persistence of official Marxism in Vietnam, China, and North Korea.

The second reason for including Vietnam is that its history has always been intertwined with that of China and, in the twentieth century, with that of Japan, and it shares with Korea the experiences of colonialism, division, and the devastation of war fought under American auspices. If one of the reasons for studying East Asian history is to provide a framework for reflection, then surely Vietnam—and by that we mean Vietnam as a nation and not just as a war—belongs in our book. We are sure that including Vietnam is the right thing to do and worry only lest we have not done it well enough.

In an age that is often called "post-modern" and even "post-post-modern," "modern" remains an elusive term with shifting meanings. What was modern in one period tends to be regarded as old-fashioned in the next, and today, in some contexts, the word *modern* is itself out of date. To compound the problem, historians studying East Asia disagree on when and how to use the term. Thus some would begin "modern" China around the year 1000 whereas others might argue that China is not completely modern even today. Much of the diversity of views depends on definition. In our case, we use the word *modern* broadly and sparingly. Its function in our title is to signal that we are not tracing the history of East Asia back to its beginnings but are covering the general period from 1600 to the present, with the focus on the period when the people of the region could no longer ignore the multifaceted power of Western, and now global, civilization. We also discuss prior developments, including events that set the stage for "modernization" in East Asia as well as features that parallel "modern" developments in the West, such as industrialization and state building. We leave open the question of how many different ways there were and are to be "modern." We hope our readers will develop their own nuanced understanding of both "East Asia" and "modern."

History is woven of many strands, and so we include economic and political history and also give much attention to social structure, thought, and the arts. We believe that it is important to provide a general map of the historical and cultural terrain so that the student can find his or her bearings and learn enough to consider further explorations in many areas, with some idea of the rewards to be gained for the effort. This book is not a catalog of cultures, but it is meant to be an introduction to the main narrative and the present state of our understanding of East Asian history.

The themes of change and continuity pervade our writing. In looking at the "modern" period in this region we have not begun with a blank slate, and like many writers before us we have faced the duty of weighing the change within the continuity, the continuity within the change. Such a determination requires, in the final analysis, as much art as science, and no assessment is ever final. This is so not only because of the continual discovery of new evidence and new techniques (for example, in the dating of materials) but also because scholars' intellectual frameworks and analytic concepts change, and we all learn to ask new questions. Even if that were not the case, history would still have to be rewritten at intervals, inasmuch as the ultimate significance of any individual historical episode depends in the final analysis on the whole story: As long as history itself is unfinished, so is its writing.

Acknowledgments

Our book is a joint effort, but the reader is entitled to know who wrote what. Donald Clark wrote everything on Korea. We divided the work on Vietnam, with Clark contributing the discourse in Chapter 14 and the discussion through the Vietnam war in Chapter 18. The Afterword is a joint effort. The rest of the book was written by Schirokauer.

We have benefited from and been challenged by an efflorescence of scholarship that has enriched our field even as it has made it impossible to read everything. This has made the role of those who have guided us all the more important. It would take a volume in itself to name everyone who has contributed by offering suggestions, criticism, and encouragement, or who has helped by suggesting references, sup plying a date or a translation of a term, or to acknowledge individually teachers, students, and colleagues who have influenced our thinking about broader issues of history, the East Asian region itself, teaching, and writing.

We do need to acknowledge our continuing indebtedness to those who contributed to Schirokauer's earlier books, but we will not repeat their names here. However, some directly involved in this book should be named. Foremost among them is Barbara Brooks, who has been a been a valued advisor from start to finish: She helped to get us started, provided invaluable guidance (especially on the treatment of Japan and on colonial Vietnam), and gave our manuscript a final critical reading before sending it off to the publisher. It is our loss that unforeseen circumstances kept her from being a co-author as originally planned. Donald Clark also wishes to thank Conrad Schirokauer for his invitation to participate in an expanded volume on modern East Asia that includes Korea and Vietnam, and Conrad Schirokauer wants to thank Don Clark for making it possible to include Korea and Vietnam.

This book is unusual in that the publisher changed in midstream. At Harcourt we want to express our gratitude to Drake Bush, our editor and anchor man. He labored long and hard and was always a source of sound advice. We also wish to thank David Tatom and those who, like Drake, contributed to the earlier books on which the present volume draws. For a smooth transition to Thomson/Wadsworth and their dedication to this project, we thank Anne Draus and everyone listed on the copyright page, but especially Clark Baxter. Without him there simply would have been no book.

We also thank our students for providing the basic stimulus for this book. Schirokauer owes a special debt to the young scholars with whom he has been co-teaching East Asian courses during the past few years: Jaret Weisfogel, Letty Chen, Naomi Fukumori, Katherine Rupp, Suzanne O'Brien, Nicole Cohen, and Yasu Makimura, listed in chronological order.

Also deserving special mention are the staff of the East Asian Library at Columbia for their help with books; Robert Scott, head of Columbia's Electronic Text Service, Butler Library, and master electronic scanner; and, for vital last-minute assistance in obtaining permissions from China, Rongxiang Zhang and Yangming Chu.

The reports of anonymous reviewers helped us to rethink and reformulate certain issues and saved us from embarrassing errors. Inevitably, some errors will remain, and we may even have produced some new ones. In all cases, the responsibility is ours.

Finally, the completion of a demanding project such as this would have been impossible without the understanding and support of our families.

Note on Names and Romanization

In East Asia surnames precede given names, and that is the order we follow in this book except for men who are commonly known by their given names (for example, Tokugawa Ieyasu and Ngo Dinh Diem). Similarly, we have transcribed them according to the standard system of romanization as indicated below, except where common usage indicates otherwise, as with Confucius, Syngman Rhee, Kim Dae-jung, Sun Yat-sen, Chiang Kai-shek, and all Chinese Taiwanese names. Except for Edo (modern Tokyo), contemporary geographical names have been used for the sake of easy identification even though this results in some anachronisms.

For Korean words and names we have used the McCune-Reischauer system. Japanese terms are rendered in accordance with the standard Hepburn system, except that macrons have been omitted for Kyoto, Osaka, and Tokyo. For Vietnamese, this book, like others intended for a general readership, omits diacritical marks and follows the Roman alphabet even when doing so conflates two separate Vietnamese letters.

Chinese is rendered in the Pinyin transcription, but we have supplied conversion tables into and from the older Wade-Giles system, which prevailed in the West prior to 1979, remains in use in Taiwan, and is still occasionally used in Western publications.

Note on the Figures in the Part and Chapter Openers

Origami, the art of paper folding, and kirigami, the art of paper cutting (seen in the bamboo art of Part III), like paper itself, originated in China but became popular throughout East Asia. The figures used in this book were folded and cut by Lore Schirokauer. After studying these arts in Kyoto, she created and diagrammed her own designs and exhibited her work. Throughout the making of this book, she has demonstrated the faith that raises pagodas, the strength of a tiger, the resilience of bamboo, and the elegance of a crane.

Note on the Authors

Donald Clark is Professor of History and Director of International Programs at Trinity University in San Antonio, Texas. He earned his Ph.D. in East Asian history at Harvard University and is a leader in the field of Korean studies. His publications include *Christianity in Modern Korea* (1986), *Culture and Customs of Korea* (2000), and *Living Dangerously in Korea, 1900-1950* (2003) as well as contributions to *The Kwangju Uprising* (1988), the Asia Society's *Korea Briefing* series, and the *Cambridge History of China*.

Conrad Schirokauer, Senior Scholar and Adjunct Professor at Columbia and Professor Emeritus at the City University of New York, received his doctorate from Stanford University. He has studied in Paris and conducted research in Japan and China. His published papers and articles deal mostly with Song intellectual history. He is co-editor, with Robert Hymes, of *Ordering the World: Approaches to State and Society in Sung Dynasty China* (Berkeley: University of California Press, 1993). His current research is on Song perceptions of and attitudes toward history. Schirokauer was associated with a New York University summer graduate program for teachers in Japan and China and remains interested in how history is taught and written. As a textbook author, he has published *A Brief History of Chinese and Japanese Civilizations*, 2nd ed. (1989), with separate volumes on China (1990) and Japan (1993), all now available from Wadsworth. Also worth mentioning is his translation of *China's Examination Hell* by Miyazaki Ichisada (New Haven: Yale University Press (1976, 1981), which he recommends to any student who feels burdened by examinations.

Hanyu Pinyin to Wade-Giles Conversion Table

Pinyin	Wade-Giles	Pinyin	Wade-Giles	Pinyin	Wade-Giles	Pinyin	Wade-Giles
a	a	chou	ch'ou	fa	fa	hua	hua
ai	ai	chu	ch'u	fan	fan	huai	huai
an	an	chua	ch'ua	fang	fang	huan	huan
ang	ang	chuai	ch'uai	fei	fei	huang	huang
ao	ao	chuan	ch'uan	fen	fen	hui	hui
		chuang	ch'uang	feng	feng	hun	hun
ba	pa	chui	ch'ui	fo	fo	huo	huo
bai	pai	chun	ch'un	fou	fou		
ban	pan	chuo	ch'o	fu	fu	ji	chi
hang	pang	ci	tz'u			jia	chia
bao	pao	cong	ts'ung	ga	ka	jian	chien
bei	pei	cou	ts'ou	gai	kai	jiang	chiang
hen	pen	cu	ts'u	gan	kan	jiao	chiao
beng	peng	cuan	ts'uan	gang	kang	jie	chieh
bi	pi	cui	ts'ui	gao	kao	jin	chin
bian	pien	cun	ts'un	ge	ko	jing	ching
biao	piao	cuo	ts'o	gei	kei	jiong	chiung
bie	pieh			gen	ken	jiu	chiu
bin	pin	da	ta	geng	keng	ju	chü
bing	ping	dai	tai	gong	kung	juan	chüan
bo	po	dan	tan	gou	kou	jue	chüeh
bou	pou	dang	tang	gu	ku	jun	chün
bu	pu	dao	tao	gua	kua		
		de	te	guai	kuai	ka	k'a
ca	ts'a	deng	teng	guan	kuan	kai	k'ai
cai	ts'ai	di	ti	guang	kuang	kan	k'an
can	ts'an	than	then	gui	kuei	kang	k'ang
cang	ts'ang	diao	tiao	gun	kun	kao	k'ao
cao	ts'ao	die	tieh	guo	kuo	ke	k'o
ce	ts'e	ding	ting			kei	k'ei
cen	ts'en	diu	tiu	ha	ha	ken	k'en
ceng	ts'eng	dong	tung	hai	hai	keng	k'eng
cha	ch'a	dou	tou	han	han	kong	k'ung
chai	ch'ai	du	tu	hang	hang	kou	k'ou
chan	ch'an	duan	tuan	hao	hao	ku	k'u
chang	ch'ang	dui	tui	he	ho	kua	k'ua
chao	ch'ao	dun	tun	hei	hei	kuai	k'uai
che	ch'e	duo	to	hen	hen	kuan	k'uan
chen	ch'en			heng	heng	kuang	k'uang
cheng	ch'eng	e	o	hong	hung	kui	k'uei
chi	ch'ih	en	en	hou	hou	kun	k'un
chong	ch'ung	er	erh	hu	hu	kuo	k'uo

Pinyin	Wade-Giles	Pinyin	Wade-Giles	Pinyin	Wade-Giles	Pinyin	Wade-Giles
la	la	na	na	qian	ch'ien	shu	shu
lai	lai	nai	nai	qiang	ch'iang	shua	shua
lan	lan	nan	nan	qiao	ch'iao	shuai	shuai
lang	lang	nang	nang	qie	ch'ieh	shuan	shuan
lao	lao	nao	nao	qin	ch'in	shuang	shuang
le	le	nei	nei	qing	ch'ing	shui	shui
lei	lei	nen	nen	qiong	ch'iung	shun	shun
leng	leng	neng	neng	qiu	ch'iu	shuo	shuo
li	li	ni	ni	qu	ch'ü	si	ssu
lia	lia	nian	nien	quan	ch'üan	song	sung
lian	lien	niang	niang	que	ch'üeh	sou	sou
liang	liang	niao	niao	qun	ch'ün	su	su
liao	liao	nie	nieh			suan	suan
lie	lieh	nin	nin	ran	jan	sui	sui
lin	lin	ning	ning	rang	jang	sun	sun
ling	ling	niu	niu	rao	jao	suo	so
liu	liu	nong	nung	re	je		
long	lung	nou	nou	ren	jen	ta	t'a
lou	lou	nu	nu	reng	jeng	tai	t'ai
lu	lu	nü	nü	ri	jih	tan	Van
lü	lü	nuan	nuan	rong	jung	tang	t'ang
luan	luan	nüe	nüeh	rou	jou	tao	t'ao
lüan	lüan	nuo	no	ru	ju	te	t'e
lue	lüeh			ruan	juan	teng	t'eng
lun	lun	ou	ou	rui	jui	ti	t'i
luo	lo			run	jun	tian	t'ien
		pa	p'a	ruo	jo	tiao	t'iao
ma	ma	pai	p'ai			tie	t'ieh
mai	mai	pan	p'an	sa	sa	ting	t'ing
man	man	pang	p'ang	sai	sai	tong	t'ung
mang	mang	pao	p'ao	san	san	tou	t'ou
mao	mao	pei	p'ei	sang	sang	tu	t'u
mei	mei	pen	p'en	sao	sao	tuan	t'uan
men	men	peng	p'eng	se	se	tui	t'ui
meng	meng	pi	p'i	sen	sen	tun	tun
mi	mi	pian	p'ien	seng	seng	tuo	t'o
mian	mien	piao	p'iao	sha	sha		
miao	miao	pie	p'ieh	shai	shai	wa	wa
mie	mieh	pin	p'in	shan	shan	wai	wai
min	min	ping	p'ing	shang	shang	wan	wan
ming	ming	po	p'o	shao	shao	wang	wang
miu	miu	pou	p'ou	she	she	wei	wei
mo	mo	pu	p'u	shen	shen	wen	wen
mou	mou			sheng	sheng	weng	weng
mu	mu	qi	ch'i	shi	shih	wo	wo
		qia	ch'ia	shou	shou	wu	wu

Pinyin	Wade-Giles	Pinyin	Wade-Giles	Pinyin	Wade-Giles	Pinyin	Wade-Giles
xi	hsi	yan	yen	zang	tsang	zhu	chu
xia	hsia	yang	yang	zao	tsao	zhua	chua
xian	hsien	yao	yao	ze	tse	zhuai	chuai
xiang	hsiang	ye	yeh	zei	tsei	zhuan	chuan
xiao	hsiao	yi	i	zen	tsen	zhuang	chuang
xie	hsieh	yin	yin	zeng	tseng	zhui	chui
xin	hsin	ying	ying	zha	cha	zhun	chun
xing	hsing	yong	yung	zhai	chai	zhuo	cho
xiong	hsiung	you	yu	zhan	chan	zi	tzu
xiu	hsiu	yu	yü	zhang	chang	zong	tsung
xu	hsü	yuan	yüan	zhao	chao	zou	tsou
xuan	hsüan	yue	yüeh	zhe	che	zu	tsu
xue	hsüeh	yun	yün	zhen	chen	zuan	tsuan
xun	hsün			zheng	cheng	zui	tsui
				zhi	chih	zun	tsun
		za	tsa	zhong	chung	zuo	tso
ya	ya	zai	tsai	zhou	chou		
yai	yai	zan	tsan				

Source: *People's Republic of China: Administrative Atlas* (Washington, D.C.: Central Intelligence Agency, 1975), 46–47.

Wade-Giles to Pinyin Conversion Table

Each entry in the Wade-Giles column represents the initial letter or letter pair of a syllable or word. Unless otherwise indicated, conversion is accomplished simply by changing that initial letter. Where other changes are necessary or the conversion is irregular, the entire word or syllable is listed.

Wade-Giles	Pinyin	Wade-Giles	Pinyin	Wade-Giles	Pinyin	Wade-Giles	Pinyin
a	a	ch'en	chen	i	yi	p'ien	pian
		ch'eng	cheng				
cha	zha	ch'i	qi	j	r	s	s
chai	zhai	ch'ia	qia	jih	ri	shih	shi
chan	zhan	ch'iang	qiang	jo	ruo	so	suo
chang	zhang	ch'iao	qiao	jung	rong	sung	song
chao	zhao	ch'ieh	qie			ssu, szu	si
che	zhe	ch'ien	qian	k	g		
chen	zhen	ch'i	chi	ko	ge	t	d
cheng	zheng	ch'in	qin	kuei	gui	tieh	dieh
chi	ji	ch'ing	qing	kung	gong	tien	dian
chia	jia	ch'iu	qiu			to	duo
chiao	jiao	ch'iung	qiong	k'	k	tung	dong
chieh	jie	ch'o	chuo	k'o	ke		
chien	jian	ch'ou	chou	k'ung	kong	t'	t
chih	zhi	ch'u	chu			t'ieh	tie
chin	jin	ch'ü	qu	l	l	t'ien	tian
ching	jing	ch'uai	chuai	lieh	lie	t'o	tuo
chiu	jiu	ch'uan	chuan	lien	han	t'ung	tong
chiung	jiong	ch'üan	quan	lo	luo		
cho	zhuo	ch'uang	chuang	lüeh	lüe	ts, tz	z
chou	zhou	ch'üeh	que	lung	long	tso	zuo
chu	zhu	ch'ui	chui			tsung	zong
chü	ju	ch'un	chun	m	m	tzu	zi
chua	zhua	ch'ün	qun	mieh	mie		
chuai	zhuai	ch'ung	chong	mien	mian	ts', tz'	c
chuan	zhuan					ts'o	cuo
chüan	juan	f	f	n	n	ts'ung	cong
chuang	zhuang			nieh	nie	tz'u	ci
chüeh	jue	h	h	nien	nian		
chui	zhui	ho	he	no	nuo	w	w
chun	zhun	hung	hong	nüeh	ne		
chün	jun					y	y
chung	zhong	hs	x	o	o	yeh	ye
		hsieh	xie			yen	yan
ch'a	cha	hsien	xian	p	b	yu	you
ch'ai	chai	hsiung	xiong	pieh	bie	yü	yu
ch'an	chan	hsü	xu	pien	bian	yüan	yuan
ch'ang	chang	hsüan	xuan			yüeh	yue
ch'ao	chao	hsüeh	xue	p'	p	yün	yun
ch'e	che	hsün	xun	p'ieh	pie	yung	yong

Modern East Asia

A Brief History

Part One

Early Modern/Late Traditional

Part I considers the last period when East Asian history flowed at its own pace, influenced, but not deflected, by outside forces. Scholars who emphasize this period's continuity with the past tend to label these centuries as "late traditional" or "late imperial." Others prefer "early modern" as they point to similarities with "early modern" European history, point to the period's considerable continuity with its future, and cite developments that prefigured or prepared the way for future developments. However assessed, clearly it was during the last traditional dynasties that the stage was set for later developments.

We begin by setting the stage ourselves. Whether we want to emphasize the immensity of change or *are more impressed by the persistence of old patterns, we need a basis for comparison. We would also do well to bear in mind that even by the sixteenth century East Asia had a very old history and a strong sense of history. For better or worse, its statesmen and theorists could draw on traditions that had stood the test of time.*

Many of these traditions were shared. For this reason, and to spare the reader repeated discussions of rice paddies or Confucianism, we begin by considering commonalities before turning to individual countries and to the first encounters between East Asia and modern Europe.

Foundations, Traditions, Commonalities

During their formative years, Korea, Japan, and Vietnam adopted salient aspects of Chinese civilization and, over long centuries of adaptation and digestion, developed them to suit conditions and proclivities very different from those of China. Each maintained and developed its own patterns and systems while looking to Chinese antiquity as the font of civilization much as Europeans and Americans long revered classic Greece and Rome—except that China could not be relegated to a distant past: it persisted as a living source of inspiration and challenge. It still does so today, except that now China, literally "the central kingdom," no longer occupies the center of the cultural and geopolitical world of anyone but itself.

Geographical Parameters

In East Asia, complex political organization, cities, and other components of civilization appeared first in China, which was separated by formidable oceans, mountains, deserts, and steppes from the other early civilizations of Eurasia. During China's formative years, its neighbors were either largely illiterate tribal peoples or cultures that derived writing and other aspects of higher civilization from China.

Unlike Korea and Japan, which by 1600 had attained their present territorial extent, China had not yet reached its present size; but then, as in later times, the overwhelming majority of the Chinese population lived in the area south of the Great Wall, where soil and climate were suitable for the intense agriculture characteristic of East Asian civilization. Within this area, known as China Proper or Inner China, the basic division was between north and south, with the dividing line roughly along the thirty-third parallel, following the Qinling Mountains and the Huai River.

The outstanding feature of the north is the Yellow River, which flows from the highlands of the west through the alluvial lowlands of the Great Plain to empty into the sea near the Shandong Peninsula. In its slow progress toward the sea, the river carries an enormous load of fine-grained, yellowish-brown silt (loess), which gives the river its color and name. It also accounts for the river's reputation as "China's sorrow," because the steady silting process has raised the bed so high that dikes are necessary to confine it to its channel. In many places the riverbed rises higher than the surrounding countryside, and a break in the dikes can have devastating effects. It may take several years of flood and famine before the river digs itself a new bed. Such a catastrophe occurred from 1851 to 1855. By the end of the devastation, the mouth of the river had shifted from the south side of the Shandong Peninsula to its present location on the north side.

The north is a region of temperate climate, cold winters, and warm summers, but rainfall is scarce. This is particularly true in the arid west, although even in the wetter areas the annual rainfall is extremely variable. Although the area is subject to drought, it benefits from thick layers of the wind-deposited dust known as loess, that is fertile, retains moisture, and is easy to work. The north is suitable for millet, sorghum (*gaoliang*), and, in the moister areas, wheat and beans, notably soybeans.

Different conditions prevail to the south, where rain is abundant and the climate is subtropical, but minerals and nutrients have been drained out of the soil. The dominant river is the Yangzi, which is about 3200 miles long, roughly 500 miles longer than the Yellow River. In 1600 it was still clean and sparkling. Unlike the Yellow River, the Yangzi is navigable for 1500 miles, all the way to Sichuan, although large modern vessels have to stop 630 miles upriver at Wuhan. Once the necessary technology was developed and land laboriously drained, a process that took centuries, the Yangzi Basin and adjoining region proved ideal for rice culture.

Farther to the south, the West River flows through a mountainous landscape, emerging in the rich delta that forms the hinterland of Canton (Guangzhou) and Hong Kong. Still farther south are the mountains and jungle of Guangxi and Yunnan, home to many ethnic minorities who have gradually been pushed into the hills by Chinese settlers.

Here China ends. South of this rugged, but not impenetrable, region lies Vietnam and the densely populated Red River Basin, cradle of Vietnamese civilization and location of Hanoi. Like the Yellow River, the Red River is restrained by dikes to prevent it from flooding. In Vietnam, as in Yunnan and Guangxi, the mountains have long provided refuge for minority peoples; also, as along the coast of China, the seas offer people in Vietnam opportunities for fishing and trade. Champa, an Indianized Southeast Asian maritime state, prevailed in central Vietnam until the Vietnamese annexed it in the fifteenth century. Historically, Vietnam stood at the frontier between two highly sophisticated and very different civilizations, but throughout their history the Vietnamese have defined themselves in Chinese terms—sometimes as equals, as when an early Vietnamese ruler claimed to be Emperor of the South, comparable to the Chinese Emperor of the North.

Vietnam's second major river delta, that of the Mekong in the south, was incorporated in modern times to form the present long and narrow state, which stretches just over a thousand miles from northwest to southeast. Even with the additional land, Vietnam remains predominantly a country of mountains, with only about a quarter of the land suitable for agriculture to feed its present population of some 80 million. In this respect it resembles Korea and Japan, where the ratio is even less: about one fifth in both cases.

In Korea and Japan, as in Vietnam, the ocean provides a rich source of nourishment as well as trade, but in all three rice is king. In Korea, 600 miles long and 125–200 miles wide, rice is grown most plentifully in the river valleys and relatively wide coastal plains of the west and south. In Japan there are just three noteworthy plains, all on Honshu, the main island, and each ending in a bay. At 500 square miles, the Kinai Plain at the head of Osaka Bay is the smallest in size but the earliest in historical importance. The 600-square-mile plain at the head of Ise Bay is home of Japan's most sacred shrine. The Kanto Plain at the head of Tokyo Bay measures around 5,000 square miles.

In modern times, Korea's border has been defined by two rivers, the Yalu, flowing westward, and the Tumen, flowing eastward from the slopes of Mount Paektu, the Koreans' sacred peak in the Ever White Mountains. Southward from the Ever White Mountains runs the backbone of Korea, the T'aebaek Mountains, which extend the length of the peninsula and divide it into a sharply defined coastal area on the east and a series of broad valleys to the west. Korea's best farmland is in the southwest; its richest mineral resources, forests, and water power potential are in the north.

In both Korea and Japan mountains have challenged the soldier and merchant, but they did not prevent the achievement of political unity in Korea in the seventh century nor the emergence of central authority in Japan at about the same time. But mountains are not just impediments—throughout East Asia, they have provided congenial settings for the sacred, a home to spirits, and a source of legends, as well as inspiration for poets and painters. China's Mount Tai, Korea's Mount Paektu, and Japan's Mount Fuji come to mind as the best known; the majestic mountain that towers over the natural and human landscape in Fan Guan's painting remains unidentified, but that enables it all the better to evoke a general sense of mountain grandeur (see Figure 1.1).

Unlike the island state of Japan, totally surrounded by water, the Korean Peninsula is defined by water on three sides only. In the north, the Yalu River and massive mountains separate it from Manchuria, home of the founders of China's last dynasty. The mountains provided a more effective barrier to Chinese immigration than did the jungles and seas to China's south. In modern times, the population flow has been from Korea into Manchuria.

Korea and Vietnam were close enough to China to experience Chinese aggression early on: during the second century B.C.E., China's Han dynasty established colonies in the Red River Delta and in Korea, where the largest occupied a site across the river from P'yŏngyang, the present capital of North Korea. Thanks to geography and military resistance, however, the Chinese never dominated, even in the north, and eventually had to withdraw entirely. This occurred much earlier in Korea than in Vietnam. In the seventh century, the Korean state of Koguryŏ successfully fought off a mighty Tang invasion and, except for a period of Mongol dominance, the Koreans retained their autonomy, although over the years there were more invasions from the north.

Vietnam freed itself from China in the tenth century, but underwent a final period of Chinese domination from 1407 to 1427. In both states admiration for Chinese civilization went hand in hand with a determination to avoid Chinese

FIGURE 1.1 *Travelers Among Mountains and Streams,* Fan Guan (Fan K'uan, d. ca. 1023). Employing the classic Chinese perspective, the picture surface divides into three planes, one near, one distant, and a middle plane of water or mist. Hanging scroll, ink and light color on silk, 129.6 × 74.9 cm.

NATIONAL PALACE MUSEUM, TAIPEI, TAIWAN, REPUBLIC OF CHINA.

political domination. By 1600 both states had long participated in China's tributary system, acknowledging Chinese hegemony while avoiding Chinese interference. Korea and Vietnam's experiences with foreigners, though painful and destructive, have helped their people develop a strong sense of self-reliance and identity.

In contrast to Korea and Vietnam, Japan has never been threatened by China. At its closest point, the island of Kyushu is about 120 miles from the continent, across the Korean Straits. During historic times it had never been successfully invaded prior to the twentieth century, and only the thirteenth-century Mongols had made the attempt. Historically, the Japanese have been free from military or political interference from abroad, and its leaders have been determined to keep it that way.

Rice

In early times people farming the dry fields of the north lived primarily on millet. By the seventeenth century the modern pattern was established with wheat and millet predominating in the north while the south was rice country. Although it remained a special treat in northern areas, the majority of East Asians lived on rice. Foremost among the advantages of growing rice is that it yields more nutrition per land unit than any other crop. Other advantages have been summarized by Francesca Bray:

> It is highly adaptable, can be grown under almost any conditions, does not necessarily require fertilizers (although it does respond well to their use) and will produce as many as three crops a year if there is sufficient water, without exhausting the fertility of the paddy field. The techniques of rice cultivation are such that farmers themselves have been able to select for desirable traits through the centuries, and so a very wide range of cultivates has been developed.[1]

These varieties include drought resistant strains, early ripening varieties, and rice suited for different tastes and/or purposes, such as brewing. The reason for its low fertilizer requirements is that flooding of the paddy brings in nutrients. A high seed-to-yield ratio and ease of transport are other advantages.

Although dry rice is grown on steep fields in the hills, it is mostly, and most productively, grown in wet paddy fields. Rice can feed many people, but, traditionally, it also requires many people working long hours to prepare the paddy fields, plant and transplant the seedlings, weed, harvest, thresh and husk. It is no accident that throughout the world the most densely populated agrarian areas are those that grow rice.

Irrigating the fields is an intricate process involving the allocation of water, which demands careful local coordination, whether provided by lineages (descent groups) as in China or by villages as elsewhere in East Asia. It also affected political geography. Except in China, the political centers of East Asian states were close to the rice-based economic centers. In China the norm was for the political center to remain in the north, linked by the Grand Canal, actually a series of canals and rivers, to the rich south. Thus in China, transportation requirements as well as the demands of agriculture contributed to the transformation of the landscape. Throughout the region dikes were built, swamps drained, hills and mountains terraced.

Material Culture

In the seventeenth century, as through most of history, life in East Asia was at least as safe and comfortable as in Europe, and technology at least as advanced. As we read this book, it is appropriate to bear in mind that paper, a Chinese invention, was just one of East Asia's gifts to the world. Others include three that are often cited as transforming Europe: the gunpowder that destroyed its castles and brought down its knights; the printing that revolutionized the circulation of ideas; and the compass that enabled the Portuguese and their successors to find their way to China and Japan. Even our vocabulary reflects the excellence of Chinese textiles and ceramics: *silk* derives from the Chinese word for that most prized of fabrics, while the source of *china* is obvious.

Just as a variety of ingenious and complex looms were invented to facilitate the weaving of cotton and silk, much thought and creativity went into the construction of pumps and other devices to raise water, ships protected by watertight compartments and steered by axial rudders, steel bits for drilling salt wells in the southwest, and steel chains for hanging suspension bridges over the steep ravines of the same region. A complete list would go on and on and would range from the Korean submarine and plated warship to the Japanese folding fan.

The delicious variety of East Asian cuisines need hardly be mentioned except that good food contributed greatly to the pleasures of life. Perhaps people ate better than they were housed, but the Japanese gave the world its first modular houses, and north Chinese and Koreans battled winter cold by devising flues— the Chinese used them to heat beds made of clay and the Koreans ran them under their floors. In all four lands items of superb workmanship decorated the lives of those who could afford them and there developed traditions of fine arts, of calligraphy and landscape painting, of furniture and garden design, just to mention a few. In these and many other areas—theater, tea, lacquer, and jade come to mind—there also developed connoisseurship that, as elsewhere, set apart insiders and outsiders, rich and poor, the elite from the vulgar, reflecting the complexity of the societies.

The most delicious food, luxurious clothes, fine houses, and art collections are lost on those who are ill. People in East Asia were as apt to become ill as people elsewhere on the globe. But, as S. A. M. Adshead has recently pointed out,[2] thanks to the urban nightsoil collector, Chinese rivers were spared the sewage polluting the rivers of London, Rome, and Paris, and the resulting spread of disease. Certainly, the Japanese addiction to the bath made for good personal hygiene.

Throughout the region bamboo supplied a natural source for pipes, used for plumbing and in salt wells.

Those who became ill had as good a chance for recovery in East Asia as in the West. During his stay in Vietnam, the Jesuit missionary Alexander de Rhodes (1591–1660) found medicine there by no means inferior to that practiced in Europe, where, at the time, bleeding was the standard treatment. The doctors who treated him practiced a form of medicine originating in China. By his time there was a rich medical tradition with treatments based both on practical experience and theory. This in turn was based on more general concepts of the structure and dynamics of nature.

Theories of the Natural Order

The Chinese and other East Asians thought of nature in dynamic rather than static terms. As illustrated by Fan Guan's painting (Figures 1.1 and 1.2), humans did not dominate but were a part of the world.

Basic to East Asian medicine is the concept of *qi*, in this context translated as "life breath" but susceptible of broader meaning and thought of as forming everything (see page 13). In the dynamic universe everything is structured and animated by *yin* and *yang*, paired complementary opposites whose interaction keeps the world going. *Yin* is associated with the feminine, the passive, the negative, the weak; *yang* with the opposite qualities and forces, the masculine, the active, the positive, the strong. *Yin* is cold and winter; *yang* hot and summer. *Yin* is response, *Yang* stimulus. Neither can do without the other, nor does either ever appear alone. As illustrated by South Korea's flag, there is a bit of each in the other (Figure 1.3). The resulting configurations can become complicated, as when a woman (*yin*) has a problem with her liver (*yang*) in the evening (*yin*) of the first day (*yang*) in a winter (*yin*) month.

The two terms appear in many contexts, from the popular to the technical, from the concrete to the abstract. For instance, the Chinese word for "landscape" is conceived in terms of water (*yin*) and mountains (*yang*); diagnosis of *yin* and *yang* are fundamental to the geomancer examining a site to determine its suitability for a house or grave.

FIGURE 1.2 Detail from *Travelers Among Mountains and Streams*. Fan Guan reduces the travelers to their proper dimensions while a road invites us to enter and contemplate nature's grandeur.

Another important concept is that of the Five Phases: wood, fire, earth, metal, and water. Because this idea recalls the four elements of Greek philosophy, it has been translated as the "Five Elements." But this translation is misleading, for it implies inertia and passivity rather than the dynamic self-movement inherent in the original conception, and it obscures the point that the processes of nature occur in a particular sequence.

The East Asian view of the world is informed by a sensitivity to change as the fundamental constant in life. *The Classic of Changes,*★ an ancient and still popular divination manual, is based on this idea. The

FIGURE 1.3   The famous circle that represents the interaction of *yin* and *yang* forms the heart of South Korea's flag.

book gives sixty-four readings, each corresponding to a different *hexagram,* or configuration of solid lines (*yang*) and broken lines (*yin*), and indicative of various, constantly shifting situations requiring different responses. Four *trigrams* (which form the upper and lower halves of the hexagrams) appear on the flag of the modern Republic of Korea (see Figure 1.3).

Language and Writing

Nothing is more fundamental to a culture than language, and speaking precedes writing in the life of a people as it does in that of an individual. In East Asia, as in Europe, many people not only used strong local dialects but also spoke mutually unintelligible languages. Even within China, speakers of the local languages of Shanghai, Canton, and Xiamen are incomprehensible to each other as well as to people from elsewhere in China. However, these languages are at least related as members of the Sino-Tibetan linguistic family. Some linguists propose that Vietnamese too is Sino-Tibetan. It resembles Chinese in distinguishing words by tones, indicating the function of a word by its placement in a sentence, and in using modifiers to express mood, tense, and so on, but it is often characterized as an Austro-Asiatic language related to Khmer and Mon, spoken in Cambodia and Burma respectively. Other scholars argue that Vietnamese does not fit into any larger grouping but is unique. Korean and Japanese belong to yet another group. As Altaic languages, they differ from Chinese in cadence and sound, and are structured by complex grammars completely alien to Chinese.

★Now romanized *Yi Jing,* the title is *I Ching* in the Wade-Giles system of transcribing Chinese. In English this book is also known as *Book of Changes.*

Box 1.1 Chinese Writing

The characters, or symbols, developed in China may be divided into four broad categories. The earliest were **pictographs** of objects increasingly abstracted over time. We may no longer recognize 馬 as a horse, but 木 still resembles a tree. Among things that cannot be seen are a few that can nonetheless be visualized and rendered as simple **ideographs**, such as 一, 二, 三, (one, two, three), or 上 (up) and 下 (down). More interesting are the complex ideographs formed by association: 林, two trees for a forest, or 好, woman and child to represent good. Another way to increase the written vocabulary was to use an already existing character to represent one or more words with the same sound. Examples of such phonetic borrowings, or **phonograms**, are 不, a flying bird, used to write the homonym "no," and 而, beard, for "and" or "but." However, this could become extremely confusing, as 馬 , for example, could stand not only for horse but also for agate, weights, leeches/locusts, panel/board, to abuse or scold, an interrogative particle, or mother/old woman, all pronounced alike. To deal with this, a signifier (or radical) was added to form a **compound character**. A tree was placed next to a horse, 檇, to signal a word pronounced like horse but having something to do with wood, hence wooden panel. A jade or gem was added for agate, 瑪, a stone for weights, 碼, and insect for leeches, 螞, etc. The majority of characters are of this kind. Unfortunately, with changes in pronunciation the phonetic is not necessarily an accurate guide to present-day pronunciation. One further change that needs to be noted is that in The People's Republic many characters were further simplified so that 馬 became 马. The Japanese also adopted some simplified characters but stayed closer to the traditional forms.

Vietnamese, Koreans, and Japanese had no script to render their diverse languages prior to the introduction of Chinese writing. Throughout East Asia the first books were written in Chinese, and until modern time, full literacy continued to be defined in terms of command of Chinese texts. Familiarity with the classical language of China was seen as a prime criterion for high status, and literacy was considered the very basis of civilization, distinguishing it from barbarism. Although the majority of Chinese symbols include a phonetic component, they are primarily units of meaning rather than sound. Thus people who spoke mutually unintelligible tongues could and did read the same canonical texts considered valid everywhere and for all ages.

In China the vernacular and the formal classical language remained separate until the twentieth century, though they did influence each other. Beyond China even people literate in Chinese had a desire to write their own languages but found it very difficult to use Chinese symbols for this purpose. It is probably more difficult to use Chinese characters to write Korean or Japanese, with their wealth of word-endings and particles, than it would be to write English in this manner! One way of rendering native words lacking a Chinese equivalent was to use Chinese characters for native sounds as well as for meaning. But this made for endless difficulties and confusion, and eventually Japan, Korea, and Vietnam turned to phonetic scripts.

The first of these was developed in Heian Japan (794–1185). It was a hybrid system, retaining Chinese characters for nouns, the stems of verbs, and adjectives, but rendering grammatical markers as well as indicators of mood, voice, tense and the like phonetically in *kana,* or more accurately, *hiragana,* since a second form called *katakana* is employed primarily for foreign words and for emphasis. As a result, a page of Japanese looks like Chinese characters afloat in a sea of squiggles. In the fifteenth century Korea devised an alphabet known as *han'gŭl* (see Figure 3.2) while Vietnam continued to use *nom,* a complex system based on Chinese characters, into the twentieth century, when it turned to the phonetic *quoc-ngu* system of transcribing Vietnamese into Latin script, devised by seventeenth-century Jesuits, most notably Alexander de Rhodes.

Even after the development of indigenous scripts, Chinese remained the language of government and of formal prose throughout East Asia. Members of the elite, who prided themselves on their command of the language and the Chinese literary and intellectual tradition continued to write poetry in Chinese. On the other hand, the poetry most valued tended to be in the vernacular. In Japan this was also the case for prose. There, the most prized diaries and novels were composed by women, who were not supposed to use Chinese. The *Tale of Genji,* written by a court woman a thousand years ago, is an outstanding example. Centered on the life and loves of its "shining prince," it occupies a very special place in Japanese culture. Not only has it inspired poets and painters, but, to quote its most recent English translator, "It is not just a book, but a cultural phenomenon. It has been turned into movies, plays, dance, modern novels, Kabuki, comic books (manga), musical theater, and opera."[3]

Confucianism

The term *Confucianism* has been used by students of thought to identify a set of texts and ideas, while social scientists employ it to refer to a way of life. This might well have pleased Confucius (between 549 and 449 B.C.E.) and later thinkers committed to a tradition much concerned with the practical consequences of ideas. However, they believed that their Way had been realized only in remote antiquity when, under the aegis of the sages, peace and harmony had prevailed throughout the world. We will therefore begin by considering Confucianism as a teaching while keeping in mind that, like other faiths, it also influenced and was influenced by how people lived.

By 1600 the teachings of Confucius had been around for two millennia! Naturally they had evolved. Most influential by the time we encounter it was the version developed in China in the eleventh and twelfth centuries and generally known in the West as Neo-Confucianism.

An earlier, core text, *The Analects,* was accepted as conveying the authentic words and conversations of Confucius. It is now regarded as consisting of layers dating from between 479 and 249 B.C.E. It formed one of *The Four Books,* selected by Zhu Xi (1130–1200) to constitute the basic curriculum of classical learning and of the civil service examination system in China, Vietnam, and Korea. In Japan *The Four Books* were equally revered. In all four lands they were internalized by youngsters who memorized the texts before they were capable of understanding their meaning.

The second of *The Four Books* was named for Mencius (387–303 B.C.E.), famed for maintaining that human beings are basically good, although their potential for goodness will turn sour if not properly nourished and cultivated. Mencius also advocated benevolent rule, with the threat that failure would cost the ruler "The Mandate of Heaven." In the common view, such loss of divine sanction would be preceded by abnormalities such as eclipses, earthquakes, floods and droughts, as well as famine and revolts. If these warnings went unheeded, the mandate would be lost. This became the standard Confucian explanation for dynastic change.

Both of the remaining books, *The Great Learning* and *The Doctrine of the Mean,* were chapters of *The Record of Rites* selected for special emphasis by Zhu Xi. Actually "rites" only captures a part of the meaning of *li,* a term also featured in *The Analects.* To be sure, it denotes sacred rites, but also includes all ceremonies, proper behavior, and good manners. The *li,* if performed in good faith, with everyone keeping to his or her proper role, were thought to produce universal harmony so that there would be no need for physical sanctions, no necessity for laws or punishments. The model for society was the patriarchal family headed by a virtuous and wise father. For mainstream Confucians, family values came first, both in terms of human development and in terms of value: according to *The Analects,* a son should not turn in a father for stealing a sheep. Confucians stressed the claims of filiality, the wholehearted obedience a child owes its parents in return for their love and concern. The parent/child relationship served as a model for the rest of the classic "Five Relationships": ruler/subject, husband/wife, elder brother/younger brother, and (junior) friend/(senior) friend. Beyond that, however, the devout Confucian should have a feeling of obligation to everyone. Zhang Zai (1020–1077), one of Zhu Xi's predecessors, took it even further:

> Everyone is my father and Earth is my mother, and even such a small creature as I find an intimate place in their midst. Therefore that which fills the universe I regard as my body and that which directs the universe I regard as my nature. All people are my brothers and sisters, and all things are my companions.[4]

Foremost among the Confucian moral values was *Ren* (仁); written by combining the symbols for *person* and *two,* it is the ground for the other virtues, the condition for being fully human in dealing with others. Translated variously as humanness, humaneness, or benevolence, it permeates all human relations—in the state as in the family. According to Mencius, we are all endowed with a sense of compassion which needs to be cultivated to produce *Ren.* Our native sense of shame is the germ of dutifulness, our sense of modesty the germ of courtesy, our inborn sense of right and wrong the germ of wisdom.

According to Confucianism, every individual can become a sage by recovering his original nature or finding his lost mind. Self-cultivation was a major theme in Confucian thought and practice, given additional psychological and philosophical depth by *The Doctrine of the Mean* as well as by Song thinkers. *The Great Learning* stressed the link between self-cultivation and government, viewing the perfection of the individual as prerequisite for the perfection of society. Good government required good officials. The implied meritocratic ideal, though rarely achieved, inspired the government examination system of China, Korea, and Vietmam, which theoretically selected men according to the breadth and depth of their Confucian learning, and went to great lengths to prevent cheating.

Neo-Confucians accepted the discourse of *yin* and *yang* and the five elements, as well as *qi*, but coupled the latter with *li* (written differently from the *li* above), usually translated "principle" or "pattern." Since Chinese does not distinguish between singular and plural, the word can be understood as a network of principles, with each *li* a part of the entire system. For Zhu Xi, the *li* constituted the underlying pattern of moral and physical reality. Nothing could exist if there were no *li* for it. But it also required *qi*, which here can be thought of as a kind of material energy that occupies space. In its refined form it is a rarefied ether, but condensed it becomes the most solid metal or rock. Zhu Xi envisioned the world as a sphere in constant rotation, so that the heaviest *qi* is held at the center by the centripetal force of the motion. The *qi* becomes progressively lighter and thinner as we move away from the center. This explains why the air at high altitude is thinner than at sea level.

Human beings, too, are composed of *li* and *qi*. The *li* assures the fundamental goodness of people, but the *qi* accounts for human imperfection. Neo-Confucianism had a moral seriousness that found expression in a variety of ways. It made especially heavy demands on women. A girl was taught to obey her father. After marriage to the husband who had been selected for her, she had to obey him as well as his mother, who usually ran the household. If she were widowed, she was not supposed to remarry but was expected to listen to her eldest son. She was required always to be modest and to help everyone in the family live up to moral principles. Woman's sphere of action was within the home, while men managed the world at large.

Confucians concerned themselves with institutions, policies, and statecraft. Some may have shown an interest in law, but as Confucians they distinguished themselves from the Legalists, advocates of punitive law, who were discredited after the harsh regime of the Qin (221–206 B.C.E.). On the other hand, since self and society, inner and outer, were seen as intimately linked, some Confucians concentrated on self-perfection. In doing so they could well adopt Daoist or Buddhist techniques, but, unlike the followers of these two teachings, the Confucians understood the self as a social self and sought sagehood within, not beyond, society. Unlike Legalism, Daoism and Buddhism not only influenced Neo-Confucianism but continued to flourish on their own.

Daoism

Daoism and Buddhism are exceedingly complex; they include texts of philosophy and of popular religious practices. Furthermore, the two main Daoist classics, *The Dao De Jing* (or *De Dao Jing*, also known by the name of its purported author, Lao Zi) and the *Zhuang Zi* were widely read and savored as literary masterpieces by people not necessarily Daoists. This is ironic, since both texts share a suspicion of language: the former begins by saying that the permanent Way cannot be spoken of and maintains that those who know don't speak and those who speak don't know. Daoists, since they don't believe in logic, are immune to the charge of self-contradiction. To grasp the Way in its entirety one has to transcend language and logic and see things not from our limited human perspective but from the total perspective of the Way (*Dao*) itself. By doing so, a person is released from social conventions and is able to regain oneness with nature.

Both texts use language poetically. *The Dao De Jing* is itself a poem—allusive and elusive. The *Zhuang Zi* delights in flights of fantasy, paradox, and evocative anecdotes as when it relates that Zhuang Zi once woke from a nap not knowing whether he was Zhuang Zi dreaming he was a butterfly or a butterfly dreaming he was Zhuang Zi. In China and beyond, Daoism was an inspiration for literature and art, the appreciation of nature and spontaneity. According to an old cliché, a Confucian in office easily turned into a Daoist when he returned home, cast off his official robes and cares, relaxed, tried out some poetry with friends over a cup of wine, perhaps even dreamed.

A link between the philosophical Daoism of the literary elite and the Daoism of the religious sects is the figure of Lao Zi, whose statue figures prominently in Daoist temples. Also, the classical texts make reference to breathing exercises to foster longevity and enable practitioners to attain a kind of immortality. In developing such ideas Daoists contributed to the advancement of chemistry/alchemy, undifferentiated in China as in medieval Europe. They took an interest in *yin* and *yang* and other concepts concerning the operation of the physical world. Daoism was also engaged with everyday life, and Daoist priests performed numerous rites for the well-being of their patrons. Reminiscent of the Chinese state, Daoism developed a rich hierarchic pantheon headed by the August Jade Emperor and welcoming local deities in China and Vietnam. Although Daoist influences can be found in Korea and Japan, Daoism did not send out missionaries and its presence there was limited. In contrast, Buddhism, introduced to the rest of East Asia mainly from China, took deep root in all four lands.

Buddhism

Gautama Siddhartha (c. 563–483 B.C.E.), the founder of Buddhism, was roughly contemporary with Confucius. (Gautama refers to his clan and Siddhartha was the name he received at birth. He is also known as Sakyamuni, sage of the Sakya tribe. After he attained enlightenment he was called the *Buddha* or the *Tathagata*.) By the time Buddhism reached East Asia, the original teachings, directed at satisfying the spiritual quest of a small group, had broadened into a universal faith with wide appeal. It took further centuries for this religion to take root in China, but it came to pervade the culture of Tang China (617–907) from which it spread to Korea and Japan. For the most part, China also served as the primary source for Buddhism in Vietnam. Throughout East Asia it became "indigenized" into the domestic religious landscape.

At the core of the Buddha's teachings are the *Four Noble Truths*. The first of these is that life is suffering. Pain and unhappiness are unavoidable. Death is not the answer. Like other Indians, Buddhists believed that living beings are subject to reincarnation. According to the law of karma, for every action there is a moral reaction. A life of good deeds leads to reincarnation at a higher level; evil deeds lead in the opposite direction. But the ultimate goal is not rebirth as an emperor or billionaire: it is to achieve *Nirvana* and never be born again.

The second Truth explains the first: the cause of human suffering is craving or desire. This leads to the third Truth: that to stop the suffering, desire must be stopped. The cause of suffering must be completely understood and dissolved. The Fourth Truth proclaims the eightfold path to accomplish this: right views, right intention, right speech, right action, right livelihood, right effort, right mindfulness, and right concentration. Most sects understood the religious life as practiced by monks and nuns to entail vegetarianism, celibacy, and abstinence from alcohol as well as positive religious practices and meditation.

As Buddhism evolved and spread, the Buddha was transformed from a teacher of superlative wisdom, but a man nonetheless, into a god whom people could worship and to whom they could pray. The image of the Buddha appeared, art and iconography developed along with ceremonies accompanied by musical chants and the burning of incense.

Many problems of doctrinal interpretation were left unanswered by the Buddha, for he was a religious teacher concerned with showing the way to salvation, not a philosopher interested in metaphysics for its own sake. As in other traditions, later commentators worked out the implications of the founder's teaching. The ultimate result was a vast literature and a rich variety of schools and sects, with a major distinction between the Theravada sects, which still predominate in Southeast Asia, and the Mahayana schools, which played the major role in East Asia.

Buddhism appealed to people in East Asia because it addressed itself to human suffering with a directness unmatched in the native traditions. It also provided a well-developed body of doctrine, art, magic and medicine, music and ritual, even heavens and hells, and a rich pantheon of deities. The historic Buddha was joined by other Buddhas: the Buddha of Medicine; Amida, the Buddha who presides over the Western Paradise; Maitreya, the Buddha of the Future whose coming would usher in a new and perfect age. Because of his messianic appeal, Maitreya was often associated with rebel movements.

One sect influential throughout East Asia was the School of Meditation, known as Zen in Japan. Even more popular were schools that offered less arduous or exclusive paths to salvation such as faith in Amida or the efficacy of the *Lotus*

FIGURE 1.4   Buddhist sculpture of Avalokitesvara, the bodhisattva embodiment of mercy, depicted with multiple hands and arms, the better to aid the multitudes.

FIGURE 1.5   *Detail of Figure 1.4.* Avalokitesvara is a favorite subject of Buddhist sculpture, including this statue, regarded as the most beautiful in Vietnam.

Sutra, a sermon attributed to the historic Buddha that became the most venerated Buddhist scripture in East Asia. Shinran (1173–1262), founder of Japan's True Pure Land sect, still the largest in that country, was convinced that salvation depended on faith in Amida, accessible to laity even more than to clergy, so he left the monastery for life in the world and married a nun.

Most beloved among Mahayana objects of worship were the bodhisattvas, beings who postponed their own salvation in order to help other living beings. Foremost among them was Avalokitesvara, the embodiment of mercy. In India and China Avalokitesvara originally appeared as a male, but over the centuries this bodhisattva gradually came to be considered a woman (Figures 1.4 and 1.5).

By 1600 Confucianism generally overshadowed Buddhism intellectually and politically. It is also fair to say that except in Vietnam and in some Japanese Zen temples, Buddhism's power to inspire artistic creativity had declined as well. But, before and after 1600, temples continued to be built and maintained, and patronage was not lacking. There were, to be sure, those who bent the rules: a local Chinese gazetteer complains about local monks taking "vegetarian wives" (1609) and the church's enemies delighted in spreading scurrilous tales, but men and women continued to enter the religious life, and Buddhism remained a living faith. The sects retained their independence even as Buddhism also contributed to religious syncretism.

Syncretism

None of the East Asian religions commands exclusivity on the part of its worshippers. There has been an underlying tendency to compartmentalize or combine Confucianism, Buddhism, and Daoism (Figure 1.6). As a matter of course people performed their Confucian duty by offering ritual homage to tablets representing their ancestors, but this did not keep them from offering incense to a Buddha, praying to a local goddess for progeny, or calling on a medium to supplement the efforts of a doctor. The human world was pervaded by the supernatural. Some deities were specialized. A fisherman would no more appeal to the smallpox deity for a bountiful catch than we would consider purchasing marine insurance at our local ice cream parlor.

FIGURE 1.6 *Patriarchs of the Three Creeds.* Attributed to Josetsu. The artist shows the three great teachers—Sakyamuni, Confucius, and Lao Zi—in harmonious agreement, yet renders each figure in its own style. In the abbreviated brushwork beloved by Zen artists, every stroke, every line, counts. Hanging scroll, ink on paper, 98.3 × 21.8 cm.
RYOSOKUIN MONASTERY, KYOTO.

Buddhism and Daoism were amenable to local deities whose presence often predated their own arrival in a community and whose goodwill was seen as essential by the local people. Every body of water had its dragon, each hollow its spirits; ancient heroes might live on as gods, while special trees or rocks were charged with numinous energy. By their nature such deities and cults were local, with great variation within as well as among the four East Asian lands. Even in Japan, where the spirits were loosely subsumed under Shinto, they did not form a unified, ordered pantheon. At the pinnacle of state and society, sovereigns gained legitimacy by claiming that the Confucian Mandate of Heaven had been bestowed on them, but beyond China they also drew on native myths, values, and traditions. By the time we begin our account, the male political elite throughout East Asia was reading the same books and professing similar values, but this hardly implies uniformity in public or private.

This chapter has stressed commonalities, but we must not lose sight of major differences even in basic institutions. That includes the family. The patriarchal family, supported by Confucianism, was the norm, and the perpetuation of the family was important everywhere, but inheritance practices differed radically. In Japan a single heir inherited by far the largest portion of an estate, but in China, after providing for dowries for unwed daughters, it was divided equally among all surviving sons. These inheritance practices not only affected the quality of life of those concerned but had a major impact on the size and economic viability of land-holdings and on the degree of social mobility.

Women were subordinate throughout East Asia; but only in China, and more in some regions than in others, did mothers wrap their daughters' feet in tight bandages, bending the four toes of each foot into the sole and bringing sole and heel as close together as possible, to form tiny feet. Thought to enhance a girl's attractiveness, tiny feet also deterred her from straying into mischief and demonstrated to the world that her family could dispense with her labors in the field.

More broadly, the need to define and delimit our generalizations also applies to such very general traits as deference to authority, stress on ritual form, and respect for scholarship and scholars (including students, scholars in the making). It is not only that one can cite major counter examples and that similar traits may appear in very different forms. They also varied according to place and changed over time. Furthermore, regarded broadly, many such traits hardly seem unique to East Asia. Perhaps they strike us now because we no longer practice or value them.

Notes

1. Francesca Bray, *The Rice Economies: Technology and Development in Asian Societies* (Berkeley: Univ. of California Press, 1994), pp. 25–26.

2. S. A. M. Adshead, *Material Culture in Europe and China, 1400–1800* (New York: St. Martin's Press, 1997), p. 161.

3. Murasaki Shikibu, *The Tale of Genji*, trans. by Royall Tyler (New York: Penguin Putnam, 2001), p. xii.

4. *A Source Book in Chinese Philosophy*, trans. by Wing-tsit Chan (Princeton: Princeton Univ. Press, 1963), p. 497 (converted to *pinyin*).

2

Qing China

Rise of Manchu Power	**Q I N G D Y N A S T Y**			**Late Qing**
Later Jin (1616–1636)	Kangxi (166–1722)	Qianlong (1736–1795)	Opium War (1839–1842)	

c. 1600 · 1644 · 1911

FIGURE 2.1   The Qing Empire, 1775.

In this chapter we will consider the Qing Dynasty (1644–1911) to around 1800. This was a century and a half of major achievements: the state reached its greatest geographical extent (Figure 2.1); the economy grew as did the population; scholars and artists were productive; popular culture flourished. In terms of cultural and political sophistication and the dynamics of economic development, China was comparable to the most advanced societies on earth, including Europe, whose "great divergence"[1] into sustained industrial growth was still to come. But by 1800 the Qing had seen its best days, even if no one could yet imagine that it was to be China's last dynasty.

The establishment of the new dynasty was a momentous event, but by no means did it represent a radical break with the past. Social and cultural transformations tend to be more gradual than political change, and, given the limitations of seventeenth-century communication and transportation technology, the new rulers could not have refashioned China had they wanted to. In recognition of the considerable continuity between the Qing and its Ming predecessor (1368–1644), scholars interested in the long view frequently include both under the rubric "late imperial" China.

Society and the State

As in most agrarian societies, local life in late imperial China was dominated by local elites. They formed an interface between society and government, represented on its lowest level by a magistrate who, from his county seat, had authority over a population which even in Ming times averaged over 50,000. Because his staff was small, his tour of duty limited to three years, and the "law of avoidance" assured that he was a stranger, he needed to work with members of the local gentry with whom he shared a world view grounded in a common education, common values, and, when the system worked smoothly, common objectives. The gentry took the lead in the construction of public works such as bridges and waterworks, in social welfare measures, in temple building, and in defense. Such activities complemented rather than challenged the state. However, the local elite could also balk at or even sabotage tax collection and resist other efforts at revenue extraction or policies that went against their interests.

Ideally, members of the elite derived their status from learning, their power from eligibility for office and the access to officials that learning made possible, and their wealth from land-owning. The most solidly established were *literati*, officials, and landlords all in one, whose learning, power, and wealth reinforced each other: Wealth allowed a family to dispense with the labors of a son in the fields and pay for his education. Education was both a source of local prestige and a prerequisite for taking the civil service examinations that led to government office, which, in turn, provided opportunities for the acquisition and retention of wealth.

These three attributes did not always overlap, however: there were learned but poor scholars as well as men of wealth who lacked the education and polish to be welcome in polite society, let alone pass examinations. Elite families frequently engaged in commerce, even though the classic Confucian view considered merchants nonproductive and relegated them to the bottom of a four-place hierarchy headed by scholars (*shi*), followed by farmers, with artisans in third place. Since status was not hereditary, elite families might fall to commoner status, while merchants and others could raise themselves by educating their sons. Economically, movement up or down was furthered by the ready transferability of land and other forms of wealth. Generational fragmentation of wealth resulted from the practice of dividing estates among male heirs after providing dowries for unmarried daughters, rather than passing on the family property intact to a single heir.

Although eligibility for office remained important, the local elite perpetuated themselves by forming marriage ties with similar families to build powerful networks. Still more basic than marriage ties was membership in common descent groups, consisting of families with the same surname who traced themselves back to a common ancestor. Especially in the wealthy Lower Yangzi and the southeast, such groups formed lineages which controlled property, most notably land to support ancestral halls and graveyards where ceremonial sacrifices for lineage ancestors were performed. Lineages frequently maintained schools. Lineage cohesion was further promoted by the compilation of genealogies, which identified those entitled to lineage membership and fostered a sense of identity. Solidarity was also protected and sustained by formal lineage rules enforced by punishments including expulsion for the most serious infractions.

In practice, as in theory, the basic social unit was the family, but the ideal joint family with "five generations under one roof," including the nuclear families of brothers, required a degree of wealth seldom enjoyed by commoners. The family was normally headed by the senior male, although a widowed matriarch could be the major force. Age prevailed over youth, but men generally outranked women. The "interior" world of the household was regarded as the women's sphere, while men dealt with the external world. Marriages were arranged by and for families, with the bride becoming a member of her husband's family, and subject to supervision and discipline by her mother-in-law. Giving birth to a child, preferably a boy, raised her standing in the family, and, in the end, "the lonely disaffected young bride became the pillar of the joint family as a mother-in-law" and "the girl who shrieked her childhood away in agony as her foot bones were crushed grew up to insist on binding her daughter's feet."[2] Women as well as men accepted prevailing norms. Dorothy Ko has pointed to the common saying "a plain face is given by heaven, but poorly bound feet are a sign of laziness" as evidence "that a pair of nicely shaped small feet represented the triumph of individual willpower and effort."[3]

We should note here the variety of lifestyles in a land as vast as China. There were regional differences: small feet were more common in the south than in the north and were a mark of status and prosperity in both regions. Poor and low-class women had hard lives but normal feet. There were differences between urban and rural, rich and poor. A criminal, say a salt smuggler, might well enjoy high standing within his community though despised by the official elite. Within China proper, in the south and southwest there were many ethnic minorities with their own ways, and beyond the Great Wall non-Chinese traditions prevailed.

Local societies moved to their own rhythms; nevertheless, the localities were part of a larger whole. G. William Skinner has proposed a pattern of market towns, 45,000 by the middle of the nineteenth century, "each the nucleus of an autonomous economic system . . . structured spatially according to the principle of centrality and temporally by the periodicity of the market days."[4] Although this theory may be overly schematic, it can help explain how local structures survived dynastic upheaval. Culturally, too, markets as forums for theatrical performances, along with itinerant peddlers and practitioners of medical and religious arts, provided for a considerable degree of cultural integration. Political integration was supplied by the state.

Supreme over state and society was the emperor, who claimed to have received heaven's mandate. Ming and Qing emperors, like their predecessors, performed all the sacred rites demanded of the "Son of Heaven," who linked the human and natural orders. Although constrained by custom and tradition, the emperor's power was absolute in theory. Under harsh emperors, officials who refused to toady to their superiors and criticized the ruler did so at the risk of torture and death. An official who became famous for his uprightness, concern for the common people, frugality and great courage was Hai Rui (1513–1587), who suffered imprisonment and torture after submitting a memorial to the emperor criticizing His Majesty's vanity and erratic conduct, while holding him responsible for the injustice, corruption, military weakness, heavy taxation and the impoverishment of the people that prevailed during his reign. The emperor was an autocrat, but his reach was limited by his need to work through a vast bureaucracy. To succeed in the long run, he had to avoid alienating the officialdom or provoking the people into rebellion.

Like all governments, that of China provided security, collected taxes, maintained large-scale projects such as the dikes along the Yellow River, and administrated a judicial system. Beyond that, in keeping with Confucian imperatives, the government joined the local elite in activities meant to assure the physical and moral welfare of its subjects. A populace panicked by the threat of starvation or spurred by "immoral" heterodox ideas to resist the status quo posed a threat equally to the gentry and the state.

A key institution, dating back to the Sui (581–617) and continued by the Qing, was the civil service examination system that linked state and society as well as political and intellectual life. With the exception of a small minority of men whose family background included criminals, brothel keepers, or other undesirables, the examinations were open to all. There were documented cases of men from truly humble backgrounds winning the coveted highest degree, but the need for years of intensive study favored candidates from elite families who could afford to dispense with the labor of their sons and to educate them. Great pains were taken to avoid dishonesty, since the credibility of the government was at stake.

To pass required a thorough command of Confucian classics and literature. Attempts to test for an ability to apply this knowledge to current problems were only sporadically successful. The tendency was to reward formal competence in composing essays along the lines of the models readily available at the local bookstore. Nevertheless, the examination system retained enormous prestige and produced China's most impressive statesmen. Dominating education, it fostered a gentlemen elite bound by a shared conceptual framework, a common set of references and ideals.

The Fall of the Ming

By the seventeenth century there were numerous signs that, after well over two centuries, the Ming was in trouble. In the 1590s the dynasty could still conduct campaigns in Mongolia and send large armies to fight the Japanese invaders of Korea (see Chapter 3). These military operations, as well as later military efforts in Manchuria, put enormous financial burdens on a government undermined by corruption, divisiveness, and incompetence in the highest places. The financial crisis was a symptom of profound malaise.

The traditional Chinese analysis of dynastic decline holds that internal decay precedes external disaster. The Ming fits the formula nicely. During its last half century it clearly lacked the vitality to renew a decaying political apparatus. The balance between the central government and the local elite was upset when the dynasty made too many concessions to the gentry. Too much was given away, too many fields removed from the tax rolls. Large landowners were able to find tax shelters through manipulation, and only peasant freeholders remained to pay taxes. Local resentment against the gentry grew, while lack of funds forced the dynasty to neglect public works. Grain stored for emergencies was sold off. Even the postal system was shut down. Finally, the regime failed to pay even its most strategically placed troops. Desperate men formed outlaw gangs that gradually coalesced into full-fledged rebel organizations. One of these, led by Li Zicheng (c.1600–1645), a former postal attendant, seized Beijing, and the last Ming emperor committed suicide. Li, however, was unable to found a new dynasty, for he had failed to take the necessary ideological and administrative steps to gain the backing of the scholar-official elite.

The Founding of the Qing

A major theme in Chinese history is the interaction between the Chinese and their nomadic and semi-nomadic neighbors whose way of life made them formidable horsemen and fierce warriors. When united under effective leadership, the Chinese, with their superior economic resources and larger population, normally had the upper hand, but they could never fully control their mobile adversaries. To deal with these troublesome neighbors, Chinese governments worked out various strategies ranging from a diplomacy of accommodation and alliance to attempts at outright military suppression. One military alternative was the kind of static defense that induced the Ming dynasty to rebuild The Great Wall into the impressive structure it is today. In the northeast, the Ming relied on the Willow Palisades, a barrier formed by lines of willows and a deep trench fortified by military checkpoints.

Beyond the Willow Palisades lay Manchuria, home of the Jurchen, who spoke a language related to Korean but not to Chinese. Although the Jurchen traced themselves back to the Jin Dynasty (1115–1234) that had once dominated north China, they had long been divided into tribes. In the north they subsisted by hunting and fishing, but in the south, where they were in contact with Chinese speakers, they farmed, raised livestock, and took pleasure and pride in their horsemanship and hunting skills. The ethnic origins of the inhabitants of the agricultural lands of Liaodong and southern Manchuria were diverse. They were not necessarily descended from Chinese settlers, but they spoke Chinese and by and large were Chinese culturally. There was also a major Mongolian presence in Manchuria, and Mongol influence on the Jurchen was strong.

To bring the various peoples of Manchuria into a state and create a regional power took Nurgaci (1559–1626), clan and tribal chief, more than twenty-five years as he fought, negotiated, and married his way to leadership and power. To facilitate state building he ordered the creation of a script, based on Mongolian, to write the Jurchen language. Originally favored by the Ming, Nurgaci came to be revered by them as the founder of the dynasty that replaced their own, but it was his successor, Hong Taiji (r. 1626–1643) who created a new ethnic identity called "Manchu," and envisioned a broader empire. In 1636, while remaining "divine khan" to his tribal subjects, Hong Taiji signaled his ambition to rule China by founding the new "Qing" (pure) dynasty. Nothing in the Chinese tradition stipulated that the imperial house had to be ethnically Chinese.

From the beginning, the new dynasty drew support from an alliance with Mongols and Chinese speakers, mostly from Manchuria. This was reflected in the organization of its armies into "banners," each with its own colors. By the time of the conquest, there were eight Manchu banners (278 companies), eight Mongol (120 companies) and eight "Chinese" (165 companies). Membership in the banners was hereditary. After the conquest, they were stationed in garrisons strategically located throughout the empire. There the bannermen lived apart from the local population under a general who reported directly to Beijing.

After Li Zicheng overthrew the Ming, the key to the military situation was in the hands of the Ming general Wu Sangui (1612–1678), whose army guarded Shanhaiguan, the strategic pass between the mountains and the sea that formed the eastern terminus of the Great Wall. When Wu threw his lot in with the Manchus, Li Zicheng's fate was sealed.

After the Manchus entered the capital, Beijing, in June 1644, the Qing ruler announced he had come to punish the rebels, buried the deceased Ming emperor and empress with full honors, and claimed to be the legitimate successor of the old dynasty. To consolidate and expand their control, the new rulers needed the support and participation of Chinese officials and the tacit assent of the Chinese populace. Even before they gained the capital, the dynasty sought to draw on the talents of Chinese scholars and reassure the Chinese elite by holding its first examinations. Also prior to the conquest they formed a political system that balanced an Assembly of Princes and High Officials composed almost exclusively of Manchus with such traditional Chinese institutions as The Six Ministries (personnel, revenue, rites, war, justice, and public works), and the Censorate, charged with reporting on the conduct of the civil service with the right and duty also to criticize the emperor.

Despite such reassuring measures, the subjugation of the rest of China, especially the south, involved long and bloody warfare including a terrible ten-day massacre in Yangzhou that left the city's gutters filled with corpses. After the capture of Nanjing, which Ming loyalists had made their capital, the Qing emperor forced all men to shave the forward portion of their heads and braid their hair in back into a long queue (pigtail). The Manchus were not the first to force their hair style on their subjects; the Ming had done the same in Vietnam.

After the fall of Nanjing, the Qing still faced prolonged resistance. For some forty years warfare, banditry, and peasant uprisings, along with periods of starvation and epidemics, took a heavy toll. From 1646 to 1658 much of the southeast coast was controlled by Zheng Chenggong (1624–1662), the son of a Chinese pirate-adventurer and a Japanese mother, widely known as Coxinga. From 1661 to 1669, in order to deprive Zheng of support and supplies, a seventeen-mile strip along the coast, extending from Zhejiang to the Vietnamese border, was completely cleared of people. Barriers, guard posts, and watch towers were erected to prevent anyone from entering. Originally based in Xiamen (Amoy), Zheng moved to Taiwan (Formosa) from which he expelled the Dutch in 1662. His son held out against the Manchus, who finally subdued the island in 1683 and placed it under the administration of Fujian Province. By then the southwest, too, was pacified, but only after the War of the Three Feudatories (1673–1681), one of whom was Wu Sangui, who had created a practically autonomous state for himself in Yunnan and Guizhou.

In their new empire, the Manchus, who comprised only about two percent of the population, and their Mongol associates formed a conquest elite who were conscious of their non-Chinese heritage, forbidden to intermarry with the Chinese, and distinguished from them in dress, family rituals, diet, and lifestyle. For example, Manchu women were not allowed bound feet. An inner circle of this elite dominated the inner court and exercised profound influence on government throughout the life of the dynasty.

While claiming to be heirs of the Ming and recipients of Heaven's Mandate, Qing emperors, as Manchus, concurrently asserted the claim to rule as khans. In addition, they demonstrated an ability to draw on Buddhist traditions to make their rule acceptable to people beyond the Great Wall. Ritual observances, the rulers solemnly acting like rulers, demonstrated that they were meant to be rulers. Potent symbolism was a major component of Qing authority and power.

China proper was divided into eighteen provinces further subdivided into circuits, prefectures, and counties, but Inner Asian affairs were handled by the Court of Colonial Affairs using the peoples' own languages and appealing to their own political traditions. The emperors themselves regularly studied Mongolian, Manchu, and Chinese. Although the trend was toward increasing bureaucratization, Inner Asians saw themselves as subjects of a universal empire. But China was the Center.

Early Qing Thinkers and Painters

While many literati accepted service under the new dynasty, the most original work came from the brushes of men who refused to serve the Qing. Among those who in these turbulent times found tranquility in a Buddhist monastery was Hongren (1610–1663; see Figure 2.2), who "represented the world in a dematerialized cleansed vision . . . revealing his personal peace through the liberating form of geometric abstraction."[5]

Although Hongren had his followers, other painters who lived through the change of dynasties were too individualistic to attract followers or perpetuate styles. One such was Zhu Da, also called Bada Shanren (c. 1626–1705), whose personal behavior was distinctly odd: he sang and laughed frequently but refused to speak. His painting was equally unusual: surging landscapes, huge lotuses, and birds and fishes with the eyes of a Zen patriarch. His handscroll "Fish and Rocks" (Figure 2.3) begins with a section (not shown here) done with a dry brush, and the brushwork becomes wetter as the painting proceeds. Although there are references to the Ming dynasty and himself in the poems on and in the painting, the work remains enigmatic. Zhu Da had to wait several centuries for his fame, but he exemplifies the self-expression favored by the aesthetic theory of his time, which regarded representation as crude and unworthy of gentlemen amateurs even if the distinction between amateur and professional was one more of theory than practice.

Like Zhu Da in the world of painting, Wang Fuzhi (1619–1704) had no followers in his own time, but late in the dynasty came to be admired as a philosopher who gave primacy to *qi,* and as a student of history who emphasized that institutions and policies of one age or culture were not necessarily applicable to another. Another Ming loyalist with trenchant political views that had to wait for centuries for a hearing was Huang Zongxi (1610–1695), who complained that in antiquity the people had been the master, the prince the tenant, but that now the situation was reversed. "Thus he who does the greatest harm in the world is none other than the prince."[6] Among the policies advocated by Huang was the restoration of the pre-Ming strong chief ministership, tax and land reforms, increasing the authority of local officials, and the strengthening of education, including the creation of independent schools.

Huang's most influential work was a great compendium of Ming thought still widely used. The writings and teachings of Huang's contemporary, Gu Yanwu (1613–1682), made a deep impression on mainstream Qing scholarship. Objecting to the abstract speculations of Song and Ming philosophers, Gu insisted on what he considered real and practical learning, solidly based on

FIGURE 2.2   Hongren's masterpiece, *The Coming of Autumn,* displays a marvelous sense of structural depth. Hanging scroll, ink on paper, 122.4 cm high.

FIGURE 2.3 *Fish and Rocks,* Zhu Da (Bada Shanren 1624–c.1705), Qing dynasty. Note the water plants and lotuses on the left and the strange rock that invites speculation. Section of handscroll, ink on paper, 29.2 × 157.5 cm.

FIGURE 2.4 *Fishermen Returning Home,* third and last panel of *Summer Mountains, Misty Rain* (1668), Wang Hui (1632–1717). Handscroll, ink on paper, 17 in. × 19 in.
ASIAN ART MUSEUM OF SAN FRANCISCO. GIFT OF THE TANG FOUNDATION. PRESENTED BY NADINE, MARTIN, AND LESLIE TANG IN CELEBRATION OF JACK C. C. TANG'S SIXTIETH BIRTHDAY (B87D8). USED BY PERMISSION.

scholarship in the original sources rather than relying on later commentaries. He himself wrote important studies on historical geography and inscriptions but is most famous for work in historical phonetics. His essays, collected under the title *Records of Daily Knowledge (Rizhilu),* discuss government, the examination system, and economics as well as the classics and history, showing a range and critical spirit representative of the best of seventeenth-century thought. He was influential in founding Qing philological scholarship and what came to be known as "evidential learning." Subsequent Qing scholars contributed greatly to textual scholarship.

Not all painters of the early Qing were eccentric or even persistently loyal to the Ming. Outstanding among the more orthodox painters were four artists all named Wang, among whom Wang Hui (1632–1717) was the most gifted. One of his paintings is a rendition of Fan Guan's *Travelers* (Figure 1.1). His *Summer Mountains, Misty Rain* (Figure 2.4) is representative in that Wang here follows the style and composition of the masters of the Song dynasty (960–1279) to create a painting very much his own. "This work," to quote Patricia Berger, "shows Wang's interest in the effect of light on form, its ability to clarify or obscure, and his virtuous talent for pictorial rhythms."[7]

In 1691 Wang Hui received an imperial command to supervise the painting of a series of scrolls commemorating Kangxi's southern tour. He was only one of a number of painters and other men of talent to enjoy the patronage of Kangxi and in turn enhance the aura of the throne and the glory of its occupant.

Box 2.1   *The Qing Emperors*

Beginning with the Ming period emperors used a single era name (*nianhao*, literally "year designation") throughout their reigns. Consequently, the emperors are often referred to by their era names rather than by their formal posthumous temple names or their personal names, although these are also employed in the scholarly literature.

Era Name	Temple Name	Personal Name	Era Dates
Shunzhi	Shizu	Fulin	1644–1661
Kangxi	Shengzu	Xuanye	1662–1722
Yongzheng	Shizong	Yinzhen	1723–1735
Qianlong	Gaozong	Hongli	1736–1795
Jiaqing	Renzong	Yongyan	1796–1820
Daoguang	Xuanzong	Minning	1821–1850
Xianfeng	Wenzong	Yizhu	1851–1861
Tongzhi	Muzong	Zaichun	1862–1874
Guangxu	Dezong	Zaitian	1875–1908
Xuanzong	none	Puyi	1909–1911

The Reign of Kangxi

Kangxi was on the throne from 1662 to 1722, and actually ruled from 1668 on. As already noted, he was able to complete the Manchu conquest of China, and did so in campaigns fought largely by Chinese troops under Chinese generals. After the incorporation of Taiwan, he turned his attention to China's borders in the North and West. In the Amur River region his army destroyed a Russian Cossack base. This success was followed by the Treaty of Nerchinsk, signed with Russia in 1689, which settled frontier problems between the two great empires and regularized relations between them. It also removed the threat of a possible alliance between the Russians and a confederation of Western Mongols. Against the latter, Kangxi personally led his troops in 1696–1697 and won a great victory. Around the middle of the seventeenth century, Western Mongols had intervened in the political-religious struggles taking place in Tibet and had remained as conquerors. In 1720 Kangxi's armies entered Tibet and installed a pro-Chinese Dalai Lama (the spiritual and secular ruler of Tibet). This was the first but not the last Qing intervention in Tibet.

Kangxi's martial exploits reflected his identification with his forebears and his desire to preserve a Manchu way of life, which he saw as essential for maintaining Manchu supremacy. Another expression of this feeling was his zest for great hunts.

To help preserve Manchu distinctiveness, one of the first acts of Kangxi's reign was the closing of Manchuria to Chinese immigration. Kangxi was very much the Manchu, but he was by no means anti-Chinese. Kangxi maintained a strict balance between Manchus and Chinese in the top central administrative posts, and in the provinces, generally, a Chinese governor was counterbalanced by a governor-general, usually placed over two provinces, who was a Manchu, a Mongol, or a Chinese bannerman. Banner garrisons continued to be the main source of security. The emperor also used his Chinese bondservants, who managed the imperial household and the emperor's personal treasury. They also performed confidential tasks such as sending in secret reports on conditions in the provinces.

Kangxi was a vigorous man. He rose well before dawn each day to go through a great stack of memorials before receiving officials, beginning at 5 A.M. (later changed to 7 A.M. to accommodate officials not living near the palace). His personal tours of inspection in the south are famous. To show his benevolence, he reduced taxes and forced Manchu aristocrats to desist from seizing Chinese lands. He was also a man of wide intellectual interests, including Western learning. He won the affection of many Chinese literati by holding a special examination in 1679, and not only patronized artists but sponsored the compilation of the official Ming history, a great phrase dictionary, a giant encyclopedia, and an exhaustive dictionary of Chinese characters. He gave special support to the philosophy of Zhu Xi.

Kangxi was one of the most successful emperors in all of Chinese history, but he was unable to provide for a smooth succession. Although he had fifty-six children, only one son was by an empress. He was designated heir apparent, but disappointed his father, who complained that he was "dissolute, tyrannical, brutal, debauched."[8] He also showed signs of mental instability, and in the end Kangxi placed him in confinement, but failed to appoint a successor. The claim that fourteen years later he named his fourth son on his deathbed looks very much like a later fabrication. During these years, various sons, suspicious of each other and each backed by his own political faction, conspired and maneuvered for the succession. The upshot was that after Kangxi's death, the throne was seized in a military coup by the fourth son, who became Emperor Yongzheng (r. 1723–1735).

Yongzheng

Yongzheng censored the record of his accession and also suppressed other writings deemed inimical to his regime or hostile to the Manchus. Like his father, he used military force to preserve the dynasty's position in Mongolia. When Tibet was torn by civil war from 1717 to 1728, he intervened militarily, leaving a Qing resident backed by a military garrison to pursue the dynasty's interests. After the dynasty came to an end in the twentieth century, this provided a basis for Chinese claims of sovereignty over Tibet.

Yongzheng was a tough, hard-working ruler bent on effective government. During the early Qing the emperor had been assisted by the Grand Secretariat, a six-man board composed of three Manchu and three Chinese, but under Kangxi the Grand Secretariat lost its influence. In a move toward greater efficiency and control, Yongzheng created a five-man Grand Council whose members linked the inner court with the outer bureaucracy, headed by the chiefs of the six ministries. By expanding the number of officials entitled to submit secret memorials and sending them confidential replies, he operated his own channel of communication apart from the general bureaucracy.

The emperor saw the need for administrative and fiscal reform and restructured the financing of local government in order to free magistrates from dependence on private and informal funding. Active in tax reform, he simplified the system of tax registers by combining the land and personal service taxes. This and other measures along with strong imperial oversight, led to increased government efficiency, though in the long run effective reform below the county level proved unattainable.

Yongzheng's reign was despotic, efficient, and vigorous. By the simple device of sealing the name of the heir-apparent in a box kept in the throne room, he was able to assure that on his death there would be no struggle over the succession. Thus he prepared the way for what was to be the dynasty's most splendid reign, that of Qianlong.

Qianlong

During Qianlong's reign (1736–1795), the Qing achieved its greatest prosperity. Expansion into Central Asia reached its greatest extent (see map, Figure 2.1). This was partly the result of Qing diplomatic skill in practicing "divide and rule" policies, their ability to work with local leaders and manipulate inner Asian symbols of authority, and the sheer power of their armies. The Qing also took advantage of the disunity and declining strength of the Inner Asian peoples. The weakening of these peoples has been subject to various interpretations. According to Morris Rossabi, the most plausible explanations include the diminishing importance of the international caravan trade in an age of developing maritime commerce, a trend toward the development of sedentary societies marked by urbanization, and Russian expansion that reduced the area to which tribes could flee in retreat, thereby reducing their mobility.[9]

Under Qianlong, Chinese Turkestan was incorporated and renamed Xinjiang. To the West, Ili was conquered and garrisoned. This brought into the empire Muslim leaders, including followers of the activist Naqshbandiyya order, difficult to convince as to the legitimacy of Qing rule. The Qing also dominated Outer Mongolia after inflicting a final defeat on the Western Mongols. Its policy there was to preserve Mongol institutions, but it allowed Chinese merchants to enter and exploit the people, thus reinforcing the anti-Chinese animosities of the animal-herding Mongols. It is no accident that after the Qing fell in the twentieth century, the Mongols promptly declared their independence. Throughout this period there were continued Mongol interventions in Tibet and a reciprocal spread of Tibetan

Lamaism in Mongolia. Qianlong again sent armies into Tibet and firmly established the Dalai Lama as ruler, with a Qing resident and garrison to preserve Qing suzerainty. Other than that, no further attempt was made to integrate Tibet into the empire after the manner of Xinjiang. To foster the loyalty of Mongols and Tibetans, Qianlong drew on the Buddhist tradition. Six tangkas (Tibetan religious paintings) survive portraying the emperor as Manjusri, boddhistava of compassion and wisdom. Tibetan records often refer to him by that name.

Further afield, military campaigns against Vietnam, Burma, and over the Himalayas into Nepal forced local rulers to accept Qing hegemony and render tribute. Qianlong's expansion involved millions of square miles and brought into the empire non-Chinese peoples, such as Uighurs, Kazakhs, Kirghiz, and Mongols, who were at least potentially hostile. It was also a very expensive enterprise. The dynasty enjoyed unprecedented prosperity and managed in the mid-1780s to accumulate a healthy financial reserve, but its resources were not inexhaustible. Yet Qianlong delighted in the glory and wealth. He built a sumptuous summer residence, partly of Western design, and undertook grand tours of the empire. In his policy toward the literati, he combined Kangxi's generous patronage of scholarship with Yongzheng's suspicion of anti-Manchu writings. The greatest project he sponsored was the *Complete Library of Four Treasuries (Siku quanshu)*, employing 15,000 copyists working twelve years to produce 3,462 complete works in 36,000 volumes. This "final affirmation of the unity of knowledge and power in Chinese history"[10] preserved many books but also merged with a campaign to ferret out and suppress writings offensive to Manchu sensibilities.

Some 80 percent of Qianlong's officials were Chinese, but the emperor was much concerned that Manchus not become Chinese. To this effect he ordered compilation of Manchu genealogies and histories, promoted study and use of the Manchu language by Manchus, and insisted on all that set Manchus apart from Chinese down to the details of feminine adornment. Three earrings in each ear were mandatory for Manchu ladies, and woe to her who made do with just one in the Chinese manner. Qianlong's measures standardized Manchu lore and practices; they reaffirmed Manchu identity but rendered the tradition inflexible.

Eighteenth-Century Governance

The eighteenth century was generally a time of prosperity, when institutions functioned as smoothly as they ever had. A system of state and local granaries ensured adequate and affordable food supplies. In the rich Lower Yangzi region, the local elite constructed and operated community granaries, but elsewhere government assumed a more active role in providing these sources of emergency food. In the eighteenth century it also performed formidable feats of information gathering and coordination over the breadth of the land.

The state's concern to promote popular morality was expressed in the promotion of village lectures based on edifying imperial pronouncements and its compilation of an officially sanctioned pantheon of local gods and spirits, although it tolerated others as long as they were not considered downright subversive. It also fostered schools. As in the case of community granaries, in the more advanced areas education was left to local initiative, but in outlying provinces officials played a more active role. Thus, a dedicated eighteenth-century governor of Yunnan provided the leadership for establishing 650 schools for the instruction of the numerous minority peoples of the province.

When the system operated effectively, as in the eighteenth century, state and society formed a continuum without a fixed boundary. Though local gentry might resist tax collection and examination candidates resent the bitter competition which left them little hope for success, essentially officials and elite shared a broad spectrum of values and ideas pushing them to cooperate rather than compete, to work in harmony rather than to conflict. As a recent study puts it:

> Because the state understood the art of ruling to include shaping people's moral behavior, it was inclined to be meddlesome, authoritarian, and censorious. But at the same time, because only people who freely choose to do the right thing can be said to have high moral standards, the state accepted and even promoted initiatives among its subjects that it saw as likely to make people take their moral and social agency seriously.[11]

Eighteenth-Century Literati Culture

Following the lead of Gu Yanwu, but without his breadth, Qing scholars engaged in "evidential research" and made important, even iconoclastic, discoveries concerning the questionable historicity of parts of such canonical texts as *The Classic of Changes*, *The Classic of History*, and *The Records of Rites*. However, the concentration on philology (historical linguistics) easily led to the view that textual studies alone were truly "solid" (in the sense that they avoided abstract speculation) and "practical." Yan Yuan (1635–1704), on the other hand, condemned both quiet meditation and book learning as standing in the way of true self-cultivation, which should lead to the capability of changing the world. He studied military science and medicine, but his chief disciple Li Gong (1659–1733) expounded his teachings in the form of commentaries on the classics.

A major eighteenth-century thinker was Dai Zhen (1723–1777), who made important contributions to linguistics, astronomy, mathematics, and geography as well as philosophy. Like most of the creative seventeenth-century thinkers, he rejected the metaphysical existence of *li*, which he considered simply the pattern of things. He also disputed Zhu Xi's dualistic theory of human nature, insisting that it contradicted the teachings of Mencius, that human nature is one whole and all good, and that moral perfection consists in fulfilling one's natural inclinations.

Dai Zhen shared his age's faith in philology, but this was not true of his contemporary Zhang Xuecheng (1738–1801), who strongly disliked philological studies and sought meaning in the study and writing of history. Zhang is perhaps most famous for his thesis that "the six classics are all history," by which he meant that they are not "empty" theoretical discussions but that they document antiquity and illustrate the Dao. A scholar must not stop at the facts but get at the meaning. Zhang once compared a work of history to a living organism: its facts are like bones, the writing is like the skin, and its meaning corresponds to the organism's vital spirit.

Along with history and philosophy, another subject of perennial concern to Chinese scholars was the function and evaluation of literature. The poet Yuan Mei (1716–1797) held that the purpose of poetry is to express emotion and that it must give pleasure; he rejected the didactic view, held by Zhang Xuecheng, among others, that it must convey moral instruction. Yuan's poetry and prose reflect the life of a talented, refined eighteenth-century hedonist, unconventional within the bounds of good taste, and marginally aware of the exotic West. One of his prize possessions was a large Western mirror much admired by his female pupils. Among Yuan's less conventional works are a cookbook and a collection of ghost stories. His interest in the latter was shared by his friend, the painter Le Ping (1735–1799), the youngest and last of the so-called Eight Eccentrics of Yangzhou, a man who claimed actually to have seen the apparitions he painted.

In the eighteenth century, painters of various schools were at work: professionals working in the meticulous and mannered "northern" style, eclectics drawing on diverse traditions and models, and individualists striving, sometimes excessively, for originality. An unusually interesting and prolific artist was the painter Gao Qipei (1660–1734). Even in the Song dynasty and earlier, artists had experimented with unconventional materials instead of using a brush, but none had gone as far as Gao (see Figure 2.5).

Qing painters and scholars generally perceived themselves as latecomers in a long and revered tradition. As such they faced a dilemma similar to that of painters, poets, and composers of our own time who no longer feel they can contribute to the traditional lines of development in their arts, that is, be another

FIGURE 2.5 *Tiger Seen from Above* (c. 1700), Gao Qipei (1660-1734). Ink and colors on paper, 105.3 × 51.5 cm. At the upper right, Gao Qipei wrote the following text: "Life with the fingers from the man from outside the Shanghai gate." Beneath it are several red stamps.

Rijksmuseum, Amsterdam AK-RK-1991-10.

Rembrandt, Beethoven, and so forth. What had been valid for one age could not serve another. Thus some literati artists cultivated the notion that the epitome of art was non-art, that is, the deliberate cultivation of innocent awkwardness. But unusual behavior was tolerated, and it became quite acceptable to sell one's paintings. Both Gao and Le did so without jeopardizing their "amateur" status. Meanwhile, openly professional artists, who did not claim literati status, sold their work to ordinary, unsophisticated folk who appreciated bright colors and verisimilitude. Colored woodblock prints also appealed to a wide audience as did popular drama and vernacular literature. The latter in particular reached new heights.

Fiction

Many of the dynasty's best writers and thinkers were men who had failed in the examination route to success, an experience which perhaps helped them to view society with a measure of critical and even satiric detachment. The examinations themselves were a favorite target. Pu Songling (1640–1715) wrote this account of the seven transformations of a candidate in the provincial examination:

> When he first enters the examination compound and walks along, panting under his heavy load of luggage, he is just like a beggar. Next, while undergoing the personal body search and being scolded by the clerks and shouted at by the soldiers, he is just like a prisoner. When he finally enters his cell and, along with the other candidates, stretches his neck to peer out, he is just like the larva of a bee. When the examination is finished at last and he leaves, his mind in a haze and his legs tottering, he is just like a sick bird that has been released from a cage. While he is wondering when the results will be announced and waiting to learn whether he passed or failed, so nervous that he is startled even by the rustling of the trees and the grass and is unable to sit or stand still, his restlessness is like that of a monkey on a leash. When at last the results are announced and he has definitely failed, he loses his vitality like one dead, rolls over on his side, and lies without moving, like a poisoned fly. Then, when he pulls himself together and stands up, he is provoked by every sight and sound, gradually flings away everything within his reach, and complains of the illiteracy of the examiners. When he calms down at last, he finds everything in the room broken. At this time he is like a pigeon smashing its own precious eggs. These are the seven transformations of a candidate.[12]

This examination was held in a labyrinthine compound, with the candidates housed in individual cells where they had to spend the night. It was an eerie place sealed off from the rest of the world, for during an examination session the great gates remained firmly shut: if a man died during the examination, his body was wrapped in straw matting and thrown over the wall. Thus it was a perfect setting for numerous tales of ghosts, usually the spirits of jilted maidens come to wreak vengeance on the men who had done them wrong.

As David Rolston points out, "neither landscape painting nor traditional Chinese fiction is structured around the use of the convention of fixed perspective or viewpoint so important in western painting or fiction."[13] *The Scholars* (*Rulinwaishi*), a novel by Wu Jingzi (1701–1754) is a good case in point. Primarily a satire on the examination system, it catches in its net an assortment of human follies and unveils the intricacies of social life in vignettes of the pompous and the ignorant, the unworldly scholar and those who cheat him, and so on. Although it is episodic in organization and somewhat uneven in quality, it incorporates certain technical advances in the art of storytelling, notably in the way it allows its characters to reveal their personalities gradually rather than labeling them at the very start.

China's most beloved and exhaustively studied novel is *The Dream of the Red Chamber* (*Honglou Meng*), also translated as *The Story of the Stone*. Like *The Scholars*, it offers priceless insights into Qing society, this time from the vantage point of a large, eminent family in decline. With rich detail and a cast of hundreds, it reveals how such a family was organized and how it functioned, the relationships between the generations and the sexes, the lives of women, the status of servants; and it does all this with fine psychological characterizations based on the personal experience of the author, Cao Zhan (d. 1763). But it is far more than a novel of manners. Conscious of its own fictionality, it prompts the reader to contemplate the distinction between the real and the unreal and to ponder the nature of desire. C. T. Hsia has written that "it embodies the supreme tragic expression in Chinese literature," and that, "the ultimate tragic conflict lies in a tug of war between the opposing claims of compassion and detachment."[14]

Despite the literary excellence of *The Dream*, neither it nor other novels ever gained Confucian legitimacy as high literature. In Japan the novel was an honored part of literary culture, but in China reading a novel was a surreptitious pleasure indulged in by students when their teacher was not looking—or vice versa.

A Buoyant Economy

During the initial forty cataclysmic years following the founding of the Qing, warfare, destruction, dislocation, and cold weather combined to bring widespread hardship, famine, disease, and population decline. But then both the economy and the population revived and went on to reach new heights. By the end of the eighteenth century, the Chinese population was around 300 million, about double what it had been around 1600. More people lived in China than in Europe. The century saw an increase in life expectancy and an all-around improvement in the standard of living.

In agriculture, increased production and commercialization went hand in hand. Yields improved with the geographical spread of crops, such as specialized strains of rice suitable to local conditions, and of improved irrigation techniques and better fertilizers, such as soybean cakes. Production was also significantly increased by the introduction of new plants from the Americas: sweet potatoes, peanuts, tobacco, and corn. These could be grown on land previously left uncultivated as unsuitable for traditional Chinese crops.

A rising population spurred demand. The economy became more complex with the expansion of markets for commercial crops such as tea, sugar, cotton, hemp, tobacco, and for other products of agricultural activity, most importantly mulberry trees for feeding silkworms. Rice was grown commercially not only to supply cities and towns but also for sale to farmers who had converted rice paddies to more profitable cash crops.

The developments in agriculture had their counterparts in manufacturing. The products of China's kilns were world famous; Chinese ceramics were copied in Europe and Japan. Brewing, paper making, mining and metal working industries thrived. China led the world in silk and cotton textile production. The demand for raw cotton exceeded what could be grown in China, so it was imported from India by way of Thailand. Until the 1770s, Chinese shipping predominated not only in coastal trade but also in foreign shipping, as Chinese junk owners took advantage of the monsoons and engaged in business dealings with a thriving overseas Chinese community.

By the end of the eighteenth century Chinese shipping no longer dominated, but China's maritime trade with the West continued to contribute to Chinese wellbeing. Throughout the century the balance of overseas trade had been in China's favor, as it had been ever since the sixteenth century, when China became the world's "sink" for silver, which flowed in from Japan and the Spanish colonies of Mexico and Peru to pay for Chinese textiles and ceramics. To quote William Atwell, writing of the 1570s:

> Within a short time Chinese silks were being worn in the streets of Kyoto and Lima. Chinese cottons were being sold in Filipino and Mexican markets, and Chinese porcelain was being used in fashioning homes from Sakai to London.[15]

The major distribution center in the intercontinental trade connecting Europe and China was Manila, in the Philippines (held by Spain since 1565), which attracted a community of Chinese traders.

While this trade was disrupted by the troubles of the seventeenth century, silver imports resumed after trade restrictions were lifted in 1683. The silver flow declined in the 1720s and again at mid-century, but it rose again after 1760. The demand for silver in China and China's ability to absorb the silver without triggering inflation attest to the productivity of the Chinese economy and to the absence of a market for European products in China.

Eighteenth-century China, like all large countries at this time, was primarily agricultural, but Beijing remained the world's largest city until London surpassed it around 1800. Increased trade fostered growth of market towns linked by empire-wide merchant groups and serviced by a sophisticated banking system. As William Rowe has concluded, "the uniquely efficient water-transport system and marketing mechanism of preindustrial China allowed it to overcome the barriers of long distance and low technology, and to develop a national market by mid-Qing, even though in Europe and elsewhere such a development may have been conditional upon the advent of steam-powered transportation."[16]

Despite the spread of a "national market," generalization about China's local social and economic foundations remains difficult and potentially misleading because conditions varied greatly from area to area then as they do today. Economic growth and transformation were most evident along the coast and along the major river arteries, with the Yangzi and Pearl River Delta areas profiting most from the new prosperity.

The population continued to increase even though Chinese families took various measures to limit the number of children. People married young but practiced sexual abstinence in the early years of marriage when living with their parents. Infanticide, especially female infanticide, as well as neglect, also reduced the number of offspring. Still the population grew. With more people there was mounting pressure on land. As an official put it in a memorial to Yongzheng, "while the population increases daily, the land does not."[17] Under Yongzheng the government actively pursued a policy of land reclamation, while under Qianlong market forces encouraged the maximum spread of agriculture up into the hills, with terraces all the way to the summits, and out into the hinterlands. In 1793 Hong Liangji (1748–1809) became the first official to warn against excessive population growth.

These developments changed the balance between the human and the natural environment. Deforestation, which began long before this period, became more acute. "The earth was loose; when the big rains came, water rushed down from the highlands and mud and silt spread out below. Fertile areas near the mountains were repeatedly covered with sand and were abandoned."[18] Another result of a long-term trend toward deforestation was the shortage of wood that already in the sixteenth century prompted salt extractors to shift from boiling to less effective solar evaporation. In the sixteenth and seventeenth centuries, highland and lowland communities frequently fought over woodlands to the point that the state had to intervene. As more accessible forests were cut down, the primary sources of timber were increasingly distant from the center; Guizhou in the southwest and the Yalu region in the northeast became the major suppliers.

The environmental history of much of China and East Asia is complex, because there were major differences within as well as between regions, and much remains to be learned. But a start has been made, revealing the frequently complex interrelations among technology, commerce, climate, government policies, and social practices. Indications are that major parts of China were heading into environmental crisis by the late eighteenth century as forests disappeared, soil eroded, rivers silted and flooded rendering human life more dire and condemning to extinction animals deprived of habitat. However, the worst was still to come. As Kenneth Pomeranz has shown, China, environmentally as well as economically, did not yet compare unfavorably to Europe, which was able to avoid intensified land use by exploiting the ecological "windfall" provided by the New World.[19]

Dynastic Decline

As the expense of military campaigns far beyond the bounds of China proper mounted, the resources of even the prosperous Qianlong regime were strained, while laxity and corruption were rendering government less effective and more expensive. The worst offender was Heshen (1750–1799), a handsome and clever Manchu who enjoyed the aging emperor's complete trust for twenty-three years, during which he built a network of corruption and amassed an enormous fortune. Although bitterly detested, he could not be removed, for he never lost Qianlong's confidence and affection. An attack on Heshen implied an attack on His Majesty's own judgment and suggested the presence of factionalism. Perhaps Qianlong was especially sensitive to any signs of factionalism since his father, Emperor Yongzheng, had written a strong critique on this subject. Like his political authority, the moral and intellectual authority of the emperor were beyond question. Qianlong abdicated after his sixtieth year as emperor in order not to rule longer than his illustrious grandfather, but he continued to dominate the government until his death in 1799. Only then was Heshen removed.

As always, the common people bore the burden of extravagance and corruption. As a result, many of them joined in the White Lotus Rebellion (1796–1804). At its height it affected Sichuan, Hubei, Henan, Gansu, and Shaanxi. The rebellion drew its following by promising the coming of Maitreya (the Buddha of the future), a restoration of the Ming, and the rescue of the people from all suffering. It gained momentum as it attracted the destitute and displaced, and proved the power of its cause. The ineffectiveness of the dynasty's response assisted the movement: government generals used the occasion to line their own pockets and bannermen proved their total incompetence. Not until after Heshen's fall did the government make real headway. A new, very capable commander was appointed, disaffected areas were slowly taken back from the rebels, and militia bands organized by the local elite proved effective in putting down insurgency.

The civil service was not expanded to keep pace with the growth of the population or the economy or to accommodate the growing number of thwarted candidates, many of them superbly qualified. Already in the Song there had been men who spent a lifetime taking examinations—when the emperor asked his age, one such man replied, "fifty years ago twenty-three." Now the aged candidate became a stock figure in literature. The government even relaxed standards for men over 70 so that, past retirement age, they could at least enjoy the psychological satisfaction of receiving a degree. In an effort to weed out candidates, new examinations were introduced. Thus in 1788 the reexamination of provincial and metropolitan graduates was introduced. That brought the total minimum number of examinations required for the final degree to eight, not counting a final placement examination. By this time the criteria for judging papers had become exceedingly formalistic. Candidates spent years practicing highly complex, artificial "eight-legged essays," required in the examinations, and bookshops did a thriving business selling model answers. In the meantime, the old battle of wits

FIGURE 2.6 *A Cheating Shirt.* Before entering the examination compound where they were to spend three days and two nights, candidates underwent a thorough body search. Absolutely forbidden to bring anything with writing on it, the wearer of this undershirt clearly hoped to beat the system.

Fujii Museum, Kyoto, Japan. Photograph © Lore Schirokauer.

between examiners and cheaters remained a draw (see the "cheating shirt," Figure 2.6). The unsatisfactory state of the examination system, and the tendency of the government to tinker and elaborate rather than reform and innovate, suggests a dangerous hardening of the institutional arteries just as China's place in the world was about to change.

Notes

1. The term is taken from Kenneth Pomeranz, *The Great Divergence: China, Europe, and the Making of the Modern World Economy* (Princeton: Princeton Univ. Press, 2000).

2. Susan Mann, "The Education of Daughters in the Mid-Ch'ing Period," in Bejamin A. Elman and Alexander Woodside, eds., *Education and Society in Late Imperial China, 1600–1900* (Berkeley: Univ. of California Press, 1994), p. 21.

3. Dorothy Ko, *Teachers of the Inner Chambers: Women and Culture in Seventeenth-Century China* (Stanford: Stanford Univ. Press, 1994), p. 171.

4. G. William Skinner, "Chinese Peasants and the Closed Community: An Open and Shut Case," in *Comparative Studies in Society and History* 13 (1971), p. 272.

5. James Cahill, *The Compelling Image: Nature and Style in Seventeenth-Century Chinese Painting* (Cambridge, Mass.: Harvard Univ. Press, 1982), p. 183.

6. W. Theodore de Bary, trans. *Waiting for the Dawn: A Plan for the Prince. Huang Tsung-hsi's Ming-i Tai-fang lu* (New York: Columbia Univ. Press, 1993), p. 92.

7. http://www.asianart.org/exhibits/collect_chin_p3.htm.

8. Jonathan D. Spence, *Emperor of China: Self-Portrait of Kang-hsi* (New York: Alfred E. Knopf, 1974), p. 128.

9. Morris Rossabi, *China and Inner Asia—From 1638 to the Present Day* (New York: Pica Press, 1975), pp. 139–40. Rossabi does not think Buddhism was a major factor, although it may have contributed to the decline (pp. 140–41).

10. R. Kent Guy, *The Emperor's Four Treasures: Scholars and the Rise of the State in the Late Ch'ien-lung Era* (Cambridge, Mass.: Harvard Univ. Press, 1987), p. 37.

11. R. Bin Wong, Theodore Huters, and Pauline Yu, "Introduction: Shifting Paradigms of Political and Social Order," in Huters, Wong, and Yu, *Culture & State in Chinese History: Conventions,* *Accommodations, and Critiques* (Stanford, Calif.: Stanford Univ. Press, 1997), pp. 4–5.

12. Quoted in Ichisada Miyazaki, *China's Examination Hell*, trans. by Conrad Schirokauer (Yale University Press, 1981), pp. 57–58.

13. David L. Rolston, *How to Read the Chinese Novel* (Princeton: Princeton Univ. Press, 1990), p. 14.

14. C. T. Hsia, *The Classical Chinese Novel* (New York: Columbia Univ. Press, 1968), pp. 246 and 264.

15. William Atwell in Frederick W. Mote and D. Twitchett, eds., *The Cambridge History of China*, vol.7 (Cambridge: Cambridge Univ. Press, 1988), p. 587.

16. William T. Rowe, *Hankow: Commerce and Society in a Chinese City, 1796–1889* (Stanford, Calif.: Stanford Univ. Press, 1984), p. 62.

17. Han Liangfu as quoted in Robert B. Marks, *Tigers, Rice, Silk, and Silt: Environment and Economy in Late Imperial South China* (Cambridge: Cambridge Univ. Press, 1998), p. 291.

18. Quoted from the Gazetteer for Chengde (Hunan) in Peter C. Perdue, *Exhausting the Earth: State and Peasant in Hunan, 1500–1850* (Cambridge, Mass.: Harvard Univ. Press, 1987), p. 88.

19. See note 1. Another major factor in Europe's "great divergence" was the proximity of coal to the center of textile production, whereas in China they were far apart.

3

Chosŏn Korea

CHOSŎN DYNASTY

1392   1592   1636   1894 1910

**Invaded
1592/1597/
1627/1636**

**Sino-
Japanese
War**

King Sejong
(1418–1450)

King Yŏngjo   King Chŏngjo
(1724–1776)   (1776–1800)

Korea's Chosŏn dynasty (1392–1910), established in the same century as China's Ming, became by far the longest-lasting regime in East Asia. As noted in Chapter 1, by 1392 Korea already had a long tradition of political independence and cultural borrowing. Though partially colonized once, during the Han dynasty, the Koreans successfully repelled attempts by China's Sui and Tang dynasties to reassert control in the seventh century. After unification under the kingdom of Silla in 668 C.E., the Koreans maintained an autonomous state that covered most of the peninsula. However, they also respected Chinese civilization, emulated many of its cultural patterns, and pursued a policy of loyal submission to the emperor on the Chinese throne.

In the centuries prior to the Chosŏn dynasty, the Korean people consolidated their unique combination of local traditions and imported institutions. The institutional and cultural continuity of the Chosŏn period makes it necessary to begin here with the founding of the dynasty in the fourteenth century and to take the story to the middle of the nineteenth century. Thus the scope of this chapter exceeds the temporal scope of the other chapters in Part I, beginning earlier as well as ending later.

Korea under the Chosŏn dynasty continued developing its own language and literature, art, social structure, economy, and many unique forms of daily life such as food, work patterns, and folk religion. On top of this cultural base, Korea studied Chinese models and adapted Chinese patterns for its higher culture, including government institutions, Confucian philosophy, the Chinese written language, Chinese patterns in art and architecture, and refinements such as the Chinese lunar calendar, Chinese herbal medicine, and Ming clothing styles. These two streams of tradition—the local and the imported—are sometimes referred to as the "Small Tradition" and the "Great Tradition," and they are found in all the nations in the Chinese cultural sphere. Korean culture offers many examples of the conflict, coexistence, and even blending of the two streams, as in Figure 3.1.

FIGURE 3.1 *Sansindo (Mountain Spirit with Tiger)*, 18th-century Korean painting. Themes from Daoism (the mountain hermitage), classical Chinese symbolism (the pine symbolizing endurance), the tiger (a Korean reference), and the mountain spirit (a figure from Korean shamanism) blend in one of the most common representations in all of Korean art. Unidentified artist, Chosŏn Dynasty, 18th Century. Inks and colors on paper.

Choson Dynasty: Foundations

At its beginning, the Chosŏn dynasty replaced the state of Koryŏ, a medieval kingdom that had been subjected to Mongol domination and had suffered serious internal corruption. In its later years, the Koryŏ kingdom's problems included excessive concentrations of power and property in the hands of a relatively few aristocratic families, some of which had ties to the Mongols, and too much influence in the hands of the Buddhist religious establishment. The aristocratic families paid no taxes on their vast estates, called *nongjang*, and their tendency to own large numbers of slaves also cut the number of active taxpayers.

In the fourteenth century, a rising faction of Confucian-educated officials in the Koryŏ capital began calling for reform. Their rise coincided with the rise of the Ming and the fall of the Mongols in China, a change that robbed pro-Mongol elements in Korea of their most important external prop. In 1392 the Koryŏ reform faction overthrew the Koryŏ ruling house and established the new state of Chosŏn. The founder, who is known to history as King T'aejo (1335–1408), moved the royal capital to Hanyang, or modern Seoul, to symbolize a new beginning. He built a new Chinese-style royal palace to symbolize his position as a king (*wang*) within the universe ruled by his superior, the Emperor of China.

Continuing Korea's long practice of submission to the Middle Kingdom, King T'aejo sent tribute envoys to the Ming emperor, and swore that Korea had cut all its ties to the Mongols and that it would not make alliances or have relations with any of China's enemies in the future. The emperor eventually rewarded the Korean monarch with "investiture," (that is, recognition, which was essential to the king's status), valuable gifts, a tacit promise of military support in case of foreign attack, and permission for a certain amount of tributary trade. By the early fifteenth century Sino-Korean relations were on firm footing.

As part of its effort to institutionalize Confucian ethics in the new regime, the government of Chosŏn adopted the Ming criminal code and a council structure for decision making in the royal court. To keep the kings mindful of Confucian values, they were tutored from boyhood and subjected to Chinese-style "royal lectures" (*kyŏngyŏn*). To enforce Confucian virtue in the officialdom, the government set up a censorate to review and criticize the actions of officials, and an inspectorate to uncover corruption and report evildoers to the authorities in the capital.

In their capital, the kings of Chosŏn were assisted by officials organized by rank in six Chinese-style ministries (Personnel, Revenue, Rites, Military, Justice, and Public Works), a number of palace officials including secretaries, advisors, inspectors, censors, tutors, and a coterie of palace staff that included eunuchs, ladies-in-waiting, guards, servants, and government-owned slaves.

The officialdom was organized into two branches, civil and military, with the civil branch exceeding the military in prestige. As in China, the civil service was Chosŏn's most prestigious profession, and families invested much in preparing sons for the examinations that they had to pass in order to qualify for appointment to the bureaucracy. Preparation involved the moral lessons of the Confucian classics, development of a refined style in classical Chinese, which was the written language for all Korean documents, and success in preliminary examinations at the local and provincial levels. Candidates who passed the mid-level literary examinations won the coveted *saengwŏn* or *chinsa* degrees and were eligible to take the capital examinations, known as the *munkwa*, which enabled them to display mastery of the high traditions of history, philosophy, and ethics. Only the most talented and disciplined candidates passed the entire series of examinations and emerged ready to govern. As in China, the Chosŏn examination system was a meritocracy, at least in theory. However, access to the examinations was much more limited than in China: the archives reveal that most of the exam passers at the *munkwa* level were members of Chosŏn's leading families. Thus it appears that Korea's landed aristocracy found ways to protect itself despite the reform impetus of the early Chosŏn period.

The Enlightened Reign of King Sejong (r. 1418–1450)

The early Chosŏn kings promoted Neo-Confucianism as their regime's official ideology. This reflected the Chosŏn founders' distaste for the inflated influence of Buddhism on the Koryŏ court. Though the Chosŏn kingdom's Confucian reforms did not succeed in every respect, they did succeed in giving the kingdom a kind of moral text on which to base all judgments. Chosŏn Neo-Confucianism put much stress on the "encouragement of learning," and there was no better example of the learned scholar-king than King Sejong (r. 1418–1450), the fourth and most celebrated of Chosŏn's twenty-seven monarchs. Sejong sponsored important new studies in history, literature, astronomy, and philosophy by scholars working in a palace institute known as the "Hall of Worthies" (Chiphyŏnjŏn).

They are best remembered for their invention of the alphabet now known as *han'gŭl* ("Korean writing"), an alphabet which has consonants and vowels that are arranged into clusters representing the sounds of word syllables in spoken Korean (see Figure 3.2). This enabled Koreans to put their language into writing accurately and phonetically, as we do with Western alphabets. Over time, Koreans learned to combine the two written styles, using Chinese symbols for words with Chinese roots and *han'gŭl* syllables for Korean-root words and Korean grammatical elements in sentences. This system resembles the mixture of *kana* and Chinese characters used in Japan.

King Sejong enjoyed convening his retinue of scholars and challenging them to explore new avenues of learning. One, Chŏng Inji, wrote an exhaustive history of the entire Koryŏ dynasty (the *Koryŏ-sa*). Others invented a clock, a rain gauge, new ways of calculating mathematics, and various musical instruments. One significant innovation was a font of movable copper type that could be rearranged to

FIGURE 3.2 Handwritten *han'gŭl* script in the thirteen-volume *Strange Encounters on Mount Hwa* (18th century). Page 1, volume 1.

print different texts. This copper font was used to print eight different works between 1403 and 1484. King Sejong's proclamation of the *han'gŭl* alphabet, in a work entitled *The Correct Sounds for the Instruction of the People* (*Hunminjŏng'ŭm* in Korean), was one of the works printed with the experimental copper type.

Chosŏn Dynasty Society

The elite class of Koreans during the Chosŏn period were called *yangban* ("of the two branches"), a term that referred to membership in the civil or military branches of the government. *Yangban* officials and their family members enjoyed public esteem by virtue of their learning, presumed moral fitness, and willingness to shoulder the heavy responsibilities of public service. They also enjoyed material privileges based mainly on land ownership, since official salaries were paid in the form of land grants at the beginning of the dynasty and there was a tradition of investing income in additional land increments. Certain *yangban* families were associated with certain places, clan seats in rural counties where they maintained primary households, often in imposing mansions that looked out over valleys where tenant farmers and slaves worked their land and provided them with income. The ideal *yangban* displayed an attitude of noblesse oblige toward common people in his jurisdiction, sometimes supplying emergency charity. But mainly the *yangban* sought to perpetuate the privileges of their families and class by educating sons to pass the examinations, rise in the officialdom, and win more wealth and power for the clan. Even when the local *yangban* landlords were not actually in office, their social access to the nearby magistrates and governors made them extensions of the power structure. Thus it was rare for any commoner, even if he were a wealthy farmer who amassed enough money to educate his sons, to win acceptance in this self-perpetuating ruling elite.

In addition to officials who passed the examinations, Korea's *yangban* class included *merit subjects,* individuals who had been rewarded by the king for loyal service during times of crisis. Chosŏn's founder, King T'aejo, for example, rewarded several groups of merit subjects for helping him overthrow the previous king and consolidate his own control. His merit subjects were close associates whom he appointed to high positions without making them pass the examinations. Their rewards included permanent tax-free grants of government land and slaves that could be inherited by their children; they became instantly wealthy. Their fast track to power was often resented by "ordinary" *yangban,* giving rise to an undercurrent of conflict between them and their descendants throughout the dynasty. And there was a third door into the *yangban* class for talented young people who could win the favor, or protection ("shade" *ŭm,* Chinese *yin*), of a high official and get recommended for direct appointment. The recommendation system was supposed to provide a way to promote the deserving, but it, too, was a problem because high officials were sometimes known to accept favors in return for their "shade."

The scholar-official-landlord *yangban* class occupied the top rank of Korean society, the rank of people who labored with their minds. Commoners labored with their hands, doing the society's productive work. They paid a share of what they produced to the government in the form of taxes, and many paid a share to their *yangban* landlords and other patrons. Commoners also did the labor service on public works and facilities that was required of every taxpayer for a set number of days every year. And they supplied sons to the military as draftees when there was trouble.

In theory, Chosŏn Korea had a four-tiered class structure along Chinese lines, with the *yangban* at the top, producers (farmers) second, specialists (artisans) third, and the "lowborn" (slaves and people who did distasteful work such as butchers) at the bottom. The Neo-Confucian ethos of the Chosŏn period made fine distinctions between people and their occupations but in practice the greatest gulf was between the *yangban* and everyone else, from peasant landowners to merchants to sharecroppers down to slaves. The incidence of slavery was dramatically higher than in China, where it was limited and largely took the form of household slavery.

Male privilege was also basic to Chosŏn society. The leading families maintained genealogies that carefully documented the history, patriarchy, and relationships of males in the lineage and the fathers-in-law of the lineage's daughters. Because male succession was so important to the continued prosperity of the family, *yangban* men often had secondary wives and concubines to help produce sons. Sons of concubines, however, were discriminated against as something less than fully entitled members of the male line. Though most had educations and many were treated like their "legitimate" brothers, when it came time to perform ancestral rituals or get married or engage in anything that represented the lineage, the sons of concubines suffered direct discrimination. In their careers they were barred from taking the civil service examinations and achieving high office. Instead they had to settle for jobs as clerks and lower-level bureaucrats in the *chung'in* class, positions for which they qualified through specialized examinations called *chapkwa*. Their marriages were arranged with partners who were from secondary lineages, making for continued discrimination that lasted for generations.

Korean patterns of patriarchy, reinforced by the teachings of Confucius, made it necessary for women to defer to the men in their families. *Yangban* women were kept secluded, protected from prying eyes and the attentions of outsiders. Their parents arranged their marriages and the custom was to keep them from meeting their grooms until the actual wedding ceremony, after which they were transferred to their husband's houses as new members of their in-laws' families. They had little say in the matter and no rights to property or decisions about how or where they would live. *Yangban* women were supposed to be models of morality and chastity, and their loyalty to their husbands lasted even into widowhood, since it was unacceptable for a widow to marry a second time.

The Problem of Legitimacy

King Sejong died in 1450 and his son King Munjong reigned only two years before his own death. King Munjong's young son was next in line, and he ascended the throne only to die in exile after a palace coup staged by his uncle, Prince Suyang, who became King Sejo, ruling from 1455 to 1468. Sejo's usurpation of the throne was widely regarded as a crime, and to consolidate his power he had to fend off condemnation by many of Chosŏn's most respected elders and reward his supporters with merit subject titles and lavish grants of land and slaves. This created an instant faction and began a rivalry between the lineages of the two brothers, Kings Munjong and Sejo. King Sejo punished many of his critics, but the controversy raged for several generations.

Sejo usurped the throne of Chosŏn at a time when the legitimacy of the dynasty itself was still in question. Its founder, King T'aejo, had been guilty of usurpation in 1392, and for more than a decade thereafter the imperial court in China had regarded him with suspicion. The first Ming Emperor never granted him investiture: it was not until 1403 that the Yongle Emperor finally recognized Chosŏn by investing the third king of the dynasty. The question of the regime's legitimacy was so sensitive a subject that King Sejong had made it a major theme of one of his reign's greatest literary works, *Songs of the Dragons Flying to Heaven*

(*Yongbi ŏch'ŏn'ga*), which compared his ancestors to the greatest of China's imperial ancestors. Much of King Sejong's emphasis on history—in particular his commissioning of the Koryŏ-sa—had been aimed at providing justification for his
grandfather's usurpation of the Koryŏ throne in 1392. Now, scarcely more than
sixty years later, the legitimacy of the ruling house was again in doubt because of
King Sejo's coup.

The collective power of the *yangban* class as they argued over this problem is
evidence of the weakness of the position of the monarchy in Korea as compared to
that of the emperor in China. The Korean king had to win and maintain support
from several quarters, beginning with the emperor but including factions of the
yangban aristocracy and his own Korean officials, whose help he needed in order
to govern. King Sejo tried to bolster the authority of the throne at the expense of
the *yangban* by packing his court with newly named merit subjects, by making it
harder for *yangban* to accumulate land through inheritance, and by subjecting the
yangban to taxation. These were unpopular moves that further alienated the country's landed elite and generated animosities that fueled factional infighting for
many years to come.

Intellectual Flowering in the Sixteenth Century

During the sixteenth century, Korea produced several significant Neo-Confucian philosophers. One of these was Yi Hwang (better known by his literary name of
T'oegye) (1501–1570), Korea's foremost proponent of the ideas of Zhu Xi, and a
scholar who occupies an analogous position to Zhu Xi in the history of Korean
thought. T'oegye is best known for his *Ten Diagrams on Sage Learning,* which ex-
plicates "the essential framework of, and linkage among, Neo-Confucian metaphysics, psychological theory, moral conduct, and spiritual discipline."[1] T'oegye,
like Zhu Xi before him, stressed disciplined study of the textual tradition to appre-
hend principle (*i*, Chinese *li*) and thus to know how to live a principled life. He is
also famous for his part in the "four-seven debate," which pertains to the origins
of and relation between, on the one hand, the "four beginnings"—humanity, righteousness, propriety, and wisdom—which Mencius had taught were inherent in all
people, and the "seven feelings" (desire, hate, love, fear, grief, anger, and joy).
T'oegye separated the "beginnings" and "feelings" at their source, and presented
an argument that is too abstract and subtle to lend itself to brief summation.

T'oegye's younger contemporary Yi I (better known as Yulgok) (1536–1584),
argued a different view, which was to place primary emphasis not on "principle" but
on "material force," or "matter" (*ki*, Chinese *qi*). The differences between T'oegye
and Yulgok reflected a highly refined version of the ancient philosophical debate in
East Asia that appears in many forms, including the complementary halves of the
symbol for *yang* and *yin.* They were struggling for a better understanding of what it
means to be human and spiritual at the same time. Their scholarship and refined

moral tone made them famous as Korean exemplars of Confucian learning, and even today their works are widely read and they are important national figures.

The second half of the sixteenth century saw the foundation of numerous local academies, or *sŏwŏn*, that were typically headed by a famous *yangban*-class teacher who taught his protégés his own theories on philosophical problems like the Four-Seven debate. The first of these was T'oegye's own *sŏwŏn* near the town of Andong, a center for scholars who were interested in his theories about the primacy of principle. The government recognized T'oegye's *sŏwŏn* by granting it a royal charter that exempted it from tax, among other privileges. Before long, other *sŏwŏn* were springing up around the country, some founded by disgruntled members of *yangban* out-factions. The founder or leading scholar of each *sŏwŏn* was regarded with reverence by his disciples, and his theories on philosophy and politics became the *sŏwŏn* scholars' central ideas, to be defended in debates with scholars from rival academies. Chosŏn-era *sŏwŏn*, like their counterparts in Ming China, became headquarters for political cliques as ambitious young scholars competed to put their teachers' versions of Neo-Confucian theory into practice by getting themselves appointed to office. The rivalries drew on philosophical differences like the ones that had occupied T'oegye and Yulgok; however, the personal loyalties and regional political conflicts that complicated the debates and turned them into petty, even violent, feuds doubtless would have displeased the two great scholars.

The Imjin War and the Manchu Invasions

The worst crisis ever to face the kingdom of Chosŏn occurred in the 1590s when Japan invaded the peninsula as part of a war to establish hegemony over Korea and China. The invasion was launched in 1592 (the year with the name "Imjin" in the Korean calendar) by Toyotomi Hideyoshi, after he had completed the unification of Japan, and it made use of experienced samurai veterans of the war for unification. In the first assault, an estimated 160,000 Japanese troops, many of them carrying firearms, landed near Pusan on the southeast coast and fought their way through southern Korea as far as Seoul. Though the Korean royal army resisted, the kingdom was caught unprepared for the invasion. King Sŏnjo (r. 1567–1608) was forced to abandon his capital and flee to the Manchurian border, where he appealed to the Ming for military assistance. Chinese armies intervened and stopped the Japanese advance at P'yŏngyang.

Korea, meanwhile, had been turned into a battlefield. The failure of Korean army defenses forced civilians to bear the brunt of the fighting. *Yangban* landlords, common farmers, and even Buddhist monks rallied villagers into informal militia units and fought heroic rear-guard actions. These "righteous troops" (*ŭibyŏng*) occupied much of the invading army and inflicted significant damage, even though they were usually defeated by the better-armed Japanese.

To keep their troops supplied and reinforced, the Japanese had to cross the straits separating the islands from the Korean peninsula (see Figure 3.3). On the south coast of Korea a *yangban* official named Yi Sunsin took advantage of Japanese vulnerability on the sea and distinguished himself with a naval campaign that

FIGURE 3.3 Korea during the Chosŏn dynasty.

sank many Japanese ships and disrupted the invaders' supply lines. To enable his boats to fend off arrows and fire bombs so they could attack at close range, he covered their decks with canopies made of copper, giving rise to the name "turtle ships" (Korean: *kŏbuksŏn*). Using oarsmen below decks, he maneuvered his turtle boats around the islands and narrow waterways of the south coast, drawing the Japanese into traps where he was able to outmaneuver and destroy them. His success in these battles earned him a reputation for great daring and military skill, and he died a hero in the last engagement of the war off Hansan Island in 1598.

Japan's invasion of the mainland stalled with the Battle of P'yŏngyang, and it was not until 1597 that Hideyoshi sent a second wave. This too was a failure, and Japan called off the war when Hideyoshi died in 1598. Korea, meanwhile, suffered greatly. Many Koreans died in the fighting or were captured or kidnapped and taken to Japan. There was much vandalism and looting. Many of Korea's remaining Buddhist temples were ransacked and burned, their precious gold-leafed images and paintings being stolen not only by the Japanese enemy but also by the "friendly" Chinese. In Seoul itself, when the king and royal court fled the city just before it fell to the invading Japanese, Korean citizens, reacting to being abandoned by their ruler, attacked the central palace and set it ablaze, after which it lay in ruins until the 1860s.

The war in Korea coincided with the rise of the Manchus under their powerful new chief Nurgaci, whose sons went on to destroy the Ming and establish the Qing dynasty in China. Part of the Manchu strategy required forcing the Koreans to break their ties with the Ming and switch their support. For a short time the Koreans managed a balancing act between their commitment as a Ming tributary state and the need to placate the Manchus. However, when the Koreans briefly tried to side with the Ming in the 1620s, the Manchus invaded. In 1627 they extorted a promise that Korea would behave like a loyal younger brother to the Manchu ruler. However, when the Koreans refused to receive a Manchu envoy and gave signs of going back on their promise, the Manchus invaded again, in 1636. In their second invasion they penetrated all the way to Seoul and forced King Injo to surrender. Chosŏn had to break relations with the Ming, send troops to help the Manchus conquer the Ming, accept the newly founded Qing empire as its suzerain and offer tribute, and give the Manchus two of the king's eldest sons as hostages.

Although the Manchus wreaked less havoc in Korea than the Japanese a generation earlier, the humiliation of being forced to submit to people whom the Koreans had always regarded as barbarians was a severe blow to the morale of the Korean monarchy and ruling class. They were never comfortable with the Manchus as their overlords, and although they carried on correct tributary relations until the 1890s, internally they continued to mourn for the Ming as their legitimate "older brother." To symbolize this they engaged in quiet forms of protest such as numbering the dates on their internal documents according to the defunct Ming calendar and wearing clothing and hair styles from the Ming period.

Struggles within the Yangban Class

Military defeats at the hands of the Japanese and Manchus caused the government of Chosŏn to reorganize its military defenses. The Office of Border Defense grew in importance and actually emerged as a key decision-making body. Much attention was paid to conscription and training, and a new system of garrisons was put in place. Though the army eventually evolved into a force devoted mainly to suppressing internal rebellion, the effort to raise an effective defense represented a positive response to the bitter experiences of the early 1600s.

The invasions of Korea happened just as its government was embroiled in a major power struggle among political factions. Before the Japanese invasion there were "Easterners" (Tong'in) and "Westerners" (Sŏ'in), so named for the location of their residences in the capital city. No sooner had the "Easterners" achieved ascendancy and purged the "Westerners" than they proceeded to divide into "Northern" (Pugin) and "Southern" (Namin) subfactions over the question of a successor to King Sŏnjo, who died without an heir in 1608. The Northerners won, and put King Kwanghae on the throne, only to see him overthrown in 1623 by the Westerners, who had been biding their time on the sidelines. The Westerners then spent most of the seventeenth century feuding with the Southerner subfaction; but when they won decisively in 1694, they too proceeded to split into sub-factions: the "Old Doctrine" (Noron) and the "New Doctrine" (Soron). The infighting was about power, but the factions took positions based on ethical interpretations. For example, one debate between the Southerners and Westerners concerned the length of time a king's mother should spend mourning the death of her son. Another concerned whether the son of a royal concubine could be named crown prince. In the competitive atmosphere of Chosŏn politics people drew little distinction between a person's political beliefs and his moral virtue. Dissent was dangerous, and criticizing a person's politics was very close to attacking his moral virtue. When political disagreements were defined in moral terms there was little incentive for compromise. Instead, the process created winners and losers, with the winners trying to purge the losers and prevent their ever returning to office. Sometimes this led to actual killing. When a group lost power it retired to the countryside, often to a *sŏwŏn*, where it brooded and plotted revenge.

Korea in the Eighteenth Century

Much is made of the factional feuding that plagued the Chosŏn dynasty's middle years and the weakness and confusion that it produced. However, the same period saw considerable intellectual vitality. The feuding cooled during the eighteenth century under two particularly able Chosŏn kings, Yŏngjo (r. 1724–1776) and his grandson Chŏngjo (r. 1776–1800). After fifty turbulent years during which the kingdom of Chosŏn seemed to reach its nadir, King Yŏngjo reinvigorated the government by asserting himself as a model Confucian sage-ruler. He mastered the classics and was recognized as a scholar in his own right. He used court ceremonies and the rituals of Confucian culture to uplift public life. He inspired people by putting his policy of *tangp'yŏng* ("pacifying-the-factions") into effect, quieting the rivalries among the four main factions—the Old Doctrine, New Doctrine, Northerners, and Southerners—by ordering proportional appointments to the bureaucracy in a way designed to prevent any one group from acquiring dominance.

King Yŏngjo also effected economic reforms, including a halving of the military cloth tax on commoners and the institution of a land tax. The years of disruption had created a serious social problem in the form of "wandering" (that is, homeless) people. One of the causes had been the crushing burden of taxation on free commoner-landlords. King Yǒngjo's reform was an attempt to spread the burden around more equally and it was partially successful. *Yangban* landlords, however, continued to find ways to pay less than their fair share.

As a strong ruler, King Yǒngjo might have gone down in history as a great king, but his reign was tainted by one shocking and controversial act. In 1762, the king put his own son, Crown Prince Sado, to death after a chain of events that showed the prince to be deranged and possibly plotting to kill Yǒngjo himself. The killing of his only son was technically within King Yǒngjo's rights as monarch, particularly since the prince was guilty of a number of murders, but the deed was not accepted by everyone in the royal court. They split into critics and defenders of the prince's execution, forming new factional combinations that launched a new era of political infighting. When Yǒngjo passed from the scene in 1776, he was succeeded by the dead prince's son, who became King Chǒngjo. King Chǒngjo complicated the issue by honoring the spirit of his dead father, making obvious his criticism of King Yǒngjo. The royal family itself was torn by these developments, and once again the dynasty suffered a legitimacy crisis.

FIGURE 3.4 Landscape, Shin Yunbok (mid-18th to early 19th centuries). Chosǒn dynasty, early 19th century. Ink and light colors on paper, 25.2 × 15.5 cm.

Ho-Am Art Museum, Seoul, Korea.

The Cultural Environment of Late Chosǒn

While these political events were occurring in the eighteenth century, Korea experienced a renaissance in fields ranging from literature to art to philosophy. While continuing to follow Chinese models, Koreans also refined their own creations. A good example is the work of the painters Kim Hongdo (b. 1745) and Shin Yunbok (b. 1758). Kim Hongdo's paintings showed children in school and at play and ordinary working people in everyday situations, some of them humorous. Shin Yunbok's favorite themes were social and romantic, and often featured *kisaeng* courtesans performing for male patrons in *yangban* costumes (see Figure 3.4). Kim Hongdo was the more formal of the two and produced classical landscapes, plums, orchids, and lotus flowers in addition to more whimsical themes such as the tiger in Figure 3.5. Koreans appreciate both artists for their honoring of their native culture. Their genre paintings are today some of the most descriptive documents of Korean life in the 1700s.

On the more formal side, Kings Yǒngjo and Chǒngjo sponsored court artists who were commissioned to produce inspirational works that encouraged reason, respect, and an aesthetic appreciation of tradition and discipline. The kings themselves led austere lives and the artists in their painting academy, called the Tohwawŏn were expected to do likewise. Their works include screens depicting the orderly rituals of court life, portraits of worthy officials, and depictions of virtuous and unselfish acts.

Ceramics also flourished as did ink painting. Bamboo, which bends but does not break, and the plum, which alone blooms in the dead of winter, were East Asian symbols of the upright and stalwart gentleman who maintains his principles even under the most dire circumstances. Thus they are fitting decorations for the accouterments found on a scholar's desk (see Figure 3.6).

The era also brought advances in literature written in *han'gŭl* script. This followed many years during which King Sejong's alphabet was little used. Korean writers, who were mainly *yangban* schooled in the Chinese classics, had actually scorned the alphabet as too simple and too limiting, and they had continued to write in the much more difficult Chinese characters. It took many years and a great deal of money

FIGURE 3.5 *Tiger and Pine Tree*, Kim Hongdo (1745–1806?). Chosŏn dynasty, late 18th century. Ink and light colors on silk, 90.4 × 43.8 cm.

Ho-Am Art Museum, Seoul, Korea.

FIGURE 3.6 Cyclindrical water-dropper with design of bamboo and prunus (plums). Water-droppers were used when mixing ink in the inkstones. An indispensable item on a Korean and East Asian scholar's desk, water-droppers formed an artistic genre of their own. Unidentified artist, porcelain, underglaze in blue, diameter 9 cm. Korean, Chosŏn dynasty, 18th century.

Gift of Colonel John R. Fox, Courtesy of Herbert F. Johnson Museum of Art, Cornell University (65.219).

to learn to write Chinese well. Few people who were not *yangban*-class men could afford this kind of education. Accordingly, the few who could write Chinese were able to use literacy and their writing ability as a social barrier, protecting their privileged position while denying basic communications skills to the less fortunate.

In the eighteenth century, however, the educated women who belonged to the royal family, along with other cultured women of the *yangban* class, began to write their own literature, not in Chinese but in the Korean *han'gŭl* alphabet. Their works were diaries, memoirs, and stories about palace life, written in the Korean language and far more expressive of the emotions and conflicts that were a part of daily life. Certain commoners also learned *han'gŭl* well enough to write stories and novels. These works survive as commentaries on life in the *yangban*-dominated Chosŏn kingdom. By the turn of the nineteenth century, *han'gŭl* had become a tool for non-*yangban* to communicate and even organize rebellions against their rulers.

The *yangban* class, however, was not without its own reformers. The Chinese Neo-Confucian philosopher Zhu Xi had taught that truth could be found through a better understanding of reality—"the investigation of things," as he called it. By the eighteenth century certain *yangban* groups had become highly critical of their own class and its grip on Korean wealth and institutions. In the seventeenth century, the *yangban* scholar Yu Hyŏngwŏn conducted extensive studies on Korean society, beginning with the agricultural system, and concluded that thorough reform was called for in the system of official appointments, national defense, and the land system. His great treatise, *Pan'gye Surok*, is a catalog of Chosŏn's institutions and their workings, and it inspired later scholars to seek their own reforms. Analysts and reformers in this school of thought came to be known as the *Silhak* ("Practical Learning") school. Taking the agricultural system as the basic enterprise of the Korean people, they concentrated their attention on the farming class of commoners who actually worked the land. The conditions in which they worked, verging on serfdom in many cases, was of great concern to the *Silhak* scholars, who began to think in terms of justice and security for workers, generating ideas that threatened the privileges of the landholding *yangban* class. Since criticism of the social and economic system amounted to an attack on the *yangban*, the *Silhak* scholars were seen as subversive.

One variant of the *Silhak* school was a group of Korean scholars who had traveled to China and were familiar with different ways of doing things in other countries. Since the road to China led northward, they were known as the "Northern School" (*Pukhak*). *Pukhak* scholars pointed out that the Chinese themselves were adaptable and not afraid of change when circumstances called for it. They attacked the nonproductive *yangban* class and the kingdom's social system. Using Zhu Xi's teaching about the "investigation of things," they sought better understandings of reality. They were open-minded enough to experiment with Catholicism, which had acquired a foothold in Beijing through the Jesuit presence that began in 1583. This window on the West suggested new ways of understanding many things, including astronomy, mathematics, health, and social ethics. It even led a small circle of *Silhak* scholars to found a secret branch of the Catholic religion in Korea, in 1784.

The Crisis of the Nineteenth Century

Conflict between reform-minded officials and established *yangban* interests in the royal court is one major theme of Korean politics in the nineteenth century. The *Silhak* scholars suffered retribution for their departures from established orthodoxy. The Catholic community especially was viewed with suspicion because of its loyalty to a foreign faith as well as its associations with out-factions in the Choson political system. Bloody anti-Catholic purges took place in 1801, 1811, 1849, and 1866 and thousands of believers lost their lives.

Throughout the Choson dynasty, Korean society experienced shifts in the social structure. In the seventeenth and eighteenth century, for example, many slaves won their freedom, either by buying it or by leaving their owners and becoming wanderers and commoners, in effect, selling their labor for wages. Another, opposite, trend was the difficulty experienced by *yangban* families in keeping their high social status when they were unable to produce sons who could find their way into government office. By 1800 there were many nominal *yangban* who had little means and had lost most of their property and prestige. In the meantime, the barriers that had prevented the sons of *yangban* men and concubines from attaining office had broken down. Significant numbers of concubines' sons had been permitted to take jobs as government specialists (for example, clerks, accountants, legal specialists) under the permissive rules of King Chongjo's administration. These specialists sparked the growth of a new class of "middle persons" (*chung'in*), who were fundamentally interested in social reform because of their own social positions. Many of Korea's earliest Catholics were from the *chung'in* class, attracted by the religious idea that all are equal before the throne of God.

The impetus to change was fueled in the early nineteenth century by the growing autonomy of large landlords in the provinces. In the southwestern Cholla provinces and in the northwest near the Chinese border, the power of local *yangban* came to exceed the power of the central government, and they sent growing numbers of sons to pass the examinations and take more prominent places in the central bureaucracy. Change was also on the minds of ordinary workers such as farmers and miners, who raised the standard of revolt several times during the early nineteenth century. While the royal court continued to be preoccupied with factional politics and the struggles between the royal line and powerful families, such as the ones that supplied queens for the successive kings, the country as a whole experienced a ripening for reform generated by many different constituencies. This pressure for change was significant by the mid nineteenth century and coincided with the arrival of Western military and cultural forces in China and Japan that served as catalysts for change in Korea's neighbors. The Koreans themselves tried for a time to resist being influenced by these outside developments. Their failure in this and the rapid intervention of foreign influence created the conditions for Choson's decline in the late 1800s.

Note

1. Peter H. Lee and W. Theodore de Bary, eds. *Sources of Korean Tradition,* vol. 1 (New York: Columbia Univ. Press, 1997), p. 350.

Tokugawa Japan

4

| 1568 | 1600 | 1651 | 1787 |

**EARLY
TOKUGAWA**

**TOKUGAWA SHOGUNATE:
THE MIDDLE YEARS**

**Period of
Unification**

| Momoyama (1568–1600 or 1615) | Persecution of Christians (1614) | Japan Closed to Foreigners (1630) | | Genroku (1688–1704) | Kyōhō Reforms (1716–1736) |

Unification (1573–1600)

Consolidation (1600–1651)

Bakufu–Han Relations

Economic and Social Change

Classes and Values

The Aesthetic Culture of the Aristocracy

Genroku Urban Culture

The Print

Theater and Literature

Intellectual Currents: Confucianism

Historiography and Nativisim

Dutch Learning

Reform and Its Limits

Art and Literature after
the Genroku Period

During its formative years Japan had drawn deeply on Chinese models, often as mediated by Korea, but by the time the Tokugawa Shogunate was founded in 1600, it had been blending the imported and the native for over a millennium, developing its own ways and institutions. Under the Tokugawa, Japan enjoyed peace, experienced economic growth, delighted in a vibrant urban culture, and engaged in an intense intellectual life. This chapter considers its origins in the period of unification, its early and its middle years. By the time the stresses inherent in the system began to tear it apart, it had developed foundations for a very different future.

Unification (1573–1600)

Although Chinese influence still ran deep in Japan, from around the middle of the ninth century, the trajectory of political and social change diverged from that of the continent as Japan, alone in East Asia, experienced the rise to dominance of a warrior class. Known as *bushi* or *samurai,* the warriors belonged to a hierarchy bonded by ties of vassalage culminating in a hereditary leader, the shogun. While the shogun's power was basically military, his legitimacy came from the emperor, who traced his descent to the Sun Goddess and retained an aura of sanctity. The emperor held court in Kyoto, his capital since 794, attended by an aristocracy that continued to set standards of refined culture long after it had lost political and economic power. Meanwhile, the shoguns administered their affairs through the *bakufu*, a term originally designating a military field-headquarters, but used for the shogun's government.

The first *bakufu* was the Kamakura Shogunate (1185–1333), located in the city of that name in Eastern Japan. It was succeeded by the Ashikaga Shogunate (1336–1573), which ruled from Kyoto and ended in a century of warfare (1467–1573) during which feudal lords (*daimyo*) strove to preserve or enlarge their domains (*han*), turning them into small states centered around castle-towns. The trend was for the samurai to become concentrated in these castle-towns, supported by stipends from their *daimyo,* rather than continuing to live on the land. Thus the fragmentation of Japan into virtually independent domains was accompanied by increased centralization within the individual domains.

The restoration of central authority leading to the establishment of a third dynasty of shoguns was a cumulative process, directed by three leaders each building on the work of his predecessors. The first was Oda Nobunaga (1534–1582), known for his ruthlessness in destroying enemies, including militant Buddhists, and for his use of firearms, first introduced by shipwrecked Portuguese in 1543. By the time he was assassinated by one of his own generals, he controlled about a third of Japan.

Toyotomi Hideyoshi, the invader of Korea (see Chapter 3), was born a peasant but rose to become one of Nobunaga's generals. After defeating his rivals for the succession, he continued to amass power, inducing *daimyo* to acknowledge his supremacy by arms, marriage politics, and diplomacy. Unable to subdue the strongest *daimyo*, Tokugawa Ieyasu, he gave his sister to Ieyasu in marriage and assigned him substantial holdings in the East (Kanto), thus assuring that Ieyasu was both content and at a distance. Hideyoshi also relocated his own vassals, placing the most trusted in strategic positions and discouraging those thought to harbor territorial ambitions by providing them with hostile neighbors. To demonstrate their loyalty, vassals were sometimes required to leave wives and children with Hideyoshi as virtual hostages. By 1590 all *daimyo* had sworn oaths of loyalty to him and he was, in effect, overlord of all Japan.

Hideyoshi was intent on keeping the *daimyo* in their places but not eliminating them. On the contrary, his policies strengthened the *daimyo* locally vis-a-vis their warriors and farmers, even as he took steps to assure their subordination. When a *daimyo* was relocated, he took many of his vassals with him into his new domain where they had no hereditary links to the land, accelerating the tendency for samurai to be concentrated in castle-towns.

In his "sword hunt" of 1588 Hideyoshi ordered all peasants who had not already done so to surrender their weapons, the metal to be used in building a great statue of the Buddha. This was followed in 1591 by class-separation edicts prohibiting fighting men from becoming peasants or townsmen, forbidding peasants from leaving their fields and becoming merchants or artisans, and preventing the latter from becoming farmers. Hideyoshi, himself risen from the peasantry to the greatest heights, sought to make sure that henceforth everyone would remain within his hereditary social status. Although in theory applicable everywhere, in practice confiscation of swords and implementation of the class-separation edicts was up to the local *daimyo*, who determined the degree and pace of compliance based on their assessment of local conditions.

Another far-reaching measure was the land survey (1582–1598) conducted to assess cultivated land in terms of average annual productivity, measured in *koku* of rice (4.96 bushels). Again, individual domains varied in the degree of implementation, but the holdings of each *daimyo* were now calculated in terms of the assessed value of his domain rather than acreage. From this time on, a *daimyo*, by definition, held land assessed at a minimum of 10,000 *koku*. Wealthy *daimyo* held much more than that. Some had several hundred thousand *koku*, and there were a few with over a million. Hideyoshi personally held 2 million, not including those of his wealthiest, most trustworthy vassals. Tokugawa Ieyasu held 2,555,000.

Hideyoshi's vision of the world and his own place in it extended well beyond Japan. He took an active interest in overseas trade and suppressed the pirates and freebooters who had long plagued the Chinese and Korean coasts. One of his two great castles was at Osaka (see Figure 4.1), which soon eclipsed nearby Sakai as a trading center, and remains today the largest city in western Japan.

But Hideyoshi looked abroad for more than trade: he thought in terms of empire. In the 1590s, he demanded the submission of the Philippines by their Spanish governor, although he never enforced this demand. He also planned to conquer China and divide it among his vassals. After China would come India and the rest of the world as he knew it. His invasion of the continent can partially be seen

FIGURE 4.1 Japan c. 1664.

as an attempt to satisfy the perpetual land hunger of his vassals or, at least, to find employment for restive samurai. It would also convince everyone of Hideyoshi's power. Another factor was his personality, but Jurgis Elisonas has suggested that "not so much megalomania as ignorance moved the entire enterprise."[1]

Whatever Hideyoshi's motivation, the outcome was a disaster. Similarly, his hopes to found a dynasty came to naught. He left his five-year-old son and heir in the care of regents who had their own ambitions. The winner in the ensuing struggle for supremacy was Ieyasu (1542–1616). He was appointed shogun in 1603, but this merely confirmed the hegemony he had established at the decisive battle of Sekigahara in 1600, a victory marking the effective beginning of the Tokugawa Shogunate.

Consolidation (1600–1651)

Ieyasu devised the essential structure of the Tokugawa political system, drawing on the heritage of Hideyoshi; his two immediate successors, Hidetada (1616–1623) and Iemitsu (1623–1651), completed it. By the middle of the seventeenth century, the system was in full operation.

Ieyasu rose to supremacy as the leader of a group of *daimyo*, each backed by his own vassals and supported by an independent power base. Appointment by the emperor as shogun gave Ieyasu legitimacy. The *daimyo*, however, were by no means all deeply committed to the Tokugawa. Hideyoshi's recent failure to establish a dynasty had demonstrated the folly of relying solely on the loyalty of such men, especially when passing on the succession to a minor. Ieyasu himself assured the smooth transfer of power to his son by resigning from the office of shogun in 1605, after holding it for only two years. But he continued in actual control until his death.

All the *daimyo* were the shogun's vassals, bound to him by solemn oath. When a *daimyo's* heir succeeded to his domain, the new *daimyo* had to sign his pledge of vassalage to the shogun in blood. Still, some vassals were more reliable than others, and the Tokugawa classified them into three groups. Least trusted and potentially the most dangerous were the "outside," or allied, *daimyo (tozama)*, who were too powerful to be considered Tokugawa subordinates. Some had supported Ieyasu at the battle of Sekigahara, but others came over to the Tokugawa only after the outcome of that battle left them no other choice. More trustworthy were the "house" *daimyo (fudai)*, most of whom had been family vassals raised to *daimyo* status by the Tokugawa and who thus were indebted to the *bakufu* for their status and domains. The third group, the "collateral" *daimyo (shimpan)*, belonged to Tokugawa branch families eligible to supply a shogun if there were no heir from the main line. The Tokugawa also had its direct retainers on its own lands. Some of these held fiefs of less than the 10,000 *koku* required for *daimyo* status, and many received stipends directly from the *bakufu*.

When Ieyasu was transferred to the Kanto region by Hideyoshi, he chose as his headquarters the centrally located village of Edo (modern Tokyo), then consisting of about a hundred houses. The shogunate also maintained castles at Osaka and Shizuoka (then called Sumpu) as well as the Nijō Castle in Kyoto, residence of a *bakufu* official responsible for governing the city and serving concurrently as the shogun's representative at the imperial court. To secure itself militarily, the Tokugawa placed its house *daimyo* strategically to dominate the Kanto, central Japan, and the Kyoto-Osaka area, while relegating the outside *daimyo* to outlying areas. To keep the *daimyo* weak, they were limited to one castle each and needed *bakufu* permission before they could repair this castle. They were allowed only a fixed number of men-at-arms and forbidden to build large ships. To prevent alliances that might threaten the *bakufu*, the *daimyo* had to obtain its assent for their marriage plans.

During the first half of the seventeenth century the shogunate further increased its strength at *daimyo* expense. In this period there were 281 cases in which daimyo were transferred from one fief to another, shuffles which strengthened some and weakened others. Another 213 domains were confiscated outright. This could happen when a lord proved incompetent or a domain was torn by a succession dispute. More often confiscation resulted from failure to produce an heir. Deathbed adoptions were not recognized. By such means the Tokugawa more than tripled their holdings to 6.8 million *koku*, about a fourth of Japan. The distribution of their holdings also favored the Tokugawa economically, as they included many important cities such as Osaka, Kyoto, and Nagoya. In the mid-Tokugawa period, collateral *daimyo* held land worth 2.6 million *koku*, house *daimyo*, 6.7 million, and outside *daimyo*, 9.8 million. Religious institutions held around 600,000 *koku*, and the emperor and the court could draw on land worth only 187,000 *koku*.

To see to it that the *daimyo* obeyed *bakufu* orders, the shogun had his own inspectors. He also kept the *daimyo* under surveillance by requiring them to spend alternate years in residence in Edo. When they returned to their domains, they had to leave their wives and children behind. This system of alternate attendance (*sankin kōtai*) forced the *daimyo* to spend large sums traveling back and forth with their retinues and to maintain suitably elaborate residences in Edo. They were also called on to support public projects such as waterworks or the repair of the shogun's castle at Edo, but such exactions were not as burdensome as the constant expense of alternate attendance. This requirement turned Edo into the capital not only of the *bakufu* but of all Japan.

The shogun's dual role as feudal overlord and the emperor's deputy made him responsible for the conduct of foreign affairs. The early *bakufu* also reserved for itself the right to issue paper money. It even issued regulations for the dress of the *daimyo* and in 1635 declared "all matters are to be carried out in accordance with the laws of Edo,"[2] though that sounds like wishful thinking. The *bakufu* usually interfered only when a *daimyo* proved incompetent or when an issue involved more than one domain.

Bakufu–Han Relations

Whatever the shogun might wish, the *daimyo* remained largely free to manage affairs in their own *han*. The tendency of *daimyo* and their samurai to identify with their own domain, at times even generating *han* chauvinism, was strongest among the outside *daimyo*, but the others also focused on managing their *han*. Thus they had a stake in maintaining and enlarging the decentralized aspect of the larger political system. Under the fourth shogun, Ietsuna (1651–1680), the *daimyo* regained much lost ground. *Bakufu* policy was reversed. There was a drastic decline in the number of *daimyo* transferred and *han* confiscated. Deathbed adoptions were recognized as legitimate. The shogunate even began permitting *han* to issue their own paper money. A proliferation of local currencies ensued. To protect their own money, some *han* in the eighteenth century prohibited the use of outside currencies—including the *bakufu*'s money!

The vigorous but eccentric fifth shogun, Tsunayoshi (1680–1709), presided over a reassertion of *bakufu* power, which earned him the enmity of the *daimyo* and lasting ignominy and ridicule. He was an easy target, for he carried to an extreme his Buddhist devotion to the preservation of animal life and especially his solicitude for dogs, sometimes even at the cost of human life. This earned him the epithet "dog shogun." Nevertheless, his period saw a great flowering of culture as well as a resurgence of centralizing activity. But this did not lead to a permanent shift in the power balance nor did it initiate a long-term trend toward greater *bakufu* control. If it had, this shogun's historical image would have been different.

Until the end of the Tokugawa, the pendulum continued to swing between the *bakufu* and the *han*. In his analysis of the history and dynamics of this process, Harold Bolitho has shown that periods of *bakufu* assertiveness tended to occur under vigorous shoguns working with trusted advisors drawn from among the shogunate's low-ranking retainers. Unencumbered by fief or vassals, totally dependent on the shogun, they became his men, free from potential conflicts of interest. Under such regimes, the high-ranking Senior Councilors, always selected from among the house *daimyo*, *(fudai)*, were treated with an outward show of respect while they were actually bypassed and disregarded. Little love was lost between the *fudai* and the new men.

When the shogun was a minor or an incompetent, control over the *bakufu* reverted to the Senior Councilors, descendants of the Tokugawa's most favored and highly trusted vassals. The service of these vassals had formed the core of Ieyasu's strength, and he relied on their descendants for continued loyal service to his house. While these men were conscious of their heritage of special obligations toward the shogunate, they also had responsibilities and opportunities as *daimyo*. The tensions between shogunate and *han* were mirrored in their own persons as they faced the often conflicting demands of *bakufu* and *han*. The usual pattern was for them to act more as *daimyo* than as bakufu officials. Such Senior Councilors were not prepared to sacrifice *han* privileges for the sake of the larger body politic. There were even cases of *han* held by incumbent Senior Councilors refusing to export grain badly needed to combat famine elsewhere. There were periodic shifts in the balance of power between the *bakufu* and the *han*, but the issue was never resolved completely in favor of one or the other. It can be argued that this proved beneficial in the long run since it allowed for considerable divergence while still maintaining a center.

The more than 250 *han* varied widely in size, natural resources, and local conditions. All the lands held by a *daimyo* were not necessarily contiguous; some domains were more easily organized than others. But in general, operating on a smaller scale than the *bakufu*, the *daimyo* were more successful in controlling their retainers. The trend for the samurai to be concentrated in the *han* capitals divorced from the land continued strong. By the last decade of the seventeenth century over 80% of the *daimyo* were paying stipends to their samurai. By the end of the eighteenth century 90% of samurai were entirely dependent on their stipends. Only 10% still retained local roots in the country.

Economic and Social Change

During the Tokugawa peace made economic growth possible. There was a rise in demand to meet the needs of the samurai and the growing expenses of the *daimyo*. The system of alternate attendance stimulated the commercialization of agriculture, and agricultural productivity increased substantially, especially in the seventeenth century. Cultivated acreage doubled thanks to vigorous irrigation and land reclamation. Technological improvements, the practice of multiple cropping, better seed strains, and improved fertilizers helped, as did the dissemination of knowledge through agricultural handbooks and manuals. The spread of market networks was accompanied by regional specialization in cash crops such as cotton, mulberry trees for the rearing of silk worms, indigo, tobacco, and sugar cane, but grain continued to be grown in all parts of Japan.

Population rose from about 18 million at the beginning of the Tokugawa to around 30 million by the middle of the period. Afterwards there were fluctuations in population, but there was no major long-term increase during the rest of Tokugawa; in 1872 the population stood at only 33.1 million. Although famine and disease took their toll, mortality rates were comparatively low, and the average life span was very likely longer than in premodern Europe, since Japan was free from war and less susceptible to epidemics. Late marriage, the custom of having only one son marry and inherit, as well as abortion and infanticide kept population growth under control. Family planning was widespread. Even when times were good, life was by no means easy for Japanese peasants who remained at the mercy of the elements. Many were poor, but, for most of the period, the standard of living rose.

With samurai now largely removed from the land, the villages were left virtually free to collect the taxes due their overlord. Within the village, neither the benefits of agricultural growth nor the burdens of taxation were shared equally: there were wide gradations in wealth, status, and power backed by the state. Since tax reassessments were infrequent, wealthy peasants who were able to open new lands and otherwise increase their yields found their incomes rising.

Traditionally, the main house of an extended family had claims on the services of the lesser households, along with some obligations to look after the poorer members. Furthermore, the heads of the main houses formed the traditional village leadership. Now with more money in circulation, wealthy villagers turned increasingly to hired laborers or tenant farmers to work their land. They also put their money to work in rural commerce, money lending, and such rural industries as processing vegetable oils, brewing sake, producing soya sauce, and making paper. Since the wealthy villagers did not necessarily belong to the old main houses, tensions ensued.

These tensions were aggravated by economic disparities, for poorer villagers and the landless did not share in the prosperity of the countryside, but suffered as contractual relationships replaced those based on family. Most often they endured in silence, but at times they gave vent to their resentment in uprisings. Peasant unrest was on the increase in the late Tokugawa. In contrast to early Tokugawa rural uprisings, often led by village headmen, those of the later period were frequently directed against those wealthy and powerful villagers. However, neither the uprisings nor the changes in agricultural technology seriously threatened the basic stability of the village. Violence was a form of protest, not a means toward revolution. Changes in agriculture increased yield but did not alter the basic pattern of rice farming, with its need for intensive labor and community cooperation. At the same time, the experience of calculating work in terms of money and time was to prove a legacy useful in the future.

Internal peace and economic vigor were conducive to expansion of the Japanese presence in the far north, homeland of the non-Japanese Ainu people who, by the end of the eighteenth century, accounted for only about half the population of Hokkaido. The Japanese presence then accelerated, partly out of concern over Russian expansion. In the early nineteenth century in eastern Hokkaido they pursued a policy of turning the Ainu into Japanese, forcing them to abandon their bear festival, to cut their hair in the Japanese manner, and to give up tattooing and ear-piercing. The decline in Ainu numbers and identity proved to be a long-term trend.

Economic expansion also left a dubious ecological legacy. In the seventeenth century both the *bakufu* and the domains promoted land clearance. Old-growth forests were cut. By the end of the century, producers and consumers were faced with a lumber shortage. In the eighteenth century there was a countervailing move to save natural resources and even to reforest cleared areas. However, government policies were inconsistent, because agriculture brought in more by way of much-needed tax revenue than did forestry. Conrad Totman concludes, "How best to balance the need for both woodland and arable was a dilemma that early modern Japan never resolved."[3]

Much of the lumber went to the cities, home not only of officials but of merchants, who became rich as the economy flourished and the political authorities found their services indispensable. Merchants supplied an economic link between the cities and the rural hinterlands as well as between localities and the capital. They handled the transport, warehousing, and sale of rice and other commodities. Frequently, they were licensed to operate *han* monopolies and organize commodity production. Important merchants acted as financial and forwarding agents for the *daimyo*, handling shipments to Osaka for exchange or to Edo for the *daimyo's* consumption. They supplied banking services, dealing in the manifold *han* currencies, transferring funds, and issuing loans to political authorities and hard-pressed samurai. They were the backbone of widespread and diverse commercial networks. The position of individual commercial establishments could be precarious—in extreme cases, a wealthy merchant with heavy loans out to the powerful might suffer confiscation so that the loans could go unpaid, as happened to a great Osaka merchant in 1705. However, these cases were exceptions. Government measures forcing creditors to settle for less than full repayment, or even cancellation, simply had the effect of raising the cost of new loans, because the authorities never found a way to eliminate the need for such borrowing.

With the *bakufu*, *daimyo*, and samurai dependent on them, the merchants prospered; in the second half of the eighteenth century there were over 200 mercantile establishments valued at over 200,000 gold *ryō*, a monetary unit worth roughly a *koku* of rice. Such merchants were fully the economic equals of *daimyo*. Some of the great modern commercial and financial empires go back to the early Tokugawa, including the house of Mitsui, founded in 1620.

By the beginning of the eighteenth century, Edo had a population of about a million, a little over half of them townspeople (*chōnin*). Osaka, too, developed as a prosperous commercial and shipping center, and Kyoto remained a major city. The capitals of the *han* also became trade centers, with merchants and artisans playing an active role in shaping the character of each city. The most prominent merchants, as City Elders, Ward Representatives, and the like, had a role in administration.

As in the villages, there were also great differences in status and wealth among the town dwellers; for every great merchant there were many more humble shop-keepers, peddlers, artisans, laborers, and servants. At the bottom of society, con-stituting under 2% of the population at the end of the Tokugawa period, were *hinin* ("non-people"), mostly beggars, and *eta*, or outcasts (today called *burakumin* be-cause *eta* is considered pejorative), who, most prominently, engaged in butchering and tanning, tasks considered unclean. The *bakufu* supported one powerful out-cast house to lord it over all outcasts in its domain in return for supplying leather goods and men to serve as prison guards and executioners. As Eiko Ikegami has pointed out, "The identical action of killing, whether human beings or animals, was, however, interpreted variously as either a source of pollution and exclusion (in the case of the outcasts) or a source of honor and power (in the case of the samurai).[4]

Classes and Values

To create an enduring order, Ieyasu followed Hideyoshi in drawing a clear line between samurai and commoners. It did happen that destitute rōnin, master-less samurai, dropped out of their class, or that through marriage an alliance was formed between a wealthy merchant family and that of an impoverished samurai, but such cases remained uncommon.

Assigned to various duties, the samurai staffed the increasingly bureaucra-tized administrative machinery of the domains and the *bakufu*. Most were now oc-cupied more with civil than with military affairs. The most visible sign of the samu-rai's privilege was his sole right to wear swords, symbols of his status even after they had ceased to be his major tools. While he was expected to acquire some pro-ficiency in at least one of the martial arts, these became "a matter of formal gym-nastics and disciplined choreography."[5] Nevertheless, the ethos of the samurai re-mained that of a loyal military vassal imbued with a strong and prickly sense of personal honor and a proclivity to violence that the bakufu needed to tame as well as exploit.

Success in civil office depended on study. Although Ieyasu patronized the Confucian scholar Hayashi Razan (1583–1657), whose family continued to supply the heads of the *bakufu*'s Confucian Academy, it was not until the end of the century that Confucianism came to prevail. The ideal was for the samurai to combine the virtues of Confucian scholar and old-time warrior. An early proponent of a fusion of Confucian and warrior values was Yamaga Sokō (1622–1695). A student of Hayashi Razan and of the martial arts, he is considered a founding father of the modern way of the warrior (*bushidō*). One of his followers became the leader of the famed forty-seven rōnin who persevered in seeking vengeance for the wrong done their dead lord. In 1703 their carefully nurtured plans were rewarded with success as they stormed into the Kyoto mansion of the offending *daimyo* and killed him. They were immediately considered heroes, and have remained popular examples of ideal loyalty. Theirs was an act of warrior courage and devotion, but it was also illegal! For a time the shogunate debated what should be done, but then found a solution which would uphold the substance of civil law while preserving the warriors' honor: they were ordered to commit ritual suicide. Playwrights lost no time in adapting the story for the stage. *Chūshingura* (*Treasury of Royal Retainers*), to give the drama its proper title, was popular with commoners and samurai alike, and has remained a Japanese favorite; in the twentieth century both the cinema and the television versions enjoyed great success.

In Tokugawa times there was much on which samurai and commoner could agree. The official morality was promoted in periodic lectures and spread by the many schools founded during the Tokugawa period so that by 1800, 40 to 50% of Japanese males were literate to some degree. Fewer girls went to school, but, as in China, special texts were published for their benefit. It is estimated that 10% of girls were in school by the end of Tokugawa in 1868.

Hierarchical principles of organization operated throughout the society, as did a tendency to rank people in grades. Like samurai, even the inhabitants of the demimonde of the urban pleasure quarters were carefully ranked. The great merchant houses resembled feudal fiefs not only in their wealth but also in their expectation of lifelong loyal service from their employees, who, in turn, were entitled to be treated with paternalistic solicitude. A similar relationship survives in Japanese industry to this day.

Although merchant and samurai held many values in common, it was a mark of samurai pride to regard financial considerations with contempt. Fukuzawa Yukichi (1853–1901), in his famous autobiography, tells how his father took his children out of school when, to his horror, their teacher began to teach them arithmetic, a subject fit only for merchants and their offspring. But business had its defenders, including the Kaitoku Academy in Osaka, which taught the importance of trade and of those who engaged in it. Also legitimating the merchants' calling was the strain of Buddhism that considered all occupations as valid forms of devotion. "Heart Learning" (Shingaku), a religion founded by the Kyoto merchant and philosopher Ishida Baigan (1685–1744), combined elements of Shinto, Confucianism, and Buddhism to create an ethic for the artisan and merchant stressing honesty, frugality, and devotion to one's trade. Diversity in classes and lifestyles made for similar diversity in the visual, literary, and performing arts as well as in thought.

The Aesthetic Culture of the Aristocracy

The aristocracy inherited a rich cultural tradition. The subtle arts of the tea ceremony and flower arranging continued, and the Nō drama that had flourished in Ashikaga times had its devotees, including the shogun Tsunayoshi, who himself performed in Nō plays. In architecture, the classic aesthetic of restraint was exemplified by the imperial villa at Katsura, outside Kyoto, but it coexisted with a love for the ornate, displayed at Nikko, the mausoleum north of Tokyo where Ieyasu's remains are interred. Here brightly painted and gilded decorations luxuriate in chaotic flamboyance, saved from empty vulgarity by their setting in a magnificent forest, creating, in Alexander Soper's words, "a serene depth of shadow into which their tumult sinks without an echo."[6]

In Kyoto, aristocratic aesthetics enjoyed a surge of vitality in a movement led by Hon'ami Kōetsu (1558–1637) who established a community of artists and craftsmen on a site granted him by Ieyasu in recognition of his prominence as a member of that city's Nichiren Buddhist community. Nichiren was a thirteenth-century religious leader whose adopted name combines the words for sun (*ni*) and lotus (*ren*) to express his faith in Japan, Land of the Rising Sun. Kōetsu was trained in his family's hereditary art of sword repair and connoisseurship, but his far-reaching talents found masterly expression in tea bowls, lacquer inlay work, and cast metal vessels as well as in painting and, above all, in calligraphy. Frequently he worked in collaboration with other artists as in the bold and free calligraphy he contributed to the handscroll "Thousand Cranes," painted by Tawaraya Sōtatsu, a highly gifted younger contemporary (Figure 4.2). The result is a deco-

FIGURE 4.2 *Thousand Cranes.* Section of a hand-scroll. Painting by Tawaraya Sōtatsu, calligraphy by Hon'ami Kōetsu. Gold and silver underpainting on paper, 341 × 1460 cm.

FIGURE 4.3 *Irises,* from a scene of *The Tale of Ise,* Ogata Kōrin. One of a pair of six-fold screens. Color on gold foil over paper, 151.2 × 360.7 cm.
Nezu Institute of Fine Arts, Tokyo, Japan.

rative elegance that does honor to an aristocratic tradition going back to the Heian period (794–1185).

The third great Kyoto artist was Ogata Kōrin (1658–1716), represented here by a pair of iris screens, which Elise Grilli has compared to Mozart's variations on a musical theme, the artist "first stating his motif, then adding variations, shifts, repetitions, pauses, leaps, intervals, changes of tempo, accents, chords, rise and fall, with changes of mood from major to minor." [7] Kōrin's color orchestration and his superb eye for the decorative are visible even in a monochrome reproduction (see Figure 4.3).

Genroku Urban Culture

Urban culture reached a high point during the Genroku Era, technically the era name for the sixteen years 1688–1704, but more broadly used for the cultural life of the fifty-year period beginning in the last quarter of the seventeenth century, when some of Japan's most creative artists were at work. These include the playwright, Chikamatsu (1653–1724); the short story writer, Saikaku (1642–1693); Moronobu (1618–1694), generally credited with developing the Japanese print; and Bashō (1644–1694), master of the haiku.

Most large cities have "pleasure districts," parts of town devoted to bohemian life, erotic activities, entertainment, and gambling. Tokugawa cities were no exception. But rarely, if ever, have such quarters produced a first-rate aesthetic as they did in seventeenth-century Yoshiwara, the home of Edo's "floating world." Here, and in similar quarters in the other large towns, there was a world that savored sophisticated stylishness in dress, coiffure, perfume, gesture, and in life itself. The tone was set by the worldly flair of the man-about-town and the elegance of the spirited courtesans who presided over this world and who looked down with disdain on the country boor.

The Print

Courtesans and actors were favorite subjects of the ukiyo-e, "pictures of the floating world," woodcut prints that were preceded by ukiyo-e paintings and by illustrations for books such as the *Yoshiwara Pillow* (1660), a combination sex manual and "courtesan critique." To produce the prints, portraits of courtesans, theater scenes, nature subjects, or scenes from urban life were carved into wood

blocks. These were then inked and printed on paper. The process was highly experimental until Hishikawa Moronobu consolidated the early efforts.

At the beginning the prints were in black and white, but soon color was added, first by hand, then by developing techniques for printing red and green, and by the eighteenth century three- or four-color prints were produced. A versatile master and major contributor to the development of the print was Okumura Masanobu (c. 1686–1764), who, in Figure 4.4, shows an eighteenth-century beauty, dressed in a characteristically sumptuous kimono, gracefully at play.

Masanobu, a master of a variety of styles, influenced other artists, including the creator of the hand-colored print shown in Figure 4.5, which conveys a wealth of information about the material culture. Depicting the interior of a house in Yoshiwara, the composition experiments with the receding perspective of European painting.

Masanobu was a publisher as well as an artist, but usually these functions were carried out by different people. Numerous people had a hand in creating a print. The publisher not only distributed and sold the prints, but also commissioned them from the artist with more or less explicit instructions on subject and style. The artist drew the picture and designed the print, but then turned it over to the engraver and the printer. The craftsmanship of these men helped determine the quality of a print, but the artist contributed the essential vision.

FIGURE 4.4 *Courtesan Striking a Shuttlecock with a Battledore*, Okumura Masanobu (1710s). Poetic verses written in calligraphic script decorate the courtesan's kimono. Woodblock print, ink on paper, 65.2 × 32.2 cm.

Theater and Literature

An unceasing source of inspiration for the print artist was the kabuki theater, whose celebrated actors enjoyed as much acclaim and attracted as avid a following as did the most elegant of Yoshiwara courtesans.

FIGURE 4.5 *A Tea House in the Yoshiwara, with a Game of Backgammon.* Attributed to Torii Kiyotada (fl. c. 1720–1750). The image shows such standard features of Japanese interior architecture as rooms separated by sliding partitions, the tatami floor, and the sense of spaciousness created by the virtual absence of furniture. Color woodcut, 43.3 × 64.1 cm.
Fine Arts Museums of San Francisco, Achenbach Foundation for Graphic Arts Purchase (A057901 1970.25.14).

Kabuki originated in the dances and skits performed in Kyoto early in the seventeenth century by a troupe of female performers. But this women's kabuki lasted only until 1629, when it was banned by the *bakufu* to put an end to the outbursts of violence that erupted as rivals competed for the favors of these ladies. For the next two decades young men's kabuki flourished, until it ran into similar difficulties and was prohibited in 1652. After that all actors were mature men. Even then kabuki continued to be under restrictions, tolerated but licensed and controlled, because, like other indecorous pleasures, it could not be suppressed.

Kabuki's spectacular scenery, gorgeous costumes, and scenes of violent passion enchanted audiences. It was very much an actor's art, dominated by dynasties of actors who felt quite free to take liberties with the texts of plays. The audience greeted the virtuoso performances of the stars with shouts of approval. Particularly esteemed was the artistry of the men who played the female roles. These masters devoted their lives to achieving stylizations of posture, gesture, and voice, conveying the quintessence of femininity, always operating in that "slender margin between the real and unreal"[8] that Chikamatsu, sometimes called Japan's Shakespeare, defined as the true province of art.

Chikamatsu wrote for the kabuki stage but preferred the puppet theater (*bunraku*), where his lines were not at the mercy of the actors. In *bunraku*, large wooden puppets, each manipulated by a three-man team, enacted a story told by a group of chanters, accompanied by three-stringed samisen. This theater became so popular that live actors came to imitate the movements of the puppets. Even after kabuki carried the day in Edo, *bunraku* continued to flourish in Osaka. The puppets, like the masks employed in Nō, assured that the action on stage would not be a mere mirror of ordinary life but would be more stylized and symbolic. It also made possible scenes of violence and fantastic stage business which, impossible for live actors, pose no problems for figures that do not bleed and are not bound by the usual limits of human physiology. Chikamatsu frequently used spectacular elements in his plays on historical subjects, such as *The Battle of Coxinga*, his most famous work in this genre.

Chikamatsu also wrote more subtle domestic plays. These center on conflicts between moral obligation (*giri*) and human emotion (*ninjō*). Feeling usually wins out over duty, but at a heavy price. One play, for example, tells of the tragic love of a shopkeeper and a lovely courtesan whom he cannot ransom from her house for lack of funds. Frequently the poetic high point of the play is the lovers' flight to death. Often the women exhibit greater strength of character than the men, but both are turned into romantic heroes through the purity and intensity of their emotions. Art imitates life, but life also imitates art: the plays produced such a rash of love suicides that the *bakufu* finally banned all plays with the words "love suicide" in the title.

Ihara Saikaku loved to write about love in his stories and books. Sometimes he wrote about samurai, but his best work deals with recognizable city types: the miser and money-grubber, the playboy who squanders his patrimony, the young beauty mismatched to an elderly husband, men and women in love with love. Exuberant and witty, he mixed humor and sex, and wrote with a robust directness. He was also a prolific composer of *haikai,* light verse that grew out of *renga,* linked verse in which one poet started off, leaving it up to friends to continue. Enlivened by infusions of everyday speech and humor, *haikai* turned its back on aristocratic refinement, as seen in this famous pair of links in a sixteenth-century anthology:

> Bitter, bitter it was
> And yet somehow funny.
> Even when
> My father lay dying
> I went on farting.[9]

Vulgar as it is, the second verse does contrast sharply with the first, as is required in this poetic form. The popularity of haikai is attested by several seventeenth-century anthologies, one containing verses by over 650 contributors.

Classical poems (*tanka*) and *renga* often began with seventeen syllables arranged in three lines five/seven/five, which, when standing alone, form a *haiku.* The greatest haiku master was Matsuo Bashō, who was born a samurai but gave up his rank to live the life of a commoner, earning his living as a master poet with pupils from all strata of society.

Not every seventeen-syllable poem is a true haiku, for the real measure of a haiku lies not in its formal structure or surface meaning but in its resonance, not in what it says but in what is left unsaid. It presents the reader with a series of images, which, when connected in the imagination, yield a wealth of associations, visions, and emotions. Consider, for example, Bashō's best known haiku:

> An old pond
> Frog jumps in
> Sound of water.

The inner spring of the poem is the juxtaposition of two contrasting natural elements, a juxtaposition that (like the frog in the water) sets off waves in the reader's mind. The old pond supplies the setting, but implies a condition of ancient stillness that contrasts with the sudden action, and results in a delightful image. It raises the question, "How does one explain the relationship between the pond which has been there for centuries and a tiny splash that disappears in a moment?" This question was posed by Professor Makoto Ueda, who responded, "Different people will give different answers, though they will all experience the same sort of 'loneliness' when they try to give an explanation. It seems that Bashō was more concerned with the loneliness than with the answer."[10] Some of his finest poems were composed on his travels and are contained in his *The Narrow Road of Oku*. One reads:

> At Yoshino
> I'll show you cherry blossoms
> Cypress umbrella.[11]

He wrote the poem on his umbrella, and there is a gentle whimsy in Bashō's idea of sharing the beauty of the cherry blossoms with his umbrella. The word translated "umbrella" can also mean "hat." Figure 4.6 is a portrait of Bashō dressed for travel, with this haiku inscribed on it.

This painting is an example of the genre known as *haiga* in which a *haiku* and a painting (*ga*) are integrated. It is by Yokoi Kinkoku (1761–1832) in the general manner of Yosa Buson (1716–1783), the most eminent artist in the literati mode. Like Chinese gentleman painters, the creators of Japanese "literati painting" (*bunjinga*, Chinese *wenrenhua*) also cultivated calligraphy and poetry as means of self-expression. They looked to China for inspiration but did not limit themselves to Chinese subjects in their art.

FIGURE 4.6 *Portrait of the poet Bashō*, Yokoi Kinkoku (1761–1832). Bashō, the greatest haiku master, composed some of his finest poems on his travels and appears here ready for his next trip with his traveling hat. Ink and color on paper, hanging scroll, 21.6 × 18.4 cm.

Intellectual Currents: Confucianism

Tokugawa Confucians were deeply influenced by developments in China, but their writings also reflect the vast differences between the two countries. In Japan there was no civil service examination system to reward mastery of Confucian texts. Most Confucian scholars came from lower samurai or commoner ranks and made their living as teachers or doctors. One attraction of Confucianism to such men was its advocacy of government by the meritorious rather than the well-born. At the same time, even the sinophiles among them took pride in Japan. Some argued that Japan came closer to Confucian ideals than Qing China, while others played an ingenious "game of one-upmanship."[12]

The beginnings of Tokugawa Confucianism are usually traced back to Fujiwara Seika (1561–1619), an aristocrat who did not find it beneath his dignity to write a letter for a Kyoto merchant sending a trade mission to Vietnam. He drew up a ship's oath which began: "Commerce is the business of selling and buying in order to bring profit to both parties." He defined profit as "the outcome of righteousness," and admonished merchants not to be greedy.[13]

In Japan as in China and Korea, Confucian teachings found a home in academies. Edo's premier Confucian academy was founded by Hayashi Razan (1583–1657) under *bakufu* patronage, but Edo did not dominate Tokugawa thought. The fragmentation of political authority made for intellectual diversity.

An outstanding early exponent of Song Confucianism was Yamazaki Ansai (1618–1682), a stern and forceful teacher who stressed "devotion within, righteousness without," and was so dedicated to Zhu Xi that he said he would follow the master even into error. When asked the hypothetical question, What should be done were Confucius and Mencius to lead a Chinese invasion of Japan? he answered that he would capture the two sages and put them at the service of his own land. Deeply versed in Shinto, Ansai attempted to fuse Confucian ethics with Shinto religion. Most Confucians justified the shogunate by incorporating it into the hierarchy of loyalty, but Ansai's contemporary Muro Kyūso (1658–1734) argued that the Tokugawa ruled by virtue of a heavenly mandate.

Muro Kyūso found it necessary to defend the thoughts of Zhu Xi against increasingly vigorous challenges from other schools. The man considered to be the founder of the rival Wang Yangming school in Japan was Nakae Tōjū (1608–1648). Like the Chinese philosopher, he stressed the inner light, and insisted on the importance of action. His lofty and unselfish character attracted the admiration of his contemporaries and of later activist intellectuals. His best-known disciple, Kumazawa Banzan (1619–1691), ran into political trouble, not because of his philosophic ideas, but for such policy recommendations as relaxing the *daimyo*'s attendance requirements to save expenses. His deep concern for the well-being of the peasantry went hand in hand with lack of sympathy for the merchant class, as reflected in his advocacy of a return to a barter economy using rice in place of money.

Like Yamazaki Ansai and Kumazawa Banzan, Kaibara Ekken (1630–1714) found much of value in Shinto, but his philosophy of nature was based on *qi* (see

Chapter 1). The writings of this remarkable man range from botany to ethics, from farming to philology, and include precepts for daily life and a primer for women. They express his breadth of mind, commitment to the welfare of society, and faith in the unity and value of knowledge.

In Japan, as in China, there were men who denied the authority of Song thinkers and insisted on going back to the foundation texts. This was the stance of Yamaga Soko, the formulator of bushidō, and of Itō Jinsai (1627–1705) who drew inspiration from the *Analects:*

> The *Analects* is like the boundless universe which men live in without comprehending its full magnitude. Enduring and immutable throughout the ages, in every part of the world it serves as an infallible guide. Is it not, indeed, great![14]

Jinsai rejected the distinction between *li* and *qi* and stressed self-cultivation with an emphasis on *Ren* (humaneness).

Another opponent of Song philosophy was Ogyū Sorai (1666–1728), who insisted on going back even earlier than the *Analects* to the Six Classics. A complex, many-sided thinker and prolific writer, he emphasized rites and institutions and wrote on many topics: philosophy and politics; literature, linguistics, and music; military science; and economics. A younger contemporary of Sorai, Goi Ranju (1697–1726), head of the Kaitokudo Academy, did not believe that the ancients had exhausted all knowledge, and even envisioned intellectual progress. A member of the next generation who studied at the academy was Tominaga Nakamoto (1715–1746), a skeptic who argued that all historical texts were unreliable. In the work of these and others were the roots for ideas which exceeded the confines of the Tokugawa order and, indeed, the normal bounds of Confucian thought. But Confucian thought too could take men's minds in unanticipated directions.

Historiography and Nativism

A perennial field of Confucian scholarship was the study of history. Hayashi Razan began work on a history of Japan that was completed by his son and accepted as the official history of the shogunate. Another major contributor to scholarship was the statesman and scholar Arai Hakuseki (1657–1725), noted for his careful attention to evidence and willingness to reexamine traditional beliefs.

A different emphasis appeared in *The Great History of Japan* (*Dainihonshi*), begun in the seventeenth century sponsored by Mito, a Tokugawa collateral house. Begun under the Lord of Mito, Tokugawa Mitsukuni (1628–1700), it was not completed until the twentieth century. Mitsukuni, a grandson of Ieyasu, enlisted the services of a Chinese émigré and Ming loyalist, Zhu Shunshui (1600–1682). The resulting history was highly moralistic and exalted the Japanese imperial house. Since the shogun derived his legitimacy from the emperor, there was nothing inherently anti-*bakufu* in this, but its focus on the emperor rather than on the shogun was potentially subversive. Indeed, it later became an emperor-centered source for nationalistic sentiments, and eventually supplied intellectual ammunition for the anti-*bakufu* movement to "restore the emperor," which culminated in the Meiji Restoration of 1868.

Interest in Japan's past often went hand in hand with a new appreciation of native traditions. Ansai had advocated both Confucianism and Shinto, but Kada Azumamaro (1669–1736) urged a return to a Shinto purified of Confucian elements. Rejection of Confucianism and celebration of the native tradition became a defining theme in the nativist thought of the National Learning (*kokugtaku*) scholars.

Frequently this was linked to a championship of Japanese literature and aesthetics. Thus Tokugawa Mitsukuni commissioned the Shingon priest Keichū (1640–1701), a great philologist, to write a commentary on the Manyoshu, the oldest anthology of Japanese poetry. Motoori Norinaga (1730–1801), a gifted philologist, enjoyed wide influence as a teacher and political advisor. His views on *The Tale of Genji*, Japan's premier classical novel, remain influential, but his life's work was the study of the *Kojiki*, one of the first histories of Japan which contains accounts of the *kami* (gods/spirits—the *shin* in Shinto). Motoori thought it wrong to try to understand these stories rationally and arrogant not to recognize the limitations of the human intellect. Indeed, the irrationality of the old legends was a sign of their truth, for "who would fabricate such shallow sounding, incredible things?"[15] Supreme among the *kami* was the Sun Goddess, and though she spread her favor everywhere, foremost among the countries of the world was the land of her birth. Motoori left a dual heritage, academic philology and ideological nativism. Of those who drew on the latter aspect of his thought, the most influential was Hirata Atsutane (1776–1843), whose narrow Japanism proved attractive to many nineteenth- and twentieth-century ultranationalists.

Dutch Learning

As the Dutch were the only Westerners allowed even limited access to Japan (see Chapter 5), it is from them that the Japanese got their information about the West. Their annual audience with the shogun allowed the Japanese to satisfy their curiosity about the exotic:

> He [the shogun, mistaken for the emperor by the Dutch chronicle] order'd us to take off our Cappa, or Cloak, being our Garment of Ceremony, then to stand upright, that he might have a full view of us; again to walk, to stand still, to compliment each other, to dance, to jump, to play the drunkard, to speak broken Japanese, to read Dutch, to paint, to sing, to put our cloaks on and off . . . I join'd to my dance a lovesong in High German. In this manner, and with innumerable such other apish tricks, we must suffer ourselves to contribute to the Emperor's and Court's diversion.[16]

This is from a report of the embassy of 1691 or 1692. "The Red-haired Barbarians," as the Dutch were commonly known, continued to be the objects of wild rumor. But they also drew the attention of serious scholars after 1720, when the *bakufu* permitted the import of books on all subjects except Christianity. These scholars wrestled with the difficulties of the Dutch language, laboriously made translations, compiled the first dictionaries, and wrote treatises on geography, astronomy, medicine, and other Western subjects. Shiba Kōkan (1738–1818), the first in Japan to produce copper engravings, was fascinated by the ability of Western art to portray objects as they appear to the eye. Arai Hakuseki had earlier recognized the practical value of Western studies, and this too is what Shiba valued. For spiritual nourishment such men continued to turn to their own heritage, thus foreshadowing the nineteenth-century formula "Eastern ethics-Western science." Because of *bakufu* policy, they knew little about Western political, philosophical, or religious thought.

By the end of the eighteenth century, there were also scholars of Dutch Learning who, alarmed by Western expansionism, discussed political, military, and economic matters at considerable personal risk. Hayashi Shihei (1738–1793) was arrested for defying a *bakufu* prohibition by publishing a book dealing with political issues: he advocated defense preparations against the threat he saw impending from abroad. Honda Toshiaki (1744–1821), who wanted to turn Japan into the England of the East complete with mercantile empire, escaped persecution by not publishing his ideas.

Implicit in the views of the scholars of Dutch Learning was dissatisfaction with the Tokugawa seclusion policy, which stood in the way of their learning more about Western civilization and prevented them from traveling overseas. Meanwhile, by stressing the royal line, Mito Confucians and National Learning scholars also helped to weaken the *bakufu* ideologically. And even orthodox Confucianism did not really require a shogun or a *bakufu*. Thus, by 1800 there were fissures in the Tokugawa's intellectual, as well as in its political and economic, foundations.

Reform and Its Limits

The underlying discrepancy between official theory and socioeconomic reality was brought home to the *bakufu* in a series of financial crises, some aggravated by poor harvests due to natural causes. Major famines during 1732 to 1733 and again after 1783 brought death and starvation as well as rural uprisings and urban riots highlighting the government's ineptness.

Repeatedly, revenue failed to keep up with government needs. Retrenchment was one standard response. Often, as in the Kyōhō Reforms (1716–1736), a spending cut was seen as morally desirable as well as fiscally necessary. Calls for reduction in government spending were accompanied by admonitions for samurai to revive warrior morality and detailed laws to limit merchant expenditure. More effective was the granting of merchant monopolies in exchange for an annual fee. To make it easier to fill high offices with capable men of low inherited rank, the practice of granting such men permanent high hereditary rank was abandoned in favor of raising their rank and stipends only during their tenure of office.

Among the sources of needed revenue were special payments imposed on the *daimyo*, programs of land reclamation, and campaigns to squeeze more taxes out of the peasantry, but in the long run these yielded diminishing returns. The same can be said of the *bakufu*'s attempts to set prices of essential commodities. Some initially successful measures backfired, as when monetary deflation quelled a destructive inflation only to bring on a deflation so severe that it provoked urban riots in 1733.

Later in the century, the *bakufu* made some additions to its reform repertoire as when, under the leadership of Tanuma Okitsugu (1719–1788), it encouraged foreign trade, tried to develop mines, created new monopolies, imposed new merchant licenses, and showed interest in developing Hokkaido. Tanuma, however, was resented for favoring the *bakufu* vis-a-vis the *han*, and his enemies emphasized his corruption. In 1787 food shortages caused by crop failures the previous year led to uprisings throughout Japan and violent rioting in Edo. Tanuma died in disgrace. Whether the *bakufu* was capable of leading the country in new directions remained a question for the future.

FIGURE 4.7 *A Flirt*, from the series *Ten Studies in Female Physiognomy*, Kitagawa Utamaro. Woodblock print, ink, color, and mica on paper, 37.8 × 25.1 cm.

Art and Literature after the Genroku Period

After the Genroku period, artists continued to work in the Genroku genres, but the classic age of the popular theater, the print, and haiku was past. Notable among the ukiyo-e artists was Tōshūsai Sharaku, famous for the psychologically penetrating and bitterly satirical prints of actors he turned out during a ten-month outburst of creativity in 1794. More in keeping with the spirit of the time was Suzuki Harunobu (1724–1770), who excelled in the subtle use of color and the freshness of his young beauties. Controversial and uneven was the prolific Kitagawa Utamaro (1754–1806), who achieved great popularity with his prints of the ladies of the "floating world" (see Figure 4.7).

With the end of the eighteenth century, there was a falling off in the quality of the figure print, but, as if in compensation, the landscape print flourished. A master of this art was the "old man mad with painting," Katsushika Hokusai (1760–1849), an eclectic genius. He is represented here by one of his depictions of Mt. Fuji (see Figure 4.8). Less versatile, but at his best producing

FIGURE 4.8 "Fuji at Torigoe" from *Fugaku Hyokkei*,
Hokusai. The instrument shown here is an orrery, a mechanical
model of the solar system.

works imbued with a delicate lyricism, was Andō Hiroshige (1797–1858), who
lived to see Commodore Perry arrive in Japan in 1853.

  Prose and poetry also continued to be produced, and was enjoyed by a wide
audience. Perhaps the best loved of the later haiku poets was Kobayashi Issa
(1763–1827). He achieved a wide identification with nature and showed sympathy for even the humblest of animals and insects.

> Lean frog,
>   don't give up the fight!
> Issa is here![17]

Notes

1. Jurgis Elisonas, "The Inseparable Trinity: Japan's Relation with China and Korea," in John W. Hall, ed., *The Cambridge History of Japan,* vol. 4, *Early Modern Japan* (New York: Cambridge Univ. Press, 1991), p. 271.

2. Harold Bolitho, *Treasures Among Men: The Fudai Daimyo in Tokugawa Japan* (New Haven: Yale University Press, 1974), p. 17.

3. Conrad Totman, *Early Modern Japan* (Berkeley: Univ. of California Press, 1993), p. 229.

4. Eiko Ikegami, *The Taming of the Samurai: Honorific Individualism and the Making of Modern Japan* (Cambridge: Harvard Univ. Press, 1995), p. 116.

5. Ronald P. Dore, *Education in Tokugawa Japan* (Berkeley: Univ. of California Press, 1965), p. 151.

6. Robert Treat Paine and Alexander Soper, *The Art and Architecture of Japan* (Baltimore: Penguin Books, 1955), p. 274.

7. Elise Grilli, *The Art of the Japanese Screen* (Tokyo and New York: John Weatherhill, 1970), pp. 111–12.

8. Attributed to Chikamatsu by his friend Hozumi Ikan. Hozumi's account of Chikamatsu's views has been translated by Donald Keene as "Chikamatsu on the Art of The Puppet Stage,"

in Donald Keene, ed., *Anthology of Japanese Literature* (New York: Grove Press, 1955), p. 389.

9. Ryusaku Tsunoda, W. Theodore de Bary, and Donald Keene, comps., *Sources of Japanese Tradition* (New York: Columbia Univ. Press, 1958), p. 454.

10. Makoto Ueda, *Matsuo Bashō* (New York: Twayne, 1970), p. 53.

11. Calvin French, *The Poet-Painters: Buson and His Followers,* exhibition catalog (Ann Arbor: Univ. of Michigan Museum of Art, 1974), p. 132.

12. See Kate Wildman Nakai, "The Naturalization of Confucianism in Tokugawa Japan: The Problem of Sinocentrism," *Harvard Journal of Asiatic Studies,* 40 (1980), 157–99.

13. Ryusaku Tsunoda et al., *Sources of Japanese Tradition* (New York: Columbia Univ. Press, 1958), p. 349.

14. Ibid., p. 419.

15. Ibid., p. 524.

16. E. Kaempfer, quoted in Donald Keene, *The Japanese Discovery of Europe* (Stanford: Stanford Univ. Press, 1969), p. 4.

17. Harold G. Henderson, *An Introduction to Haiku,* (New York: Doubleday, 1958), p. 133.

East Asia and Modern Europe: First Encounters

Key Dates

1514	Portuguese reach China
1543	Portuguese reach Japan (shipwreck)
1549	St. Francis Xavier lands in Kyushu
1571	Spanish conquest of Philippines
1601	Matteo Ricci received by Emperor of China
1614	Persecution of Christians in Japan
1630	Japan closed to foreigners
1700	300,00 Christian converts in China
1742	Pope decides against Jesuits in Rites Controversy

The Portuguese in East Asia

The Jesuits in Japan

The Impact of Other Europeans

The "Closing" of Japan

The Jesuits in Vietnam

The Jesuits in China

The Rites Controversy

The Decline of Christianity in China

*Trade with the West and
the Canton System*

The story of the early contacts between post-Renaissance Europe and East Asia can be conceived as an overture setting the tone, introducing basic themes, and establishing the harmonics of the history to come. We have already noted the trade nexus, and turn now to consider more direct encounters. The general failure of the early intermediaries to build viable bridges of mutual understanding made it all the harder to do so later when East Asia had to deal with a Europe transformed by the French and Industrial revolutions.

The Portuguese in East Asia

The pioneers of European global expansion were the Portuguese, who reached India in 1498, China in 1514, and Japan in 1543. Having wrested control of the seas from their Arab rivals, they established their Asian headquarters in 1510 at Goa, a small island off the coast of West India. In 1511 they captured Malacca, a vital center for the lucrative spice trade located on the straits separating the Malay Peninsula from Sumatra (see Figure 5.1). The desire to break the Arab spice monopoly supplied the economic motive for this initial European expansion. Spices were highly valuable relative to their bulk and weight. Easily transported and fetching a high price, they formed an attractive cargo. And there was an assured market for them in Europe, where they added flavor to an otherwise dull diet and made meat palatable in an age when animals were slaughtered in the

FIGURE 5.1   Eastern Europe and Asia in the 16th and 17th centuries.

fall for want of sufficient fodder to sustain them through the winter. They were also used in medicine and in religious ceremonies.

Prospects for trade were hampered, however, by the absence of any European commodities that could be marketed in Asia. Lacking access to silver, the Portuguese initially financed themselves by a mixture of trade and piracy, taking advantage of their superior ships, weapons and seamanship. They derived income from transporting goods from one Asian country to another: Southeast Asian wares to China, Chinese silk to Japan, and Japanese silver to China. They used their profits from this trade to purchase spices and other products for European markets. But before this trade could prosper, they had to secure entry into China and Japan. This posed problems quite different from those they had encountered in seizing a small island off the coast of politically divided India or in driving the Arabs from Malacca.

In China they got off to a very bad start. Not waiting for official permission to trade, they engaged in illegal commerce and even built a fort on Lintin Island, located at the mouth of the river that connects Canton to the sea. Their unruly behavior did not endear them to the Ming authorities, and served to confirm the opinion that these "ocean devils" were a new kind of barbarian. The outrageous behavior of the Portuguese traders was further embellished by the Chinese imagination. When the Portuguese bought kidnapped Chinese children as slaves, the Chinese concluded that their purpose was to eat them. The Chinese long continued in the firm belief that they were dealing with barbarous child-eaters. More than just a popular rumor held by the ignorant, this belief found its way into the official history of the Ming dynasty.

The first Portuguese envoy to China not only failed to obtain commercial concessions; he ended his life in a Cantonese prison. It was a most inauspicious beginning. But the Portuguese would not leave, and their superiority on the seas made it impossible for the Chinese to drive them out. In 1557 an arrangement was reached permitting the Portuguese to establish themselves in Macao in exchange for an annual payment. There the Portuguese administered their own affairs, but the territory remained under Chinese jurisdiction until Macao was ceded to Portugal in 1887.

The Jesuits in Japan

Trade and booty were not the only objectives of the Europeans who ventured into Asian waters. Missionary work was also important: mid-sixteenth-century Goa boasted some 80 churches and convents. From the beginning, the missionary impulse provided a strong incentive as well as religious sanction for European expansion; and it was the missionary rather than the trader who served as prime intermediary between the civilizations of East Asia and the West from the sixteenth to the twentieth centuries.

Among the early missionaries, the great pioneers were the Jesuits, members of the Society of Jesus. Founded in 1540, this tightly disciplined religious order formed the vanguard of the Catholic Counter-Reformation. They were the "cavalry of the church," prepared to do battle with Protestant heretics in Europe and/or the heathen in the world beyond. Along with its stress on martial discipline and intensive religious training, the Society was noted for its insistence on intellectual vigor and depth of learning. The latter included secular as well as sacred studies, and the ideal Jesuit was as learned as he was disciplined and devout.

In 1549, less than ten years after the founding of the Jesuit order, St. Francis Xavier (1506–1552), one of the original members of the Society, landed on Kyushu, the most accessible of Japan's four major islands. This was just six years after the Japanese had first encountered Europeans, some shipwrecked Portuguese who had landed on the island of Tanegashima. Xavier was well received and was soon able to establish relations with important men in Kyushu. First impressions on both sides were favorable. The Japanese were impressed by the strong character and dignified bearing of the European priests. The Jesuit combination of martial pride, stern self-discipline, and religious piety fitted well with the ethos of sixteenth-century Japan. Nor did the Christian religion seem altogether strange. On the contrary, initially Christianity, brought to Japan from Goa, seemed like just another type of Buddhism. It was similar in some of its ceremonies, and it was difficult for the early priests to convey the subtleties of theology, to explain the difference between God and the cosmic Buddha, for example, or to distinguish Paradise from the Buddhist Pure Land. At last the Jesuit fathers concluded that the devil, in all of his malicious cleverness, had deliberately fashioned Buddhism to resemble the true faith so as to confound and confuse the people.

The initial meeting of the Jesuits and the Japanese was facilitated by similarities in their feudal backgrounds. In Japan, the Europeans found a society that resembled their own far more than did any other outside Europe. "The people," wrote Alessandro Valignano (1539–1606), "are all white, courteous and highly civilized, so much so that they surpass all the other known races of the world."[1] Only the Chinese were to receive similar praise—and, indeed, to be regarded as "white." Donald Lach has summarized the qualities the Jesuits found to admire in the Japanese: "their courtesy, dignity, endurance, frugality, equanimity, industriousness, sagaciousness, cleanliness, simplicity, discipline, and rationality."[2] On the negative side, besides paganism, the Jesuits were appalled at the prevalence of sodomy among the military aristocracy and the monks. They criticized the Japanese propensity to suicide and also found fault with the "disloyalty of vassal to master, their dissimulation, ambiguity, and lack of openness in their dealings, their bellicose nature, their inhuman treatment of enemies and unwanted children, their failure to respect the rule of law, and finally their unwillingness to give up the system of concubinage."[3] Nevertheless, the similarities between Japanese culture and their own gave the Jesuits high hopes for the success of their mission.

In their everyday behavior the Jesuits tried to win acceptance by adapting themselves to local manners and customs, as long as these did not run counter to their own creed. "Thus," Valignano observed, "we who come hither from Europe find ourselves as veritable children who have to learn to eat, sit, converse, dress, act politely, and so on . . ."[4] They learned how to squat Japanese style, learned to employ the Japanese language with its various levels of politeness, and mastered the art of tea—the Jesuit dwelling was usually equipped with a tea room so that their guests could be properly entertained. C. R. Boxer has pointed out that the Christian monks came from a land with rather different standards of personal cleanliness: "Physical dirt and religious poverty tended to be closely associated in Catholic Europe where lice were regarded as the inseparable companions of monks and soldiers."[5]But in Japan the devoted monks even learned to wash, a major concession to Japanese sensibilities. Still there were limits: Valignano could not bring himself to endorse the Japanese custom of taking a hot bath every day. That would really be going too far!

Careful attention to the niceties of etiquette was required of the Jesuit fathers in their strategy of working from the top down. It was their hope to transform Japan into a Christian land by first converting the rulers and then allowing the faith to seep down to the populace at large. The purpose of their labors was not to Europeanize Japan or China, but to save souls. They realized that the enthusiastic support of the ruling authority would be an invaluable asset, while without at least the ruler's tacit approval they could do nothing.

This approach met with considerable success in Kyushu, where they converted important local lords, who ordered their people to adopt the foreign faith. Although there were numerous cases of genuine conversion, some lords simply saw the light of commerce, adopting a Christian stance in the hope of attracting the Portuguese trade to their ports. On at least one occasion it happened that when the great Portuguese ship did not appear, they promptly turned their backs on the new faith. The Jesuits themselves became involved in this trade and also in politics. For seven years they even held the overlordship of Nagasaki, granted to them by a Christian lord.

Xavier and the monks who came after him realized that real progress for their mission depended on the will not only of local Kyushu lords but of the central government. Xavier's initial trip to Kyoto came at an unpropitious time—the city was in disorder. But Nobunaga (1532–1584), the first of Japan's three great unifiers after a century of division, soon became a friend of the Jesuits. Attracted by their character and interested in hearing about foreign lands, perhaps he was also happy to talk with someone not part of the hierarchical order which he himself headed. This personal predilection coincided nicely with reasons of state. It was consistent with his hostility toward the Buddhist orders and with his desire to keep the trading ships coming in. Hideyoshi (1536–1598), Nobunaga's successor, was at first similarly well disposed toward the foreign religion. He liked dressing up in Portuguese clothes, complete with rosary, and once said that the only thing that kept him from converting was the Christian insistence on monogamy.

The political and economic success of the Jesuits helped the spread of Christianity, but power, or the semblance of power, always entails risks. There was the danger that the ruler might perceive the activities of the monks not as assets bolstering his own position but as liabilities, actual or potential threats to his authority. A portent of future disaster came in 1587 when Hideyoshi issued an order expelling the monks. Eager to encourage trade and not really feeling seriously

FIGURE 5.2 "Southern Barbarians" in Japan. Namban screen.
Courtesy of the Freer Gallery of Art, Smithsonian Institution, Washington, D.C. (F1965.22).

threatened, he did not enforce the decree, but it foreshadowed the persecutions that were to begin in earnest 36 years later.

Meanwhile, there was a surge of popularity for things Western, for instance, "Southern Barbarian Screens," showing the giant black ships of the foreigners and the foreigners themselves (see Figure 5.2). Other scenes, based on paintings from Europe, depicted various barbarian topics: the battle of Lepanto, an Italian court, European cities, maps of the world, not to mention religious subjects. While some artists painted European subjects Japanese style, others experimented with Western perspective and techniques of shading to produce three-dimensional effects. Nor were Western motifs limited to painting. Western symbols were widely used in decoration: a cross on a bowl, a few words of Latin on a saddle, and so forth.

The Impact of Other Europeans

Despite the order of 1587, Western influences continued to enter Japan. The situation was further complicated when the Portuguese were followed by other Europeans. The first of these to reach Japan were the Spanish, whose conquest of the Philippines (named after Philip II) was completed in 1571. To the Japanese, Manila presented a new source of profitable trade, but the colonization of the Philippines also alerted them to the imperialist ambitions of the Europeans and revealed connections between Christian evangelism and colonialism. With the arrival of the Dutch and English Protestants in the early 1600s, there were also Europeans in Japan who broke the link between trade and missionary activity and did their best to fan Japanese suspicions of their Catholic rivals. Now, as later, the "West" did not represent a single interest nor did it speak with a single voice.

The Spanish empire differed from that of Portugal in kind as it did in scale. Whereas the Portuguese maintained themselves by the proceeds from the inter-Asia trade, the Spanish commanded the precious metals of the New World, especially the silver which reached China by way of Manila to pay for Chinese silks. The immediate effect on Japan of the coming of the Spaniards was to complicate the situation of the Jesuits. The Spanish were every bit as committed to the missionary enterprise as were the Portuguese, but they patronized Franciscan monks rather than Jesuits. The first Franciscan arrived in Japan from Manila in 1587. Much less well-informed about conditions in Japan than the Jesuits, the Franciscans were less discreet in their work. They rejected the Jesuit strategy of working from the top down, and, instead of associating with the elite, worked among the poor and forgotten, the sick and miserable, those at the very bottom of society. The Jesuits did not disguise their contempt for the ignorance and poverty of the Franciscans, the "crazy friars" (*fraile idiotas*) as they called them, and these sentiments were heartily reciprocated by the friars, who scoffed at Jesuit pretensions.

The "Closing" of Japan

It was an omen of things to come when, in 1597, Hideyoshi crucified six Franciscan missionaries and eighteen of their Japanese converts after the pilot of a Spanish ship driven ashore in Japan reportedly boasted about the power and ambitions of his king. Like Nobunaga and Hideyoshi, Tokugawa Ieyasu, the third and last of Japan's three unifiers, was at first friendly to the Christians, but he too turned against them. In 1606 Christianity was declared illegal, and in 1614 he undertook a serious campaign to expel the missionaries.

By 1614 there were over 300,000 converts in Japan. The destruction of Christianity was long and painful. Tortures, such as hanging a man upside down with his head in a pit filled with excrement, were used to induce people to renounce their faith. Before it was all over, there were more than 3,000 recognized as martyrs by the Vatican, of whom fewer than seventy were Europeans. Others died without achieving martyrdom. From 1637 to 1638 there was a rebellion in Shimabara, near Nagasaki, against a lord who combined merciless taxation with cruel suppression of Christianity. Fought under banners on which Christian slogans were written in Portuguese, and led by some masterless samurai, it was a Christian version of the rural uprisings characteristic of the century of warfare before Nobunaga. In its suppression, some 37,000 Christians lost their lives.

Persuasion as well as violence was employed in the campaign against Christianity. Opponents of Christian dogma argued that the idea of a personal creator was absurd and asked why, if God were both omnipotent and good, he should have tempted Adam and Eve and devised eternal punishment in Hell for non-Christians even though they led exemplary lives. According to Christian teaching, even the sage emperors Yao and Shun would end in hell. The First Commandment was attacked as leading to disobedience of parents and lord; a loyal retainer should accompany his lord even into hell.

Such arguments suggest that the Japanese saw Christianity as potentially subversive, not only of the political order, but of the basic social structure, for it challenged accepted values and beliefs and demanded a radical reappraisal of long-revered traditions. Its association with European expansionism posed a threat from abroad, and, as exemplified by the Shimabara Rebellion, it also harbored the seeds of radical disruption at home. Thus the motivation for the government's suppression of Christianity was secular, not religious. The government was not worried over the state of its subjects' souls, but it was determined to wipe out a dangerous doctrine.

New restrictions followed. The Spaniards were expelled in 1624, one year after the English had left voluntarily. In 1630 Japanese were forbidden to go overseas or to return from there or to build ships capable of long voyages. The Portuguese were expelled after the Shimabara Rebellion on the grounds of complicity with that uprising. When they sent an embassy in 1640, its members were executed. The only Europeans left were the Dutch (see Figure 5.3), who kept other

FIGURE 5.3 *A Dutch Dinner Party.* Prints such as this satisfied the public's curiosity about the strange customs of the Westerners—and may or may not have been accurate portrayals. Color print, 22 × 33 cm.

Europeans from trying their luck in Japan until the English and Russians challenged Dutch naval supremacy in the late eighteenth and early nineteenth centuries. In 1641the Dutch themselves were moved to a tiny artificial island of Deshima in Nagasaki Harbor, where they were virtually confined as in a prison. The annual Dutch vessel to Deshima was all that remained of Japan's contact with Europe, but it sufficed to spark the "Dutch Learning" discussed in Chapter 4.

Japan's "closing" was far from complete. Trade and diplomatic contacts with Korea and the Ryukyu Islands continued. Japan refused to participate in the Qing tribute system, but this did not prevent an annual average of almost 26 Chinese ships from coming to Nagasaki.

The Jesuits in Vietnam

As elsewhere, the first Europeans to arrive in Vietnam were Portuguese adventurers and traders. In 1525 they established a trading center at Hoi An which attracted a community of Japanese and Chinese merchants and developed into a thriving international port. Although the Portuguese first brought Dominicans to Vietnam, the most lasting impact was made by Father Alexander de Rhodes, the Jesuit who developed a phonetic script for Vietnamese (see Chapter 1). Born into a Portuguese family in Avignon, then under papal rule, he was well connected in Paris and Rome.

The Jesuit activities in China, Japan, and Vietnam were closely linked. Rhodes was originally bound for Japan. When staying in Japan was no longer possible, he was transferred to Vietnam after spending a year in Macao. The account of his travels provides a good reminder of the hazards of the voyage from Europe via Goa to and within East Asia, and of the dedication and courage demanded of these hardy travelers, sustained by faith in their sacred mission, obeying the will of a God who would not abandon them. Rhodes attributed narrow escapes at sea to the magical efficacy of his most treasured possession, a hair of the Virgin.

By the time Rhodes arrived in Vietnam in 1624, a church had already existed in Danang for nine years, founded by a Jesuit trained in Macao. Like his confreres in Japan, Rhodes was enthusiastic about the people and impressed with the steadfast faith of the converted. His account also includes details which might otherwise have gone unrecorded, such as what happened to a woman caught in adultery:

> The punishment inflicted on her is to lead her into a field; she is laid on
> the ground completely bound; an elephant is commanded to throw her
> into the air with his trunk, to catch her on his tusks, and finally trample
> her underfoot.[6]

Control over Vietnam at this time was divided between the Trinh lords in the north and the Nguyen in what is now central Vietnam but then constituted Vietnam's south (see Chapter 6). Although the Jesuits sought to work from the top down, and did convert a Nguyen princess, government policy in both the Nguyen-ruled central Vietnam and in the north under the Trinh vacillated from tolerance, often motivated by desire for trade and military technology, to suppression, lax at times but at others escalating to outright persecution, as when two Vietnamese catechists were executed in 1645.

Much of the time Rhodes himself had to work clandestinely, traveling and meeting the faithful at night. Several times he was expelled, but managed to smuggle himself back. Among those converted by Rhodes were Japanese merchants residing in Hoi An, many of their Vietnamese wives, and their headman or governor. By 1640 there were a reported 39,000 converts in central Vietnam and 82,000 in the north.

In 1658, the French, disregarding Portuguese objections that Vietnam lay within the sphere the Vatican had assigned to them for missionary work, sponsored the Société de Mission Etrangère. Two years later this body sent out its first French priest, who opened a seminary in Ayutthaya (Thailand) as part of an ongoing effort to foster development of a native clergy. In 1664, the French showed their interest in developing trade with the area by founding the Compagnie des Indes de l'Indochine, chartered to foster French commerce. Thus the French strengthened their early presence and laid foundations for what was to become French Indochina.

The Jesuits in China

Xavier had hoped to begin the work in China himself, considering this not only a great project in itself but also a major step in the Christianization of Japan, providing an answer to the question he was constantly asked there: "If yours is the true faith why have not the Chinese, from whom comes all wisdom, heard of it?"[7] Xavier died before he could reach his goal, and three further Jesuit attempts to enter China also failed. Then Valignano established a special training center in Macao so that missionaries could study the Chinese language and culture in preparation for work in China. As elsewhere, it was Jesuit policy in China to concentrate on gaining the support and, if possible, the conversion of the upper classes. To this end, they once more went as far as possible to accommodate themselves to native sensibilities and ways of doing things.

Again, the strong character and attractive personalities of the first missionaries were of great importance in gaining them entry. The outstanding pioneer was Matteo Ricci (1551–1610). A student of law, mathematics, and science, he also knew a good deal about cartography and something of practical mechanics. Once in the East, he was able to master the Chinese language and the classics. Slowly Ricci made himself known in Chinese officialdom, impressing scholars and officials with his knowledge of mathematics, astronomy, and cartography, his command of Chinese classical learning, and his prodigious memory. At last in 1601, after eighteen strenuous years, Ricci was received in an imperial audience and won permission for himself and his colleagues to reside in the capital. (By this time they had discarded the Buddhist robes worn by Jesuits in Japan and had adopted the gowns of Confucian scholars as more acceptable to the Chinese.) In Beijing he was able to win over and convert a number of prominent men. By the time Ricci died in 1610, the mission was well established in the capital and accepted by the government. Ricci's body was laid to rest in a plot donated by the emperor.

During the period when the Japanese were persecuting Christians with increasing ferocity, the Jesuits in China labored fruitfully, building on the foundations laid by Ricci. They were particularly successful in demonstrating the superior accuracy of European astronomical predictions. Thereby they succeeded in displacing their Muslim and Chinese competitors, and established themselves in the Bureau of Astronomy, an important and prestigious office. Jesuit gains in this area were solidified by the work of Adam Schall von Bell (1591–1666), a German Jesuit who was a trained astronomer and served as chief government astronomer in Beijing. Schall von Bell also assisted in casting cannon for the Ming, although it did not save the dynasty.

The Jesuits made some notable converts among the literati, particularly during the troubled years of the declining Ming. Most notable was Xu Guangqi (Paul Hsu, 1562–1633), who translated Euclid's *Elements* and other works on mathematics, hydraulics, astronomy and geography, thereby becoming the first Chinese translator of European books. With the help of such men, Western science and geography were made available to China, but European influence remained limited. Thus, when Li Zhi (1527–1602), one of the most forceful and independent Late Ming thinkers, met Ricci, he was impressed with the Jesuit's personality but saw no merit in his proselytizing mission. The triumph of the Manchus did not seriously disrupt Jesuit activity. Schall von Bell was retained by the new dynasty as their astronomer. He was followed by the Belgian Jesuit, Ferdinant Verbiest (1633–1688), the last of the trio of great and learned missionary fathers. Verbiest, like Schall von Bell, cast cannon and in other ways won the favor of Kangxi. A good account of Jesuit activities at court comes from the emperor's own brush:

> With Verbiest I had examined each stage of the forging of cannons, and made him build a water fountain that operated in conjunction with an organ, and erect a windmill in the court; with the new group . . . I worked on clocks and mechanics. Pereira taught me to play the tune "Puyanzhou" on the harpsichord and the structure of the eight-note-scale, Pedrini taught my sons musical theory, and Gheradini painted portraits at the Court. I also learned to calculate the weight and volume of spheres, cubes, and cones. . . .[8]

The Emperor accepted the Jesuits' science with alacrity and took their quinine for the sake of his health. He also discussed religion with them, but here they were less successful: "I had asked Verbiest why God had not forgiven his son without making him die, but though he had tried hard to answer I had not understood him."[9] In China, as in Japan, the fathers found it most difficult to explain the central tenets of their faith to people with very different ideas about the nature of the universe and of the divine.

The high point for early Catholicism in China came in the middle years of Kangxi's reign, but by 1700 there were no more than 300,000 Christians in China, roughly the same number as in much smaller Japan a century earlier. In both cases the missionaries were there on sufferance, dependent on the good will of the authorities. And in China, as earlier in Japan, divisions between the Europeans themselves strongly contributed to their undoing.

The Rites Controversy

The controversy that brought an end to the missionary activity in China centered on the Jesuit policy of accommodation, which was opposed by rival orders, particularly and vigorously by the Dominicans. It revolved around the question of the proper attitude a Christian should adopt toward Confucianism, its doctrines, and practices. This kind of dispute also undermined the Jesuits in Vietnam but not in Japan, where Catholic fathers of all orders agreed in their condemnation of Buddhism and Shinto and in their absolute refusal to allow their converts to have anything to do with such heathen religions.

In China, however, the basic strategy used by Ricci and followed by his successors was to accept the teachings of Confucius, "the prince of philosophers." They argued that they had come not to destroy Confucius, but to make his teachings complete, capping his doctrines with the truths of revealed religion. Like Chinese thinkers intent on using Confucius in new ways, the Jesuits also discarded and condemned previous interpretations and commentaries on the classics. They attacked Neo-Confucianism and developed new theories of their own. In their enthusiasm for the classics, the Jesuits turned Confucius into a religious teacher. Some members of the order went as far as to trace the origin of the Chinese people to the eldest son of Noah. The most extreme even claimed to find Christian prophecies in the *Classic of Changes*. Meanwhile, the Dominicans held that the ancient Chinese were atheists, and argued against the Jesuit portrayal of Confucius as a deist. The resulting literature greatly influenced Western understanding of Chinese philosophy. At its best it was a serious effort by Europeans to understand Chinese thought in what they believed to be universally valid terms.

The status of Confucius and the acceptability of the classics were major issues for missionaries operating in a society dominated by the Confucian examination system. Even more troublesome, however, was the related problem posed by Confucian observances. Were the ceremonies in veneration of Confucius, held in the temples of Confucius throughout the land, acts of religious devotion and therefore anathema to a Christian? Or were they social and political in character, secular expressions of respect for China's greatest teacher? Even more important, what about the rites performed by every family in front of the tablets representing its ancestors? Was this a worship of the departed spirits and thus the most iniquitous idolatry? Or did these acts of commemoration for one's forebears merely convey a deep sense of filial piety? Were the two kinds of ceremonials civic and moral in nature, or were they religious, and therefore sacrilegious? Consistent with their stand on Confucianism, the Jesuits claimed the ceremonies were nonreligious and therefore permissible. The Dominicans disagreed.

The issue was fiercely debated, for much was at stake. Theology aside, it is easy to see the practical reasons for the Jesuit standpoint. To exclude Christians from performing the ceremonies for Confucius would be to exclude them from participation in Chinese political life. Worse still, to prohibit the ritual veneration of ancestors would not only deprive Chinese Christians of their sense of family but would make them appear as unfilial, immoral monsters in the eyes of their non-Christian fellows. If Christianity rejected the classics and advocated this kind of nonconformist behavior, it would be turned into a religion subversive of the Chinese state and society. Persecuted and condemned, Christianity would be unable to reach many souls, who would thus be deprived of their chance for salvation.

But the Dominicans could muster strong counterarguments. Why should a church that condemned Protestant Christianity condone Confucian Christianity? The issue was not the acceptability of Christianity to the Chinese but whether the salvation of souls would be fatally jeopardized by tolerating false Confucian doctrines. In their eyes, nothing could be allowed to interfere with the Christian's sacred duty to maintain the purity of the faith.

The Decline of Christianity in China

The question, When does Christianity cease to be Christianity? was to reappear in the nineteenth century and is not all that different from the question, "when does Marxism cease to be Marxism?" which agitated some thinkers in the twentieth century. Such questions are never easy to resolve, and perhaps only true believers need grapple with them. Be that as it may, in the papacy, the church had a source of authority that could rule on what was acceptable and what was not. The process of reaching a decision was complicated and involved. What is important here is that the outcome went against the Jesuits. In 1704 the pope condemned Chinese rituals, and in 1742 a decree was issued that settled all points against the Jesuits. This remained the position of the Catholic Church until 1939. Grand and powerful emperors like Kangxi, however, resented Rome's claims of authority over their subjects and saw no reason to abide by the papal judgment as to what was fitting for their realm. They naturally favored the Jesuit point of view. In the end, the pope would send only those missionaries the emperor of China would not accept.

Some missionaries remained in China after the break, including the Jesuit Giuseppe Castiglione, who served as court painter for half a century, from 1715 to 1766. Among other things, he designed a miniature Versailles for the Summer Palace, destroyed in the nineteenth century. Michael Sullivan has described his fusion of artistic traditions as a "synthetic style in which with taste and skill and the utmost discretion, Western perspective and shading, with even an occasional hint of chiaroscuro, were blended to give an added touch of realism to painting otherwise entirely Chinese in manner."[10] Figure 5.4 shows a painting in the European manner done at the Chinese court. Just as Louis XV of France sometimes amused himself by having his courtiers and their ladies assume Chinese dress, the

FIGURE 5.4 A lady's portrait in Western-style costume (inspired by Daiyu). Anonymous, mid 18th century.

Collection of the Palace Museum, Beijing, China.

Qing emperor Qianlong enjoyed exotic Western costume on occasion. Meanwhile western perspective appeared in color prints intended for a broad popular market.

Regardless of the Rites Controversy, the Christians also had opponents in China itself, motivated by the usual combination of self-interest and conviction. There was no Chinese counterpart to Nagasaki: instead, Canton and the surrounding area, the part of China most exposed to the Europeans, already at this time took a negative view of the foreigners. Christianity was proscribed in 1724. Some churches were seized and other acts of persecution occurred, but the suppression of Christianity was not as thorough as that which had taken place in Japan. This was probably because there was no Chinese equivalent to the Shimabara Rebellion—at least not yet. Not until the nineteenth century did the potential of Christianity as an ideology of peasant rebellion become evident in China. By the end of the eighteenth century, the number of Chinese converts had been reduced to about half what it had been at the beginning of the century.

Western contact did influence some areas of intellectual life, such as astronomy and cartography, but remained peripheral, far removed from the mainstream of Chinese intellectual life. There was no revolution in thought or art. Those of the Qing elite who came in touch with things Western rarely progressed much beyond the appreciation of European exotica, such as clocks and other mechanical devices. Ricci himself lived on as the patron saint of clockmakers. The influence was much stronger in the other direction, for the Jesuit reports on China were well received in Europe and helped to create the image of an ideal China dear to the philosophers of the European Enlightenment.

A major difference between the course of events in China and Japan was that in China trade considerations did not influence government decisions concerning missionary policies.

Trade with the West and the Canton System

After 1683, the Qing, recognizing that the flourishing maritime trade with Southeast Asia was of great economic importance to coastal communities and posed no security problems for the empire, basically left its management to local authorities. Though Kangxi instituted some restrictions on foreigners trying out the Chinese market, it was Qianlong who restricted them to Canton, where a special area was set aside for the warehouses (called "factories") of the foreign traders, who were allowed to reside there but not to bring their wives and settle down (see Figure 5.5).

FIGURE 5.5 The Canton waterfront, c. 1760. Artist unknown. One of four panels creating a panorama of the waterfront. Notice the flags of Western nations in front of their respective warehouses. Gouache on silk, 47.7 × 73.7 cm.

There were other restrictions under this Canton System (1760–1842). In all their transactions foreign traders were required to deal with a group of Chinese merchants who had been granted a monopoly of foreign trade. These merchants belonged to the Cohong, an association of firms (or *hong*) established for that purpose. In theory the Cohong was composed of a maximum of thirteen *hong*, but in practice there were only seven or eight such establishments, supervised by an imperial official who usually squeezed a good deal of personal profit out of his position. Each foreign ship was placed under the responsibility of a particular *hong*, which handled not only commercial matters but also saw to it that duties were paid and that the foreigners conducted themselves properly.

Under this system, the foreigners were not granted direct access to Chinese officials, nor were there any provisions for government-to-government relations. On the British side, the prime agent was the East India Company, which, under government charter, enjoyed a monopoly of trade between England and China and governed much of India, an arrangement not challenged until the nineteenth century, when the idea and forces of free trade triumphed.

The Qing taxed foreign maritime trade more heavily than that of Chinese ships, but both were administered separately from the tributary system of conducting foreign relations. Consequently, when Macartney, in 1793, and Lord Amherst, in 1816, came to China to try to expand trade and open European-style diplomatic relations, they ran head-on against a well-established dynastic practice that the Qing court saw no reason to change. The system continued to operate until China faced a Europe that could no longer be contained.

Korea has not figured in our account because it was only marginally involved. Koreans first learned of Christianity through a Chinese book written by Matteo Ricci. This aroused keen interest among a small group of Korean scholars who persuaded the son of the tribute envoy to Beijing to accompany the mission and learn more. Converted in Beijing, he returned with books, crucifixes, and images, and in 1784 organized a lay congregation. Ten years later they obtained the services of a Chinese priest, but he was put to death in 1801 by the government, intent on wiping out what it considered a dangerous heresy. Korea's initial encounter with Christianity was a story of enthusiasm and suppression.

Along with enthusiastic participation in the trade opportunities offered by the Chinese tributary system, Koreans continued to trade with Japan regardless of political changes there. Like China and Japan, Korea used silver as an ultimate standard of value and to store wealth. But it did not participate directly in world trade, nor did a Korean port serve as an international transshipment site as Manila and Hoi An did. Thus it was only indirectly affected by the world silver flow.

Notes

1. C. R. Boxer, *The Christian Century in Japan* (Berkeley: Univ. of California Press, 1951), p. 74.

2. Donald F. Lach, *Asia in the Making of Europe,* vol. 1, *The Century of Discovery* (Chicago: Univ. of Chicago Press, 1965), p. 728.

3. Ibid.
4. Quoted in Boxer, *The Christian Century in Japan,* p. 214.
5. Ibid.
6. *Rhodes of Viet Nam: The Travels and Missions of Father Alexander de Rhodes in China and Other Kingdoms of the Orient,* trans. by Solange Hertz (Westminster, Md.: The Newman Press, 1966), p. 61.
7. A. H. Rowbotham, *Missionary and Mandarin* (Berkeley: Univ. of California Press, 1942), p. 46.
8. Quoted in Jonathan Spence, *Emperor of China* (New York: Alfred A. Knopf, 1974), pp. 72–73.
9. Ibid., p. 84.
10. Michael Sullivan, The *Meeting of Eastern and Western Art* (New York: New York Graphic Society, 1973), pp. 60–67.

Part Two

The Nineteenth Century

In the nineteenth century the whole world came to feel the might of Europe, where intellectual, political, and economic forces at work since the Renaissance were producing unprecedented wealth and power. This process was accelerated in the late eighteenth century by the Industrial and French Revolutions, gaining momentum with the emergence of new technologies, new appetites, new ideas, new values, and new problems setting off tremors that were to reverberate throughout the globe. It was a tumultuous period of intense economic competition, stringent national rivalries, bitter class conflicts, and sharp clashes between old and new values and ideas. Yet few Europeans questioned the superiority—moral, intellectual, economic, and political—of their civilization or, indeed, of their century.

A major development still with us was that the nation-state won unprecedented and enthusiastic acceptance as the "natural" and uniquely legitimate political entity worthy to be the primary object of political loyalty. Though just what constitutes a "nation" remained ill-defined; nevertheless, the nation-states were able to mobilize human and natural resources to an unprecedented degree, as demonstrated in World War I, which, triggered and fueled by nationalism, brought an end to Europe's global predominance while destroying Czarist Russia and Austro-Hungary, Europe's last old-style multinational empires.

Nineteenth-century nationalism prompted European patriots to revolt against foreign rule, and it also glorified commercial, military, and cultural expansion abroad. Reflecting the accelerating pace of change in East Asia as in Europe, we devote two chapters to the first two thirds of the century (with the terminal dates adjusted to the history of the individual countries) and two chapters to the last third of the century, when the emergence of a unified Germany changed the map of Europe, and the intensified competition for new colonies known as "the new imperialism" changed the map of the world. Although in terms of European and even global history, the century came to a close with World War I, the pivotal event in East Asia occurred twenty years earlier, for the Sino-Japanese War radically affected Korea, China, and Japan.

The West was never uniform, nor its course of events smooth. It helps to place East Asian turbulence in perspective if we keep in mind that the forces of nationalism and republicanism erupted in revolutions on the European continent in 1830 and 1848, that in 1839 English Chartists took to the streets demanding political reforms, that warfare played a crucial role in the creation of Italian and German national states (completed by 1870), that Americans slaughtered each other in civil war, and that bitter fighting and strife marked the transition from Napoleon III, through the Paris Commune, to the establishment of the conflicted Third Republic in France (1870). The violence of the nineteenth century is matched only by that of its successor.

Vietnam and China: Internal Crises and Western Intrusion

In 1800 the Chinese were busy suppressing the White Lotus Rebellion, while in Vietnam the Tay Son Uprising (1771–1802) was in its final phase. Both upheavals were fueled by the widespread discontent of impoverished peasants alienated by government corruption and ineptitude while drawn by the vision of a better world sanctioned by the divine. Both revealed deep fissures in government and society. Both failed. However, while in China the White Lotus foreshadowed the much greater conflagration to come, in Vietnam the defeat of the Tay Sons led to the founding of the Nguyen dynasty (1802–1945), the first to control the entire territory of the country as we know it today. Although its last emperor did not officially abdicate until 1945, the dynasty was only an empty shell after the French effectively seized control in 1883. Accordingly, our periodization of Vietnamese differs from that of the rest of East Asia.

I. Vietnam

Historical Background: The Later Le Dynasty
(1428–1788)

The Tay Son Uprising (1771–1802)

The Nguyen as Rulers of All Vietnam (1802–1867)

Scholarship and Literature

The Loss of Independence

Historical Background: The Later Le Dynasty (1428–1788)

The Le dynasty was founded in 1428 by Le Loi (1385–1430), who put an end to thirteen years of Ming rule. In his youth Le Loi had passed the civil service examinations under the brief Ho dynasty (1400–1407) and, after founding the new dynasty, continued a policy of looking to China for institutional models. The later Le reached its greatest success in the fifteenth century, particularly under Emperor Le Thanh Tong (1460–1497), who reformed and strengthened the Chinese-style six ministries (Rites, War, Justice, Interior, Public Works, and Finance) and the bureaucracy, thereby weakening the landed aristocracy. He promulgated a new legal code that combined Confucian and Vietnamese traditions, including those giving women greater rights. While the code stipulated that all land belonged to the emperor, it followed the policy of Le Loi in setting limits, based on status, rank, profession, and age, on the amount anyone could actually hold. Neo-Confucianism was firmly established as the state orthodoxy, and the emperor effectively patronized scholarship. Forceful abroad as well as at home, Le Thanh Tong invaded Champa in 1471, annexed some of the old kingdom, and reduced the rest to a protectorate.

In the sixteenth century the dynasty suffered a severe reversal. The future seemed to be with the new Mac dynasty (1527–1592), but, as it turned out, the Le were able to regain the throne, thanks to the support of Trinh military leaders. However, the Le remained dependent on the Trinh ever after. The Trinh lords resembled Japanese shoguns, except that a dynasty of rival lords belonging to the Nguyen family controlled central Vietnam. Thus, for the remainder of the dynasty, a Le Emperor in Hanoi, controlled by the Trinh, was recognized in Beijing as a tributary and accepted as legitimate sovereign in Vietnam, but for all practical purposes Vietnam was divided in two. Trinh rulers prevailed in the traditional Vietnamese heartland centered on the Red River Basin but were unable to prevent the Nguyen from ruling the lands south of the eighteenth parallel from their capital in Hue (see Figure 6.5).

Confined by mountains and the sea, neither the Trinh nor the Nguyen could expand east or west. The north, known as Tonkin, was also hemmed in by the Chinese to the north and the Nguyen to their south. The Nguyen state, however, faced only weaker obstacles to its south, and Vietnamese expansion had always been to the south. During their ascendancy, the Nguyen continued this process, pushing south at the expense of the Chams and Khmers. Frequently, Vietnamese from the North were encouraged to farm southern lands, as were Chinese, including 3000 Ming loyalists who fled from the Qing and were settled by the Nguyen into the northeast Mekong Delta, incorporating and transforming what had been Cambodian lands.

Expansion at the expense of Cambodia remained a recurrent theme. Champa was fully incorporated in 1692. Beginning in 1658, Vietnamese troops frequently intervened in Cambodian succession disputes as rival princes sought either Vietnamese or Siamese support. In 1674 Vietnamese forces entered Saigon (then Cambodian) before going all the way to seize Phnom Penh. Other incursions took place in 1699, 1747, 1753–1755, and 1771–1772, leading to cession of territory in what a Nguyen general described as "the policy of slowly eating silkworms."[1] Six provinces of present Vietnam were obtained in this manner by 1750.

While the south was being incorporated into a Vietnamese state, influence also worked in the other direction, creating "a new way of being Vietnamese."[2] People living in the Nguyen territory were deeply influenced by the customs and beliefs of local Cham and other cultures. Accustomed to a world filled with numerous spirits and supernatural beings, newcomers readily paid their respects to resident deities. For example, the polyandrous Cham goddess Po Nagar acquired a Vietnamese name, but retained her naturalism and sexuality. In the 1880s she was honored with many titles by a pious ruler, and today the polyandrous deity, properly draped, is venerated by Vietnamese as intensively as by Chams (see Figure 6.1).

Southerners were more mobile than the inhabitants of the long-settled north. They differed in cuisine and dress, lifestyle and in poetry. In keeping with Southeast Asian traditions, the Nguyen kings were attributed aspects of divinity. They did adopt Chinese institutions, but not until the eighteenth century, and then only slowly. For instance, after Chinese-style civil service examinations were instituted in 1740, they were suspended for twenty-six years. Southeast Asian ways were particularly strong in the military, with special attention paid to the use of elephants, abundant in the south, rare in the north. Used effectively in warfare, they were also employed in administering capital punishment: women guilty of adultery were not the only ones to suffer death by elephant (see Chapter 5).

We should also bear in mind that the Nguyen territory ranged from older, more northern lands in central Vietnam to the recently incorporated Mekong delta, and from the ocean to the mountains. Local cultures retained their diversity. For example, inlanders were ignorant of "The Great Fish of the Southern Seas" venerated only along the coast, where annual ceremonies continue to be performed. However, this whale cult was limited to the former Cham area: in the north the whale remained only a fish. Both the east-west and the north-south divisions were significant.

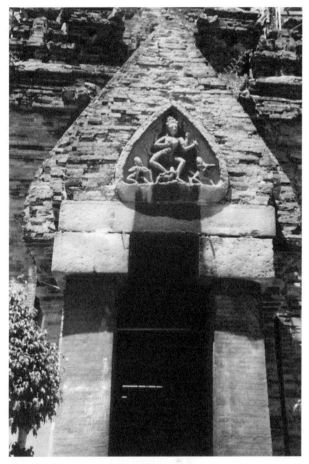

FIGURE 6.1 Temple of Po Nagar in Nah Trang. The figure of the dancing Siva that graces the temple originated in India, as did much of the old Cham culture.
PHOTOGRAPH © LORE SCHIROKAUER.

The Tay Son Uprising (1771–1802)

In the eighteenth century people under both the Trinh and Nguyen suffered from misgovernment, political divisiveness, excessive taxation, corruption, and the privatization of communal land. Exacerbating conditions in the north were natural disasters resulting in famine and disease. The south was better off, but also had problems, including the economic dislocations associated with a failed attempt by the government to impose a zinc currency in place of traditional copper. The harsh conditions in the north fueled numerous rebellions, but the most significant one began in the central-southern mountains around the village of Tay Son, from which it derived its name. Led by three brothers and fortified by signs of supernatural support (some fabricated), it attracted both people living in the hills and disaffected peasants in the lowlands. It also found support among small merchants, gained the backing of four wealthy merchants—two of them Chinese—and even of a Cham princess.

During these turbulent years of almost uninterrupted fighting, the Tay Son gave top priority to military matters, with emphasis on army recruitment, weapons procurement, and the like. They also encouraged commerce and fostered education. Displaced people were returned to their villages, where communal land was restored. We cannot tell what they might have accomplished given stability and more time, but they did not solve the problem of corruption, and failed to develop an original ideology or compelling program.

The rebellion put an end to the Trinh. In 1789 the Qing intervened with 200,000 troops on behalf of the Le emperor, but the expedition turned into a disaster for the Chinese and marked the end of any hopes for a Le restoration. In the south, the Nguyen were thoroughly defeated, and seemed on the verge of extinction. But, in the end, Nguyen An, a prince who had been driven to seek shelter in Siam, was able to defeat the Tay Son, for he proved to be "an opponent who lost battle after battle but always came back, an opponent with an eye to the long-term campaign rather than the single confrontation, for whom success came not from armed combat but was the result of organization, training, the marshalling of resources, preparation, planning, and waiting, waiting, waiting . . ."[3] By utilizing men from many lands, he achieved naval supremacy and was able to transport armies by sea, while in Saigon he gained the backing of Chinese and other commercial interests. Among his foreign supporters were a small number of French mercenaries and two ships paid for by funds raised by Pigneau de Behaine, a French cleric long active in central Vietnam, who earlier had taken Nguyen An's son to Paris in pursuit of an ambitious plan to gain French government support. The spread of Catholicism had enjoyed French patronage ever since the pope founded the Société de Mission Etrangère at the urging of Father Alexander de Rhodes, but the French government had other priorities. When he failed to gain official support, Pigneau de Behaine acted on his own. Nguyen's cause had already made considerable progress by the time the French contingent joined in, but this was a harbinger of future French military involvement.

The Nguyen as Rulers of All Vietnam (1802–1867)

After his victory, Nguyen An proclaimed himself Emperor Gia Long (r. 1802–1820) and ruled a unified empire with its capital at Hue. The emperor's name, combining the first syllable of Gia Dinh, the largest city in the south, and the second syllable of Thang Long, the original name for Hanoi, signified the unification of north and south. Vietnam now assumed its present form, which has been compared to a pole carrying a basket at each end, representing the fertile and wealthy Red River and Mekong Deltas, north and south. To sustain this entity required a sturdy pole and a strong back. Whereas earlier "the south" referred to everything below the Tonkin, we now and hereafter need to differentiate between the narrow central region including Hue, and the south, dominated by Saigon and the Mekong Delta. Another image, reflecting less happy times, describes Vietnam as "a slightly bent half-moon country shaped like a starved sea horse trapped inside the sky."[4]

In assuming the imperial title, Gia Long was claiming the legacy of the Le and the Confucian legitimization that supported it. At the same time, he was keenly aware of his Nguyen heritage, and claimed to have restored Nyugen rule, thanks to the cumulative spirit-influence of a long line of rulers. This self-image had nothing to do with a Confucian mandate of Heaven, but appealed to people of the south in terms with which they were familiar.

Gia Long was succeeded by Minh Mang (1820–1841) an equally vigorous emperor, who did all he could to model his regime on that of China. He transformed Hue into a typical Chinese capital complete with forbidden city, six ministries, and censorate. The Vietnamese legal code copied that of the Qing. The examination system, complete with the eight-legged essay, flourished. The emperor's tomb is approached by a Chinese-style spirit-way with statues of military and civil officials and animals standing guard. Along with the other structures, it serves as a reminder of the continued power of the Chinese imperial tradition to serve as a compelling model (Figures 6.2 and 6.3). At the same time, included within the

FIGURE 6.2 Tomb of Minh Mang (1820–1843): Gate. The tomb for the emperor and his empress is reached through the Hien Due Gate, one of a number of gates and other structures displaying the wealth and power of the Nguyen dynasty as well as its Chinese orientation—for a gate such as this would not be out of place in an imperial Chinese tomb.

FIGURE 6.3 Tomb of Minh Mang: Spirit-Way. Statues of officials and animals line the "spirit-ways" of imperial Chinese tombs. Minh Mang's array is relatively modest, but imperial nonetheless.

PHOTOGRAPH © LORE SCHIROKAUER.

walls of the forbidden city and departing from the Chinese model were temples to predynastic ancestors, placed there "to enshrine the Restoration myth,"[5] first promoted by Gia Long.

Minh Mang sponsored many Chinese institutions, not all of them suitable for a smaller country. He brought northerners into the government, but also continued to sponsor Buddhism and native cults. The central political elite, based near the capital, was able to manipulate the examination system so that by the 1860s only three southerners had won the top degree.

This suggests inadequate integration of the south. However, the Nguyen had ambitions in Cambodia, where they remained deeply involved. For seven years, 1834–1841, they even reduced Cambodia to a Vietnamese province administered in a Sino-Vietnamese manner. However, they had bitten off more than they could chew, even with Chinese-style teeth. The Cambodians revolted, throwing off Vietnamese rule, only to be dominated by Siam from 1841 to 1845. The Cambodian kings, pressured on both sides, then tried to assert some independence by declaring vassalage to both Bangkok and Hue, until the French took control in 1863.

Scholarship and Literature

Under the Nguyen, the north remained the center of serious Confucian scholarship and of the promotion of strict Confucian morality. A notable northern scholar was Phan Huy Chu (1782–1840) who spent the years 1809–1819 on his massive *Survey of the Institutions of Successive Courts,* in which he included categories such as geography and classical literature, and treated political principles without partiality for one regime or another.

Northern elites had a reputation for puritanism, but a very different ethos flourished elsewhere. Many stories (but few facts) relate to the life of Ho Xuan Huong, born around 1775–1780 and deceased by the 1820s. The following may be autobiographical, but we cannot be sure.

On Sharing a Husband

Screw the fate that makes you share a man.
One cuddles under cotton blankets, the other's cold.
Every now and then, well maybe or maybe not.
Once or twice a month, oh, it's like nothing.
You try to stick to it like a fly on rice
but the rice is rotten. You slave like the maid,
but without pay. If I had known how it would go
I think I would have lived alone.[6]

Writing in the native *nom* script (see Figure 6.4), Ho is known for her skillful use of double meanings, frequently sexual. Beloved for its free spirit, her poetry remains widely popular. To quote a modern appreciation:

Ho Xuan Huong's poems are so effortless in construction, so simple and spontaneous, that they rank as the most charming in Vietnamese. . . . Her daring has won her a reputation as an early feminist. She preaches free love, equality of the sexes, and the cause of unmarried mothers; she derides social conventions, ignorant scholars and high officials and impious monks.[7]

Poetry remained the heart of Vietnamese literature, and the greatest poet of the century was Nguyen Du (1765–1820). He was not related to the royal house—Nguyen is a common name, even shared by the brothers who led the Tay Son Uprising. Nguyen Du belonged to a Northern scholar–official family that supported the Le dynasty to the end. During the Uprising, he avoided

FIGURE 6.4 "On Sharing a Husband" by Ho Xuan Huong, written in the native *nom* script.

SOURCE: *SPRING ESSENCE: THE POETRY OF HO XUAN,* ED. AND TRANS. HOHN BALABAN (PORT TOWNSEND, WA: COPPER CANYON PRESS), P. 24.

office, but then reluctantly served the new Nguyen dynasty. His experiences of humiliation, political debasement and of suffering wrongs are echoed in *The Tale of Kieu,* a long narrative poem written in *nom.* Based on a Chinese novel and cast in powerful, evocative verse, it relates the sufferings of *Kieu,* who, in order to rescue her father from debtor's prison, agrees to a marriage for money. She is sold into a brothel, from which she is eventually rescued, only to fall again. But throughout, she remains pure at heart, and in the end overcomes adversity. The beauty of the poem's language as well as empathy for *Kieu* were to stir the hearts of many Vietnamese, including men who, like Nguyen Du, felt forced to prostitute their political beliefs and serve an illegitimate master (see pp. 254 and 423).

The Loss of Independence

Situated at the border between the Southeast Asian cultural sphere and that of China, the new Vietnam was a diverse place in just about every respect. To keep it together called for an effort—political and cultural, economic and military—that proved beyond the capacity of the dynasty. To maintain a regime based in Hue in Vietnam's narrow middle required the support of at least one of the rich and populous lands to the north or south, but the government failed to win strong backing in either region. Threatened by internal rebellion and confronting French commercial and territorial ambitions, the dynasty "almost inevitably maneuvered themselves into a deadly crossfire—hostile subjects challenging them on the one hand and French imperialists encroaching on the other."[8]

As already noted, French expansionists included missionaries as well as naval officers and commercial types. Earlier, although Christianity was outlawed by both Trinh and Nguyen, missionaries had been tolerated, especially by the Nguyen, who were eager for trade. Gia Long combined uneasy tolerance for the missionaries with suspicion of French commercial and political intentions. Minh Mang, aware of missionary and local Catholic support for internal rebellion and foreign intervention, issued increasingly severe decrees, beginning with the proscription of Christianity in 1825, by which time there were already an estimated 300,000 converts. Proscription turned into repression. In 1832 he had a missionary strangled to death for being involved in a rebellion.

Relations deteriorated further under Emperor Thieu Tri (1841–1847), whose efforts at settling disputes over missionaries were undermined by the French bombardment of Danang in 1847. The fourth Emperor, Tu Duc (1847–1883), faced internal rebellion and, in 1858, a French-Spanish invasion. Several years of fighting were concluded with the Treaty of Saigon (1862), under which the Vietnamese agreed to lift restrictions on religion and trade, to give France a major voice in the conduct of foreign policy, and to cede Saigon along with three neighboring provinces. To these the French added another three in 1867 to form a colony they called Cochin China (Fr. Cochinchine). (The origin of this name is in dispute. According to one popular theory, "Cochin" was derived from an old Chinese term for the Red River delta, and "China" added to distinguish it from Cochin in India.)

Under the French Third Republic (1870–1914), French politicians sought to compensate for the loss of territory and national pride in the Franco-Prussian War of 1870–1871 by imperial conquest overseas, but the initiative for the next phase in Vietnam was taken by Frenchmen on the spot. First, in 1873, a French merchant–adventurer seized part of Hanoi. Then, to restore order, the Vietnamese government permitted a French force into the area; but the French commander, Francis Garnier (1839–1873), sent by the Governor of Cochin China, Admiral Jules-Marie Dupré (1813–1881), made common cause with his fellow countrymen. Garnier's gunboats went marauding down the northern rivers and streams between Hanoi and the sea until he was killed in a surprise battle. This episode led to serious debates in Paris and the forced resignation of Dupré. French encroachment continued, but at a slower pace. Under the Treaty of 1874 the French withdrew, but the Red River was opened to foreign trade; Vietnam recognized Cochin China as a French colony, and promised to follow France in its foreign policy.

The south was now permanently lost, and the north was precarious, as local armed forces (usually led by the elite), Chinese fleeing the suppression of the Taiping Rebellion, armed Vietnamese Catholic units, rebellious mountain tribes, Chinese and Vietnamese bandits organized as the "Black Flags" under a Chinese secret society leader, as well as Qing border troops and French consular troops, all pursued their own agendas. Meanwhile, the French determined not to allow any other power to dominate the north. When they seized Hanoi in 1882, the Nguyen court responded by seeking help from both the Qing and the Black Flags. The Qing sent troops, but after losing the Sino-French War (see Chapter 9), they were eliminated as a factor in Vietnam, leaving the French supreme, but loyalist Vietnamese bitterly resentful.

According to a treaty signed in 1883, Tonkin in the north and Annam in central Vietnam, like Cambodia, became French "protectorates." In 1887 the addition of Laos completed the formation of French Indochina. "Protectorate" is an official euphemism, since power over all Vietnam was in the hands of a French governor-general in Hanoi. However, while Cochin China was governed according to French law administered by Frenchmen and Frenchified Vietnamese, the "protectorates" were under dual jurisdiction, with French citizens responsible to French authority, but the old Vietnamese bureaucracy still in place, their officials surviving "as traumatized, moldering tokens of the classical past."[9]

FIGURE 6.5 French Indo-China.

II. China

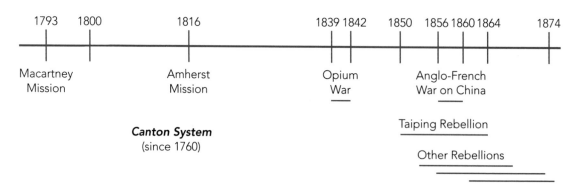

The Opium War (1839–1841) and Its Causes

The Treaty of Nanjing and the Treaty System

Internal Crisis

The Taiping Rebellion (1850–1864)

Zeng Guofan and the Defeat of the Taiping

China and the World from the Treaty of Nanjing to the End of the Taiping

Nineteenth-century China was beset by internal and external difficulties, each contributing to the severity of the other. Opium, for example, came from abroad, but its spread in China was made possible by official corruption, and the appeal of the drug to bannermen did not bode well. The Qing now faced long-term problems that would have taxed the ingenuity and energy of even an honest and effective government. Foremost were the problems created by population pressures, for the population continued to increase in the nineteenth century as it had in the eighteenth. By 1850 the number of inhabitants in China had risen to about 430 million, without any comparable increase in productivity or resources. As the pressures of the struggle for survival strained old humanistic values to the breaking point, it left little room for honesty, let alone charity. Life became brutish and hard. As ever, the poor suffered most, and they were legion, for the uneven distribution of land left many people landless, destitute, and despairing. The situation was made worse by government neglect of public works.

Emperor Jiaqing (1796–1820) tried to remedy the government's financial problems by cutting costs and selling official posts and titles, but was unable to solve the underlying fiscal and economic problems, reform the bureaucracy, or help the people, who ultimately supplied the funds. Emperor Daoguang (1820–1850) continued his father's policy of frugality but could not stem the decay. Internal pressures were building, but external crisis preceded internal eruption.

The Opium War (1839–1841) and Its Causes

Before turning to the opium crisis that triggered the war, we need to consider the long-range factors that made it a turning point in China's foreign relations. Underlying the tensions between China and the West was the incompatibility of the Chinese and Western views of themselves and the world. Both were supremely self-confident and proud of their own civilizations. Both were narrowly culture-bound. Thus, when the Macartney mission arrived in Beijing in 1793 in the hope of broadening the terms of trade and initiating treaty relations, the presents sent to Emperor Qianlong by England's George III were labeled as "tribute" by the Chinese. Qianlong responded to the English monarch by praising his "respectful spirit of submission" and, in the gracious but condescending language appropriate for addressing a barbarian king residing in the outer reaches of the world, turned down all his requests, political and economic. He saw no merit in the British request for representation in Beijing nor did he favor increased trade: "As your Ambassador can see for himself, we possess all things. I set no value on objects strange or ingenious, and have no use for your country's manufactures."[10]

The sources are inconsistent on whether or not Lord Macartney performed the ceremonial kowtow expected of inferiors and performed by emperors themselves toward Heaven, but he was confident that the Chinese would perceive "that superiority which Englishmen, wherever they go, cannot conceal."[11] The English sent another mission to China in 1816, headed by Lord Amherst, but he was not granted an audience at court.

The British motive for coming to China remained primarily economic. In contrast to China's self-sufficiency and Emperor Qianlong's disdain for foreign products, there was a Chinese product in great demand in Britain. This was tea. First imported in tiny quantities in the late seventeenth century, tea was initially taken up as an exotic beverage with medicinal properties, then popularized as a benign alternative to gin, and finally was considered a necessity of English life. The East India Company, which enjoyed a monopoly of trade with China until 1834, was required by Act of Parliament to keep a year's supply in stock at all times. Tea imports reached 15 million pounds in 1785, and double that amount in the decade preceding the Opium War. Not only did the East India Company depend on the income from tea trade, the British government also had a direct stake in tea, since about one-tenth of its entire revenue came from a tax on Chinese tea.

Not until the 1820s did the Company begin experimenting with tea growing in India, and it was many years before Indian tea would provide an alternative to the tea of China. The importance of Chinese tea extended even to American history: it was Chinese tea that was dumped from East India Company ships in the famous Boston Tea Party (1773).

The British problem was how to pay for this tea. There was no market for British woolens in China, and the "singsong" trade in clocks, music boxes, and curios was insufficient to strike a balance of trade. Until the last third of the eighteenth century, the sale of British imports covered 10 percent or less of the cost of exports, with the rest paid for in cash and precious metals. Unable to find anything European that the Chinese wanted in sufficient quantity, the English turned toward India and the "country trade" between India and China, conducted under East India Company license by the private firms of British subjects. Money obtained in Canton by the "country traders" was put on deposit there for the Company against bills of exchange on London. In this way, England, India, and China were connected by a trade-and-payments triangle.

Until 1823 the largest commodity imported to China from India was cotton, but this never reached the volume necessary to balance the trade. That was accomplished by opium. Opium had long been used for medicinal purposes, but the smoking, or more accurately, the inhaling of opium fumes through a pipe, began in the seventeenth century. The spread of the practice was sufficient to provoke an imperial edict of prohibition in 1729, but this and subsequent efforts to suppress the drug were unsuccessful, and opium consumption continued to increase. Distributed partly through older salt-smuggling networks, and protected by the connivance of corrupt officials, it spread steadily and proved particularly attractive to soldiers and government underlings. The drug was debilitating and habit forming (see Figure 6.6). Withdrawal was excruciatingly painful. Over time the addict developed a tolerance for opium and needed more and more of the drug to achieve a "high." Thus, to pay for tea, the Chinese were sold a poison. Since the opium was brought to China by private "country traders," the East India Company disclaimed responsibility for the illegal traffic in China. At the same time, however, it profited from the sale of opium in India. However, within India, where the British, as the paramount power, felt a certain sense of responsibility, consumption of opium for nonmedicinal purposes was strictly prohibited.

The Chinese market for opium developed at such a pace that the balance of trade was reversed. During the 1820s and 1830s silver seems to have left China in large quantities to pay for opium imports. This caused an increase in the number of copper coins needed to buy a specific amount of silver, thereby destabilizing the Qing monetary system. What began as a public health problem now became a fiscal problem as well. In 1834, the Company's monopoly of the China trade was abolished by the British government. This opened the gates of trade still wider on the British side, resulting in an increased flow of opium to China, and an increased flow of silver out of China.

Abolition of the Company's trade monopoly was a victory for English advocates of free trade, who were as antagonistic to restraints on trade abroad as at

FIGURE 6.6 *Opium Smokers.* Those who could afford to do so indulged in high-quality opium prepared for them by servants at home. The less affluent had to prepare their own. But the least fortunate were left to smoke opium ash or refuse on rudimentary benches in shoddy surroundings in dismal opium dens.
PHOTOGRAPH © MANSELL/TIMEPIX COLLECTION (838558).

home. The immediate effect in China was to put an end to the system of Co-hong–Company relations in Canton. Now in place of the Select Committee of the East India Company, the British side was represented by an official of the crown. To initiate the new relations, Britain sent out Lord Napier as First Superintendent of Trade with instructions to establish direct contact with the Qing viceroy, to protect British rights, and to assert jurisdiction over Englishmen in Canton. To accomplish these aims, he was ordered to use a moderate and conciliatory approach. Napier, however, more ambitious than diplomatic, immediately took an adamant stand on the issue of direct communication with the viceroy. He violated Chinese regulations by not waiting in Macao for permission to proceed to Canton and by sending a letter rather than petitioning through the *hong* merchants. With neither side willing to back down, the impasse developed into a showdown. All Chinese employees were withdrawn from the British community, food was cut off, and trade was stopped. Napier finally withdrew to Macao, where he died. This all took place in 1834. Unfortunately, in the ensuing lull, no progress was made toward finding a new modus vivendi between the two sides.

For a brief moment the Chinese considered legalizing opium, but in 1836 the emperor decided on suppression. In doing so, he sided with the Spring Purification Circle of reform-minded literati officials, who were seeking influence in government decision making. Thus an "Inner Opium War," to use James Polachek's formulation, developed parallel to and intertwined with the external conflict.[12]

Opium dealers and addicts were prosecuted with great vigor, and imprisonments and executions were widespread, with the result that the price of opium dropped precipitously. This program was well under way when the vigorous and determined reformer Lin Zexu (1785–1850) arrived in Canton in March 1839. As imperial commissioner, he was charged with stamping out the drug trade once and for all.

Lin conducted a highly successful campaign against Chinese dealers and consumers. He also severely punished corrupt officials who had connived at the trade. To deal with the foreign source of the opium, he appealed to Queen Victoria: "Suppose there were people from another country who carried opium for sale to England and seduced your people into buying and smoking it; certainly your honorable ruler would deeply hate it and be bitterly aroused."[13] He also admonished the foreign merchants, and he backed moral suasion with force. He demanded that the foreigners surrender all their opium and sign a pledge to refrain from importing the drug in the future at the risk of confiscation and death. To effect compliance, he used the same weapons of isolating the foreign traders employed successfully in 1834 against Napier. Elliot, the British Superintendent of Trade, took a fateful step in response when he ordered the British merchants to turn their opium over to him for delivery to the Chinese authorities. By this act he relieved the merchants of large amounts of opium they had been unable to sell because of the efficacy of the Chinese prohibitions, and he made the British government responsible for eventual compensation. No wonder that the merchants enthusiastically dumped their opium: 21,306 chests were delivered to Lin Zexu. It took twenty-three days to destroy it all.

In England, firms interested in the China trade exerted great pressure on the government for prompt and vigorous military action. Lin, meanwhile, pleased with his victory, continued to press Elliot on the issue of the pledges, but here he did not succeed. The Superintendent of Trade argued that it was against British law to compel the merchants to sign the pledges and that the imposition of the death penalty without the benefits of English judicial procedure was also contrary to British law. What was at stake here was the issue of British jurisdiction over British subjects, a source of Anglo-Chinese friction since 1784, when the British had refused to submit to Chinese justice. The issue came to the fore again in the summer of 1839, when a group of English sailors killed a Chinese villager in the Canton hinterland. Refusing to turn the men over to Lin Zexu, Elliot tried them himself, but when they were returned to England the men were freed, since the home court ruled that Elliot had exceeded his authority.

The first clash of the war took place in November 1839, when the Chinese tried to protect one of the only two ships whose captains had signed the bond despite Elliot's stand and who now wanted to trade. When a British ship fired a shot across the bow of the offending vessel, the Chinese intervened with twenty-one war junks, which, however, were no match for the foreign ships. In December, trade with the British was stopped, and on January 31, 1840, a formal declaration of war was announced by the governor-general of India acting in the name of the home government.

In June 1840, the British force, consisting of 16 warships, 4 armed steamers, 27 transports, a troop ship, and 4,000 Irish, Scottish, and Indian soldiers, arrived in China. First the British blockaded Canton and then they moved north. Lin and his associates remained confident of victory, holding that the British, like their maritime pirate predecessors, depended on the spoils of war to finance their military operations, and thus had grossly overextended themselves.

The British were fired on at Xiamen (Amoy) while trying to deliver a letter from Prime Minister Palmerston under a white flag of truce, a symbol the Chinese did not understand—just one example of mutual cultural misunderstanding. They then seized Chusan Island, south of the Yangzi estuary, and Dinghai, the chief city there. The main body of the fleet sailed another 800 miles north to Beihe, near Tianjin, where Palmerston's letter was accepted. By this time the emperor had lost confidence in Lin Zexu, whose tough policy had led to the military retaliation. Lin was dismissed, disgraced, and exiled to Ili in Central Asia. His place was taken by the Manchu prince Qishan (d. 1854), who, in September 1840, by flattery and accommodation, got the British to return to Canton for further negotiations. When these came to naught, the British resumed military operations, with the result that in January 1841 Qishan was forced to sign a convention that provided for the cession of Hong Kong, payment of an indemnity to Britain, equality of diplomatic relations, and the reopening of Canton. Both Qishan for the Qing and Elliot for the British thought they had done very well, but neither government accepted their work. The Chinese emperor was indignant at how much had been conceded, while Palmerston fumed that Elliot had demanded too little. The reactions of the Chinese and British governments showed all too clearly how far apart they still were. Caught in the middle were the negotiators. Like Lin Zexu earlier, now Qishan came to feel the imperial displeasure: his property was confiscated and he was sent to exile on the Amur. Elliot too was dismissed; his next position was as consul-general in Texas.

In the renewed fighting, the British besieged Canton in February 1841, but the siege was lifted on payment of a ransom of 6 million Spanish silver dollars. However, before their departure, the British experienced the growing hostility of the local population. They were attacked by a body of troops organized by the local gentry. Although militarily ineffective, the attack was an indication of popular sentiment, and its results were embellished by hard-liners to support their advocacy of continued intransigence toward the British. In August, Elliot was relieved by Pottinger, and the last phase of the war began when the British moved north, occupying Xiamen in August and Dinghai in October. Reinforcements were sent from India, increasing the naval force and bringing troop strength up to 10,000. With this force, Pottinger continued the campaign, advancing up the Yangzi until his guns threatened Nanjing. There on August 29, 1842, the treaty was signed that ended the war. It was a dictated peace imposed by the Western victor on the vanquished Chinese.

The Treaty of Nanjing and the Treaty System

The Treaty of Nanjing (together with the supplementary Treaty of the Bogue, October 1843) set the pattern for treaties China later signed with the United States and France in 1844, established the basic pattern for China's relations with the West for the next century, and supplied the model for similar treaties imposed on Japan. The Canton System and the Cohong monopoly were abolished. Five ports—Canton, Xiamen, Fuzhou, Ningbo, and Shanghai—were opened to British trade and residence. Britain received the right to appoint consuls to these cities. The treaty also stipulated that henceforth official communications were to be on a basis of equality.

The Qing was forced to pay an indemnity of 21 million Spanish silver dollars. Of this, 12 million was for war expenses, in keeping with the European practice of forcing the loser to pay the costs of a war. Another 6 million was paid as reparations for opium handed over to Commissioner Lin, while the remaining 3 million went to settle the debts owed by the *hong* merchants to British merchants.

An important provision of the treaty established a moderate Chinese tariff of from 4 to 13 percent on imports, with an average rate of 5 percent. The Chinese, whose statutory customs had been even lower, did not realize that by agreeing to this provision they were relinquishing the freedom to set their own tariffs. On the British side there was the conviction that, as Adam Smith had taught, the removal of constraints on trade would benefit all by allowing everyone to concentrate on what he did best.

The British, having acquired an empire in India, with all the burdens of government that it entailed, did not seek to create another in China. Trade, not territory, was their aim. But they did demand and obtain a Chinese base. Hong Kong Island, at that time the site of a tiny fishing village, was ceded to them in perpetuity. Well located and with an excellent harbor, it developed into a major international port.

The issue of legal jurisdiction over British subjects was settled by the Treaty of the Bogue, which provided for extraterritoriality—that is, the right of British subjects to be tried according to British law in British consular courts. Having only recently reformed their own legal system, the British were convinced of its superiority. There were precedents in Chinese history for allowing "barbarians" to manage their own affairs, but in the context of modern international relations, extraterritoriality amounted to a limitation on Chinese sovereignty.

The Treaty of the Bogue also provided for most-favored-nation treatment. This obliged China to grant to Britain any rights China conceded in the future to any other power. Its effect was to prevent China from playing the powers off against each other. It meant that once a nation had obtained a concession, it was automatically enjoyed by all the other states granted most-favored status. In the

1844 treaties, the United States and France gained this status. In the American treaty, China agreed to allow for the maintenance of churches in the treaty ports and to treaty revision in twelve years, while the French won the right to propagate Catholicism.

The status of the opium trade was left unsettled in the original treaties. An agreement to outlaw smuggling did not slow down the growth of the traffic, which was legalized under the next round of treaty settlements, 1858–1860, and opium even functioned as a kind of money. From the annual 30,000 chests prior to the Opium War, the trade expanded to reach a high of 87,000 chests in 1879. It then declined as Chinese production of opium increased. British opium imports were down to about 50,000 chests when, in 1906, the Qing took strong measures against the drug. British imports finally came to a stop in 1917, but opium smoking remained a serious social problem until the early 1950s.

For China, the treaties solved and settled nothing. A particularly ominous development was the permission granted foreign gunboats to anchor at the treaty ports, for when additional ports were opened, it gave foreign powers the right to navigate China's inland waterways. Today, with the benefit of hindsight, it is apparent that the cumulative effect of the treaties was to reduce China to a status of inequality unacceptable to any modern nation.

Although it is now universally regarded as a milestone, the treaty settlement did not seem so to the Qing authorities who, as John Fletcher has shown, had made many of the same concessions as recently as 1835 in reaching a settlement with the tiny Central Asian state of Kokand. This treaty involved an indemnity, a tariff settlement, the abolition of a merchant monopoly, and a special position exceeding that of most-favored-nation status, and seen by the Qing as simply a case of "impartial benevolence."[14] From the vantage point of Beijing, Hong Kong seemed as remote as Kokand.

Foreign policy remained deeply imbedded in political conflicts revealing deep lines of division in the body politic. When the Manchu-led centralizers, who advocated peace, came into power, they purged their opposition so thoroughly that Chinese scholar–officials of various intellectual persuasions found common ground in pressing for open discussion in official channels, administrative decentralization, and a policy of determined resistance against the foreigners. Few men had any inkling of the dimensions of the challenge facing the empire. For example, Wei Yuan (1794–1857), author of the influential *Illustrated Treatise on the Sea Kingdoms* (first version, 1844), limited himself to incorporating new information into old categories, and felt no need to break with tradition. Despite his geopolitical orientation, he persisted in underestimating the British threat.

Under the circumstances, the best that experts could suggest was for China to acquire "barbarian" arms and to employ the old diplomacy of playing off one "barbarian" against another. Less well-informed officials suggested that future military operations take advantage of the supposed physical peculiarities of the "barbarians," for example, their stiff waists and straight legs, which made them dependent on horses and ships, or their poor night vision.

Internal Crisis

The encroachments of the foreign powers was ominous, but the internal crisis was even more dangerous. Government leadership remained totally inadequate. Earlier, Emperor Daoguang's partial success in reforming the official salt monopoly system had not compensated for his failure to reinvigorate the Grand Canal or Yellow River managements. The former was impassable by 1849, after which tax grain had to be shipped by sea. The abandonment of the canal cost thousands their jobs. Emperor Daoguang did not live to see the Yellow River disaster of 1852. Since 1194, the greater river had flowed into the sea south of the Shandong Peninsula, but now it shifted to the north, spreading flood and devastation over a wide area.

The next emperor, Xianfeng (1851–1861), was nineteen when he inherited the throne and proved equally incapable of dealing with an increasingly menacing situation. Even while rebellion threatened the dynasty, a major scandal involving bribery and cheating shook the examination system.

Famine, poverty, and corruption gave rise to banditry and armed uprisings, as had so often happened in the past. The most formidable threat to the dynasty came from the Taiping revolutionaries. To aggravate the crisis, the dynasty also had to contend with rebellions elsewhere. In the border regions of Anhui, Jiangsu, Henan, and Shandong, there was the Nian Rebellion (1853–1868) led by secret societies, probably related to the White Lotus Society. There was also a Muslim rebellion in Yunnan (1855–1873) and the Dongan Rebellion in the Northwest (1862–1875). Yet it was the Taiping who came closest to destroying the Qing, in a civil war that, in terms of bloodshed and devastation, was the costliest in human history. It is estimated that more than 20 million people lost their lives.

The Taiping Rebellion (1850–1864)

The founder of the Taiping movement was a village school teacher named Hong Xiuquan (1814–1864), who belonged to the Hakka, ethnically a Han subgroup, which many centuries earlier had migrated from the north to the southeast, where they remained a distinct ethnic group. Originally, Hong hoped for a conventional civil service career, and four times went to Canton to participate in the civil service examination, only to fail each time. In 1837, shocked by his third failure, he became seriously ill, and for forty days was subject to fits of delirium during which he experienced visions. These visions he later interpreted with the aid of a Christian tract he picked up in Canton, where Protestant missionaries had made a beginning in their effort to bring their faith to China. He also received some instruction from an American Southern Baptist missionary. On the basis of his limited knowledge of the Bible and Christianity, he proceeded to work out his own form of Sinicized Christianity.

Central to Hong's faith was his conviction that in his visions he had seen God, who had bestowed on him the divine mission to save humankind and exterminate demons. He also met Jesus, and was given to understand that Christ was his own elder brother. This recasting of Christianity into a familistic mode had its appeal for Hong's Chinese audience, but dismayed Western Christian missionaries, who were further appalled by Hong's claims that he himself was a source of new revelation. The emphasis in Taiping Christianity was on the Old Testament—on the Ten Commandments, not the Sermon on the Mount. Hong's militant zeal in obeying the first commandment by destroying "idols" and even Confucian ancestral tablets soon cost him his position as a village teacher. He became an itinerant preacher among the Hakka communities in Guangxi, gaining converts and disciples among the downtrodden and dispossessed, whom he recruited into the Association of God Worshippers. To the poor and miserable, he held out a vision of the Heavenly Kingdom of Great Peace (*Taiping tianguo*), an egalitarian, God-ordained utopia.

In keeping with both Christianity and native traditions, the Taiping stressed a strict, even puritanical, morality. Opium, tobacco, gambling, alcohol, prostitution, sexual misconduct, and foot binding were all strictly prohibited. Women were made equal to men in theory and, to a remarkable extent, also in practice. Consonant with both Christian egalitarianism and native Chinese utopian ideas was a strong strain of economic egalitarianism, a kind of simple communism. Property was to be shared in common, and in 1850 the members of the Association were asked to turn over their funds to a communal treasury that would provide for everyone's needs.

The Taiping land program was based on a system of land classification according to nine grades found in *The Rites of Zhou*, long a source of Chinese radical thought. The idea was that everyone would receive an equal amount of land, measured in terms of productivity of the soil. Any production in excess of what was needed by the assignees was to be contributed to common granaries and treasuries. The system did not recognize private property.

The basic political structure was a unit of twenty-five families consisting of five groups of five families each. The leaders of these and larger units were to combine civil and military duties and look after the spiritual welfare of their people by conducting Sunday religious services. The Taiping developed their own hymns, primers, and literature, which served as the subject matter for a new examination system open to women as well as men. Similarly, there were female as well as male military units. Marriages took place in church and were monogamous.

What stood in the way of realizing this utopia were the "demons," mostly Manchus. By July 1850 the Association had attracted 10,000 adherents, primarily in the remote and neglected province of Guangxi. In defiance of the Qing, they now cut off their queues, the long braids of hair hanging down from the back of the head, which had been forced upon the Chinese by the Manchus as a sign of subjugation. Since they also refused to shave the forepart of their heads, the government called them the "long-haired rebels." Millenarian religious beliefs, utopian egalitarianism, moral righteousness, and hatred of the Manchus proved a potent combination when fused into a program of organized armed resistance. In November 1850 there were clashes with government troops, and on January 11, 1851, Hong's thirty-seventh birthday, his followers proclaimed him "Heavenly King," thus formally defying the Qing.

At this stage, the Taiping enjoyed good leadership. One of the outstanding secondary leaders was Yang Xiuqing, originally a charcoal burner, who was a talented organizer and strategist. Starting from their base in Guangxi, the Taiping forces made rapid military progress. One of their favorite tactics in attacking cities was to use their contingent of coal miners to dig tunnels to undermine the defending walls. The incompetence of the government forces also helped. As the Taiping armies advanced, they picked up strength. It has been estimated that their number reached over one million by the time they took Nanjing in 1853.

After such a quick advance, with their ranks swollen by new adherents only partially versed in Taiping tenets, it was time to call a halt and consolidate. They had formally been proclaimed the Heavenly Kingdom of Great Peace in 1851. Now, with its capital at Nanjing, they attempted to turn it into a solid regime. To continue military operations, two expeditions were sent out. A small force was dispatched north and came within twenty miles of Tianjin before suffering reverses and defeat. Large forces went west and enjoyed considerable success until 1856, but they too were eventually defeated.

Taiping treatment of Westerners was cordial but clumsy. They lost much good will by employing condescending language and expressions of superiority not unlike those used by Beijing. After the British failed to obtain Taiping recognition of their treaty rights, they decided on a policy of neutrality, and the other powers soon followed suit. This remained the policy of the foreign powers through the 1850s.

A turning point for the Taiping regime came in 1856 in the form of a leadership crisis they could ill afford. Yang Xiuqing had increased his power to the point of reducing Hong to a mere figurehead. Yang, too, went into trances, and claimed to be acting on God's orders, but he was unable to convince the other leaders. When he over-reached, they turned on him. Yang, along with his family and thousands of followers, was killed, but no strong successor appeared to take his place. By the time Hong's cousin Hong Rengan (1822–1864) came into prominence in 1859, it was too late to restructure the regime. Hong Rengan was the most Westernized of the Taiping leaders, but had neither the time nor the power to build the centralized and modern state he had in mind. His leadership lasted only until 1861. Hong Xiuquan himself was immersed in his religious mission, occupied in writing elaborate comments on the Bible, and totally lost to the world.

Failure of the leadership was one source of Taiping weakness. Inadequate implementation of stated policies was another. Practice did not conform to theory. For example, Hong Xiuquan himself, as well as other Taiping leaders, kept numerous concubines despite the Taiping call for monogamy. Moreover, there were many missed opportunities: the failure to strike before the dynasty could regroup; the failure to cooperate with secret societies and other opponents of the regime who did not share the Taiping faith; the failure to cultivate good relations with the foreign powers.

To make matters worse, Taiping revolutionary ideas repelled all those Chinese who identified with the basic Confucian way of life and understood that the Taiping program was not merely anti-Manchu but anti-Confucian, and thus subversive to the traditional social order. Consequently the Taiping not only failed to recruit gentry support, but they antagonized this key element in Chinese society. To the literati, rule by "civilized" Manchus was preferable to rule by "barbarized" Chinese.

Zeng Guofan and the Defeat of the Taiping

What ultimately prolonged the Qing dynasty's life was a new kind of military force organized by Zeng Guofan (1811–1872), a dedicated Confucian and a product of the examination system. Unlike the old armies organized under the Qing banner system (see p. 25), Zeng's army was a strictly regional force from Hunan, staffed by officers of similar regional and ideological background personally selected by him. They, in turn, recruited soldiers from their own home areas or from members of their own clans. A paternalistic attitude of officers toward their men, a generous pay scale honestly administered, careful moral indoctrination, and common regional ties all helped to produce a well-disciplined force high in morale. Qing statesmen were aware that strong regional armies such as Zeng's threatened the balance of power between the central government and the regions, and were ultimately dangerous to the authority of the dynasty. But the traditional armies of the regime had proved hopelessly inadequate, and the Manchu rulers had no choice but to trust their defense to Zeng. Although organized in Hunan, where it began its operations, the army also fought the Taiping in other provinces. It was not always victorious: twice Zeng suffered such serious reverses that he attempted suicide. But in the long run a well-led and highly motivated army, honestly administered and true to its purpose, proved superior to the Taiping forces.

The dynasty also benefited from the services of two other remarkable leaders. Zuo Zongtang (1812–1885) and especially Li Hongzhang (1823–1901) whose Anhui Army became the strongest anti-Taiping force. After the treaties of 1860, the Western powers sided with the regime that had made such extensive concessions to them, and Western arms were of great assistance, particularly to the Anhui Army. An American adventurer was succeeded by a British officer as leader of four or five thousand Chinese in the "Ever Victorious Army." Meanwhile, French officers commanded the "Ever Triumphant Army," composed of Chinese and Filipino mercenaries. Customs revenues helped loyalists purchase foreign arms and steamers and establish arsenals.

After a series of victories, the loyalist armies laid siege to Nanjing. When the situation became desperate, Hong Xiuquan relied on divine intervention, ordering the starving people to eat manna. According to a Taiping general, "The Sovereign himself, in the open spaces of his palace, collected all sorts of weeds, which he made into a lump and sent out of the palace, demanding that everyone do likewise."[15] The same source attributes Hong's subsequent fatal illness to his eating of these weed concoctions. Shortly after Hong's death, on July 19, 1864, the city fell to an army commanded by Zeng Guofan's brother. As had happened often in this bitter war, the fall of Nanjing was followed by a bloodbath. Hong's son managed to flee,

FIGURE 6.7   Ren Xiong. In a self-portrait unlike any ever painted before, Ren depicts himself with a military haircut and expresses both belligerence and anxiety. Hanging scroll, ink and color on paper. 177.5 × 78.8 cm.
<small>COLLECTION OF THE PALACE MUSEUM, BEIJING, CHINA.</small>

but was discovered in Guangxi and executed. The Taiping, once so close to victory, were completely eradicated. Similarly, the loyalist forces succeeded in quelling the Nian, Muslim, and other rebels.

The Taiping's example was to inspire future revolutionaries, while conservatives continued to admire Zeng Guofan. That others were restless and defiant is suggested by the famous life-size self-portrait of **Ren Xiong** (1820–1857), who served in a military headquarters but did not rest easily with his choice (Figure 6.7). Painted in Shanghai, which was beginning to assume its role as a major meeting place between China and the West, this original, unsettling work of art mirrors the stress of its time and foreshadows future conflict and distress.

China and the World from the Treaty of Nanjing to the End of the Taiping

As we have seen, the Treaty of Nanjing established a pattern, but satisfied neither side. Frustrated in attempts at local negotiation, the British demanded direct representation in Beijing. They also pressed for treaty revision, because the opening of the new ports had not led to the anticipated increase in trade. Behind the demands for freer trade was the persistent belief that only artificial restrictions prevented the development of a giant market in China for British textiles and other products.

One cause of friction between the English and the Chinese was the repeated postponement of the opening of Canton because of the strong antiforeign feeling of its people. The continuation of the opium trade did not help matters, nor did the development of a new commerce in Chinese laborers. These men were often procured against their will, crowded into dismal "coolie" vessels, and transported as contract laborers to work the plantations of Cuba and Peru. The boom set off by the discovery of gold in California in 1848 also brought Chinese immigrants to the United States, but they came as free laborers, their passage organized by Chinese merchants. By 1852 there were 25,000 Chinese in the American West, and by 1887 there were twice that number in California.

There were some efforts at cooperation during these years, as the foreign powers sided with the dynasty rather than the Taiping. With Chinese consent, the

British set about suppressing piracy. More important was the establishment of the Foreign Inspectorate of Customs in Shanghai in 1854 after the Qing officials had been ejected by rebels. The Inspectorate became responsible for the collection of tariffs and the prevention of smuggling. By the new treaties of 1858, its authority was extended to all treaty ports. It remained an important source of support for the dynasty during and after the Taiping Rebellion.

Nevertheless, there was more discord than harmony, and in 1856 war broke out once more. The immediate cause of war was the Arrow Affair. The Arrow was a Chinese-owned but Hong Kong registered vessel which, although flying the British flag, was boarded by Chinese officials, who seized twelve Chinese men whom they charged with piracy. When the viceroy returned the men but refused to apologize and guarantee that it would not happen again, the British responded by seizing Canton. There was a lull in the fighting while the British were occupied fighting a war in India set off by the Mutiny of 1857. When the war in China was resumed in December 1857, the English were joined by the French.

As in the first war, the Europeans again moved north, and in Tianjin the British and French negotiated the Treaties of Tianjin, providing for permanent residency of diplomats in Beijing, the opening of ten new ports, foreign travel throughout China, reduction of inland transit dues, an indemnity, and freedom of movement for all Christian missionaries. However, hostilities resumed after the British envoy discovered that the Qing planned to exchange ratifications in Shanghai rather than Beijing. Although the Chinese defeated the British at Taku, where the river leading to Tianjin enters the sea, victory went to the allies who entered Beijing, where Elgin, the British commander, vented his anger by burning down the imperial summer palace of around two hundred buildings northwest of Beijing. In October the Conventions of Beijing, were signed to supplement the Treaties of Tianjin, which now also took effect. In addition to the usual indemnity, China was forced to open eleven new ports, to grant rights to travel in the interior, and to allow foreign envoys to reside in Beijing. In 1860 the French also surreptitiously inserted into the Chinese text a provision granting missionaries the right to buy land and erect buildings in all parts of China.

The peace agreements were secured through the mediation of the Russian ambassador to Beijing, who used the opportunity to consolidate the gains Russia had made to date and to obtain new concessions for his country. Under Peter the Great and Catherine the Great, Russia's land empire had expanded into the area west of the Pamirs then known as Russian Turkestan, and in 1851 Russia obtained trading privileges and the right to station consuls at Kuldja and Chuguchak (Dacheng) in the Ili region of Chinese Turkestan (now Xinjiang) east of the Pamirs. Now areas southwest of Kuldja and Urga (Ulan Bator) in Outer Mongolia were also opened to them, but, having suppressed Muslim rebellions, the Qing were able to retain their position in Central Asia.

Meanwhile, Russia made massive gains in the northeast. In the Amur region Nikolai Muraviev, governor-general of Siberia, began putting pressure on the Qing in 1847. In 1860, the entire area north of the Amur was ceded to the Russians, who also received the lands east of the Ussuri River, which were incorporated into the Russian Empire as the Amur and Maritime Provinces. In the latter, Muraviev founded Vladivostok ("Ruler of the East," in Russian). Russia also now received most-favored-nation status. The gains Russia made at this time remain a source of conflict between the Russians and Chinese.

Notes

1. Quoted in Alexander B. Woodside, *Vietnam and the Chinese Model: A Comparative Study of Vietnamese and Chinese Government in the First Half of the Nineteenth Century* (Cambridge: Harvard Univ. Press, 1988), p. 247.

2. Li Tana, *Nguyen Cochinchina* (Ithaca: Southeast Asia Program, Cornell University, 1998), Chapter 5.

3. K. W. Taylor, "Surface Orientations in Vietnam: Beyond Histories of Nation and Region," in *The Journal of Asian Studies 57,* No. 4 (Nov. 1998), p. 965.

4. Lan Cao, *Monkey Bridge* (New York: Penguin Putnam, 1997), p. 150.

5. Nola Cooke, "The Myth of the Restoration: Dang-trong Influences in the Spiritual Life of the Early Nguyen Dynasty (1802–47)" in Anthony Reid, ed., *The Last Stand of Asian Autonomies* (New York: St. Martin's Press, 1997), p. 277.

6. Hohn Balaban, ed. and trans., *Spring Essence: The Poetry of Ho Xuan Huong.* (Port Townsend, WA: Copper Canyon Press, 2000), p. 35.

7. Maurice M. Durand and Nguyen Tran Huan, *An Introduction to Vietnamese Literature,* translated from the French by D. M. Hawke. (New York: Columbia Univ. Press, 1985), p. 99.

8. David G. Marr, *Vietnamese Anticolonialism 1885–1925* (Berkeley: Univ. of California Press, 1971), p. 26.

9. Alexander B. Woodside, *Community and Revolution in Modern Vietnam* (Boston: Houghton Mifflin, 1976), p. 3.

10. Franz Schurmann and Orville Schell, *The China Reader: Imperial China* (New York: Vintage Books, 1967), pp. 105–13, which reproduces Harley F. MacNair, *Modern Chinese History, Selected Readings* (Shanghai: Commercial Press Ltd., 1923), pp. 2–9.

11. John K. Fairbank, *Trade and Diplomacy on the China Coast: The Opening of the Treaty Ports, 1842–1854* (Cambridge: Harvard Univ. Press, 1953), p. 59, which quotes H. B. Morse, *The Chronicles of the East India Company Trading to China, 1635–1834,* 5 vols. (Oxford, 1926, 1929) 2: 247–52.

12. James M. Polachek, *The Inner Opium War* (Cambridge: Harvard Univ. Press, 1992).

13. Ssu-yü Teng and John K. Fairbank, *China's Response to the West: A Documentary Survey, 1839–1923* (Cambridge: Harvard Univ. Press, 1954), p. 26.

14. John Fletcher, *The Cambridge History of China,* vol. 10, ed. John K. Fairbank (Cambridge: Cambridge Univ. Press, 1978), pp. 375–85.

15. Quoted in Jonathan D. Spence, *God's Chinese Son: The Taiping Heavenly Kingdom of Hong Xiuquan* (New York: W. W. Norton, 1996), p. 325.

Japan from Tokugawa
to Meiji: *1787–1873*

1787 1793 1800   1837   1853   1868 1873

Osaka Uprising   Perry's Arrival

(1789–1791)

LATE TOKUGAWA   **MEIJI**
                                                                 (First Phase)

Kansei
Reforms   Famine   Mizuno Tadakuni Ii Naosuke
                          (1833–1836) (1841–1843)   (1858–1860)

The Bakufu 1787–1841

Economy and Society

Reforms

Intellectual Currents

The Opening of Japan

Domestic Politics

Sonnō Jōi

Mixed Responses to the West

Last Years of the Shogunate, 1860–1867

Formation of a New Government:
The Meiji Restoration

The Charter Oath

Dismantling the Old Order

Disaffection and Opposition

The Crisis of 1873

The Meaning of the Restoration

Internal crisis and Western intrusion are the main themes of this chapter, as of the last. Although prior to the 1830s there were some good years, the Tokugawa system was showing many symptoms of stress even before challenges from abroad put the old order to a final test. However, the dynamism of the forces subverting Tokugawa state and society ultimately helped Japan to develop into a modern country.

The Bakufu 1787–1841

Nature rescued the land from the famine of the 1780s, but it took government action to relieve the *bakufu*'s financial distress. The Kansei Reforms (1789–1791) were led by Matsudaira Sadanobu (1787–1793), an earnest Confucian who served a young shogun and owed his position as head of the *bakufu* to the support he received from an inner circle of *daimyo*. Matsudaira encouraged a return to simpler times. He launched a much-needed campaign against corruption and made an effort to improve public services in Edo, but his fiscal and economic program relied on edicts mandating lower prices for rice, restrictions on merchant guilds, cancellation of some samurai loans, and rent control. Matsudaira also sought to freeze foreign policy, reducing contact with the Dutch and proposing to leave Hokkaido undeveloped as a buffer to foreign intervention.

To improve administration, he not only sought to advance "men of ability" but tried to control what they thought by furthering education and by making the Neo-Confucianism of Zhu Xi the official doctrine. He proscribed heterodoxy from the official *bakufu* school, but this had little effect elsewhere. There was also a hardening of censorship. All told, these measures "institutionalized and hardened tradition . . . and left a regime less flexible and more concerned with preserving a tradition that had now been defined."[1]

It did not take long for the *bakufu*'s systemic fiscal ills to reappear. By 1800 its annual budget showed a small deficit, the beginning of a trend. Forced loans and nineteen currency devaluations between 1819 and 1837 brought only temporary relief. The political authorities remained dependent on the market and the merchants who understood and manipulated the market. The government could not simply borrow, because there was no system of deficit financing. When famine struck again, beginning in 1833 and reaching a crescendo in 1836, the *bakufu*'s response was once again inadequate. Once again reform was urgently needed.

Economy and Society

Reflecting Japan's geographical and political diversity, there were major local differences in the economy and society. Fortunately, a number of local studies are currently helping to correct overemphasis on the center, which was less central then than now. Thus in his study of the herring fisheries in Hokkaido, which supplied fertilizer to the rest of Japan, David L. Howell found "a vibrant proto-industrial complex of commodity production for distant markets, dominated by merchant capitalists who used their ties to the local feudal authorities to good advantage."[2] A number of other domains pursued market-oriented policies, and commercial networks developed that linked communities in ways beyond the control of individual political authorities.

Change varied geographically and was complex socially. Some flourished; others suffered. Among the losers were lower-ranking samurai who had to convert a substantial portion of their rice stipend into cash and who were constantly at the mercy of a fluctuating market that they did not understand and would not study. When *daimyo*, burdened with periodic attendance in Edo and the need to maintain establishments in both Edo and their own *han* capitals, found themselves in financial difficulty, they frequently reduced samurai stipends. This hurt even the small minority of high-ranking men with large stipends, but was downright devastating for the bulk of samurai, who ranked low in status and stipend.

Some samurai married daughters of wealthy merchants, but many lived in increasingly desperate circumstances. They pawned their swords, worked at humble crafts such as umbrella making and sandal weaving, and tried to hide their misery from the world. A samurai was taught that his mouth should display a toothpick even when he had not eaten. The samurai were not dissatisfied with the premises of a social system in which, after all, they formed the ruling class, but they were enraged by the discrepancy between the theoretical elevation of their status and the reality of their poverty. Not only was their poverty demeaning, but the spectacle of merchant wealth hurt their pride. It seemed the height of injustice that society should reward the selfish money-makers and condemn to indigence the warrior whose life was one of service. They harbored deep resentment against incompetence and corruption in high places, and called on governments to employ more capable men from the lower samurai ranks.

City merchants and rural entrepreneurs flourished, but the increasing scope of the market had diverse effects on ordinary folk. In the Kanto there were villages left with untilled fields as people fled rural poverty in the hope of a better life in industry or commerce, but the market often proved a hard taskmaster. Consolation when things turned out badly and hope in a better future were offered by charismatic religious teachers and by cults such as Fujiko, which was centered on pilgrimage to Mount Fuji and worship of Maitreya, associated in Japan as elsewhere with millenarianism (see Chapter 1).

When, as during a famine, things became unbearable, people resorted to violence. The best estimate has it that during 1830–1844 there were 465 rural disputes, 445 peasant uprisings, and 101 urban riots. A great impression was made by the 1837 uprising led by Ōshio Heihachiro (1793–1837), a low-ranking *bakufu* official and follower of Wang Yangming's philosophy of action. Although poorly planned and quickly suppressed, the uprising expressed a general sense of malaise and of the disintegration of authority. This was the case also in the countryside, where, in earlier conflicts, villagers had united behind their headmen, but now the gap between the rich and poor had reached the point where interests diverged too widely for the village to speak with a single voice.

Reforms

In response to the financial and social crisis, there was one more concerted effort at reform both in the domains and at the center. On both levels, large doses of antiquated remedies such as economic retrenchment, bureaucratic reform, and moral rearmament were administered, but there were also some innovative policies. In the *bakufu*, reforms began in 1841 under Mizuno Tadakuni (1793–1851), a house *daimyo* (*fudai*) who rose to *bakufu* leadership. His measures included recoinage, forced loans, dismissal of officials to reduce costs, and sumptuary laws intended to preserve morals and save money. Censorship became stricter. An effort (by no means the first) was made to force peasants to return to their lands. This was in keeping with the Confucian view of the primacy of agriculture as well as with the Tokugawa policy of strict class separation—but it hardly solved any problems.

A program to create a solid area of *bakufu* control around Edo and Osaka called for the creation of a *bakufu*-controlled zone of 25 square miles around Edo and 12 square miles around Osaka by moving certain *daimyo* and direct retainers out of these areas. This could have rationalized administration and strengthened the shogunate, but the plan proved too ambitious and could not be carried out. In the hope of fighting inflation, merchant monopolies were broken up and an attempt was made to bar the *daimyo* from engaging in commercial monopolies. Despite the retrenchment policy, an expensive and ostentatious formal procession to the Tokugawa mausoleum at Nikko was organized in an effort to reassert the *bakufu*'s preeminence. But the *daimyo* were not easily bridled, and the reform lasted only two years.

Various domains, faced with similar problems, attempted local reform programs of their own. Here and there *han* government machinery was reformed, stipends and other costs were cut, and some domains even rewarded the expert assistance of outstanding members of the merchant community by promoting them to samurai status. Agriculture was encouraged and commercial policies were changed. Generally, in the *han* as in the *bakufu*, the reforms ended, "some whimpering their way into oblivion, others culminating in an explosion in which the reformers were dismissed . . . and sometimes thrown into prison as well. . . . Whatever the end, they were ignored until their resurrection as models for fresh reforms in the 1850s and 1860s."[3]

A major domain in which the reforms did take hold was Satsuma in Kyushu (see Figure 7.1). Subsequently, Chōshū in southwest Honshu enjoyed similar success. In important ways these were untypical domains. For one, they were both large, outside *han* (*tozama*) which had accepted Tokugawa supremacy only when they had no other alternative. Both had had their domains transferred and reduced in size. One consequence was that they kept alive an anti-Tokugawa tradition. Another was that the reduction in the size of their domains left them with a higher-than-average ratio of samurai to the land. In Satsuma, this led to the formation of a class of samurai who worked the land *(goshi)* and maintained a tight control of the countryside, which experienced not a single peasant uprising

FIGURE 7.1   Map showing Satsuma in Kyushu and Chōshū in southwest Honshu, 1850s–1860s.

throughout the Tokugawa period. Satsuma backwardness was also an asset to the domain in the sense that it worked against the erosion of samurai values found in economically more advanced and urbane regions. Both Chōshū and Satsuma also had special family ties with the court in Kyoto, the most likely focus for any anti-*bakufu* movement.

In both *han*, finances were put in order and a budget surplus was built up, although by different means. In Chōshū, rigorous cost-cutting was initiated, major improvements were made in *han* financial administration, and the land tax was reformed. Most monopolies were abolished, since they were unprofitable for the government and unpopular among the people. Only the profitable shipping and warehouse monopolies at Shimonoseki were continued. Otherwise, commodity transactions were turned over to merchants for a fee. Satsuma, in contrast, derived much of its income from its monopolies, especially the monopoly on sugar from the Ryukyu Islands, a Satsuma dependency, which was directed to continue sending tribute to China in order to foster trade. Thus the Ryukyus served as a source of Chinese goods for Satsuma. The sugar monopoly was strictly enforced: private sale of sugar was a crime punishable by death. The sugar was brought to market in Osaka in the *han*'s own ships, and at every stage, from production to sale, everything was done to maximize profit for the Satsuma treasury.

These programs required vigorous leadership, because they naturally ran up against the opposition of merchants and others who benefited from doing things the old way. Both Chōshū and Satsuma were fortunate in having reform-minded *daimyo* who raised to power young samurai of middle or low rank, men who tended to be much more innovative and energetic than conservative samurai of high rank. Particularly in Chōshū, such differences in background and outlook among the samurai class led to bitter antagonisms and political turbulence.

The fact that reform was more successful in Chōshū and Satsuma than in the *bakufu* suggests that it was easier to implement reform in a well-organized, remote domain than in the central region, where the economic changes were most advanced and political pressures and responsibilities were far greater. Reform attempts in other *han* varied in success, but Chōshū and Satsuma are particularly important, since these two large and wealthy domains were to play a crucial role in the eventual overthrow of the Tokugawa.

Intellectual Currents

Economic, social, and political changes were accompanied by intellectual restiveness. Perceptions and ideas advanced by Shinto Revivalists of the School of National Learning, the Mito school with its emphasis on the centrality of the emperor, followers of Dutch Learning, and advocates of social restructuring ate away at the intellectual foundations of Tokugawa rule.

From the world of Osaka merchants came the bold ideas of Yamagata Bantō (1748–1821), a great Osaka financier with a well-established place in society. Yamagata based his ideas on astronomy, and formulated a view of the world that allowed for achievements to occur anywhere on the globe. He had great regard for utility and trust. One of his recommendations was to make written Japanese more accessible by using only the phonetic *kana* script and eliminating all Chinese characters. An even more unorthodox thinker was Kaihō Seiryō (1748–1821), who spent his life traveling all over Japan free from encumbrances of status or family, and saw all relations, including that between lord and samurai, in economic terms: the samurai sells his service to the lord in exchange for a stipend. For Kaihō Seiryō this was merely accommodating to *li* (principle). Here a key Neo-Confucian concept is employed to structure a new theory of social conduct. The old bottles were capable of holding remarkably new wine.

In political thought, the respective roles of emperor and shogun continued to be subjects of discussion. In Mito, noted for its work on history (see Chapter 4), scholars emphasized that the emperor ruled by virtue of his unique descent and that the shogun's legitimacy came from the mandate he derived from the emperor. Aizawa Seishisai (1782–1863), a leading Mito thinker, combined Confucian values and *bushidō* with Shinto mythology in discussing Japan's unique polity (*kokutai*). In 1825 he wanted the emperor to create in Japan the kind of unity that he saw as the basis for the strength of Western states and attributed to (iniquitous) Christianity. As Bob Wakabayashi has indicated, in 1825 Aizawa's "argument for using the emperor's religious authority to bolster *bakufu* political supremacy was sensible and compelling."[4] But thirty years later the emperor and shogun had grown so far apart that this would have been inconceivable, However, Aizawa's glorification of the emperor was to outlast the very idea of a *bakufu*.

Attitudes toward the West varied widely. Hirata Atsutane (1776–1843), for example, drew on the ideas of Motoori Norinaga (see Chapter 4, p. 78) and advocated an irrational and frequently naive nativism, but as a physician he admired Western medicine and studied Dutch medical texts. To reconcile his adulation of Japan with his appreciation for the foreign science, Hirata maintained that Japan had originally been pure and free of disease: the need for a powerful medical science arose only after Japan was infected by foreign contacts.

Most students of Dutch Learning took a more positive attitude. Interest in practical Western sciences such as astronomy, medicine, and mathematics continued to grow. The *bakufu* itself, in 1811, set up a bureau to translate Dutch books even while it maintained its closed door policies toward the West. Takano Chōei (1804–1850) and Watanabe Kazan (1795–1841), persecuted for disagreeing with the *bakufu*'s seclusion policy, ended as suicides.

Outstanding among the students of Western science was the Confucian scholar Sakuma Shōzan (1811–1864), who conducted experiments in chemistry and glassmaking, and later became an expert in the casting of guns; he was a serious thinker about the principles as well as the products of Western technology. There was ample room in his thought for Western learning, which he saw as part of the ultimate unity of *li* as taught by Zhu Xi, supplementing, not supplanting, his own tradition. His formula, "Eastern ethics and Western science," conveying the primacy of Japanese values as well as the compatibility of Western science, became an influential slogan after the Meiji Restoration. But Sakuma did not live to see the day, for he was murdered by an antiforeign extremist from Chōshū in 1864.

Sakuma's intellectual strategy was essentially one of compartmentalization. The basic framework was left intact, with native and foreign traditions assigned different functions. Each had its distinct role. Most students of Dutch painting would have agreed, for they valued Western techniques more for their practical results than for any aesthetic merit. Yet, like all generalizations, this demands qualification. Hokusai, who lived until 1849, once contrasted the use of shading for decorative purposes in Chinese and Japanese art with its employment to create an effect of three-dimensionality in the West. He concluded, "One must understand both methods: there must be life and death in everything one paints."[5]

The Opening of Japan

The opening of China to the West was a result of the Opium War and subsequent treaties with the European powers. In Japan, the opening resulted from an armed mission by Commodore Matthew C. Perry of the United States Navy in 1853 (see Figure 7.2). The treaties that followed that momentous event ended the Tokugawa policy of seclusion. This undermined not only the authority of the *bakufu* but of the entire Tokugawa system.

Before 1853 there were a number of Western attempts to induce the Japanese to broaden their foreign policy, but these efforts were sporadic, because they were not supported by substantial economic and political interests of the kind at work in China. Regarded as poor and remote, Japan was considered a low priority by the great powers. The first approaches came from Japan's nearest Eurasian neighbor, the Russian Empire, and took place in the north, in the Kurile Islands, Sakhalin, and Hokkaido. In 1778 and again in 1792 the Russians requested trade relations in Hokkaido, and in 1804 a similar request was made in Nagasaki. All were refused. British ships seeking trade or ship's stores were also turned away. British whaling ships sometimes requested supplies, but in 1825 the *bakufu* ordered that all foreign ships should be driven from Japanese waters. In 1837 a private American-British attempt to open relations with Japan fared no better. But in 1842 the shogunate relaxed the edicts of 1825 and ordered that foreign ships accidentally arriving in Japan were to be provided with water, food, and fuel before being sent on their way.

China's defeat in the Opium War and the opening of new ports increased the number of Western vessels in East Asia, and hence the pressure on Japan. This changing situation could not be ignored. To begin with, the lessons of Chinese weakness and Western strength were not lost on Japanese observers. Information concerning Western science, industry, and military capabilities continued to be provided by scholars of Dutch Learning and by the Dutch at Nagasaki. Information also came from China: Wei Yuan's *Illustrated Treatise on the Sea Kingdoms* was widely read after it appeared in a Japanese edition in 1847. Furthermore, the Japanese were making progress in mastering Western technology. By the 1840s Mito, Hizen, and Satsuma were casting guns using Western methods. In 1850 Hizen possessed the first reverberatory furnace needed to produce iron suitable for making modern cannons. As

FIGURE 7.2 *Commodore Matthew C. Perry* (1794–1858) of the United States Navy. Artist unknown. In 1853–1854, Perry successfully led an armed mission to force isolationist Japan's agreement to open trade and diplomatic relations with the United States. Woodcut, nineteenth century, 26 × 24.5 cm.
Photograph courtesy Peabody Essex Museum, Salem, Massachusetts.

already noted, a few courageous students of the West had suggested abandoning the policy of seclusion well before the arrival of Perry. The Dutch, too, had warned the *bakufu* of the designs of the stronger Western nations.

In 1846 an American mission to Japan ended in failure, but, with the acquisition of California in 1848, the interest of the United States increased, since Nagasaki, 500 miles from Shanghai, was a convenient fueling stop for ships bound from San Francisco to that port. Thus the United States, rather than Britain or Russia whose interests remained marginal, took the lead, sending out Commodore Perry with four ships. Perry and his fleet reached Japan in July 1853, forced the Japanese to accept a letter from the American president to the emperor, and announced that he would return for an answer the following spring.

No match militarily for the American fleet, the *bakufu* realized that it would have to accede at least in part to American demands. In preparation for that unpopular move, it took the unprecedented step of soliciting the opinions of even the outside *daimyo*. This turned out to be a serious miscalculation, for instead of hoped-for support, the *bakufu* received only divided and unhelpful advice and seriously undermined its exclusive right to determine foreign policy.

When Perry returned in February 1854 with eight ships, an initial treaty was signed that provided for the opening of Shimoda and Hakodate to ships seeking provisions, assured that the shipwrecked would receive good treatment, and permitted the United States later to send a consul to Japan. Similar treaties with Britain and France followed in 1855, and the Dutch and Russians negotiated broader agreements in 1857. The task of negotiating a commercial treaty was left to the first American consul, Townsend Harris, who arrived in Japan in 1856 and gradually succeeded in persuading the shogunate to make concessions (see Figure 7.3). The resulting treaty was signed in 1858, and another round of treaties with the Dutch, Russians, British, and French followed.

At the end of this process, Japan's international situation was essentially that of China under the unequal treaty system. First there was the matter of opening ports. This began with Shimoda on the Izu Peninsula and Hakodate in Hokkaido; it was extended to Nagasaki and Kanagawa (for which Yokohama was substituted); dates were set for the opening of Niigata, Hyogo (modern Kobe), and admission of foreign residents, but not trade, into Osaka and Edo. As in China, the treaties gave foreigners the right to be tried by their own consular courts under their own laws (extraterritoriality). Japan lost its tariff autonomy and was limited to relatively low import duties. Most-favored-nation treatment obliged Japan to extend to all states any concession it granted to any one of the others.

Domestic Politics

For the *bakufu*, forced to accede to the foreign demands without enjoying support at home, these were difficult years. Each concession to the powers provided additional ammunition to its domestic enemies. Compounding its difficulties, the *bakufu* was itself divided by factionalism and policy differences. An

FIGURE 7.3 *Harris's Procession on the Way to Edo.* Artist unknown. Townsend Harris, first American consul to Japan, traveled to Edo (Tokyo) in 1856 to negotiate a commercial treaty with Japan—a treaty that contained terms unfavorable to Japan. Watercolor, 53.5 × 38.8 cm.

attempt was made after Perry's arrival to broaden the shogunate's base by drawing on the advice of non-house *daimyo*. The Lord of Mito, Tokugawa Nariaki (1800–1860), a persistent advocate of resistance to the West, was placed in charge of national defense. These measures, however, failed to strengthen the *bakufu*— too many men were pulling in opposite directions.

When the shogun died without an heir in 1858, a bitter dispute took place over the rival claims of two candidates for the succession. One was still a boy, but had the strongest claim by descent. He also had the backing of most of the house *daimyo* (*fudai*) including that of Ii Naosuke, greatest of the *fudai*. The other candidate was Tokugawa Yoshinobu (then known as Hitotsubashi Keiki), the capable son of the Lord of Mito.

The immediate issue in the succession dispute concerned control over the *bakufu*, for Keiki's accession was seen as a threat to the continued control over the shogunate by the *fudai*. At the same time, foreign policy was involved, for the *bakufu* officials, as men on the spot, were inclined to make concessions to the foreigners. The great lords, however, demanded a vigorous defense policy against the intruders from the West. Furthermore, the Lord of Mito and some of his peers envisioned their own *han* as playing important roles in building up military strength. Thus his advocacy of a strong foreign policy was consistent with his desire to strengthen his own domain at the expense of the center. Meanwhile, the split in the *bakufu* increased the political importance of the imperial court. Nariaki even appealed to Kyoto for support for his son's candidacy. And when the shogun tried to obtain imperial approval for the treaty negotiated with Harris, he failed.

The crisis of 1858 was temporarily resolved when Ii Naosuke took charge of the *bakufu* as Grand Councilor (*tairo*), a high post more often than not left vacant, and one that had previously been held by several members of the Ii family. The effective power of this position depended on the authority of the incumbent, and the strong-minded Ii Naosuke used it to dominate the shogunate. He proceeded to sign the treaty with the United States without prior imperial approval, vigorously reasserted *bakufu* power, purged his enemies, forced into retirement or house arrest the *daimyo* who had opposed him and were on the losing side in the succession dispute, including the Lord of Mito, and punished some of the court nobles and Mito loyalists. For a moment the *bakufu* was revitalized. But only for a moment: in March 1860 Ii was assassinated by a group of samurai, mostly from Mito. They were advocates of *Sonnō* —"Revere the Emperor"—and *Jōi*—"Expel the Barbarians."

Sonnō Jōi

As we observed earlier, Mito was the home of an emperor-centered school of historiography and political thought, and its lord was one of the most fervent advocates of a strong military policy to "expel the barbarians." It is therefore not surprising that Mito thought influenced the passionate and brilliant young man who became the main spokesman and hero of the Sonnō Jōi movement. This was Yoshida Shōin (1830–1859), the son of a low-ranking Chōshū samurai. Yoshida was influenced by *bushidō* in the tradition of Yamaga Sokō, by books on military science, and by Confucianism. From Sakuma Shōzan he learned about the West. Then he became acquainted with Mito ideas on a study trip to northern Japan, which, since it was unauthorized, cost him his samurai rank. Apprehensive of the West and convinced of the importance of knowing one's enemy, he tried to stow away on one of Commodore Perry's ships, but was caught and placed under house arrest in Chōshū. After his release he started a school there and attracted disciples, including Kido Kōin (or Takamasa, 1834–1877), one of the three leading statesmen of the Meiji Restoration, and the future leaders Itō Hirobumi and Yamagata Aritomo. Yoshida condemned the *bakufu* for its handling of the foreign problem. He charged that its failure to expel the barbarians reflected incompetence, dereliction of duty, and a lack of proper reverence for the throne. Like many men of lower samurai origins, he resented a system that rewarded birth more than ability or talent, and blamed the *bakufu*'s inability to reject the foreigners on this system. What was needed to redress the situation were pure and selfless officials who would act out of true loyalty rather than mindless obedience. Thus Yoshida's teaching combined elements of moral revival at home, opposition to the foreigner, and championship of the throne.

Initially, Yoshida favored the appointment of new men to the *bakufu*, but after the signing of the treaty with the United States in 1858, he concluded that the *bakufu* must be overthrown. Both personal fulfillment and national salvation required an act of unselfish self-sacrifice by a national hero. In 1858 Yoshida, seeking to achieve both aims, plotted the assassination of the emissary sent by the shogun to the imperial court to persuade the emperor to agree to the commercial treaty with the United States. Word leaked out. Yoshida was arrested and sent to Edo, where he was beheaded the following year.

Mixed Responses to the West

In this turbulent era, Japanese reactions to the West varied widely. Some Japanese, like the Confucian Shinoya Tōin (1810–1867), had an absolute hatred for everything Western. He even belittled the script in which the foreigners wrote, describing it as

> confused and irregular, wriggling like snakes or larvae of mosquitoes. The straight ones are like dog's teeth, the round ones are like worms. The crooked ones are like the forelegs of a mantis, the stretched ones are like slime lines left by snails. They resemble dried bones or decaying skulls, rotten bellies of dead snakes or parched vipers.[6]

It is not surprising that a culture which prized calligraphy should find the strictly utilitarian Western script aesthetically unappetizing, but Shinoya's invective goes beyond mere distaste. Every word betrays, indeed is meant to express, horror and disgust at the beasts that had now come among them.

But there were others who were determined to learn from the West, even if only to use that knowledge to defeat the foreigner. Their slogan was *kaikoku jōi:* "open the country to drive out the barbarians." The learning process continued. In 1857 the *bakufu* opened the "Institute for the Investigation of Barbarian Books" near Edo Castle. Not only the *bakufu* but some of the domains sent men on study trips abroad; in the case of the *han* this was often done illegally. The process of adopting Western technology, begun even before Perry's arrival, was accelerated. An indication of the people's receptivity to the new knowledge is provided by the popularity of the writings of Fukuzawa Yukichi (1835–1901), who went abroad twice in the early sixties and published seven books prior to the Restoration, beginning in 1866 with the first volume of *Conditions in the West (Seiyō jijō)*, which appeared in 1866 and promptly sold 150,000 copies. Another 100,000 copies were sold in pirated editions. These works, written in a simple style easy enough for Fukuzawa's housemaid to read, were filled with detailed descriptions of Western institutions and life: hospitals and schools, tax systems and museums, climate and clothes, cutlery, beds, and chamberpots. Fukuzawa went on to become a leading Meiji intellectual, but the turbulent years just prior to the Restoration were dangerous for men of his outlook.

Unlike Yoshida Shōin, some people hoped for a reconciliation of the court and *bakufu,* and there were some who still hoped the *bakufu* could transform itself and take the lead in creating a more modern state. These issues, at work during the sixties, were finally buried in the Restoration.

Last Years of the Shogunate, 1860–1867

After the assassination of Ii Naosuke in 1860, the *bakufu* leadership tried compromise. An effort was made to effect a "union of the court and military" that was confirmed by the shogun's marriage to the emperor's sister. In return for affirming the emperor's primacy, the *bakufu* obtained assent for its foreign policy. It also sought to win *daimyo* support by relaxing the requirements for attendance at Edo. However, this policy ran into the opposition of Kyoto loyalists, activists of the *Sonnō Jōi* persuasion, samurai, and voluntary rōnin who had escaped the bonds of feudal discipline by requesting to leave their lords' service. Psychologically this was not difficult, as their loyalty to their lords had become bureaucratized and they now felt the claims of a higher loyalty to the throne. Men of extremist dedication, ready to sacrifice their lives for the cause, terrorized the streets of Kyoto in the early sixties and made the capital unsafe for moderates, who risked losing their heads and having them displayed as a warning to others.

This also happened to statues: their location in a temple did not save the statues of Ashikaga shoguns from decapitation at the hands of some followers of Hirata Atsutane who, unable to reach prominent living targets, exercised vengeance on the Ashikaga for wronging the emperor in the fourteenth century. Mito, too, was unsafe for moderates.

For ordinary people this was a time when their frustrations came to a head, a time of messianic visions and religious fervor, of amulets falling from the sky, and of people finding temporary escape from misery by dancing wildly in the streets, shouting "*ee ja nai ka*" ("ain't it great," or "what the hell"), barging into the houses of the rich and powerful demanding food and drink, forcing them to join the dance, and wreaking general havoc. Beginning in the cities of central Japan and spreading along the Tōkaido, these riots showed that the Tokugawa order was falling apart. George M. Wilson says of the Meji Restoration that "a pervasive urge to remedy distress at home was just as compelling to most participants as the patriotic intent to elevate Japan in the international area."[7]

Westerners, too, were blamed for the distress, for the opening of the ports was followed by a marked rise in the price of rice, causing great hardship and reinforcing nativistic hatred of foreigners. Several foreigners were assassinated by fervent samurai in 1859, and in 1861 Townsend Harris's Dutch interpreter was cut down, and the British legation in Edo was attacked. In 1862 a British merchant lost his life at the hands of Satsuma samurai. When the British were unable to obtain satisfaction from the *bakufu,* they took matters into their own hands. In

August 1863 they bombarded Kagoshima, the Satsuma capital, in order to force punishment of the guilty and payment of an indemnity.

A similar incident involving Chōshū took place in the summer of 1863. By that time extremists had won control of the imperial court and, with Chōshū backing, had forced the shogun to accept June 25, 1863, as the date for the expulsion of the barbarians. The *bakufu*, caught between intransigent foreigners and the insistent court, interpreted the agreement to mean that negotiations for the closing of the ports would begin on that day, but Chōshū and the loyalists interpreted it more literally. When Chōshū guns began firing on foreign ships in the Straits of Shimonoseki, the foreign ships fired back. First American warships came to shell the fortifications, then French ships landed parties that destroyed the fort and ammunition. Still Chōshū persisted in firing on foreign vessels, until in September 1864 a combined French, Dutch, and American fleet demolished the forts and forced Chōshū to come to terms. These losses, plus a defeat inflicted on Chōshū adherents by a Satsuma-Aizu force in Kyoto in August 1864, stimulated Chōshū to overhaul its military forces. It had already undertaken to purchase arms and ships. Now peasant militia were organized, and mixed rifle units were formed, staffed by commoners and samurai, a radical departure from Tokugawa practice and from the basic principles of Tokugawa society. One of these units was commanded by Itō Hirobumi, recently returned from study in England.

Satsuma's response to defeat, although not as radical as Chōshū's, was similar in its appreciation of the superiority of Western weapons. With British help, the domain began acquiring Western ships, forming the nucleus of what was to become the Imperial Japanese Navy. The British supported Satsuma partly because they were disillusioned with the *bakufu* and partly because the French were supporting the shogunate with arms, hoping to lay the foundations for future influence in a reconstituted shogunate. By now many *bakufu* officials appreciated the need for institutional change as well as modernization. During the closing years of the Tokugawa, the issue was no longer one of preserving the old system but of who would take the lead in building the new. In Chōshū and Satsuma too there was now less talk about "expelling the barbarians" and more about "enriching the country and strengthening the army," at least among the leaders.

The politics of these years were even more than usually full of complications and intrigues, and, as long as Chōshū and Satsuma remained on opposite sides, the situation remained fluid. Traditionally unfriendly to each other, competing for power in Kyoto, and differing in their policy recommendations, they were nevertheless unified in their opposition to a restoration of Tokugawa power. There were two wars against Chōshū. In the first, 1864–1865, a large *bakufu* force with men from many domains defeated Chōshū. This in turn set off a civil war in Chōshū from which the revolutionaries, with their mixed rifle regiments, emerged victors. This led to a second *bakufu* war against Chōshū, but before this second war began, in 1866, Chōshū and Satsuma made a secret alliance. When war did come, Satsuma and some other powerful *han* remained on the sidelines. Although outnumbered, the Chōshū forces, better trained, better armed, and high in morale, defeated the *bakufu*.

After this defeat by a single *han*, the *bakufu*, under Tokugawa Yoshinobu (who inherited the position of shogun in 1866), tried to save what it could. There were attempts to work out a *daimyo* coalition, and calls for imperial restoration. In November the shogun accepted a proposal that he resign in favor of a council of *daimyo* under the emperor. According to this arrangement, he was to retain his lands and, as the most powerful lord in Japan, serve as prime minister. However, this was unacceptable to the *sonnō* advocates in Satsuma and Chōshū and to the restorationists at court, including the court noble Iwakura Tonomi (1825–1883), a master politician. On January 3, 1868, forces from Satsuma and other *han* seized the palace and proclaimed the restoration. The shogunate was destroyed. Tokugawa lands were confiscated, and the shogun himself was reduced to the status of an ordinary *daimyo*. A short civil war ensued. There was fighting in Edo and in northern Honshu, but no real contest. Last to surrender was the *bakufu* navy in May 1869.

Formation of a New Government: The Meiji Restoration

The men who overthrew the Tokugawa in January 1868 did not subscribe to any clear and well-defined program. There was general agreement on the abolition of the shogunate and "restoration" of the emperor, but this meant no more than that the emperor should once again be at the center of the political system, functioning as the source of legitimacy and providing a sense of continuity. It definitely did not mean that actual power should be given to the sixteen-year-old Meiji Emperor (1852–1912; r. 1867–1912),* nor did it necessarily imply the destruction of feudalism, for there were those who envisioned the restoration in terms of a new feudal system headed by the emperor. On the other hand, Japanese scholars had long been aware that the Chinese system provided a bureaucratic alternative to feudalism. This, very likely, eased the shift to bureaucratic centralization.

The new leaders did not always see eye to eye, but they did share certain qualities: they were all of similar age (35–43) and rank, and came from the victorious *han* or the court aristocracy, although the *han* coalition was soon broadened to include men from Tosa and Hizen. The three most eminent leaders in the early years of the restoration were Ōkubo Toshimichi (1830–1878), Kido Kōin (1833–1877), and Saigō Takamori (1827–1877). Both Ōkubo and Kido had risen to leadership in their own domains (Satsuma and Chōshū), through their influence in the domain's bureaucratic establishment and among the loyalist activists. Of the two, Ōkubo was the stronger personality—disciplined, formal, and somewhat intimidating, completely dedicated to the nation, cautious, and practical. Kido was more lively but also more volatile, less self-confident but more concerned than Ōkubo

---

*His name was Mutsuhito but, as in the case of the Qing emperors in China, it is customary to refer to him and his successors by the designation given to their reign periods.

with strengthening the popular base of the government. But he was just as devoted to building a strong state.

Ōkubo's was the single strongest voice in government during 1873–1878. One
of his initial tasks was to retain the cooperation of Saigō, the military leader of the
Satsuma forces who had joined with Chōshū to overthrow the Tokugawa. Saigō
was a man of imposing physique and great physical strength. He was known for
his outstanding courage, and possessed many of the traditional warrior virtues,
such as generosity and contempt for money. More conservative than the others,
he was devoted to Satsuma and its samurai, but worked with the others at least
until 1873. They were united in their conviction that the country must be strengthened to resist the West.

For the sake of national self-preservation, the leaders were prepared to enact
vast changes, but it took time to plan and carry these out, and indeed, to consolidate their own power in a land where, as Kido complained, "we are surrounded
on four sides by little *bakufu*."[8] To insure that the emperor would not become a
focus of opposition to reform, Ōkubo argued that he should be moved to Edo, renamed Tokyo (Eastern Capital) in September 1868. This took place the following
year when the emperor moved into the shogun's former castle, which in 1871,
after much debate, was renamed the "imperial palace."

The Charter Oath

Even before the move, in April 1868, while the emperor was still in Kyoto, a
Charter Oath was issued in his name to provide a general, if vague, statement of
purpose for the new regime. It consisted of five articles:

1. An assembly widely convoked shall be established and all matters of state
   shall be decided by public discussion.

2. All classes high and low shall unite in vigorously promoting the economy
   and welfare of the nation.

3. All civil and military officials and the common people as well shall be allowed to fulfill their aspirations, so that there may be no discontent among
   them.

4. Base customs of former times shall be abandoned and all actions shall conform to the principles of international justice.

5. Knowledge shall be sought throughout the world and thus shall be
   strengthened the foundation of the imperial polity.[9]

Although the government was reorganized to provide for an assembly in keeping with the first article, power remained with the original leadership, and the attempt to implement this provision was soon abandoned. In contrast, the end of
seclusion, the acceptance of international law, and the openness to foreign ideas
conveyed by the last two articles did take place. Symbolic of this shift was the audience granted representatives of the foreign powers by the emperor in Kyoto just

a month before the Charter Oath was issued. The document itself was drafted by two men familiar with Western thought; it was then revised by Kido. The ramifications of the Charter Oath were far from clear, but the last article, to seek for knowledge "throughout the world," was taken very seriously. Furthermore, with its call for an assembly and its strong internationalism, the entire document illustrates the gulf between Japanese and Chinese leaders at this time. No Chinese government would have issued such a document in an attempt to gain political strength.

Dismantling the Old Order

While the machinery of the central government underwent various reorganizations, the prime need was for the government to extend and consolidate its authority and ability to collect taxes. Since the continued existence of the feudal domains was a major obstacle to this, the government leaders undertook the delicate but essential task of abolishing the *han*. In March 1869, Kido and Ōkubo were able to use their influence to induce the *daimyo* of Chōshū and Satsuma to return their domains to the emperor. They were joined in this act by the lords of Tosa and Hizen. Many others followed suit, anxious to be in the good graces of the new government and expecting to be appointed governors of their former domains, which they were. The real blow came in 1871 when, in the name of national unity, the domains were completely abolished and the whole country was reorganized into prefectures. This was made palatable to the *daimyo* by generous financial arrangements. They were allowed to retain a tenth of the former domain revenue as personal income while the government assumed responsibility for *han* debts and financial obligations. The *daimyo* were also assured continued high social standing and prestige. Finally, in 1884, they were elevated to the peerage.

By background and experience, the new leadership was keenly sensitive to the importance of military power. Initially, the new government was entirely dependent on forces from the supporting domains, but this would hardly do for a government truly national in scope. Accordingly, the leaders set about forming a new army freed from local ties. Rejecting the views of Saigō, who envisioned a samurai army that would ensure the warrior class a useful and, he hoped, brilliant role in Japan's future, the leaders decided in 1872 to build their army on the basis of commoner conscription. In January 1873, the new measure, largely the work of Yamagata Aritomo (1838–1922), "father of the Japanese Army," became law.

The restoration had a profound effect on the samurai. The new army, by eliminating distinctions between commoners and samurai, cut right to the heart of the status system. Anyone could become a warrior now. Other marks of samurai distinctiveness were eliminated or eroded. In 1870 commoners were allowed to acquire surnames and were released from previous occupational and residential restrictions. In 1871 the wearing of swords by samurai was made optional; five years later it was to be prohibited entirely.

The samurai's position was further undermined by the abolition of the *han*, which left them without any political or social function. Furthermore, continued payments of their stipends at the customary rate was more than the central government could afford. Accordingly, they were pensioned off. But in view of their number, the government could not afford to treat them as generously as it did the *daimyo*. At first, samurai stipends were reduced on a sliding scale from half to a tenth of what they had been, then they were given the right to commute these into 20-year bonds (1873), and finally they were forced to accept the bonds (1876).

Reduction and commutation of samurai stipends was only one of the measures taken to establish the new government on a sound financial basis. In addition to monetary and banking reform, a tax system was created (1873). The fiscal measures were largely the work of Ōkuma Shigenobu (1838–1922), a man from Hizen who was to remain prominent in Meiji politics, and Itō Hirobumi (1841–1909) of Chōshū. The main source of government revenue was, as before, agriculture, but in place of the old percentage of the crop payable by the village to the *daimyo*, the tax was now collected by the government in money in accordance with the assessed value of the land. It was payable by the owner, and for this purpose ownership rights had to be clearly established. This was not done in favor of the absentee feudal interest long divorced from the land, nor did ownership pass equitably to all peasants. Instead, certificates were issued to the cultivators and wealthy villagers who had paid the tax during Tokugawa times. In this way tenancy was perpetuated. Since poor peasants, often unable to meet their taxes, were forced to mortgage their land, the rate of tenancy increased, rising from about 25% before the new system to about 40% twenty years later.

Disaffection and Opposition

The creation of a modern political, military, and fiscal system benefited the state but hurt some of the people. The peasantry was unhappy not only about the land system but also about forced military service, and showed its bitter displeasure by staging uprisings with increasing frequency from 1866 to 1873. Many of the large merchant houses that had developed symbiotic relationships with the *bakufu* or *daimyo* also suffered during these years and some went bankrupt.

More serious for the regime was samurai discontent. The new government was itself led by former samurai, and for many men the new order meant a release from old restrictions and the opening of new opportunities. Since the samurai were the educated class with administrative experience, it was they who supplied the personnel for local and national government, provided officers for the army, teachers for the schools, and colonists for Hokkaido. Casting aside tradition, some entered the world of business and finance. Yet there were many who did not make a successful transition, who were unable to take advantage of the new vocations now opened to them or to use their payments to establish themselves in new lines of endeavor. And among the leaders as well as the supporters of the Meiji government were men who firmly believed that its purpose was literally the restoration of the old, not the creation of the new. A split between conservatives and modernizers developed early in the Restoration and came to a head in 1873.

The Crisis of 1873

The crisis of 1873 centered on the issue of going to war with Korea in order to force it to open its doors to Japan. Those who advocated war, such as Saigō and Itagaki Taisuke (1836–1919) from Tosa, did so not only out of nationalist motives but also because they saw war as a way to provide employment for the samurai, an opportunity to give them a greater role in the new society, a means to preserve their military heritage. Saigō, a military leader with great charisma and devotion to the way of the warrior, asked to be sent to Korea as ambassador so that he could get himself killed and provide a cause for going to war.

A decision for war was made in the summer of 1873, in the absence of Ōkubo, Kido, and other important leaders who were abroad, in America and Europe. They were on a diplomatic and study mission headed by Iwakura Tonomi, the noble who had played a leading role at court in bringing about the Meiji Restoration. The purposes of the Iwakura mission were to convey the Meiji Emperor's respects to the heads of state of the treaty powers and build good will, to discuss subjects for later treaty revision, and to provide its distinguished members with an opportunity to observe and study the West at first hand. It took 631 days, including seven months in the United States, four in England, and seven in continental Europe. The Japanese leaders did not just have audiences with heads of state and observe parliaments and courts. They were interested in everything.

> They toured cotton mills, iron foundries, shipyards, newspaper plants, breweries, prisons, banks, stock exchanges, cathedrals, telegraph offices, military fortifications, lunatic asylums, libraries and art galleries . . . [They] visited zoos; attended the theater and opera; and took in endless concerts, ballets, and an occasional masked ball, circus performance, and fox hunt.[10]

They returned home in September 1873 with a new appreciation of the importance and complexity of modernization and new realization of the magnitude of the task facing Japan in its quest for equality. They were convinced of the urgent priority of domestic change.

When the mission returned, Ōkubo led the opposition to the Korean venture on the grounds that Japan could not yet afford such an undertaking. Ōkubo, Kido, and Iwakura prevailed, with the support of many officials and the court. In October it was decided to abandon the Korean expedition and to concentrate on internal development. The decision split the government. Bitterly disappointed, the war advocates, including Saigō and Itagaki, resigned. They provided leadership for those who were disaffected by the new government and its policies, an opposition which would prove troublesome to those in power. But their departure left the government in the hands of a group of men unified by a commitment to modernization. Most prominent among them were Ōkubo, Itō, Ōkuma, and Iwakura.

By 1873 the Meiji government had survived the difficult period of initial consolidation. It had established the institutional foundations for the new state, had found a means of defense and national security, and with the resolution of the 1873 crisis, had charted the basic course of development at home and peace abroad that was to dominate Japanese policies during the next twenty years.

The Meaning of the Restoration

Like other major historical events, the Meiji Restoration meant and continued to mean different things to different people. Most visible was increased openness to the West in matters small and large. Already in the early 1870s the gentleman of fashion sported a foreign umbrella and watch and, as recommended by Fukuzawa Yukichi, strengthened his body by eating beef. Faddish Westernism was satirized in one of the best-sellers of the day, *Aguranabe (Sitting around the Stew Pan)* (1871) by Kanagaki Robun (1829–1903). Ōkubo ate bread, drank dark tea for breakfast, and wore Western clothes even at home. In 1872 Western dress was made mandatory at court and other official functions. The Gregorian calendar was adopted the same year. After the Tokyo fire of 1872, the city's main avenue, the Ginza, was rebuilt under the supervision of an English architect. It boasted brick buildings, colonnades, and gas lamps (see Figure 7.4).

FIGURE 7.4   The Ginza, 1873. The Ginza's facade and lamp posts represent the Meiji Restoration's most visible feature—an increased openness to the West in matters small and large.

Photograph © Tsisei Corporation, Japan. Used by permission.

The inhabitants of Tokyo could take pleasure and pride in the Ginza, but the glitter of the capital was not shared by the countryside. Already in 1874 the widening contrast between the prosperous modern capital and the hinterland prompted Fukuzawa Yukichi to warn:

> The purpose [of the government] seems to be to use the fruits of rural labor to make flowers for Tokyo. Steel bridges glisten in the capital, and horse-drawn carriages run on the streets, but in the country the wooden bridges are so rotten one cannot cross them. The cherry blossoms bloom in Kyōbashi [in Tokyo] but weeds grow in the country fields. Billows of smoke such as rise from city stoves do not rise from the farmer's furnace. . . . We must cease making Tokyo richer and concentrate on rural districts.[11]

Unfortunately for those at the bottom of society, this was not to be.

Ideologically, the main thrust was to use the old to justify the new, a process which produced a new vision of the past as well as of the future. Invoking the name of the emperor, a symbol of continuity with the old, the Meiji leaders were able to innovate even as they assured the survival, in new forms, of old values and ideas.

Along these lines, there was an effort to turn Japan into a Shinto state. In 1868 Shinto was proclaimed the basis for the government and a Department of Shinto was established, with precedence over the other departments. There was a drive to purify Shinto, to eliminate Buddhist influences that had steadily seeped into Shinto, and to make Shinto the only religion of Japan. This drive, however, ran into opposition from Buddhists, and conflicted with Western pressures for the legalization of Christianity. In 1872 the Department of Shinto was abolished, and in 1873 the ban on Christianity was lifted. Settlement of the legal status of Shinto had to wait until 1882 (see Chapter 8).

The restoration was revolutionary in that it destroyed the old system and created a centralized state. It eliminated the old class lines and legally opened all careers to all men. In all areas of human activity it prepared the way for the profound changes that, during the next century, were to transform the very countryside of Japan. But if it was a revolution, it was a revolution from above, an "aristocratic revolution," to borrow a term from Thomas C. Smith.[12] Though popular unrest helped undermine the Tokugawa, the restoration was not the product of a mass movement nor of a radical social ideology. It did not radically change the structure of village life or the mode of agricultural production. It eliminated the samurai elite as a legally defined, privileged class, but, led by men who were themselves samurai, did so in terms samurai could understand.

The legacy of the restoration was complex and perhaps is not even yet fully played out, for it provided a base for both the successes and the failures that were to come.

Notes

1. Marius B. Jansen, ed. *The Cambridge History of Japan,* vol. 5: *The Nineteenth Century* (Cambridge: Cambridge Univ. Press, 1989), p. 60.

2. David L. Howell, *Capitalism from Within: Economy, Society and the State in a Japanese Fishery* (Berkeley: Univ. of California Press, 1995), p. 91.

3. Harold Bolitho in Howell, *Capitalism from Within,* p. 159.

4. Bob Tadashi Wakabayashi, *Anti-Foreignism and Western Learning in Early Modern Japan: The New Theses of 1825* (Cambridge, Mass.: Harvard Univ. Press, 1986), p. 134.

5. Michiaki Kawakita, *Modern Currents in Japanese Art, Heibonsha Survey of Japanese Art,* vol. 24, trans. by Charles S. Terry (New York and Tokyo: Weatherhill/Heibonsha, 1974), p. 29.

6. Marius B. Jansen, ed., *Changing Japanese Attitudes Toward Modernization* (Princeton: Princeton

Univ. Press, 1969), pp. 57–58; quoting van Gulik, "Kakkaron: A Japanese Echo of the Opium War," *Monumenta Serica 4* (1939): 542–43.

7. George M. Wilson, *Patriots and Redeemers in Japan: Motives in the Meiji Restoration* (Chicago: Univ. of Chicago Press, 1992), p. 2. For *ee ja nai ka,* see p. 98.

8. Albert Craig and Donald Shively, eds., *Personality in Japanese History* (Berkeley and Los Angeles: Univ. of California Press, 1970), p. 297.

9. Ishii Ryosuke, *Japanese Legislation in the Meiji Era,* trans. William J. Chai (Tokyo: Pan-Pacific Press, 1958), p. 145.

10. John Hunter Boyle, *Modern Japan: The American Nexus* (Fort Worth: Harcourt Brace Jovanovich, 1993), p. 92.

11. Quoted by Mikiso Hane, *Peasants, Rebels, and*

Outcastes: The Underside of Modern Japan (New York: Pantheon Books, 1982), p. 33.

12. See Thomas C. Smith, "Japan's Aristocratic Revolution," *Yale Review 50* (Spring 1961), 370–83. Also see Marius B. Jansen, "The Meiji State: 1868–1912," in James B. Crowley, ed., *Modern East Asia: Essays in Interpretation* (New York: Harcourt Brace Jovanovich, 1970), pp. 95–121, which cites Smith on p. 103.

8

The Emergence of Modern Japan: 1874–1894

1868	1877	1889	1890	1894	1912
The Restoration	Satsuma Rebellion	Promulgation of the Constitution		Start of the Sino-Japanese War	

Rescript on Education

MEIJI JAPAN

After the Meiji leaders consolidated their new regime, their top priority was to transform Japan into a modern nation accepted as an equal by the powers of the world. During the next twenty years, a new political framework was devised, the foundations for a modern economy were laid, profound change occurred in institutions as in values and ideas. Just as tradition meant different things to different people, throughout the nineteenth and twentieth centuries there were diverse (and changing) versions of modernity. Rather than attempting a substantive definition of the modern, we use the term in a purely temporal sense, to mean "up to date." During the nineteenth and twentieth centuries, modernity was largely defined by the West, by virtue of its great power.

Change was neither smooth nor simple. In the intricate interweaving of old and new, some old customs went the way of the samurai's sword and topknot, but others were retained or transformed and put to new uses. Early Meiji saw the appearance not only of what was patently new, and seen as such, but also the emergence of new versions of the past. As John Downer, summarizing a body of recent scholarship, has written:

> Thus they [recent scholars] called attention to the careful and adroit manner by which elites and molders of popular opinion, in Japan as elsewhere, routinely create modern myths under the rubric of "tradition" or cultural uniqueness—whether these be myths involving the emperor, or an idealized hierarchical "family system," or a code of "obedience and filial piety," or a harmonious "traditional employment system," or a simple and egalitarian rural community, or a pure "national essence" rooted in the past before the corruption of foreign influences from China and the West.[1]

As we have seen, myths centered on a "national essence" could draw on Tokugawa nativist thought, but they became modern myths participating in Japan's process of becoming modern. That process knows no end, but Japan's victory over China in 1895 marked the conclusion of the crucial initial phase, for by then it had achieved many of its initial objectives: a centralized government, a modernizing economy, and sufficient military strength to warrant international respect.

Political Developments

Acting in the name of the emperor, a small inner circle dominated the government during the 1870s and 1880s, but not without opposition. To mollify those disappointed by the abandonment of the Korean expedition so earnestly sought by Saigō and his friends, in 1874 Japan sent a military force to Taiwan, ostensibly to punish aborigines who had killed some shipwrecked Okinawans. This expedition was a smaller and less dangerous undertaking than a military confrontation with Korea. It was successful, with the result that China was forced to pay an indemnity and to recognize Japanese sovereignty over the Ryukyu Islands, thus ending the ties that the Ryukyus had maintained with China even while they were Satsuma vassals.

The success of the expedition, however, did not alleviate the situation of disoriented and embittered samurai who felt betrayed by the Meiji leaders. Such men resorted to arms in an uprising in Hizen in 1874, Western Kyushu in 1876, and, most seriously, in Satsuma in 1877. The Satsuma Rebellion was led by Saigō Takamori, who had withdrawn from the government after the 1873 decision against the Korean expedition. The number of those who threw in their lot with the rebellion rose as high as 42,000. Its suppression strained the military resources of the Restoration government, but after half a year the rebellion was crushed.

The Satsuma Rebellion was the last stand of the samurai. When the military situation became hopeless, Saigō committed ritual suicide. His was a martyr's death for a lost cause. Saigō died under official condemnation as a traitor, but the Meiji government soon rehabilitated him, and government leaders joined in expressions of admiration and acclaim. Not only conservatives but representatives of the most diverse political persuasions praised the magnanimity of his spirit and transformed Saigō into a legendary hero, celebrated in poems and songs (including an army marching song), portrayed on stage and in an extensive literature, depicted in portraits and prints, even identified with the planet Mars.

Protest against the government continued, on occasion, to take a violent turn. Less than half a year after Saigō's death, some of his sympathizers assassinated Ōkubo Toshimichi, also from Satsuma, who had worked so hard and successfully to create the new Japanese state. There were other assassination attempts, both successful and not. More important in the long run, however, was the formation of nonviolent political opposition, animated not only by objections to one or another aspect of government policy, but also in protest against the political domination exercised by a few men from Chōshū and Satsuma who had exclusive control over the centers of power. Basing their position on the first article of the 1868 Charter Oath, early in 1874 opposition leaders demanded the creation of an elected legislature. Prominent among them was Itagaki Taisuke, the Tosa leader who, along with Saigō, had left the government over the Korean issue.

In Tosa and then elsewhere, antigovernment organizations voiced the discontent of local interests, demanding political rights, local self-government, and formation of a national assembly. The advocates of a constitution and the leaders of what became known as the movement for popular rights drew upon Western political theories. Constitutionalism itself was an idea with wide currency and a long pedigree in the West, where it was associated with ideas concerning the supremacy of law, a "social contract," and human rights highlighted in eighteenth-century political thought. In the West, constitutions limited the powers exercised by heads of state by providing for representative institutions to share in governing, but a strong argument advanced in Japan was that representative institutions would create greater unity between the people and the emperor. In this view, a constitution was needed not in order to limit the emperor's powers, but to control his advisors. The men in power were not averse to some kind of constitution as a necessary and even desirable component of modernization. Indeed, Kido, as a participant in the Iwakura mission to Europe, became persuaded of the need for a constitution.

By 1878, Kido, Ōkubo, and Saigō were all dead. Of the older men only Iwakura remained important, and three younger men who had already contributed significantly to the Meiji state now assumed leadership: Itō Hirobumi and Yamagata Aritomo, both from Chōshū, and Ōkuma Shigenobu from Hizen. Yamagata was the creator of the new army, while Itō took the lead in political modernization, and Ōkuma served as Finance Minister. They agreed that Japan should have a constitution, but not on the structure of the constitution, nor on a schedule for drawing it up and implementing it. Tensions between Itō and Ōkuma came to a head in 1881 when the latter wrote a memorandum advocating the adoption of an English-style political system. His proposals that the majority party in parliament form the government, that the cabinet be responsible to parliament, and that the first elections be held in 1883 clashed with the conservative and gradualist views of his colleagues. First his proposals were rejected; then, when Ōkuma joined in public criticism of the government over its sale of a certain government project in Hokkaido, the emperor consented to having Ōkuma ousted from the government. At the same time the government announced that the emperor would grant a constitution to take effect in 1890.

Formation of Parties

In response, Itagaki and his associates formed the Jiyutō (Liberal party), and Ōkuma followed by organizing the Kaishintō (Progressive party). Both parties advocated constitutional government with meaningful powers exercised by a parliament, but they differed somewhat in ideology and especially in composition. The Jiyutō, linked to Tosa, drew much of its support from rural areas, where peasants and landlords were unhappy that their taxes were as high as they had been under the Tokugawa, and resented bearing a heavier tax burden than that required of commerce and industry. The Jiyutō proclaimed itself as "devoted to the expansion of liberty, protection of rights, promotion of happiness, and reform of society."[2] Ōkuma's party (linked to Hizen) was, in contrast, more urban and more moderate, advocating English-style liberalism and setting forth more specific proposals. It had the backing of merchants and industrialists. Although both opposed the government and advocated representative government, the two parties fought each other energetically. At the same time, the parties were troubled by internal factionalism; party splits were based on master–follower and patron–client relations rather than on differences in programs.

The organized opposition was further hampered by the need to operate under restrictive laws, including those promulgated to control political criticism. One source of such criticism was the press. The first newspaper appeared in 1871. Early papers had a small but elite readership and focused on politics, but restrictive press laws enacted in 1875 and revised in 1877 gave the Home Minister power to suppress publications and fine or imprison offenders. The 1880 Public Meeting Law placed all political meetings under police supervision. Included among those prohibited from attending such meetings were teachers and students. Nor were political associations allowed to recruit members or to combine or correspond with similar bodies. Finally, the 1887 Peace Preservation Law increased the Home

Minister's powers of censorship and gave the police authority to expel people from a given area: 570 were shortly removed from Tokyo.

The Liberal party was hurt not only by differences among its leaders but even more by antagonism within its membership, including conflicts between tenants and landlords. It proved impossible to contain within one party both radicals who supported, and even led, peasant riots and the substantial landowners who were the objects of these attacks. In 1884 the party was dissolved. At the end of the same year Ōkuma and his followers left the Progressive party, although others stayed to keep it in existence. Criticism of the government continued, but this initial attempt to organize political parties turned out to have been premature.

While suppressing its critics, the government was also taking steps to increase its effectiveness. A system of centralized local administration was established that put an end to the Tokugawa tradition of local self-government. Villages and towns were now headed by officials appointed by the Home Ministry in Tokyo, which also controlled the police. In the late seventies (1878–1880), local assemblies were created as sounding boards of public opinion, but their rights were limited to debate and their membership restricted to men of means. The details of bureaucratic procedure were worked out and a civil service system fashioned. A new code of criminal law was enacted, and work was begun on civil and commercial codes.

For the parties and the government alike, the promulgation of a constitution was seen as an essential component in fashioning a modern state uniting the people and the nation, as exemplified by the advanced countries of the West. However, the West offered a range of ways to accomplish this with varying degrees of popular participation and power. To prepare for drawing up a constitution, Itō spent a year and a half in Europe during 1882–1883, mostly studying German theories and practices as most in keeping with the kind of constitution he and the other oligarchs wanted. After his return, a number of steps were taken in preparation for the constitution: a new peerage was created in 1884 composed of the old court nobility, former daimyo, and some members of the oligarchy; in 1885 a European-style cabinet was created with Itō as premier; and in 1888 the Privy Council was organized as the highest government advisory board.

The Emperor and the Constitution

In the last chapter we noted the abandonment of the original effort to turn Japan into a Shinto state and the granting of religious tolerance, but this did not settle how such tolerance was to coexist with the belief in the divine descent of the emperor and in the legends in which it was grounded. The matter was settled in 1882 with the division of Shinto into Shrine Shinto and Sect Shinto. Most Shinto shrines, including the most prominent, such as Ise and Izumo, sacred to the Sun Goddess and her brother, respectively, came under Shrine Shinto. Thus they were transformed into state institutions operating on a higher plane than the merely "religious" bodies, such as the various forms of Buddhism, Christianity (legalized in 1873), and ordinary Shinto shrines subsumed under Sect Shinto. This formula

FIGURE 8.1 *Portrait of the Meiji Emperor,* Takahashi Yuichi. Oil, 1880. Emperor Meiji—the reign name of the emperor of Japan from 1867 to 1912 (his given name was Mutsuhito)—ascended the throne when he was fifteen. He is depicted here in a modern medium, dressed in a manner appropriate to an emperor appearing on the world stage during the "long nineteenth century" that ended in 1914.

COLLECTION IMPERIAL HOUSEHOLD, TOKYO, JAPAN.

permitted the government to identify itself with the Shinto tradition from which it derived the mystique of the emperor, source of its own authority, while at the same time meeting the demands for religious tolerance voiced by Japanese reformers and Western nations.

In the name of the "restoration" of the emperor, strands of nativist thought and notions of modern monarchy were combined to form an image of the emperor—promoted by careful manipulation of the emperor himself and spread by word and picture. In his person, he represented both old and new: he was a divine being embodying a timeless spirit, but this was a modern divinity, resplendent in his flashy, new, world-class uniform (see Figure 8.1).

In 1889, after work on the constitution was completed, it was promulgated as a "gift" from the emperor to his people. The Meiji constitution remained in force until 1945. The emperor, "sacred and inviolable" father of the family state, was supreme. He was the locus and source of sovereignty: the land and people belonged to him. He had the power to declare war, conclude treaties, and command the army. He also had the right to open, recess, and dissolve the legislature, the power to veto its decisions, and the right to issue his own ordinances. The ministers were responsible not to the legislature, but to the emperor. The legislature, called the Diet (derived from *dieta,* Late Latin for public assembly) consisted of two houses, the House of Peers and the House of Representatives. The latter was elected by a constituency of tax-paying property owners amounting to about 450,000 men, or 1.1% of the total population. The most consequential power of the Diet was the power of the purse, but, following the example of the Prussian constitution, the Meiji constitution provided for automatic renewal of the previous year's budget whenever the Diet failed to pass a new budget.

Only the emperor could take the initiative to revise the constitution. The emperor was the final authority, but he was also above politics; the actual exercise of imperial authority was divided between the Privy Council, the cabinet, the Diet, and the general staff. Since the constitution failed to provide for coordination between these bodies, this was done by the men who had been governing in the emperor's name all along. Gradually, the practice developed of deciding on the selection of prime minister and other major questions by consulting the *genrō*—elder statesmen and leaders of the Meiji Restoration, such as Itō and Yamagata, who talked things out in private. Obviously, this could work only as long as there were *genrō* to consult.

The oligarchs who framed the constitution viewed the government, like the emperor in whose name it functioned, as above the divisive and unedifying world of party politics. But the parties turned out to be stronger than the oligarchs had expected. In the first election of 1890, the reconstituted Liberal party (Jiyutō) won 130 seats, the Progressives (Kaishintō), led once again by Ōkuma, won 47, while only 79 members favoring the government were elected. As a result of this growing party strength, there was a stiff parliamentary battle over the budget in the first session of the Diet, which was resolved only after the premier, Yamagata, resorted to bribery and force. When the budget failed to pass the following year, the Diet was dissolved. During the subsequent elections (1892), the government used the police to discourage the opposition, but failed to obtain a more tractable Diet. Imperial intervention in 1893 worked only temporarily. Another election was held in 1894, but the majority remained opposed to the government, and the Diet was dissolved after only a month and a half.

It was the war with China over Korea that broke the political deadlock and provided temporary unity in the body politic. During the war, the government enjoyed enthusiastic support at home. By that time, Japan was quite different from what it had been twenty years earlier, when the oligarchs rejected intervention in Korea. The political developments were just one dimension of the transformation of Japan.

Western Influences on Values and Ideas

Enthusiasm for aspects of Western science and technology went back, as we have seen, to Tokugawa proponents of Dutch Learning, and, from the very start of Meiji, there was a fashion of Western styles, including styles of dress. Representative of Japanese attitudes, the Meiji Emperor himself wore Western clothes and dressed his hair in the Western manner, as in his portrait by Takahashi Yuichi (1828–1894), shown in Figure 8.1. Not only the subject but also the artist was influenced by Western styles. Takahashi was very conscious of his precursors: he revered Shiba Kōkan. Like Shiba and his own teacher, the prominent Western-style painter Kawakami Tōgai (1827–1881), Takahashi placed great value on realism. Most of his works, unlike the emperor's portrait, were still-life studies of familiar objects, and his most famous work is a realistic painting of a salmon. A major difference between Kawakami Tōgai and Takahashi is that whereas the former saw Western art as no more than a necessary component of Western learning to be mastered for technical reasons, Takahashi also valued it as art.

Similarly, men turned to the West in other fields, not only for practical reasons but because they were attracted by the intrinsic nature of Western achievements. Prominent among such men were the intellectuals who, in 1873, formed the Meirokusha, a prestigious society devoted to all aspects of Western knowledge. These same men led what was known as the movement for "civilization and enlightenment" (*bummei kaika*). A leading theorist of this movement was Fukuzawa Yukichi, whose books on the West were mentioned earlier.

"Civilization and Enlightenment"

In eighteenth-century Europe, the intellectual movement known as the Enlightenment sought to put all traditional ideas and institutions to the test of reason. Impressed by the achievements of science as exemplified in the work of Sir Isaac Newton (1642–1727), such philosophers as Voltaire (1694–1778) and Diderot (1713–1784) believed that reason could produce similar progress in solving human problems, and that the main obstacles to truth and happiness were irrationality and superstition. Their greatest monument was the encyclopedia compiled by Diderot and his associates, a summation of the accomplishments of reason in all fields of human knowledge.

Japanese intellectuals like Fukuzawa Yukichi were strongly influenced by the European Enlightenment, particularly the emphasis on reason as an instrument for achieving progress. Their faith in progress was also confirmed by influential Western historians such as H.T. Buckle (1821–1862) and Francois Guizot (1787–1874). Firm belief in progress remained widespread during the nineteenth century, even after faith in reason had faded.

A corollary to this new concept of historical progress, in Japan as in the West, was a negative reevaluation of Chinese civilization, now regarded as unchanging, and therefore decadent. No longer did the Japanese look up to China as the land of classical civilization; on the contrary, China was now a negative model, and, as China's troubles continued, the Japanese tended to regard it with condescension as well as concern. Now the source of "enlightenment" was in the West.

One of Fukuzawa's prime goals in advancing the cause of "civilization and enlightenment" was to stimulate in Japan the development of an independent and responsible citizenry. "It would not be far from wrong," he complained, "to say that Japan has a government but no people."[3] Tracing the lack of individual independence back to the traditional family, Fukuzawa advocated fundamental changes in that basic social institution. Ridiculing the ancient paragons of filial piety, he urged limitations on parental demands and authority. While he viewed the role of women in terms of family and home, Fukuzawa also, on occasion, recommended greater equality between the sexes, championed monogamy, argued that women should be educated and allowed to hold property, and compared the Japanese woman to a dwarfed ornamental tree, artificially stunted.

According to Fukuzawa, history was made by the people, not by a few great leaders, and he thought it wrong to place too much faith in government or to give the political authorities too much power. His view of the role of government resembled the concept of the minimal state held by early European liberals. Consistent with these ideas, he did not enter government himself, but disseminated his views in books and through a newspaper he founded. He also established what became Keiō University, a distinguished private university in Tokyo whose graduates played an important part in the world of business and industry.

In Fukuzawa's mind, the independence of the people and the independence of the country were linked; indeed, the former was a prerequisite for the latter. This view was widely held among the proponents of "enlightenment." For instance, the translator of the best-seller *Self-Help* by Samuel Smiles, whose Japanese version was published in Tokyo in 1871, explained that Western nations were strong because they possessed the spirit of liberty. John Stuart Mill's *On Liberty* appeared in Japanese translation the same year; Rousseau's *The Social Contract* was published in installments during 1882–1884. Fukuzawa, with his faith in progress, believed that the ultimate universal movement of history is in the direction of democracy, and that individual liberty makes for national strength.

Fukuzawa's liberalism of the early seventies was based on the Western Enlightenment concept of natural law, that is, that human affairs are governed by inherent concepts of right just as the physical world is governed by the laws of nature. This belief resembled the Neo-Confucian concept of *li* ("principle") in linking the natural and human orders, but the European doctrine, unlike the Chinese, included the affirmation of innate human rights. It postulated an affirmative body of law stating the inherent rights of people in society, in whose name societies could overthrow unjust governments and establish new ones. It was to natural law that the American colonists appealed when they declared their independence in 1776, and this was also the case when the French revolutionaries promulgated their Declaration of the Rights of Man in 1789.

Social Darwinism

After the "civilization and enlightenment" of the 1870s, discourse became more many-sided, but the concept of natural law was soon displaced by another, more recent Western import: Social Darwinism. There were various versions of this doctrine, most notably those developed by the enormously influential Herbert Spencer (1820–1903), but all were based on the theory of evolution by natural selection presented in Darwin's famous *On the Origin of Species* (1859). Darwin held that over time the various forms of life adapt to changing natural conditions and that those which adapt best are most likely to survive. This theory was summarized by the catch phrase "survival of the fittest." Social Darwinism was the application of these doctrines to the human realm. Applied to the success or failure of individuals within society, it justified brutal competition. Similarly, applied to the rise and fall of nations, it focused on military as well as civil competition. In both cases, "the fittest" were those who came out on top and thereby contributed to human progress.

Social Darwinism, purporting to have a scientific basis, offered a persuasive explanation of the present, while holding out hope for a different future. It explained why Japan had been unable to resist the Western powers, but held out the promise that a nation did not have to accept permanent inferiority. Thus it justified Japanese efforts to develop national strength by mastering the learning and techniques of the West. Unlike natural law with its moral rules, it turned strength itself into a moral criterion, and justified not only resisting foreign aggression but also engaging in aggressive expansionism of one's own.

In the mid-seventies Fukuzawa first became skeptical of natural law, and then abandoned it. He lost confidence in international law and formed a new view of international relations as an arena in which nations struggle for survival. In 1876 Fukuzawa remarked, "a few cannons are worth more than a hundred volumes of international law."[4] By 1882 he was willing to accept even autocracy if it meant strengthening the nation. Furthermore, he favored imperialist expansion both to assure Japan's safety and to bring the benefits of "civilization" to neighboring countries such as Korea. Thus he welcomed the war when it came in 1894.

Fukuzawa found words of praise for some aspects of the Japanese tradition, including the samurai value of loyal service, but continued to look primarily to the West for his models and ideas. However, he avoided the extremes of Westernization. In early Meiji some thinkers allowed their enthusiasm to get the better of their judgment, and there were all kinds of extreme proposals for radical Westernization, including one to abolish the national language and another to intermarry with Europeans. However, not all supporters of Westernization were genuine enthusiasts. Many desired to impress Westerners in order to be accepted as equals and to speed treaty revision. This was the motive behind a variety of movements, ranging from a drive to reform public morals to the revision of the legal code. It also accounts for one of the symbols of the era, the Rokumeikan, a hall completed in 1883 to accommodate mixed foreign and Japanese social gatherings. Designed by an English architect in the elaborate manner of the European Renaissance, it provided the setting for dinners, card parties, and fancy dress balls.

The Arts

In the arts, Western influence was both audible and visible. It affected music taught in the schools and that performed in military bands. In literature, the seventies and eighties have been defined as "the age of translation,"[5] during which Japanese versions of European novels were published and read with great enthusiasm to be joined, in the mid-eighties, by the first modern Japanese novels, worthy forerunners of great achievements to come. In painting, we have already noted the work of Takahashi, but the impact of the West was visible also in more traditional genres. Sometimes called the last of the major ukiyo-e artists was Kobayashi Kiochika (1847–1915). He introduced Western light and shading into ukiyo-e, using the principles of Western perspective, but retaining a traditional Japanese sense of color (see Figure 8.2).

Western styles of painting were advanced by foreign artists who taught in Japan and by Japanese who studied abroad, particularly in France, bringing back new styles and ways of looking at the world. Kuroda Seiki (1866–1924) studied in France from 1884 to 1893, and it was there that he painted *Morning Toilet* (Figure

FIGURE 8.2 *Train at Night*, Kobayashi Kiyochika. Woodcut. This was the great age of the railway, a force as well as symbol of technological and economic transformation. With his unique techniques of light and shadow, the artist sets his train rushing through the night against a calm, seemingly eternal Japanese landscape.
PHOTOGRAPH COURTESY COLLECTION R. O. MULLER.

8.3), which caused a stir when exhibited in Tokyo in 1894, and unleashed a storm of controversy when shown in more conservative Kyoto the following year. Japan and East Asia had no tradition of painting the nude. There were protests that Kuroda's painting was pornography, not art. But Kuroda won the battle, and went on to become one of Japan's most influential Western-style painters.

The initial enthusiasm for Western art led to the neglect of, and even disdain for, traditional art. This shocked the American Ernest Fenollosa (1853–1908) when he came to Japan in 1878 to teach at Tokyo University. Fenollosa did what he could to make the new generation of Westernized Japanese aware of the greatness of their artistic heritage. He, himself, was an admirer of the last of the masters of the China-influenced Kano school, Kano Hōgai (1828–1898), and, together with the younger Okakura Tenshin (1862–1913), sparked a revived interest in traditional styles. Meanwhile, Japanese art fascinated such Western artists as Gaugin, Van Gogh, and Whistler.

Conservatism and Nationalism

The reaction against the enthusiasm of the early Meiji Westernizers was not limited to the arts. Starting in the late eighties, there was a tide of conservative thought. Many were attracted by the old formula, "Eastern ethics; Western technology," a concept earlier advanced by Sakuma Shōzan.

FIGURE 8.3 *Morning Toilet,* Kuroda Seiki. Kuroda learned an academic style under the French painter Louis-Joseph-Raphael Collin, but also acquired an Impressionist vision that incorporated bright outdoor light. Oil, 1893, 178.5 × 98 cm.

NATIONAL RESEARCH INSTITUTE OF CULTURAL PROPERTIES, TOKYO.

Some feared that acceptance of a foreign culture was a step toward national decline, and sought for ways to be both modern and Japanese, to adopt universalist aspects of Western culture while retaining what was of value in their own past. The educated and sensitive were especially troubled by the tensions inherent in a program of modernization under traditionalist auspices. Western scientific rationalism could, by questioning the founding myth, undermine the throne itself. In 1892 a Tokyo University professor was forced to resign after he wrote that Shinto was a "survival of a primitive form of worship."[6] That was sacrilege. Similarly, Western individualism, fostered by the policy of modernization, clashed with the old family values that, Fukuzawa notwithstanding, continued strong and remained in official favor.

Drawing on German thought, new conservative voices affirmed Japanese uniqueness along with their belief in national progress, arguing that change should come about gradually, growing organically out of past traditions with emphasis not on the individual but on the state. There was talk about a national "essence," though little agreement on how it should be defined. Akira Iriye has drawn attention to the weakness in Japan of the liberal elements that Western nationalism inherited from its origins, when it "had been part of the democratic revolution in which national identity was sought less in a country's ethnic and historical uniqueness than in the belief that it embodied certain universal values such as freedom and human rights." Such a nationalism "could often be transformed into internationalism because a nation could envision a world order that embodied some of the universalistic principles that it exemplified itself."[7] Japanese particularism often took a benign form, but was also prone to lead to cultural exceptionalism and political chauvinism, even if Japanese nationalists were hardly unique in celebrating (and exaggerating) the uniqueness of their nation. Such views could easily lead to a sense of special national mission.

Some Japanese intellectuals, notably Okakura, soon went on to define a wider world role for Japan by emphasizing Japan's Asian roots. Thus, in a book bearing the revealing title, *The Ideals of the East* (1902), Okakura presented the nation's mission in terms of preserving an "Asian" cultural essence. Not only Japan's cultural place in the world but also its political mission remained key issues throughout modern times.

Education

Japanese intellectual and political leaders were quick to realize the importance of education in fashioning a new Japan capable of competing with the West. In this, as in other areas, they showed great interest in the practices and institutions of European countries and of the United States. One member of the Iwakura mission paid special attention to education, and wrote fifteen volumes on the subject after his return from abroad.

At the beginning of the Meiji period, Japan sent many students overseas to obtain the advanced training it could not provide at home. One-eighth of the Ministry of Education's first budget (1873) was designated for this purpose, and 250 students were sent to the United States and Europe on government scholarships that year. Furthermore, many foreign instructors from the same countries were brought to Japan to teach in various specialized schools. However, these were temporary expedients to be used until Japan's own modern educational system was in operation. By the late 1880s, the number of foreign instructors was down, and only fifty to eighty students were being sent abroad by the government annually. A landmark in the history of higher education was the establishment of Tokyo University in 1877, with four faculties: physical science, law, literature, and medicine.

Considerable progress was made in building a complete educational system to replace the uncoordinated network of now-outdated academies and *han*, temple, and family schools. Yet actual accomplishments fell short of the ambitious plan drawn up in 1872 calling for 8 universities, 256 middle schools (equivalent to American high and junior high schools), and 53,760 elementary schools. Thirty years later, in 1902, there were only 2 universities, 222 middle schools, and 27,076 elementary schools. Similarly, the government had to retreat from its 1872 ordinance making four years of education compulsory for all children. Among the difficulties this program encountered were money problems (elementary education was locally financed), teacher shortages, and the reluctance of rural parents to send their children to school. However, by the time four years of compulsory education were reintroduced in 1900, the great majority of children who were supposed to be in school were in actual attendance, and in 1907 the government was able to increase the period to six years. By that time the teachers were predominantly graduates of Japanese Normal Schools (teacher training institutes), the first of which was established in Tokyo in 1872 with the assistance of Marion M. Scott, an American educator.

When the Ministry of Education was first established in 1871, the French system of highly centralized administration was adopted. Although local schools were locally financed, the ministry not only determined the general direction of education but prescribed textbooks, supervised teacher training, and generally controlled the curriculum of schools throughout the country. Government educational policy therefore was decisive in determining what was taught.

There was wide agreement among political leaders that an essential function of the educational system was to provide the people with the skills necessary for modernization. They realized that not only factories and businesses but also armies and navies require a certain level of literacy and command of simple arithmetic among the rank and file, as well as higher education for managers and officers. Beyond that, the leaders recognized that schools foster values, and looked to them to help mold the Japanese people into a nation. On the question of specific moral content, however, there were intense disagreements reflecting different visions of Japan's future. In the seventies, when enthusiasm for the West ran high, even elementary readers and moral texts were frequently translated from English and French for use in Japanese schools. But there were also critics who insisted that the schools should preserve traditional Confucian/Japanese values. Another influential position was opposed to both Western liberal values and to traditionalist ideals, but looked to the schools to indoctrinate the populace with modern nationalist values. An influential proponent of this last position was Mori Arinori (1847–1889), Minister of Education from 1885 until he was assassinated by a nationalist fanatic in 1889.

Although Mori had a strong hand in shaping the educational system, the most important Meiji pronouncement on the subject was drafted under the influence of Motoda Eifu (1818–1891), the Emperor's lecturer on Chinese books who for twenty years provided Confucian guidance and advice. This was the *Rescript on Education,* issued in 1890. For half a century it remained the basic statement of the purpose of education, memorized by generations of school children. It begins by attributing "the glory of the fundamental character of Our Empire" to the Imperial Ancestors who "deeply and firmly implanted virtue," calls on His Majesty's subjects to observe the usual Confucian virtues beginning with filiality toward their parents, and enjoins them to "pursue learning and cultivate arts" for the sake of intellectual and moral development, and "to advance public good and promote common interests." Furthermore, "should emergency arise, offer yourselves courageously to the State, and thus guard and maintain the prosperity of Our Imperial Throne coeval with heaven and earth."[8] In this document, Confucianism is identified with the throne (no mention is made of its foreign origins), and a premium is placed on patriotic service to the state and the throne. These values were further drummed into school children in compulsory ethics classes. Education was to serve to prepare Japan for the future in the name of the past.

Modernizing the Economy

In the twenty years that followed consolidation of the Meiji regime, Japan laid the foundations for a modern industrial economy. The nation was still primarily agrarian, but Western experience had shown that capital accumulated through the sale of surplus agricultural production and labor obtained through the migration of surplus rural population to the cities were necessary conditions for industrial development. Both conditions existed in Meiji Japan.

Japanese agriculture had become more efficient due to the introduction of new seed strains, new fertilizers, and new methods of cultivation. New land for farming was being opened, especially in Hokkaido. New applications of science to agriculture were being tried at experimental stations and agricultural colleges. In consequence, during the fourteen years preceding the Sino-Japanese War, rice yields increased by 30 percent, and other crops showed comparable gains; per capita rice consumption increased. Agriculture was further stimulated by the development of a substantial export market for silk and tea, and a growing domestic demand for cotton. Thus trade also helped generate capital needed for investment in manufacturing.

Increased agricultural production did not result in major changes for the grower. Village government and the organization of village labor remained largely the same. Rents remained high: it was not unusual for a peasant's rent to equal half his rice crop. Profits resulting from the commercialization of agriculture went to the landlord, who handled the sale, rather than to the tenant. Even the creation of factory jobs did little to relieve population pressure on the land. Much of the factory labor was performed by peasant girls sent to the city to supplement farm incomes for a number of years before they were married. Housed in company dormitories and strictly supervised, they were an inexpensive work force. When times were bad and factory operations slowed down, they could be laid off and returned to their villages. It was a system advantageous to both the landlord and the industrialist.

In Western countries, the industrial revolution was largely carried out by private enterprise. In Japan, however, where it was government policy to modernize so as to catch up with the West, the government took the initiative. The Meiji regime invested heavily in the economic infrastructure—those basic public services that must be in place before an industrial economy can grow: education, transportation, communication, and so forth. As previously mentioned, students were sent abroad at public expense to study Western technologies and techniques, and foreigners brought to Japan to teach in their areas of expertise. A major effort went into railroads. The first line was completed in 1872, running between Tokyo and Yokohama. By the mid-nineties there were 2,000 miles of track, much of it privately owned, for government initiative was followed by private investment once the feasibility, and especially the profitability, of railroads had been established. Transportation within cities began to quicken as Kyoto, in 1895, became the first Japanese city to have trolleys.

This sequence of state initiative followed by private development can also be observed in manufacturing. The government took the lead in establishing and operating cement works, plants manufacturing tiles, textile mills (silk and cotton), shipyards, mines, and munitions works. The government felt these industries were essential, but private interests were unwilling to risk their capital in untried ventures, with little prospect of profits in the near term. Thus, if such ventures were to be started, the government had to start them and finance the initial period of operations.

The Zaibatsu

The expenditure of capital required for this effort, the payment due to samurai on their bonds, the costs of the Satsuma Rebellion, and an adverse balance of trade combined to create a government financial crisis. Rising inflation damaged the government's purchasing power and hurt the samurai, whose income depended on the interest paid on their bonds. These problems came to a head in 1880. The government's response was mainly to cut back on expenditures, leading to a deflation that is generally seen as preparing the way for a period of economic growth sustained to the end of World War I.

As part of its economy move, the government decided, late in 1880, to sell at public auction all its enterprises, with the exception of the munitions plants. Most of the buyers were men who were friendly with government leaders and who recognized the long-term advantages of buying the factories, which were selling at bargain prices. These enterprises did not become profitable immediately, but when they did, this small group of well-connected firms enjoyed a controlling position in the modern sector of the economy. These were the *zaibatsu*, huge financial and industrial combines.

The *zaibatsu* were usually organized by new entrepreneurs, for most of the old Tokugawa merchant houses were too set in their ways to make a successful transition into the new world of Meiji. The outstanding exception to this generalization was the house of Mitsui, originally established in Edo as a textile house, and also enriched by its banking activities. When it became apparent that government initiatives were creating new economic opportunities in commerce and industry, Mitsui brought new men into the firm to take advantage of them. The new leadership was vigorous and capable, establishing first a bank and then a trading company. These institutions became important factors in Japan's foreign commerce; they also engaged in domestic transactions, profiting handsomely from handling army supply contracts during the Satsuma Rebellion. In 1881 Mitsui bought government coal mines, which ultimately contributed greatly to its wealth and power. By that time the traditional drapery business had been relegated to a sideline and delegated to a subordinate house.

A contrast to Mitsui is offered by the Mitsubishi *zaibatsu*, founded by Iwasaki Yataro (1834–1885), a former Tosa samurai, bold and ruthless in the wars of commerce. Iwasaki developed a strong shipping business by obtaining government contracts, government subsidies, and, for a time, even government guarantee of its dividend payments. At one point the government lent the company ships, a loan that eventually became a gift. Mitsubishi also benefited greatly from doing government business during the Taiwan expedition of 1874, and again during the Satsuma Rebellion. The firm grew strong enough to displace some of its foreign competitors, and around its shipping business it developed banking and insurance facilities and entered foreign trade. It also went into mining, and its acquisition of the government-established Nagasaki shipyard assured its future as the leader in shipbuilding and heavy industry, although Iwasaki did not live long enough to see the shipyard turn a profit. Iwasaki ruled the combine like a personal domain, but he also recruited an able managerial staff composed largely of graduates of Fukuzawa's Keiō University.

For Iwasaki, personal ambition and patriotism were fused. As he conceived it, his mission was to compete with the great foreign shipping companies, and he was convinced that whatever benefited his company was also good for the nation. Not everyone, however, agreed with this assessment. For a time Iwasaki had to face the competition of a rival company, one of whose organizers was Shibusawa Eiichi (1840–1931), one of the great Meiji entrepreneurs and bankers, founder of the Tokyo Chamber of Commerce and Bankers' Association, a believer in joint-stock companies, in competition, and in business independence from government. Iwasaki won this battle, but Shibusawa remained enormously influential, not only because of his economic power but also because of his energetic advocacy of higher business standards and the view that business could contribute to public good by remaining independent of government.

The success of such men as Iwasaki and Shibusawa should not obscure the fact that new ventures continued to entail risk. Not all new ventures were successful. For example, the attempt to introduce sheep-raising into Japan was a failure. Initial attempts at organizing insurance companies were similarly ill-conceived, since they used rates and tables appropriate for European rather than Japanese conditions. But insurance companies were finally established, and altogether successes outnumbered failures.

One reason for the success of the *zaibatsu* and other new companies was their ability to attract capable and dedicated executives. Formerly, many capable members of the samurai class had refused to enter the business world because concern with money making was considered abhorrent. But this obstacle was largely overcome after the Restoration, not merely because these were now ex-samurai families, but because commercial and industrial development were required for the good of the state. Those who helped build a strong bank, trading company, or manufacturing industry were seen as rendering a service to the emperor and to Japan. Indeed, the government's initial sponsorship of many enterprises lent them some of the prestige of government service. The fact that many companies were created by men of samurai origins also helped make business socially acceptable.

The association of business with government also influenced business ideology in Japan. From the beginning, the ethos of modern Japan business focused on its contributions to the Japanese nation, not on the notions of economic liberalism that prevailed in the West. The company did not exist only, or even primarily, to make a profit for its shareholders. Likewise, provisions were made in the internal organization of the business to encourage group solidarity and mutual responsibility, to give participants in the venture a strong sense of company loyalty, and keep workers in their place. The association of business and government also helped to justify the government's influence on business, and helped to account for continued acceptance of policies that kept consumption low even as national income rose.

In somewhat similar fashion, in the 1890s the argument first appeared that Japanese factories were "exceptional sites of warm-hearted social relations,"[9] a contention that grew more insistent in the early twentieth century as movements for legislation concerning factory conditions, working hours, child labor, and so on, gained momentum.

In discussing the *zaibatsu* and other modern firms, it should not be supposed that large-scale trading, mining, and manufacturing represented the whole of Japanese business. On the contrary, many small-scale establishments continued to function well past the early Meiji era. But the new firms did represent major growth and change in economic activity, and signaled a change in Japanese perceptions of Japan's role in international affairs as well. This was reflected in economic terms by efforts to preserve economic independence—for example, by protecting home markets, conserving foreign exchange, and avoiding dependence on foreign capital so as to assure Japanese ownership of railways and other large-scale enterprises. It was reflected, also, in Japanese foreign policy and especially in the modernization and deployment of the Japanese military.

The Military

Japanese military forces engaged in three major operations in the twenty years following the Restoration: the Taiwan expedition of 1874, the Satsuma Rebellion of 1877, and the Sino-Japanese War of 1894–1895. The first two operations were fought primarily for domestic purposes, as the new Meiji government sought to consolidate its power. The Sino-Japanese War, on the other hand, was an outward-looking venture from the start, a test of strength with China on the Korean Peninsula. An even more striking difference was in the quality of Japanese military organization, armament, and tactical skill in 1874–1877 and 1894.

The Taiwan expedition of 1874 was far from brilliant. The landing was poorly executed, hygiene was so defective that disease took a great toll, and equipment had to be abandoned because it was unsuitable for use in a tropical climate. Similarly, the force that suppressed the Satsuma Rebellion did so because of its superiority in numbers and equipment rather than its military excellence.

To improve the quality of the army, Yamagata directed a major reorganization in 1878. He established a general staff along German lines, and Germany became the overall model for the army, which had previously been influenced by France. By strengthening the reserves, the military potential was greatly increased. During the ten or fifteen years before the Sino-Japanese War, generous military appropriations enabled the army to acquire modern equipment, mostly manufactured in Japanese arsenals and plants, while the creation of a Staff College and improved training methods further strengthened the army and made it more modern. Like Yamagata, most of the leading generals were from Chōshū.

Naval modernization was similar to that of the army, except that England was the model, and continued to be a source from which some of the larger vessels were purchased. In 1894 the navy possessed 28 modern ships with a total displacement of 57,000 tons, and also 24 torpedo boats. Most important, Japan had the facilities to maintain, repair, and arm its fleet. From the start, most of the naval leadership came from Satsuma.

The military is a good example of the way in which the various facets of modernization were intertwined and supported each other, for the armed forces both benefited from and contributed to the process. Not only did they stimulate new industries, ranging from armaments to tin cans, but it was also in the army that the rural conscript was for the first time exposed to a wider and more modern world. Indeed, when conscription was first introduced, many men from backward districts were quite bewildered by the accouterments of modern life. There are reports that some bowed in reverence to the stove in their barracks, taking it for some kind of god. For many men, the army provided the first introduction to shoes. Before the spread of education, some men learned to read and write in the army. All were exposed to the new values of nationalism and loyalty to the emperor. Most also learned to smoke (cigarettes were first reported in 1877) and to drink native alcoholic beverages as well as excellent Japanese beer, first brewed in the 1870s, and they had their first experience with the modern city. Soldiers enjoyed a better diet, receiving more meat than the average Japanese. But discipline was very harsh, and draft dodging was rampant. Nevertheless, the majority did serve.

In this and other ways life was changing for that majority, but compared to later, it was changing very slowly. There were changes in style, such as glass replacing paper inside the house, or the use of Western umbrellas outside, but, as Susan B. Hanley has shown, the essential consumption patterns and basic components of the material culture of the Japanese people remained traditional and stable.[10]

Notes

1. John W. Downer, "Sizing Up (And Breaking Down) Japan," in Helen Hardacre, ed., *The Postwar Development of Japanese Studies in the United States* (Leiden: Brill, 1998), p. 14.

2. First article of the party platform as quoted by Kyu Hyun Kim, "Political Ideologies of the Early Meiji Parties," in Hardacre, *Postwar Development,* p. 400.

3. Quoted in Carmen Blacker, *The Japanese Enlightenment: A Study of Fukuzawa Yukichi* (London: Cambridge Univ. Press, 1964), p. 111.

4. Ibid., p. 128.

5. Donald Keene, *Dawn to the West: Japanese Literature of the Modern Era: Fiction* (New York: Holt, Rhinehart and Winston, 1984), Chapter 3, "The Age of Translation."

6. Quoted in Kenneth Pyle, *The New Generation in Meiji Japan: Problems in Cultural Identity,*

1885–95 (Stanford: Stanford Univ. Press, 1969), p. 124.

7. Akira Iriye in Marius Jansen, *The Cambridge History of Japan,* vol. 5, p. 754.

8. "Rescript on Education," in John Lu, *Sources of Japanese History* (New York 1974), vol. 2, pp. 70–71.

9. Andrew Gordon, "The Invention of Japanese-Style Labor Management," in Stephen Vlastos, *Mirror of Modernity: Invented Traditions of Modern Japan* (Berkeley: Univ. of California Press, 1998), p. 19.

10. Susan B. Hanley, "The Material Culture: Stability in Transition," in Marius Jansen and Gilbert Rozman, eds., *Japan in Transition: From Tokugawa to Meiji* (Princeton Univ. Press, 1986), pp. 467–69 and passim.

China and Korea:
1870–1894

9

While the Meiji government brought about major changes in Japan, governments on the continent were less successful in preparing their people to come to grips with a new world. As we have seen, Vietnam lost its independence in 1883 (see Chapter 6) despite the Qing war with France (1884–1885). Attempts at dynastic renewal and "self-strengthening" in China and Korea, while not negligible, in the end failed to solve problems of dynastic decay. Meanwhile, the histories of the three Northeast Asian powers increasingly intertwined, ending with China and Japan at war over Korea.

I. China

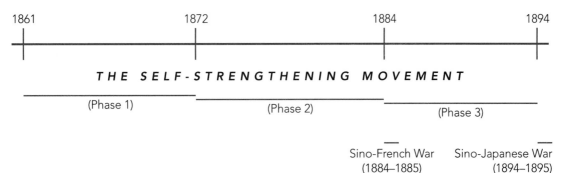

The Post-Taiping Revival

Self-Strengthening—the First Phase

Self-Strengthening—the Theory

The Empress Dowager and the Government

Education

Economic Self-Strengthening

The Traditional Economic Sector

Missionary Efforts and Christian Influences

Old and New Wine in Old Bottles

The Post-Taiping Revival

During the Tongzhi period (1862–1874), Zeng Guofan, Li Hongzhang, and other leaders in the victory over the Taipings sought to cope with the dislocations wrought by warfare and to revive the dynasty by launching a program of Confucian reformism: expenses and taxes were cut in the ravaged south, relief projects were instituted, public works projects initiated, land reclaimed and water controlled, granaries set up. As always, agriculture had priority.

An aspect of the revival dear to its Confucian sponsors was a strengthening of scholarship by reprinting old texts, founding new academies, opening libraries, and the like. Examination system reform was similarly a high priority as was the elimination of bureaucratic corruption. Questions dealing with practical issues of statecraft were introduced, and attempts were made to limit the sale of degrees and offices. By such measures the reformers sought to raise the level of honesty.

However, the reforms did not penetrate to the crucial lower level of the bureaucracy—many county magistrates continued to gain office through purchase—and nothing effective was done to curb the rapacity of the solidly entrenched and notoriously corrupt sub-bureaucracy of clerks and underlings. Furthermore, with the leadership for the reforms coming primarily from provincial governors, the dynasty was powerless to reverse the trend toward regionalism. The disruption of old bonds with the central government removed many of the political constraints on local wealth and power, and set in motion a restructuring of local society that ultimately proved dangerous for both the state and the social order.

Self-Strengthening—the First Phase

The aim of the Self-Strengthening Movement was to fortify the Qing through selective borrowing from the West. It began in the Tongzhi period with a focus on military modernization and international relations, and was expanded in its middle phase (1872–1885) to encompass transportation (shipping and railways), communications (telegraph), and mining. Finally, after China's defeat by France in 1885, it was further broadened to include light industry.

During the first phase, Li Hongzhang created gun factories in Shanghai (1862) and Suzhou (1864), established an arsenal in Shanghai with Zeng Guofan (1865), and founded another in Nanking (1867). In 1870, Li also expanded machinery works first built in Tianjin in 1867. Another leader in Fuzhou founded a shipyard with machinery from France with a shipbuilding and a navigation school attached, one teaching French, the other English.

With the emperor a minor, foreign policy was largely under the direction of Prince Gong, who expressed the regime's order of priorities thus:

> The situation today may be compared (to the diseases of a human body). Both the Taiping and the Nian bandits are gaining victories and constitute an organic disease. Russia, with her territory adjoining ours, aiming to nibble away our territory like a silk worm, may be considered a threat at our bosom. As to England, her purpose is to trade, but she acts violently, without any regard for human decency. If she is not kept within limits, we shall not be able to stand on our feet. Hence she may be compared to an affliction of our limbs. Therefore we should suppress the Taipings and the Nian bandits first, get the Russians under control next, and attend to the British last.[1]

It was apparent to Prince Gong that new approaches to foreign policy were required to meet these objectives. In 1861, to deal with the foreign powers and related matters, he sponsored the establishment of the Zongli Yamen (Office of Gen-

FIGURE 9.1   Three members of the Zongli Yamen and statesmen of the
Tongzhi period. Left to right: Shen Guifen, President of the Ministry of
War, Dong Xun, President of the Ministry of Finance, Mao Changxi,
President of the Ministry of Works.

eral Management), as a subcommittee of the Grand Council, to supervise a number of offices (see Figure 9.1). Since its influence depended on that of its presid-
ing officer and his associates, it was most influential during the 1860s, when Prince
Gong was at the height of his authority. An important innovation introduced by
the Zongli Yamen was appeal to international law, using Henry Wheaton's *Elements of International Law,* a standard text translated by the American missionary
W. A. P. Martin.

Prince Gong, recognizing that Chinese officials would be at a disadvantage in
dealing with foreigners unless they had a better understanding of foreign languages
and learning, was instrumental in having the Zongli Yamen establish a school for

foreign languages and other nontraditional subjects in 1862. The language staff was foreign, and included Martin, who became the school's president in 1869. By that time astronomy and mathematics had also been introduced, despite the objections of the distinguished Mongol scholar, General Secretary Woren (d. 1871) who memorialized: "From ancient down to modern times your slave has never heard of anyone who could use mathematics to raise the nation from a state of decline or to strengthen it in time of weakness."[2] Woren was not alone in his objections to this extension of "barbarian" influence.

Nevertheless, similar schools were established at Shanghai, Canton, and Fuzhou. Foreigners were relied on to run both the military and educational establishments. In this way the foundations of self-strengthening and modernization were laid, but the emphasis remained heavily military. This was true even of Feng Guifen (1809–1874), an advocate of learning from the barbarians, who had the audacity to propose that examination degrees be presented to men demonstrating accomplishment in Western mechanical skills.

During the 1860s an important area of Chinese cooperation with the foreign powers was the Maritime Customs Service. Its first director, Horatio Nelson Lay, had acquired a fleet of eight gunboats for the Chinese in England. Although these were paid for by the Chinese, he arranged that the captain of the fleet should receive all his orders through and at Lay's own discretion. This was unacceptable to the Qing, and there were protests. China's first effort to acquire a modern navy ended with disbandment of the little fleet, and Lay was pensioned off. Matters improved, however, when Robert Hart succeeded Lay in 1863. Hart's attitude was the opposite of Lay's. He insisted that the customs was a Chinese service, that Chinese officials were to be treated as "brother officers," and he gave the Qing government well-intentioned and frequently helpful advice on modernization, while building the service into an important source of support for the dynasty.

Cooperation between the Qing and the powers produced the first Chinese diplomatic mission to the West, which was headed by the retiring American minister to Beijing, Anson Burlingame, on Robert Hart's recommendation. For a multi-ethnic Confucian state like the Qing to employ a trusted foreigner on such an important mission did not appear as extraordinary as it would have later, after nationalism took hold. Accompanied by a Manchu and a Chinese official, Burlingame left China in 1867 for a trip to Washington, several European capitals, and St. Petersburg, where he died. Carried away by his own eloquence, he told Americans that China was ready to extend "her arms toward the shining banners of Western civilization"[3] In Washington, he concluded a treaty rather favorable to China.

The most important negotiations for treaty revision were conducted in Beijing by the British. These culminated in the Alcock Convention of 1869, which included some concessions to the Chinese on duties and taxes, and stipulated that, under the most-favored-nation clause, British subjects would enjoy privileges extended to other nationals only if they accepted the conditions under which those privileges had been granted. It also allowed China to open a consulate in Hong Kong. These concessions may appear minor, but the English merchant community felt threatened by them, and their opposition proved strong enough to prevent ratification of the convention.

A fatal blow to the policy of cooperation came in 1870 in Tianjin. A Catholic nunnery there had made the mistake of offering small payments for orphans brought to the mission. Rumors spread that the children had been kidnapped and that the sisters removed the children's hearts and eyes to make medicine. The tense situation erupted into violence. A mob took the life of the French consul and twenty other foreigners, including ten nuns, in what came to be known as the Tianjin Massacre. The powers mobilized their gunboats. Diplomacy finally settled the issue, largely because France's defeat in the Franco-Prussian War the same year deprived France of military power and forced the French to concentrate on domestic problems.

Self-Strengthening—the Theory

Confucian pragmatism was nothing new. Willingness to adopt new means to strengthen and reform the state had animated a long line of Confucian scholars from the Song on, and, as it became clear during the early years of the nineteenth century that the Qing was in serious trouble, some scholars turned against philology to focus on what today would be called policy studies. The *Anthology of Qing Statecraft Writing (Huangchao jingshi wenbian)*, published in 1827, is a case in point. It is a collection of essays on social, political, and economic matters written by Qing officials and published by He Changlin (1785–1841), with the actual work done by Wei Yuan (see Chapter 6). Concern for reform and willingness to take a hard, critical look at financial and political institutions characterized the writings of leading intellectuals, and Wei Yuan began to merge these concerns with an interest in the West. The first person to see the West as a source for solving the problems it had created was Feng Guifen, who urged China to use "barbarian techniques" against the "barbarians," the hallmark of the Self-Strengthening Movement.

Although self-strengthening was well established by the 1870s, its classic formulation came in 1898 from the brush of Zhang Zhidong (1837–1909), a governor-general and practitioner of self-strengthening. Like Sakuma Shōzan earlier in Japan, Zhang wanted to preserve traditional values while adopting Western science and technology. The idea was that Chinese learning would remain the heart of Chinese civilization, while Western learning would have a subordinate, supporting role. This was expressed in terms of the traditional Neo-Confucian dichotomy of *ti* (substance) and *yong* (function): Western means for Chinese ends. The basic pattern of Chinese civilization was to remain sacrosanct, but it was to be protected by Western techniques.

Conservative opponents of self-strengthening feared that Chinese civilization would be contaminated by borrowing from the West, since ends cannot be separated from means. In the Confucian formulation, *ti* and *yong* are aspects of a single whole. The Confucian tradition had always been concerned with means as well as ends, and generations of scholars had insisted that the Way did not consist merely of "empty" abstractions, but concerned practical realities. There was no essence apart from application. And there was a great deal more to the West than mere techniques. It was fallacious to believe that China could merely borrow techniques from the West without becoming entangled in manifestations of Western culture. If China went ahead with efforts to adopt Western techniques while preserving traditional culture, the best that could be hoped for would be an uneasy compartmentalization. To preserve tradition in a period of modernization, the country would have to be protected from the kind of radical social reappraisal hailed in Japan by champions of "reason" like Fukuzawa Yukichi.

The contrast with Japan is instructive, for there social change was sanctioned by an appeal to nationalism as symbolized by the throne, whereas in China Confucianism was much too closely associated with the social structure to allow for a similar development. Meiji Japan demonstrated that elements of Confucianism were compatible with modernization, but also that modernization involved changes reaching into the very heart of a civilization.

FIGURE 9.2 The Empress Dowager Cixi (1835–1908) seated on the Imperial Throne. Scholars, too, grew long fingernails to show the world that they worked with their minds, not their hands.

The Empress Dowager and the Government

The dominant figure at court from the mid seventies until her death, just three years before the demise of the dynasty, was the Dowager Empress Cixi (1835–1908) (see Figure 9.2). The intelligent, educated daughter of a minor Manchu official, she entered the palace as a low-ranking concubine, and had the good fortune to bear the Xianfeng emperor his only son. After that emperor's death, she became coregent for her son, the Tongzhi emperor, whom she dominated. It was also rumored that she encouraged him in the debaucheries that weakened his constitution and brought him to the grave in 1875 at age nineteen. She then manipulated the succession in order to place on the throne her four-year-old nephew, the Guangxu emperor (r. 1875–1908), and continued to make the decisions even when he ostensibly assumed the imperial duties in 1889. At first Prince Gong had provided a counterforce, but his power declined in the seventies, and in 1884 he was removed from the government altogether.

The Empress Dowager was a strong-willed woman, an expert at political infighting and manipulation. One of her most reliable supporters was the Manchu bannerman Ronglu (1836–1903), to whom she gave important military commands. Yet, it was an anomaly to have a woman in control of the court, and her prestige was not enhanced by rumors that she was responsible for the murder of her rivals. Corruption in high places also took its toll. The powerful eunuch Li Lianying (d. 1911) was totally loyal to his mistress, but also totally corrupt, using his influence to amass a fortune. Cixi herself accepted payments from officials and misspent funds. The most notorious case of financial abuse was her use of money intended for the navy. The Navy Department, established in 1885, became a branch of the imperial household, and China's most famous and magnificent "ship" was made of marble (see Figure 9.3).

Cixi's prime political aim was to continue in power. She had no aversion, but neither did she have any commitment, to the policy of selective modernization advocated by the champions of self-strengthening, and her understanding of the West was very limited. It was to her immediate political advantage to avoid dependence on any single group of officials and to manipulate a number of strong governors-general who had gained in power while suppressing the Taiping Rebellion. These indispensable provincial administrators could no longer be controlled

FIGURE 9.3 On the shore of Kunming Lake, the Marble Pavilion has become a popular recreational site attracting ordinary Chinese visitors as well as foreign tourists—the kind of folk it was intended to exclude. Summer Palace, Beijing.

Photograph © Dmitri Kessel/Timepix (651809).

by the court at will, but fortunately for Beijing, they remained absolutely loyal to the dynasty. The governors-general operated their own political and financial machines and commanded substantial military forces, but they were still dependent on Beijing's power of appointment. Major policy decisions continued to be made in Beijing. The central government was also strengthened financially by receipts from the Maritime Customs. Thus the West helped to preserve the dynasty even as it was undermining its foundations.

Most powerful of the governors-general was Li Hongzhang, from 1870 firmly established in Tianjin, where he commanded an army, sponsored self-strengthening efforts, and successfully avoided transfer. A protégé of Zeng Guofan, he shared his master's devotion to the dynasty, but not his Confucian probity. From his headquarters, not far from Beijing, Li dominated China's policy toward Korea, but he could not control its foreign policy elsewhere. Arguing for the priority of maritime defense, he objected to overemphasis on inner Asia and unsuccessfully opposed two military campaigns conducted there during the 1870s.

In the next decade he failed to prevent the war of 1884–1885 with France over Vietnam. In this war, fought not only in Vietnam but also on Taiwan and the Pescadores, the Qing suffered the destruction of the Fuzhou dockyards as well as the loss of the fleet built there. Since the defeated dynasty was forced to relinquish all claims to Vietnam, Li was vindicated, but his opposition to going to war against France earned him the denunciations of his enemies, who castigated him as an arch traitor.

Li, however, survived these attacks and remained the most important patron of Self-strengthening, now broadened to include light industry in the hope for better results.

Education

Crucial to every phase was the need for officers, managers, and technical personnel such as scientists and engineers. The fastest way to fill this need was to send students abroad. However, this approach had a mixed success. The most extensive effort of this sort was made between 1872 and 1881, when 120 students were sent to the United States under the supervision of Yung Wing (Rong Hong, 1828–1912), Yale class of 1854, and the first Chinese to graduate from an American university. The boys were between fifteen and seventeen years old, young enough to master new subjects, but also immature and easily swayed by their foreign environment. To assure continued Confucian training, they were accompanied by a traditional Confucian mentor. Nevertheless, they soon adopted American ways, participating in American sports, dating and in some cases eventually marrying American girls, and in a few instances even converting to Christianity. Yung Wing himself married an American and ended up living in Hartford, Connecticut. The mission had been launched with the backing of Zeng Guofan and Li Hongzhang, but Li withdrew his support when the students were denied admission to West Point and were fiercely attacked by Beijing officials for neglecting their Confucian studies. The mission, poorly managed from the start, was abandoned. Among its participants were some of the first, but by no means the last, Chinese students who, during their overseas stay, became alienated from their culture.

The obvious alternative to study abroad was to supply instruction in modern subjects at home. This was the purpose of the language school established by Prince Gong, and other schools at several arsenals and the Fuzhou dockyard. By 1894 a telegraph school, a naval and military medical school, and a mining school were also in operation. The curriculum of these schools typically encompassed both the classical studies required for success in the examination system and the new subjects. Since command of traditional learning remained the key to entry into government service, the students naturally tended to concentrate on that, for otherwise their career opportunities were very limited. The most famous graduate of the Fuzhou dockyard school was Yan Fu (1853–1921), who was sent to England to continue his studies at the naval college in Greenwich, but after returning home to China was unable to pass the provincial examination, and gained fame not as an admiral, but as a writer and translator.

It did occur to some reformers to broaden the content of the examinations and allow candidates credit for mastering modern subjects, but suggestions along such lines encountered formidable opposition, since they affected the Confucian core of the civilization. A minor concession was finally made in 1887. Three out of some 1500 provincial examination candidates might now be granted that degree after being examined in Western along with (not in place of) traditional subjects. They would then be eligible for the highest examination (the *jinshi*) on the same terms as the other candidates!

Economic Self-Strengthening

The accomplishments of the second phase of self-strengthening included a shipping company, textile mills, the beginnings of a telegraph service, and the Kaiping Coal Mines. Li Hongzhang took the lead in sponsoring and protecting the new ventures. During the first phase, the new factories, arsenals, etc., run by officials with the help of foreigners, had suffered from bureaucratic corruption and poor management. To avoid this, Li enacted a policy of "government supervision and merchant operation." Capital came from both the public and private sectors. Private financing was very much desired, but capital was scarce, and other forms of investment were more lucrative and prestigious. Private investment came primarily from Chinese businessmen residing in the treaty ports and familiar with modern-style business ventures and techniques.

The records of these companies were mixed. The China Merchants Steam Navigation Company is a good example. When private capital proved insufficient to finance the company, Li Hongzhang put up the rest from public funds. To help the company make a go of it, Li secured the shipping line a monopoly on the transport of tax grain and official freight bound for Tianjin. He obtained tariff concessions for the company and protected it from its domestic critics and enemies. In exchange, Li exercised a large measure of control, appointing and dismissing its managers, employing its ships to transport his troops, and using its payroll to provide sinecures for political followers. He also used its earnings to buy warships. To advance his policy in Korea, Li had the company lend money to the Korean government.

In the end, the investors made money and their political sponsor benefited, but, after an initial spurt, the companies stagnated. Moreover, they failed to train Chinese technical personnel, and were plagued by incompetent managers, nepotism, and corruption. Even their political sponsors exploited the companies, regarding them as sources of patronage and revenue rather than as key investments for the modernization of the country. By the mid-nineties, there was a modern sector in the Chinese economy, but it was largely limited to the periphery of the empire, where Chinese merchants were able to hold their own successfully against foreign competition.

The Traditional Economic Sector

While the new enterprises proved disappointing, developments in the traditional sector were hardly encouraging. Chinese tea merchants, despite sophisticated institutions and techniques adequate to sustain dominance of the domestic market, found it increasingly difficult to compete internationally against tea grown in India and Sri Lanka (Ceylon). The large-scale producers of these countries had an advantage over the small Chinese growers in their ability to sustain a high-quality product by investing in fertilizer, replacement bushes, and labor at the crucial picking time. Furthermore, the elaborate structure of the Chinese collection system, that worked so well internally, was too unwieldy to organize an adequate response to international competition. After 1887, with the decline of exported tea, raw silk became China's main export. In the mid-1890s China was the world's largest exporter of silk, although by 1904 Japan had supplanted her in that respect.

Beyond the treaty ports and their immediate hinterlands, the penetration of foreign imports appears to have been slow, and their impact varied. Statistics are hard to come by, and there is no consensus about the ways in which the world economy interacted with forces already at work in the Chinese countryside. Thus Philip Huang's study of an area of North China where farmers had been growing cotton for a long time remains controversial as well as suggestive. According to Huang, since cotton brought a better price than grain but, being susceptible to drought, also entailed larger risks, the gap between the successful rich and those pushed into poverty by failure increased. Combined with population pressure and an absence of other opportunities for employment, this set in motion an invidious process of "agricultural involution," a term first applied by the anthropologist Clifford Geertz to Java, where poor peasants worked the land for marginal and diminishing returns. According to Huang, while the men farmed, their wives and daughters supplemented family income by laboring at spinning wheel and loom, often at less than subsistence wages. Whereas spinning was practically eliminated by machine-made thread, the low prices paid to the weavers kept the price of native cloth below that of the factory-made product, which had to be shipped into the interior. "The world economy thus did not undermine the rural economic system or stimulate new departures but accelerated processes already underway. The incorporation of Chinese agriculture into the world economy telescoped and greatly accelerated change in the small peasant economy."[4]

Missionary Efforts and Christian Influences

The Western presence in nineteenth-century China was no more confined to trade and politics than it had been during the Late Ming encounter. Once again, missionaries were drawn to China, but now there were Protestants as well as Catholics. An early Protestant arrival was Robert Morrison of the London Missionary Society. He reached Canton in 1807, learned the language, brought out a Chinese-English dictionary and a Chinese version of the Bible (later used by the Taipings), founded the school where Yung Wing received his early education, and set up a printing press. Other missionaries, many of them Americans, brought modern medicine and other aspects of Western secular knowledge to China.

The missionaries made a notable effort in education: by 1877 there were 347 missionary schools in China with almost 6,000 pupils. Such schools helped spread knowledge about the West as well as propagate the religion. A notable missionary–educator was W. A. P. Martin, who contributed to the Self-Strengthening Movement and became the first president of Beijing University. The first foreign language newspaper published in China was a missionary publication, and missionaries also contributed to scholarship. Outstanding among the missionaries who became Sinologists was James Legge, a master translator who rendered the Chinese classics into sonorous Victorian prose. In this and other ways, missionaries with varying degrees of sophistication and self-awareness served as cultural intermediaries.

As indicated by the growth of their schools, the missionaries met with some success, but their strength was largely in the treaty ports, and the results were hardly commensurate with their efforts. By the end of the century, the number of Catholic missionaries in China had climbed to about 750, and there were approximately half a million Catholics in China, up from around 160,000 at the beginning of the century. The Protestants had less success. In 1890 there appear to have been only slightly over 37,000 converts served by roughly 1,300 missionaries, representing 41 different religious societies. The Tianjin Massacre of 1870 had demonstrated the potential fervor of antimissionary sentiment, and nothing happened to reduce hostilities during the next quarter of a century.

The reasons for the poor showing of Christianity are many and various. They include difficulties in translation and communication analogous to those that plagued Buddhist missionaries a millennium and a half earlier. The most important concepts of Christianity, such as sin or the Trinity, were the most difficult to translate, none more so than the most sacred idea of all, the idea of God. Agreement on how to translate "God" into Chinese was never reached; three versions, one Catholic and two Protestant, remained current. As before, differences in culture compounded the difficulties in communication.

The nineteenth-century missionary, however, also encountered problems that he did not share with his predecessors, for the Chinese associated Christianity with both the Taiping Rebellion and the unequal treaties. The former showed Christianity as subversive to the social and political order, while the latter brought the missionaries special privileges. Both were resented. Furthermore, the aura of power also attracted false converts, individuals attracted by the possibilities of a treaty port career, and opportunists out to obtain missionary protection for their own ends. Popular resentment of the missions was fired by scurrilous stories and bitter attacks (see Figure 9.4). This hostility was encouraged by the elite, who saw in Christianity a superstitious religion that threatened their own status and values. It was no accident that anti-Christian riots often occurred in the provincial capitals during examination time, when they were filled with candidates committed to the status quo.

FIGURE 9.4   *The [Foreign] Devils Worshipping the Incarnation of the Pig [Jesus].* This print employs a homonym for the transliteration of "Jesus" to depict Christ as a pig.

FROM *CHINA AND CHRISTIANITY* BY PAUL A. COHEN (CAMBRIDGE: HARVARD UNIVERSITY PRESS, 1963). COURTESY DEPARTMENT OF EAST ASIAN STUDIES, HARVARD UNIVERSITY.

Here there is an interesting contrast with the situation in Japan, where 30 percent of Christian converts during the Meiji period were from samurai backgrounds. Christianity served the spiritual needs and provided a vehicle for social protest for samurai who found themselves on the losing side of the Restoration struggle. As a result, in the 1880s and 1890s a prestigious native clergy was developing in Japan, and Christianity remained more influential than the slow growth of the churches would indicate. In post-Taiping China too, Christianity continued to appeal to people dissatisfied with the status quo, and it counted among its converts some notable protesters, including Sun Yat-sen. But the elite remained hostile, and the real cutting edge of protest was to be elsewhere: too radical for the nineteenth century, Christianity turned out to be insufficiently radical for the twentieth.

In the meantime, missionaries contributed to the Western perception of China. Working in the treaty ports, dealing not with Confucian gentlemen but with men on the margin of respectable society, the missionaries frequently developed a negative view of China and its inhabitants, an image the reverse of the idealistic picture painted earlier by the Jesuits.

Old and New Wine in Old Bottles

In this difficult age, as in most, there were artists and poets who aimed at "transcending turmoil"[5] by working within the rich tradition to which they were heirs. Their accomplishments can give much pleasure, but others more directly convey a sense of the anxieties and hopes of an age. For example, the poetry of Wang Pengyun (1848–1904), an official who served as a censor, sounds notes of uncertainty, apprehension, and regret in an age of dynastic decay.

In Reply to a Poem from Cishan, Thanking Me for the
Gift of Song and Yuan Lyrics I Had Had Printed
>   (To the tune "The Fish Poacher")
>   Now that the lyric voice wavers in wind-blown dust
>   Who is to speak the sorrows of his heart?
>   Two years of carving, seeking from each block
>   The truest music of the string unswept,
>   Only to sigh now
>   Finding my grief in tune
>   With every beat that leaves the ivory fret!
>   I sigh for the men of old
>   Pour wine in honor of the noble dead:
>   Does any spirit rhymester
>   Understand my heartbreak?
>
>   The craft of letters
>   Furnishes kindling, covers jars:
>   True bell of tinkling cymbal, who can tell!

Du Fu,* who lifelong courted the perfect phrase
—Did his verse help him, though it made men marvel?
Take what you find here,
See if an odd page, a forgotten tune
Still has the power to engage your mind.
My toiling over
I'll drink myself merry, climb the Golden Terrace,
Thrash out a wild song from my lute
And let the storms rage at will.[6]

Late Qing writers were much given to writing sequels, new versions, and parodies of China's classic novels, often at great length. *The Dream of the Red Chamber* was a favorite (see the discussion in Chapter 2). Publication of *The Dream of the Green Chamber* (about a brothel) in 1878 was preceded by *A Precious Mirror for Judging Flowers* (1849), a homosexual romance. *Quell the Bandits* (1853), characterized by David Der-wei Wang as anticipating China's modern political novel,[7] plays off *The Water Margin* (also translated as *All Men Are Brothers*), a classic novel recounting the deeds of 108 bandit heroes driven by the cruel corruption of a decadent government to take justice into their own hands. Such works, for all their flaws, looked toward the future.

A literary man and political reformer hopeful of the future was Huang Zunxian (1845–1905), who spent 1877–1879 in Tokyo as part of the Chinese legation. A collection of his poems describing Japan was published by the Zongli Yamen in 1879. He also wrote a history of Japan, and served as a diplomat in San Francisco, Singapore, and London. Rejecting the conventional poetic genres, he sought to preserve tradition through innovation.

Among those who welcomed the winds from the West were a small group of remarkable men, some with experience abroad in official or unofficial capacities. Guo Songdao (1818–1891) was China's first minister to England and the first Chinese representative to be stationed in any Western country. Wang Tao (1828–1897) spent two years in Scotland assisting James Legge in his translations, and also visited Japan. One of the founders of modern journalism in China, he favored the adoption of Western political institutions as well as science and technology. Another remarkable man was Zheng Guangyin (1842–1921), a famous scholar–comprador, modernizer, and writer. Such men were interested in Western "substance" (not just "function"), while remaining committed to the Confucian tradition.

Important for the future were a number of younger men whose formative years fell into this period, although they did not become influential until the late nineties. There are three names in particular to which we will return: Yan Fu, born in 1853; Kang Yuwei, born in 1858; and Sun Yat-sen, born in 1866. The discussion of their ideas must wait, however, for it was not until China was jolted by her defeat in the Sino-Japanese War that they came to the fore.

*Du Fu (712–770), along with Li Bo (or Li Bai, 701–763) was one of China's most revered poets.

II. Korea

Key Dates

1866	General Sherman
1875	Clash with Japan
1876	Treaty with Japan
1882	Chinese Intervention
1885	Li Hongzhang and Itō Hirobune agreement
1894–1895	Sino–Japanese War
1895	Treaty of Shimonoseki

The Politics of Reform

The Incursion of the Powers

Gradualists versus Advocates of "Enlightenment"

Christianity and Western Thought

The Tonghak Rebellion and the Sino-Japanese War

The Treaty of Shimonoseki (1895)

The Politics of Reform

In Korea, as in China, the period opens with a program of dynastic restoration conducted under a regency for a minor sovereign. With the accession in 1864 of the twelve-year-old king, Kojong (r. 1864–1907), his father, Yi Ha'ŭng (1821–1898) became regent. Known to history by his princely title as the Taewôn'-gun, he was determined to fight corruption at court and to boost the power of the throne. To combat corruption, he punished officials guilty of robbing the treasury and made appointments based on merit and ability rather than family or factional ties. To put an end to decades of "in-law politics" that had resulted from the special position of the queens' relatives, he chose for his son a consort from the less-powerful Min clan of Yŏhŭng. To fight corruption in the bureaucracy, he punished officials who had been skimming the country's grain reserves. To diminish the power of the strongest *yangban* outside the capital, he struck at the *sŏwŏn* academies (see Chapter 4), taxing their lands and ordering them closed. And to display

FIGURE 9.5 *Orchids*, Yi Ha'ŭng (1821–1898). Better known as the Taewŏn'gun (Prince Regent), Yi Ha'ŭng was a student of the Chusa style that revolutionized Korean calligraphy. Ink on paper. 117.3 × 29.8 cm.

FROM *KOREAN PAINTNG* BY KEN VOS (LONDON: BAMBOO PUBLISHERS, 1992), P. 53.

the importance of the king, he ordered the enormously expensive reconstruction of the Kyŏngbok Palace, the original Chosŏn dynasty palace in Seoul that had lain in ruins since the Japanese invasions of the 1590s.

The Prince Regent Taewŏn'gun's personal prestige was confirmed by his command of the brush, for he was a skilled calligrapher and ink artist whose orchids (see Figure 9.5) were widely appreciated. Although he established himself as one of the strongest courtiers of the late Chosŏn dynasty, he soon discovered that he had a rival. His daughter-in-law Queen Min and her male relatives almost immediately assumed a stance opposing him. Not surprisingly, the Taewŏn'gun also encountered strong opposition from the *yangban* class in general, since his reforms threatened the privileges of the landed aristocracy. But opposition also came from merchants who resented being assessed to pay for the rebuilding of the royal palace. Commoners, too, suffered from the aggregate burdens of forced labor, taxation, and inflation caused by the government's excessive minting of cash to pay the bills.

The Incursion of the Powers

It was during the Taewŏn'gun's regency that Chosŏn first experienced military pressure from the West. Though the Koreans were well aware of China's losses in the Opium War and under the unequal treaty system, for decades they had managed to fend off attempted visits by Britishers, Americans, Germans, Frenchmen, and Russians, earning for their country the nickname of "Hermit Kingdom." When approached, the Koreans refused to open relations with the foreigners, citing their special relationship with China under the terms of the tributary system. The single exception to Korea's closure to the West was the continuation of French missionary activity and the resilience of the Korean Catholic community despite waves of official persecution. By the 1860s the heterodox ideas of Catholicism, together with its tendency to attract the discontented, once more caused such concern at court that it brought forth a final, full-scale attack on the foreign faith. When the Taewŏn'gun ordered the massive purge of 1866, there were more than 20,000 Catholic believers in Korea. By year's end, more than 8,000 converts had been killed along with nine of the twelve French missionaries known to be residing in the country.

France responded by sending part of its Asiatic naval squadron to seek redress and "open" Korea to French commerce and missionary work. The French flotilla entered the mouth of the Han River and was fought off by a determined Korean defense. This apparent success emboldened the Korean court in its opposition to contact with the West. The Taewŏn'gun proclaimed, "The barbarians are attacking us. We must fight or surrender. Whoever advises conciliation betrays his country. Let this be a warning to our people and all future generations!" (now inscribed on a stone monument on the palace grounds).

Coincidentally in 1866, an American merchant vessel, the *General Sherman*, tried to open contact with Korea by sailing into the mouth of the Taedong River as far as P'yŏngyang. The authorities were outraged by this bold intrusion, and ordered the ship out of Korean waters. The crew disregarded this order, and made threatening gestures toward local officials, whereupon the *General Sherman* was attacked, set afire, and destroyed, with the loss of all hands.

In 1871 the United States government responded to the destruction of the *General Sherman* by sending a naval force to investigate and, it was hoped, to "open" Korea, as Commodore Matthew Perry had "opened" Japan in 1853–1854. When the American squadron approached the mouth of the Han River it was met by Korean defenders determined to repel the Westerners as they had the French in 1866. The Americans landed Marines on Kanghwa Island, however, and there was a brief but bloody battle. Though the Korean side suffered heavier casualties than the Americans, the U.S. side failed to win its objective, and was obliged to depart without a treaty or apology for the destruction of the *General Sherman*. The Koreans thus reaffirmed their seclusion policy with renewed confidence.

As the Koreans learned of the changes surrounding the Meiji Restoration in Japan, they redoubled their determination to "resist heterodoxy and uphold orthodoxy" *(chŏksa wijŏng)* in their own country. They continued the ban on Christianity, renewed their pledge to maintain the purity of Confucian civilization, and bolstered their coastal defenses. Korean thinkers such as Yi Hangno (1792–1868) recommended an all-out nationwide resistance to further foreign incursions, including any from China and Japan, which were no longer "pure." The Korean court even sent a message to the Japanese government chiding the Meiji leaders for their craven willingness to copy the Western barbarians.

Such insults were part of the inspiration for the "conquer Korea" debate *(seikan ron)* that raged within Japan in the 1870s. The Japanese made their move in 1875 when they sent a naval vessel, Perry-style, to the mouth of the Han River. When Korean shore batteries opened fire, the Japanese organized a show of force, and demanded that the Koreans sign a modern-style international treaty, their first with any foreign state, on Kanghwa Island. There was considerable argument in Seoul over whether to sign the treaty, which contained language defining Korea as a sovereign state independent of China, opened additional ports to Japanese trade, permitted Japanese citizens to live and work in Korea, and allowed a Japanese ambassador to take up residence in Seoul. As a disciple of Yi Hangno pointed out, "The Japanese who come nowadays dress in Western clothes, use Western guns, and sail in Western ships—clear evidence of the Japanese being one with the Westerners."[8] Ultimately, however, Japanese military force prevailed, and the Koreans signed. One byproduct was the rise in Seoul of a reform faction, or "progressive party," of younger *yangban* who recommended studying the new Meiji system and adapting elements of Japan's modernization program to the Korean scene.

As regent, the Taewŏn'gun had campaigned to upgrade the power of his son, King Kojong, expecting him to remain steadfast in the conservative mold after he reached the age of majority. However, after the king came of age and started making decisions on his own, he displayed an unexpected independent streak by showing an interest in some of the progressive faction's ideas. Kojong also took the advice of China's Li Hongzhang to seek "self-strengthening" through controlled reform. The result was a significant policy shift that combined the traditional close relations with China, the tracking of reform in Meiji Japan, the opening of relations with Western nations, and limited toleration for Western ideas, including Christianity. In 1882, with Li Hongzhang's blessing, Chosŏn signed a treaty with the United States, its first with a Western power. The following year it received its first Western diplomat, U.S. Minister Lucius Foote. Negotiations leading up to the U.S.-Korean treaty in 1882 were difficult, and the treaty itself was written with great attention to Korean sensibilities. For example, Americans did not get the right to send missionaries to Korea. They did promise to use their "good offices" to assist Korea in relations with other states, a provision that later became an issue when Koreans accused the United States of failing in its duty to protect Korea from Japanese imperialism in the early 1900s. However, when Great Britain, France, Russia, Germany, Italy, and Belgium signed treaties with Korea in the mid-1880s, the door swung wide open to missionary work, exploration, trade and investment. By the mid-1890s Protestant and Catholic missionaries, traders, concessionaires, speculators, teachers, mining engineers, and even a few random expatriates had taken up residence in Korea, forever ending the era of Chosŏn as "the Hermit Kingdom."

The spate of treaties with foreign powers triggered the escalation of an already existing conflict between conservative and progressive factions in the Korean court. King Kojong's dispatch of study missions to Japan and diplomatic missions to the West exacerbated the conflict and sparked a reactionary backlash. In 1881 there was an abortive attempt to replace King Kojong with a more cooperative prince. In 1882, soldiers of the old Korean army staged a mutiny to oppose the creation of Japanese-style modern military units. King Kojong was obliged to call his father back from retirement to get control of the situation, and the old regent then proceeded to dismantle not only the modern army units but also the T'ongni Kimu Amun, Korea's newly established version of China's foreign office, the Zongli Yamen. Japan reacted by sending troops, ostensibly to collect reparations for damages to its diplomatic mission during the soldier's mutiny. Seeing Japan's forces in Korea, China responded by sending a larger force and establishing military supremacy in Korea. Upset with the Taewŏn'gun for provoking chaos and military confrontation in Korea, the Chinese engineered his kidnapping and removal to China under virtual arrest.

This began a period of intense Chinese meddling in Korea's internal affairs. The Chinese "recommended" advisors, both Chinese and Western, to direct various aspects of Korean policy and to administer foreign affairs and the newly-founded Customs Service. In a departure from tradition, the Qing government stationed a permanent representative, or "resident," in Seoul to protect Chinese interests and act as a special advisor. This was Yuan Shikai, the protégé of Li Hongzhang, who was destined eventually to become President of China after the revolution of 1911–1912. His presence in Seoul in the early 1880s encouraged a wave of Chinese merchant immigration to the Korean peninsula.

Gradualists versus Advocates of "Enlightenment"

Chinese interference in Korea thwarted some of the more radical proposals that were emanating from the progressives at court, who started calling themselves the "Enlightenment Party" (*kaehwa dang*). The mild reformers were interested in preserving the Korean class system, and they saw Chinese military backing as a way to stave off fundamental change. The enlightenment party, on the other hand, included people who had been abroad and were determined to strengthen Korea in the style of Meiji Japan rather than Li Hongzhang's China. Like their Japanese mentors, they were ready to challenge the political and social structure in fundamental ways. They proposed the abolition of classes, a sweeping revision of Korea's educational system, and liberation from Qing influence, which they saw as an obstacle to progress.

Certain members of the enlightenment party had studied with the great Meiji intellectual Fukuzawa Yukichi. Fukuzawa did not want his protégés to provoke a full-scale confrontation between China and Japan over Korea, and he gave only tepid support to the enlightenment faction's more militant ideas. Nevertheless, the enlightenment group staged a violent coup in December 1884 that took the lives of several of the gradual reform group. They actually seized control of the palace for several days before being routed by counterattacking Chinese troops. In the aftermath of the coup, the surviving enlightenment group members fled to Japan. The following spring, Li Hongzhang and Itō Hirobumi signed an agreement committing both China and Japan to withdraw their forces from Korea, to refrain from giving military aid to Korea, and to consult before acting in the future if intervention appeared again to be necessary. With the Li–Itō Convention, otherwise known as the Treaty of Tianjin, the dangerous Sino-Japanese military rivalry over Korea came to a standstill that lasted until 1894.

Christianity and Western Thought

Despite Korea's new international contacts, many Korean *yangban* remained steadfastly opposed to Western heterodoxies that competed with orthodox Neo-Confucianism, and insisted that Korea maintain its ideological purity. However, in April 1885, the same month as the Li–Itō Convention, Korea received its first Protestant missionaries. In the decade that followed, American Presbyterians and Methodists founded numerous churches in and around Seoul and the ports that had been opened for trade. A clinic founded in 1885 later developed into a leading modern hospital and medical school. A Presbyterian boys' school that was founded in the same year and a Methodist girls' school founded in 1886 evolved into Yonsei and Ewha, two of contemporary Korea's greatest universities. Paejae Academy, a Methodist boys' school, produced several of Korea's most important modern leaders, including Syngman Rhee (1875–1965).

Though Western missionaries at first had difficulty recruiting converts and students, they were unhampered by the association with gunboat diplomacy and violent Taiping-style revolution that repelled and frightened many people in China. By 1900 the Korean Protestant community was growing rapidly and attracting many who were curious about modern life in the West as well as many who became authentic spiritual converts. Catholic missions also returned in the 1890s, reinvigorating Korea's earlier Christian community. The central cathedral in Seoul, completed in 1898, became one of the city's defining landmarks.

The positive response of many Koreans to foreign ideology owed much to the genuine disillusionment that gripped many Korean intellectuals at the end of the nineteenth century. Though the Chosŏn dynasty and its institutions had lasted so long that it seemed inconceivable that there could ever be a Korea without them, even pedigreed *yangban* were tired of the reaction and corruption that were so much a part of the country's political culture. One young *yangban* who had an extraordinary opportunity to study abroad, first in China under American missionaries and then in the United States at Vanderbilt and Emory Universities, was Yun Ch'iho (1865–1945). As he was leaving America to return to Asia in 1893, he reflected on his homeland with criticism and concern:

> It suffocates me (literally) to think that there is a country of 80,000 square miles where millions of souls cannot think or say or act as they please; where talents have no market; ambition, no sphere; patriotism, no play; where infernal despotism breeds and nurses generations of slaves, beggars, and idiots; where men are dying in life and living in death; where moral and material putrefaction and filth are destroying thousands every year. How long will this political hell last?[9]

The Korea to which Yun Ch'iho was returning was caught in a true political whirlpool, weakened by internal factions and feckless leadership, and surrounded by larger countries that had designs on its future. Since the Li–Itō Convention of 1885, China had tightened its grip on Korea, thwarting King Kojong's feeble attempt to conduct an independent foreign policy, and supervising the country's internal affairs through pro-Chinese officials in key positions. Queen Min's male relatives had created an oligarchic faction for themselves, controlling the tax system, the civil service examination system, official appointments and promotions, and the issuing of licenses for every kind of private enterprise.

The Japanese, meanwhile, had created their own sphere of operations in Korea centering on the ports, where they dominated trade and transport. Japanese merchants busied themselves penetrating the domestic market, overwhelming Korean small businesses with better-quality textiles from Japan and daily use items such as matches. The treaty system limited the Seoul government's ability to use customs duties to protect the Korean market from Japanese sellers. Meanwhile, itinerant Japanese buyers gathered up rice and other foodstuffs in Korea and exported them to Japan, creating scarcity and high prices for Korean consumers. As the intrusion of foreign influence started affecting daily life across the country, the government's essential weakness was revealed in its inability to manage the imbalances.

The Tonghak Rebellion and the Sino-Japanese War

As Sino-Japanese rivalry over Korea simmered in the early 1890s, events within Korea began setting the stage for war. The catalyst was an uprising in southwestern Korea called the Tonghak Rebellion. Tonghak, meaning "Eastern Learning" was a religious movement founded earlier in the century that joined concepts from Buddhist tradition and beliefs and practices common in Chinese and Korean folk religion. As with so many popular movements in East Asian history, what began as a religion quickly took on political significance, serving as a vehicle for protest against excess taxation, official corruption, and a national regime in decay. Though its founder was arrested and executed in the 1860s and the movement lost its way, it reemerged during regional riots in 1893 and became a major rebellion the following year when Korea was struck by famine. When the Seoul government had difficulty dealing with the rebels, it fell back on the ancient relationship with China, and called for Chinese military assistance. When Li Hongzhang dispatched a contingent of 1,500 troops, Japan answered with a comparable force. These entered Seoul and seized control of the royal palace, in effect arresting King Kojong and Queen Min.

When the Sino-Japanese War over Korea began in July 1894, most observers expected China to prevail. All parties, including the Japanese, were therefore surprised when Japan decisively defeated China on both sea and land during nine months of fighting. The Japanese crushed Li Hongzhang's army in a battle at P'yŏngyang, invaded Manchuria, and completely destroyed Qing seapower. Dalian and Port Arthur were captured by land from the rear, rendering useless the artillery pointing to the sea and the naval bases financed at great cost by Li.

In retrospect, the reasons for the outcome are easy to see. Japan was better-equipped, better-led, and more united than China. Chinese battle tactics were astonishingly inept: for example, in the Battle of Korea Bay, the general in charge of the Chinese fleet arranged his ships in cavalry formation, like horses, thus opening them to destruction by the Japanese admiral, who was using a disciplined modern naval formation. But China's greatest disadvantage was its officials' disinterest in defending their stakes in Korea. Regional governors in southern China saw the war not as a national struggle, but as a project of the northern viceroy Li Hongzhang, and they withheld their forces.

The Treaty of Shimonoseki (1895)

The war ended with a peace treaty that was signed at Shimonoseki on the western tip of the Japanese main island of Honshu. In the Treaty of Shimonoseki, China renounced its traditional special role in Korea, and recognized it as a fully independent state. In addition, China ceded to Japan the island of Taiwan and the nearby Pescadores Islands, a significant increase for the Japanese empire. As if to recognize that Japan was now a world power on a par with the Western imperialist nations, China paid Japan a large indemnity, granted Japan most-favored-nation status, and opened seven additional ports to Japanese trade. The treaty also granted Japan control of the Liaodong Peninsula at the northern end of the Yellow Sea, a foothold on Manchuria that would have opened the way for Japanese development on the continent beyond Korea. However, Russia, France, and Germany reacted with diplomatic pressure to block this transfer, in what is known as the "Triple Intervention" of 1895, and China paid Japan a supplemental indemnity instead. The Sino-Japanese War thus resulted in a dramatic shift in the East Asian balance of power from China to Japan, a condition that was to continue until Japan's defeat in the Second World War. The world learned that China was even weaker than previously believed. Korea became a pawn in the great game of empire, with the enlightenment clique in the ascendancy and Japanese officials pulling strings in the background. To the north, Czarist Russia was consolidating its presence in Siberia and Manchuria with railroads and bases. Japan, therefore, turned from its victory against China to face a new continental rival, Czarist Russia.

Notes

1. Ssu-yu Teng and John K. Fairbank, *China's Response to the West: A Documentary Survey, 1839–1923* (Cambridge: Harvard Univ. Press, 1954), p. 48. Parentheses inserted by the translation.

2. W. Theodore de Bary and Richard Lufrano, eds., *Sources of Chinese Tradition*, 2nd ed. vol. 2 (New York: Columbia University Press, 2000), p. 238. Adapted from Ssu-yu Teng and John K. Fairbank, *China's Response to the West*, p. 76.

3. Quoted in Immanuel C. Y. Hsu, *China's Entrance into the Family of Nations: The Diplomatic Phase, 1858–1880* (Cambridge: Harvard Univ. Press, 1960), p. 168.

4. Philip C. C. Huang, *The Peasant Economy and Social Change in North China* (Stanford: Stanford Univ. Press, 1985), p. 137.

5. Claudia Brown and Ju-hsi Chou, *Transcending Turmoil: Painting at the Close of China's Empire*

1796–1911 (Phoenix: Phoenix Art Museum, 1992).

6. Cyril Birch, ed., *Anthology of Chinese Literature* (New York: Grove Press, 1971), vol. 2, p. 294.

7. David Der-wei Wang, *Fin-de-siecle Splendor: Repressed Modernities of Late Qing Fiction, 1849–1911* (Stanford: Stanford Univ. Press, 1997), p. 125.

8. Ch'oe Ikhyŏn quoted in Peter H. Lee, ed., *Sourcebook of Korean Civilization*, vol. II (New York: Columbia University Press, 1996), p. 333.

9. *Yun Ch'iho Ilgi (Yun Ch'iho's Diary)*, vol. 3 (Seoul: National History Compilation Committee, 1974), p. 182.

Part Three

Continental East Asia and Imperial Japan: 1895–1945

During this half-century, interaction between the world's civilizations increased in intensity and complexity until all became involved in World War II, which brought in its wake drastically redrawn mental as well as physical landscapes in East Asia as elsewhere. Earlier, World War I had encouraged ethnic nationalism but failed to achieve a stable multinational state system. Resulting directly from the war, the Russian Revolution and the establishment of the Soviet Union offered a radical vision of equality and world revolution. The mostly prosperous twenties gave substance to the claim that the war had ended in a "victory for democracy," but the thirties were to show how precarious a victory that was, as Fascism, also rooted in the debacle of the war, gained ground, and the advances in international cooperation achieved in the twenties were negated.

World War I shattered old European verities and led to a period of cultural and intellectual ferment. Einstein, Freud, and Picasso achieved major breakthroughs prior to the war, but it was in the twenties that their ideas became current. Now people read and argued over Joyce and Pound, delighted in or sneered at Bauhaus architecture, applauded or were puzzled by surrealism, futurism, the antics of the Dadaists, and the sounds of Schoenberg, Hindemith, and Stravinsky. It was also a time of the de-

velopment of popular culture, spread not only in print but through radio and film.

The twenties seemed to prove Henry Ford a better visionary than Karl Marx, but in 1929 came the great crash followed by the Great Depression. Both Communism and Fascism made great gains when the depression discredited prewar capitalism and, to varying degrees in different countries, the political systems in which it had been nourished. The legitimacy of existing states was challenged not only by Marxists longing for "the withering away of the state" after the triumph of the proletariat, but equally by Fascists and other ethno-nationalists advocating a special destiny for their "people," "nation," or "race." These terms meant different things to different people, but were no less powerful on that account during a decade when economic crisis intensified ideological passions to an extent difficult to imagine in the present time of economic prosperity and political apathy.

As we will see, World War I had major repercussions also in East Asia, but there Japan's defeat of China in 1895 looms even larger, for it marked the beginning of a half-century of Japanese empire building that had a profound effect throughout and beyond the region.

10

China: Endings and Beginnings, 1895–1927

| 1895 | 1898 | 1900 | | 1905 | 1908 | 1911 | 1914 | 1916 | 1918 | 1921 | 1927 |

Demise of the QING DYNASTY

THE WARLORD ERA

- 100 Days of Reform
- Revolutionary Alliance
- Revolution
- World War I
- C.C.P. Founded
- Nationalist Government

- Boxer Rebellion
- Death of Cixi
- The May Fourth Incident (1919)

- Death of Yuan Shikai

China's defeat by Japan ushered in a period of accelerating changes as the forces of reform, reaction, and revolution interlocked in complex patterns in an international environment full of menace. After the demise of the Qing, it proved easier to do away with the old than to create the new.

I. The Last Years of the Last Dynasty

The New Reformers

The Scramble for Concessions

The Boxer Rising

Winds of Change

Stirrings of Protest and Revolution

Eleventh-Hour Reform

The Revolution of 1911

The New Reformers

The shock of defeat allowed new voices to be heard. They differed from the proponents of self-strengthening both in the scope of the changes they advocated and in a willingness to reexamine basic assumptions. At the same time, the radicals of this generation still had received a Confucian education and had a command of traditional learning.

A major influence was Yan Fu, the one-time naval student at Greenwich, who voiced the bitter resentment of many:

> We thought that of all the human race none was nobler than we. And then one day from tens and thousands of miles away came island barbarians from beyond the pale, with bird-like language and beastly features, who floated in and pounded our gates requesting entrance and, when they did not get what they asked for, they attacked our coasts and took captive our officials and even burned our palaces and alarmed our Emperor. When this happened, the only reason we did not devour their flesh and sleep on their hides was that we had not the power.[1]

Emboldened by the more open atmosphere, Yan publicized his ideas, first in a series of essays, and then in a number of extremely influential translations, notably Thomas Huxley's *Ethics and Evolution* (1898), Adam Smith's *Wealth of Nations* (1900), and John Stuart Mill's *On Liberty* (1903). Yan argued that Western learning was needed to release Chinese energies, and rejected much of Chinese tradition including even Confucius. He was especially attracted to Social Darwinism, with its dynamic view of history as evolutionary and progressive, and the hope it held out, on a supposedly modern scientific basis, for those who would struggle.

Yan Fu was no political activist, but others, notably Kang Yuwei (1858–1927) and his followers Tan Sitong (1865–1898) and Liang Qichao (1873–1929), not only spread their ideas through their writings and in study groups but tried to implement political programs. Kang, an original thinker deeply grounded in Buddhism as well as Confucianism, elaborated a highly original theory to construct a Confucian basis for ideas that went well beyond the Confucian tradition. Drawing on an unorthodox school of classical interpretation, he argued that Confucius was not merely a transmitter of ancient teachings but a prophet whose language was full of hidden meanings. Kang's Confucius saw history as a universal progress through three stages, each with its appropriate form of government: the Age of Disorder (rule by an absolute monarch), the Age of Approaching Peace (rule by a constitutional monarch), and the Age of Great Peace (rule by the people). His Confucius was a seer and prophet not only for China but for the entire world. Tan Sitong went beyond Kang to argue that the monarchy should be replaced by a republic, and attacked the traditional Confucian family distinctions in the name of *ren*, the central Confucian virtue. Neo-Confucian thinkers had earlier given *ren* a cosmic dimension, but Tan drew on modern scientific concepts in identifying *ren* with ether. Kang Youwei, too, equated *ren* with ether and electricity.

In their political program, Kang and his followers sought to transform the government into a modern and modernizing constitutional monarchy along the lines of Meiji Japan. Thanks to a sympathetic governor, they were able to carry out some reforms in Hunan, but their greatest opportunity came during the "Hundred Days of Reform" (actually 103 days, June 11th to September 20th), when Emperor Guangxu asserted his authority to issue a flood of edicts aimed at reforming the examination system, remodeling the bureaucracy, and promoting modernization. It was an ambitious program, but the edicts remained more significant as expressions of intent than as indicators of accomplishment, for most were never implemented.

The reforms were initiated by moderately experienced statesmen, but later accounts exaggerated the influence of Kang and his associates and the degree to which there was, from the start, a struggle between a progressive emperor and a supposedly reactionary Empress Dowager (see Figure 9.2). However, rumors of Kang's allegedly extremist influence on the emperor helped to solidify the opposition and pave the way for Cixi, backed by General Ronglu, to stage a coup. She placed Emperor Guangxu under house arrest and turned him into a figurehead for the remaining ten years of his life.

After the coup, Tan Sitong remained in China and suffered martyrdom. Kang Yuwei and Liang Qichao managed to flee to Japan, where they continued to write and work for renewal and reform. Kang, elaborating on his utopia, dreamed of a future when the whole world would be united in love and harmony under a single popularly elected government, which would operate hospitals, schools, and nurseries, administering a society in which all divisive institutions would have disappeared, including even the family. Meanwhile, Liang continued to expand his horizons as well as those of his numerous readers. Like many of his contemporaries everywhere, he championed evolution and progress, processes which he conflated and, contrary to Darwin, saw as products of human will. But this will had to serve the group. Like most Chinese and Japanese thinkers, Liang was not an individualist.

The Empress Dowager's coup sent China's most advanced thinkers into exile, but did not spell a wholesale reaction against reform. She approved moderate reforms, including military modernization and reforms in education and the monetary and fiscal systems. That little was accomplished was due to the weakness of the central government and the magnitude of the problems facing the dynasty. By no means the least of these came from abroad.

The Scramble for Concessions

China's display of weakness in the war against Japan set in motion a scramble for special rights and privileges in which Russia, France, Britain, Germany, and Japan pursued their national interests and jockeyed for position in case China collapsed completely, as seemed quite likely at the time. The concessions extracted from China were economic and political. Loans were forced on the Qing, secured by tax revenues, such as maritime customs. Long-term leases of Chinese territory were granted, including the right to develop economic resources such as mines and railroads. Germany leased territory in Shandong; Russia leased Port Arthur in the southern Liaodong Peninsula; France held leases on land around Guangzhou Bay; and Britain obtained Weihaiwei and the New Territories, adjacent to the Kowloon area of Hong Kong. The powers frequently obtained the right to police the leased areas. Often they combined leaseholds, railroad rights, and commercial rights into a "sphere of interest," where they were the privileged foreign power, as, for example, Germany was in Shandong. Finally, there were "nonalienation" pacts in which China agreed not to cede a given area to any power other than the signatory: the Yangzi Valley to Britain, the provinces bordering French Indochina to France, Fujian to Japan. Russia received special rights in Manchuria.

Britain, as the prime trading nation in China, pursued an ambiguous policy, concerned to retain access to all of China but also to obtain a share of the concessions. The United States at this time was acquiring a Pacific empire. In 1898 it annexed Hawaii and, after war with Spain, the Philippines and Guam. At the urging of Britain, the United States then adopted an open-door policy enunciated in two diplomatic notes. The first of these (1899) merely demanded equality of commercial opportunity for all the powers in China, while the second (1900) also affirmed a desire to preserve the integrity of the Chinese state and Chinese territory. This was a declaration of principle, not backed by force; neither its altruism nor its effectiveness should be exaggerated.

The Boxer Rising

The Boxers, members of the *Yihequan* (Righteous and Harmonious Fists), developed in response to harsh economic conditions. Popular anxieties were also fueled by anti-foreignism, stemming from alarm over the spread of railways, which cut across the land regardless of the graves of ancestors or the requirements of geomancy, railways along which stood telephone poles carrying wires from which rust-filled rainwater dripped blood-red. As a counterforce, the Boxers relied on *qigong* (ritualized exercise), spells, and amulets to endow them with supernatural powers, including invulnerability to bullets. In 1898 flood and famine in Shandong, combined with the advance of the Germans in that province, led to the first Boxer rising there in May of that year; but it was drought in the spring and summer of 1900 that brought many new members and wide popular support.

Originally antidynastic, the Boxers changed direction when they received the support of high Qing officials prepared to use the movement against the foreign powers. Thus encouraged, the Boxers spread, venting their rage on Chinese and foreign Christians, especially Catholics. On June 13, 1900, they entered Beijing. Eight days later the court issued a declaration of war on all the treaty powers. The Boxers were officially placed under the command of imperial princes. There followed a dramatic two-month siege of the legation quarter in Beijing, where 451 guards defended 473 foreign civilians and some 3,000 Chinese Christians who had fled there for protection. The ordeal of the besieged was grim, but they were spared the worst, for the Boxers and the Chinese troops were undisciplined, ill-organized, and uncoordinated. The city was full of looting and violence, but the legation quarter was still intact when an international relief expedition reached Beijing on August 15 and forced the court to flee the capital.

During these dangerous and dramatic events, southern governors-general ignored the court's declaration of war, claiming it was made under duress. The powers, nevertheless, demanded from the Qing court a very harsh settlement. It included a huge indemnity (450 million taels, or 67.5 million pounds sterling) to be paid from customs and salt revenues. Other provisions required the punishment of pro-Boxer officials and of certain cities, where the civil service examinations were suspended. The powers received the right to station permanent legation guards in the capital and to place troops between Beijing and the sea. The Boxer rising also provided Russia with an excuse to occupy Manchuria, where some Russians remained until Russia's defeat by Japan in the war of 1904–1905.

The Boxer rising became a source of literature focusing on one of its leading figures, Sai Jinhua (1874–1936), who was a courtesan, the concubine of a Chinese diplomat in Europe, and supposedly the mistress of the German field marshall who commanded the allied forces occupying Beijing. Depraved strumpet to some, selfless heroine to others, she fills both roles in *A Flower in a Sea of Sins* (*Niehai hua*, 1907) by Zeng Pu (1872–1935).

Winds of Change

Between 1895 and 1911, the modern sector of the Chinese economy continued to grow, but it was dominated by foreign capital. Extensive railway concessions were granted to the treaty powers, and Chinese railroads, like that linking
Beijing and Hankou, were financed by foreign capital. Foreigners also controlled
much of China's mining and shipping, and were a major factor in manufacturing,
both for export (tea, silk, soybeans, and so on) and for the domestic market (textiles, tobacco, and so on). Modern banking was another area of foreign domination, prompting the Qing government in 1898 to approve the creation of the Commercial Bank of China as a "government operated merchant enterprise." Two
more banks were formed in 1905 and 1907.

Except for railways and mines, foreign investments were concentrated in the
treaty ports. It was also there that Chinese factories gradually developed, taking
advantage of modern services and the security found in foreign concession areas.
Chinese enterprises were particularly important in textile manufacturing. Most
remained small (by 1912 only 750 employed more than 100 workers), but they
were an important part of China's economic modernization. It was during this
time that Shanghai became China's largest city.

In Shanghai and, to a lesser extent, in other treaty ports, changes in social
structure occurred. During the last five years of the dynasty there emerged a bourgeoisie, "a group of modern or semi-modern entrepreneurs, tradesmen, finan-
ciers, industrial leaders, unified by material interests, common political aspirations, a sense of their collective destiny, a common mentality, and specific daily
habits."[2] There were also the beginnings of an urban working class, who at times
expressed their resentment over terrible working conditions by going on strike. In
the city, too, the old family system lost some of its economic underpinnings, and
an audience developed receptive to new ways of looking at things.

There were now 170 presses supplying 2 to 4 million readers for the "depravity novels," "chivalric/court case novels," "exposé," and "science fantasy" novels
studied by David Der-wei Wang. More often than not they took a jaundiced view
of those in power, though few were as blunt as the prostitute in the "depravity
novel" *Nine-tailed Turtle* who tells her customer, "The whole of officialdom is just
like a big whorehouse."[3] In *The New Story of the Stone* (1908), Wu Jianren
(1866–1910) brings back the main protagonist of *Dream of the Red Chamber*, and
at one point has him arrested as a dissident, but also takes him to "The Civilized
World," filled with technological wonders, a utopia (unlike Kang Yu-wei's) not to
be taken as actually attainable.

Meanwhile, out in the real world a strong influence on provincial affairs was
exercised by a semi-modern urban elite composed of merchants and bankers
(more or less traditional), military and professional men (among them journalists)
trained in modern methods, and absentee landowners, an elite whose interests
and even values often differed from those of the landed gentry on the one hand
and from the central government on the other. The very definition of elite status

was changed forever when the examination system was abolished in 1905, putting an end to a key institution that had linked government and society, thought and action, the local and the central for well over a thousand years.

The government had taken this radical step in recognition of the need for more modern specialists, but also to secure the loyalty of graduates of new schools by reassuring them in their career expectations.

Stirrings of Protest and Revolution

Some were caught off balance by the winds of change, others trimmed their sails, but there were also those who looked to the future with hope, and organized attempts to induce further changes. An early and notable example was the formation of the first antifootbinding movement in 1894, which resulted in a law banning the practice in 1902. However, even in the cities the law was largely ignored. Footbinding persisted longest in rural areas, and old women with bound feet can still be seen in remote areas. Other expressions of public opinion included a flurry of criticism at what appeared to be a maneuver to depose the emperor (1900), protests at Russia's refusal to leave Manchuria (1903), a boycott against the United States protesting exclusionary immigration laws (1905), and a boycott against Japan (1908), as well as movements to regain railway rights.

Readers of the political press that emerged after 1895 were now exposed to articles and cartoons linking dissatisfaction with the government to resentment against foreign exactions (see Figure 10.1.) Politically, the defeat of 1895 opened the way not only for radical reformism but also set Sun Yat-sen (1866–1925) on the path of revolution. Sun was born into a Guangdong peasant family, received a Christian education in Hawaii, and studied medicine in Hong Kong. He founded his first revolutionary organization in 1894. Throughout his life overseas, Chinese communities remained an important source of moral and financial support. Over the years he elaborated his "Three Principles of the People"—nationalism, democracy, and the people's livelihood. He called for the overthrow of the dynasty and the establishment of a republic, principles broad enough to attract the varied and loosely organized membership of Sun's Revolutionary Alliance (Tongmenghui), formed in Tokyo in 1905 by the merger of a number of revolutionary groups. His supporters now included students, many from elite families.

Many looked to political revolution to solve China's ills, but some more radical voices sought social revolution as well. One such was the pioneer feminist Qin Jin, born in 1877 and executed as a revolutionary in 1907. In 1904, shortly after she had left not only the husband her family had selected for her but also a son and a daughter, she wrote the following poem:

Regrets: Lines Written en Route to Japan
> Sun and moon have no light left, earth is dark;
> our women's world is sunk so deep, who can help us?
> Jewelry sold to pay this trip across the seas,

FIGURE 10.1   "A record of the situation in China." Cartoon in *Shibao*, August 26, 1907. The ladle in the center repesents officials scooping from the jug of the people (on the right) and pouring their resources through a government funnel into the foreigners' teapot.

FROM *PRINT AND POLITICS: "SHIBAO" AND THE CULTURE OF REFORM IN LATE QING CHINA*, BY JOAN JUDGE (STANFORD: STANFORD UNIVERSITY PRESS, 1996), P. 184. REPRINTED COURTESY STANFORD UNIVERSITY PRESS.

> Cut off from family I leave my native land.
> Unbinding my feet I clear out a thousand years of poison,
> With heated heart arouse all women's spirits.
> Alas, this delicate kerchief here
> Is half stained with blood, and half with tears.[4]

Eleventh-Hour Reform

The abolition of the examination system was only the most drastic of a series of reforms by which the Empress Dowager hoped to save the dynasty after the failure of the Boxers. Some, like the drive against opium, accomplished much, but the program as a whole failed to inspire officials to change their ways. The momentum was all downhill. In *Modern Times: A Brief History of Enlightenment* (*Wen-ming xiaoshi*, 1905) Li Boyuan (1867–1906), a widely read author of exposé novels, depicts officials whose venality is matched only by the ignorance and arrogance of purveyors of the new Western learning. According to David Der-wei Wang, "Li Boquan saw in this campaign for reform and modernization less a promise of new economic and political structure than an omen of collective self-delusion, incompetence, and procrastination."[5]

Frequently, measures taken to save the Qing ended up undermining it. The educational reforms are an example. By 1911 even remote provinces boasted new schools, teaching new subjects and ideas. Students also studied abroad in record numbers, especially in Japan where, by 1906, there were at least 8,000 Chinese students, many supported by their provincial governments. There, away from home, they enjoyed new personal and intellectual liberty. Even those who did not manage to complete their education drank in the heady wine of new ideas. From the writing of the highly influential Liang Qichao, many learned about the major events of world history and were introduced to Western social and political thought. The example of Japan was itself a powerful influence, as were books translated from Japanese. More books were translated into Chinese from Japanese than from any other language. Many Japanese loanwords entered the Chinese language, thus reversing the flow that had taken place over a millennium earlier.

Chinese students thus learned about Western history, law, science and logic, became convinced of the truths of Social Darwinism, and were inspired by the visions of nationalism. As non-Chinese, the Manchus were an obvious target. The Japanese example showed that nationalism was compatible with the preservation of elements of traditional culture, but a commitment to nationalism entailed a willingness to jettison those elements of tradition that failed to contribute to national development. Toward the end of the decade students became increasingly restive and revolutionary.

Manchu political reform included restructuring the government along modern lines and developing a constitution. After a study mission abroad (1905–1906) and subsequent deliberations, in 1908 the government announced a nine-year plan of constitutional reform, beginning with provincial assemblies in 1909. Although elected on a limited franchise, these assemblies, as well as the central legislative council convened in 1910, became centers of opposition rather than sources of popular support.

Nothing was more urgent than the creation of a modern military, but here too the reform program backfired. The new forces proved unreliable because they were either influenced by new, subversive ideas or were loyal to their commanders rather than to the throne. The main beneficiary of military modernization turned out to be Yuan Shikai, who, after his service in Korea (see p. 187), had advanced his career by siding with Cixi in her coup and by standing firm against the Boxers. He became commander of the New Army in 1895 and, as governor-general of Zhihli from 1901 to 1907, continued to build up the army with which he retained ties even after he was dismissed from the government in 1909.

The government had some foreign policy success, especially in reasserting sovereignty over Tibet, but failed to emerge as a plausible focus for nationalism. Not only was it handicapped by its non-Han ethnic origins, but at this critical juncture, there was general confusion and disorganization after the Empress Dowager and Emperor Guangxu both died in 1908. Since the Emperor had seemed in good health, there were rumors that his death one day before that of the Empress Dowager was due to poison. The rumors were never proven, but this was not a propitious way to start a new reign. The new emperor was an infant, and the regent was inept, but bitterly resentful of Yuan Shikai, who was fortunate to be allowed to retire in 1909.

The Revolution of 1911

In its program of modernization, the dynasty was handicapped by its financial weakness. This became painfully apparent in its handling of the railway issue. In order to regain foreign railway concessions, a railway recovery movement was organized by provincial landed and merchant elites, who created their own railway companies. The Qing government, however, wanted to centralize, and in 1911 decided to nationalize the major railway lines. Lacking the necessary financial resources, it was able to do so only by contracting foreign loans, inevitably with strings attached. The loans and the subsequent disbanding of provincial railway companies caused a furor, nowhere more so than in Sichuan, where the local investors felt cheated by the price the government was willing to pay for their shares. Provincial interests resented the threat to provincial autonomy. Nationalists were indignant over the foreign loans that financed the transaction. This was the prelude to revolt. The insurrection that set off the revolution took place when a New Army regiment mutinied in Wuchang on October 10. It was carried out by men only very loosely connected with the Revolutionary Alliance, the main revolutionary organization in the land. Its leader, Sun Yat-sen, was traveling in the United States raising money, but rushed home when he heard the news.

After the October 10 incident, province after province broke with the dynasty. It turned for help to Yuan Shikai, who had served as Grand Councilor and Foreign Minister in 1907–1908, but had been dismissed after the death of his patron Cixi in 1908. Yuan was the obvious man to turn to, for he enjoyed foreign support as well as the loyalty of China's best army, and he had prestige as a reformer. However, he was not about to sacrifice himself for a losing cause, but he was not strong enough to impose his will on all of China. The revolutionaries had in the meantime formed a government at Nanjing with Sun Yat-sen as provisional president. A compromise between Yuan and the revolutionaries was clearly called for if China was to avoid prolonged civil war and the nightmare of direct foreign intervention. An agreement was reached. The Manchu child-emperor formally abdicated on February 2, 1912, bringing an end not only to a dynasty but to a political system whose foundations had been laid in 221 B.C.E. China became a republic.

II. From Yuan Shikai to Chiang Kai-shek

Yuan Shikai

After the Qing abdication, Sun Yat-sen stepped aside, and Yuan accepted the presidency of a republic with a two-chambered legislature. He also agreed to move the capital to Nanjing, but once in office he evaded this provision, and Beijing remained the capital of the Republic. In the absence of well-organized political parties or deep-rooted republican sentiment among the public, there was little to restrain Yuan from rapidly developing into a dictator. To be sure, elections were held in February 1913 with about 5 percent of China's population entitled to vote.

The Guomindang (GMD or Nationalist party), the successor to the Tongmenghui, was the largest party in the new parliament. Yuan, however, was not about to share power. He bullied the elected parliament, and in March 1913, Song Jiaoren (1882–1913), architect of the constitution and leader of the parliamentary GMD, was assassinated on Yuan's orders. That summer Yuan forced a showdown by ordering dismissal of pro-Nationalist southern military governors. When they revolted in what is sometimes known as the Second Revolution, Yuan crushed them easily. For the next two years, the other military governors remained loyal, but Yuan remained dependent on military authority.

Yuan basically sought to continue the late Qing program of centralization, but to do so he had to struggle against the forces of reformist provincialism as well as revolutionary nationalism. Often the two combined, because to finance a program regarded with suspicion by provincial interests, Yuan needed funds, and, in the absence of a radical social revolution, this meant obtaining foreign loans. This antagonized nationalists because the loans came with foreign strings and "advisors." The *Shibao* cartoon rang truer than ever (Figure 10.1).

In 1915, taking advantage of the great powers' preoccupation with World War I, Japan presented China with the notorious Twenty-One Demands, divided into five groups: (1) recognition of Japanese rights in Shandong; (2) extension of Japanese rights in Mongolia and Manchuria; (3) Sino-Japanese joint operation of China's largest iron and steel company; (4) China not to cede or lease any coastal area to any power other than Japan; and (5) provisions that would have obliged the Chinese government to employ Japanese political, financial, and military advisors, to give the Japanese partial control over the police, and to purchase Japanese arms. Yuan managed to avoid the last and most onerous group of demands, which would have reduced China to a virtual Japanese satellite. However, with the other powers preoccupied in Europe, Yuan was forced to accept Japan's seizure of Germany's holdings in Shandong, grant Japan new rights in southern Manchuria and Inner Mongolia, and acknowledge her special interest in China's largest iron and steel works, which had previously served as security for Japanese loans. The domestic result was a wave of anti-Japanese nationalist outrage, which expressed itself in protests and boycotts.

Yuan made no attempt to harness nationalist feelings to his own cause, but prepared for restoration of dynastic rule with himself as emperor. According to an American advisor to Yuan, China was not ready for a republic. Yuan probably was not off the mark in believing that bringing back the emperorship would follow the preferences and meet the expectations of the vast majority of China's population, but he did nothing to tap or mobilize mass support or to mollify the resentment of the educated. He just went ahead. The new regime was proclaimed in December 1915, to begin on New Year's Day. Hostility to the new dynasty was so overwhelming that in March 1916 Yuan gave way and officially abandoned his imperial ambitions. He never regained his old prestige, and died a failure in June of that year.

The Warlord Era

After the fall of Yuan Shikai, the pattern of Chinese politics became exceedingly complex, as military men came to the fore. In 1917 there was even a two-week restoration of the Qing. In August of that year China, under the premier and warlord Duan Qirui (1865–1936), entered Word War I by declaring war on Germany. During the next year the Chinese government received loans of some 145 million yen from Japan (the Nishihara loans), ostensibly to strengthen the Chinese ally, but actually siphoned off to support Duan's military and political plans.

Although a national government ruled in Beijing, actual power lay in the hands of regional strongmen (warlords) who came to dominate civil administration in the areas under their control largely through force of arms, and who struggled with each other to enlarge or protect their holdings. They constantly made and unmade alliances with each other, while the foreign powers (especially Japan and the Soviet Union), fishing in these troubled waters, sought to play the warlords off against each other for their own benefit.

Some of the warlords, including Duan, had been generals under Yuan Shikai; others had begun their careers as bandits, and more or less continued to behave as such. One of the most notorious was the "Dog-Meat General" of Shandong, with his entourage of White Russian guards and women. A huge brute of a man, greedy and cruel, he decorated his telegraph poles with the severed heads of secret society members. Other warlords showed a genuine interest in social welfare and education, and tried to build up their areas economically, but they lacked the vision and organization to clear a way for the future. Conditions varied widely, but for many these were years of great insecurity and suffering.

Internationally, the 1920s were peaceful, but China's sovereignty was more impaired than ever. Its customs and salt revenues were committed to paying foreign obligations, and tariffs were kept artificially low. China's major cities were designated as treaty ports, some—most notably Shanghai—with foreign concession areas under foreign jurisdiction. In these enclaves foreigners led privileged lives. They also continued to enjoy extraterritoriality wherever they went. While the foreigners' economic impact should not be exaggerated, both commercial travelers and missionaries used British steamers to travel inland on waterways, policed if necessary by foreign gunboats, to service churches and clinics. Foreigners were everywhere. It was politically offensive and profoundly degrading.

Economically, the modern sector expanded during the global postwar boom so that 1917–1923 has been called "the golden age of Chinese capitalism."[6] The influence of the world economy on China expanded, with, for example, the sale of kerosene spreading into interior villages. Over all, these economic developments were insufficient to destabilize the economy enough to bring about either a fundamental breakdown or a breakthrough to growth. However, economic activity can never be separated from other aspects of life. We may speculate that with the state too weak to exert pressure, the examination system no longer in place to reward Confucian learning, and the old paternalistic ideology tarnished, there was increasingly little to prevent former gentry families from turning into landlords pure and simple. If so, this suggests fragmentation of the social fabric analogous to the political fragmentation produced by the warlords. Meanwhile, the shattering of the old world was most visible in the intellectual arena.

Intellectual Ferment

It did not take the fall of the Qing to produce iconoclasm and protest. Revolutionary ideas had already been current among Chinese students in Tokyo and were discussed in magazines and schools in China itself. We have already noted the beginnings of feminism. In China, as in Japan, radicals were drawn to the teachings of anarchism—especially the ideas that the state is inherently oppressive and that natural human social tendencies can create a just society. The abolition of the examinations and the collapse of the Qing opened the floodgates to new ideas, but destroyed neither the respect accorded scholars and intellectuals nor their commitment to society and their sense of their own importance.

A major landmark was the founding in 1915 of *New Youth,* the journal that came to stand at the core of the new intellectual tide. In the first issue, its founder, Chen Duxiu (1879–1942) issued an eloquent call for the rejuvenation of China, accompanied by an equally strong denunciation of tradition. The new intellectuals castigated Confucianism as responsible for all that was found wanting in the old state and society, for stifling human creativity and suppressing women, for standing in the way of freedom and progress. Few were convinced by Kang Youwei, who tried to cast Confuciansm in a new role as the official state religion. Unsuccessful in his earlier attempt to construct a Confucian justification for modernization that would persuade scholars grounded in the classics, he now failed to make Confucianism acceptable to those whose primary loyalty was to the nation. He was not the only intellectual whom time passed by as ideas once considered radical appeared conservative in a changed world. Confucianism was not destroyed, but it was put very much on the defensive.

New Youth opposed not only the traditional teachings but also the language in which they were written. The journal opened its pages to Hu Shi (1891–1962), a former student of the American philosopher John Dewey, and China's leading champion of the vernacular language *(baihua)*. Hu Shi argued that people should write the spoken language, not the language of the classics, and that the vernacular should be taught in the schools. He praised the literary merits of the old novels written in the vernacular, which had long been widely read but had not been considered respectable. The campaign for the vernacular was a success, although classical expressions had a way of creeping into the vernacular and newly borrowed terms stood in the way of easy comprehension. Nevertheless, the new language was both more accessible and more modern than the old. Introduced into the elementary schools in 1920, it was universally used in the schools by the end of the decade.

New Youth was also the first magazine to publish Lu Xun, pen name of Zhou Shuren (1881–1936), who became China's most acclaimed twentieth century writer. Lu Xun had gone to Japan to study medicine, but decided to devote himself to combating not physical ailments, but China's spiritual ills. His bitter satire cut like a sharp scalpel, but a scalpel wielded by a humanist who hoped to cure, not kill. The protagonist in "A Madman's Diary" (*New Youth,* 1918) discovers the reality underneath the gloss of "virtue and morality" in the old histories: a history of man eating man. He ends with the plea, "Perhaps there are still children who have not eaten men? Save the children. . . ."[7]

Chen Duxiu and many other intellectual leaders taught at Beijing University. Their ideas found a ready following among the students at this and other universities. On May 4, 1919, some 3,000 students staged a dramatic demonstration in Beijing to protest the assignment at the Versailles Peace Conference of Germany's former possessions in Shandong to Japan, even though China, like Japan, had entered World War I on the allied side and sent labor battalions to France. The students were outraged. Their demonstrations became violent. The house of a pro-Japanese minister was burned and another minister was beaten badly. In clashes with the police one student died. There were arrests followed by more protest, a wave of strikes, and a show of merchant and labor support for the students. In the end the government had to retreat. Those arrested were released, and those who had ordered the arrests were forced to resign. China never signed the ill-fated Treaty of Versailles.

The May Fourth incident came to symbolize the currents of intellectual and cultural change first articulated in *New Youth,* and gave rise to the broader term "May Fourth Movement" (c. 1915 to early 1920s). After the incident, there was a new sense of urgency. What had been a trickle of protest became a tide of attacks on just about every aspect of Chinese culture in a total rejection of the past—including such basic institutions as the family. Simultaneously, the movement introduced a host of new and radical ideas. New journals appeared, and there was much heady and excited talk, but also action, as young people spurned arranged marriage and engaged in increased social action, including organizing labor unions. The May Fourth movement had long-term revolutionary consequences, both in what it destroyed and in what it introduced. In the short term, although the current of nationalism ran deep and strong, there were intense disagreements over the future direction of Chinese culture, and a tremendous variety of ideas, theories, and styles swelled the eddies of intellectual and cultural life.

Intellectual Alternatives

Europe's self-destruction in war and the failure of liberal principles at Versailles prompted Liang Qichao to turn back to the Chinese tradition in the hope of synthesizing the best of China and the West, with Chinese elements predominating. An important debate began in 1923 between the proponents of science and those of metaphysics, involving different evaluation of Chinese and Western cultures. Among the advocates of the latter were proponents of scientism, who believed that science holds the answers to all problems and that the scientific is the only method for arriving at truth. Their opponents argued that science is applicable only to a narrow field of study and that moral values have to be based on deeper metaphysical truths that by their very nature are beyond the reach of scientific methodology. Since similar problems agitated the West at this time, Chinese thinkers drew on the ideas of such classic European philosophers as Immanuel Kant and also on the thought of contemporaries widely different in methodology and results. For example, some promoted the ideas of John Dewey (1859–1952), the American pragmatist who would replace "absolute truth" with truths which worked as solutions to problems; but others turned to Henri-Louis Bergson (1859–1941), the French exponent of vitalism, a doctrine centering on life as a force that cannot be explained in material terms.

Those who identified with the Chinese tradition further drew on the insights of Neo-Confucianism and Buddhism, particularly the former. One of the most noteworthy defenders of tradition was Liang Shuming (1893–1988), who put his Confucian principles into action by working on rural reconstruction. Another was Zhang Junmai (1887–1969), later the leader of a small political party opposed to both the Communists and the Nationalists. Other philosophers such as Feng Yulan (Fung Yu-lan, 1895–1990) and Xiong Shili (1885–1969) drew on Neo-Confucian thought, but the trend of the times was against them.

Among the champions of science and Western values were the scientist Ding Wenjiang (1887–1937) and the father of the vernacular language movement, Hu Shi. Hu Shi was a leading liberal who advocated a gradualist, piecemeal problem-solving approach to China's ills in the face of attacks both from the traditionalists on the right and from the left. His message increasingly fell on deaf ears, for his approach required time, and time was precisely what China lacked. More often than not, this included time to digest the heady dose of new intellectual imports or, for that matter, to study the old traditions in depth.

Cultural Alternatives

Qi Baishi (1863–1957), probably the most beloved painter of the century, was singularly unaffected by the turmoil of the times. Qi began as a humble carpenter and did not turn to painting until his mid-twenties, but his industry and longevity more than made up for a late start. It is estimated that he produced more than 10,000 paintings. Qi was a great admirer of the seventeenth-century individualist Zhu Da, but followed his own inner vision. He was not given to theorizing, but did express his attitude toward representation: "The excellence of a painting lies in its being like, yet unlike. Too much likeness flatters the vulgar taste; too much unlikeness deceives the world."[8] His works show, to quote a Chinese critic, "a loving sympathy for the little insects and crabs and flowers he draws," and have "an enlivening gaiety of manner" so that "his pictures are really all pictures of his own gentle humanism"[9] (see Figure 10.2).

There were other painters and calligraphers who remained uninfluenced by the West, but many felt that the new age required a new style. Among those who tried to combine elements of the Chinese and Western traditions were the followers of a school of painters established by Gao Lun (Gao Jianfu, 1879–1951). Gao sought to combine Western shading and perspective with Chinese brushwork, and was also influenced by Japanese decorativeness. He sought to bring Chinese

FIGURE 10.2 *Grasshopper and Orchid Leaves,* Qi Baishi (Qi Huang, 1863–1957). Although Qi also painted landscapes and portraits, he excelled in depicting the humble forms of life, such as rodents and insects, with a loving and gentle humor reminiscent of the haiku of Kobayashi Issa. Ink on paper, 21.5 × 30.5 cm., signed Baishi.

painting up to date by including in his works new subject matter, such as the airplanes in Figure 10.3.

In Shanghai, meanwhile, a small group of artists tried to transplant French-style bohemianism into that international city. Xu Beihong (1895–1953), for example, affected the long hair and general appearance popular in the artists' quarter of Paris. When he returned from that city in 1927, Xu also brought back a thorough mastery of the French academic style. Somewhat more advanced in his Western tastes was Liu Haisu (1896–1994), founder of the Shanghai Art School (1920), where he introduced the use of a nude model. This was also one of the first schools to offer a full course of instruction in Western music. Liu was inspired by French postimpressionists like Matisse and Cezanne. Later, however, Liu returned to painting in a traditional manner, and Xu, too, abandoned his Western dress for a Chinese gown. Today Xu is perhaps most appreciated for his paintings of horses (see Figure 10.4).

Modern Chinese literature had its origins in the novels of the late Qing. A very popular but superficial genre was "Butterfly" literature, named after poems inserted into a novel, comparing lovers to pairs of butterflies. Between 1910 and 1930, around 2,215 such novels offered a literate but unlearned public amusement and escape. Also going back to the late Qing there was a steady and swelling stream of translations. Lin Shu (1852–1924), the most famous and prolific early

FIGURE 10.3 *Flying in the Rain*, Gao Lun (Gao Jianfu), 1932. Chinese painters, like writers and intellectuals throughout East Asia, devised different ways to combine traditionalism and modernism in style and subject matter, but lyrical landscapes with airplanes bouncing through the sky are rare anywhere. Ink and color on paper.

ART MUSEUM, CHINESE UNIVERSITY OF HONG KONG, CHINA.

FIGURE 10.4 *Standing Horse*, Xu Beihong. 1935.

XU BEIHONG MEMORIAL GALLERY, BEIJING, CHINA. USED BY PERMISSION.

translator, rendered into classical Chinese the novels of Charles Dickens, Walter Scott, and others in an opus that grew to some 180 works. Thanks to the labors of Lin and other translators, soon all the major European literary traditions as well as that of Japan were available in translation.

The May Fourth movement had a strong effect on literature. The intellectual revolution was accompanied by a literary revolution. This brought with it experiments, such as those of Xu Zhimo (1896–1931), who modeled his poetry on English verse, complete with rhyme. More widespread was a tendency toward romantic emotionalism, an outpouring of feelings released by the removal of Confucian restraints and encouraged by the example of European romanticism. One strain, as analyzed by Leo Ou-fan Lee, was the passive-sentimental, presided over by the hero of Goethe's *The Sorrows of Young Werther,* read in China and Japan as "a sentimental sob story." The subjectivism of these writers was not unlike that of the writers of "I novels" in Japan. Another strain was dynamic and heroic. Its ideal was Prometheus, who braved Zeus's wrath and stole fire for mankind. Holding a promise of release from alienation, it was compatible with a revolutionary political stance. For Guo Moruo (1892–1978), once an admirer of Goethe, Lenin became beyond all else a Promethean hero. Perhaps the strongest expression of Promethean martyrdom came from Lu Xun, "I have stolen fire from other countries, intending to cook my own flesh. I think that if the taste is good, the other chewers on their part may get something out of it, and I shall not sacrifice my body in vain."[10]

Controversies and rivalries stimulated the formation of literary and intellectual societies as like-minded men joined together to publish journals advocating their causes and denouncing the opposition. Revolutionaries were not alone in arguing that literature should have a social purpose, but as the years passed without any improvement in Chinese conditions, the attractions of revolutionary creeds increased. Writers of revolutionary persuasion such as the Communist Mao Dun (Shen Yanbing, 1896–1981) depicted and analyzed the defects in the old society and portrayed the idealism of those who were out to change things. Such themes appeared not only in the work of Communist writers like Mao Dun, but also in the work of the anarchist Ba Jin (Li Feigang, 1905–), best known for his depiction of the disintegration of a large, eminent family in the novel appropriately entitled *Family* (1931), a part of his *Turbulent Stream* trilogy (1931–1940). Such works provide important material for the student of social as well as literary history.

Marxism in China: The Early Years

Marxism was not unknown in China, but had little appeal prior to the Russian Revolution. The few who were drawn to socialism were attracted more by its egalitarianism than by concepts of class warfare. The writings of Marx and Engels offered the vision of a perfect society, but their thesis that socialism could only be achieved after capitalism had run its course suggested that Marxism was inappropriate for a society only just entering "the capitalist stage of development."

The success of the Russian Revolution (1917) changed all that. Faced with a similar problem in applying Marxism to Russia, Lenin amended Marxist theory to fit the needs of his own country, and thereby also made it more relevant to the Chinese. His theory that imperialism was the last stage of capitalism gave new importance to countries such as China, which were the objects of imperialist expansion and the places where capitalism was particularly vulnerable. Also most significant was Lenin's concept of the Communist party as the vanguard of revolution, for now party intellectuals could help make history even in a precapitalist state.

Furthermore, Marxism was modern, and claimed "scientifically" valid doctrines. It shared the prestige accorded by Chinese intellectuals to Western and "advanced" ideas, even as it opposed the dominant forms of economic and political organization in the West. A Western heresy to use against the West, it promised to undo China's humiliation, and persuaded its converts that "dialectic materialism" assured that Communism was the wave of the future. Thus China could once again be in the forefront of world history. The Russian Revolution demonstrated that it worked.

Li Dazhao (1888–1927), professor and librarian at Beijing University, was initially attracted by its promise as a vehicle for national revolution, while Chen Duxiu turned from science and democracy to Marxism as a more effective means of achieving modernization. Others were drawn to it for a mixture of reasons, high among them the promise it held for solving China's ills. By spring of 1920, when Grigorii Voitinsky arrived in China as an agent of the Communist International (Comintern), a core of Marxist intellectuals was available as potential leaders for the organization of the Chinese Communist party (C.C.P.) that took place the following year.

At its first gathering in July 1921, the C.C.P. elected Chen Duxiu its Secretary General. Despite considerable misgivings, the party submitted to a Comintern policy of maximum cooperation with the Guomindang. A formal agreement was reached in 1923 which allowed C.C.P. members into the GMD as individuals, subject to GMD party discipline. The C.C.P. leaders found it difficult to accept the Comintern's theoretical analysis of the GMD as a multiclass party, but submitted to Comintern discipline and the logic of the situation where the few hundred Communists were outnumbered by the thousands of GMD members, and had little contact with the masses. This initial period of cooperation lasted until 1927. The C.C.P. grew, but the GMD remained the senior partner.

The Guomindang and Sun Yat-sen (1913–1923)

After the failure of the "second revolution" of 1913, Sun Yat-sen was again forced into exile in Japan, where he tried to win Japanese support for his revolution. After the death of Yuan Shikai, Sun was able to return to China and establish a precarious foothold in Canton, where he depended on the good will of the local warlord. Denied foreign backing from Japan and elsewhere, Sun was also handicapped by the weakness of the GMD party organization, which was held together only loosely, largely through loyalty to Sun himself. The success of the Russian Revolution provided a striking contrast to the failure of Sun's revolution. Sun was also favorably disposed to the U.S.S.R. by the Soviet Union's initial renunciation of Czarist rights in China. This corresponded to a new anti-imperialist emphasis in his own thought and rhetoric, after the end of Manchu rule had not led to marked improvement in China's position in the world. Also, he was impressed by the mass nationalism of the May Fourth Movement.

Sun was therefore ready to work with the Communists, and in 1923 concluded an agreement with the Comintern that concurred with Sun's view that

China was not ready for socialism, and that the immediate task ahead was the achievement of national unity and independence. Through this pact, Sun received valuable assistance and aid. Under the guidance of the Comintern agent Mikhail Borodin (originally named Grusenberg), the GMD was reorganized into a more structured and disciplined organization than ever before, while General Galen, alias Vassily Blyukher (or Blücher), performed the same service for the army. Sun made some minor ideological compromises, but did not basically depart from his previous views.

GMD and C.C.P. Cooperation (1923–1927)

For both sides this was a marriage of convenience. At first it worked. The GMD gained guidance and support. C.C.P. members rose to important positions in the GMD, and the party grew. A good example of a C.C.P. leader occupying an important GMD office is Zhou Enlai's (1898–1976) service as chief of the political department of the Whampoa Military Academy under Chiang Kai-shek (1887–1975). Here the cream of the GMD officer corps was trained and prepared to lead an army to reunify China and establish a national regime.

The C.C.P. devoted itself mainly to organizing the urban labor movement, which had already won its first victory in the Hong Kong Seamen's Strike of 1922. Shanghai and Canton were particularly fertile grounds for labor organizers, since in these cities the textile and other light industries continued their pre–First World War growth, assisted by the wartime lull in foreign competition. Of some 2.7 million cotton spindles in China around 1920, 1.3 million were in Chinese-controlled factories, and 500,000 were owned by Japanese. In Chinese and foreign plants alike, wages were very low, working hours long (averaging nine and one-half hours in Shanghai, up to thirteen in the provinces), and all-around conditions remained very harsh. Under these circumstances, the C.C.P.'s work met with substantial success. It gained greatly by its leadership during and following the incident of May 30, 1925, when Chinese demonstrators were fired on by the police of the International Settlement in Shanghai, killing ten and wounding more than fifty. A general strike and boycott followed; in Hong Kong and Canton the movement held out for sixteen months. The strike did not achieve its goals, but C.C.P. party membership increased from around 1,000 in early 1925 to an estimated 20,000 by the summer of 1926.

Sun Yat-sen did not live to witness the May 30 incident, for he died of cancer in March 1925. He was an energetic speaker and tireless visionary, glorified as the father of the revolution, but he left no clearly designated heir, and an ambiguous ideological legacy. His last major statement, "Three Principles of the People" (1924), stressed the first principle, nationalism—now directed against foreign imperialism—and provided for self-determination for China's minorities. The second principle, democracy, contained proposals for popular elections, initiative, recall, and referendum, but full democracy was to come only after a preparatory period of political tutelage. He emphasized the need for a disciplined people and believed that the Chinese people had too much freedom, not too little. The state would be a republic with five branches of government: legislative, executive, judicial (as in the West), plus an examination branch to test applicants for government posts, and a censorial branch to monitor government officials and control corruption, as under the emperors.

Finally, the principle of the people's livelihood aimed at both egalitarianism and economic development. It incorporated a proposal by the American reformer Henry George (1839–1897) to tax the unearned increment on land values in order to equalize holdings. An additional refinement was a land tax based on each landowner's assessment of the value of his land. To prevent underassessment, the state was to have the right to purchase the land at the declared value. Beyond that, Sun had a grandiose vision of "building the wealthiest, most powerful and happiest nation on earth,"[11] but his plan for Chinese industrialization was unrealistic. More realistic was a proposal for state ownership of major industries, but he remained critical of Marxist ideas of class struggle.

After Sun Yat-sen's death, Wang Jingwei (1883–1944) was well placed to succeed to the GMD leadership, for he had been associated with Sun in Japan and was considered a revolutionary hero for his attempt to assassinate the Manchu Prince Regent in 1910. But in 1926 it became apparent that he had a formidable challenger in Chiang Kai-shek. In 1923, Sun had sent Chiang to Moscow to study the Soviet military. On his return to China, Chiang became head of the Whampoa Military Academy, where he was highly successful, esteemed alike by the Soviet advisors and by the officer candidates

While Wang Jingwei loosely presided over the GMD, the C.C.P. steadily gained influence in the party, much to the alarm of the GMD right and of Chiang Kai-shek. In March, 1926, Chiang decided to act: he declared martial law, arrested Soviet advisors, and took steps to restrain the C.C.P. influence in the GMD, yet managed to retain the cooperation of both the C.C.P. and of its Soviet supporters, whose assistance he needed for the military unification of the country. This he began in the summer of 1926 by launching the Northern Expedition (see Figure 10.5), setting out with his army from Canton. Although there was some heavy fighting against warlord armies, the force made rapid headway on its march to the Yangzi, and some warlords decided to go over to the Nationalist side. In the fall of 1926, the Nationalist victories enabled them to shift the capital from Canton to more centrally located Wuhan. There, Wang Jingwei headed a civilian government, but could not control Chiang and his army.

The Break

On its march north to the Yangzi, the army was assisted by popular support, and nowhere was this support more enthusiastic than among the Communist-led workers of Shanghai, where the General Labor Union seized control even before

FIGURE 10.5 China and the Northern Expedition, 1926–1928.

the arrival of the troops. Elsewhere, too, there was an increase in labor activity. This alarmed Chinese bankers and industrialists, who, ready to support a national but not a social revolution, financed the increasingly anti-Communist Chiang Kai-shek. In April, 1927, Chiang finally broke with the C.C.P. completely by initiating a bloody campaign of suppression in Shanghai, which then spread to other cities. Union and party headquarters were raided; those who resisted were killed; suspected Communists were shot on sight. C.C.P. cells were destroyed and unions disbanded in a devastating sweep that left the urban C.C.P. shattered.

The C.C.P.'s emphasis on city factory workers was entirely consistent with Marxist theory, but the majority of the Chinese people continued to work the land.

Marx, as a student of the French Revolution, despised the peasantry as "the class which represents barbarism within civilization."[12] But Lenin, operating in a primarily agrarian land, assigned the peasantry a supporting role in the Russian Revolution. The C.C.P., although it concentrated on cities, had not neglected the peasants. In 1921, China's first modern peasant movement was organized by Peng Pai (1896–1929), and by 1927 the C.C.P. was at work in a number of provinces, most notably Hunan, where the young Mao Zedong (1893–1976) wrote a famous report urging the party to concentrate on rural revolution and predicting, "In a very short time . . . several hundred million peasants will rise like a mighty storm, like a hurricane, a force so swift and violent that no power, however great, will be able to hold it back." In another famous passage in the same report, he defended the need for violence, saying, "A revolution is not a dinner party."[13]

In Hunan, as in other rice areas, tenancy rates were high, and the poorer peasants were sorely burdened by heavy rental payments and crushing debts. Tenants had few rights and faced the recurring specter of losing their leases. It was, as Mao saw, a volatile situation, fraught with revolutionary potential. But the Chinese party and its Soviet advisors remained urban-minded.

After Chiang's coup, the C.C.P. broke with him, but continued to work with the government at Wuhan, which also broke with Chiang, but still depended for military support on armies officered largely by men of the landlord class, the prime object of peasant wrath. In this situation Comintern directives were wavering and contradictory, reflecting not Chinese realities but rather the exigencies of Stalin's intraparty maneuvers back in Moscow. The end result was that in June the C.C.P. was expelled from Wuhan. Borodin and other Soviet advisors were sent back to the U.S.S.R. The C.C.P. entered on a difficult period of regrouping and reorganization.

Establishment of the Nationalist Government

After Chiang Kai-shek's coup in Shanghai, he established a government in Nanjing, which remained the capital until 1937. The Northern Expedition resumed in 1928, by which time the Wuhan leaders, bowing to the inevitable, had made their peace with Chiang, as had a number of warlords whose forces now assisted the Nationalist drive north and actually outnumbered Chiang's own troops. In June 1928, after a scant two months of fighting, Beijing fell. China again had a national government, but the often only nominal incorporation of warlord armies into the government forces meant that national unification was far from complete. Warlordism remained an essential feature of Chinese politics until the very end of the Republican period in 1949.

In 1927 anti-imperialist mobs attacked British concessions in two cities, and violence in Nanjing left six foreigners dead, a number wounded, and foreign businesses and homes raided. Such incidents were officially attributed to Chiang Kai-shek's leftist rivals. The powers concluded that he was the most acceptable leader, who would negotiate rather than expropriate their holdings. Chiang's victory reassured all the powers except Japan, which had plans of its own for Manchuria and Inner Mongolia. Japan had restored its holdings in Shandong to

Chinese sovereignty in 1922, but now sent troops to Shandong, claiming they were needed to protect Japanese lives and property. In 1928 they clashed with Chinese soldiers. Still more ominous was the assassination that year of the warlord of Manchuria, Zhang Zuolin, by a group of Japanese army officers who acted on their own, hoping this would pave the way for seizure of Manchuria. The Japanese officers did not get their way in 1928, but their act was to serve as a prelude to the Japanese militarism and expansionism that threatened China during the thirties, even as the Nanjing government tried to cope with warlords and revolutionaries at home, in its attempt to achieve stable government.

Notes

1. Quoted in James Reeve Pusey, *China and Charles Darwin* (Cambridge, Mass.: Harvard Univ. Press, 1983), p. 50.

2. Marianne Bastid-Bruguiere, "Currents of Social Change," in John K. Fairbank and Kwang Ching Liu, eds., *The Cambridge History of China,* vol. II (Cambridge: Cambridge Univ. Press, 1980), pp. 558–59.

3. David Der-wei Wang, *Fin-de-siecle Splendor: Repressed Modernities of Late Qing Fiction, 1849–1911* (Stanford: Stanford Univ. Press, 1997), p. 216.

4. Quoted in Jonathan D. Spence, *The Gate of Heavenly Peace: The Chinese and Their Revolution, 1895–1980* (New York: Viking, 1981), p. 52.

5. David Der-wei Wang, *Fin-de-siecle,* p. 223.

6. Marie-Claire Bergere, in John K. Fairbank, ed., *The Cambridge History of China,* vol. 12 (Cambridge: Cambridge Univ. Press, 1983), pp. 745–51.

7. Joseph S. M. Lau and Howard Goldblatt, *The Columbia Anthology of Modern Chinese Literature* (New York: Columbia Univ. Press, 1995), p. 15.

8. See the biographical entry for Ch'i Pai-shih in Howard L. Boorman, ed., *Biographical Dictionary of Republican China* (New York: Columbia

Univ. Press, 1967–71), vol. 1, pp. 302–304. Qi's statement is quoted on p. 302.

9. Michael Sullivan, *Chinese Art in the Twentieth Century* (Berkeley: Univ. of California Press, 1959), p. 42.

10. Quoted in Leo Ou-fan Lee, *The Romantic Generation of Modern Chinese Writers* (Cambridge, Mass.: Harvard Univ. Press, 1973), p. 74.

11. Quoted in David Strand, "Calling the Chinese People to Order: Sun Yat-sen's Rhetoric of Development," in Kield Erik Brødsgaard and David Strand, eds., *Reconstructing Twentieth-Century China: State Control, Civil Society, and National Identity* (Oxford: Oxford Univ. Press, 1998), p. 155, citing Lu Fangshan, *Zhu Zhixin yu Zhongguo geming (Zhu Zhixin and the Chinese Revolution)* (Taibei: Sili dongwu daxue, 1978), p. 236.

12. Karl Marx quoted in Lucien Bianco, *Origins of the Chinese Revolution, 1915–1949,* trans. by Muriel Bell (Stanford: Stanford Univ. Press, 1971), p. 74.

13. Mao Tse-tung, "Report on an Investigation of the Peasant Movement in Hunan," in *Selected Works of Mao Tse-tung* (Peking: Foreign Language Press, 1967), vol. 1, reprinted in Ranbir Vohra, *The Chinese Revolution: 1900–1950* (Boston: Houghton Mifflin, 1974), pp. 115–17.

Imperial Japan
1895–1931

1895   1912   1926   1931

LATE MEIJI   **TAISHŌ**   **EARLY SHOWA**

Between the founding of empire in 1895 and the advent of militarism in 1931, Japan increasingly participated in world history. It was in many respects a success story, but later history was to reveal the potential for disaster. The death of the Meiji emperor in July 1912, while not as momentous as the abdication of China's last emperor earlier that year, marked something of a watershed, and was experienced as such. People at the time felt that the passing of the emperor, who had presided over Japan's transformation for over forty years, signified the end of an era, a judgment with which many later scholars have concurred. We have divided this chapter accordingly.

I. Late Meiji, 1895–1912

Foreign Policy and Empire Building

Economic and Social Developments

Politics

Literature and the Arts

Foreign Policy and Empire Building

From the very beginning, Meiji foreign policy aimed to achieve national security and equality of national status. But how were these to be defined and how attained? As Louise Young put it, "In an international order where the 'strong devour the weak,' Japanese concluded they could either join with the West as a 'guest at the table' or be served up with China and Korea as part of the feast."[1] Both the army's German advisor and Yamagata, the hard-headed, realistic architect of Japan's modern army, held that Korea was the key to Japan's security, and in 1890 propounded the thesis that Japan must defend its "line of sovereignty" and secure its "line of interest," which ran through Korea. At the same time, the Japanese navy, heavily influenced by the ideas of Admiral Alfred T. Mahan (1840–1914), an American advocate of the importance of sea power, demanded Japanese naval domination of the surrounding seas. Colonies were desired both as "the ultimate status symbol" and for strategic reasons. Economic and other considerations also played a part, but an authority on the subject concluded "no colonial empire of modern times was as clearly shaped by strategic considerations."[2]

Equality was as elusive a concept as security, but at a minimum it required the end of extraterritoriality and the restoration of tariff autonomy. In the 1870s work began on revision of the law codes to bring them into line with Western practices, so that the powers would no longer have reason to insist on maintaining jurisdiction over their own subjects. Even before the lengthy process of revising the codes had been completed, there was strong and vociferous public demand for an end to extraterritoriality. One result was that in 1886 the government was forced to back down from a compromise it had negotiated providing for mixed courts under Japanese and foreign judges. The intensity of public pressure also helped to induce the British to agree in 1894, shortly before the start of the Sino-Japanese War, to give up extraterritoriality when the new legal codes came into effect (1889). Other countries followed suit. In return, foreign merchants were no longer limited to the treaty ports. These treaties also secured tariff autonomy, and in 1911 Japan regained full control over its customs duties.

By that time, Japan, under the most-favored-nation clause of the Treaty of Shimonoseki, was enjoying extraterritorial rights in China and benefiting from China's lack of tariff autonomy. As a result, Japan's exports to China increased both absolutely and in proportion of total exports, rising from less than 10% prior to 1894 to 25% by World War I. A commercial treaty negotiated with China in 1896 gave Japan and other nations enjoying most-favored-nations treatment the right to establish factories in the treaty ports, spurring investment in China, but limiting China's ability to nurture its own industries.

The acquisition of Taiwan gratified the navy, but most of the public shared the army's disappointment and outrage when French, German, and Russian intervention forced Japan to give up the strategic Liaodong Peninsula. The government's response to this setback was to follow a prudent foreign policy while increasing military spending. Accordingly, Japan exercised careful restraint during the Boxer Rebellion (1900) and earned respect for the disciplined behavior of its soldiers.

Japan's chief rival in northeast Asia was Russia, which had demonstrated its intent to become a major power in the area by constructing the Trans-Siberian Railway (1891–1903). In 1896 Russia had obtained permission to run tracks across northern Manchuria directly to Vladivostok, and in 1898 it obtained the lease of Port Arthur on the Liaodong Peninsula, thereby acquiring a much-needed warm-water port, but further alienating the Japanese, who had so recently been denied the peninsula, and were concerned to hold their own in the scramble to gain concessions from China .

Russia also interfered in Korea, allying itself with conservative opponents of Japanese-backed reformers. Agreements reached in 1896, 1897, and 1898 kept the Russo-Japanese rivalry from exploding into immediate war, but Russian use of the Boxer Rebellion to entrench its interests in Manchuria intensified Japanese apprehensions.

Japan was not alone in its concern over Russian expansion. Great Britain, which had not joined in the intervention after the Sino-Japanese War, had long been alarmed over Russia's eastward expansion. In 1902 it abandoned its policy of "splendid isolation" to form an alliance with Japan. Great Britain recognized Japan's special interest in Korea, and each nation recognized the other's interests in China. Britain and Japan agreed that each would remain neutral in any war fought by the other against a single enemy in East Asia, and that each would assist the other if either were attacked by two powers at once. This meant that if Japan and Russia went to war, British forces would join Japan if France or Germany supported Russia. Japan would not have to face a European coalition alone. This alliance with the foremost world power gave Japan new prestige and confidence. But Russia remained determined to maintain and expand its position in East Asia.

These conflicting ambitions led to the Russo-Japanese War of 1904–1905, fought both on land (mostly in Manchuria, which of course was Chinese territory) and at sea. For both belligerents the cost was heavy, but victory went to Japan. Despite some hard fighting, Russian troops were driven back on land, while

FIGURE 11.1   *Sea Battle near Port Arthur, March 10, 1904: A Sailor from the Sazanami Jumps to the Russian Ship and Kicks Its Captain into the Sea,* Migita Toshihide (1866–1905). Woodcut print triptych, ink and color on paper, 1904.

ARTHUR M. SACKLER GALLERY OF ART, SMITHSONIAN INSTITUTION, WASHINGTON, D.C.. GIFT OF GREGORY AND PATRICIA KRUGLAK (51999.1319-C).

in two separate naval actions the Japanese destroyed virtually the entire Russian navy. The naval war was spectacular, and much celebrated back in Japan (see Figure 11.1). Japan attacked the Russian Pacific fleet at Port Arthur, just before the declaration of war. Russia's Baltic fleet then embarked on an 18,000-mile trip, sailing all the way around Africa because Britain refused passage through the Suez Canal. Its destination was Vladivostok, but it was demolished by the Japanese in a decisive battle in the Tsushima Straits, between Japan and Korea. Only four of the thirty-five Russian ships reached Vladivostok.

Not only in Japan, but throughout Asia people were deeply impressed by this first victory of a non-Western nation over a European power. In Russia, these defeats had fateful consequences. The failed Revolution of 1905 was a precursor of the successful Revolution of 1917. Though victorious, the Japanese were thoroughly exhausted. Thus both sides were happy to accept the offer from the United States to mediate and to participate at a peace conference in Portsmouth, New Hampshire.

In the resulting Portsmouth Treaty, Japan gained recognition of its supremacy in Korea, the transfer of Russian interests in Manchuria (railways and leaseholds on the Liaodong Peninsula), and cession of the southern half of Sakhalin Island (north of Hokkaido). Japan had demanded all of Sakhalin and a war indemnity, but Russia successfully resisted these demands. This aroused the anger of the Japanese public, which, drunk on victory and uninformed of their country's inability to continue the war, had expected more. In Tokyo the treaty was greeted by three days of rioting.

One immediate result of Japan's victory was economic expansion in Manchuria, where the semiofficial South Manchurian Railway Company was soon engaged in shipping, public utilities, and mining, as well as railroading. From the start the Japanese government held half of the company's shares and appointed its officers. Although private Japanese firms also entered Manchuria, it has been calculated that in 1914, 79% of all Japanese investments in Manchuria were in the South Manchurian Railway. Furthermore, 69% of all Japanese investments in China prior to the First World War were in Manchuria. Japan's economic reach stretched beyond its formal empire.

Economic and Social Developments

Both the Sino-Japanese and the Russo-Japanese war stimulated the Japanese economy. Both wars were followed by an outburst of nationalist sentiment that gave a strong boost to heavy industry (for example, the Yawata Steel Works, established in 1897) and to armaments, including shipbuilding. After 1906, Japan produced ships comparable in size and quality to any in the world. Japanese technology continued to progress, with advances in new fields such as electrical engineering. Light industry, particularly textiles, continued to flourish and dominate the modern sector. The single most important item of export, amounting to nearly half the total, was in partly finished goods, especially silk. (Because of superior quality control, Japanese silk exports overtook those of China.) Trade figures revealing an increasing emphasis on the import of raw materials and the export of manufactured goods are indicative of economic change, and in 1912 the industrial sector accounted for 36% of the GNP (gross national product). Other statistics indicate increases in labor productivity and in urbanization, widening the gulf between city and country. The government, guided by pragmatic conservative reformers, sponsored a program of rural cooperatives, which were established by an act of the Diet in 1899. Through the cooperatives, which helped with credit, marketing, and production and through intense propaganda, the government hoped to avoid class conflict.

Not everyone in the industrial sector benefited from economic growth. Those working in the numerous small, traditional establishments experienced little change in their living conditions. Especially harsh were the working and living conditions of those who labored in the factories and shops. These were comparable to those in Western countries at a similar early stage of industrialization. During the first decade of the twentieth century, 60% of the work force was still female. An act promulgated in 1900 outlawed strikes, but when conditions became too bad, male workers, for whom a factory job was not an interlude prior to marriage but a lifelong occupation, rebelled, sometimes violently. Thus in 1909, three infantry companies were required to quell violence in the Ashio Copper Mines. Another labor action that made a deep impression was the 1912 Tokyo streetcar strike.

Conservative reformers, mindful of the social legislation of Bismarckian Germany, insisted early on that the government had the responsibility to ensure a balance between capital and labor, but the first factory laws were not passed until 1911. Efforts to improve the lot of women and children working in the factories also made headway only slowly. Not until 1916 did a law take effect giving them some protection, such as limiting their working day to eleven hours.

The distress of the workers was much on the minds of radicals. Beginning in the early nineties, there was a small group of radicals composed of Christian socialists and anarchists. They courageously opposed the war with Russia, holding antiwar rallies in the Tokyo YMCA even after the war began. However, barred by the government from forming a political party, and facing government repression, they were unable to expand their influence beyond the world of intellectuals and college students. In 1911, twelve of their leaders were convicted, on most flimsy evidence, of plotting the death of the emperor, and were executed.

Among the main beneficiaries of economic growth were the huge industrial-financial combines (*zaibatsu*), which retained close ties with government. The dominant political party during this period, the Seiyūkai (Association of Friends of Constitutional Government), also had a stake in economic development, because projects for railway and harbor development were a major means by which it won regional support and built local power.

Politics

During the Sino-Japanese War the oligarchs and the party-controlled Diet were united in pursuit of common national aims, but after the war, political struggles resumed. A handful of men, enjoying the prerogatives of elder statesmen (*genrō*), advised the emperor on all major matters. They tended to see themselves as guardians of the general public good in contrast to the private interests represented by the parties, and to stress the need for unity in face of a hostile world. As participants in fashioning the new state and architects of its major institutions, they enjoyed great prestige as well as the support of their protégés and associates. The party politicians, on the other hand, resented the perpetuation of the *genrō*'s power and their propensity to limit political decision making to a few hand-picked insiders.

The politicians' main weapon against a prime minister who defied them was that under the constitution only the Diet could authorize increases in the budget. Complicating the political situation were divisions within both the oligarchy and the party leadership. Among the former, Yamagata, a disciplined, rather austere military man, was committed to "transcendental government"—dedicated to emperor and nation and above political partisanship. His main *genrō* rival was Itō, the more flexible conservative who had supervised the writing of the constitution. Itō was more willing than Yamagata to compromise with the parties. Similarly, not all Diet members were adamantly opposed to collaborating with the *genrō*. Some lost their enthusiasm for opposing a government that could dissolve the Diet and thereby subject them to costly reelection campaigns. Also, the oligarchs could trade office for support. Accommodation had its appeal, but initially it was an uneasy accommodation; there were four dissolutions of the Diet between 1895 and 1900.

Another political factor was the influence of the military. As stipulated by the constitution, the chief of the general staff reported directly to the emperor concerning command matters, thus bypassing the Minister of War and the cabinet. In 1900 the military's power was further strengthened when Yamagata obtained imperial ordinances specifying that only officers on active duty could serve as Minister of the Army or Minister of the Navy. In effect, this gave the military veto power over any cabinet, for it could break a cabinet simply by ordering the army or navy minister to resign. Still, control over funds for army expansion remained in the hands of the lower house.

Up to 1901 the oligarchs themselves served as prime minister, but after that date Yamagata's protégé Katsura Tarō (1847–1913) and Itō's protégé Saionji Kimmochi (1849–1940) alternated as prime minister for the remainder of the Meiji period. Katsura, like Yamagata, was a general from Chōshū; Saionji was a court noble with liberal views, but little inclination to political leadership.

Katsura and Saionji were able to govern because they had the cooperation of the Seiyūkai, which Itō had founded in 1900 as a means to obtain assured support in the Diet. In 1903 Itō turned the presidency of the party over to Saionji, but the real organizing force within the party was Hara Kei (1856–1921), an ex-bureaucrat who became the leading party politician of his generation. Hara greatly strengthened the party by building support within the bureaucracy during his first term as home minister (1906–1908), and also used his power to appoint energetic partymen as prefectural governors. He linked the party to the provinces and freely resorted to the pork barrel to build up constituencies among the local men of means who formed the limited electorate.

The business community, including the *zaibatsu,* was interested in maintaining a political atmosphere favorable to itself, while political leaders welcomed business support. Thus Itō, when he organized the Seiyūkai, obtained the support of Shibusawa Eiichi and other prominent business leaders, although many remained aloof. The head of Mitsui was so intent on establishing his firm's independence from government that he even discontinued the practice of extending loans to Itō without collateral. However, the trend was toward closer association between the *zaibatsu* and politics, as exemplified by the relationship between Mitsubishi and Katsura after 1908. During Katsura's second ministry (1908–1911), his chief economic advisor was the head of the Mitsubishi Bank.

The relative strength of the participants in the political process did not remain unchanged. The *genrō* enjoyed great influence as long as they remained active, but theirs was a personal, not an institutional, power. It tended to diminish with time. As the number of living participants in the Restoration decreased, the power of the oligarchs to orchestrate politics declined. As prime minister, Katsura did not always follow Yamagata's advice. Furthermore, the *genrō* lost an important source of support when a new generation of bureaucrats came to the fore. These men did not owe their positions to *genrō* patronage, for, after 1885, entrance to and promotion in the bureaucracy were determined by examinations. As servants of the emperor, bureaucrats enjoyed high prestige and considerable influence.

Political compromise eroded much of the idealism found in the early movement for people's rights, but the Seiyūkai prospered. Its strength in the Diet alarmed the parliamentary opposition, which was divided and diverse. It included not only men opposed in principle to the Seiyūkai's compromises, but also small and shifting groups of independents, and a series of "loyalist" parties that habitually supported the cabinet. Decision making was complicated, as government policies were determined by the interaction of various power centers, none of which could rule alone. The arrangement functioned as long as funds were sufficient to finance both the military's and the Seiyūkai's highest priority projects and as long as none of the participants felt their essential interests threatened. When that ceased to be the case, it brought on the Taishō political crisis.

Literature and the Arts

The beginnings of modern Japanese literature can be traced to Tsubouchi Shōyō (1859–1935), a translator and the author of *The Essence of the Novel* (1885), in which he opposed both didacticism and writing solely for entertainment, and advocated Western realism, that is, the view that literature should portray actual life. During 1887–1889, Futabatei Shimei (1864–1909) followed with *Drifting Cloud* (1887–1889), a psychological study of an ordinary man told in a style more colloquial than usual.

Following the introduction of realism came Western romanticism, with its emphasis on expression of feelings and on naturalism, which aimed at scientific detachment as advocated by the French writer Emile Zola. Although in Europe naturalism was hostile to romanticism, this was not necessarily the case in Japan, where Shimazaki Tōson (1873–1943) won fame for his romantic poetry as well as for *The Broken Commandment* (1906), a naturalistic account of a member of the pariah class (*burakumin*; see Chapter 4) who tries to keep his pledge to his father never to reveal that he was born into this group, which continued to suffer discrimination and contempt even though not subject to legal restrictions.

Two Late Meiji writers, Mori Ōgai (1862–1922) and Natsume Sōseki (1867–1916), produced works of lasting literary merit. Ōgai identified with his family's samurai heritage, while Sōseki was a proud son of plebeian Edo. Their writings differed in substance and style, but both men, though deeply influenced by the West, achieved greatness by drawing on their Japanese heritage. Both spent time abroad. Ōgai was sent by the army to study medicine in Germany. After returning to Japan, he had a distinguished career as an army surgeon, rising in 1907 to the post of surgeon-general. He was both a modern intellectual profoundly influenced by his time in Europe and a samurai-style army officer, not an easy combination, but one that stimulated major achievements. Admired for the masculine, restrained style of his original works, he was also a prolific and excellent translator. Among his finest translations are his renderings of Goethe, including the full *Faust*, and of Shakespeare, which he translated from the German. He also translated modern German poetry, with the result that more modern German verse was available in Japanese translation than in English. Furthermore, he introduced

German aesthetic philosophy to Japan and influenced the development of modern Japanese theater; the performance of his translation of an Ibsen play in 1908 was a major cultural event.

Ōgai's first story, "Maihime" ("The Dancing Girl," 1890), recounts the doomed romance between a Japanese student sent by his government to Germany and a German girl named Alice. It became a precursor of the many "I novels," thinly disguised autobiographical works, which became one of the standard genres of modern Japanese fiction and also owe something to the Heian tradition of literary diaries. After his initial romantic period, Ōgai went on to write works of increasing psychological insight and philosophical depth. He turned more and more to Japanese themes, as in his novel *The Wild Goose*. Ōgai was greatly moved when his friend General Nogi (1849–1912), hero of the Russo-Japanese War, followed the Meiji Emperor into death by committing ritual suicide along with his wife. Afterwards Ōgai published painstakingly researched accounts of samurai. A particularly acclaimed late work is his *Chibu Chūsai*, an account of a late Tokugawa physician with whom Ōgai identified.

Natsume Sōseki studied in England, where a meager government stipend forced him to live in poverty, and he had virtually no friends. Later he described himself as having been "as lonely as a stray dog in a pack of wolves."[3] Both this experience of loneliness and the extensive reading he did while in England were reflected in his subsequent work. Sōseki returned from Europe to teach English literature at Tokyo Imperial University, before resigning this position to devote himself wholly to writing. He was acclaimed not only for his fiction but also for his poetry in Chinese, his haiku, and his literary criticism. He once described his mind as half-Japanese and half-Western, and his early novels reflect English influence, particularly that of George Meredith, but in his mature work the Japanese element predominates.

Sōseki's early novels, *I am a Cat* (1905) and *Botchan* (1906), present slices of Meiji life with affectionate good humor. Also in 1906, in a mere week, he wrote the remarkable painterly and diarylike *The Grass Pillow*, also translated as *The Three-Cornered World*, for "an artist is a person who lives in the triangle which remains after the angle which we may call common sense has been removed from this four-cornered world."[4] Travel in that world was by railway train:

> It is an unsympathetic and heartless contraption which rumbles along, carrying hundreds of people crammed together in one box. . . . People are said to board and travel by train, but I call it being loaded and transported. Nothing shows greater contempt for the individual than the train. Modern civilization uses every possible means to develop individuality and then having done so, tries everything to stamp it out. It allots a few square yards to each person within that area. At the same time, it erects railings around him, and threatens him with all sorts of dire consequences if he should dare to take but one step beyond their compass.[5]

The main theme of Sōseki's mature works is human isolation, studied in characters given to deep introspection. Like Ōgai, Sōseki was stricken by the death of the Meiji Emperor and General Nogi's suicide, which entered into *Kokoro* (1914),

FIGURE 11.2 *Tao Qian* (Chinese poet, 365–427). Detail from one of a pair of six-fold screens, *Master Five Willows,* by Yokoyama Taikan. Taikan favored tradition, but his style resonates with his own time. Color on paper, 1912, 169.4 × 361.2 cm.

a novel concerning the relationship between a young man and his mentor, called "Sensei" (master or teacher). Sōseki links Sensei's personal tragedy and suicide to the deaths of the emperor and general, and to the larger tragedy of the passing of a generation, and with it the loss of the old ethical values. Sensei perceives he has become an anachronism.

Painters, like writers, were grouped in several schools. The disciples of Okakura Tenshin, for example, continued to avoid the extremes of formalistic traditionalism and imitative modernism, while seeking a middle ground that would be both modern and Japanese. One such was Yokoyama Taikan (1868–1958). His screen shown in Figure 11.2 depicts the Chinese poet Tao Qian (365–427), whose blend of regret and relief at withdrawal from public life continued to strike a responsive chord.

Among the artists working in European styles was Kuroda Seiki, whose nude had so shocked Kyoto in the nineties. Kuroda continued to paint in a Western manner, and he had many students. At the time of his death in 1924, he had come

FIGURE 11.3 *Concert Using Japanese and Western Instruments*, Sakaki Teitoku (1858–1925). Playing the violin while kneeling must have taken much practice—one can only hope the ensemble's music was as charming as the painting. Oil, 1910.
PHOTOGRAPH © LORE SCHIROKAUER.

to be "the Grand Old Man of Western painting in Japan."[6] Some attempts at rendering Japanese themes in Western style produced paintings that are little more than historical curiosities, but in other cases there was a happier result. The painting by Sakaki Teitoku (1858–1925) shown in Figure 11.3 was executed in oil around 1910. While young men blow traditional bamboo flutes, two young women play violins.

Western influence on the visual arts was often direct and immediate, as it was for Umehara Ryūzaburō (1888–1986), who studied in France, met Renoir in 1909, and became his favorite pupil. The strongest influence on Japanese sculpture during this period was Rodin, who enjoyed a great vogue in Japan, especially after a major exhibition of his work in Tokyo in 1912.

Music also changed. The Meiji government early on sponsored Western military music, and in 1879 the Ministry of Education agreed to a proposal made by Izawa Shūji (1851–1917) to combine Japanese and Western music in the schools. Izawa had studied vocal physiology in the United States, and persuaded the Ministry of Education to bring Luther Whiting Mason (1828–1896) from Boston to Japan to help develop songs for use in elementary schools. The first song book (1881) consisted half of Western songs supplied with Japanese words ("Auld Lang Syne," for example, turned into a song about fireflies) and half of Japanese pieces harmonized in the Western manner.

Meiji popular music was more freely eclectic than that taught in schools. Beginning during the last decade of the nineteenth century, Japanese composers began working with sonatas, cantatas and other Western forms, and, thanks to the Tokyo School of Music, good performers were available on the piano and violin, as well as on the koto and other traditional instruments taught at the school. However, performers made greater progress than composers. As suggested by William

P. Malm, training in Western harmonics "created a series of mental blocks which shut out the special musical potentialities of traditional styles."[7] The rediscovery of the latter and their creative employment did not take place until after the Second World War.

II. The Taishō Period (1912–1926) and the Twenties

The Taishō Political Crisis, 1912–1913

Japan during the First World War

Politics and Policies, 1918–1924

Party Government, 1924–1931

Popular Culture

Fine Arts

Mingei

Literature

Intellectual Trends

The Taishō Political Crisis, 1912–1913

The Taishō period began with a political crisis, when financial conditions forced a cutback in government spending that made it impossible to fund both the Seiyūkai's domestic program and two new divisions for the army. Although the Seiyūkai won support at the polls, Prime Minister Saionji was forced out of office in December 1912, when the army ordered the Minister of the Army to resign. While the *genrō* deliberated about a successor to Saionji, a number of politicians, journalists, and businessmen organized a movement "to protect constitutional government." The ensuing mass demonstrations were reminiscent of those protesting the Portsmouth Treaty in 1905.

Called on to form a government once more, Katsura, no longer willing to compromise with the Seiyūkai, attempted to organize a party strong enough to defeat it, but failed. When the Seiyūkai threatened a vote of no confidence, Katsura tried to save the situation by obtaining an imperial order forcing the Seiyūkai to give up its planned no-confidence motion. This was a stratagem previously employed by embattled prime ministers, but this time it did not work: the Seiyūkai turned down the order. The crisis ended with Katsura's resignation. Such use of an imperial order was discredited and never tried again.

For the first time a party majority in the Diet, backed by public opinion and a vociferous press, had overthrown a cabinet. Katsura died in 1913, but the coalition he had created held together under the leadership of Katō Komei (Katō Takaaki, 1860–1926) whose background included graduation from Tokyo Imperial University, service in Mitsubishi, and a career in the Foreign Office capped by an appointment as Foreign Minister at the age of forty. He enjoyed a financial advantage from his marriage into the family that controlled Mitsubishi. A capable and determined man, he was personally reserved. But this was no handicap, for there was no need for party leaders like Katō or Hara to cultivate mass support. The power of a party leader depended on his strength within his party, although this was influenced by the party's showing at the polls.

The emergence of a strong second party meant that now the Seiyūkai faced a rival for control of the lower house. The parties represented a cross section of skills and resources needed to make participation in government viable. To quote Arthur E. Tiedemann, "Each party had associated with it the three essential ingredients for achieving political power: professional politicians to do the nitty-gritty of day-to-day party management; former bureaucrats who had the administrative talents required to form a viable alternative government acceptable to the *genrō*; and businessmen who could supply the funds and influence essential to successful election campaigns."[8]

Although the Taishō political crisis confirmed the importance of the Diet and the parties, they were not the only power center. Again there were compromises: not until Hara became prime minister in 1918 did the top government post go to a man who had made his career as a party politician. Before Hara, there were three prime ministers: Admiral Yamamoto Gombei (1913–1914), a military bureaucrat from Satsuma whose government was brought down by a scandal in naval procurement; the septuagenarian Ōkuma Shigenobu (1914–1916), who was intent on destroying the Seiyūkai but failed; and Terauchi Masatake (1916–1918), a Yamagata-backed Chōshū general who had been governor-general of Korea. It was the Ōkuma and Terauchi governments that guided Japan during the First World War.

Japan during the First World War

When the Western powers became immersed in war, new opportunities opened up for Japan. In August 1914 Japan declared war on Germany, and within the next three months seized German holdings in Shandong and the German islands in the

Pacific. In January 1915 the Ōkuma government presented the Twenty-One Demands to China. As we have seen (see p. 205), Japan obtained additional rights, but at the cost of stirring up strong Chinese resentment. A prominent critic of this policy was the pro-German Yamagata, who wanted Japan to be on good terms with China in order to prepare for the war he anticipated against the West.

Much larger and more costly than the military effort against Germany during the First World War was Japan's attempt to prevent the extension of Bolshevik power over territory that had belonged to the Russian Empire but had become a battleground after the Revolution of 1917. Russia and Japan had been wartime allies, but in March 1918 the Bolsheviks signed a separate peace with Germany (the Treaty of Brest-Litovsk). Complicating the situation in the East was the presence of Czech troops fighting their way out of Russia and determined to continue the war against Germany.

The Japanese intervened and by mid-summer 1918 controlled the eastern Trans-Siberian Railway and Vladivostok. The United States then changed its earlier opposition to intervention, although President Wilson envisioned only a limited military operation. The Japanese, however, sent 75,000 troops, triple the number sent by the Allies (United States, Britain, France, and Canada). Faced with Russian Communist victories and the absence of a viable alternative, the United States withdrew its forces in January 1919. The other Allies soon did likewise, leaving only the Japanese, who continued their efforts in the vain hope of at least keeping the Bolsheviks from controlling eastern Siberia. Though failure was apparent by 1920, the last Japanese troop did not withdraw until 1922.

Japan could pay for such a costly undertaking largely because its economy boomed during the war, which brought an unprecedented demand for its industrial products and the withdrawal of European competition. Old industries expanded, new ones grew up, and exports surged, turning Japan from a debtor into a creditor. But while some prospered, others suffered. The sudden economic expansion produced inflation, but workers' wages, as well as the income of those in fishing and other traditional occupations, failed to keep pace. The price of rice rose until people could no longer afford this most basic food. In August 1918, rice riots erupted in cities, towns, and villages all over Japan. Even as Japanese troops were setting off for Siberia, other soldiers were firing on hungry people rioting at home. The bitter irony was not lost on Japanese radicals. The immediate effect of the turbulence was to bring down the Terauchi government. When the *genrō* met to choose the next prime minister, they settled on Hara Kei.

Politics and Policies, 1918–1924

Hara Kei had spent his career building up the Seiyūkai in preparation for the day of party rule, but by 1918 he was too set in his ways to embark on significant new policies or initiate meaningful change. From then until his assassination by a demented fanatic in November 1921, he initiated only minor changes, and remained partisan in his concerns. Democratic intellectuals, students, and the leaders of labor and farmer unions were disillusioned when the government turned a deaf ear to their demands for universal suffrage, and instead passed an election law that retained a tax qualification for voting and reconstructed local electoral districts to favor the Seiyūkai. Abuse of office, financial scandals, and narrow partisanship had damaged the public image of the parties for years, and the record of the first party prime minister did nothing to alter this. Liberals who had placed their hopes in parliamentary reform either became cynical or looked elsewhere, while the public at large was apathetic.

In foreign affairs Hara's prime ministership began with the peace conference at Versailles, where Japan failed to obtain a declaration of universal racial equality but did gain acquiescence to its claims in China and the Pacific. His government then adopted a policy of cooperation with the United States, the only possible source for capital badly needed by Japanese industry facing difficult adjustments after peace brought an end to wartime prosperity. The first product of the new policy was the Washington Conference of 1921–1922, as a result of which Japan's alliance with Britain was replaced by a Four Power Pact signed by France, Great Britain, Japan, and the United States. The signatories also agreed to limit construction of capital ships (ships over 10,000 tons with guns over eight inches) so as to maintain the existing balance of naval power at a ratio of three-five-five for Japan, the United States, and Britain, calculated in tonnage. In February 1922 Japan further agreed to a Nine Power Treaty, acceding to the American Open Door Policy. In October 1922, Japan agreed to withdraw from Siberia.

That October Japan also reached an agreement with China, where nationalist sentiment had turned bitterly anti-Japanese. At Versailles, Japan had agreed, in principle, to the restoration of Chinese sovereignty in Shandong, provided that it retained economic rights there. This was now officially agreed upon. To secure and advance Japanese interests in Manchuria, Zhang Zuolin, the local warlord, was supported by the Japanese army. However, Shidehara Kijūrō followed a general policy of getting along with the United States and conciliating China during his tenure as foreign minister from 1924 to 1927 and again from 1929 to December 1931.

The purpose of this policy was to avert another anti-Japanese outburst and costly boycotts of Japanese goods, which would hinder continued Japanese economic expansion. After 1914, Japanese investments in China accelerated. By 1931 over 80% of Japan's total foreign investments were in China, where they amounted to 35.1% of all foreign investments in that country.* In 1930, 63% of Japanese investments in China were in Manchuria, and another 25% in Shanghai, where Japanese engaged in trade, banking, and textile manufacturing. In 1930 Japanese owned 39.6% of the Chinese textile industry (calculated in number of spindles). They were also a major factor in China's iron industry, with interests in Hankou and Manchuria.

*Great Britain accounted for 36.7% of foreign investment in China, but this was only 5 to 6% of all British overseas investments. Three other countries each accounted for over 5% of foreign investment in China: The U.S.S.R. for 8.4%, the U.S.A. for 6.1%, and France for 5.9%.

Hara was succeeded by his finance minister, but this man lacked political skills and lasted only until June 1922. Three non-party prime ministers followed, two admirals and one bureaucrat who organized his cabinet entirely from the House of Peers but resigned when faced by a three-party coalition in control of the Diet. The leader of the strongest of these parties, the Kenseikai (Constitutional Government Association, established 1916) was Katō Kōmei, who had last served as foreign minister under Ōkuma during the war. He was now called upon to form a new government.

The most momentous event of the years between Hara and Katō was geological, not political: in September 1923 the Tokyo-Yokohama area was devastated by a severe earthquake followed by a conflagration, which came close to leveling the area. The red sky was visible all night from a distance of a hundred miles. Around 100,000 people lost their lives. As so often in a disaster, the earthquake and fires brought out the best and the worst in people. While some courageously and selflessly helped their fellows, others joined in hysterical racist mobs rampaging through the city killing Koreans. The police reacted to the emergency by rounding up socialists, anarchists, and Communists as a "security measure," and there were cases of police torture and killing.

Party Government, 1924–1931

The increase in the power of the parties signified a shift in the balance of power rather than a systemic reordering of power centers. It was the power of the parties that induced Tanaka Giichi, a Chōshū general much favored by Yamagata, to accept the presidency of the Seiyūkai in 1925 when it was out of power. But the party's choice also confirmed the willingness of the parties to work within the existing parameters, and highlighted the continued prestige and influence of the army, even during the peaceful twenties.

The main accomplishments of party government came while Katō was prime minister (1924–1926). Foremost among them was passage of a "universal" suffrage act, which gave the vote to all males twenty-five and over. To still the fears of conservatives apprehensive over the possible spread of radical ideas, a Peace Preservation Law was also passed. This made it a crime to advocate change in the national political structure or to urge the abolition of private property. The Katō government never invoked the law, but it was available to later, less liberal regimes.

Katō also tried to reform the House of Peers (changing its composition and reducing its powers), but succeeded in making only minor changes. His government was more successful in introducing moderate social reforms, including the legalization of labor unions, the establishment of standards for factory conditions, the setting up of procedures for mediating labor disputes, and the provision of health insurance for workers. There was, however, no similar program to alleviate the problems of the rural poor.

Katō soon became embroiled in difficult political negotiations with other parties and the House of Peers, among others. When Katō died in 1926, he had not transformed Japanese politics, but he did leave a record of accomplishment that might, under different circumstances, have served as a basis for building a strong system of party rule. That this did not happen is partly the result of the kinds of problems Japan had to face during the next five years, but it also reflects the weakness of the parties. Even the increased suffrage was a mixed blessing, for the larger electorate made election campaigns costlier and politicians more open to corruption.

From 1927 to 1929 the government was led by Tanaka. In foreign policy Tanaka departed from Shidehara's conciliatory approach. When, in 1927, Chiang Kai-shek resumed the military expedition to unify China, Tanaka, under political pressure at home, sent an army brigade to Shandong, where clashes with Chinese soldiers ensued. (See Chapter 10.) Still more ominous was the assassination, in June 1928, of Zhang Zuolin by a group of Japanese army officers who did not think him sufficiently pliant and hoped their action would pave the way for the seizure of Manchuria. This did not happen—at least not then. Instead, Manchuria was brought under the new Chinese government by Zhang's son, and Tanaka had to recognize the Guomindang regime in Nanjing as the government of China. Tanaka's government itself collapsed when he incurred the displeasure of the Showa Emperor (r. 1925–1989) and court by failing to obtain from the army suitable punishment for Zhang's murderers. This episode was a harbinger of future unilateral army actions, but first, party government had one more chance.

In 1929, Hamaguchi Ōsachi became prime minister, and in 1930 his party, the Minseitō, won the election. Shidehara once again became foreign minister, and resumed his policy of reconciliation with China. He cooperated with Britain and the United States in negotiating the London Naval Treaty of 1930, which provided for a ten:ten:seven ratio for other than capital ships. The treaty was ratified only after heated debate and the forced resignation of the naval chief of staff. It generated bitterness among the military and members of patriotic societies, such as the young man who shot the prime minister in November, 1930. Hamaguchi never recovered from his wounds, but hung on in office until April 1931. From then until December 1931, the Minseitō cabinet continued under Wakatsuki Reijirō (1866–1949), who earlier had served as home minister under Katō and as prime minister from January 1926 to April 1927. He was an experienced politician, but during 1931 the government lost control over the army.

The restlessness of the military was not government's only problem. During most of the twenties, Japan was beset by persistent economic difficulties, including an unfavorable balance of payments, failure of jobs to increase fast enough to keep up with population growth, and a sharp decline in the price of rice, which helped consumers but hurt farmers. The giant *zaibatsu* profited from new technology, the economics of scale, and the failure of weaker firms, but times were hard on small operators. In 1921 a dramatic dockyard strike in Kobe resulted in an eight-hour day, which was extended to other heavy industries, but by and large the union movement progressed only slowly. This was also the case for unions of tenants, many of whom now worked for landlords who had moved to the city.

Carol Gluck aptly summed up the situation when she characterized Japan as being in "a hiatus between a traditional agrarian paternalism that was disintegrating and a modern industrial paternalism that was still in its formative stages. The landlords were no longer offering succor to distressed tenants, and the companies were not yet acting in a paternalist role on any significant scale."[9]

To solve the balance-of-payments problem, there were calls for the government to cut expenses and retrench in order to reduce the cost of Japanese goods and improve their competitive position in international trade. This was the policy followed by Hamaguchi, who also strengthened the yen by returning to the gold standard. Unfortunately, he initiated this program just as the Great Depression was getting under way, and persisted in it despite great economic dislocations and suffering. From 1925 to 1930 the real income of farmers declined by about a third. The poorest were, as always, the hardest hit. As in earlier periods of famine, there were cases of peasants eating bark and digging for roots, or maintaining life by selling daughters into brothels.

The government's economic failure undermined the credibility of the political parties, which even in normal times had little public esteem. No mass movement arose directed against them, but there was also little in their record to inspire people to do battle in their defense. Their enemies included those dissatisfied not only with their policies and politics but with just about every facet of twenties liberalism, internationalism, and "modernity."

Popular Culture

During the twenties a wave of Western influence affected lifestyles, diet, housing, and dress, particularly in Tokyo and other great cities, where there was a boom in bread consumption, Western dress became prevalent in public, and fashionable houses included at least one Western room. On the Ginza the "modern boy" (*mobo*) and "modern girl" (*moga*) dressed and coiffured in the latest imported styles might be on their way to listen to jazz or see a movie. Although there was always an audience for films filled with melodrama and swordplay, others dealt with the problems and joys of daily life.

Western sports gained ground, including baseball, although the first professional teams date from the thirties. People began playing golf and tennis. Friends met in cafes, or a fellow could practice the latest steps with a taxi dancer at The Florida or another of Tokyo's dance halls. The old demimonde dominated by the geisha, a world fondly chronicled by Nagai Kafū (1879–1959), was on the decline, and modern mass culture was in the ascendancy.

Centered in the cities, the new popular culture was steadily diffused, as even the remotest village became accessible by train and car, not to speak of the radio, introduced in 1925. Mass circulation magazines, some directed at a general audience, others written especially for women or young people, catered to the unquenchable thirst of the Japanese public for reading matter.

Fine Arts

Internationalism was represented not only in politics but also in the arts. Tokyo was not far behind Paris or London in experimenting with the latest styles and techniques. Indeed, it sometimes led the other capitals, as when in 1922 Frank Lloyd Wright built the Imperial Hotel in Tokyo, a break with Japan's own version of the European Art Nouveau. The American architect, himself influenced by the Japanese tradition, was not the only stimulating visitor from abroad during the Taishō and early Showa years. Japanese scientists, for example, could converse with Einstein on his visit to their country in 1919, and music lovers enjoyed concerts by eminent foreign performers: both Kreisler and Heifetz gave concerts in Tokyo in 1923. Bach, Mozart, and Beethoven were becoming as much a part of the musical life of Japan as of any other country, foreshadowing the time when, after the Second World War, the Japanese pioneered in teaching young children to play the violin and also became the world's foremost manufacturers of pianos.

A grand piano dominates the four-panel screen (see Figure 11.4) painted in 1926 by Nakamura Daizaburō (1898–1947), which is representative of the followers of the Okakura school. Conversely, there were Japanese artists who, like Xu Beihong in China, depicted traditional subjects in Western style.

FIGURE 11.4 *At the Piano*, Nakamura Daizaburō. Not only the traditional dress of the young woman playing by the light of an electric lamp but the technique and aesthetics of the painting recall the earliest Japanese art rather than contemporary Western styles. Four-fold screen, color on silk, 1926, 164.5 × 302 cm.
KYOTO MUNICIPAL MUSEUM OF ART.

FIGURE 11.5 *Saltimbanques*, Tōgō Seiji. The title of this cheerful, decorative picture is French for "traveling showmen," and it would take a very keen eye, not to say considerable imagination, to detect a particularly Japanese element. Oil, 1926, 114 × 71 cm.

© TOGO TAMAMI. COURTESY TOGO TAMAMI AND THE NATIONAL MUSEUM OF MODERN ART, TOKYO.

A major influence for modernism was the *White Birch* (*Shirakaba*) journal (1910–1923) one of whose editors was Shiga Naoya (1883–1971). In contrast to the school of naturalism and the advocates of proletarian literature, the *White Birch* group was dedicated to the exploration of the inner self, the pursuit of deeper personal understanding and self-expression, as in the "I novel" or in individualistic art. Seeking to become "children of the world," they introduced many European writers and published articles on the work and theories of such artists as Van Gogh—whose suicide for art's sake they praised as superior to that of General Nogi.

Much of the art produced during this period was imitative, but one artist who developed his own style was Umehara Ryūzaburū. A disciple of Renoir, Umehara also owes something to his childhood in Kyoto, where he became thoroughly familiar with the styles of Sōtatsu and Kōrin as still practiced in his family's silk kimono business (see Figures 4.2 and 4.3).

European pointillism, cubism, futurism, dadaism, surrealism all had their impact on the Japanese avant-garde, here represented by a painting dated 1926 (Figure 11.5). Tōgō Seiji (1897–1978), in Europe at the time, was influenced by French and Italian futurism and dadaism, but here shows an inclination toward cubism.

Mingei

Many trends converged in the "folk craft" or "folk arts" movement promoted by Yanagi Muneyoshi (or Sōetsu, 1889–1961), who coined the term *mingei* in 1926. His deep belief in the creative genius of the people was in tune with Taishō democracy, while his rejection of machine mass production and his devotion to the strong, honest beauty created by anonymous craftsmen working together to create objects for daily use are reminiscent of John Ruskin (1819–1900) and William Morris (1834–1896), founder of the late Victorian Arts and Crafts Movement. Yanagi, like Morris, championed the dignity of the craftsman, and linked the aesthetic beauty of folk art to the ethical qualities under which it was produced. His attempt to establish a commune for *mingei* artists failed, but he succeeded in inspiring a new appreciation for traditional woodcarving, housewares, woven and dyed cloth, and all kinds of articles made of bamboo, straw, handmade paper, wood (including furniture and traditional buildings), metal, and leather. The list goes on and on to include virtually all the products of traditional workmanship. Such works found a home in the museums, such as the Japan Folk Art Museum in Tokyo (1936), where they continue to be displayed, studied, enjoyed, and celebrated.

Yanagi's interest in folk culture was shared by Yanagida Kunio (1875–1962), Japan's foremost scholar of folklore. The massive survey he directed in the thirties laid the foundations for a whole field of studies. Beyond preserving and studying the folk craft (his preferred translation of *mingei*) of the past, he also strove to further the production of *mingei* as a living force. Foremost among his associates in the *mingei* movement were four potters: Tomimoto Kenkichi (1886–1963), the British potter Bernard Leach (1887–1979), Kawai Kanjirō (1890–1966), and Hamada Shōji (1894–1978). Others worked in textiles and other crafts. Among the woodcut artists influenced by Yanagida was Munakata Shikō (see p. 386).

Literature

Naturalism, symbolism, social realism, neo-perceptionsim—in literature as in the visual arts, a multitude of agendas had their proponents and special vocabulary, "pushing this or that 'ism,' this or that school and inflicting on the reader who wishes to comprehend the book's argument prior belief in this jargon." These words were written in 1930 by Kobayashi Hideo (1902–1983), Japan's foremost modern critic, who went on to say, "I don't trust the jargon. I believe that not trusting jargon is the mark of the critical spirit."[10]

Kobayashi admired Shiga Naoya, already mentioned as a member of the *White Birch* group, master of the autobiographical short story and "I novel," and of a concise, unaffected (though carefully crafted), sensitive style. Shiga was much admired and imitated, but he also had his detractors. Prominent among those who rejected the autobiographical mode were the advocates of proletarian literature exemplified by such novels as *The Cannery Boat* (1929) by Kobayashi Takiji (1903–1933), in which the workers revolt against a brutal captain. Although much of this literature was propagandistic, it did make the reader and writer more sensitive to social conditions.

A gifted writer who defies classification was Akutagawa Ryūnosuke (1892–1927), author of some 150 short stories between 1917 and 1927, many of them modern psychological reinterpretations of old tales. Because of the famous film of the same name released in 1950 by Kurosawa Akira, he is probably best known in the West for "Rashomon," which presents the story of a murder and rape as told from the viewpoint of three protagonists and a witness. In doing so, it raises questions about all our perceptions of historical truth. Akutagawa's stories are frequently eerie, but are saved from being merely macabre by the keenness of his psychological portrayals. Pessimistic, given to self-doubt, and distressed at the changing world about him, he committed suicide in 1927, citing "a vague unease."

In poetry as in art, some dedicated themselves to new experiments, while others continued working with the old forms. In the nineteenth century, Masaoka Shiki (1867–1902), known primarily as a haiku poet, contributed toward revitalizing traditional poetry, which continued to be written and published throughout the twentieth century. Others, however, looked to the West, and some even employed the Roman alphabet (*rōmaji*). Foreign influence did not necessarily produce timeless verse; one poet proclaimed, "My sorrow wears the thin garb of one-sided love."[11] The most admired master of free verse was Hagiwara Sakutarō (1886–1942) whose collection *Howling at the Moon* (1917) caused a sensation. Moving from the canine to the feline, he published *Blue Cat* in 1923—using "blue" in the sense of the blues. *Age of Ice* (1934), his last book of new free verse, includes a poem in which he identifies with a caged tiger.

A major prose writer was Tanizaki Junichirō (1886–1965), who began with a fascination with the West, but turned increasingly to the Japanese tradition. The protagonist of *Some Prefer Nettles* (1917), unhappily married to a "stridently" modern wife, finds comfort in the arms of a Eurasian prostitute, symbolic of the West, but, as the novel unfolds, he is increasingly attracted to a traditional Kyoto beauty. Tanizaki himself moved to Kyoto following the great earthquake of 1923. Some of his best work still lay in the future, including his masterpiece, *The Makioka Sisters*, written during the Second World War. One theme in this long, panoramic novel is the contrast between two of the sisters, one traditional in appearance and mentality, the other modern. Tanizaki's devotion to tradition also led him to translate *The Tale of Genji* into modern Japanese.

A similar trajectory from avant-garde to tradition was followed by Kawabata Yasunari (1899–1972), whose main works and fame were still to come. A very different writer then also at the beginning of her career was Uno Chiyu (1897–1996), whose persona and writings were more in tune with the twenties and the post–World War I years than with the thirties when she published her best-known novel, *Confessions of Love* (*Iro Zange*, 1935), based on the well-known failed love suicide attempted by Tōgō Seiji (see Figure 11.5) in 1929. Uno's interview with Tōgō a month later led that same night to a famous liaison that lasted five years.

Intellectual Trends

Philosophers and political theorists, like artists and writers, were challenged by claims that modern Western ideas possessed universally valid principles, and by their need to make sense of and find value in their own tradition. On the left, there was a revival of interest in anarchism and socialism, suppressed in 1911, and Marxism enjoyed new prestige after the Russian Revolution. Some were active in the labor movement, but the labor parties formed after passage of the universal suffrage act suffered from an excess of factionalism and a lack of mass participation. This was also true of the Japanese Communist party, which was dominated by intellectuals, some of great personal status. There was also a fledgling feminist movement, which campaigned for equality and women's rights, particularly the right to vote, for at the time women were legally minors and remained completely excluded from the political process.

Most widely read among liberal theorists were Minobe Tatsukichi (1873–1948) and Yoshino Sakuzō (1878–1933), both deeply versed in German thought. Minobe was a legal scholar who followed his teacher at Heidelberg, Georg Jellinek, in making a distinction between sovereignty, which belongs to the whole state, and the power to rule, which is supervised by the emperor. In this sense, the emperor becomes the "highest organ" of the state, limited by the other components of the state and by the constitution. The constitution, furthermore, in Japan as elsewhere (according to Minobe), allows, and indeed requires, continuing change in the direction of increasing rationality, responsible government, and popular participation. Minobe's work gained wide currency, and his book was the most frequently assigned text in courses on constitutional law. In 1932 he was appointed to the House of Peers, but his prominence was to cost him dearly later on.

Yoshino did not obtain such Establishment approval, but his many articles were widely read. A Christian populist and a democrat, he was a philosophical idealist who argued for democracy as an absolute rather than on utilitarian or pragmatic grounds. He also held an idealistic view of the nation and rejected any suggestion that democracy was incompatible with the Japanese tradition: "Those who argue that democracy is not compatible with the national spirit believe in the anachronistic and erroneous notion that the Emperor and people are mutually exclusive of each other."[12] Democracy would fulfill, not diminish, the emperor's role.

After the First World War, Japanese intellectuals were attracted to Hegel, Kant, and Nietzsche, the phenomenalism of Husserl, the hermeneutics of Heidegger and the vitalism of Bergson and Eucken. Outstanding among the philosophers who digested Western philosophy and assimilated it into their own original work was Nishida Kitarō (1870–1945), strongly steeped in Buddhism and best known for his philosophy of transcendent nothingness. Other theorists used Western philosophy to differentiate an authentic Japaneseness from the West and what they perceived as the diluted or hybrid culture that they disliked and dismissed. Nishida was not alone in refraining from discussing politics, but others defined Japanism in political terms, and demanded political action.

Some ideologues, conscious of the hardships suffered by the countryside, condemned the life and values of the cities and called for a return to virtuous agrarianism. Among the most severe critics of the parties and *zaibatsu* was Kita Ikki (1883–1937), who combined advocacy of imperialistic assertiveness abroad with a call for egalitarianism at home to bring emperor and people together. Unhappy with Japan's political organization and its stance in the world, he looked not to the electorate or a mass popular movement for salvation, but placed his faith in change from above enacted by a few dedicated men. Accordingly, his ideas found a friendly reception in small societies of superpatriots and among army officers who saw themselves as continuing in the tradition of the rōnin who had selflessly terrorized Kyoto during the closing days of the Tokugawa. Kita also found more recent exemplars among the ex-samurai who, after Saigō's death, had formed the Genyōsha (Black Ocean Society, 1881) and the Kokuryūkai (Amur River Society, also translated Black Dragon Society, 1901). The former was dedicated to expansion in Korea; the latter concentrated on Manchuria. Both employed intimidation and assassination.

The story of the attempts made by these men to effect a "Showa Restoration" belongs in the thirties, but Kita Ikki's most influential book was written in 1919. The rejection in the thirties of party government and internationalism that had prevailed in the twenties revealed that these had as yet shallow roots.

Notes

1. Louise Young, *Japan's Total Empire: Manchuria and the Culture of Wartime Imperialism* (Berkeley: Univ. of California Press, 1998), p. 21.

2. Mark R. Peattie in Ramon H. Myers and Peattie, eds., *The Japanese Colonial Empire, 1895–1945* (Princeton: Princeton Univ. Press, 1984), p. 8. See p. 10 for colonies as "the ultimate status symbol."

3. Quoted in Sōseki Natsume, *Ten Nights of Dream–Hearing Things–The Heredity of Taste*, trans. by Aiko Ito and Graeme Wilson (Rutland, Vt., and Tokyo: Charles E. Tuttle, 1974), p. 12.

4. Natsume Sōseki, *The Three-Cornered World*, trans. by Alan Turney (Chicago: Henry Regnery, 1965), p. iii.

5. Ibid., p. 181.

6. Shuji Takashina and J. Thomas Rimer, with Gerald D. Bolas, *Paris in Japan: The Japanese Encounter with European Painting* (St. Louis: The Washington Univ. Press, 1987), p. 105.

7. William P. Malm, "The Modern Music of Meiji Japan," in Donald H. Shively, ed., *Tradition and Modernization in Japanese Culture* (Princeton: Princeton Univ. Press, 1971), p. 300.

8. Arthur E. Tiedemann, "Big Business and Politics in Prewar Japan," in James W. Morley, ed., *Dilemmas of Growth in Prewar Japan* (Princeton: Princeton Univ. Press, 1971), pp. 278–79.

9. Carol Gluck, *Japan's Modern Myths* (Princeton: Princeton Univ. Press, 1985), p. 282.

10. Quoted in *Literature of the Lost Home: Kobayashi Hideo—Literary Criticism 1924–1939*, ed. and trans. by Paul Anderer (Stanford: Stanford Univ. Press, 1995), p. 108.

11. Quoted in Donald Keene, ed., *Modern Japanese Literature: An Anthology* (New York: Grove Press, 1956), p. 20.

12. Tetsuo Najita, "Some Reflections on Idealism in the Political Thought of Yoshino Sakuzo," in Bernard Silberman and H. D. Harootunian, eds., *Japan in Crisis: Essays on Taishō Democracy* (Princeton: Princeton Univ. Press, 1974), p. 40.

12

Vietnam, Korea, and Taiwan under Colonial Rule

All East Asian countries experienced imperialism, to varying degrees. Macao and Hong Kong were the first to be taken over by European powers, but they differ in scale as well as in their maritime character from Vietnam, Korea, and Taiwan. As colonies, these three large territories came to be more or less completely and—at least from the colonizers' perspective— permanently under foreign jurisdiction, ruled primarily for the benefit of the "home" countries. Though colonialism was a worldwide phenomenon, its forms and dynamics differed depending on time, place, and the parties involved. For example, when Japan acquired Taiwan, it took a lightly populated island that had been only recently and incompletely sinicized, but when it took Korea it seized a foreign civilization in its entirety, complete with its own history, language, and customs. In Indochina, the French were overlords to people who were entirely different from themselves linguistically, racially, and culturally, but in Korea, the Japanese took over a neighboring people with whom they were able to communicate readily via Chinese characters and with whose culture they already had much in common.

Nevertheless, French colonialism in Vietnam, and Japanese colonialism, especially in Korea, offer several intriguing points of comparison. One obvious similarity was the use of force and intimidation in the process of taking over the colony, and the maintenance of enough military and police power to overwhelm any possible local resistance. Another was the establishment of a colonial administration that employed colonial people in the lower ranks of the bureaucracy, police, and educational systems, and provided avenues for limited advancement to colonized people who were willing to identify with the colonial regime. And a third was the spontaneous development of anti-colonial resistance movements. The resistance grew out of a burgeoning nationalism that manifested itself in violent acts of resistance. But it also had more subtle origins. One of the most volatile was the anger felt by Vietnamese or Koreans who tried sincerely to mold themselves into authentic French or Japanese but found that no matter how hard they tried, the binary divide between colonizer and colonized always kept them in the status of second-class citizens.

I. Vietnam under the French

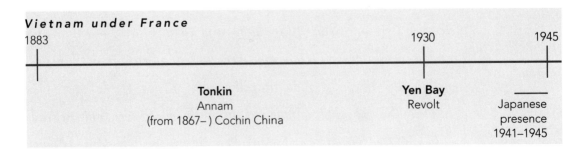

Economic Policy

Social Change

Education

New Stirrings of Opposition

The Twenties and Thirties

The Rise of Ho Chi Minh

We begin with Vietnam because it was the first of the three considered here to experience colonization. As we have seen (Chapter 6), France's annexation of the south, called Cochin China, begun in 1862 and completed in 1867, was followed by the establishment of protectorates over Annam in the center and Tonkin in the north in 1883–1884 (see Figure 6.4). In 1887 the French added the protectorates of Cambodia, under their control since the 1860s, to form the Indochinese Union, expanded in 1893 to include Laos.

Overseeing the entire Union was a governor-general residing in Hanoi. Cochin China was directly administered by the French colonial service, but in Annam and Tonkin the French retained the Vietnamese emperor and court at Hue as well as the old "mandarin" bureaucracy. However, after 1897 a French resident superior controlled the Tonkin mandarinate. In Annam, too, the authority of the emperor was increasingly limited. There also, beginning with Governor-General Paul Doumer (1897–1902), the French assumed administrative control, including tax collection.

The French also controlled the emperor, his succession, and even his physical movements. There had been resistance from the beginning of French encroachments on the Nguyen Dynasty, but attempts by the elite to use the throne to rally opposition to the French, such as the "Save the King" Movement (Can Vuong) begun in 1885, were suppressed. A 1916 insurrection marked the last such attempt. Emperors found they had to go along.

While a minority of the old elite resisted, in Annam and Tonkin a generation of traditional scholar-officials continued their old-fashioned devotion to the court and served in its now collaborative bureaucratic structures. Despite their direct experience of modern Western colonialism and the scientific inventions that had overwhelmed their traditional society, these men struggled to maintain the tradition of Sino-Vietnamese scholarship, and participated in the examination system, which continued until 1915 in Tonkin and 1919 in Annam, fifteen years after it had been abolished in China.

Economic Policy

From the beginning of the Cochin China colony in 1862, the French authorities favored the formation of large, and preferably French, landholdings. Initially, they gave out enormous grants of land, much of it confiscated from people who had resisted or fled when France invaded. The unequal distribution of land persisted to the end of French rule, with many people left landless or nearly so. The trend in the protectorates was similar in favoring large landowners. The Nguyen had taxed indirectly through the villages and done so lightly and in kind, but the French taxed family heads directly and in cash. Many small farmers lost their land. As Ngo Vinh Long points out, "A common technique used by the French was to exploit traditional Vietnamese court law in depriving the peasants of their rights of landownership and then to apply French laws to assert the rights of ownership to the same lands."[1]

In keeping with the French policy of having its colonies supply raw materials for the factories back home, Doumer initiated a major program of building railroads, roads, harbors, ports, and bridges so that the production of the country's mines (mainly coal), farms (especially rice), and plantations (mainly rubber) would find their way to France (see Figure 12.1). Under the French, work on dikes, drainage, and irrigation facilities increased agricultural production. Between 1918 and 1930, French investment, primarily in rubber, coffee, tea, and sugar plantations but also in mining and industry, increased over 600 percent, but a small group of French syndicates controlled almost all operations and profits. A handful of Frenchmen within the colonial administration and in the private sector of the colonial economy exerted near-total control. France's order of priorities was demonstrated when Cochin China exported rice abroad rather than shipping it north to alleviate rice shortages there.

France also valued the colonies as markets, and thus discouraged the formation of local industries that might compete in that market. When the Great Depression of the 1930s resulted in a decline in world trade, it merely reinforced a system in which the colonies provided secure markets "favoring the survival in France of the least modern sector and preventing economic progress in the colonies."[2]

Until the mid-1920s, the colonial regime derived as much as 70 percent of its tax income from monopolies over the production and sale of commodities such as opium, wine, and salt. The French only encouraged, but did not require, Vietnamese to purchase opium imported and sold at a profit of 400–500 percent. However, they forced villagers who had previously consumed home-brewed rice wine to buy set quotas of foreign-tasting, high-priced alcoholic beverages. Heavy demands for *corvée* labor further added to peasant burdens. In 1908 this led to local demonstrations and riots in central Vietnam that were severely repressed by the colonial police. The French also trafficked in coolie labor, shipping large numbers of peasants from the overpopulated north to work on southern rubber plantations or in Tahiti and other French possessions in the South Pacific. At best, colonial rule brought mixed benefits to the Vietnamese people. Although not widely avail-

Pont Doumer, à Hanoï.

FIGURE 12.1 *The Pont Doumer*, drawn by Georges Fraipont. Named after Governor-General Paul Doumer (1897–1902), who facilitated rapid exports to France by modernizing transportation networks throughout Indochina. The bridge, like the French colonization, did not last (see Figure 18.1).

FROM *HANOI, BIOGRAPHY OF A CITY*, BY WILLIAM S. LOGAN. COURTESY UNIVERSITY OF NEW SOUTH WALES PRESS, SYDNEY. QUOTED FROM *INDO-CHINE FRANÇAIS (SOUVENIRS)* (PARIS: VIUBERT ET NONY EDITEURS, 1905), P. 312.

able, Western medicine did lengthen life expectancy and raise birth rates, and there was sufficient improvement in agriculture to increase food production. However, population increases outstripped opportunities for raising living standards for Vietnamese at all levels. Most people experienced declining living standards in the 1920s and the 1930s. There were cases of acute impoverishment in the countryside.

Life changed more rapidly in the cities than in the country, but Vietnamese villagers who had traditionally relied on a largely self-sufficient subsistence economy now entered into wider and more modern market networks and participated in the new material culture. As described by one writer depicting life in the Red River delta region in 1938:

> In the countryside life has not changed as it has in the city. But farmers used to grow rice to eat, weave clothing to wear, use bamboo from their gardens to build their houses; now they have to take their rice and sell it in order to purchase in turn other things they need which are brought to them from the city by merchants and peddlars. . . . The rural folk no longer find the French to be a terrifying race of people, nor do they find their artifacts to be miraculous or fantastic any longer.[3]

FIGURE 12.2   The Cathedral at Phat Diem, about 81 miles south of Hanoi and 17.5 miles from Ninh Binh, was built on land that was originally marsh. An architectural hybrid, it is topped by a cross proclaiming its religious affiliation.

<small>PHOTOGRAPH © LORE SCHIROKAUER.</small>

Some even converted to Catholicism. By the time of the French conquest about 5 percent of the population had been converted, and the church continued to emphasize the development of a native clergy. Although architecturally most of the churches were clearly European transplants, the massive cathedral at Phat Diem is very much a local product. Built between 1875 and 1899 under the direction of a Vietnamese priest, it follows the overall plan of a Roman church, but its curling roofs, massive interior columns, and the scarlet red lacquer work on its altar are more commonly found in Sino-Vietnamese Buddhist temples. There are also overtones of Vietnamese community houses (*dinh*). On the cathedral's roof, a great bell and a large gong stand ready to sound the message of the faith. (See Figure 12.2.)

Social Change

As elsewhere in East Asia, most Vietnamese continued to work the land. Increasingly, this was not their own land, as even in the north wealthy landowners increased their holdings by extending credit and foreclosing on the less fortunate. Meanwhile, ownerships of newly opened lands in Cochin China went to the wealthy and well-connected absentee landlords to be tilled by sharecroppers at rents as high as 60 percent.

Much of this rice was exported through Saigon, which grew to supplant Hanoi as Vietnam's, and indeed Indochina's, largest and richest city. It also became a center for rubber export, textile mills, a cement industry, and fish-sauce and other food-processing plants.

Enjoying this newly found wealth was a class of Vietnamese, French, and Chinese entrepreneurs. Although a good number of the Chinese who immigrated in the eighteenth and nineteenth centuries intermarried with the Vietnamese, many others retained their identity. This was facilitated by both the French and the Nguyen treating the Chinese as separate communities with their own leaders, schools, and clan organizations. Favored by the French, many engaged in commerce and manufacturing: the Chinese section of Saigon is still called Cholon, meaning "Big Market." Others worked as miners, longshoremen, or fishermen.

Some of the most successful Vietnamese and Chinese obtained French citizenship, but there was also a small but growing lower bourgeoisie. The more well-to-do segment engaged in business or pursued professional careers in such emerging professions as engineering and medicine. Many of them were self-made, without the historic connection to the scholar-officials that had ruled Vietnam's past. Less well-off than members of this social stratum were an urban intelligentsia including teachers, journalists, students and clerks, who were often from elite families that had a tradition of Confucian emphasis on public service and education and had maintained their distance from the French.

In Saigon and elsewhere leadership for the emerging anticolonial movements and protests came overwhelmingly from members of this urban intelligentsia, but, for many years, the diversity in their views stood in the way of their forming a coherent movement. Regional differences in historic background and experience under colonialism made for disagreement and disunity. Furthermore, as William Duiker has pointed out, these elites lacked a common religion to help build national bonds or provide a basis for a national consciousness.[4]

The success of Cao Dai, founded in 1926 by an official in the French service with a deep interest in spiritism and séances, showed that at least in the south many were ready to embrace a new religion. Cao Dai, literally "high platform," a Daoist epithet for the highest god, got its name from Daoism, fostered Confucian morals, endorsed Buddhist belief in karma and reincarnation, modeled its organization on that of the Roman Catholic Church, and included Confucius, Jesus, and Mohammed in its pantheon. (See Figures 12.3 and 12.4.) It was similarly synthetic in its choice of more modern exemplars, paying special reverence to Sun Yat-sen, Victor Hugo, and Nguyen Binh Khiem (1491–1587), whose poetry was marked "by a strange combination of resigned fortitude, robustness of character, and irony which explodes at times into outrage, as in 'The Hated Rats,' but most often expresses itself in patient humor." Depicting officials as rats goes back to the Chinese *Classic of Poetry*, but it did not require much effort for twentieth-century Vietnamese to find in their own world rats who gorge on taxes with "those yellow teeth whose hunger maims our flesh."[5]

FIGURE 12.3   The Great Temple of Cao Dai in the sacred city
Tay Ninh, southwest of Ho Chi Minh City (Saigon). Here, as in
other Cao Dai temples, rituals are performed four times a day.
PHOTOGRAPH © LORE SCHIROKAUER.

FIGURE 12.4   *Window of the Great Temple of Cao Dai.* The omnis-
cient and omnipresent eye emanating sunrays is the central symbol
of Cao Dai, a fitting design for the windows of the great hall of
worship (note the rays and the trees visible through the glass).
Within the hall, dragons curl up the pillars and vivid colors prevail.
PHOTOGRAPH © LORE SCHIROKAUER.

Education

In Vietnam, as elsewhere, education helped mold people's values and ideas. In French Indochina change came only slowly. This was particularly the case in the protectorates, especially in Annam, where the court was located and where, during the first fifty years of colonial rule, changes in curriculum were inhibited by voices at court insisting that education remain geared to the traditional examination system. Meanwhile, in Cochin China education was in French along with *quoc ngu*, the phonetic script devised in the seventeenth century. However, throughout Vietnam, primary education was scarce, limited to urban centers. *Lycées* (French secondary academic schools) were extremely few.

The French seem never to have quite decided between a policy of assimilation, designed to make Vietnamese French in every way, and a policy of association, "which considered that colonies and the colonized people are distinct entities with their own cultures and institutions, albeit ultimately convertible to 'civilization' and to the high status enjoyed by France and the French."[6] Albert Sarraut, governor-general from 1911 to 1913 and 1919 to 1923, pursued the latter policy, and attempted to expand education—but he was equally intent on having Vietnam contribute to France's economy (see Figure 12.5). He ordered schools built in the villages—at village expense. However, his successor, Martial Merlin, reversed this policy in the 1920s, restricting secondary and post-secondary education, shutting down traditional schools that remained in Tonkin and Annam, and seeing to it that village schools would provide only three years of primary instruction in Vietnamese, taught by minimally qualified and poorly paid instructors. All in all, by 1930 only about 10% of school-age Vietnamese children actually went to public or private schools, and the next decade saw only modest increases.

Only a small number of Vietnamese youths received education beyond the primary level. Up to 1940, at any given time approximately 500 students found places in the *lycées*, and only a dozen or so graduated from university per year—this out of a population which in 1936 amounted to 18.6 million. Those who ventured to France for higher education experienced a far freer social and intellectual atmosphere.

FIGURE 12.5 His Excellency M. Albert Sarraut, governor-general of Indochina, and His Majesty Khai-Dinh, emperor of Annam (central Vietnam). Governor-general from 1911 to 1913 and again from 1919 to 1923, Sarraut attempted to expand education in village schools throughout the Indochinese Union.

FROM *L'INDOCHINE FRANÇAIS* (HANOI: GOVERNMENT GENERAL DE L'INDOCHINE, 1931).

There they were able to absorb French culture, and were exposed to the ideals of the French Revolution and leftist political philosophies, but when they returned home, they had to endure demeaning employment and prejudicial treatment. Their objections to colonialism grew in confidence and definition during the first decades of the twentieth century, strengthened by French anti-colonial discourse and hardened by the insensitivities of the French authorities.

Educated youths, however small a fraction of the overall population, were to be at the vanguard of nascent revolutionary movements that took the place of older, less radical movements.

New Stirrings of Opposition

From the beginning of French rule, some scholar-officials, mindful of Vietnam's struggles for independence in the past, resisted collaboration and maintained honor even at the price of family ruin and death. But, even after exposure to modern nationalism, many more chose to serve the emperor, hoping to preserve their status and scholarship while passively upholding French rule. A few, however, were attracted to ideas subversive both to colonial rule and to the traditional order, which they saw as an obstacle to a better society and to political independence. France was one source of such ideas, but other examples were closer at hand. By the turn of the century, Vietnamese scholars were reading texts by such Chinese reformers as Kang Yuwei and Liang Qichao, as well as Yan Fu's translations of works of Spencer and Mill. A movement sprang up to reform Vietnam through the "new learning." Phan Boi Chau (1867–1940) and Phan Chu Trinh (1872–1926), unrelated though they bore the same surname, represented two facets of "learning from the West." Both men received classical educations and passed the important regional examination in 1900, but both attacked the status quo, and were subjected to exile and imprisonment.

When Phan Boi Chau traveled to Japan in 1905, he immediately found himself in the midst of Chinese reformers with whom he shared a profound Confucian background and an intense distress at the state of government back home. In 1905 Liang Qichao himself expressed his sympathy for the plight of the Vietnamese under colonialism by publishing and contributing a preface to Phan's *History of the Loss of Vietnam.* This book not only advocated the "new learning" but also conveyed an intense nationalism and contained veiled incitements to armed uprising against the French.

Phan Boi Chau had his deepest impact as organizer and leader of a "Travel East" movement that influenced scores, perhaps hundreds, of young Vietnamese to study in Japan. He did not formulate a coherent ideology or program, but focused on expelling the French, and increasingly advocated doing so through violent revolution. He did this from Japan until the French succeeded in having him deported, and continued doing so from China, where he sought the support of successful Chinese revolutionaries after 1911. In 1913 he masterminded terrorist incidents in Vietnam that killed two French army officers and a high-placed collaborator. Sentenced to death in absentia, he remained abroad until, in 1925,

French authorities finally brought him back under arrest to face a new trial that produced a new death sentence.

One of those who heeded the call to "travel east" was Phan Chu Trinh, who was politically more moderate, but culturally more radical than Phan Boi Chau. His hero was Fukuzawa Yukichi, Japan's foremost proponent of "enlightenment" Western-style. In 1907 Phan Chu Trinh helped found a school in Hanoi modeled on the one established by Fukuzawa that eventually became Keiō University. Phan Chu Trinh, more than Phan Boi Chau, was a master of reasoned debate and the use of symbolic gestures to defy colonial rule. He took care to dress fashionably in Western clothes made from local Vietnamese materials. In one lecture at the school, he skillfully chided the Vietnamese for their subservience to both Chinese and Western domination when he urged Vietnamese men to cut their traditional Chinese-style chignons in favor of short haircuts:

> It was not until the Ming invaders came in and . . . compelled us to imitate them that our men began to let their hair grow and wore it in a bun. . . . But today . . . Heaven has opened our minds. We have awakened and the whole nation is modernizing. So go out and cut your hair! Don't leave any more land for that stupid gang of parasites to colonize on top of your heads, from which they can suck your blood![7]

In the wake of such arguments, short haircuts for men became subtly defiant of French rule, and the French were helpless to protest.

The Hanoi school and similar endeavors did not survive government repression, but the work of both Phans showed young Vietnamese how, in pursuit of a new identity, they could selectively borrow from the West along the lines of Chinese and Japanese predecessors. Meanwhile, Trinh, the nonviolent reformer, was arrested in the wake of anti-tax rioting in Annam in 1908, and sent to the penal island of Con Son, notorious for its "tiger cages." His sentence was commuted to house arrest in 1911, but then he was allowed to leave for Paris, where he wrote articles attacking French rule and welcomed anti-French Vietnamese to his home. After his death and funeral in 1926, the incoming French governor-general responded to widespread demonstrations and strikes led by thousands of enraged students and others mourning the fate of the two leaders, by commuting Chau's death sentence to house arrest. By this time, the two Phans, despite their differences, "had become linked in the popular mind as the towering symbols of scholarly patriotism, revered symbols of fortitude and continuity with the past."[8]

The Twenties and Thirties

In Vietnam, as in China, the twenties were years of ferment, particularly among young people struggling to redefine what it meant to be Vietnamese even as they rejected much of the old culture and lived under a colonial regime that proclaimed the virtues of the French Revolution but did not grant its Vietnamese subjects equality, liberty, or fraternity. It even happened that at the 1926 trial of Nguyen An Ninh (1900–1943), his translation of Jean-Jacques Rousseau's *Contrat*

Social was presented as evidence of sedition. The prosecution in this case may have been unusually obtuse, but the contradiction in French policies had been there all along. After his release from prison, Ninh was drawn to, though he did not join, Cao Dai. He remained politically active and ended by being killed in prison by the French, apprehensive that the Japanese might use him.

A burgeoning vernacular press reflected and promoted intellectual and cultural change. While some preferred to publish in the less strictly controlled French language newspapers and periodicals, many sought a wider audience by writing in the *quoc ngu* press, whose origins go back to 1865, but which now came into its own. A new literary style influenced by French literature called for the purging of Chinese expressions and references. Confucianism, religion, and the purpose of art were among topics hotly debated, as was the role of women. New styles of dress and hair took hold, while satirists mocked old customs and realists depicted the lives of rickshaw pullers, servants, and other members of the urban underclass.

Cultural radicalism did not necessarily entail political radicalism. Nguyen Van Vinh (1882–1936), for instance, was a widely read translator, journalist, and essayist who even in his most acerbic writings never turned against the French politically. One of his many publications was a translation of *The Tale of Kieu* (see Chapter 6, p. 110) from *nom* into *quoc ngu*. This set off a storm of controversy over the appropriateness of Kieu as a symbol for Vietnam or a model for Vietnamese womanhood. Among those most ardently championing Kieu was Pham Quynh (1892–1945), a prominent neo-traditionalist journalist intent on preserving a Vietnamese essence as well as an advocate of educating women of the upperclass. Loyal to the old court, he became head of the imperial cabinet and minister of education (1932).

Others became increasingly radical, joining such organizations as the Vietnamese Revolutionary Youth League, founded in 1925 by Ho Chi Minh, or the Nationalist Party of Vietnam, started in 1927 and deeply influenced by Sun Yat-sen. After a major revolt in Tonkin in 1917 led by prisoners in a penitentiary and mutinous Vietnamese troops, violence had been small scale, but that changed in 1930 when Vietnamese troops mutinied at Yen Bay not far from Hanoi. After the mutiny was suppressed, thousands were sent to brutal, overcrowded, mismanaged prisons where they became radicalized. As the prison authorities themselves realized, "inmates at Saigon Central Prison are receiving a comprehensive communist education."[9] The same happened at other prisons, and a period in prison was to become almost a requisite for the top Vietnamese Communist leadership. Ho Chi Minh was exceptional only in that he served his prison time outside the country.

The Rise of Ho Chi Minh

The Nationalists suffered a grievous blow when thirteen of their leaders were guillotined following the uprising at Yen Bay. One lesson drawn from this fiasco was the need for careful organization, analysis, planning, and guidance such as could be provided by the Comintern, and for an inspiring leader who could unify the different groups.

That leader was the man born a Nguyen but later known as Ho Chi Minh (1890–1969), who was almost forty at the time he presided over the founding of the Vietnamese Communist Party in February 1930 (name changed to Indochinese Communist Party in October 1930). Ho (then known by another name) had left Vietnam in 1913 and first gained public attention by his unsuccessful attempt to petition the Versailles Peace Conference (1919) to grant Vietnam self-determination. His bitter disappointment in the treaty resembled that of the Chinese participants in the May Fourth Movement. As it did with some Chinese leaders, it induced him to seek more radical solutions and more effective means. In Paris he joined the French Socialist Party and in 1920 was a founding member of the French Communist Party. He then spent over a year in Moscow (June 1923–November 1924), where he studied at the University of the Toilers of the East and participated in the Fifth Comintern conference. After going to Canton in 1924, he spent the next six years primarily organizing revolutionary activities among Vietnamese expatriates in various parts of Asia. Imprisoned in Hong Kong in June 1931 at the request of the French, he managed to get released in December 1932 and to reach Moscow in the spring of 1934. In the fall of 1938 he was able to return and resume operations, first from China and finally from a base within Vietnam itself—but not before experiencing life in a Chinese prison. The dramatic story of Ho's revolutionary career, his voluminous writings (poetry as well as prose), his powers of persuasion, devotion to the cause, personal affability and good humor under trying circumstances, along with his skill at strategy and inclination to move gradually at home and abroad gave him a solid reputation. His stature was to be further enhanced by his conduct during and after World War II, ultimately securing his place in the eyes of many Vietnamese as the wise and benevolent father of the revolution. However, on the eve of the war, much of his work still lay ahead.

II. Korea under Japanese Colonial Rule

Setting the Stage for Conquest

The Japanese Takeover

Japanese Colonial Rule

The Independence Movement

The Origins of Korean Communism

The Nineteen-Thirties

The Second World War in Korea

Effects and Legacies of Japanese Rule

Korea's period as a colony, 1910 to 1945, was shorter than that of Vietnam, but is remembered with equal anger and regret. In both cases it began with the collusion of the traditional authorities. In Korea this occurred when Korea's own government signed the peninsula over to the Japanese in return for favored treatment and emoluments. This fact still disturbs Koreans today, just as Japan's treatment of the Korean people during the colonial era continues to cloud relations between the two countries.

Japan's reasons for taking Korea were not limited to national security. The Japanese believed their country to be overpopulated, and the mainland of Asia was one obvious place to send people and seek resources for their continuing economic modernization. As they were taking Korea, certain Japanese planners had their eye on Manchuria to the north and even dreamed of moving into China and eventually creating a Japanese-led empire of "Asia for Asians." In this context, the annexation of Korea may be seen as one step in the process that culminated in the Pacific War.

Setting the Stage for Conquest

The Treaty of Shimonoseki that ended the Sino-Japanese War in 1895 defined Korea as a sovereign state and formally ended China's historic role as Korea's suzerain and protector. At the beginning of the war, Japanese stationed in Seoul had lost no time taking control of the Korean government. Working through the enlightenment faction (*kaehwadang*) of young Koreans who saw Japan as a model for their own country's modernization, they had promulgated changes known as the Kabo Reforms ("kabo" being the Korean name for the year 1894). These had included dissolution of all traditional ties to China, a thorough restructuring of the Korean government as a constitutional monarchy, and a catalog of social reforms that outlawed slavery, ended the centuries-old civil service examination system, abolished class distinctions, and alienated the ruling *yangban* establishment. Japanese forces virtually occupied the Kyŏngbok Palace throughout the war, warding off objections to the reforms. However, a backlash developed as members of the Queen's political faction persuaded the royal court to try to use Russian influence to check Japan. When this policy became evident following the Shimonoseki Treaty, the

Japanese struck back by sending attackers into the palace to murder Queen Min. The murder shattered politics in Seoul and sent King Kojong fleeing from the palace to live for more than a year in the Russian legation as the guest of the Russian minister. This was the peak of Russian influence in Korea, from 1896 to 1898.

Though the excessive ambition of Japanese officials in Korea had backfired, Koreans could not agree on a program to bolster defenses and assure Korea's survival as an independent country. As soon as it appeared that Russia was in the ascendancy, other Western powers demanded and got economic concessions from King Kojong to let them profit from mining, electric power, railroad construction, and other modern investments. One response came from a group of Western-educated intellectuals who started an "Independence Club" and published Korea's first modern newspaper, arguing that trying to play foreigners off against each other with concessions was not the best way to assure the country's independence. Rather, the leadership should resist foreign encroachment and look to building up its military defenses and reforming its institutions. The Independence Club advocated modern freedoms and used public rallies to generate support. This brought countermeasures from the Establishment. When squads of hired market "peddlers" used violence to break up one of the rallies, the club went into a steep decline. By the end of 1898 it was out of business.

The Japanese Takeover

When King Kojong left the Russian legation in 1897, he moved to a new palace facility that was located in close proximity to the Western legations. For several years he enlisted the help of the Western diplomatic community to counteract Japanese pressure. In 1897 he declared that Korea was now an "empire" (to be known as Taehan Cheguk, the "Great Han Empire"), and for the first time in Korean history declared himself an "emperor" with the right to offer sacrifices to Heaven, a prerogative theretofore reserved to the Emperor of China. Meanwhile, more Koreans were discovering the outside world, as government emissaries, as students assigned to higher studies, and as laborers, such as the ones who were hired to work in the canefields of Hawaii.

However, in 1902 England and Japan concluded an alliance that essentially eliminated British objections to Japanese expansion in Korea. In 1904 Japan attacked the Russian naval squadron at Port Arthur on the Liaodong Peninsula, and opened the Russo-Japanese War. This conflict, which brought Russian and Japanese armies to Korea and eventually centered on battlefields in Manchuria, wore down both sides until, in May 1905, the Japanese were able to win a decisive naval engagement in which Russia's main battle fleet was sunk in the Tsushima Strait. Japan's victory in the Battle of Tsushima Strait led to a peace conference at which U.S. President Theodore Roosevelt brokered a treaty at his summer home in Portsmouth, New Hampshire.

The Portsmouth Treaty ended the Russo-Japanese War by dividing the area of the war into spheres of influence. The Russians were allowed to keep their railroad interests in northern Manchuria. Japan was to gain the South Manchurian Railroad running from Harbin to Port Arthur/Dairen (today's Luda) and to have an exclusive sphere in Korea, where its "paramount interests" were recognized both by Russia and, in effect, by the United States, which had mediated the agreement. Russia thus withdrew from Korea; and with England in a formal alliance with Japan and the United States recognizing the terms of the Portsmouth Treaty, there was no one to oppose Japanese forcible imposition of a protectorate on the Korean government in November 1905. Indeed, the Japanese waited until they had guaranteed American nonintervention through the Taft-Katsura Agreement of 1905, whereby the United States promised not to interfere in Korea in return for Japan's pledge to accept U.S. colonization of the Philippines.

From 1905 until 1910, Japan made Korea a "protectorate," taking charge of its foreign relations and defense in 1905, and then taking over its finances and legal system in 1907. The great Meiji statesman Itō Hirobumi was sent to rule Korea as its Japanese "resident-general," and after Itō's assassination by a Korean in 1909, the Tokyo government moved to take full control through the treaty of annexation that was signed on August 22, 1910.

The Korean people did not simply accept the events leading up to the Japanese protectorate. Prince Min Yŏnghwan (1861–1905), a member of the late queen's family, committed suicide in protest. Local leaders raised irregular militia units to resist the presence of Japanese in their area, calling themselves *ŭibyong* ("righteous troops") after the spontaneous local militia that had fought the Japanese invaders in the 1590s. Their violent resistance was augmented by angry Korean farmers who saw Japanese land developers conduct surveys, uninvited, with the obvious intention of buying up their land and selling it to Japanese. Koreans founded voluntary associations and started newspapers in attempts to rally the populace for "self-strengthening." Korean educators started modern schools in hopes that studying modern subjects could prepare the younger generation to restore Korea and recover its independence. In 1907, as waves of despair swept Korea, many joined the recently legalized Christian church, associating themselves with Western religion and mission education in the same hope. Indeed, one reason for the growth of Christianity in Korea was its appeal as an alternative to Japanese ideas regarding reform and social transformation.

Korean resistance grew significantly in 1907 when Resident-General Itō Hirobumi ordered the disbanding of the royal Korean army. Many soldiers refused to lay down their arms, and joined the "righteous troops," bringing forth new waves of Japanese repression. King Kojong attempted a last-minute appeal to the world community protesting his country's complete loss of independence, but the appeal, which was aimed at diplomats meeting at The Hague in the Netherlands, was discovered and blocked by the Japanese. Japan then proceeded to extend its control over Korea, forcing the abdication of King Kojong and giving Resident-General Itō Hirobumi authority over Korea's Finance, Justice, and Home ministries. Itō's control of Korea's defenses, finances, courts, police forces, and internal administration made him Korea's *de facto* ruler. There only needed to be an occasion to take Korea outright. The occasion came with An Chunggŭn's assassination of Itō on the platform of the railroad station in the Manchurian city of

FIGURE 12.6   Hwanggung-u Pavilion (Temple of Heaven), site of the proclamation raising Korea to the status of empire. (Photograph c. 1925.)
Collection Donald N. Clark.

Harbin in 1909. The following year, after arranging pensions, payments, and honors for Korea's leading *yangban* noblemen, Japan annexed Korea on August 22, 1910, via a treaty that dissolved the Chosŏn dynasty monarchy as Korea's government and Korea itself as a nation. Korea acquired a new Japanese name, Chōsen, and the Japanese governor-general of Chōsen was its new ruler.

Japanese Colonial Rule

With their annexation to Japan as a colony, the Koreans not only lost the right to govern themselves but also the right to assemble, to join groups that were interested in politics, to publish or speak freely. Many lost their lands through Japan's manipulation of a land survey that vested much good farmland in the hands of the colonial regime and of Japanese land development companies that were designed to transfer it to Japanese investors. They lost their right to participate in local affairs through the reorganization of all government affairs and the appointment of Japanese bureaucrats to administer the provinces, counties, townships, and villages. Their most significant part in the new colonial structure was as hired policemen who assisted in the control of their own people.

At the top of the Japanese colonial structure, the governor-general was a uniformed army general, Terauchi Masatake, appointed by the Prime Minister of

朝鮮總督府 （京城名所）
The Government General of Chosen, Keijo.

FIGURE 12.7   Government-General Building, Seoul, built in 1926 and demolished in 1996. Large enough to house a new bureaucracy, this site held the administrative ministries that Japan imposed on its Korean colony.
COLLECTION DONALD N. CLARK.

Japan, but in fact a law unto himself in Korea. The governor-general was the colony's chief executive, chief justice, and its only legislator. He had personal command of the Chōsen Army, a military force headquartered in Seoul with units spread across the peninsula. He had personal command of the police, who were actually military police, or gendarmes (infamously known as the *kempeitai*). Under his direction the colony acquired a bureaucracy divided into ministries that mirrored the structure of the home government in Tokyo, though it was a completely separate and autonomous structure (Figure 12.7). And the colony financed itself through its own system of revenue collection in a separate currency denominated in yen, like that of Japan proper, but issued through the Bank of Chōsen.

Governor-General Terauchi moved to break all forms of Korean resistance as quickly as possible. After forbidding political activity, he went after groups and individuals who were potential rallying points, imprisoning writers, teachers, and religious leaders as examples, even when the charges against them were flimsy and obviously trumped up. Then, partly as a way of modernizing procedures, the government-general promulgated many types of laws and regulations, requiring licenses for many kinds of enterprise. The imposition of standards for licenses to teach, or practice medicine, or handle money was a way of standardizing procedure. However, the power to grant or withhold licenses was also a key tool of the colonial bureaucracy as it sought to punish and reward Koreans according to their degree of cooperation. As Mark R. Peattie has written:

> Korea now entered the dark epoch known to its chroniclers as the "period of military rule," a term that in English hardly conveys the crushing impact of the Japanese army and police on every aspect of Korean life. "Regulations of every kind poured forth wildly and were as harshly enforced," noted a Japanese journalist in Korea at the time, adding that "so completely were the people's liberties restricted that the entire peninsula could be said to have been militarized"[10]

The land survey that was conducted between 1910 and 1918 mapped the peninsula and classified the land according to use and type (forest land, farm land, coastline, and so on) and required owners to produce proof of ownership. This presumably simple requirement trapped many squatters, tenant farmers and sharecroppers—Korea's poorest peasants—into losing their livelihoods when they could not produce documents or failed to understand Japanese instructions. Better-prepared Koreans who were able to prove their titles, however, kept their land and, along with many newly-arrived Japanese buyers, even increased their holdings, thus adding to the pattern of rural land concentration. The gap that had always existed between rural landlords and poor peasants was thus widened by colonial policy, helping set the stage for the violent left-right confrontations that followed the liberation of Korea in 1945.

Japan took charge of Korea's modern facilities as well, controlling transportation, communications, banking, and manufacturing. Japanese firms quickly came to dominate mining, construction, chemicals, and other modern industries. Japanese goods flooded the Korean retail market, driving many Koreans out of business. Only the biggest Korean companies, backed by large Korean fortunes concentrated in family holdings, were well enough positioned to survive Japanese competition. Most found it necessary to align themselves with the government-general and the Japanese market. In effect, they became part of the Japanese power structure in the colony.

In place of traditional Korea's highly informal educational system, which had consisted of tutors and small village academies that fostered literacy in classical Chinese and prepared students for the civil service examinations, the Japanese introduced a plan to deliver mass education at the elementary level. For this they needed teachers, and they encouraged middle schools and private academies to meet government standards for elementary teacher training. The plan was to produce "loyal and obedient" subjects of the Japanese emperor through primary schools (four years) and secondary schools (four years for boys, three for girls). However, the process of building and equipping schools and training teachers for a wholly new Korea-wide educational system took a very long time. By 1919 only 3.7 percent of Korea's school-age children were enrolled in government schools, while three times that number were still studying in village *sŏdang*. In 1929 the regime adopted a plan to establish an elementary school in every Korean *myŏn* (township) and one high school in each of the thirteen provinces. By the end of the colonial period, however, only a small percentage of Korean children had ever

FIGURE 12.8 Nandaimon-dōri (today's Namdaemun-no), a main square of colonial-era
Seoul with key Japanese institutions (Bank of Chōsen on the left, main post office on the right).
Collection Donald N. Clark.

been to a government school. Rather, the schools served mainly the children of
Japanese residents in Korea by a ratio of two to one. Their language of instruction
was Japanese, and their curriculum, especially in the 1930s as war approached,
aimed at fostering respect for the emperor and Japan's national heroes.

The Independence Movement

The high point of Korean resistance to Japanese colonial rule came in 1919,
when a coalition of religious leaders signed a declaration of independence and
started a nationwide wave of protests that lasted for more than a year. The Korean
independence movement was influenced in part by external events—the Russian
Revolution, the Versailles conference and President Woodrow Wilson's Fourteen
Points, and the May Fourth movement in China—and by Korean students who
had gone to Japan for higher studies and reflected on the plight of their home
country. The government-general of Chōsen was caught off balance by the independence movement, and responded with great violence, using the *kempeitai*, the
army, the police, and even firemen wielding pikes against the demonstrators. The
movement, which was meant to be nonviolent, had its violent moments. Koreans

attacked *kempeitai* units and Koreans in the colonial police force. Japanese forces even felt obliged to enter southeastern Manchuria in pursuit of Korean settlers who were attacking Japanese border stations. The Korean independence uprising did not end until late 1920, and cost the lives of more than a few Japanese as well as thousands of Koreans.

Korea's independence movement embarrassed many Japanese. Although Koreans who wanted countries like the United States to condemn Japan were disappointed by the lack of interest or response abroad, the Tokyo government was sufficiently chastened to try a new approach in Chōsen. Instead of an army general ruling under "military rule," Korea got an admiral, Saitō Makoto (1919–1927), who ushered in a period of "cultural rule" whose goal was to persuade Koreans to support the colonial program and accept Japanese direction. An important part of Admiral Saitō's program was to grant concessions that were highly symbolic but did not seriously undermine Japanese power. He allowed Koreans to start their own Korean-language newspapers and magazines. He granted a demand to establish a government university in Korea so Korean students could have access, at least in principle, to higher studies in their own country. Saitō relaxed many of the more obnoxious regulations and allowed Koreans to associate in a wide variety of civil society organizations. One of the most interesting of these was the Korean Products Promotion Society begun by Cho Mansik (1882–?), following Gandhi's example in India, to persuade Koreans to buy only things made in Korea by Koreans. Another thread was the study of Korean history and culture, an outgrowth of the efforts at self-strengthening through education that had begun in the protectorate period. Research into the Korean language led to spelling standardization, the production of a national dictionary, and even the writing of modern novels in Korean.

Saitō even allowed the formation of a national organization to discuss politics—albeit under close surveillance. Koreans used this period to discuss how they should continue pushing for independence. Some argued that the Japanese were too strong to be defeated and would have to be accepted while Koreans tried to preserve their culture through studies of history and literature and by educating young Koreans to work toward liberation. Using language approximating ordinary speech, Yi Kwangsu (1892–1950?) published novels such as *Heartless* (1917), conveying national pride, and the poet Yi Sanghwa asked "Does Spring Come to Stolen Fields?" Publication of such literature was itself a political act.

An organization called the Sin'ganhoe (New Korea Society) brought together people from across the political spectrum. At one end were the "cultural nationalists," conservatives who wanted to preserve the culture of Korea without necessarily overthrowing the colonial regime or the social and economic relations permitted by the Japanese. At the other end were left-wing socialists and even a few revolutionaries who advocated violence not only to overthrow the government-general but also to restructure Korean society and redistribute wealth.

Admiral Saitō's decade of "cultural rule" had moments of disturbance as Koreans showed that they had not accepted the essence of Japanese domination. Korea's last "emperor," the prince who had reigned symbolically from 1907 to

1910, died in 1926, and his funeral was an occasion for muted protest. In 1929 in Kwangju, fighting broke out between Korean and Japanese students over an incident in which a Korean girl had been molested by a Japanese boy in a train station; when the colonial police tried to break up the fights, the people in general rose up in rioting.

The Origins of Korean Communism

The Korean Communist party (better known as the Korean Labor party, or Chosŏn Nodongdang) began as several factions in several places, first in 1918 among Koreans in Irkutsk, in Siberia. In 1920 in Shanghai, the exile Yi Tonghwi (1872–1935) founded a Korean Communist Party based on an earlier socialist group. The two Korean communist organizations fought each other in a bloody confrontation in the town of Alekseyevsk, Siberia, in 1921; and though many Korean leftists were disgusted at their rivalry, the movement grew as an amalgam of elements committed to revolutionary change in their homeland. Korean students in Japan, such as the ones who had helped inspire the 1919 independence movement, were also attracted to left-wing ideas that pointed to armed struggle.

The idea that violence was necessary to preserve Korean identity offended the "cultural nationalists" in the Sin'ganhoe during its existence between 1927 and 1931. One reason is that many of the cultural nationalists were beneficiaries of privileges to be had under the colonial system as it existed: that is, Japanese education and Japanese-sanctioned family wealth. Another is that while the Society's national leadership was in the hands of the cultural nationalists, the branch organizations across the country tended to be led by leftists. These groups proposed going much further than liberating Korea from Japanese rule. They advocated a redistribution of wealth and privilege through a social revolution, as well. The two wings of the nationalist movement were therefore at odds, and it was no surprise when their short-lived attempt at cooperation collapsed with the end of the Sin'ganhoe in 1931. The two wings of Korean nationalism were never again to work together.

The united front of the Sin'ganhoe had afforded Korea's communists a certain shelter. Their isolation after 1931 forced them into a life-or-death confrontation with the Japanese authorities, who were themselves anti-communist, but were also embarked on a program of militarization and expansion on the continent after the Manchurian Incident of 1931. There was no place for toleration of communists in the Japanese plan, and the colonial government in Korea made a concerted effort to annihilate all factions of the Korean Communist party. In order to survive, the Korean left wing had to go underground or leave the country. Some groups went into exile in China, first in Shanghai, and later, when the Chinese Communist party ended its Long March in Yan'an, with the C.C.P. in Shaanxi Province. Others migrated to the Soviet far east, seeking safety in the maritime province by living as ethnic Koreans in Russia. Still others attempted to carry on a guerrilla war in the mountains of the Korea-Manchurian border, raiding Japanese outposts and creating mayhem wherever possible. This was the faction of Korean communists in which the future North Korean leader Kim Il-sung (1912–1994) made his reputation.

The Nineteen-Thirties

Japan itself abandoned democracy in the 1930s and chose militarism and war in an effort to expel Western imperialism and widen its control over an "Asia for Asians." (See Chapter 13.) Korea was transformed into a staging area for this effort as Japanese armed forces invaded Manchuria in 1931 and north China in 1937. Korea's first sense of this situation came with the replacement of Admiral Saitō with a new ruler, army general Ugaki Kazushige (1868–1956), in 1931. Ugaki's economic task was to organize the infrastructure of Korea to supply the Japanese military in Manchuria and China. For example, he started developing the east coast of Korea as an integral part of the metropolitan Japanese economy. Ch'ŏngjin, on the northeast coast of the peninsula, was turned into a major port and railhead for transportation directly from the Sea of Japan (or "Eastern Sea" as it is known in Korea) to Jiandao, the area of southeastern Manchuria whose population is largely Korean, and onward to Mukden (Shenyang) and the Manchurian railroad network. A Japanese oil refinery went up at Wŏnsan, a chemical factory was built at Hamhŭng, and elaborate waterworks were built in the mountains and along the Yalu River to generate electrical power. Much Korean cropland was turned to cotton and wool production to help equip the military forces—and to reduce the threat of Korean competition for Japanese food growers. The result was a trend away from food production in Korea, which harmed the Koreans, and toward manufacturing, which supported Japanese military expansion.

In political terms, General Ugaki began the complete acculturation of the Korean people as Japanese citizens and subjects of the emperor. To this end he launched propaganda campaigns, matching those already underway in Japan, telling people to regard Korea and Manchuria as historically one, to think of Japan and Korea as united in a single body, and to think of the self as a part of the great national entity, or *kokutai*. As good imperial subjects, Koreans were exhorted to speak only the "national language" (*kokugo*), which was Japanese. Korean schoolchildren were taken to Shinto shrines that had been built originally for Japanese residents on the peninsula and made to bow to the spirits of the nation's heroes, including Japanese soldiers who had died in the wars to subjugate Korea.

General Ugaki's successor was another army general, Minami Jirō (1874–1956), who carried the program much farther. While continuing Ugaki's economic program, he initiated outright repression of Koreans in a program that approached cultural genocide. It became a crime to speak Korean in school or to refuse to attend "patriotic" ceremonies at Shinto shrines. Studies of the Korean language were deemed subversive, and cultural nationalists who were devising standards for spelling words in *han'gŭl* were rounded up and imprisoned. Civil society groups, both secular and religious, were subjected to police surveillance and their leaders were arrested, interrogated for long hours, and often jailed to guarantee loyalty. Ultimately, all organizations in Korea were required to amalgamate into federations whose primary purpose was avowed to be support for the emperor and the war.

The Second World War in Korea

Mobilization laws in 1938 began labor drafts that shipped many Koreans to Japan against their will and even drafted young women into the infamous "comfort women" corps, who were transported to forward army units to serve as sex slaves for Japanese soldiers. As part of the mobilization, trusted Korean men were recruited for the first time to serve in the Japanese armed forces, a consequence of the increased manpower requirements of the full-scale invasion of China. In the full-employment wartime economy of Japan, Koreans were drafted and sent to Japan to do the dirtiest and most dangerous industrial work, such as coal mining. As materials and commodities became scarce, Koreans experienced ever-stricter rationing of everything from food, fuel, and medicine to newsprint and building supplies. Destitute Koreans scratched for food on the desiccated mountainsides of "fire-lands" (*hwajŏn*) created by the most primitive slash-and-burn farming methods. The colonial government made the Koreans donate their pots and pans and wedding rings in metal-collection drives, and cash in special civilians' collections to pay for warplanes. Leather was so scarce that bankers and professors lined their shoes with fresh newspaper scraps each morning. During the war the speaking of Korean was forbidden altogether, and Koreans were required to choose Japanese surnames for themselves, trading their hallowed ancestral Kims and Yuns for Japanese names like Kanemura and Yamaguchi. Under a strict news blackout, little news reached Korea apart from the glowing reports of victories generated by the national Domei News Agency. Near the end of the war, when B-29 contrails appeared in the air as American bombers headed for Manchuria, Koreans concluded that the war was ending in defeat for Japan. After the Cairo conference in December 1943, there were also reports of an Allied agreement to liberate Korea. Nevertheless, the collapse of Japan came as a surprise to most Koreans. It was a special shock to Koreans who had cast their lot with the Japanese when they realized that there was likely to be a reckoning between those who had suffered most under Japan and those who had found ways to get along and even to prosper.

Effects and Legacies of Japanese Rule

Economic Misdevelopment. Koreans, like Vietnamese, take offense at assertions by their former colonizers that they should be grateful at least for the physical improvements that were made in their country by the colonial government. When Japanese cite the hydroelectric dams, ports, railroads, highways, schools, mines, factories, and myriad buildings that were left behind for Koreans to use when Japan was forced to withdraw from the peninsula, Koreans argue that none of these things were constructed for their benefit but rather to make their colony more profitable for the Japanese. No doubt the Koreans did use much that the Japanese left behind after 1945. But the Koreans are correct in noting that Japan rather misdeveloped Korea—for example, creating a chemical industry that was geared to munitions, a banking system that was aimed at providing for Japanese investors, and a land system that favored big landowners and destroyed small farms.

Fear and Coercion. As in Vietnam, coercion was a basic feature of colonial rule in Korea. The Japanese would have preferred to see Koreans voluntarily accept their control and guidance, but it was enough merely to make them obey. Attempts to convert the Koreans and turn them into loyal subjects of the Japanese emperor were a dismal failure. Admiral Saitō failed to co-opt them with his "cultural policy" in the 1920s, and General Minami was only able to win sullen acquiescence at gunpoint in the late 1930s. Fear was an essential element of Japanese rule in Korea, and Koreans were kept in a constant state of worry that they or their family members would be targeted by the colonial police. The arbitrariness of Japanese arrests was proof that the colonial authorities would not hesitate to punish some Koreans to intimidate the rest.

Social and Psychological Disruption. As was the case in all colonies to a greater or lesser extent, Japanese rule was highly disruptive to Koreans, socially and psychologically. As the shapers of modern life for Korea, Japan introduced modern methods of government, education, industry, and mass communication. Koreans thus were given a taste of modern systems and a desire to participate in them. However, while they were exposed to new structures and opportunities, Koreans were by and large confined to lower levels within those structures. The Japanese began a system of mass education, for example, but only at the elementary level. A Korean student had to go to Japan and "become Japanese" if he or she wanted training beyond middle school. The more Korean identity a person retained, the less likely he or she was to advance into positions of responsibility—or more rarely still, of authority. This was logical from a Japanese point of view, but it was deeply troubling to Koreans.

Instilling the Idea of Japanese Superiority. As a rule, no colonial system accepted the colonized people as equals of the colonizers. The Japanese in Korea regarded themselves as innately superior to the Koreans, and they made much of their own efforts to "civilize" and "improve" the Koreans, who, it was said, were incapable of governing themselves. One of the tragedies of colonialism is that many of the colonized accept this premise and learn to regard themselves as inferior. Many Koreans became conditioned to looking up to the Japanese and admiring their manifest sense of purpose and their political, military, and economic skills. Koreans learned to do many modern things from their Japanese rulers. The postwar years offer many examples of Koreans continuing to do things the Japanese way, from school uniforms to popular music to police and army methods. South

Korea's late twentieth-century economic prosperity was patterned on Japanese models, and the famous Korean conglomerates such as Hyundai and Samsung are called *chaebŏl*, the Korean version of the Japanese term *zaibatsu*.

The Bitter Fruits of Collaboration. These accumulated social, economic, and institutional distortions were part of the legacy of colonial rule that Japan left behind in Korea after being defeated in 1945. Korean politics exploded as Koreans accused each other of collaboration and betrayal, particularly during the war years when the Japanese had pushed hard to get Koreans to support the war effort in public. Koreans who had served in the Japanese colonial bureaucracy and police organizations were condemned as national traitors. Intellectuals who had supported Japan in public statements were condemned, even though some of them, like Ch'oe Namsŏn (1890–1957), the primary author of the 1919 Independence Declaration, and Yi Kwangsu, the country's leading novelist, had towering reputations as cultural nationalists. Wealthy businessmen and landowners stood accused of supporting the Japanese in order to save their fortunes. And Christians fought each other over the fact that some had bowed to government pressure and worshipped at Shinto shrines while others had refused and gone to jail. The collaboration issue was also central to the separation of North and South Korea under left- and right-wing Korean political factions after the war. In the north, the Soviet-backed leftist regime of Kim Il-sung sought out collaborators of every type and identified them as enemies of the people, in some cases divesting them of the assets that they had managed to maintain through the colonial period. North Korea got considerable propaganda value out of the fact that collaborators were relatively safe in the south and even protected under the U.S. military occupation and, later, under the Republic of Korea, as we shall see in Chapter 14.

III. Taiwan

Taiwan

1883   1895   1945

Under Qing Rule | Colonial Taiwan

When Japan acquired Taiwan as its first colony in 1895, it did so with many of the same objectives that subsequently prompted it to seize Korea, and the Japanese implemented many of the same policies in both colonies. Consequently, the inhabitants of the island shared many of the experiences of their fellow colonials, but, in the final analysis, the differences between Taiwan and Korea, then as now, loom at least as large as the similarities.

One difference was that in 1895 the people on Taiwan were given two years in which to decide between staying on as Japanese colonials or moving to the mainland as subjects of the Qing. The latter choice proved attractive to a good number of the local elite. This included men who had staked their future on the examination system, for by the time of the Japanese takeover, the "gentrification"[11] of what had once been a frontier elite was well advanced. It was to serve their needs that between 1860 and 1893, fourteen academies had been established on the island, which only in 1885 had been elevated to provincial status.

The departure of 6400 people, about 2.3 percent of the population, no doubt removed some potential leaders of resistance, but, as it was, the Japanese occupation began with five months of fighting. The Taiwanese, however, lacked coordination. The "Republic of Taiwan," declared by the last Qing governor, lasted only twelve days. Until 1902 the Japanese faced occasional scattered attacks. Even after Japanese authority had been firmly established over the Han (ethnic Chinese) population (2,890,455 according to the 1905 census) armed clashes continued with Taiwan's original inhabitants (estimated at 122,000 in 1909), who occupied the central highlands and continued to lose ground as they had under the Qing. It was their misfortune that their forest contained camphor trees. Camphor, turned into a government monopoly by Japan, was a prime export, in great demand for use in the manufacture of smokeless gunpowder.

As in Korea, the governor-general of Taiwan was the supreme administrative and judicial authority. Until 1919 he was a military man, but from 1898 to 1906 civil administration was in the hands of Gotō Shimpei (1857–1929), a medical man responsible for much of the basic framework of the Japanese colonial system. A major objective, accomplished by 1905, was for Taiwan to pay for itself despite continuing heavy government expenditures. To rationalize their administration, the Japanese conducted a land survey and a census. As later in Korea, the colonial authorities relied heavily on the police for a wide range of services, including tax collection, agricultural, hygiene, water supply and sanitation service, but in Taiwan, unlike Korea, the Japanese controlled these matters by cleverly adapting an old Chinese system of mutual responsibility (*baojia*), under which the population was organized into groups of (theoretically) a hundred households, each composed of units of ten. In contrast to the ineffectiveness of this system on the mainland, in Taiwan the *hokō* system (pronouncing the term the Japanese way) became the instrument by which the state reached down into the villages to affect each individual, something beyond the ability of all Chinese mainland governments prior to 1949. Only the Han population was organized in this manner.

The *hokō*, along with earlier guard units composed of Han settlers and acculturated aborigines, supplied the manpower for a local militia who acted as police auxiliaries. They not only provided security and surveillance, but undertook road repair and even railroad maintenance, as well as contributing to various rural campaigns. They also constituted a heavy burden on the population, who, in addition to the regular taxes, were saddled with *hokō* dues, and had to supply labor when needed. Though nominally the *hokō* leaders were elected by the households, the system was controlled by the police, which came to include 20 to 30 percent Taiwanese, but remained firmly under Japanese command.

As in Korea, the Japanese developed the Taiwan economy, but did so to meet their own needs and serve their own purposes. A central bank (The Bank of Taiwan, 1899) issued currency and sought to manage the economy. By the time Japan acquired Taiwan, it was an exporter of tea and sugar as well as camphor, but the sugar industry was faltering. The Japanese changed that, turning Taiwan into a major producer of sugar, able to fulfill their domestic needs and thus saving foreign exchange that otherwise would have gone for sugar imports. Along with tea, the Japanese also fostered rice cultivation and initiated irrigation projects. They also did much to develop the network of roads and railways, and improved the harbors for ocean shipping. Modern postal and telegraph system were established. Beginning with Gotō, they were also very active in public health. The death rate was reduced, and by 1945 the population just about doubled.

Consumer industries included food processing, logging and textiles—but not until Japan began preparing for total war did heavy industry get started. The completion of the Sun Moon Lake Electrical Generation Plan (1935) was a milestone. Aluminum, textiles, iron, cement, and chemical industries grew in what nevertheless remained an essentially agrarian economy.

As in Korea, there were local people of wealth and education who worked with the Japanese-dominated establishment. There was the ambivalence about education that we have already noted in Indochina and Korea. True, schools were established, but initially there were only lower-level and inferior schools for the Taiwanese, in contrast to the higher levels of education available to Japanese who settled in Taiwan. In 1928, an imperial university was established in Taipei, but it had three times as many Japanese students as it did Taiwanese. In 1945 there was only one Taiwanese professor on its faculty.

As shown by the establishment of the university, in Taiwan as in Korea, there was a relaxation of control in the twenties followed by the severity of the thirties. In the twenties, Japanese liberals talked of eventual assimilation, and there was a temporary and limited loosening of the colonial reins, with greater tolerance for Taiwanese to express their own views at home as well as in Tokyo. In 1921 a Taiwanese intellectual even demanded the abolition of the *hokō* system. Although some changes were made, it was not abolished until two months before Japan surrendered in 1945. To follow Siomi Shunji's analysis, from 1895 to 1920 the police were the prime movers, but during the next quarter of a century they were a background force.[12]

Stimulated by developments in China and Japan, there was a quickening of intellectual life in Taiwan and among Taiwanese in Tokyo, with movements to forge a new and modern culture and to write in the vernacular about current concerns. The main character of the first novel written by Lai Ho (1894–1943), often considered the father of modern Taiwanese literature, was a Taiwanese vegetable seller whose small manual scale for weighing out his sales was broken in two by Japanese policemen. A central issue facing Lai and a new generation of younger writers trying to forge a Taiwanese identity was that of language, as classical Chinese was rapidly becoming obsolete, and the new literary language that gained currency on the mainland after the May Fourth Movement was based on a vernacular incomprehensible to the people of Taiwan. Lai Ho himself was really most at home in classical Chinese, which he had to translate into the local vernacular.

One solution was to write in Japanese. From the start, the Japanese had encouraged people to learn Japanese, and by the thirties there was a substantial audience for writers such as Wu Cho-liu (1900–1976), whose *An Orphan of Asia* expressed a sense that Taiwan had been abandoned by its Chinese parents and never become a full-fledged member of the Japanese household in which it now found itself. The problem of defining Taiwan's place in the world was to persist long after the Japanese were gone.

As in Korea, during the thirties and especially during the war, there were campaigns to have Taiwanese adopt Japanese names and worship at Shinto shrines, but these did not make them into first-class subjects of the Emperor. Taiwanese men did fight in the imperial army, and Taiwanese living on the China coast enjoyed status as Japanese subjects, forming an imperial vanguard much as Korean settlers did in Manchuria. However, many Taiwanese suffered under the heavy hand of Japanese rule. Like the people in Japan itself, they were totally surprised by the defeat of Japan, but welcomed reversion to Chinese rule, even though they had not been consulted.

Notes

1. Ngo Vinh Long, *Before the Revolution: The Vietnamese Peasants Under the French* (New York: Columbia Univ. Press, 1973), p. 14.
2. Andrew Hardy, "The Economics of French Rule in Indochina: A Biography of Paul Bernard (1892–1960)" in *Modern Asian Studies*, vol. 32, no. 4 (10, 1998), p. 813.
3. Dao Duy Anh, as quoted in Neil Jamieson, *Understanding Vietnam* (Berkeley: Univ. of California Press, 1993), pp. 91–92.
4. William Duiker, *The Communist Road to Power in Vietnam* (Boulder: Westview, 1996), pp. 11–13.
5. Ngyuen Ngoc Bich, ed. and trans., *A Thousand Years of Vietnamese Poetry* (New York: Alfred A. Knopf, 1975), pp. 82, 84–85.
6. Truong Buu Lam, *Colonialism Experienced: Vietnamese Writings on Colonialism 1900–1931* (Ann Arbor: The Univ. of Michigan Press, 2000), p. 11.
7. Quoted in Jamieson, *Understanding Vietnam*, pp. 59–60.
8. Hue-Tam Ho Tai, *Radicalism and the Origins of the Vietnamese Revolution* (Cambridge, Mass.: Harvard Univ. Press, 1992), p. 146.

9. Peter Zinoman, *The Colonial Bastille: A History of Imprisonment in Vietnam, 1862–1940* (Berkeley: Univ. of California Press, 2001), p. 218, quoting materials in the Centre des Archives d'Outre-Mer, Aix-en-Province.
10. Mark H. Peattie, "The Japanese Colonial Empire, 1895–1945," in Peter Duus, ed., *The Cambridge History of Japan*, vol. 6: *The Twentieth Century* (Cambridge: Cambridge Univ. Press, 1988) p. 231.
11. Robert Gardella in Murray A. Rubinstein, ed., *Taiwan: A New History* (Armonk, N.Y.: M. E. Sharpe, 1999), p. 180.
12. Hui-yu Caroline Ts'ai, *One Kind of Control; The Hokō System in Taiwan Under Japanese Rule, 1895–1945* (PhD Dissertation, Columbia University, 1990), pp. 494–95, citing Shunji's essay as translated into Chinese by Chou Hsien-wen in *T'ai-wan yin-hang chi-kan*, comp. T'ai-wan Yin-hang Ching-chi Yen-chiu-shih (Taipei: Bank of Taiwan) vol. 5, no. 4 (1953), pp. 267–68.

13

East Asia: The Thirties and World War II

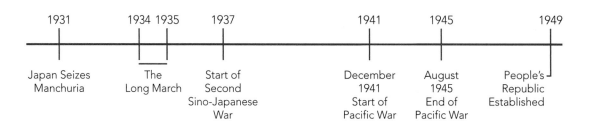

1931 — Japan Seizes Manchuria

1934 1935 — The Long March

1937 — Start of Second Sino-Japanese War

December 1941 — Start of Pacific War

August 1945 — End of Pacific War

1949 — People's Republic Established

The fate of Nationalist China and Imperial Japan became fatally intertwined when Japan seized Manchuria in 1931, entering into what in Japan is now called "a dark valley." These were dark years also in much of the rest of the world. In the wake of the Great Depression, people in many countries, desperate for vigorous action, accepted dictatorship of one kind or another as the most effective way of pulling through. While the Soviet Union (USSR) claimed to be on the road to communist utopia, it was not only in Italy and Germany that there were people who viewed Fascism as the wave of the future. In Japan, militarists seized power from the political parties, and in China, too, the military gained in power and prestige.

During most of the thirties the Western Democracies were preoccupied with domestic problems, and the strongest, the United States, was committed to isolationism. International statesmanship was at a low ebb. The failure of the League of Nations to respond to Japanese aggression in Manchuria revealed the inability or unwillingness of any government to do more than pay lip service to the principles of collective security.

The Manchurian Incident and Its Consequences

The Japanese government derived its legitimacy from the emperor, but the ruling political parties confronted charges that they were betraying their sacred trust. In the name of the emperor, the enemies of constitutional government criticized the political manipulations of the Diet leaders, their ties to business, and their policy of accommodating the West and conciliating China, exemplified by the Washington Conference of 1921–1922. Such sentiments animated the members of various patriotic organizations and prevailed in the army, chafing from the cuts made in its budgets and restrictions imposed by civilian administrations. Military leaders' dissatisfaction with the political ethos and government policies fused with their sense of being charged with a separate mission for which they were responsible to the emperor alone. There were calls for a "Showa Restoration" and much talk of the divinity of the emperor as the embodiment of the national polity (*kokutai*), a term which became an "incantatory symbol"[1] all the more powerful for being vague.

Among the most vehement critics of party government were radical egalitarians like Kita Ikki, who favored nationalizing industry, and radical agrarians like Gondō Seikyo (1868–1937), who would have abolished industry altogether and returned Japan to rural simplicity. Although their visions of the future differed, they agreed on two things: that the existing government obtruded on the imperial will and must be swept away, and that Japan had a divine mission overseas. Such ideas formed the agenda for small societies of extremists given to direct action, such as the Cherry Society, which planned an unsuccessful military coup in Tokyo in March 1931. The membership of this society consisted entirely of army officers, none higher in rank than lieutenant colonel.

The assassination of the Manchurian warlord Zhang Zuolin in 1928 was the work of men such as these. They hoped that Zhang's murder would trigger a war in which this vast, strategic, and potentially wealthy area would be conquered for Japan. This did not happen, but another attempt to start a war appealed to the superpatriots, not only because it might gain Manchuria, but also because it would strengthen their support in the army, increase the army's power and popularity at home, and undermine the government they so detested.

Emphasis on Manchuria was also consistent with the thought of more analytical army men, like Ishiwara Kanji (Ishihara Kanji, 1886–1949), who worked out the plan of attack. He and other students of World War I wanted Japan to control the economic resources of Manchuria as a step toward attaining the economic independence required for waging total war. Many officers, concerned with the possibility of war with the Soviet Union, were also mindful of Manchuria's strategic value.

In the fall of 1931 the time seemed ripe, for China was hampered by floods in the Yangzi Valley and the Western powers were neutralized by the depression. The seizure was masterminded by Ishiwara and other officers serving with the Japanese Army on the Liaodong Peninsula. These officers, none higher than colonel, fabricated a supposed Chinese attempt to sabotage the South Manchuria Railway Company as an excuse for hostilities, and then made sure the fighting continued until the army controlled Manchuria. Although certain high army officials in Tokyo very likely knew of the plot, it was carried out without the knowledge, let alone the authorization, of the civilian government in Tokyo, which, once informed, tried to halt the operations, but found itself powerless to do so. An attempted military coup in Tokyo in October did not immediately topple the government, but did succeed in intimidating civilian political leaders. The Wakatsuki government, divided and helpless, resigned in December. It was followed by a Seiyūkai government under Inukai Ki (Inukai Tsuyoshi, 1855–1932), which for another half year tried to maintain a semblance of party control.

Events moved swiftly on the continent and at home. In Manchuria, the army consolidated its hold and established a puppet state, which early in 1932 declared its independence from China. Manchukuo, as it was known, was placed under the titular rule of Puyi who, as an infant, had been the last emperor of China—but it was actually controlled by the army. Meanwhile, the fighting had spread to China proper; for six strenuous weeks, Japanese and Chinese fought around Shanghai until a truce was arranged. However, Japanese efforts to reach a general settlement with China and obtain recognition of Manchukuo were rebuffed. Japan was condemned by the League of Nations, and withdrew in March 1933. The failure of the League to do anything more than talk was not lost on Mussolini and Hitler.

After Japanese troops crossed the Great Wall in the spring of 1993, a truce was concluded in May 1933 that left Japanese troops in control of the area north of the Wall and provided for a demilitarized zone whose boundaries were marked by the railway line running between Beijing, Tianjin, and Tanggu—but it did not prevent the Japanese from setting up a puppet regime in that area nor from exerting continuous pressure on North China. In December 1935, Japanese army officers failed in their plans to engineer a North Chinese puppet regime, and full-scale war broke out in the summer of 1937. In the meantime, in Manchuria, and now also in Korea, the Japanese concentrated on the development of heavy industry, building up an industrial base on the continent under army control.

Japanese Politics and the Road to War

At home, too, 1932 was an eventful year, as members of the patriotic societies continued to further their cause by assassinating prominent men, including the head of the house of Mitsui. On May 15 they raided the Tokyo power station, a bank, Seiyūkai headquarters, and the official residence of the prime minister. They assassinated Inukai in his home.

When the men responsible for the May 15 violence were brought to trial, they were treated with great respect. They were allowed to expound their doctrines for days at a time and given a national podium from which to proclaim the selflessness of their patriotic motives. In this way they largely succeeded in portraying themselves as martyrs. The light sentences meted out at the conclusion of the lengthy trials further discouraged those who hoped for a return to civilian rule. Instead, power shifted away from the political parties and into the hands of civilian bureaucrats and, especially, the military. In 1936 the leftist Social Mass Party managed to win half a million votes. The following year that party's total climbed to 900,000 votes, and it captured thirty-seven seats in the lower house of the Diet. In that same election the Seiyūkai and Minseitō together polled some seven million votes, giving them 354 out of a total of 466 seats. But their showing in the polls was to little avail. The parties were too weak to control the military. Those who wished to preserve constitutional government chose to compromise with the military establishment in the hope of averting a complete overthrow of the existing order.

Efforts to achieve political stabilization through a national union government, in which all the power centers were represented, were fostered by Saionji, the last of the *genrō*, who hoped to protect the throne from involvement in politics. But these met with only partial and temporary success. The next two cabinets, in office from May 1932 to March 1936, did include party men, but were headed by admirals, who were considered more moderate than certain potential prime ministers from the army.

A prime source of continued instability were the divisions within each of the power centers. Within the bureaucracies there was rivalry between ministries, as well as disagreement between conservative officials and technocrats who envisioned radical restructuring of state and society.

The military, too, was divided. The army and navy frequently clashed, and the breakdown in discipline during the actions in Manchuria and the violence at home reflected disunity in the army itself. The lines of army factionalism were complex: for example, there was a division between those who had studied at the Central War College and those who had attended officers' training school. However, two main groups stood out. The more extreme faction, led by Generals Araki

Sadao (1877–1966) and Mazaki Jinzaburō (1876–1956), was known as the Kōdōha or "Imperial Way faction," because it emphasized the imperial mystique and advocated an ill-defined doctrine of direct imperial rule. Like the radical civilian theorists of the right, it opposed existing political and economic institutions, and sought a moral and spiritual transformation that would assure a glorious future for both army and country. In contrast, the Tōseiha, or "Control faction," led by General Nagata Tetsuzan (1884–1935), the leading proponent of total war, and including Ishiwara and Tōjō Hideki, gave priority to the long-range buildup of the economy and the transformation of Japan into a modern military state.

For a few years the advantage lay with the Imperial Way faction, but it suffered a setback in 1935 when General Mazaki was dismissed from his post as director-general of military education. A lieutenant-colonel retaliated by assassinating General Nagata. The Control faction responded by arresting the officer and laying plans for the transfer of other firebrands to Manchuria. The lieutenant colonel's trial was still in progress when, on February 26, 1936, a group of junior Kōdōha officers, commanding over a thousand men, seized the center of the capital and killed a number of prominent leaders, although some of their intended victims, including the prime minister, Admiral Okada Keisuke (1868–1952), managed to elude them. The young officers hoped that their action would bring down the old system and that generals Araki and Mazaki would take the lead in restructuring the state, but these senior generals remained aloof. As in 1928, the emperor intervened, and the navy responded to the crisis with vigor. On the third day of the insurrection, the rebels surrendered. This time the leaders were tried rapidly and in secret. One of those who perished at the hands of a firing squad was Kita Ikki, who had not participated in the mutiny, but was too closely associated with the young officers and their movement to escape punishment.

The elimination of the Imperial Way faction actually increased the army's political power because it could now threaten a second mutiny if it did not get its way. The army still had to consider the wishes of other components of the power elite, but was able to secure a substantial increase in military spending. Japan now withdrew from the naval limitation agreement, opening the possibility that it might have to confront the combined might of the Western powers and the U.S.S.R. The army's strategic planners thought primarily in terms of a war with the latter, thus providing a strong inducement for Japan to sign an anti-Cominterm Pact with Hitler's Germany in December 1936.

Domestically, there ensued an intensification of propaganda and indoctrination, coupled with a continuation of repression directed at the radical left and those whose ardor for emperor and national polity *(kokutai)* was deemed insufficient. The most notorious case took place in 1935 when Minobe Tatsukichi, the distinguished legal theorist, was charged with demeaning the emperor by considering him merely "the highest organ of the state." Minobe defended himself with spirit, but was forced to resign from the House of Peers. Even so, in 1936, while living in seclusion, the old man suffered an attempt on his life that left him wounded. By that time, his books had been banned. Censorship became more severe, and expressions of intense national chauvinism filled the media.

The abandonment of the gold standard and the military buildup stimulated the economy and enabled Japan to recover from the depth of the depression, but agriculture remained depressed, and small firms benefited much less than did the *zaibatsu*.

China: The Nanjing Decade— an Uneasy Peace

From 1927 to 1937, the Nationalist government in Nanjing avoided war with Japan, but these were hardly peaceful. years. Even after the completion of the Northern Expedition in 1928, the government actually controlled only the lower Yangzi Valley. Elsewhere it was dependent on the unreliable allegiance of local powerholders. In 1930 the government secured its authority in the North after waging a costly campaign with heavy casualties against the combined armies of two warlords. Nanjing was strengthened by this victory, but still lacked the power to subdue the remaining warlords once and for all. That some of these could claim to stand for national goals reinforced the Nationalists strong tendency to give highest priority to building military strength, even before Japan's seizure of Manchuria and the threat of further Japanese aggression made such a policy imperative.

At home, the Nanjing regime had to deal with warlords and Communists. The government's policy toward the warlords was to temporize, try to prevent the formation of antigovernment warlord coalitions, and to settle for expressions of allegiance until it could establish central control. Its power and prestige were increased when it defeated a rebellion in Fujian in 1933–1934, and especially after it obtained control over Guangdong and the submission of Guangxi in 1936. Its campaigns against the Communists provided occasions for the dispatch of central government troops into warlord provinces, especially after the Communists began their Long March in 1934 (see below), and similarly the Japanese threat proved useful in eventually bringing certain warlords into line. Thus the trend favored Nanjing, but the actual balance between central and local power varied widely in different parts of China. The tenacity of the warlord phenomenon in certain regions is illustrated by Sichuan, in parts of which warlords remained powerful even after the Nationalists moved their wartime capital to that province. Similarly, Xinjiang, in the far west, remained virtually autonomous.

The Nanjing Decade—Domestic Policies

The regime's military emphasis was reflected in government spending, with 60 to 80 percent of the annual outlay going to military expenses and debt service. The latter amounted to about a third, reflecting heavy government borrowing, but military considerations were also paramount in such civil projects as road and railway construction. Taking the place of the ousted Russian military advisors were a series of German military men, who tried to introduce German military doctrines (including concepts of military organization not necessarily suitable to the Chinese situation) and helped arrange for the import of German arms and munitions. In 1935, at the height of their influence, there were seventy German advisors in China, but their number decreased after Germany and Japan signed the anti-Comintern pact in December 1936. The last were recalled in 1938. Noteworthy within the army were the graduates of the Whampoa Military Academy, particularly those who completed the course during Chiang Kai-shek's tenure as director, for they enjoyed an especially close relationship with their supreme commander.

It was Whampoa graduates who, during 1931, formed the Blue Shirts, a secret police group pledged to complete obedience to Chiang Kai-shek. They and the so-called CC clique (led by two Chen brothers trusted by Chiang) were influenced in ideology and organization by European fascism. The Blue Shirts were greatly feared because of their spying and terrorist activities, including assassinations. The CC clique, too, had considerable power, but failed in its prime aim, which was to revitalize the Guomindang. After the split with the Communists in 1927, the Guomindang purged many of its own most dedicated revolutionaries. One result was that young activists, often from the same modern schools that had earlier supplied recruits for the Guomindang, were drawn to the Communist party. Another result was the creation within the ruling party of an atmosphere attractive to careerists who, concentrating on their own personal advancement, were disinclined to rock the boat. Meanwhile, Chiang saw to it that the party remained just one of several centers of power.

The deterioration of the party was a particularly serious matter, because the Nanjing government suffered from factional politics and favoritism as well as from bureaucratic overorganization, which spawned departments with overlapping functions and countless committees grinding out lengthy reports and recommendations, detailing programs that consumed vast quantities of paper but were rarely implemented. Coordination was poor. It sometimes happened, for example, that government censors suppressed news items deliberately issued by the government itself. The conduct of official business lumbered along unless quickened by the personal intervention of Chiang Kai-shek, whose power was steadily on the increase. His power was based on the loyalty of the military, the Blue Shirts, and core partisans such as the CC clique, the financial backing of bankers and businessmen (including the relatives of Chiang's wife), and on Chiang's manipulation of various political cliques and factions. The Soong family deserves special mention, for it included not only Sun Yat-sen's widow, who was politically inactive during the thirties, but also the decidedly active wife of Chiang Kai-shek, another sister who married the notoriously corrupt H. H. Kung, and T. V. Soong, a brother who was a reformist finance minister. Chiang was indispensable, but lacked the charisma to inspire his officials, who feared rather than loved him. Nor did he have the gift of eloquence with which to rouse the people had he so desired. Negative sanctions, such as the executions sporadically ordered by Chiang when an exceptionally flagrant case of corruption was brought to his attention, were not enough: the regime lacked drive and direction.

The regime was also weak ideologically. Sun Yat-sen became the object of an official cult, but his ideas were not further refined or developed. Nor was political tutelage enacted. Instead, emphasis was shifted toward a revival of Confucianism. In contrast to Sun's admiration for the Taipings, Chiang sought to emulate Zeng Guofan, who in his day had crushed the Taipings by revitalizing Confucian values. Chiang's regard for Confucius and Zeng was already apparent during his days at Whampoa, but became even more obvious in 1934 when he launched an extensive program to foster traditional values known as the New Life Movement. He exhorted the populace to observe four vaguely defined Confucian virtues and spelled out the criteria for proper behavior in detailed instructions. The people were to sit and stand straight, eat quietly, refrain from indiscriminate spitting, and so forth, in the hope that they would thus acquire discipline. It did not work. Officials and commoners continued to act much as before. The government never did devise an ideology able to arouse the enthusiasm of its own personnel, command the respect of the people, or convince intellectuals. Censorship clearly was not the answer, although even foreign correspondents were subjected to it, some complaining that China was worse than Japan.

Local government under the Nationalists was equally ineffective. They restructured county government and established four bureaus charged with education, construction, public security, and finance, and even attempted to reach down below that level by assigning officials to the wards into which they divided the counties; but they failed to wrest control over taxes and local security from the entrenched local elite, who, in practice, continued to wield actual power. Like its predecessors, the Nanjing regime failed to mobilize the financial or human resources of the village. With income from land taxes remaining in the provinces, the government was financed primarily from the modern sector.

Despite early links with the business community, the Guomindang tended to treat business as a source to be exploited for revenue rather than as an asset to be fostered as a component of national strength. During 1928 and 1929, China at long last regained the tariff autonomy lost in the Opium War, but this was of little help to China's industries, because exports were subjected to the same tariffs as imports, and imported raw materials were taxed as heavily as were finished goods. In 1933, heavily in debt to the banks, the government took control of the banking system in a move that benefited the treasury but not the private sector. Overall, the modern sector grew during the first ten years of Nationalist rule, but only at roughly the same pace as during the years between the fall of the Qing and the establishment of the regime in Nanjing.

During the early thirties, the traditional agrarian sector of the economy, which accounted for most of China's production and employed the vast majority of its people, was afflicted by severe weather conditions, the exactions of the tax collector piling on surtax after surtax (later changed to special assessments), and the decline in commodity prices brought on by the Great Depression. Not only climate, but taxation and exposure to international markets varied widely, making generalization very risky. Even in provinces like Jiangsu and Zhejiang, firmly controlled by the government, taxes paid by one district often far exceeded those paid by another. When the international price of silk collapsed, peasants dependent on sericulture, such as those of Wuxi County in Jiangsu, were badly hurt. Parts of the north were no better off. Statistics for parts of northern China indicate that by 1934–1935 nearly half of the peasant households were farming less than ten mu (1 mu = .167 acres), when fifteen were needed for subsistence, reflecting a deepening agrarian crisis. Everywhere, since the government did nothing to change the status quo in the villages or on the land, the poorest and the weakest suffered most. Like so much legislation promulgated during those years, a law passed in 1930 limiting rents to 37.5 percent of the harvest was not enforced. Payments of 50 percent were common and 60 percent was not unusual. Programs for developing cooperatives and fostering rural reconstruction were organized, but their benefits rarely filtered down to the rural poor. In 1937 there was a price recovery, and harvests were good, but by that time millions had suffered bitter poverty and despair.

Chiang Kai-shek and his supporters wanted to unify the country and stabilize society. They wished to consolidate the revolution that had brought them into power, not expand it. Consequently, they put a premium on suppressing forces pushing for continued revolution, and were intent on destroying the Communists, who maintained that the revolution was unfinished and proclaimed their determination to lead it to completion. To Chiang Kai-shek nothing was more urgent than the elimination, once and for all, of his old enemies. For the C.C.P., too, these were crucial years.

The Chinese Communists, 1927–1934

The Shanghai massacre and the subsequent suppression of the C.C.P. and its associated labor movement effectively eliminated the party as an urban force, altered its geographical distribution, and profoundly affected its strategy and leadership. For some years it remained unclear just what direction it would take. Neither the Comintern in Moscow nor its Chinese followers were willing simply to write off the cities. Urban insurrection was tried but failed: the Canton Commune (December 1927), met with profound popular apathy and lasted only four days. The use of armed force to capture cities such as Changsha in Hunan in 1930 also failed. Although no one was ready to say so, at least in public, Moscow clearly did not have the formula for success. Meanwhile, in China various groups and factions contended for power and the adoption of their policies.

One of these groups was the C.C.P. military force, reorganized in the mountains on the Hunan-Jiangxi border, where, in the spring of 1928, Zhu De (1886–1976) joined Mao Zedong, who had arrived the previous fall. In command of some 2,000 troops, the two men laid the groundwork for the Red Army, with Zhu in military command and Mao in charge of political organization and indoctrination. As Mao was to say in 1938, "Political power grows out of the barrel of a gun. Our principle is that the Party commands the gun; the gun shall never be allowed to command the Party."[2] Through indoctrination, the recruitment of soldiers into the party, and the formation of soldiers' committees, Mao secured the control of the party over the army. On the military side, Zhu and Mao empha-

sized guerrilla warfare, which put a premium on mobility and surprise, rapid retreats to avoid battle with superior enemy forces, lightning strikes to pick off small
contingents of the enemy, and constant harassment to keep the enemy off balance. Essential to this type of warfare is popular support to provide intelligence,
supplies, and recruits, as well as cover for guerrillas under enemy pursuit. Peasant
participation and support were secured by redistributing land and furthering the
revolution in the countryside.

This strategy focused on the development and expansion of rural C.C.P.-
controlled bases. In the early thirties there were a number of such areas, with the
largest in Jiangxi, where the founding of the Chinese Soviet Republic was proclaimed in December 1931. The basic agrarian policy was "land to the tiller," involving the confiscation of large holdings for reassignment to the poor, with "middle peasants" left largely unaffected. But there was a good deal of disagreement
over definitions, as well as wide variations in the degree of local implementation of
the program. In Jiangxi, Mao and Zhu were strong, but they had by no means
won complete acceptance of either their program or their leadership, even after
party headquarters were moved from Shanghai to Jiangxi in recognition of the
new C.C.P. power center, a defeat for those oriented toward the Comintern in
Moscow. Factionalism continued to threaten party unity, but the most severe challenge was external.

Chiang Kai-shek's first three "annihilation campaigns," 1930–1931, helped
strengthen rather than weaken the C.C.P., as the Red Army employed its tactics
to good effect, capturing weapons, men, and land. The fourth campaign,
1932–1933, again ended in defeat for the Nationalists. In the fifth campaign,
begun late in 1933, Chiang, on German advice, changed his strategy. Deploying
some 750,000 men supported by 150 airplanes, he surrounded the Jiangxi Soviet
and gradually tightened the circle of his blockade. When, in the fall of 1934, their
situation became untenable, the Communist forces abandoned their base, broke
through a point in the blockade manned by former warlord armies, and began
their Long March (see Figure 13.1).

The Long March

When the Communists left Jiangxi, their first priority was survival, their destination unclear. That was settled in January 1935 in an important conference
held at Zunyi in Guizhou, where it was decided to proceed to Shaanxi, where a
small soviet was already in place. In Shaanxi the C.C.P. would be out of easy reach
of Guomindang armies. They would be able to act on their declaration of war
against Japan and might even hope for some aid from the U.S.S.R. At Zunyi, Mao
gained a new prominence, although he did not actually control the party until the
forties.

The march itself was a heroic vindication of Mao's belief in the power of
human will and determination. In just over a year, the marchers covered some
6,000 miles, traversing snow-covered mountain passes where they froze in their

FIGURE 13.1   China, 1930—Spring 1944. The Long March.

thin clothes and crossing treacherous bogs and marshes. To the hardships provided by nature was added the hostility of man, for there was rarely a day without some fighting. At one point they had no alternative but to cross a mountain torrent spanned by a thirteen-chain suspension bridge from which the enemy, armed and waiting on the other side, had removed the planks.

The six- or seven-day crossing of grasslands in the Chinese-Tibetan border region was a terrible ordeal. Here heavy rainfall and poor drainage had created a waterlogged plain on which green grass grew on multiple layers of rotting grass beneath. First a vanguard was sent to chart the way, and in the central grasslands they could find no place dry enough to sleep, so the marchers had to remain standing all night long, leaning against each other. The rest of the army followed through the slippery, treacherous terrain, trudging on despite hunger and fatigue, trying to ward off rain and hail and survive the unbearable cold of the nights. Since the men and women carried only a very small amount of grain, they subsisted mostly on wild grasses and vegetables eaten raw because there was no firewood for cooking. Sometimes the vegetables turned out to be poisonous, and the stagnant water reportedly smelled of horse's urine.

The marchers succeeded in overcoming this and other obstacles. Some of the women even gave birth. But many perished. Of about 100,000 who set out from Jiangxi, less than 10% completed the march. Some were left behind to work in various areas, but many more perished. The loss was only partially offset by new recruits who joined along the way. After completion of the march, including those already in Shaanxi, the Communists, led from Mao's headquarters in the caves of Yan'an, were about 20,000 strong.

The survivors of the march emerged toughened and filled with a sense of solidarity forged by shared hardships. There was also a heightened self-confidence, a conviction that the movement would surmount all obstacles. Something of this spirit is conveyed in a poem Mao wrote shortly before reaching Shaanxi:

> Lofty the sky
> and pale the clouds—
> We watch the wild geese
> south till they vanish.
>
> We count the thousand
> leagues already travelled.
> If we do not reach
> the Great Wall we are not true men.
>
> High on the crest
> of Liupan Mountain
> Our banners billow
> in the west wind.
>
> Today we hold
> a long rope in our hands.
> When shall we put bonds
> upon the grey dragon?

The saga of the Long March remained a source of heroic inspiration for decades. The last veteran of the March did not leave the stage until the death of Deng Xiaoping in 1997.

United Front and War

With the Communists in Shaanxi, Chiang remained as determined as ever to crush them, but their call for a united front against Japan had special appeal for the troops of Marshal Zhang Xueliang, who had been ordered to end resistance against the Japanese in Manchuria in 1931 and move south with his armies to Xian. Zhang's forces were less than enthusiastic in fighting the C.C.P. To breathe life into the anti-Communist campaign, Chiang Kai-shek flew to Xian in December, 1936. But he had misjudged the situation. Instead of pledging themselves to renewed anti-Communist efforts, Marshal Zhang and some of his men seized Chiang and held him prisoner for two weeks while his fate was negotiated. Exactly what transpired is not clear, but the C.C.P., agreeing with Stalin's policy of forming a worldwide united front against fascism, intervened with Marshal Zhang. Chiang was finally released after agreeing to terminate his campaign against Yan'an and lead a united front against Japan. He was at the time China's most distinguished military man, the leader of the government recognized as legitimate at home and abroad, the heir to the mantle of Sun Yat-sen. Even his enemies saw him as the only man possessing the political, military, and ideological authority to lead China in an effort to stop the Japanese.

Following Chiang's 1936 success against Guangdong and Guangxi, the formation of the Chinese united front in 1937 dismayed Japanese army officers intent on dominating China. Ever since 1933 there had been a constant danger that an unplanned military incident might escalate into a major war. This is, in effect, what happened when the Chinese held firm and refused further concessions following a clash between Chinese and Japanese soldiers on the Marco Polo Bridge outside Beijing in July 1937. Thus began the second Sino-Japanese war that in 1941 merged into the Second World War, although this is not what Japan intended in 1937.

The fighting went badly for the Chinese. By the end of July the Japanese were in possession of Beijing and Tianjin, and in August Japanese forces attacked Shanghai, the main source of Nationalist revenue. Here Chiang used some of his best German-trained troops in three months of heroic and bloody fighting with very heavy casualties. After Shanghai fell, the Chinese retreated in disarray, failed to take a stand at Wuxi as planned, but poured into Nanjing, which fell in December. The Nanjing Massacre followed. Japanese soldiers, backed by their superiors, went on a rampage, terrorizing people, killing and raping, burning and looting for seven weeks. Sixty years later the number of people who perished remains a matter of bitter contention—as though sheer numbers can measure the horror. The figure inscribed in the memorial erected in Nanjing (1985) is 300,000, but "whether 200,000 or 240,000 people were killed does not alter the dimension of the horror."[3] How and why it happened, and the lessons to be drawn therefrom continue to generate intense controversy and stimulate reflection. The Japanese acquired a reputation for terrible cruelty, which stiffened the Chinese determination to resist and continued to cast a pall long after the war.

After Nanjing the Japanese maintained and continued their offense, taking Canton in October and Wuhan in December, while Chiang, refusing to submit, adopted a strategy of trading space for time." As the war escalated, so did the Japanese government's aims and rhetoric. What had begun as a search for a pro-Japanese North China turned into a holy crusade against the West and Communism. In 1938, unable to obtain Chinese recognition of Manchukuo, the government of Prime Minister Prince Konoe Fumimaro (1891–1945) declared Chiang's regime illegitimate, and vowed to destroy it. In November Konoe proclaimed Japan's determination to establish a "New Order in East Asia" to include Japan, Manchukuo, and China in a political, economic, and cultural union, a bastion against (Western) imperialism and against Soviet Communism. Those who did not see the light were to be brought to their senses by force. Originally, in the summer of 1937, Japanese plans had called for a three-month campaign by three divisions, at a cost of 100 million yen, to destroy the main Chinese force and take possession of key areas while waiting for Chiang to ask for peace. But by the following spring they were preparing orders for twenty divisions, and had appropriated over 2.5 billion yen with promise of more to come and no end in sight.

The Nationalist government moved its wartime capital to Chongqing in Sichuan. Many refugees followed the government to the southwest (see Figure 13.2). Not only universities but hundreds of factories were transported piecemeal to help the war effort in Chongqing, where Chiang held on gamely. Before the Japanese attack on Pearl Harbor (December 1941), China obtained financial assistance from the U.S.A. and U.S.S.R., and Stalin sent some pilots stationed in Gansu Province. During 1939–1941 Chongqing suffered repeated bombings. Not until August 1941 did help come in the form of the Flying Tigers, volunteer American pilots later incorporated into the Fourteenth U.S. Air Force, commanded by General Claire L. Chennault. However, the West's support remained primarily moral, and the U.S.S.R. alone sent some official assistance. Meanwhile, during 1939–1941, fighting on the ground was limited to skirmishes, with both sides working to consolidate their positions.

In 1940 the Japanese established a puppet regime in Nanjing headed by Wang Jingwei, the erstwhile follower of Sun Yat-sen and leader of the left wing of the Guomindang. However, like a similar regime established earlier in Beijing, it was all too clear to the Chinese populace that the Japanese were pulling the strings.

FIGURE 13.2 *Refugees Crowding onto Trains Bound for Guilin,* Cai Dizhi. Chinese refugees escaping from Japanese-occupied territory followed the Chinese Nationalist government southwest to its temporary wartime capital in Chongqing. Scenes like this were common in 1937 to 1938. Woodcut.
FROM *WOODCUTS OF WARTIME CHINA, 1937–1945,* YONGHUA IINGXIN, ED. (TAIWAN: L. MING CULTURAL ENTERPRISES, DIST.).

Expansion of the War into a Pacific War

A major Japanese foreign policy concern during the thirties was relations with the U.S.S.R. During 1938–1939 there were several military clashes in the border area along Russia's frontier with Korea and Manchukuo. In these operations, quite large in scale and involving the deployment of armor, Japan was defeated. During 1937–1940 there were three military confrontations along the Russian frontier with Korea and, far more seriosuly, along the Mongolian border with Manchukuo. These operations, which increased in scale, involved the deployment of armor, artillery, and aircraft. The Japanese fought well, but the Soviets proved more than a match. The last and most severe conflict cost Japan 180,000 men and resulted in an armistice.

Japan was caught off guard diplomatically when Germany, without any warning, came to terms with the Soviet Union in August 1939. Japan was therefore neutral when the Second World War began in Europe shortly thereafter. However, the dramatic success of the German blitzkrieg strengthened the hands of those in Tokyo who favored a pro-German policy, and in September 1940, Konoe signed the Tripartite Pact, forming an alliance with Germany and Italy.

The Germans again surprised the Japanese in June 1941 when Hitler invaded Russia. Some army men wanted Japan to join the attack on the U.S.S.R. As Alvin D. Coox pointed out, they saw this as a way out of the China impasse, "apparently convinced that the best way to climb out of a hole was to widen it."[4] However, the navy wanted to advance into the oil- and mineral-rich south. Officially, Japan claimed its mission to be the creation of a "Greater East Asian Co-Prosperity Sphere," but the underlying perception was that the resources of Southeast Asia were essential for Japan's economic security.

Konoe hoped that, armed with the Tripartite Pact, he would be able to reach his aims without going to war with the United States, but the American government was becoming increasingly alarmed over Japanese expansion. When in the summer of 1941 Japan moved troops into southern Vietnam, the United States, Britain, and Holland (then in control of the East Indies, modern Indonesia) retaliated by applying the economic sanctions they had withheld in 1931. An embargo on scrap iron was serious, but the crucial product cut off from Japan was oil. America and Japan were on a collision course. To quote Michael Barnhart, "The Japanese Empire was determined to retain the rights and privileges it considered necessary for its economic and political security. The United States thought these rights and privileges contrary to its own deeply held principles and to the survival of what were now in effect its allies in the struggle against global aggression."[5] The United States was determined that Japan should withdraw from China as well as Indochina. For Japan, this would have meant a reversal of the policy pursued in China since 1931, and the relinquishment of the vision of primacy in East Asia. Dependent on oil and rubber from Southeast Asia, the Japanese were in no position to carry on protracted negotiations. They had to fight or retreat. It is a bitter irony that Japan now prepared to go to war to attain the self-sufficiency that its proponents of total war had once considered a precondition for war.

When it became clear to Konoe that the situation had reached an impasse, he resigned, to be followed by General Tōjō Hideki (1884–1948), prime minister from October 1941 to July 1944. When last-minute negotiations proved fruitless, the Japanese decided on war as the least unpalatable alternative. It began on December 7, 1941, with a surprise attack on Pearl Harbor, in Hawaii, that destroyed 7 American battleships and 120 aircraft, and left 2,400 dead. With the United States and Japan at war, Hitler, too, declared war against the United States, but German-Japanese cooperation during the war remained limited.

The Course of the War

At first the war went spectacularly well for Japan. By the middle of 1942 Japan controlled the Philippines, Malaya, Burma, and the East Indies. Japan was also in charge in Indochina (officially under the jurisdiction of Vichy France), and enjoyed the cooperation of a friendly regime in Thailand. However, contrary to hopes in Tokyo, the United States, far from being ready to negotiate a quick peace, mobilized for full-scale war.

In June 1942 Japan suffered a major defeat when it was checked at the battle of Midway, 1,200 miles northwest of Hawaii (see Figure 13.3). The Americans, taking advantage of advance knowledge of Japanese movements obtained from breaking the Japanese secret code, destroyed many Japanese planes and sank four Japanese aircraft carriers while losing only one of their own. Three more years of intense warfare, including bloody hand-to-hand combat, lay ahead, but the American use of aircraft carriers and the extensive deployment of submarines, which took a tremendous toll of vital Japanese shipping, were two of the factors contributing to Japan's ultimate defeat. Another was the island-hopping strategy whereby the American forces seized islands selectively for use as bases for further advances, bypassing others with their forces intact but out of action. One consequence of this strategy was that while the Allies wanted Japan to remain bogged down in China, China itself was not a major war theater.

China at War

The conviction that eventually the United States would enter the war sustained Chiang Kai-shek during the long years when China faced Japan virtually alone. When, after Pearl Harbor, this did happen, it buoyed the spirit of the Chinese, now allied to the one country powerful enough to crush Japan. More material forms of support were soon forthcoming, although there was never enough, because in 1942 Japan cut off Chongqing's last land route to its allies by seizing Burma and closing the Burma Road. Thereafter, supplies had to be flown in from India to Yunnan over the Himalayas (the "hump"). In addition, China ranked low in the American war effort. The Allies decided first to concentrate on the defeat of Germany, and the island-hopping strategy adopted against Japan largely bypassed

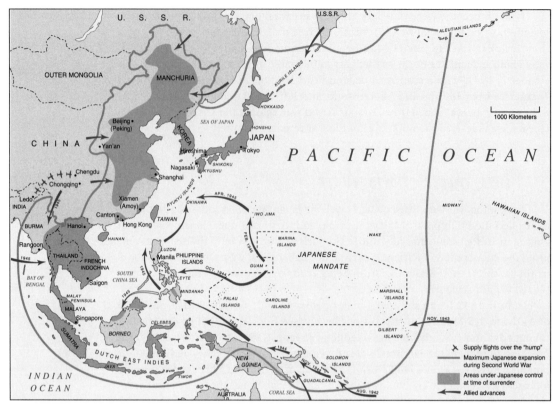

FIGURE 13.3   The Pacific War.

China, although the Allies appreciated the fact that China tied down vast numbers of Japanese troops that otherwise might have been used elsewhere (see Figure 13.3).

The top American military man in China was General Joseph Stilwell, who in 1942 became Chiang's chief-of-staff as well as commander of American forces in the China-Burma-India theater. Stilwell was a fine soldier. Chennault disregarded his warnings against building airbases unprotected by ground troops, bases from which, in early summer 1944, heavy bombers attacked industrial facilities in Kyushu and Manchukuo, airfields in Taiwan, and oil refineries in Sumatra. However, Stilwell was proven right when later that summer Japan launched their Ichigo (Number One) campaign into Hunan and Guangxi and captured the airfields. A heavy blow for the GMD, it proved a hollow victory for the Japanese.

Stilwell had high regard for the ordinary Chinese fighting man, but scarcely concealed his irritation and impatience with the inefficiencies and corruption he encountered in Chongqing, and his disgust at Chiang's policy of preparing for a postwar showdown with the C.C.P. rather than joining in a single-minded effort against the Japanese enemy. The relationship between the two men deteriorated until Chiang requested and received Stilwell's recall in 1944.

Stilwell was replaced by General Albert Wedemeyer, who was more friendly to Chiang but equally critical of conditions in the Chinese army, which were, by all accounts, horrendous. Induction was tantamount to a death sentence. Those who could possibly afford to do so bribed the conscription officer. The remainder were marched off, bound together with ropes, to join their units, often many miles and days away. Underfed and exhausted, many never completed the trip. Those who did found that food was equally scarce at the front and medical services almost completely lacking.

Misery and corruption were not unique to the military. Even in times of famine (as in Henan during 1942–1943) peasants were sorely oppressed by the demands of the landlord and the tax collector, while the urban middle class suffered from mounting inflation, which had reached an annual rate of 40 to 50 percent between 1937 and 1939, climbed to 160 percent for 1939–1942, and mounted to an average of 300 percent for 1942–1945. By 1943 the purchasing power of the salaries paid to bureaucrats was only one-tenth what it had been in 1937, while teachers were down to 5 percent of their former earnings. The result was widespread demoralization of the military and civilian populations under Nationalist control. The secret police were unable to root out corruption. Government exhortations and the publication of Chiang Kai-shek's book *China's Destiny* (1943) failed to reinvigorate ideological commitment to the government and party.

A major reason for the wartime deterioration of the Guomindang was that Japan's seizure of the eastern seaboard and China's major cities deprived the Nationalists of the great business centers of eastern China (especially Shanghai). In Sichuan, they were dependent on the elements in society that were most resistant to change and reform. Moreover, Chiang, hoarding his strength for the coming showdown with the C.C.P., was unwilling to commit his troops to battle with the Japanese more than was absolutely necessary. As a consequence, he missed whatever opportunity existed for building a modern Chinese force with American assistance, and for translating anti-Japanese nationalism into support for his own regime.

The shortcomings of the Chongqing government were highlighted by the accomplishments of the Communists, headquartered in Yan'an (see Figure 13.4). From 1937 to 1945, the party expanded its membership from roughly 40,000 to over 1 million, and its troop strength increased tenfold to an estimated 900,000, not counting guerrillas and militiamen. Furthermore, the Communists enjoyed widespread peasant support in northern China, where they established themselves as the effective government in the countryside

FIGURE 13.4 Jiang Qing (left) and Mao Zedong in Yan'an, 1960. After the Long March and during the war, the Chinese Communist Party leaders lived and worked in the Yan'an caves.
REVOLUTIONARY WORKERS ONLINE.

behind the Japanese lines. The Japanese, concentrated in the cities and guarding their lines of supply, did not have the manpower to patrol the rural areas constantly and effectively.

In the areas nominally under Japanese control, the Communists skillfully pursued policies to fuse national resistance and social revolution. The key to their ultimate success was mass mobilization of the peasantry, but the mix of policies and the pace of change varied according to local conditions. Carefully avoiding premature class warfare, they frequently began by organizing the peasants to wage guerrilla war, enlisting support from the village elites for the war effort, and manipulating them into going along with rent and interest reduction. Building up their military power, they enlisted elite support even as they undermined elite power.

Crucial was the creation of new mass organizations led by poor peasant activists, who, freed from the exactions of landlords and given a voice in government, became enthusiastic supporters of the party and government. The peasant associations and local party branches took the lead in effecting changes in taxation and reducing rent and interest payments, thus destroying the economic foundations of the old system. Similarly, new energies were released by organizing women and young people in an attack on traditional family authority. Actual or potential rivals such as secret societies or bandits were attacked and eliminated. The twin lessons of nationalism and revolution were brought home to the people through indoctrination programs and a campaign to combat illiteracy, conveying new ideas to the peasantry even as they gained access to the written word, shattering the old monopoly on learning.

The Japanese patronized puppet armies and even tolerated trade with the Guomindang-controlled areas of China, but the Wang Jingwei regime was too obviously controlled by the Japanese ever to gain credibility. At best, life in occupied China went on as usual, but Japanese arrogance alienated many Chinese. Humane behavior on the part of some individuals was overshadowed by acts of cruelty that evoked Chinese hatred and resistance. An example is the notorious "kill all, burn all, destroy all" campaign carried out in 1941 and 1942 in parts of northern China in retaliation for a C.C.P. offensive. Implemented literally, the Japanese hurt the C.C.P. badly, but they also helped turn apolitical peasants into determined fighters.

The policies and record of the C.C.P. also helped to attract urban intellectuals. To insure discipline and preserve the cohesion of the movement, swollen by new adherents, the party under Mao (now firmly established as leader) organized a rectification campaign to assure "correct" understanding of party ideology and to bring art and literature into line. Art for its own sake or for self-expression was condemned, and those guilty of being insufficiently mass-oriented were induced to confess their faults. Many were sent to work in villages, factories, or battle zones to "learn from the masses."

From the war, the C.C.P. emerged stronger than it had ever been before. The outcome of the civil war that followed was by no means obvious to observers at the time, but it is one of the ironies of the war that the Japanese, who proclaimed that they were combating communism in China, instead contributed to its ultimate victory.

Japan at War

Well before Pearl Harbor, the effects of the continued war in China were felt by the Japanese people as militarization and authoritarianism increased at home. The National General Mobilization Law of 1938 strengthened the prime minister at the expense of the Diet, and the government began to place the economy on a war basis, with rationing, economic controls, and resource allocations administered by a technological and bureaucratic elite drawn from the most prestigious universities. Getting the various centers of economic and political power to pull together remained a problem, but a precedent was set for government to direct the economy, institutions for this were founded, and Japan gained a cadre of economic and social bureaucrats.

The war entailed a greater role for government not only in industry and commerce but also in agriculture. The war years were hard on rural landlords, already hurt by the depression, while ordinary tenant farmers benefited from measures to control inflation, such as rent control (1939), as well as government efforts to increase production by allocating fertilizer. In the last years of the war, the government paid much larger bonuses to farm operators than to noncultivating landlords, who emerged from the war much weakened. As Ann Waswo has shown, "in purely economic terms and in terms of local political influence, ordinary farmers made significant gains."[6] As ever, war proved a potent catalyst for change.

In October 1940, the political parties were merged into the Imperial Rule Assistance Association, which, however, did not become a mass popular party along the lines of European fascism, but served primarily as a vehicle for the dissemination of propaganda throughout Japan. Similarly, labor unions were combined into a single patriotic organization. Great pressures were exerted to bring educational institutions and the public communications media into line so that the whole of Japan would speak with one collective voice.

To effect the "spiritual mobilization" of the country, the government tried to purge Western influence from Japanese life. As one writer put it, "While the black ships that represent the material might of the West have left, a hundred years later the Black Ships of thought are still threatening us."[7] Prominent intellectuals insisted on Japanese uniqueness and exceptionalism, and drew on German concepts of irony and angst, nostalgia for the past, and the aesthetics of death, subjectivity, and poetry to attack the "modern" at home and abroad. Not only were foreign radical and liberal ideas banned from theoretical discourse, but popular culture was purged. Permanent waves and jazz, so popular during the twenties, were now banned. Efforts were made to remove Western loanwords from the language, and the people were bombarded with exhortations to observe traditional values and revere the divine emperor. Heterodox religious sects with no ostensible political agenda were suppressed, and in a "triumph of religious stateism"[8] all religions were subordinated to the imperial cult. To mobilize the public down to the ward level, the people were formed into small neighborhood organizations.

Colonial East Asia during the War

Japan's attempt to win over the population of the conquered areas by encouraging their native religious traditions, exploiting their resentment against Western imperialism, and teaching them the Japanese language was more than offset by Japan's own imperialistic exploitation, by the harshness of its rule, and by the cruelty of its soldiers. The slogan "Asia for the Asians" did not disguise the realities of what Mark R. Peattie has characterized as a "mutant colonialism." In his words, "the tightening demands on the energies, loyalties, and resources of Japan's colonial peoples by a nation at war with much of Asia and most of the West transmogrified an authoritarian but recognizably 'Western' colonial system into an empire of the lash, a totalitarian imperium, that dragged along its peoples as it staggered toward defeat."[9]

As indicated in Chapter 12, conditions were particularly harsh in Korea, but in Taiwan, too, there was a campaign to assimilate the population and turn them into people who spoke Japanese, had Japanese names, and even worshiped at Shinto shrines. Although Taiwanese were regimented and controlled at home, Taiwanese entrepreneurs took advantage of new opportunities in Manchuria and elsewhere, and young people responded positively to efforts to recruit them into the Japanese military. The largest contingent served on Hainan island, where many perished. However, on the whole, people in Taiwan as well as Korea welcomed Japan's defeat. When Nationalists forces arrived in October 1945, they were welcomed as liberators.

Japanese forces dominated Vietnam, although, until the fall of Vichy France in March 1945, they left the Vichy French colonial administration in place. The Japanese conducted a cultural campaign claiming that they had come as liberators from all European colonialism and seeking support especially among Buddhists, while the French encouraged and gave new freedoms to Catholics. Resisting both Japanese and French were the Viet Minh (short for Viet Nam Doc Lap Dong Minh or "League for the Independence of Vietnam"), established in the northwest by Ho Chi Minh when he returned to Vietnam in 1941. Viet Minh policy was to postpone the Marxist revolutionary agenda for the sake of forming a broad nationalist coalition and in the hope of gaining assistance from the Allies. Established in 1941, the policy resulted in Ho's cooperation with the American Office of Strategic Services in 1944. That the United States would support the reimposition of French colonialism was not yet apparent by war's end.

Elsewhere in Japan's bloated empire the colonial authorities were replaced by Japanese-controlled puppet regimes. The history of Southeast Asia is beyond the scope of our text, but we should note that while Japan won no friends, they shattered once and for all the myth as well as the actuality of Western hegemony and paved the way for the end of colonialism—ultimately throughout the globe.

The End of the War

The closer the American forces came to the Japanese homeland, the easier it was for them to bomb Japan itself. Such raids were aimed not only at military and industrial installations, but also at economic targets and population centers. Incendiary bombs were dropped in order to sap the morale of the people, who by the last years of the war, were suffering from scarcities of all kinds, including food and other daily necessities, many of which were available only on the black market.

In July 1944, after the fall of Saipan, largest of the Mariana Islands, General Tōjō was forced out of office, but there was no change, either in the fortunes of war or in policy, under his successor, General Koiso Kuniaki (1880–1950). Koiso remained in office until April 1945, when he was succeeded by Admiral Suzuki Kantarō (1867–1948). Some civilian leaders sent out peace feelers to the Allies, but their efforts were hampered by the noncooperation of the Soviet Union, anxious to have the war continue long enough to allow it to participate, and by the demand issued at Potsdam in July 1945, insisting on Japan's unconditional surrender. This demand reflected the Allied belief that it had been a mistake to allow the First World War to end in an armistice rather than in a full capitulation, permitting Hitler to claim that Germany had been "betrayed" into defeat, not beaten on the field of battle. Determined not to commit a similar mistake, the Allies now demanded an unconditional surrender, which stiffened the resistance of Japanese leaders concerned over the fate of the emperor.

The last year of the war was especially terrible; on one night in March 1945, some 100,000 people died as the result of a firebomb raid on Tokyo, and a similar raid in May devastated another large part of Japan's capital city. Meanwhile bombers created an "iron-storm" over Okinawa, sending local people to seek refuge in caves, where some would perish after Japanese soldiers forced them into "compulsory group suicide."[10] Short of resources, and with its cities in ruins, during the last months of the war Japan was reduced to desperate measures, such as the use of flying bombs directed by suicide pilots, called "kamikaze" after the "divine wind" that once had saved the land from the Mongols.

Tokyo and other major cities had been practically leveled by conventional bombing, but on August 6 the United States dropped an atomic bomb on Hiroshima (see Figure 13.5) in southwestern Honshu, razing over 80 percent of the buildings and leaving some 200,000 people dead or injured and countless others to continue their lives under the specter of radiation sickness. Two days later, on August 8, the U.S.S.R. entered the war, and the next day the United States dropped a second atomic bomb, this time on Nagasaki.

FIGURE 13.5 *Hiroshima.* Through the vault over the Memorial Cenotaph for the Atomic Bomb Victims can be seen the Atomic Bomb Memorial Dome. The steel skeleton of the dome and the gutted building (formerly the city's Industrial Promotion Hall) have been left standing unaltered, in witness to the tragedy.
PHOTOGRAPH © TIMEPIX (6032641).

Recent scholarship shows that all along the Emperor paid careful attention to the war without intervening in actual military operations. But now his throne was at stake. According to Edward J. Drea:

> In the face of total defeat, he valued the imperial institution more than his people, his army, and his empire. . . . Perhaps more than fire raids, atomic bombs, the Soviet entry into the war against Japan, and the specter of invasion, it was the threat to his imperial ancestors, and there-fore the survival of the imperial institution itself, that provided the steel otherwise missing from Hirohito's regal backbone.[11]

In any case, twice during these fateful days a government deadlock was bro-ken by the personal intervention of the emperor, each time in favor of peace. Even after the final decision for peace, diehards tried to continue the war by a last re-sort to violence in the tradition of the terrorists who had first helped steer Japan toward militarism and war. They set fire to the homes of the prime minister and president of the privy council and invaded the imperial palace in search of the recording of the emperor's peace message, but they failed. When all was lost, sev-eral leaders, including the war minister, committed ritual suicide.

On August 15, the imperial recording was broadcast over the radio, and throughout Japan the people, for the first time, heard the voice of their emperor.

In the formal language appropriate to his elevated status, he informed them that the war was lost. This is how Ōe Kenzaburō, the future winner of the Nobel Prize for literature, ten years old at the time, recollects the impact of the broadcast:

> The adults sat around their radios and cried. The children gathered outside in the dusty road and whispered their bewilderment. We were most confused and disappointed by the fact that the Emperor had spoken in a human voice, no different from any adult's. None of us understood what he was saying, but we had all heard his voice. One of my friends could even imitate it cleverly. Laughing, we surrounded him—a twelve-year-old in grimy shorts who spoke with the Emperor's voice. A minute later we felt afraid. We looked at one another; no one spoke. How could we believe that an august presence of such awful power had become an ordinary human voice on a designated summer day.[12]

Notes

1. The term "incantatory symbol" comes from Masao Maruyama, in Ivan Morris, ed., *Thought and Behavior in Modern Japanese Politics,* expanded edition (New York: Oxford Univ. Press, 1969), p. 376.

2. Stuart R. Schram, *The Political Thought of Mao Tse-tung* (New York: Frederick A. Praeger, 1963), p. 209.

3. Joshua A. Fogel, Introduction to *The Nanjing Massacre in History and Historiography,* ed. Joshua A. Fogel (Berkeley: Univ. of California Press, 2000), p. 6.

4. Alvin D. Coox, in Peter Duus, ed., *The Cambridge History of Japan,* vol. 6: *The Twentieth Century.* (Cambridge: Cambridge Univ. Press, 1988), p. 324.

5. Michael A. Barnhart, *Japan Prepares for Total War: The Search for Economic Security, 1919–1941* (Ithaca: Cornell Univ. Press, 1987), p. 234.

6. Ann Waswo in *The Cambridge History of Japan,* vol. 6, p. 104.

7. Kamei Katasuichiro, quoted in Kevin Michael Doak, *Dreams of Difference: The Japan Romantic School and the Crisis of Modernity* (Berkeley: Univ. of California Press, 1994), p. 101.

8. Sheldon Garon, *Molding Japanese Minds: The State in Everyday Life* (Princeton: Princeton Univ. Press, 1997), pp. 84–87.

9. Mark R. Peattie in *The Cambridge History.* vol. 6, p. 269. For "mutant colonialism," see p. 234.

10. Norma Field, *In the Realm of a Dying Emperor* (New York: Vintage Books, 1993), p. 61.

11. Edward J. Drea, *In the Service of the Emperor: Essays on the Imperial Japanese Army* (Lincoln: Univ. of Nebraska Press, 1998), p. 215.

12. Ōe Kenzaburō, *A Personal Matter,* trans. by John Nathan (New York: Grove Press, 1968), pp. vii–viii.

Part Four

East Asia in the Second Half of the Twentieth Century

Throughout East Asia, as across the globe, the Second World War was followed by a period of change unprecedented in its rapidity and scope, affecting the direction of civilization, economic systems and social structure, and the lives of millions of people. The war destroyed the Japanese Empire, confirmed the eclipse of the Western European powers begun by the First World War, and hastened the end of the old colonialism. In Asia, the British empire was dismantled as India and Burma attained independence (1947) followed by the Malay Peninsula (1957), leaving only Hong Kong as a Crown Colony—and it was scheduled to revert to Chinese rule in 1997. However, the Dutch in Indonesia and, especially, the French in Indochina resorted to military means in a futile attempt to preserve their colonies.

The war left only two superpowers, the United States and the Soviet Union, with the capacity to exercise major influence over events in East Asia. By 1947 they had developed a bitter rivalry and a "cold" war. To quote I. M. Roberts:

> Even if the Cold War stopped short of actual armed conflict between the two principals, subversion, bribery, murder, espionage, propaganda and diplomatic quarrelling long gave fresh colour to the basic premise, that it was impossible for communist and non-communist societies to cooperate and relate to one another in the way civilized societies had once believed to be normal*

As announced by President Truman in 1947, the American policy of "containment" was determined to prevent the extension not only of the U.S.S.R. but of Communism everywhere. All too often this policy was pursued without regard for local conditions, about which the American public and even policy makers were ill-informed.

*I. M. Roberts, *Twentieth Century: The History of the World, 1901–2000* (New York: Viking, 1999), p. 462.

14

The Aftermath of World War II

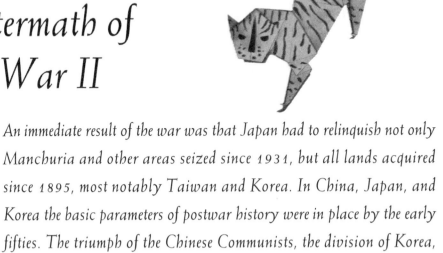

An immediate result of the war was that Japan had to relinquish not only Manchuria and other areas seized since 1931, but all lands acquired since 1895, most notably Taiwan and Korea. In China, Japan, and Korea the basic parameters of postwar history were in place by the early fifties. The triumph of the Chinese Communists, the division of Korea, and the remolding of Japan all occurred within those years. Only the future of Vietnam remained in doubt, but because this too had its immediate roots in the war and postwar periods, we have included it in this chapter.

I. China: Civil War and Communist Triumph, 1946–1949

1945　　　　　　　　　　　　　1949　　　　　　　　　　　　　　　　　1956

People's Republic of China

When Japan surrendered, Chiang Kai-shek, with American concurrence, directed Japan's generals in China to submit only to Nationalist forces. To enable the Guomindang armies to accept the Japanese surrender, the United States transported them by water and by air to those parts of the country then occupied by Japan. However, they were not allowed into Manchuria until January 1946. Manchuria had been occupied by the U.S.S.R. during the last days of the war, and the Soviets, intent on harvesting the Japanese military and industrial assets there, did not completely withdraw their troops until May 1946. By that time they had allowed the C.C.P. to gain substantial control of the Manchurian countryside. Chiang Kai-shek, determined to recover the territory where the Japanese had begun their aggression in 1931, disregarded American warnings against overextending his forces and dispatched almost half a million of his best troops to Manchuria.

During the year or so immediately after the war, the Nationalists appeared to have superior resources, at least on paper. Recognized as the legitimate government of China by all the Allies, including the Soviet Union, they had three or four times as many men under arms as their Communist rivals and enjoyed a similar advantage in armament. They were, therefore, in no mood to make concessions to the C.C.P. The Communists, on the other hand, had come through the war battle-hardened, with well-established support in the countryside, and high morale. Their leaders, too, were convinced that victory would ultimately be theirs in the coming struggle. It was against this background that in December 1945, President Truman sent General George C. Marshall to China to attempt to mediate between the two parties. Given their history of conflict, divergence of views, and confidence in their respective causes, the American initiative was probably doomed from the start. Marshall's efforts were also undercut by American support of the Nanjing government, even though President Truman stipulated that large-scale aid to China was contingent on a settlement. As during Mao's visit to Chongqing in August–October (see Figure 14.1), there was a show of cordiality, but the Marshall mission produced only a brief breathing spell before fighting broke out in earnest in mid-1946.

FIGURE 14.1   Mao Zedong (left) and Chiang Kai-shek exchange toasts at Chongqing during a welcoming party for Mao Zedong. August–October 1945.
© Bettmann/Corbis (BE046254).

Initially, until July 1947, the Guomindang armies enjoyed success, even capturing the wartime C.C.P. capital at Yan'an. However, these were hollow victories. Like the Japanese before them, in northern China and Manchuria the Guomindang controlled only the cities in the midst of a hostile countryside. Moreover, the military efficacy of the armies was undermined by the rivalries between their commanders, by Chiang Kai-shek's penchant for personal decision making even when he was far removed from the scene, and by his abiding concern to prevent any possible rival from amassing too much power. Also much in evidence were the harshness and corruption that had sapped the soldiers' morale during the war against Japan and were even more demoralizing now that they were supposed to fight fellow Chinese.

In other respects too, far from stimulating reform, the defeat of Japan resulted merely in the transfer to the rest of China of the ills that had been incubating in wartime Chongqing. A nation badly in need of political, economic, and social reconstruction was subjected to a heavy dose of autocracy and to a galloping inflation. Liberal reformers, disillusioned by the corruption and alarmed at the prospect of civil war, tried to rally the opposition. One leader of this non-Communist opposition to the Guomindang was Wen Yiduo (1899–1946), a professor at Qinghua University on its wartime campus in Kunming who tried to encourage those who hoped for a rebirth of democracy and greater freedom to criticize the government. However, the Guomindang responded to these calls for reform by assassinating the critics. In 1946, Guomindang agents assassinated Wen Yiduo himself just after he gave a fiery eulogy for one of his murdered colleagues. Wen's death shocked China and served to expose the depths to which the ruling group had sunk in its desperation to retain power.[1]

Intellectuals and students were not the only ones disenchanted with the regime, for many suffered from the arrogance of the Nationalist soldiers and the rapacity of those with political connections. The situation was particularly bad in Taiwan, where carpetbaggers from the mainland enriched themselves at the expense of alleged Taiwanese "collaborators"—a convenient charge against any uncooperative Taiwanese who had done well during the preceding half-century of Japanese rule. When the Taiwanese rioted in protest in 1947, the Nationalist government responded with brutal and bloody repression. The exact number of casualties is not known; however, Taiwanese leaders in exile claimed that over 10,000 were killed.

The government, inefficient as well as autocratic, proved unable to halt rapidly accelerating inflation that threatened all those whose incomes did not keep up with rising costs. Toward the end, people in the cities had to carry enormous bundles of paper money on their daily rounds of shopping for the necessities of life.

In the C.C.P. areas, in contrast, a disciplined and well-organized political and military leadership offered credible leadership. Unlike the Guomindang, which promised reform only after the fighting was finished, the C.C.P. implemented one change after another. A crucial and impressive demonstration of their expertise in mass mobilization took place in Manchuria, where they made the most of the window of opportunity granted them by the Soviet Union before it withdrew. Here, once their military presence was established, they were able in a mere eighteen months to transform indifferent, suspicious peasants into ardent participants in and supporters of the party and of the military campaigns directed by the brilliant general Lin Biao (1907–1971). Cooperation was secured by a mixture of hope and fear that varied with groups and individuals. Party cadres led a series of carefully orchestrated campaigns attacking and systematically displacing the old local elite that could no longer summon support from a provincial or regional elite undermined and compromised during the preceding fourteen years of Japanese rule. The campaigns culminated in land redistribution (see Figure 14.2), which revolutionized the local power structure.

The contrast between C.C.P. dynamism and Guomindang decay helps explain not only the outcome but also the unexpected rapidity of the course of events. The military turning point came in July 1947 when Communist armies attacked along several fronts in northern China. In Manchuria, Lin Biao commanded a campaign that put the Guomindang forces on the defensive and ended in October 1948 by completely routing them. During that same month and into November, the last great battle of the war was fought at the strategic city of Xuzhou on the Huai River where the Beijing-Nanjing Railway line joins the Longhai line that runs from Shaanxi to the sea. Around half a million men on each side were involved in this battle, generally known as the battle of Huai-Hai after the Huai River and the Longhai Railway. When it was all over, the Nationalists, under Chiang Kai-shek's personal command, had lost 200,000 men and no longer had any way to supply their forces to the north. In January 1949, Nationalist generals surrendered Beijing and Tianjin. Throughout the campaigns, the Communist army gained not only military advantages from its victories, but also captured valuable military equipment and supplies and increased its manpower

FIGURE 14.2 *Seizing the landlord and transporting his movable property. Dongbeizhibao,* October 9, 1947. Energized by the Chinese Communist Party's campaign for land redistribution, local populations reversed the traditional power structures.
FROM *ANVIL OF VICTORY: THE COMMUNIST REVOLUTION IN MANCHURIA, 1945–1948*, BY STEVEN LEVINE. COURTESY COLUMBIA UNIVERSITY PRESS.

as Nationalist soldiers defected or surrendered and were incorporated into the People's Liberation Army.

During 1949 the Communists continued their advance. They crossed the Yangzi in April, took Nanjing the same month, and were in control of Shanghai by the end of May. On October 1, Mao Zedong, in a great ceremony in Beijing, formally proclaimed the establishment of the People's Republic of China. There was still some fighting in the south, but clearly the C.C.P. had won control of the Chinese mainland. Meanwhile, Chiang Kai-shek and the Nationalists took refuge on Taiwan and vowed continued resistance.

The triumph of the Communists in 1949 began a new chapter in China's long history. It was the result of a long revolutionary process that had started well before the founding of the C.C.P., but in terms of the party's own programs and goals, the revolution had only just begun.

II. Japan: The Occupation, 1945–1952

1945

1952

1956

End of Occupation

The war left Japan in ruins, its cities largely destroyed, the economy wrecked. About forty percent of Japan's total urban area was wiped out, including 65% of residential housing in Tokyo, 57% in Osaka, and 89% in Nagoya, Japan's third largest city. At the time of the surrender there were nine million homeless. There was hunger, despair, psychic shock, and fear. In preparation for the arrival of the victors, the Japanese evacuated many women to the countryside and even the government ordered its female employees out of town. It is not difficult to imagine people's relief when such measures turned out to have been unnecessary.

Means and Ends

Officially, the Occupation was under the authority of the Far Eastern Commission, which sat in Washington. Its members included representatives of all the countries that had fought Japan, but actual control was in American hands. The Japanese government continued to function, but did so according to the directives and "suggestions" of the Occupation authorities, headed by General Douglas MacArthur, Supreme Commander for the Allied Powers (SCAP). Despite the "Allied Powers" in the title and the presence of some British and Commonwealth officials, the Occupation was essentially American. In MacArthur it had a leader who won easy credibility, a commanding figure, a "blue-eyed shogun," convinced of his historic mission, a military man who commanded respect, exuded confidence, and had a flair for drama. The process of policy formation was complex, involving Washington, the Occupation bureaucracy, and the Japanese, and reflecting divisions within as well as among these groups; but MacArthur had a strong hand in fashioning and interpreting as well as administering policy.

The Occupation's mission to demilitarize Japan and turn the country into a peaceful and democratic state was accepted with enthusiasm by a staff composed partly of New Dealers and by MacArthur himself, who regarded the Japanese as an immature people ready for and in need of tutelage. Despite or because of their lack of preparation, the Americans were convinced they had the answers, and their conviction of the righteousness of their values and policies remained firm, even after the onset of the Cold War induced them to change course.

At the outset, the Occupation faced the pressing tasks of disarming the Japanese military and providing enough relief to prevent famine. The widespread destruction of capital goods and industrial plants, a soil starved for lack of fertilizers, the loss of the natural resources from the former empire and of the entire merchant fleet, and the need to feed around six million Japanese expatriates and refugees from overseas threatened economic catastrophe. In this situation, suffering was unavoidable. By supplying food and medical supplies, the Occupation authorities helped to avert the worst, but the alternative to the black market was starvation. It was not until 1947 that the United States became seriously concerned with rebuilding the Japanese economy. Even in 1948 a magazine editorial complained, "in today's Japan, the only people who are not living illegally are those in jail."[2]

Demilitarization entailed the dismantling of the military establishment and a purge from positions of political and economic leadership of those most closely associated with leading the country to war. Outside of Japan—and excluding the U.S.S.R. and parts of China controlled by the C.C.P.—5,700 individuals were tried by 50 military tribunals with the result that 984 were sentenced to death, among them 173 Taiwanese and 148 Koreans. Twenty-eight top leaders charged with responsibility for the war were tried in Tokyo by an international tribunal of eleven judges that sat in Tokyo from May 1946 to April 1948 and included a Chinese, a Filipino, and an Indian jurist, but no Korean. When the sentences were handed down in November 1948, seven leaders were condemned to die, including Tōjō, the rather colorless general who had headed Japan's wartime government. His role during the war had been more like a chairman of the board than a dictator, but wartime propaganda had cast him as a Japanese Hitler. The lengthy judicial proceedings produced voluminous records, but never attained the legal clarity nor the moral authority achieved by the trial of Nazi leaders at Nuremberg.

In the end, around 200,000 persons were purged, about half of them from the military. However, most of these men were later reinstated, and some became very prominent. The military elite lost the most, but the decision of the Occupation to operate through, rather than replace, the existing government made for a high level of continuity within the bureaucracy. This contributed to the continuing importance of the bureaucracy even after a new constitution placed government on a new footing.

Although he had sanctioned a war fought in his name, the emperor was not charged with war crimes, nor was there a judicial inquiry into the part he had played. Instead SCAP's policy was to use the emperor's authority while demystifying his person and throne. He was pressured to substitute a more open lifestyle (akin to that of the British monarch) for the secluded and ritualized existence traditionally led by Japanese emperors. An example of the demystification process was the emperor's unprecedented visit to MacArthur at SCAP headquarters. The resulting photograph (Figure 14.3), showing the stiffly formal emperor standing next to the open-shirted general, caused considerable shock and dismay throughout Japan. In his New Year's message of 1946, the emperor publicly denied his divinity, and under the new constitution he became a symbol of the nation. For the remainder of his life he never acknowledged any responsibility for the war, setting an example not lost on his subjects.

This constitution, which went into effect in May 1947, was drafted and practically dictated by the Occupation. It stipulated that sovereignty belongs to the people, placed the highest political authority in the hands of the Diet (to which the executive was now made responsible), and established an independent judiciary.

Another noteworthy set of political changes were those decreasing the power of the central government, particularly the Home Ministry, and fostering local self-government. Accompanying these structural changes were provisions for universal suffrage and human rights, including the equality of women. A unique feature was the renunciation of war. Article IX stipulates, "The Japanese people forever renounce war as a sovereign right of the nation and the threat or use of force as a means of settling international disputes" and goes on to say, "land, sea, and air forces, as well as other war potential, will never be maintained."[3] In this way the authors of the constitution sought to incorporate peacefulness into the very framework of the new Japanese state.

Social Policies

The authorities at SCAP headquarters knew that Japan could not be turned into a democracy simply by changing the political system. Consequently, they tried to change Japanese society itself. Since many American officials lacked previous study or experience in Japan, they tended to rely excessively on American prototypes without taking into sufficient account Japan's own experience and situation. Thus they restructured the educational system to conform to the American sequence of elementary school, junior high school, high school, and college, and forced the Japanese to eliminate their old technical schools and special higher schools, which previously covered the eleventh to thirteenth years of education and prepared students for university study. Under the old system, only the student elite had access to a university education, but under the new, all students were to be given equal educational opportunities through high school. In an effort to expand opportunities for higher education, many of the old technical and higher schools were upgraded to become universities. But these new universities were not of a quality comparable to the old established schools like Tokyo University. Competition for admission to this and other prestigious universities remained brutal. Students found themselves embroiled in a veritable "examination hell."

In order to reform the content of education, the Occupation abolished the old ethics courses and purged textbooks fostering militaristic and authoritarian values. Its attack on these old values was rather successful, especially since they

FIGURE 14.3   General Douglas MacArthur, Supreme Commander for the Allied Powers (SCAP) occupation forces, and Emperor Hirohito of Japan, soon to publicly deny his divinity.

© AP/WIDEWORLD PHOTOS (APA5163982).

had already been largely discredited by defeat. Similarly, language reform found ready acceptance: the list of standard characters, many of them simplified, issued by the cabinet in 1946 (1,850 *tōyō kanji*) required only minor modifications and additions when revised in 1981 (the current system of 1,945 *joyō kanji*).

The Occupation was rather less successful in its attempts to create a positive sense of individual civic responsibility and citizenship. Social change entails a transformation of values, and thus naturally takes longer than institutional change, but changes in the legal system can encourage social change. Among the Occupation's notable efforts in this direction were measures to enhance the status of women and limit the powers and privileges of the family's male head. The new constitution stated explicitly in Article XXIV, "Marriage shall be based upon the mutual consent of both sexes, and it shall be maintained through mutual cooperation, with equal rights of husband and wife as a basis." The presence of many thousands of Americans in their country also gave the Japanese an unusual opportunity to observe foreign mores. It may have encouraged them to become somewhat more relaxed toward authority, and also stimulated a measure of cosmopolitanism.

Economic Policy

It was generally recognized that the desired political and social changes demanded an economic foundation, and the authorities set about restructuring the Japanese economy. Most successful in this respect was the program of land reform. This prohibited absentee landlordism and restricted the amount of land a resident landowner could hold to a maximum of seven acres to work himself and another two acres to rent out (except in Hokkaido, where the average farm was twelve acres, because the climate precludes intensive rice cultivation). Anything in excess had to be sold to the government, which resold it to former tenants. There was provision for compensation for the landlords, but inflation made this meaningless. The old inequity in the countryside was eliminated. In terms of productivity, too, the land policy was a success, for the agrarian sector was the first to recover.

In the urban industrial sector, the Occupation began by trying to eliminate, or at least reduce, the concentrations of economic power, which Americans viewed as a major component of Japanese authoritarianism. One policy was to foster labor unions. The constitution guaranteed the right of workers to organize and to bargain and act collectively. As intended, a vigorous union movement developed, but contrary to American wishes, the Japanese unions did not, like the American AFL and CIO, limit themselves to economic demands. Much like European unions, they were political in orientation, developing into labor arms of the Socialist and Communist parties. In February 1947, the Occupation banned a planned general strike, and thereafter was less friendly toward the unions. Laws prohibiting public employees from striking followed.

On the management and ownership side, the Occupation did break up the old holding companies and purged the old *zaibatsu* families from positions of economic leadership. Contrary to initial expectations, however, this did not lead to genuine decentralization. Where old systems were broken up, new and equally pervasive patterns of trade and finance developed, bearing a marked resemblance to the old. Furthermore, a plan to break up operating companies petered out: of 1,200 companies initially considered, only 28 were, in the end, broken up. Economic power and decision making remained concentrated. The reasons for this are instructive for understanding the accomplishments and failures of the Occupation as a whole, for they include both a Japanese and an American component.

On the Japanese side, strong support for land reform contrasted with a marked lack of enthusiasm for American-style trust busting. Few shared the American faith in the ultimate benefits of maximum competition. Instead, the feeling was that Japanese companies needed to be large in order to compete in the international market. Radicals and conservatives disagreed about ownership and control, not about the structure of industry and commerce.

Decentralization of the economy also faltered because it was abandoned in line with a shift in American policy already signaled by the ban on the 1947 general strike. In an atmosphere of mounting Cold War tension and in line with what is frequently called the "reverse course," economic and strategic considerations came to prevail. Increasingly, the United States saw Japan, called by the Secretary of State "the workshop of Asia," as a potentially valuable and much-needed ally after the victory of the Chinese Communists in 1949. On the advice of Joseph Dodge, a Detroit banker sent out by Washington in 1949, in April of that year the value of the yen was set at 360 to the dollar—low even then—to encourage exports by making Japanese goods inexpensive abroad, and to promote frugality at home. In May, the Ministry of International Trade and Industry (MITI) was formed by merging the Ministry of Commerce and Industry and the Board of Trade, "constituting a greater centralization of economic authority than had been achieved at the peak of Japan's mobilization for war."[4] Meanwhile, the Ministry of Finance exercised paramount sway over budgets and monetary policy. Both would continue playing these roles long after the Occupation came to an end.

Not only labor and economic policies were affected by the policy shift. Communists were purged (1949–1950), and others who had earlier been purged were allowed to reemerge in public life. Since an armed ally, capable at least of self-defense, would be more valuable than one unarmed, the United States had second thoughts about Japan's renunciation of military force.

Dodge's deflationary policies led to economic decline until the outbreak of the Korean War in June 1950 brought a flood of orders for equipment and supplies, a procurement boom that gave an enormous boost to the faltering economy. Even after the war, orders to supply American troops and bases continued to benefit the Japanese economy. Under American encouragement, Japan also created a paramilitary force of 75,000.

The End of the Occupation

The ending of the Occupation, a subject broached by General MacArthur as early as 1947, was delayed largely because of Soviet opposition. Although the Occupation continued, by the time MacArthur took command in Korea in July 1950, its work was practically complete. Dismissed by President Truman, he departed from East Asia for good in April 1951. Though in his subsequent testimony to Congress he spoke glowingly of the Japanese, they were distressed to hear him compare them to children.

Under the Occupation, electoral politics was reintroduced, and political parties representing a broad range of ideas and a variety of interests battled for votes. The Diet again became the central arena for national politics. The leading political personality to emerge during the Occupation was Yoshida Shigeru (1878–1967), a former diplomat who had opposed the military leadership in Japan during the thirties. Yoshida dominated Japanese politics for the better part of a decade, serving as prime minister in 1946–1947, and again from 1948 to 1954. A coalition of conservatives and socialists of various shades of radicalism held power briefly in 1947–1948, but was unable to create a viable government, partly because of divisions within its own ranks, and partly because of Occupation hostility toward socialism. Upon reassuming the prime ministership, Yoshida called a new election. Held in 1949, it provided his Liberal party with an absolute majority.

It was Yoshida who signed the peace treaty in San Francisco in September 1951, which was ratified the following April and accompanied by a defense treaty that provided for American bases in Japan and continued occupation of Okinawa. At the insistence of the U.S. Senate, Japan signed a parallel treaty with the Chinese Nationalists on Taiwan and agreed to follow the American policy of nonrecognition and containment of the People's Republic of China (P.R.C.). The U.S.S.R. was not a party to the San Francisco treaty. Formal diplomatic relations were established in 1956, but Moscow and Tokyo could not agree on the disposition of four small islands, and entered the twenty-first century without ever signing a peace treaty to conclude World War II.

Assessments of the Occupation must naturally take into account later history, as so many institutions and practices of contemporary Japan are rooted in this period. What came to be known as the Japanese model of bureaucratic capitalism has been dubbed the "SCAPanese model."[5] There are people who think the reforms went too fast and too far, and others who deplore the "reverse course" taken in response to the Cold War and the persistence of certain traditional institutions and patterns. These include the treatment and retention of the emperor, the role of the bureaucracy, the relationship between government and business, and failure to adhere strictly to Article IX.

What seems clear is that the Occupation did bring about major changes, but it was most successful in areas where there were Japanese precedents and substantial support. This was true of much of the political program, the land reform, and the advocacy of liberal values. Representative institutions, after all, went back to the nineteenth century, and demands for land reform, for equality, and opposition to authoritarianism all predate the rise of militarism. The movement for women's rights had begun in the 1910s. Despite misconceptions and mistakes, and despite the contradiction inherent in a plan to foster democracy by command, much of what the Occupation attempted did actually take hold.

The Occupation also had unplanned side effects, including the influx of foreign culture. Intellectuals who were eager to catch up with the recent Western developments devoured translations of Western books. Many turned to Marxism, but the whole spectrum of ideas found translators and readers. Popular culture was more open than ever to foreign influence. In some respects, the scene resembled that after the First World War. It did not take the Occupation to introduce the Japanese to baseball and jazz. However, this time change went deeper, and there was to be no radical turning away such as took place in the thirties. If anything, the doors and windows opened by defeat and occupation are even more widely open today.

III. Korea: Liberation, Division, and War, 1945–1953

Liberation and Division

The Birth of Rival Republics

The North-South Civil War

International Intervention in the Korean Civil War

The Korean Armistice

Liberation and Division

Japan's forced withdrawal from Korea did not put an end to foreign rule on the peninsula. Koreans who were expecting to be liberated to run their own affairs after Japan's defeat were to be gravely disappointed. The Soviet Union's entry into the Pacific War on August 8, 1945, led American planners to realize that Korea, like Manchuria, was about to fall under Soviet occupation, thus positioning communist forces dangerously near Japan. To block the Soviet advance, American planners suggested dividing Korea along the 38th parallel, allowing Soviet occupation of the territory north of the line, but holding the south for occupation by the United States Army. The Soviet Army, which was concentrating on occupying Manchuria, agreed.

Though there were Korean exile groups in the Soviet Union, China, and the United States that wanted to return immediately and compete for leadership, neither the Soviets nor the Americans were prepared to turn the newly-liberated peninsula over to them. Since they assumed that the long-defunct monarchy was in no position to return to power, and the exiled groups lacked legitimacy, the Allies deemed Korea to be unready for self-government, and gave little heed to the fact that in the last moments of the war volunteers in the country's valleys, villages, and towns had stepped forward to keep their local markets and farming routines going, and to make administrative decisions for the places where they lived. These committees soon became widely known as "people's committees" (Korean: *inmin wiwŏnhoe*). They sprang from many types of organizations that had existed during the colonial era: old-style village elders; young politically-active students; and labor organizers who once had tried to set up unions called *chohap*. Whatever their origins, they reflected a spontaneous effort by Koreans to take charge of their own lives. Their politics were leftist: that is, they wanted to reorganize the social and economic system that privileged the wealthy, particularly landlords and big businessmen, many of whom were accused of having profited through collaboration with Korea's Japanese rulers. In Seoul, a coalition of national leaders formed themselves into an umbrella organization called the "People's Republic," seeking to knit the People's Committees together into a national system of self-rule. A separate coalition of conservatives was also formed, aimed at maintaining the economic system as it was. Behind this was a largely Japanese-educated elite that included wealthy Koreans from established lineages that had survived the fall of the Korean monarchy and thirty-five years of Japanese rule, many of whom retained extensive landholdings and owned modern businesses. This property-owning class was disinclined to allow a free discussion of social classes and Japanese collaboration; rather, they wanted a political system that would allow them to maintain their economic position.

The American military men who arrived to occupy South Korea in September 1945 suffered from a nearly total ignorance about Korea and the political cauldron that was boiling there by the time they arrived. The Americans assumed that the Koreans were a primitive people unfit to govern themselves, notwithstanding their long tradition of autonomy prior to the Japanese takeover in 1910.

During the war, American planners had discussed putting Korea under an international trusteeship after the defeat of Japan, but no proper plans had been developed. When Korea was hurriedly divided along the 38th parallel between U.S. and Soviet forces, it was hoped that the two "trustees" would cooperate to find a way to launch Korea as an independent country. No one knew how this might be done, or which Korean leaders might be best qualified to form a Korean government. When the Americans discovered that most Koreans in the southern zone were bitterly opposed to the idea of foreign "trusteeship," believing that it was just another form of colonial domination, the U.S. tried to abandon the trusteeship formula. The Soviets, however, maintained that trusteeship was a sound policy, and they accused the Americans of changing the arrangements so they could create an anti-Communist state in South Korea, thereby making the country's division permanent.

The Americans and Soviets argued over these points in Korea as the Cold War was breaking out, and the United States went from thinking of the Soviet Union as a wartime ally to regarding it as a worldwide rival bent on conquest. When in 1947 President Truman announced the doctrine of containment, the United States pledged to block the expansion of Communism and vowed to fight Communist attempts to undermine "democratic" governments, that is, governments friendly to the United States. The presence of Soviet forces in North Korea therefore came to appear as a menace, not only to the non-Communist territory in South Korea, but also to American-occupied Japan. American policy assumed the goal of protecting South Korea from Communist control, thus angering the Soviets and their left-wing Korean Communist allies, and leading to a hardening of the 38th parallel into a permanent boundary between two rival Korean states in the north and south.

The Birth of Rival Republics

The alienation between the Korean political left and right that had developed under Japanese rule was also to be seen in North Korea, where the Soviet occupation forces pushed aside centrist political leaders and installed left-wing Communist Koreans in their stead. The Korean government that took form under Soviet occupation was led by the ethnic Korean known as Kim Il-sung (Kim Ilsŏng, 1912–1994), who had spent the war years as an officer in a Korean unit of the Soviet Red Army. Among Korean Communists, Kim was known as a long-time guerrilla fighter who had engaged in numerous raids and small battles with the Japanese along Korea's Manchurian border during the 1930s, before finally being driven into Russian territory. With Russian backing, Kim's interim regime launched an attack against those who had collaborated with the Japanese and against all elements of Korean society that had maintained or gained wealth under the Japanese colonial system. These included large landholders, businessmen, former employees of Japanese enterprises, and others seen as socially privileged. Also labeled "class enemies" of the Korean working people were many Christians, intellectuals, and small capitalists whose ideologies conflicted with the vision of a Communist-ruled Korea. After being identified as "enemies of the people," many were stripped of their property and left with little choice but to leave the area ruled by the Communists. With poverty and civil war raging to the north in Manchuria, most chose to go south.

The Americans and anti-Communist Koreans in the south made much of the fact that so many northerners were "voting with their feet" by migrating south to live in "freedom." As the left-wing regime consolidated its control in the north with Soviet backing, and the right-wing consolidated its control in the south under American sponsorship, the two Koreas drew apart. The conflict between their two visions for Korea's future was the basis for the protracted national division that has continued for more than half a century. It also appeared to merge with the worldwide conflict between Capitalism and Communism, making Korea a kind of unfortunate testing ground in the Cold War. When the United States decided to end its military occupation of the south, it turned the problem of creating a "free" Korean government over to the United Nations. In 1948, the U.N. attempted to organize a national election for a representative assembly to draft a constitution and create a government. In North Korea, however, this was interpreted as a ploy to use the larger population of the south to create a government in which the left would be a disadvantaged minority. The Kim Il-sung regime, with Soviet support, refused to allow U.N. teams into North Korea to set up the election. The election went ahead only in the southern zone. It created a constitution-drafting body that founded a republic whose legislature elected the American-educated Syngman Rhee (Yi Sŭngman, 1875–1965) as first president of the "Republic of Korea" (R.O.K.). The following month the Soviet-backed left-wing assembly in North Korea created the "Democratic People's Republic of Korea" (D.P.R.K.) and confirmed Kim Il-sung as its Supreme Leader.

The North-South Civil War

The "Korean Conflict" is usually said to have started with North Korea's invasion of the South on June 25, 1950, and ended with the armistice at P'anmunjŏm on July 27, 1953. However, that three-year period might be better understood as the international phase of a civil war between the Korean left and right that began in 1946 and did not end until the U.S.-backed R.O.K. Army had eliminated the last Communist guerrillas in the South in 1955.

During the initial phase of the war, between 1946 and 1949, the Communists in the northern zone tried to keep left-wing elements alive and active in the south. As the Soviets gradually handed power over to the Korean Workers Party (K.W.P.) under Kim Il-sung, the K.W.P. pursued its belief that the common people of the south were eager for revolution. It was thought that they only needed the right kind of opportunity to rise up against South Korea's conservative elites and their American protectors. However, though there were many strikes and other manifestations of social and economic discontent, the Americans were able to suppress them by using Koreans from the former colonial police force, the former Japanese imperial armed forces, and their own military police. The most serious rebellions were aimed at blocking the 1948 election and the creation of a separate state in South Korea. The worst, on Cheju Island, cost an estimated 30,000 lives.

Koreans in the south were deeply troubled by all these events. The R.O.K. Army and National Police did not get along, and on occasion even fought each other. In October 1948 leftist elements within the R.O.K. Army mutinied at the southern port of Yŏsu, calling down repression at the hands of army elements loyal to Seoul. By the end of 1949, however, the Seoul government had managed to reduce the left wing in South Korea to a sullen acquiescence. The country's Communist leaders were forced to gather in the north and ponder other ways to reunite the country.

In the early months of 1950, Kim Il-sung settled on a plan to invade the south in hopes of sparking the uprising that he thought would be the key to reunification. It is likely that he was encouraged by external developments, particularly the Communist victory in China and signals from the United States that it would not use force to defend the Seoul regime. He consulted with leaders in Beijing and Moscow and received pledges of military aid. He calculated that his own troops, many of whom had acquired battle experience while helping the Chinese Communists fight Japan and the Guomindang, would easily overwhelm the inexperienced R.O.K. Army. He also counted on the advantage of surprise. He thought he could take Seoul within a few days and cause the Syngman Rhee regime to collapse. The rest of the country would then fall quickly under his control.

International Intervention in the Korean Civil War

Contrary to Kim Il-sung's expectations, however, the United States met North Korea's invasion of the south on June 25, 1950, with a rapid and resolute response. Though the invading forces did in fact take Seoul within three days, the United States persuaded the United Nations Security Council to confront North Korea with a resolution branding it as an aggressor and demanding an end to the fighting. At the time, the Soviet Union was boycotting the U.N. in protest over its refusal to admit the P.R.C. as the legal representative of China, and with the Soviet ambassador absent, the Security Council resolution on Korea passed without a veto. When the North Koreans ignored the U.N. action, the Security Council passed a second resolution creating a United Nations peacekeeping force to repel the North Korean invasion and restore the 38th parallel as the line between the Korean north and south. The Security Council delegated to the president of the United States the authority to appoint the U.N. Commander-in-Chief, and President Truman named General Douglas MacArthur, in Tokyo, to lead the counterattack.

In the summer of 1950, D.P.R.K. forces proved to be almost strong enough to overrun all of South Korea. As U.N. troops reached Korea, they concentrated in the southeastern corner of the peninsula, helping the remaining defenders maintain what was called the "Pusan Perimeter." In this area General MacArthur began to rebuild the R.O.K. Army and to introduce the foreign soldiers and equipment that were meant to roll back the invasion. Though the North Koreans defeated the first American units that came to oppose them, many weeks of bitter fighting at the Naktong River halted the invasion and bought time for a United Nations Command.

North Korea's view of the invasion was that reunification was an internal Korean matter and therefore unimportant to outsiders. The United States, on the other hand, saw the attack across the 38th parallel as an international issue. The Americans' decision to intervene was based on a number of factors. First, the Truman Administration saw the D.P.R.K. attack as a Soviet ploy to enhance Communist influence in East Asia. A Communist victory in Korea would surely put great pressure on Japan, encouraging left-wing elements there and making it harder to reconstruct Japan as an American ally. Second, the U.S. saw the invasion as a test of the Containment doctrine, an act of aggression that could not go unanswered without casting doubt on the promise that America had made to defend pro-Western governments against Communism. These doubts would surely raise worries among its allies as far away as Europe and weaken the newly-founded NATO alliance. Third, the Truman Administration was itself under attack in Washington for "allowing" China to "go Communist" the previous year. With congressional elections due in November 1950, the Democratic party knew that it could not let the Republicans add Korea to their list of Democratic foreign policy disasters. Fourth, the D.P.R.K. attack was seen as a blatant violation of the United Nations Charter, which required a resolute response from the United Nations to punish acts of aggression. It was considered important to prove that the United Nations, unlike the League of Nations after World War I, had enforcement power and would not tolerate an open attack by one nation-state upon another. And finally, many American leaders felt that they had a moral obligation to uphold the government that the U.S. had established in Seoul and to defend the people in the southern zone from forced submission to Kim Il-sung's regime.

Sixteen member nations of the U.N. contributed troops to the United Nations Command in Korea. The biggest contingents, of course, were the R.O.K. Army and forces from the United States. President Truman referred to the U.N. intervention in Korea as a "police action," though to the soldiers on the ground it looked and felt like a full-scale war.

A decisive shift in the war occurred on September 15, 1950, when General MacArthur commanded an amphibious landing at the port of Inch'ŏn, 22 miles west of Seoul, and recaptured the southern capital within two weeks. The geography of Korea is such that he effectively blocked the escape of the North Korean invaders in the south and captured them by the thousands. It appeared that the U.N. peacekeeping force had succeeded in its mission, to restore the Republic of Korea and reestablish the 38th parallel as its boundary with the D.P.R.K. Buoyed by this success, however, the United Nations decided to expand the mission to invade the north. U.N. forces crossed the 38th parallel in early October, took the

D.P.R.K. capital of P'yŏngyang, and advanced as far as the Manchurian border, triggering fears in China that they were not only about to destroy the D.P.R.K. but might continue their advance into China.

In Beijing, Chinese leaders sought assurances that this would not happen, and although President Truman repeatedly said that he did not want the Korean War to turn into World War III, the Chinese were not convinced that MacArthur would not try to roll back the Communist revolution in their country. With American leaders making statements that threatened China and talking loosely about using nuclear weapons to win a decisive victory against Communism in Asia, the P.R.C. prepared to intervene on the Korean peninsula. Adding to their concerns over the fighting in Korea was the fact that the United States had positioned the U.S. Seventh Fleet in the Taiwan Strait to defend the defeated Chinese Nationalists on Taiwan. Indeed, the Korean War brought a renewed American commitment to maintaining Taiwan, using U.S. military forces and aid to interfere in what the Chinese Communists regarded as an internal affair—the secession of a Chinese province under "rebel" Guomindang control. Perceiving a broad threat from the United States under cover of the United Nations, the P.R.C. positioned a force exceeding 250,000 in the mountains of northern Korea and near the end of November 1950 attacked R.O.K., U.S., and other U.N. forces in North Korea. The result was a debacle for many U.N. units, which actually had to fight their way back across the 38th parallel. By January 1951 the combined Chinese and North Korean armies had taken Seoul once more. It was only with difficulty that the United Nations Command was able to push them back, to a battle line that was north of the city not far from the original north-south boundary.

The Korean Armistice

In the spring of 1951, truce negotiations began in a tent on the battlefront and continued for two years during which the warring armies fought bloody engagements along the width of the Korean peninsula. American aircraft pounded targets in North Korea, reducing the major cities to rubble and obliterating North Korean agriculture and industry. Believing that aerial bombing would break North Korea's will at the negotiating table, American commanders destroyed dams and dikes in a way that caused floods and famine. Much of the D.P.R.K. government and surviving small industries were driven into caves and tunnels while ordinary people remained exposed in places that were bombed to break North Korean morale even when they had no military significance.

Meanwhile streams of refugees collected in South Korea's cities where there was no bombing but also no employment and little food. International relief agencies did much to alleviate the worst suffering, but when the war ended with a hard-fought truce in July 1953, Korea's economy and morale, North and South, had been shattered. The truce was signed at the village of P'anmunjŏm by representatives of North Korea, China, and the United Nations. An American general signed for the United Nations, representing all the armies that had fought on the U.N. side, including the R.O.K. Army. No representative of the Republic of Korea signed the truce document, a fact that the D.P.R.K. has always used as a reason to label the Seoul government as a puppet of the United States. Indeed, under a 1950 agreement, the Commander-in-Chief of the United Nations Command, who was always an American general, retained operational control of R.O.K. forces in wartime and authority over R.O.K. forces that were assigned to defend against North Korean attack for the rest of the twentieth century.

Estimates of Korean War casualties vary widely. More than two million Koreans, most of them civilians, lost their lives in the north and south. Among them were an estimated half-million D.P.R.K. and 300,000 R.O.K. soldiers. Chinese battle deaths were at least 320,000, though some estimates range as high as 900,000. The United States suffered 54,246 dead, including 33,629 killed in action. The British Commonwealth and other United Nations contingents lost nearly 5,000 killed in action. Estimates of the wounded and others who died from causes related to the war number in the millions. The United States alone suffered 103,284 wounded.

IV. The Vietnamese Struggle for Independence, 1939–1956

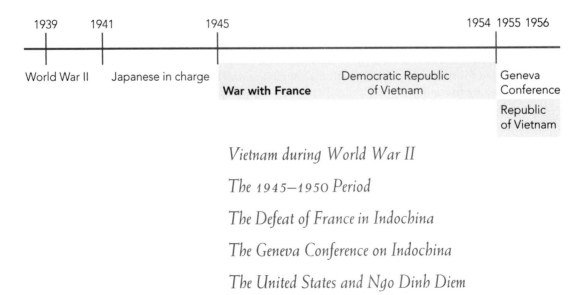

Vietnam during World War II

The 1945–1950 Period

The Defeat of France in Indochina

The Geneva Conference on Indochina

The United States and Ngo Dinh Diem

As previously noted (Chapter 12), there are many similarities between the post-colonial situations in Korea and in Vietnam. One of the most obvious is the importance of the American role in a country that was divided between competing left- and right-wing factions. Related to that is the astonishing lack of knowledge on the part of the Americans who made decisions that shaped events in Korea and Vietnam. Indeed, at the height of the Vietnam War, even after decades of American involvement, a senior American official acknowledged that, "There has never been an official of Deputy Assistant Secretary rank or higher (including myself) who could have passed in office a midterm freshman exam in modern Vietnamese history, if such a course existed in this country."[6]

Vietnam during World War II

America committed ground combat forces to Vietnam in 1965, but American involvement in Vietnam can be traced to 1940, when France fell to the Nazis and the French colonial apparatus in Vietnam started collaborating with the Axis, opening North Vietnam to incoming Japanese forces. The United States protested the expansion of Japanese military power into Indochina at that time and began clearing the decks for war in the Pacific, evacuating American civilians and increasing economic sanctions against Japan. In 1941, when Japan moved into southern Vietnam, the United States cut off all economic relations with Japan and, in effect, set the stage for the events at Pearl Harbor and beyond.

During World War II, President Franklin Roosevelt several times asserted his belief that French rule in Indochina had been brutal and should not be reestablished. At the Tehran Conference in 1943 and again in discussions with the British in 1944, he argued that the people of Indochina should be put under an international trusteeship. However, as with Korea, there was no planning for this trusteeship, and the British, having many colonies of their own, were annoyed by Roosevelt's push for decolonization. Thus, at the end of the war, the Allies were ill-prepared to do anything but reassert the status quo ante, disregarding wartime developments within Indochina and the rise of nationalism in Vietnam.

In July 1941 Japanese imperial forces took control of all five *pays* of French Indochina—the three areas of Vietnam (Tonkin, Annam, and Cochin China) plus Laos and Cambodia. Of these, Tonkin and Annam were nominally under the figurehead emperor Bao Dai, scion of the Nguyen dynasty, Cochinchina was under direct French rule, and Laos and Cambodia were under "protected rulers" of their own. The Japanese kept Bao Dai in place in Tonkin and Annam, letting him believe that they were positioning him to lead a renewed Vietnamese empire (De Quoc Viet Nam). Bao Dai thus transferred his cooperation to the Japanese, who, to his great disappointment, ended up manipulating him as a puppet ruler during the war years. In Cochinchina, for most of the war, the Japanese allowed French officials to continue working under their direction.

Meanwhile, Ho Chi Minh made contact with American intelligence officials in China and developed a relationship that he hoped might encourage the Americans to support him after the eventual expulsion of Japanese forces from Indochina. He transferred his base of operations from China to northern Vietnam, returning home for the first time in thirty years. There, in the mountains, he created a nationalist organization that he called the League for the Independence of Vietnam— the Viet Nam Doc Lap Dong Minh Hoi, better known as the "Viet Minh."

On March 9, 1945, the Japanese military in Indochina took complete control, removing the French from their positions in Cochinchina. No doubt this was a step in contemplation of the imminent Allied victory, but it is important to note that for several months in 1945 there was no French administration at all in Indochina. While the Japanese used Bao Dai in Vietnam, Ho Chi Minh, believing he had American support, tried to influence Allied policy in favor of his own movement. When Japan announced its surrender in August, Ho Chi Minh and his Viet Minh forces marched into Hanoi, took control of government buildings, installed themselves in office, and successfully demanded the abdication of Bao Dai in the old imperial capital of Hue.

In Europe, however, the Allies were making different arrangements for postwar Indochina. With the death of President Franklin Roosevelt, the U.S. Government muted its criticism of colonialism in general, and at the Potsdam Conference in July, President Harry Truman agreed to a British plan to accept the surrender of Japanese forces in southern Vietnam while the Chinese Nationalists accepted it in the north, above the sixteenth parallel. Like the trusteeship formula for Korea, the plan for Vietnam took no notice of Vietnamese wishes and ignored the emerging nationalist appeal of the Viet Minh. Rather, the British took the lead in reasserting Western control, preparing the way for a return to French colonial rule.[7]

The arrival of British forces in August and September created considerable chaos in southern Vietnam. The city of Saigon was wracked with violence as French legionnaires, liberated by the British from Japanese detention, turned guns on Vietnamese collaborators and confronted agents of the Viet Minh. Angry Vietnamese struck back, no longer respectful of the French after seeing their humiliation during the war. In October, French forces, assisted by the British, landed in the Mekong River delta and ejected the Viet Minh from Saigon—or so they thought. Viet Minh agents quickly returned. French historian Philippe Devillers later wrote,

> If we departed, believing a region pacified, the Viet Minh would arrive on our heels. . . . There was only one possible defense, to multiply our posts, fortify them, arm and train the villagers, coordinate intelligence and police. What was required was not [our] thirty-five thousand troops but a hundred thousand. . . . [8]

The 1945–1950 Period

In northern Vietnam, after a short-lived intrusion of Chinese forces sent to exercise their part of the bargain at Potsdam, Viet Minh operatives retained control. On September 2 in Hanoi, Ho Chi Minh proclaimed the founding of the

Democratic Republic of Vietnam (D.R.V.) under Viet Minh leadership, quoting from the American Declaration of Independence that "all men are created equal" and that the new government stood for "life, liberty, and the pursuit of happiness."

The world, however, did not respond. The United States did not recognize the D.R.V., and by the end of the year it was plain that it had opted to support France. Officials in the European Bureau of the State Department, arguing that France's postwar recovery required the rebuilding of its overseas empire, prevailed over officials in the Far Eastern Bureau who warned that French rule would soon prove untenable in Indochina and that the colony would turn out to be an unbearable burden.

During 1945 and 1946 the French fought their way back into control over the towns and villages of southern Vietnam. Though there were periodic pauses in what amounted to a war between the French and the Viet Minh, Ho Chi Minh appeared certain that his own people would prevail in establishing their independence. The French, on the other hand, trusted in their superior weaponry to re-establish their control. Accordingly, the cease-fires were always short-lived, with France and the D.R.V. repositioning themselves for renewed hostilities. In March of 1946, for example, France and the D.R.V. agreed that the D.R.V. should join the French Union subject to a nationwide vote by the Vietnamese people. The deal called for France to transform Cochinchina into a separate state, meaning that the D.R.V. would have to give up claims to uniting the entire country under its sway, and that France would keep forces in southern Vietnam until 1952. When the Viet Minh decided that the price was too high, the agreement broke down. By the end of the year the two sides were at war once again.

By 1947, the cost of the fighting in Indochina had become intolerable for France. In Paris, government officials started searching for a way out of the conflict. In order to save face and to maintain their economic position in Vietnam, they were determined not to allow Ho Chi Minh a complete victory. They began searching for a non-Communist alternative to Ho who could create a rival government that the people might actually prefer if given a choice. They wanted the former emperor, Bao Dai, who was living in Hong Kong at the time, to return and head their alternative government. Though Bao Dai had abdicated in September 1945, ending the Nguyen dynasty as well as his own reign, the French hoped that his residual cachet would serve to rally Vietnam's non-Communists. When, after considerable turmoil, France created the Associated State of Vietnam in 1949, Bao Dai became its *chef d'état* (chief of state). As a member of the French Union, the Associated State of Vietnam had the right to manage its internal affairs, but French officials retained control of its finances, the economy, and such vital functions as law enforcement. France thus succeeded in transforming at least the southern part of its colony into a puppet state—one that claimed sovereignty over all of Vietnam, including Annam and Tonkin as far north as the Chinese border.

The outside world reacted coolly to the new French client government in Saigon. In Washington, State Department factions resumed arguing about whether French colonialism or Asian nationalism was more deserving of American support. Some wondered if the Bao Dai government was sufficiently autonomous to deserve recognition.

In 1948, U.S. Secretary of State George Marshall had proclaimed that "the objectives of the United States can only be obtained by such French action as will satisfy the aspirations of the people of Indochina."[9] However, not long after the Communist victory in China, both the People's Republic of China and Soviet Union recognized the D.R.V. under Ho Chi Minh. This made Vietnam an urgent foreign policy problem for the Truman Administration by appearing to be another "defeat" in a long series of "losses" to Communism. Dean Acheson, Marshall's successor as secretary of state, declared that Soviet and P.R.C. recognition of the D.R.V. "should remove any illusions as to the 'nationalist' nature of Ho Chi Minh's aims, and reveals Ho in his true colors as the mortal enemy of native independence in Indochina."[10] Putting anti-Communism ahead of all other considerations in Indochina, the U.S. immediately recognized the Associated State of Vietnam. Acheson explained the step as a way of expressing "displeasure with Communist tactics which are obviously aimed at eventual domination of Asia, working under the guise of indigenous nationalism."[11] In May 1950 the United States went further by granting France US$10 million for military operations against the Viet Minh.

Throughout the late 1940s fighting continued throughout Indochina, in Laos and Cambodia as well as Vietnam, as French forces struggled to reassert their colonial regimes. In areas of northern Vietnam that were fully under their control, the Viet Minh instituted economic reorganization along socialist lines. This involved a certain amount of violence as the D.R.V. dealt with former collaborators, but Ho Chi Minh put the anti-imperialist cause ahead of the antifeudal struggle, and postponed large-scale land reform. Production and efficiency increased in areas that were free of fighting, and though some people dreaded conscription, much of the population supported the Viet Minh not only for their resistance against the French but also for their domestic policies.

The Defeat of France in Indochina

Viet Minh planners knew that their war would be long and costly. They recognized that the French would have the early advantage but that as the Viet Minh recruited and trained their troops, the advantage, in the north at least, would pass to those who better knew the terrain, language, and aspirations of the people, who, on the whole, hated French rule. Early in 1950, the Viet Minh commander Vo Nguyen Giap won an important battle in the Red River Valley. More victories followed through the year, with French forces being decimated by effective Viet Minh tactics backed by an increasing supply of weapons from China.

After recognition by the Soviets and Chinese Communists, and under conditions of warfare during which Chinese advisors tried to nudge the D.R.V. farther to the left, life in the Communist-controlled area took on a more political coloration. Stresses increased as the former Indochinese Communist Party regrouped along national lines, creating separate movements in Vietnam, Laos, and Cambodia. In the D.R.V., the government stepped up enforcement of ideological purity and encouraged open class criticism of landowners, intellectuals, and other elite members of society, people who might have supported the independence effort if it had not cost them so much personally.[12]

As the war in Korea heightened American fears about the "march of Communism," the U.S. government stepped up its military aid to the French in Indochina. In 1952, after the battlefront had settled down somewhat in Korea, Americans turned their attention to other parts of Asia. Planners thought about the danger that if the Communists were successful in Vietnam, neighboring countries would also succumb to Communist conquest or revolution, making for a chain reaction that was likened to a row of falling dominoes. This "domino theory" raised the stakes in Vietnam. The United States disliked supporting colonialism, but it seemed that American-backed military action against the Viet Minh was the only way to keep the first domino from falling. With luck it might buy time for the Associated State of Vietnam to develop into a viable nation. In the Philippines and Malaya, Western-backed anti-Communist counterinsurgency campaigns appeared to be defeating the local Communists. Perhaps the same result could be achieved in Vietnam.

Until 1953, the French had relied on their better weapons to defeat the Viet Minh and had been unable to field a very large army in Indochina. In that year, however, the new French commander in Vietnam, General Henri Navarre, devised a plan whereby more than 300,000 troops would be recruited from the local population. This "yellowing" of forces, as it was called, would enable the French to blunt the Viet Minh's home-ground advantage while enabling them to confront the Viet Minh in force with troops and weapons paid for by the United States. Enthusiastic about this plan, the Eisenhower Administration pledged $384 million, bringing total U.S. support for France in Vietnam to $500 million per year.

In May 1954 the Navarre Plan met its test in Dienbienphu, a fortified point near the Laotian border in western Tonkin. For many months the Viet Minh had been trying to draw French forces westward, away from their strongholds in the Tonkin delta. As the Communists pulled westward, the French became concerned about Viet Minh expansion into Laos, and ordered General Navarre to provide protection for the Laotian capital of Luang Prabang. Navarre decided to do more than block Viet Minh expansion: he decided to set the stage for a battle that would turn the tide and deal the D.R.V. a decisive defeat. For many weeks in early 1954, French forces ostentatiously occupied the Dienbienphu valley, setting up artillery at will and reinforcing their main post for the battle. The Viet Minh did not interfere, preferring not to waste their efforts against superior firepower. Instead they bided their time, recognizing that the French were digging into positions that they would be hard pressed to defend or reinforce once the battle began.

General Giap then did something that the French had not thought possible: he gathered a force of 100,000 men and had them haul disassembled heavy artillery and anti-aircraft pieces into the mountains around Dienbienphu. Winter clouds provided cover and much of the work was done at night. On March 12, 1954, Giap opened fire on the French fort and started capturing French outposts throughout the valley. As shells rained down on Dienbienphu, attempts to resupply the French fort by air were met by withering antiaircraft fire from the hills. In Washington, French representatives begged the United States for a quick and massive American intervention, and Eisenhower Administration officials briefly considered using nuclear weapons. The battle went on for six weeks until, on the night of May 6–7, D.R.V. forces overran the French garrison, forcing surrender. The Dienbienphu debacle was universally seen as the endgame for France in Indochina. The Navarre Plan had failed, and although the fighting continued elsewhere in Vietnam, the election of Socialist Premier Pierre Mendes-France in June tilted the Paris government toward complete withdrawal.

The Geneva Conference on Indochina

The French flag fell at Dienbienphu on the day before the great powers were to convene a conference at Geneva to discuss the future of Indochina. When the conference began on May 8, 1954, the United States was still hoping for a military victory over the Communists in Vietnam. But the Americans had also become disillusioned with French methods and capabilities. They would have been glad to see France ejected from Indochina if it had not meant a certain victory for the Communists. Fearing that the Geneva Conference would conclude by providing for a French exit in exchange for handing too much to the Viet Minh, the Eisenhower Administration refused to participate as a regular member of the conference. Instead the United States sent an "observer" delegation so that it would not be bound to support the conference's decisions. The Associated State of Vietnam likewise attended as an observer. With Washington and Saigon on the sidelines, the participants were the United Kingdom and Soviet Union (as co-chairs), France, China, the D.R.V., and the other two "Associated States of Indochina," which were Cambodia and Laos.

The delegation from the Democratic Republic of Vietnam arrived at Geneva expecting to be recognized as winners of the Vietnamese fight for independence. In this they were supported by the Soviet Union and China. However, the British and French, backed by the Americans, refused to give the D.R.V. more than its forces had won on the battlefield; that is, Tonkin. It was only after many weeks of difficult negotiations that the conferees produced a series of agreements on July 21 that set the stage for the next phase of Vietnamese history. The provisions included:

- An immediate cease-fire between French and D.R.V. forces in Vietnam, Cambodia, and Laos, withdrawal of all combatants to their respective zones, and the return of all refugees.

- The division of Vietnam into northern and southern zones at the 17th parallel, with the D.R.V. in control in the north and the Associated State of Vietnam controlling the south.

- The promise of national elections in both zones within two years, to create a unified government for all of Vietnam by popular consent; a French force to remain in Vietnam to guarantee the election followed by a complete French withdrawal.

- Creation of an International Control Commission made up of Canada, India, and Poland to supervise implementation of the agreements.

■ No new foreign bases to be allowed in either zone, and no membership in any externally controlled military alliance.

Although the United States did not sign the Geneva Accords, American observer Walter Bedell Smith gave a statement pledging the United States not to use force to oppose the implementation of the agreements.[13] The Eisenhower Administration was distressed that the D.R.V. had been granted control as far down as the 17th parallel. To make the best of the situation, the U.S. turned its attention to supporting the Associated State of Vietnam in the south.

The United States and Ngo Dinh Diem

While the conference was taking place in Geneva, change had overtaken the government in Saigon. Chief of State Bao Dai had appointed a new prime minister named Ngo Dinh Diem (1901–1963), commissioning him to create a new post-Geneva government. Diem had once served the French, but had resigned in protest in the 1930s. In 1945 the Japanese had briefly tried to recruit him, as had Ho Chi Minh. In 1950 he was invited to Michigan State University where he began an ultimately successful public relations campaign to win the notice of American politicians and Catholic leaders. With the backing of such figures as Supreme Court Justice William O. Douglas, Senators Mike Mansfield and John F. Kennedy, and New York's Francis Cardinal Spellman, Diem appeared to Bao Dai to be someone who could win American support in place of the French.

Diem's family home was near Hue, in Annam, and his family had had ties to the old imperial court. He was not well known in the south—indeed, he thought southerners as a group lacked the kind of discipline that was needed for victory over the D.R.V.[14]—and he installed many associates in cabinet and other high positions who lacked political followings in the south. He also installed his brother, Ngo Dinh Nhu, as head of the country's internal security forces. In 1955, the Ngo government wrote a constitution, and Ngo Dinh Diem became president of the Republic of Vietnam (R.V.N.).

When Ngo Dinh Diem arrived in Vietnam in 1954 he had to struggle to win public acceptance. He was not well known in the south, and his years abroad further clouded his legitimacy as a national leader. He was single in a country that prized family lineages, a Catholic in a country most of whose people practiced a mixture of Confucianism, Buddhism, and animism, and he owed his appointment to foreigners, in this case Americans. There were attempts to overthrow him from the beginning, by army elements and political challengers. American officials, though they privately expressed doubts about his capabilities, could not afford to let him fail. They stepped up aid, both covert and overt, funneling hundreds of millions of dollars into his treasury and introducing weapons and military assistance in violation of the spirit of the Geneva Accords. Seeing time as the enemy— the elections were to be held in two years—they labored to boost Diem's government in public esteem. President Eisenhower pledged full American cooperation in return for "reforms," meaning democratization. But democracy was not notably in Diem's nature. Moreover, the U.S. Central Intelligence Agency helped Washington send mixed signals to Diem, using various illegal and unethical means to help him maintain power without needing to build democratic support. In the 1955 referendum that created the Republic, for example, CIA agents showed Diem's government how to fix the vote by printing the antimonarchy ballots in red, the color of good luck, and the pro-monarchy ballots green, the color of bad luck. In some cases holdouts who insisted on voting with green ballots were attacked by Diem's police. The rampant vote tampering means that it is impossible to tell what the voters actually wanted, but the will of Diem and the Americans prevailed.

American efforts to promote the Saigon government and undermine the D.R.V. had started immediately after the Geneva Accords. During the interval in the summer of 1954 when people were allowed freely to migrate from one zone to the other, American propaganda emphasized that Catholics in the D.R.V. zone would be persecuted by the Communists. As a result, Catholics were an important part of the estimated 800,000 refugees who poured from the north into the south, enabling the Americans to point to the huge number of Vietnamese "voting with their feet." CIA operatives used fortunetellers to predict dire things for the D.R.V. zone, and dropped leaflets with propaganda messages intended to frighten northerners into migrating to the south. In other instances, CIA teams ran guns to anti-Communist guerrillas in the north, sabotaged the Hanoi city bus system, instructed Saigon police interrogators in torture methods, and organized English lessons for the mistresses of high Vietnamese officials.[15] However, these things did little to win popularity for the Ngo Dinh Diem regime, which increasingly was seen as corrupt and unworthy of support.

However, in the Democratic Republic of Vietnam, conditions were also depressed. Ho Chi Minh's regime had a hard time delivering the promised benefits of socialism. After the deprivations of World War II and the long war with France, the infrastructure of the northern economy was badly dilapidated. The D.R.V. had to import food and accept foreign aid from other socialist states. In addition, there was real opposition to the D.R.V.'s Communist methods as it set about redistributing land and punishing landlords and businessmen who had exploited the working class. To consolidate their control, the Viet Minh rounded up, tried, and executed many "class enemies" who had done nothing worthy of such extreme punishment. This in turn generated great bitterness that undermined the legitimacy of Ho Chi Minh and gave the Republic of Vietnam grounds to accuse the D.R.V. of injustice and tyranny. Ho himself admitted that his government had made many mistakes, and as the time for the 1956 election that had been arranged at Geneva approached, he vowed to do better.

However, the election never took place. President Eisenhower later wrote in his memoirs the he believed that "had elections been held as of the time of the fighting, possibly 80 percent of the population would have voted for the Communist Ho Chi Minh as their leader rather than the Chief of State Bao Dai."[16] This fact had not changed in 1955, when Ngo Dinh Diem elevated himself to the presidency of the R.V.N., and there was little hope of defeating Ho Chi Minh in 1956.

Under the circumstances, when the D.R.V. proposed consultations with Diem regarding the election, Diem refused. The United States briefly fretted that Diem was making the R.V.N. side look bad, but ultimately went along, saying that for the time being conditions for the election "were not ripe."

Notes

1. For the eulogy, in which Wen Yiduo attacked Chiang Kai-shek personally and predicted that the Guomindang leaders would meet the same fate as Mussolini and Hitler, see Pei-kai Cheng and Michael Lestz with Jonathan D. Spence, *The Search for Modern China: A Documentary Collection* (New York: W.W. Norton, 1999), pp. 337–38.

2. Quoted in John W. Dower, *Embracing Defeat: Japan in the Wake of World War II* (New York: W.W. Norton, 1999), p. 97.

3. Article IX of the Constitution. A convenient source is David John Lu, *Sources of Japanese History* (New York: McGraw-Hill, 1975), vol. 2, pp. 193–97.

4. Dower, p. 544.

5. Dower, p. 558.

6. Daniel Ellsberg, *Papers on the War* (New York: Simon Schuster, 1972), p. 28, quoted in Stanley Karnow, *Vietnam: A History* (New York, Penguin Books, 1984), pp. 150–51.

7. For Great Britain's role in the return of the French to Vietnam at the end of the war, see David G. Marr, *Vietnam 1945: The Quest for Power* (Berkeley and Los Angeles: Univ. of California Press, 1995), particularly Chapter 5, pp. 297–346.

8. Quoted in Karnow, p. 171.

9. Quoted in Chester Cooper, *The Lost Crusade: America in Vietnam* (New York: Fawcett, 1972), p. 85.

10. Quoted in Robert D. Schulzinger, *A Time for War: The United States and Vietnam, 1941–1975* (New York: Oxford University Press, 1997), p. 42.

11. Karnow, p. 223.

12. William J. Duiker, *Ho Chi Minh: A Life* (New York: Hyperion, 2000), pp. 434–39.

13. Robert F. Randle, *Geneva 1954: The Settlement of the Indochinese War* (Princeton: Princeton University Press, 1969), pp. 343–44.

14. Duiker, p. 468.

15. Neil Sheehan, ed., *The Pentagon Papers as Published by the New York Times* (New York: Bantam, 1971), pp. 13–21.

16. Dwight D. Eisenhower, *The White House Years: Mandate for Change* (New York: Signet Books, 1963), p. 449.

15

China under Mao

When Mao Zedong proclaimed the People's Republic on October 1, 1949, it marked a watershed in the history of modern China. After a century of internal disintegration and foreign aggression, China made a new beginning under leaders deeply committed to the revolutionary transformation of the nation. Mao and his associates were determined to create an egalitarian society and make China strong and prosperous.

In taking control of the entire country and then restructuring Chinese society, the new leaders faced problems as immense as China itself. They were dedicated Marxists, and in their march to power had brilliantly adapted the foreign ideology to Chinese conditions. The challenge that now awaited them of transforming China in the spirit of that ideology proved a formidable one, and the course they took was anything but smooth.

PEOPLE'S REPUBLIC OF CHINA

| 1949 | 1957 1958 | 1960 1961 | 1964 1965 | 1969 | 1972 | 1976 |

The Great Leap Forward

"Hundred Flowers" Movement

First Atomic Bomb Explosion

The Great Proletarian Cultural Revolution

Nixon Visit

Death of Mao

Withdrawal of Soviet Technicians

I. Consolidation and Construction Soviet Style, 1949–1958

Government and Politics

Foreign Relations and the Korean War

Economic Policies

Thought Reform and Intellectuals

The People's Republic of China (P.R.C.) began with an initial period (1949–1952), during which the regime consolidated its rule and forged the basic framework of a new sociopolitical order. This was followed by a period of Socialist Construction (1953–1958), initiated by the first Soviet-style five-year plan—begun in 1953, but not published until 1955.

Government and Politics

Following the example of the Soviet Union (U.S.S.R.), the Chinese formed parallel government and party structures with high party officials appointed to top government posts. Thus Mao headed the party as Chairman of the C.C.P. Central Committee and, until 1959, was also officially head of state. High party members also held positions of leadership in various quasi-official organizations such as trade unions; and, as earlier, party members served as political commissars in the army, which reported to the Military Affairs Commission headed by Mao.

Administratively, China was divided into provinces, which remained the primary political subdivisions after an additional governmental level between the provinces and the central government was tried but discarded. The three most highly populated metropolitan areas, Shanghai, Beijing, and Tianjin, were placed directly under the central government, and "autonomous regions" were created in areas inhabited by a significant number of minority people. One such "autonomous region" was Inner Mongolia. (The new government recognized the independence of Outer Mongolia, where the Mongolian People's Republic had been established in 1924, under Soviet sponsorship.) The other autonomous regions were Guangxi, Ningxia (southeast of Inner Mongolia), and the vast western regions of Xinjiang and Tibet. The latter was incorporated into the People's Republic after Chinese troops entered that mountainous land in October 1950, but Tibet did not receive autonomous region status until 1965. Aside from their strategic importance, the Inner Asian territories were significant because the government had to deal with the interests and sensitivities of their ethnic minorities.

A major step toward realizing the egalitarian aims of the revolution was taken in 1950 with the promulgation of a marriage law that gave women political and economic equality as well as equal rights to divorce. Women were free to participate in the work force and pursue careers, although, in practice, this did not release them from their traditional household responsibilities.

An important factor in making the new system work was the cohesiveness of the Party leadership forged during years of struggling side by side. The only political conflict to erupt openly was an attack on Gao Gang, the C.C.P. leader in Manchuria who was accused of separatist ambitions. Additional factors were Gao's ties with the Soviet Union and the issue of Soviet influence in Manchuria. Gao's suicide was reported in 1955. At this juncture Rao Shushi, who was based in Shanghai, was also purged. Both leaders, in charge of prime industrial centers, were accused of "operating independent kingdoms" and of forming a political alliance.

To achieve its goals, the leadership launched massive national campaigns in what became a pattern. Thus, during 1951–1952 there was a "three antis" campaign against waste, corruption, and bureaucratism, aimed at disciplining the greatly enlarged C.C.P. membership, and a "five antis" campaign against bribery, tax evasion, fraud, the stealing of state property, and the theft of economic secrets. As a result, many wealthy men had to pay heavy fines. In line with Mao's *On the New Democracy* (1940), members of the "national bourgeoisie" were initially tolerated, and only capitalists with Guomindang or foreign ties were labeled enemies of the revolution. Gradually, however, private companies were turned over to the state, although their former owners often remained as managers.

Not all drives were directed against human evildoers; there was also a concerted attack on the Four Pests: a war against rats, sparrows, flies, and mosquitoes. Although the inclusion of sparrows was misconceived, it was partly by such campaigns that the P.R.C. achieved enormous improvements in public health. Furthermore, by involving all the people in these campaigns, the leadership not only made use of China's greatest asset (manpower) but also gave the people a sense of participation and pride in the resulting accomplishments.

Foreign Relations and the Korean War

The Communist victory was hailed with enthusiasm in Moscow and bitterly deplored in Washington. Partly for ideological reasons and partly in response to continued, even if unenthusiastic, American support for the Nationalists, the C.C.P. adopted a policy of "leaning to one side," formally aligning itself with the U.S.S.R. in a treaty in February 1950, a product of Mao's first visit to Moscow and, in fact, his first trip outside China. However, relations between the two allies were not easy, for Stalin drove a hard bargain and was slow to relinquish special interests in Manchuria and Xinjiang. Still, the relationship with the U.S.S.R. was very important to China because the Soviet Union provided a model for economic and political development as well as moral, political, and economic support.

On the American side, although some observers had taken the measure of Chiang Kai-shek, large sectors of the American public continued to view him as China's savior, a view fostered by wartime propaganda and the efforts of ex-missionaries, politicians, and other supporters. Many, in and out of government, failed to appreciate that the C.C.P. were nationalists as well as Communists. All this stood in the way of easing tensions between Washington and Beijing, but it is clear that "both Chinese and American leaders were interested in and groping uneasily toward accommodation."[1] However, time ran out with the beginning of war in Korea in June 1950 (see Chapter 14).

The Korean War did not alter the international configuration of power in East Asia, but it did embitter Sino-American relations. Both sides were now more convinced than ever of the enmity of the other. In the United States, proponents of a moderate China policy were removed from influence and subjected to slander. The Nationalist regime on Taiwan was given economic and military assistance, and in 1954 the United States signed a mutual defense treaty with the government of Chiang Kai-shek. Meanwhile, American troops remained in Korea and on bases in Japan and Okinawa. The Chinese, alarmed by these developments, were confirmed of the wisdom of allying themselves with the U.S.S.R. While the Chinese viewed America as an imperialist aggressor, throughout the 1950s many people in the United States, even those in high places, considered the People's Republic to be little more than a Soviet satellite.

If the Korean War merely froze the participants into their Cold War postures, it also enhanced China's international status by demonstrating the ability of its peasant army, a bare year after the triumph of the revolution, to resist the formidable armed might of the United States. Within China, the Korean War helped the government to mobilize the people under the banner of national resistance and created its share of national heroes. Above all, it meant that the revolution had now been tested in foreign as well as domestic war.

Abroad, Beijing's representatives played an important role in the Geneva Conference on Indochina (1954) and at the conference of Asian-African states held at Bandung (Indonesia) in 1955. However, the Nationalists retained the China seat at the United Nations, and the United States prevailed on most of its allies to join it in withholding recognition of the P.R.C. The buildup of Nationalist strength on Taiwan rankled Beijing, but with the U.S Seventh Fleet patrolling the Taiwan Strait, actual fighting was limited to sporadic shelling of two Nationalist-held islands off the coast of Fujian Province.

Economic Policies

Economic matters were of central concern to the new government right from the start. It had inherited a land ravaged by war and floods, with both agricultural and industrial output badly down from prewar levels, and the monetary system wrecked by inflation. In addition, the underlying economy had serious structural weakness. In the agrarian sector, the prevalence of small, uneconomical, scattered landholdings and uneven land ownership helped to perpetuate traditional farming techniques and discouraged investment and capital formation. The industrial sector, on the other hand, consisted primarily of light industry concentrated around Shanghai and heavy industry in Manchuria. The latter had been developed to meet the requirements of foreign capital rather than the needs of China and its people.

Any government would have had to restore and strengthen the economy, but as Marxists, China's new leaders were also committed to the transfer of the means of production from private to public ownership and the creation of an egalitarian system of distribution. Their aim was to create a socialist state with a strong proletarian (working-class) base. The necessary precondition for this was vigorous industrialization, and because this was also required for the attainment of national strength, economic ideology and patriotism pointed to the same end.

By 1952, despite the strains of the Korean War, the economy had been restored to prewar levels. Factories had been put back into operation, railway lines had been repaired, and inflation brought under control. In the cities, the private sector was temporarily retained and even encouraged, but control over materials and marketing, as well as wages, prices, and working conditions, was in the hands of the state. Meanwhile, in the countryside, land redistribution was carried out not by government decree but by mobilizing the suppressed fury of the rural poor. Landlords were denounced and humiliated in public trials and at mass "speak bitterness" meetings. The more fortunate ones were allowed to retain enough land to support themselves, but many lost their lives. The campaign became associated with a general suppression of potential counterrevolutionaries during the Korean War. The end result was not only a more equitable distribution of land but a change of village leadership, now drawn from the poor peasantry.

The achievements of the first three years of the People's Republic were viewed as merely a preamble for further socialization and economic development. A planning organization was established, as was a statistical bureau, and in 1953 China took its first modern census, showing a total population of 582,600,000 on the mainland. Although its accuracy has been questioned, this figure is accepted as a general indication of the size of China's population at the time.

China's First Five-Year Plan followed the U.S.S.R. model of economic development in stressing heavy industry, with some 85 percent of total investments going into this sector. The Soviet Union supplied technical assistance (plans, blueprints, and so forth), helped train Chinese technicians (28,000 Chinese technicians and skilled workers went to the U.S.S.R. for training during the fifties), and sent about 11,000 of its own experts to work in China. Development was accelerated by importing entire plants from the Soviet Union. Most of what was left of the private sector was now eliminated. Control over the plants was given to professional managers and technocrats, whose prime responsibility was to carry out government economic directives. To enable them to do this, they were placed firmly in charge of their factories.

Since loans advanced by the Soviet Union amounted to only 3 percent of China's total state investments, the financing of this industrialization effort was predominantly Chinese. These funds came out of the government's budget. The government, in turn, derived much of its revenue from taxes and from the income of state enterprises. Ultimately, a considerable portion of investment capital came from agriculture, which remained the heart of the Chinese economy.

To increase output and channel agricultural surplus more effectively into capital formation, the government in 1953 began a program of more radical transformation of the pattern of land management. To replace the existing system of small fields, individually owned and worked, the government planned to collectivize agriculture by pooling land, labor, and other resources. The change was not to be accomplished all at once. First, "mutual-aid" teams, which shared labor, tools, and work animals, were organized. The next stage was to create village producers' cooperatives in which land also was pooled.

Initially, agricultural collectivization was planned as a gradual program, because the Chinese leadership wanted to avoid the terrible bloodshed and suffering that had accompanied Stalin's rapid collectivization in the U.S.S.R. Mao, however, in a major speech delivered in July 1955, drew on the experience of the Chinese as distinct from that of the Russian Revolution, and reaffirmed his faith in the revolutionary spirit of the Chinese peasantry. Just as the peasantry had been in the vanguard of the revolution that gave birth to the People's Republic, it would now lead the nation to socialism. In Mao's view it was the party, not the people, that was dragging its feet. The immediate effect of Mao's speech was an acceleration in the agricultural collectivization program, so much so that is was largely accomplished within a single year (1955–1956); and the timetable for full collectivization was set ahead. This speech marked the emergence of a radical Maoist strategy of economic development. In 1957 the process of collectivization was completed.

At the end of the First Five-Year Plan, the Chinese viewed the results with considerable satisfaction. The government was now firmly in control of the industrial sector: agriculture had been reorganized; iron, coal, and steel production targets had been exceeded; industrial output doubled from 1953 to 1957; and, altogether, remarkable progress had been made on the road to industrialization. There were problems, to be sure. One was the widening gap between city and country, a problem that has plagued all industrializing countries, but was of special concern in China, where the peasantry remained the majority and where the party leaders identified with it. Another problem was the reemergence of bureaucracy and the transformation of a revolutionary party into the mainstay of the establishment.

Thought Reform and Intellectuals

The leaders of the People's Republic were convinced not only of the scientific correctness of their doctrine but also of its moral rightness, and they believed that virtually everyone could be brought to share their vision and act accordingly. They were optimistic not only about the course of history but also about human nature. In keeping with tradition, they had faith that everyone could attain moral perfection, now redefined in terms of an ideal socialist person. It was their belief that given the proper environment and correct guidance, people would become selflessly devoted to revolution and community.

Naturally, the most promising were the young, uncontaminated by the old society, and the government saw to it that they were educated in the new values. Special attention was paid to the political awareness of Communist Party members and cadres, who were relied on to set examples of personal conduct and lead the people. To further the thought reform and moral transformation of even the most unpromising individuals, the authorities devised techniques of group discussion, self-criticism, and public confession. By using the individual's own feeling of moral inadequacy and guilt, and by applying external pressures, the authorities induced people to renounce old values, and prepared them for conversion to the new faith. Perhaps the most famous example of such a change of heart, accomplished in the controlled environment of a correctional institute, was provided by Puyi. As an infant he had been the last occupant of the Qing throne, and more recently he had served the Japanese as puppet ruler of Manchukuo. After undergoing thought reform, he reemerged as a citizen in good standing.

Not only prominent personages but also ordinary people now spent much time in small discussion groups, analyzing their lives as well as problems or incidents at their places of work. In this way the new ideology was transmitted to the people, and they were taught to use it in analyzing everyday problems. At the same time, social pressures were applied to everyone to conform to generally accepted standards of behavior.

The thought reform of intellectuals, already a target of Mao's wartime rectification campaign (see Chapter 13), remained difficult. Highly trained and educated people were a rare and precious resource for a nation bent on industrialization and modernization. Yet few came from peasant or worker backgrounds. More serious than their class background was the persistence of traditional elitist attitudes among intellectuals, as well as their critical habits of mind. They tended to resent taking directions from party cadres less well educated than themselves. Their special knowledge and skills were needed, but could they be trusted?

With education and the media under tight party control, the arts too were meant to serve the revolution. While Western style artists were taught "Socialist Realism," a style intended to inspire, not to mirror life (Figures 15.1 and 15.4), artists working in traditional styles (*guohua*) were accepted as furthering national glory, but urged to incorporate modern subjects in their work (Figure 15.2).

The integration of artists and intellectuals into the new society remained problematic. When, in May 1956, Mao invited writers and thinkers to "let a hundred flowers bloom; let a hundred schools contend," there was little response from intellectuals, wary of exposing themselves to attack. But in February 1957, Mao said in a speech, "On the Correct Handling of Contradictions Among the People," that nonantagonistic contradictions should be resolved by persuasion rather than force. After some further reassurance, the floodgates of criticism were opened.

FIGURE 15.1 *Chairman Mao Standing with People of Asia, Africa, and Latin America*, Wu Biduan (b. 1926) and Jin Shangyi (b.1934). Notice the new artistic style of Socialist Realism. Oil on canvas, 143 × 156 cm.
COLLECTION NATIONAL ART GALLERY OF CHINA, BEIJING. © JINN SHANGYI. USED BY PERMISSION.

Criticism was directed not only against the behavior of individual party functionaries and at specific party policies but also at the C.C.P. itself for seeking "to bring about the monolithic structure of a one-family empire."[2] Intellectuals and writers asked for independence from the party's ideological control. Academic problems should be left for professors to solve: "Perhaps Mao has not had time to solve these problems for us,"[3] one history professor suggested.

Mao had intended the campaign to rectify the party, but the criticism was more than he had bargained for. Weeds grew where he had invited flowers. A full-fledged anti-Rightist campaign developed, beginning in June 1957. Not only did prominent intellectual, literary, and artistic figures disappeared into labor camps, but so did over 400,000 others, with the government announcing a target of 5 percent per organization and the campaign quickening to include a massive purge of party members and cadres. Under these pressures some saved themselves by denouncing their friends. The upshot was that people with negative entries in their files had their lives ruined. Many of the victims were not fully rehabilitated until after Mao's death. By 1958 few were left to dare object when Mao launched his Great Leap Forward.

An underlying issue was how to balance the demands for ideological purity and revolutionary fervor with the professional competence required to operate a modern state and build an industrial system. Without the former, a new elite of experts, technocrats, and managers would pursue its own aims, and the revolution would be jeopardized. Mao believed that progress toward Communist egalitarianism and the building of national strength went hand in hand, but put his faith in Redness, often at the expense of expertise.

II. The Revolution Continued, 1958–1976

The Great Leap Forward

The Sino-Soviet Split

Domestic Politics, 1961–1965

The Great Proletarian Cultural Revolution: The Radical Phase, 1966–1969

The Winding Down, 1969–1976

By the end of the First Five-Year Plan there were indications that following the Soviet model was not producing the desired economic or social results, but there was no agreement on what should be done. While the party establishment saw a need for only relatively minor adjustments, Mao advocated a far more radical line. In the subsequent complicated, often turbulent years, he did not always get his way, but he did prevent the revolution from settling down into comfortable routines.

The Great Leap Forward

The Great Leap Forward was initiated in January 1958, but lost momentum the following year. After 1959 it continued, but without vigor, until terminated in January 1961. On Mao's initiative, the gradualism of Soviet-style central planning was abandoned in favor of reliance on the energies of the masses imbued with revolutionary consciousness. Mao believed that ideology was a force that could motivate people to heroic accomplishments. History was not confined to a series of well-defined objective stages of economic and sociopolitical development, but could be turned into a process of "permanent revolution" driven by the subjective will transforming the objective world. The P.R.C. had made use of massive manpower in labor-intensive projects all along, projects such as the building of waterways, roads, and other giant construction works. Now the glorification of labor became more intense:

> Labor is joy; how joyful is it?
> Bathed in sweat and two hands full of mud,
> Like sweet rain my sweat waters the land
> And the land issues scent, better than milk.

Labor is joy; how joyful is it?
Home from a night attack, hoe in hand,
The hoe's handle is still warm,
But in bed, the warrior is already snoring.[4]

The author of these lines, written in 1958, was Yuan Kejia (1921–), who had once been an admirer of T.S. Eliot.

All of China's human resources were to be focused in a giant leap. Through Redness and revolutionary fervor, Mao hoped to accelerate China's economic development and speed the advance toward socialism. The spirit of the people was to be the driving force for continued economic growth and social transformation. Through the catharsis of intense participation, the Great Leap Forward mobilized the emotional involvement of many people in the creation of a new order. They were made to feel that building a strong China was not something to be left to experts and technocrats; it was to be done by, as well as for, the people.

As the prime vehicle for this effort, rural communes were formed by combining the already existing cooperatives. By the end of 1958 there were 26,000 rural communes in which 98 percent of China's rural population lived. Each averaged about 25,000 people. The communes were divided into production brigades, each corresponding roughly to the traditional village, and these, in turn, were divided into production teams. The communes were intended to function as China's basic political as well as economic and social units, integrating all aspects of life. As economic units they supervised agricultural production and distribution, provided banking services, and ran small factories and machine shops, which were operated at the commune- or production-brigade level, depending on the size and degree of specialization of the plant. The communes were further responsible for police functions, and they ran schools and hospitals, provided day-care facilities and mess halls, took care of the aged, and staged plays and other entertainments. They represented an ambitious attempt to create new, large-scale communities. But they turned out to be too large, and the cadres who ran them too far removed from the realities of farming. Their size was therefore reduced, so that by the end of the Great Leap Forward the original number of communes had almost tripled to 74,000, with a corresponding decrease in the size of their memberships. Later the communes lost many of their functions to the smaller production brigades and peasants were given great discretion.

There was also a movement to establish communes in the cities by combining or transforming earlier street associations that included the inhabitants of one street (or of several small streets, or of a section of a large street) originally organized for security and welfare. They were now given additional responsibilities for economic enterprises as well as for educational and medical facilities. In general, the formation of urban communes involved the transfer of authority over factories from central and provincial ministries to the local party committee that controlled the communes. Some of the communes consisted of workers in one large factory, others included the residents of one part of a city, still others, located on the outskirts of cities, included some farmland along with an urban sector. Whatever the form of urban organization, an effort was made to release women for work by establishing mess halls, nurseries, homes for the aged, and service facilities such as laundries.

To enlist popular enthusiasm and encourage local initiative, local authorities were granted substantial leeway in deciding how to implement government directives. The central government still set general economic policy and retained control over the largest heavy industrial plants, but 80 percent of all enterprises were decentralized. No longer was there to be reliance on experts in far-off Beijing making all the decisions and operating with a centralized bureaucracy as in the U.S.S.R.

As far as possible, literature and the visual arts were to be not only for but also by the people. Teams were sent out to collect the people's literature and to encourage peasants to compose poetry and otherwise participate in the creation of art. In Shanghai alone some 200,000 people participated in producing five million poems. Many thousands undoubtedly were exhilarated at achieving recognition in a field previously reserved for an exclusive elite.

High social as well as economic expectations were raised by the creation of the communes. According to Communist theory, the achievement of a truly communist society entails a change from paying people according to their productivity to paying "each according to his needs." In line with this, experiments were conducted in paying people approximately 70 percent of their wages in kind (produce to satisfy their needs) and the rest in cash according to their productivity. Meanwhile, impressive production targets were announced, including the goal of catching up with British industrial production in fifteen years. To the Chinese leaders, the social and economic goals seemed entirely compatible.

If the Great Leap Forward achieved some of its political and psychological goals, it also produced an economic disaster. This did not become apparent for some time; the initial statistics of production were impressive, but they turned out to have been grossly inflated. An unanticipated consequence of the Great Leap Forward was a breakdown in China's statistical services, and serious mistakes were made because the government accepted the exaggerated figures forwarded by overenthusiastic local authorities. Some projects originally pursued with enthusiasm later had to be abandoned as unworkable. Perhaps the best known was the campaign to use local villagers and materials to build and operate backyard furnaces for making iron and steel. Since this fitted in well with the policy of decentralization and relying on the masses, the plan was vigorously implemented. All over China small furnaces were set up and utensils were melted down, but the furnaces proved incapable of turning out iron of acceptable quality, let alone steel.

The most serious failure of the Great Leap Forward was in agriculture. Misconceived irrigation projects leached nutrients from the soil and mass mobilization for work projects exhausted and demoralized the people. Here, too, the government worked with misleading statistics, as local units vied with each other in reporting productivity gains. The harvest of 1958 was seriously exaggerated. Relying on faulty expectations and inflated reports, the government took so much grain that in many areas practically nothing was left for the peasants. Massive famine resulted. The number who perished is difficult to determine, but 16 to 27 million is a conservative estimate. The Great Leap ended in a stupendous crash.

The Sino-Soviet Split

From the beginning of the People's Republic there were areas of tension and potential conflict between China and the Soviet Union. As we have seen, the C.C.P. came to power only after going its own way, independent of Moscow. Furthermore, the Chinese leadership was as determinedly nationalistic as the Soviets, who, under Stalin, operated on the principle that what was good for the Soviet Union was good for world Communism. This equation had some plausibility as long as there was only one great Communist state in the world, but it was a thesis that the Chinese, sooner or later, were bound to challenge.

Initially, the forces holding the alliance together were stronger than those pulling it apart. These included not only ideological ties but also shared Cold War enemies. However, around the mid-1950s serious cracks in the alliance began to appear. One cause of friction was territorial. The Chinese reluctantly accepted the independence of Outer Mongolia, whose historical status resembled that of Tibet, but they were very unhappy about their northern and western boundaries with the Soviet Union. These borders had been drawn in the nineteenth century and thus formed part of the history of imperialism that China's new government was pledged to undo. As early as 1954 Chinese publications indicated the country's refusal to accept vast regions of Central and Northeast Asia as permanently belonging to the U.S.S.R.

Another source of trouble was the Chinese desire for recognition as leaders of world Communism, as suggested in Figure 15.1. After the death of Stalin in 1953, they expected that Mao would be honored as the leading living contributor to Marxist ideology and the architect of strategies to advance the cause in the "Third World." Instead, Khrushchev went his own way by denouncing Stalin in a famous speech in 1956 that implied the illegitimacy of all "personality cults," including that forming around Mao. Figure 15.1 shows Mao as a world figure. Stylistically, it exemplifies a turning away from Soviet models and "the nationalization of oil painting," a term applied to "any means of imbuing oil painting with recognizably Chinese aesthetics." As illustrated here, one way of doing so was by forgoing the effects of light and shadow and favoring "flat patches of unmodulated color rather than painterly textures."[5]

Khrushchev's theory of peaceful coexistence and the U.S.S.R.'s new international stance further irritated the Chinese. Even Mao's opponents within the C.C.P. felt insulted that Chinese leaders had not been consulted before these major shifts in Soviet policy were announced. For their part, the Soviet leaders could hardly be expected to welcome Chinese claims, made during the Great Leap Forward, that their communes represented a higher stage on the road to the ideal society than anything achieved in the Soviet Union after forty years of Communist rule.

Despite efforts toward reconciliation, such as Chinese support for the Soviet suppression of the Hungarian uprising in 1956, Mao's visit to Moscow in 1957, and Khrushchev's to Beijing in 1958 and 1959, the strains in the alliance continued to mount. Contributing to this was the U.S.S.R.'s unwillingness to exploit its temporary supremacy in rocketry to support a possible Chinese attack on Taiwan, an attack that would have had no hope for success unless the United States were neutralized by Soviet threats. Khrushchev's relatively unbelligerent stance toward the United States seemed to the Chinese like a cowardly betrayal, while Mao's belittling of the dangers of nuclear warfare made him appear to the Soviets as a dangerous adventurer gambling with the lives of millions. No wonder the Soviets were hesitant about sharing nuclear secrets with the Chinese.

The split became unbreachable in the summer of 1960, when the Soviets withdrew their technicians from China. They even took their blueprints with them. After that, despite limited cooperation during the Vietnam War, relations remained bitter, as China and the U.S.S.R. denounced each other's policies and challenged the Marxist legitimacy of each other's revolutions. While the Chinese charged that the Soviets had deviated from the true revolutionary path, Russian and East European ideologists depicted Chinese aberrations as arising from their lack of a firm proletarian base as well as an inadequate understanding of Marxism.

An aspect of this situation was the Soviet Union's support of India in its disputes with China. Relations between China and India became tense in 1959, after the Chinese, asserting their rights under international law, imposed their rule on Tibet and used their soldiers to suppress Tibetan resistance. India's welcome of Tibetan refugees, including the Dalai Lama, the spiritual and sometime secular leader of Tibet, was resented in Beijing. As it was, China and India, the world's two most populous nations, were natural rivals for Asian leadership. The resulting tensions would not have led to outright hostility, however, had it not been for a border dispute over a remote area through which China had built a road linking Xinjiang with Tibet. The result was a short border war in 1962 in which Chinese quickly humiliated the Indian troops. The Soviet Union continued its policy of friendship with India, and China cultivated good relations with India's arch rival, Pakistan. Meanwhile, within the Communist world, China defended and allied itself with the bitterly anti-Soviet regime of Albania.

Militarily, the Soviet Union remained much the stronger of the two powers, but the People's Republic was also developing its armed strength. A milestone was reached in 1964 when it exploded its first atomic bomb. Although, as indicated by its title, the painting reproduced as Figure 15.2 was understood as celebratory, it may have been an ironic response to relentless pressures on Wu Hufan (1894–1970) to produce art that would serve the revolution and the state, for Wu was a highly sophisticated and sensitive traditional-style painter and a careful student of the paintings of the Four Wangs, who had delighted the court of Kangxi (see Chapter 2). To quote Julia Andrews, "As incongruous as it seems, this painting of the mushroom cloud is one of the most beautiful demonstrations of brushwork to be found during the period." She goes on to cite its "casual lively strokes and subtly varied ink tones."[6]

The bomb did not soften relations between the two Communist giants. Numerous border clashes endangered the peace between them, and both feared that the situation might escalate into full-fledged war. Beijing built an extensive system of underground shelters for use in case of an attack by air. The hostility of the Soviet Union was one of the principal factors that led to a gradual rapprochement between China and the United States during the 1970s.

Domestic Politics, *1961–1965*

The failure of the Great Leap Forward led to retrenchment in domestic policies, a willingness to accept, at least for a while, more modest interim social and economic goals. It was a serious setback for Mao's personal authority as well as plans. He remained party chairman, but in December 1958 had to resign as head of the government. That post was filled by Liu Shaoqi (1898–1969), a hard-working organization man long associated with Mao. Liu had supporters in high party and government positions, but the supervision of the state's administrative machinery, including the various ministries, remained under the direction of the head of the State Administrative Council, who had the title of premier. This position ha0d been held since 1949 by another trusted party veteran, Zhou Enlai. Zhou also served as foreign minister until 1959, and continued even after he left that post to act as China's main spokesman in foreign affairs. By all accounts, Zhou was one of the most capable and versatile of all the C.C.P. leaders, a superb political and military strategist, a truly gifted administrator and negotiator.

FIGURE 15.2 *Celebrate the Success of Our Atomic Bomb Explosion*, Wu Hufan. Hanging scroll, ink and color on paper, 1965.
SHANGHAI INSTITUTE OF CHINESE PAINTING. © WU HUFAN. USED BY PERMISSION WU YUANJING.

Another important government position was that of minister of defense. In 1959 Peng Dehuai (1898–1974), a veteran general, was ousted from this post for going too far in criticizing Mao and the Great Leap Forward. He was further accused of pro-Soviet tendencies, and held responsible for overemphasizing professionalism and failing to imbue the troops with sufficient ideological spirit. His successor as minister of defense was another distinguished general, Lin Biao (1907–1971) who was favored by Mao.

Under the direction of Liu Shaoqi, the government relaxed the tempo of social change. There was now greater appreciation of expertise and less reliance on the revolutionary enthusiasm of the masses. There was an increased use of economic rather than ideological incentives: in the communes the more productive workers could earn extra work points, and in the factories there were wage increases, bonuses, and promotions to be earned, measures later castigated as "economism." Peasants, while still under the obligation to produce a fixed amount of grain for the state, were allowed small private plots and permitted to sell on the free market whatever they could grow on them.

No longer able to rely on the U.S.S.R. in the international arena, China in 1964 channeled investments into creating a "Third Front," described as "a crash program to build heavy industry in inland provinces away from the militarily vulnerable coastal and northeast areas."[7] Despite political turmoil, this effort continued until 1971, augmenting the damage already inflicted on the environment by misguided dam building and other abuses during the Great Leap Forward. From the beginning, as in the campaign against sparrows, Mao and his followers advocated and pursued the conquest of nature.

After the great exertions and the disappointments of the Great Leap Forward, there was a natural slackening not only of the pace of change but also of revolutionary fervor. This alarmed Mao, who sought to combat this trend by initiating a socialist education movement in 1962 without, however, much effect. Furthermore, there now appeared in print thinly veiled attacks on Mao himself. Among them was the historical play, *Hai Rui Dismissed from Office*, written by the deputy mayor of Beijing. In this play the sixteenth-century official (see Chapter 2) was portrayed sympathetically as an honest minister who stood up for the peasants and was dismissed by a foolish and autocratic emperor. What was implied was a critique of Mao's own dismissal, in 1959, of Minister of Defense Peng Dehuai. In November 1965 an article was published in the Shanghai press denouncing this play. Thus began the Cultural Revolution.

The Great Proletarian Cultural Revolution: The Radical Phase, 1966–1969

The Cultural Revolution was profoundly ideological and strongly political. It was cultural in the broadest sense, for it sought to remold the entire society and to change the consciousness of the Chinese people. Utopian in its aims, it was disastrous in its results. Its moving force was Mao himself, determined not to allow the revolution to drift into Soviet-style revisionism, resolved to combat the reemergence of old patterns of bureaucratic arrogance and careerism, convinced that drastic measures were necessary to prevent the entrenchment of new vested interests in state and party, and hungry to resume personal control. Now an old man,

Mao was unwilling to rest on his laurels as the father of the revolution. He actively involved himself in the Cultural Revolution and dramatically displayed his physical vigor by publicly swimming some ten miles across the Yangzi River five months before he turned 74 in 1966.

The obstacles to the Cultural Revolution were formidable, because it affected the interests of a majority of party functionaries both at the center and in the provinces. But among Mao's assets were not only his unequaled prestige but also the support of the People's Liberation Army, which, under Lin Biao, emphasized guerrilla-style revolutionary spirit and fostered solidarity among officers and men by deemphasizing rank. In the summer of 1965, insignia of rank were abolished and uniforms in no way differentiated officers and men. Mao and other leaders hoped similarly to reduce or, if possible, to eliminate the distinctions and privileges of rank in society at large.

To accomplish this required the destruction of the Establishment. To carry on the battle, the country was inundated with copies of *Quotations from Chairman Mao,* the omnipresent Little Red Book cited on all occasions as the ultimate source of authority. Mao himself was glorified as never before. His sayings and pictures were everywhere; his writings were placed on family altars, his name filled the air; some villages began meetings by people holding hands and dancing to the tune of "Sailing the Seas Depends on the Helmsman, Making Revolution Depends on Mao Zedong's Thought."

The vanguard and shocktroops of the Cultural Revolution were the Red Guards, young people mostly born since the founding of the People's Republic. Mao hoped that their youthful spirit would revitalize the revolution and rescue it from sinking into comfortable revisionism. In his view it was not enough for these young people merely to read theoretical and historical works and to sing revolutionary songs. They must actually live and make revolution, so that they would be molded by direct personal revolutionary experience. As Mao had said, "a revolution is not a dinner party" (see p. 217). Going on their own "long marches" was not enough. The Red Guards were responsible for many excesses as they organized public humiliations of prominent people, administered beatings and took captives, ransacked houses and destroyed books, art, and anything old or foreign. Many people were beaten to death or committed suicide while countless others were imprisoned or sent to labor on the land. Among the most enthusiastic participants were urban youths of questionable class background proving to others and themselves their revolutionary purity.

Opposition to the Red Guard and the Cultural Revolution was considerable. In many places the local authorities were able to draw on popular support. There was rioting, and pitched battles were fought between rival groups, each claiming to represent the thought of Mao. Much of the information on these struggles comes from numerous posters written in large characters. Mao himself, in August 1966, wrote such a poster, "Let Us Bombard the Headquarters."

Many party headquarters were attacked, and the party was crippled. Leaders of the government, from Liu Shaoqi down, were made to confess their sins in public and then removed from public view. Universities were closed, scientific and scholarly journals ceased publication (although nuclear development went on apace), intellectual and cultural life was disrupted, and there was turmoil in the cities. However, Zhou Enlai managed to keep the basic machinery of government working, and was able to protect some from attack. Meanwhile, Mao's wife, Jiang Qing (c. 1914–1991), and Mao's secretary, Chen Boda (1904–1989), emerged as leaders of the Cultural Revolution group.

Writers and artists were prominent among the victims of the Cultural Revolution, and a narrow orthodoxy was also enforced in the other arts. Jiang Qing, herself once an actress, championed revolutionary operas. In place of traditional Chinese opera, audiences were now treated to dances on the theme, "We Are So Happy Because We Are Delivering Grain to the State," or expressing joy at the completion of an electric power plant.

The Cultural Revolution reached its most radical phase in early 1967. At the beginning of that year a dramatic series of events in Shanghai led to the triumph of a workers' movement that was able to overthrow the local party apparatus by overcoming factional divisions. In February the workers formed a People's Commune, which lasted only nineteen days, because Mao, thinking it too radical, did not endorse it. He preferred the formation of "revolutionary committees" in which the army played a leading role. With the party out of commission and the country badly divided, the army grew in importance as the single organized and disciplined institution capable of forceful action on a national scale. However, the revolution developed a new "ultraleft" intensity before the army was called in to calm things down. In the summer of 1967, hundreds of thousands demonstrated in Beijing against Liu Shaoqi and Zhou Enlai. Radicals even occupied the foreign ministry for two weeks. Outside of the capital the army killed countless numbers in clashes with opponents. The most dramatic events took place in July, when the army intervened to suppress insurgents in Wuhan. Further violence ensued elsewhere. Finally, in September, Mao and the leadership turned toward the army to restore order. The Red Guards were disbanded in July 1968.

Military men were prominent on the various revolutionary committees set up to administer provinces, factories, and communes as the Cultural Revolution continued, increasingly under army auspices. The revolution came to an end in 1969. In April of that year, a party congress officially confirmed the new prominence of the army by adopting a new constitution designating Lin Biao as Mao's successor. An important official criterion for party membership was class background. "Bad elements," such as the descendants of landlords, rich peasants, capitalists, and "rightists" continued to face obstacles in career advancement.

Earlier, party cadres and intellectuals had been "sent down" to work the land among the peasants, and now thousands of Red Guards were similarly removed from the cities for a stint of labor in the fields. This was not only a practical measure for restoring order but also had a theoretical basis in the "mass line," which embodied Mao's conviction that the people were the source of valuable ideas and that the function of leaders was to obtain these ideas from the masses, to concentrate and systematize them, and then take them back to the masses. The function of leaders was to learn humbly from the masses and also to teach them. The idea was that leaders would identify with the common people, but the actuality was that for ten years most of China's best and brightest had to suffer physical hardship and mental anguish and despair. Some were never to make it back to the cities, and numerous others would never be able to make up for years lost in education and training. China as a whole was to pay a heavy price for the loss of ten years of educational, intellectual, and technological advance.

The Cultural Revolution saw the resumption of Great Leap Forward trends that had been discarded during the early 1960s. A policy of economic decentralization and provincial self-sufficiency was emphasized as consistent with the Third Front program as well as with Maoist ideology. Again, Redness was emphasized over expertise and private economic incentives. Again, the focus was on the rural sector, which benefited from programs that extended medical care and education. Plants were built in rural areas to manufacture and repair farm machinery, produce fertilizer, or process local products, thereby diminishing the distinction between city and country. There were experiments in calculating work points for farm work on the basis of political criteria rather than in terms of an individual's productivity. Similarly, in urban factories there were provisions for greater worker participation in factory management and programs to lessen the distinction between workers and managers and between mental and manual labor.

The Winding Down, 1969–1976

Although the Cultural Revolution was officially ended in 1969, Jiang Qing and her associates retained control over the media and cultural affairs. During the next seven years radical Maoists remained influential in national politics and had some victories. Nevertheless, there was a gradual turn to moderation. The party was rebuilt, and moderate leaders reappeared. Mao himself wanted to curb the power of the military and turned against Lin Biao, whose downfall came in the autumn of 1971. Allegedly, Lin tried to save himself by staging a coup, and, when that failed, he attempted to flee in an airplane that crashed in Mongolia.

The fate of Liu Shaoqi and Lin Biao demonstrated the hazardous position of those marked for the succession, but Zhou Enlai, as usual, was on the winning side. Zhou continued as premier, and, with Mao aging, he was more influential than ever. Army influence decreased and more moderate economic policies were adopted. There was a general relaxation of emphasis on revolutionary fervor. For example, when universities were first reopened in 1970, after a four-year hiatus, admission was based on recommendations from comrades in the candidate's work unit and the approval of the appropriate revolutionary committee, but in 1972 academic criteria for admission were reintroduced. Also in that year, the first scientific periodicals reappeared but with an emphasis on applied science. Public exaltation of Mao was toned down. There were even attacks on the Little Red Book; C.C.P. members were now urged to pursue a thorough study of Marxist writings.

During 1973 to 1974, Lin Biao, though dead, was further denounced in a campaign linking him with Confucius. Both men were portrayed as "political

FIGURE 15.3 *Repudiating Lin Biao and Confucius*, Yang Zhixian. Like many peasant paintings, this one employs bright colors. Here vivid red predominates. Peasant painting exhibited in Beijing in 1973.

FROM *PEASANT PAINTINGS FROM HUHSIEN COUNTY.* COMPILED BY THE FINE ARTS COLLECTION SECTION OF THE CULTURAL GROUPS UNDER THE STATE COUNCIL OF THE PEOPLE'S REPUBLIC OF CHINA (PEKING, 1974).

swindlers" and sinister reactionaries. Confucius was depicted as representing a declining slaveowner class, while Lin Biao was charged with wanting to restore capitalism, each man exerting himself to reinstate an outdated system. The campaign against Confucius and Lin Biao was a sign of the continuing influence of the Cultural Revolution leaders' attack on the past, but the ancient philosopher and modern general made a strange pair, and very likely Confucius was actually a surrogate for Zhou Enlai.

The politics and ethos of the time are illustrated in Figure 15.3. The slogan spanning and dominating the entrance reads, "Workers, Peasants, and Soldiers

Are the Main Force Criticizing Lin and Criticizing Confucius." Parking their bicycles and small tractors outside the gate, people have entered the compound to peruse wall posters spelling out the case against the two villains while loudspeakers, high on their poles like their counterparts everywhere, blare out announcements, slogans, and revolutionary music.

Most peasant paintings do not serve overt political campaigns but celebrate rural life and work. Their urban counterparts were paintings showing people working in factories. Many show women at work, for China was determined that women were to become fully equal with men (see Figure 15.4). In China, as in the Soviet Union, the challenges and triumphs of a socialist society were the main topics of art and literature, depicted in a style usually designated "socialist realism," though intended to inspire, not to mirror life.

Peasant and "social realist" painting represent a break with old styles of painting, but others artists painted new subjects in a traditional way (Figure 15.1) or placed modern subjects in an essentially traditional setting rendered in a traditional manner, as in Qian Songyan's *Ode to Ya'an* paying homage to the place where the victory of the Chinese Communist Party was forged and the revolutionary Yan'an spirit supposedly held sway (see Figure 15.5).

During the sixties and seventies, workers and peasants continued to be encouraged to participate in the creation of art. There were efforts at collective writing and painting. Another arrangement was for part-time authors to get a day off from their factory jobs in order to write. Professional writers were periodically "sent down" to factory or commune so that they would not lose touch with the people. As a matter of routine, they invited popular criticism of their work and responded to suggestions for changes. For example, before *The Golden Road* (1972) was published, 200 copies were sent to communes and factories for criticism. This novel by Hao Ran (Liang Jinguang, 1932–), which went on to sell four million copies, dealt with the change from individual farming to the formation of mutual aid teams. In all the arts, the same themes occur over and over: the ideals and struggles of the revolution, the wisdom of Mao, the heroism of soldiers, the triumph of socialist virtue over selfishness, the glory of work.

During and after the Cultural Revolution, Chinese relations with the Soviet Union remained tense, even though both powers supported North Vietnam in its war against the Saigon regime and the United States. Concern over Soviet intentions was heightened to alarm when the U.S.S.R. invaded Czechoslovakia in 1968 and Party Secretary Leonid Brezhnev announced that the U.S.S.R. had the right to intervene in socialist countries, which he accorded only "limited sovereignty."

FIGURE 15.4 *Wo shi haiyan (I Am a Seagull)*, Pan Jianjun (designer/artist), c. 1973. Chinese poster showing a strong, exuberant woman defying the elements to bring modernity to the countryside.

PHOTOGRAPH © STEFAN R. LANDSBERGER.
(CHINESE PROPAGANDA POSTER PAGES, ONLINE EXHIBIT, HTTP://WWW.IISG.NL/~LANDSBERGER.)

FIGURE 15.5 *Ode to Yan'an,* Qian Songyan (1898–1985). A pagoda and a transmission station face each other across a space defined, as in traditional landscapes, by mist and clouds rendering just barely visible the entrances to Yan'an's famous caves. Print.

COLLECTION CONRAD SCHIROKAUER. PHOTOGRAPH © LORE SCHIROKAUER.

Fears of a Soviet nuclear strike, actual troop deployments along the lengthy Sino-Soviet frontier, and armed clashes in Manchuria induced China to seek broader diplomatic contacts with the United States. Although Chinese personnel did assist the North Vietnamese, there was no repetition of Korea. Chinese terrain was not threatened and no massive intervention by Chinese troops took place. Meanwhile, a channel of communication was maintained with the United States through periodic meetings of the ambassadors of the two countries, held first in Geneva and later in Warsaw. The fall of Lin Biao and the emergence of Zhou Enlai increased the prospect for improved Sino-American relations.

A contributing factor on the American side was the intention of President Nixon, elected in 1968, to withdraw the United States from the war in Vietnam. As long as China and the United States were committed to the opposing sides of a war that was raging at full force and threatening to escalate still further, substantial improvement in Sino-American relations remained highly unlikely. Nevertheless, a high-level Sino-American dialogue did not have to wait for the actual end of the war—a shift in direction toward peace was enough. By 1971 both sides were ready to talk. A new approach to China was deemed a logical corollary of the Kissinger-Nixon concept of international balance-of-power politics. The Chinese were receptive. The Sino-American rapprochement began informally with a Chinese invitation of an American ping-pong team, whose members were personally greeted by Zhou Enlai. Then came President Nixon's visit to Beijing in February 1972, and the Shanghai Communiqué, which provided for partial normalization and paved the way for the resumption of full formal diplomatic relations in 1979. In 1971, even before the Nixon visit, the United Nations had voted to admit the People's Republic in place of the Nationalists, and the new American stance now removed the last obstacle to recognition by most countries.

Two deaths dominated the news in 1976. When Zhou died in January of that year, his enemies banned public mourning, but were unable to prevent a massive gathering at the Martyrs' Memorial in Beijing's great Tiananmen Square on China's Day of Mourning in April. This expression of reverence for the late premier was tantamount to a rejection of the Cultural Revolution. Mao, aged and ailing, still had sufficient authority to designate Hua Guofeng (1920–) as Zhou's successor.

Hua was soon called upon to demonstrate his administrative talents, for in July China's worst earthquake in four centuries devastated Tangshan, an industrial and mining city a hundred miles from Beijing. In old China, people would have interpreted this as a signal of further shocks to come—and they would have been right, for on September 9 Mao died. Architect of the triumph of the C.C.P., Mao presided over the successes of the revolution, but was also responsible for its failures and for needless suffering, hardship and dying. His passing marked the end of an era.

Notes

1. Warren I. Cohen, ed., *New Frontiers in American–East Asian Relations* (New York: Columbia Univ. Press, 1983), p. 144.
2. Quoted in Merle Goldman, *Literary Dissent in Communist China* (Cambridge, Mass.: Harvard Univ. Press, 1967), p. 192.
3. Quoted in Goldman, p. 193.
4. Hsu Kai-yu, *The Chinese Literary Scene—A Writer's Visit to the People's Republic* (New York: Vintage Books, Random House, 1975), p. 227.
5. Julia F. Andrews, "The Victory of Socialist Realism: Oil Painting and the New Guohua," in Julia F. Andrews and Kuyi Shen, *A Century in Crisis: Modernity and Tradition in the Art of Twentieth-Century China* (New York: Guggenheim Museum, 1998), p. 230.
6. Julia F. Andrews, *Painters and Politics in the People's Republic of China, 1949–1979* (Berkeley: Univ. of California Press, 1994), p. 303.
7. William A. Joseph, Christine P. W. Wong, and David Zweig, *New Perspectives on the Cultural Revolution* (Cambridge, Mass.: The Council on East Asian Studies/Harvard University, 1991), Introduction, p. 2.

16

The Chinese World since Mao

1976	1978		1989	1992		1997	2002

Death of Mao · Four Modernizations · Tiananmen · Death of Deng / Recovery of Hong Kong

Era of Deng Xiaoping · Jiang Zemin 1992–2002

After the death of Mao Zedong, China embarked on a profound change of course. Many of the policies of the previous quarter of a century were reversed, and new measures adopted that bore scant resemblance to either those of Mao or of his more conventional opponents. The economy changed dramatically, and by 2000 China was growing at the fastest rate in the world, creating new problems and opportunities. All spheres of life were affected, but in different ways and at different speeds. Artistic and intellectual change was most intense; politics and its institutions lagged.

China's relationships to the external world, both in East Asia and beyond, also changed. One factor initially spurring China's leaders to adopt new policies was the recognition that it had fallen behind the impressive achievements of the rest of East Asia. That included not only Japan and Korea but Hong Kong (returned to China in 1997) and especially Taiwan, whose twentieth century continued to be so different from the mainland as to demand separate treatment.

Deng Xiaoping and the Four Modernizations

After a period of adversity (1977–1978), it became clear that Mao's true successor was not, as he had intended, Hua Guofeng but Deng Xiaoping (1904–1997). Deng was a party veteran who, during the Cultural Revolution, had been removed from office and denounced as second only to Liu Shaoqi in "taking the capitalist road," but more recently Deng had enjoyed the backing of Zhou Enlai. In July 1977, Deng became first deputy premier, and from 1978 on was clearly China's most powerful political figure. Blamed for all the ills of the Cultural Revolution were the "Gang of Four," led by Jiang Qing, Mao's widow, who insisted, in vain, that she had simply been carrying out Mao's directives. By November 1980 the new leadership under Deng felt sufficiently secure to put the Gang of Four on trial and have it televised. In January 1981 Jiang Qing and another leader were given suspended death sentences, later commuted to life imprisonment. Hua Guofeng was soon shunted into political obscurity.

Deng's program was epitomized by the slogan "The Four Modernizations," first introduced by Zhou Enlai in 1975. Directed at agriculture, industry, science, and defense, the aim was to turn China into a modern industrial state. The years since 1952 had seen considerable economic progress, but China remained an underdeveloped country. Furthermore, the Cultural Revolution had taken a heavy toll in lost educational and technological progress. Now, under Deng, merit, not revolutionary virtue, was rewarded. Professionalism and individual initiative were encouraged, and market forces were allowed greater play.

There were drastic changes in the countryside as agriculture was decollectivized. In 1982 communes lost their social and political authority, and their economic power was also curtailed. Under the "responsibility system," peasants were assigned land on contracts to produce a certain amount of grain, and increasingly won the right to decide on just how to do this and to dispose of any surplus produce on the open market. The amount of land to be assigned was to depend on the number of people in each family, an arrangement that seemed new but actually resembles both the 1951 Land Reform and the "equal-field system" enacted in 486 and discarded in the eighth century! Gradually, restrictions on commercial activities were eased, and enterprising peasants did notably well.

Similar changes took place in light industry and commerce, but at a slower pace. Official enterprises were expected to justify their existence by making a profit, government regulation was decreased, and individuals were allowed to open restaurants and workshops. Under a new open door policy welcoming foreign companies, special economic zones were established, where foreign investment was encouraged. At the same time, the skylines of first Beijing, then Shanghai, and more recently even cities in the interior, were being transformed by high-rise buildings, among them international luxury hotels where the affluent traveler could savor China in luxury and at an antiseptic distance.

Mao Zedong had once seen China's large population as an asset, but even before his death it became clear that China's future would be dim if the population continued to grow without restraint. In the early 1970s, China adopted a vigorous birth-control program. Even so, the population continued to increase, topping 1 billion in 1982. In the cities, the birth rate had fallen even before severe pressures insured virtually full compliance with the one-child-per-couple law. But this was not the case in the countryside, where children, in the absence of a public safety net, continued, with good reason, to be regarded as an asset to a family.

Industrialization and population growth put additional strains on China's already hard-pressed environment. We will return to them in our discussion of the nineties, but note here that air and water pollution were on the rise, and that land erosion had already turned the Yangzi River into a second Yellow River. In the mid-1980s topsoil loss of more than 5 billion tons annually deprived China of more soil nutrition than that produced by its entire synthetic fertilizer industry. Major programs of reforestation were one positive response, but in general the environmental degradation accelerated. The state's obligation to protecting the environment did find its way into the 1982 constitution, and a body of law ensued, but environmentalism did not figure in the Four Modernizations.

From early on some, mostly elderly, party leaders objected to the pace of change, but there were also voices at the opposite end of the political spectrum calling for more rapid liberalization. They found expression in postings on Beijing's "Democracy Wall," where, for a time, people could freely state their views. Especially notable was a poster put up in December 1978 by Wei Jingsheng (1949–), a young man who worked as an electrician and had four years of army service under his belt. In his poster Wei called for democracy as a Fifth Modernization absolutely necessary for the attainment of the other four.

This was too much for Deng and the political leadership. The wall was abolished. In May 1979 Wei was arrested. Subsequently, he received a fifteen-year sentence. Instead of a fifth modernization, Deng, in March 1979, proclaimed "four cardinal principles" as guides for the future.

The Four Cardinal Principles

The four principles consisted of "the socialist road," "the dictatorship of the proletariat," "the leadership of the C.C.P.," and "Marxism-Leninism and Mao Zedong Thought." In practice, as in theory, all four were vague at best. In 1981 "socialism with Chinese characteristics" was adopted as the official policy, but clearly the attainment of utopian egalitarianism was postponed into the distant future. The "socialist road" was to be a long one, with China deemed to be only in the "initial stage of socialism," as Premier Zhao Ziyang (1919–) put it at the Eleventh Party Congress in 1987. That same year the mayor of Shenyang was quoted as saying, "When used to promote the development of China's socialist economy, bankruptcy, leasing, shareholding and these sorts of things are no longer capitalist."[1]

Of the other cardinal principles, the leaders took "the leadership of the C.C.P." most seriously, and brooked no challenge to the political dominance of their party, which they equated with "the dictatorship of the proletariat," the orthodox Marxist label for the stage between revolution and the withering away of the state that would usher in true communism.

The status of "Marxism-Leninism and Mao Zedong Thought" was more problematic. Nineteenth-century self-strengtheners had once firmly believed in the Confucian ends they meant to serve with novel and foreign means, but China's new leaders conveyed no similar depth of conviction. To many it seemed that the official ideology commanded little more than lip service, while acquiring and enjoying personal wealth became the order of the day. China took on a new look as revolutionary posters and slogans gave way to commercial advertisements on billboards and in the media, clumsy at first but then "gradually transmogrified into slavish imitations of Hong Kong, Taiwanese and Japanese models." Geremie R. Barmé goes on to point out, "The world presented in such advertising was one nearly entirely divided from the ideological landscape constructed by the party." Referring to the vision projected by international consumerism and playing off Marx's denunciation of religion, he concludes, "During the early 1990's, this vision of the consumer's paradise, rather than the state religion of Marxism-Leninism and Mao Thought, became the true opiate of the masses."[2]

Intellectual Life and the Arts in the Eighties

It was a heady time, stimulated by a deluge of new ideas, forms and styles. The period began with the "literature and art of the wounded," as artists and writers gave expression to their suffering during the Cultural Revolution. This was followed by a "search for roots," expressed not only in literature but in films, such as "Yellow Earth," directed by Chen Kaige (1952–), who, along with his fellow "fifth generation" director, Zhang Yimou (1952–), won international acclaim for Chinese film. One of the many writers expressing similar sentiments was Mo Yan

(Guan Moye, 1956–) whose *Garlic Ballads* depicts, with great human sympathy, the bitter life of peasants suffering at the hands of arrogant party cadres. He also wrote *Red Sorghum,* in which the villains are the Japanese military in China during World War II. Made into a movie directed by Zhang Yimou, it shocked the Chinese audience, but won the best picture award at the Berlin Festival in 1988.

Some writers turned more to psychological themes or to the interplay of human feelings, and engaged in stylistic experiments such as the flow of consciousness technique used by Wang Meng (1934–), Minister of Culture 1987–1989. Others favored the magic realism of Gabriel Marcia Marquez. Meanwhile, Chinese intellectuals in all fields rejoined the international intellectual community and undertook a reexamination and reevaluation of their own past. Foreign scholars too were welcomed, as at conferences on Confucius and Zhu Xi (1987) held in the philosophers' home provinces (Shandong and Fujian, respectively). Temples and monuments were restored, as were mosques and churches. Jiang Qing's revolutionary operas disappeared from the stage, and Arthur Miller was invited to help prepare a Chinese performance of *Death of a Salesman* (1985).

Now, too, the Chinese public had its first look at modern artists ranging from Picasso to Jackson Pollock. While members of the Obscure School of Poetry expressed their alienation in verse, avante-garde painters depicted faceless figures set in endless, barren space. Some determined nonconformists, such as the Dada group of Xiamen, Fujian's largest city, sought to smash all frames. Like the original proponents of Dada in post–World War I Europe, they mocked all art. Proclaiming the end of art, they ended their 1986 exhibit by burning all the works on display, frames and all. A kindred spirit was Xu Bing (1955–) who devoted three years of hard work to compose his *Book from the Sky* that no one can read, thus challenging the viewer to reflect on the nature of writing, language, art, and life in a postmodern world (Figure 16.1).

The spirit of iconoclasm and revolt was not limited to the highbrow. Many aspects of western popular culture found a following in China, where Japanese and Taiwanese pop tunes were widely enjoyed and rock and roll gained an ardent audience. In the mid-eighties Beijing's own Cui Jian (1961–), "the John Lennon of China,"[3] formed a rock group whose records were best-sellers, much to the puzzled dismay of the Establishment.

While raucous music and critical writings continued to find a ready hearing among students and intellectuals, the regime, guided by Deng, was concerned not to let matters get out of hand, but for some ten years refrained from strong-arm measures that could alienate the intellectuals whose cooperation was needed for modernization. Thus campaigns against "cultural pollution" (1983) and "bourgeois liberalism" (1987) were relatively mild.

Still, pressure for change mounted. An outspoken advocate of openness in government, free speech, and political pluralism was the astrophysicist, party member, and university vice president Fang Lizhi (1936–1986), who encouraged his students to campaign for genuine local elections in Anhui, where his university was located. The movement spread from Anhui. In December, some 30,000 stu-

FIGURE 16.1 Detail view of the nonsense characters on the printed pages of the books from *Book from the Sky* (1987–1991) by Xu Bing. Mixed media installation: hand-printed books, ceiling and wall scrolls from intentionally false letter blocks. At first glance the writing looks like Chinese, for the characters are composed of elements found in traditional writing. They are, however, nonsense characters invented by the artist.

© XU BING. USED BY PERMISSION OF THE ARTIST.

dents demonstrated in Shanghai, and there were further demonstrations in Tianjin, Nanjing, and Beijing. In response, the government removed Fang from his job and expelled him from the C.C.P. Over a million students were sent to spend the following summer recess in the countryside.

For some ten years Deng successfully orchestrated the pace of change, and in 1987 he had the satisfaction of seeing the Thirteenth Party Congress affirm the general directions of his policies, including the primacy of economic development. This session also marked the retirement of a substantial number of the old guard, who were generally replaced by men more inclined to "seek truth from facts," an expression found in the *History of the Han* (*Han Shu*, first century C.E.), taken up by Mao, and used as a slogan by Deng. Deng now felt sufficiently confident to resign as deputy premier although, significantly, he retained his chairmanship of the Military Commission for two more years.

Tiananmen

The policy of mild repression of demands for democracy and human rights failed to deter student activism or dampen student demands for greater freedom of speech and of the press, an end to favoritism and government corruption, the right to form their own organizations, and for the people to have a greater say in government. In the spring of 1989 the government was caught off guard when students demonstrated, boycotted classes, held sit-ins, and occupied Beijing's huge Tiananmen square in their determination to be heard.

With the approach of the seventieth anniversary of the May Fourth Movement, students and officials alike were aware of the historical significance of the occasion, as was the press, now including international television as well as print media. Marches and demonstrations on May 4th quickened the movement, but did not settle anything. On May 13, two days before the state visit of Premier Mikhail Gorbachev, over two hundred students began a hunger strike supported by thousands of Beijing residents. When Gorbachev arrived, the government had to change the program and avoid Tiananmen. By May 16, the number of hunger strikers had mounted to over 3000. Meanwhile, as the movement gathered steam, students in many other cities demonstrated in support. Most alarming to the government, ordinary people, including factory workers, increasingly became involved.

Opposition within the government prevented even a mild compromise with the students, who were not well organized and did not speak with a single voice. When Deng Xiaoping asserted his leadership, the government moderates, including Premier Zhao, lost out. On May 20th martial law was declared, and 250,000 soldiers were brought into Beijing, where they were greeted by roadblocks and demonstrations. On May 29th, in a show of determination, radical students erected a large statue of the Goddess of Democracy holding high the torch of freedom to serve as the symbol of their movement (see Figure 16.2). Cui Jian's "Long March Rock" can be considered their anthem.

The end came early on June 4th when, shortly after midnight, columns of tanks and armored cars charged into the city and on to Tiananmen, crushing barriers and shooting anyone in the way. After the soldiers destroyed the student encampments and the statue on the square, the violence escalated. Many student and civilians were shot down and some soldiers died too. The carnage overwhelmed Beijing's hospitals, many of which were forbidden to treat civilian casualties. Nor could they or anyone else compile statistics of the dead and wounded.

Military suppression was followed by the arrest, and in some cases execution, of student leaders in the capital and elsewhere. Others found their way into exile in the West, where some continued as leaders of a non-unified and contentious political/intellectual community. Fang Lizhi, too, found freedom abroad. In 1997, after a second imprisonment, Wei Jingshen also found sanctuary abroad. After 1989 Chinese voices in many parts of the world presented alternatives to the ideology and policies proclaimed by Beijing. In the eighties the telephone, photocopier, and fax helped undermine the government monopoly on information, which proved even more difficult to sustain with the spread of email, the cell

FIGURE 16.2 *Goddess of Democracy*, Tiananmen Square, Beijing, May 30, 1989. Radical students erected the statue to democracy, and tanks and soldiers destroyed it six days later in their violent assault on Tiananmen Square.
© Peter Turnley/Corbis (TL009252).

phone, and the Internet toward the end of the century. The leadership's credibility now depended not on the old ideology but on its performance, especially its economic performance.

State, Economy, and Society in the Nineties

An immediate result of Tiananmen was that Deng's leading protégé, Premier Zhao Ziyang, was forced out of office and placed under house arrest. His place was taken by Jiang Zemin (1926–). In 1992 the octogenarian Deng made a dramatic tour of the south, proclaiming his determination to continue the pragmatic economic policy. After this trip, though still considered China's paramount leader, Deng faded into the background, allowing Jiang to establish himself and ensure a smooth transition when Deng died in 1997. Essentially, Jiang continued Deng's policies of economic liberalization without relaxing C.C.P. control over politics and public discourse. Economic liberalism without relaxation of political control became the hallmark of Jiang's leadership and legacy. Indicative of this dual policy was his speech of July 1, 2001, declaring that capitalists should be welcomed into the Communist Party and the subsequent closing of a publication named *The Pursuit of Truth* for criticizing this extraordinary departure from Marxist practice. Jiang redefined the role of the party as representing "advanced productive forces, advanced Chinese culture, and the fundamental interests of the majority."[4] These "Three Representations" were billed as major theoretical contributions, and seen as a bid by Jiang to gain status as a thinker before relinquishing his post as General Secretary of the Chinese Communist Party in November 2002. It remained unclear whether he would give up his position as chairman of the Military Commission, but the appointments to positions of leadership of many of Jiang's protégés suggest that he may attempt to remain the country's paramount leader as had Deng Xaioping after his "retirement." Similarly, the record of the new general secretary, Hu Jintao (1942–), includes some grounds of encouragement for both hard-liners and reformers while a *New York Times* headline announced, "China's New Leader Promises Not to Sever Tether to Jiang."[5] Only time will tell in which direction he will try to lead the party and the country.

Whatever it represented, the C.C.P. still controlled the state, but, with the state no longer "commanding" the economy, the relationship between state, economy, and society had changed. The direction of economic change remained much as before, though there were times of pause and hesitation. Under the direction of Zhu Rongji (1928–), like Jiang an engineer by background, and a former mayor of Shanghai, the economy weathered bouts of inflation peaking in 1988 and 1995, and the government continued to encourage foreign investment and trade, negotiating its way into the World Trade Organization in 2000. Whereas previously people had depended on their work unit to supply everything from housing to entertainment, these functions were now privatized, with the result that in Shanghai and other eastern cities a hundred stores blossomed, a thousand restaurants contended, and advertisements urged, "buy a house and become a boss."[6] The private sector prospered, but not everyone could become a boss.

The government reduced the scope of the state-run sector and announced its determination to continue doing so, because these enterprises were inefficient, frequently lost money, drained funds, and weakened the state banks on which they depended. However, the government had to proceed gradually because of the threat of social unrest posed by workers deprived of the security of their "iron rice-bowls." The labor market was already swollen by about 60 million peasants who were annually leaving their villages in search of better pay. The urban and rural unemployed formed a "floating population" that appeared in China's major cities looking for a day's work.

In the countryside, peasants received longer leases on their land, but continued to be required to sell a quota of grain to the state, which was anxious to maintain grain self-sufficiency. At the same time, many peasants now engaged in rural industries, which came to account for 60 percent of China's industrial output but did not solve the problem of rural poverty. Like other governments at the time, the P.R.C. authorities accepted a widening income gap as the price of economic growth.

Similarly in line with global trends, China moved in the directions of market economics, but the government often gave mixed political and economic signals. Heavy taxes, land requisitions, autocratic and corrupt officials, and/or severe water pollution elicited peasant petitions (70,000 in 1995) and demonstrations, some large and violent. One response was the provision for village elections "as a safety valve to let the peasantry vent their dissatisfaction." Jean C. Oi goes on to point out that different constituencies and different agendas left China "a country riddled with policy contradictions."[7]

That the new relationship between state and society is unstable and difficult to define is reflected in the proliferation of labels proffered by Western academics, including, but by no means limited to, "capitalism with Chinese characteristics," "capital socialism," "state-socialist corporatism," "symbiotic clientism," "Confucian Leninism," and "bureaupreneurialism." The proliferation of terms reflects the inadequacy of traditional categories as well as the blurring of the line between state and society. It also reflects the variety of relationships between state and society to be found in China. One reason for this is that the initiative to a considerable degree passed to local, especially county levels. Following the penchant for fours favored in the post-Mao years, Richard Baum and Alexei Shevchenko have characterized local governments as "Entrepreneurs, Patrons, Predators, and Developers." One of their major conclusions is that the situation "augurs neither the continued potency of the central party state nor the emergence of a pluralistic civil society but the proliferation of quasi-autonomous (and potentially corrupt) local economic empires."[8]

The potential for corruption was fully realized in what Lionel Jensen has aptly termed a "hybrid political economy" and in "the moral confusion wrought by a contradictory ideology."[9] The country was riddled with corruption, and crime was on the increase. Nor was malfeasance by any means purely local. In August 1999 China's auditor-general reported that one fifth of China's annual revenue had been "misappropriated," that all eighteen provincial governments were guilty, and that the Ministry of Water Resources was building luxury office buildings rather than much-needed dams and dikes.

The Environment

Industrialization and the efforts to meet the needs and some of the aspirations of a population reported at 1.248 billion in 1998 placed great strains on the environment. Air and water quality both posed health threats. China's major cities were shrouded in permanent haze, and people breathed polluted air not only outside but even indoors, where it especially threatened women cooking over stoves burning raw coal. Most coal remained untreated, and most women, though theoretically the equals of men, remained unliberated from the stove. China was well on the way to replacing the United States as the planet's foremost producer of greenhouse gases.

Water, too, can be lethal in China. Irrigation water is often contaminated by discharge. In the case of a village in Gansu inhabited by descendants of Confucius, the village leaders were able to obtain some redress only after challenging managers of a fertilizer plant to drink some water from a stream they had poisoned. Whether a farmer near Beijing whose geese all died after imbibing poisonous water will obtain legal redress is not yet known, but at least the courts have agreed to hear his case.

Pollution is not the only water problem. In the north water tables have sunk alarmingly and water shortages are severe. The diversion of Yellow River water for irrigation has reduced the transport of silt to the sea. Instead it is deposited on the river bed, raising it above the surrounding countryside and posing a threat of devastating floods as of old. Meanwhile, recurrent floods inundated southern regions. Not until 1999 did the government officially acknowledge that chopping down trees in the headlands of the Yangzi had something to do with this. There have been people in and out of government who were aware of the problem, but environmental policies formulated in Beijing were often ignored locally, especially when the problem mostly affected people downriver or far away.

However, the government too contributed to the destruction of the environment. In 1992 it approved a major project to dam the Three Gorges of the Yangzi River in order to address China's need for clean energy and flood control and to open Sichuan, China's most populous province, to oceangoing vessels. The waters of the river were diverted in 1997, and the dam is scheduled for completion in 2009. It is to be 170 meters high and run for 2 kilometers, comparable to a four-story building a mile wide, and will cost much more than the $25 billion of the very optimistic official estimate. It will displace well over a million people and inundate priceless cultural sites. The government discounted warnings about the potential disasters posed by the buildup of silt behind the dam, unpredictable geologic effects, the dangers of forming a lake even more polluted than the present river, and possible adverse effects downstream. Nor was it impressed by the turning of world opinion against megadams. While energy generation and water control could be achieved more cheaply and less dangerously by a series of small dams, these would not provide maritime access to Sichuan, where Chongqing is growing into a huge metropolis.

Whether and to what degree the laws on the books and increased awareness can avert the worst environmental destruction remains to be seen. The example of what the wealthy nations do will be a factor. Meanwhile, in some places local gods have sometimes been enlisted to defend the local environment.

The Revival of Religion

One response to the loosening of central government reins was the reemergence of religion, condemned not only by Cultural Revolution enthusiasts but denounced by Karl Marx himself as the "opiate of the people." Village temples to local and lineage deities were rebuilt, traditional burial practices resumed, and traditional beliefs and practices such as geomancy (*fengshui*; see Chapter 1) resurfaced. These cults and practices were still denounced as "superstition" by the political and intellectual establishment, which distinguished them from "legitimate" religions such as Buddhism, Daoism, Islam, and Christianity. As Stephen Feuchtwang attests, partly on the basis of personal observation, " In some places new religious buildings were tolerated, in others the Public Security forces periodically destroy them."[10] Much depended on local authorities and circumstances. For example, at Black Dragon Pool in northern Shaanxi the head of the officially sanctioned Cultural Management Institute also heads the temple association, and the Institute is responsible for the upkeep of the Black Dragon god's temple and the conduct of its main annual festival, featuring a tour by the god around the dry land to bring rain.

During the Cultural Revolution there was a tendency to elevate Mao to a status far beyond that of ordinary humans, and now tens of thousands of pilgrims have visited a monastery in Hunan, Mao's native province, where:

> some pray for the safety and harmony of family members while others ask Mao to cure chronic diseases. [Members of] the latter group are given a glass of "holy water" after their prayers. Those who feel Mao has listened to their prayers thank him for the kindness received.[11]

Some mosques and churches, converted to factories during the Cultural Revolution, were returned to their congregations and became once again places of worship sanctioned and supervised by the state. Chinese Catholics remained separated from Rome, as the government refused to let them obey the pope, and neither Catholic nor Protestant missionaries were permitted into the country. Unsupervised worship in private houses was also prohibited. But the loss of credibility of official materialism provided fertile ground for those seeking something beyond the quest for wealth and the passing satisfactions of consumerism.

The state remained suspicious of religion as an alternate source of authority and potential nucleus of resistance. They were particularly wary of Vajrayana Buddhism in Tibet and Islam in Xinjiang and Qinghai. But the government's concerns were not limited to peripheral minorities such as these. They were taken aback, and the security apparatus was caught by surprise, when 10,000 followers of *Falungong* quietly assembled in Beijing to protest the outlawing of their sect. Led from New York by its exiled founder, the sect, estimated by the government to have 70 million adherents, offered spiritual and physical health through dance-like *qigong* exercises and mental concentration. Its leader insisted from the start that it was nonpolitical, but the authorities were alarmed at its abilities to mobilize thousands, and troubled that its membership was largely middle-aged and well-integrated members of the community, some even belonging to the C.C.P. It was outlawed, and periodic arrests and trials followed.

The suppression of religious expression and the arrest of political dissidents continued in the face of international concern over human rights. While avoiding a second international outrage like Tiananmen, the regime continued to try to stamp out any sparks of separatism it feared might catch fire in Tibet or elsewhere. In international relations, particularly with the United States, the human rights issue continued to smolder, only to be doused by geopolitical and geoeconomic considerations. This was all the more the case when, after Semptember 2001, China gave its support to the American war on terror.

Foreign Relations and Hong Kong

Foreign relations during the late 1970s and 1980s remained within the pattern set earlier, and China remained at peace except that conflicting ambitions in Cambodia prompted an unsuccessful invasion of Vietnam in 1979. Sino-Vietnamese relations remained tense for some time. There were border clashes in 1985, but relations improved in the late nineties. China did not engage in any further military combat, but concentrated on modernizing its military.

China's relations with the Soviet Union became more cordial, especially after the U.S.S.R. withdrew from Afghanistan in 1988, while the fall of Communism in Eastern Europe and the disintegration of the Soviet Union were taken by China's rulers as warnings of what could befall them and their country.

Full diplomatic relations with the United States were established on January 1, 1979. Although Chinese wariness of the only remaining superpower was balanced by American unease over an emergent giant, relations remained generally cordial while trade grew and Americans entered into joint ventures with Chinese partners. With its business community enthralled by the old Western dream of an unlimited Chinese market, the United States tolerated widening trade deficits, and in the first year of the new century agreed to forgo annual reviews of China's generally unsatisfactory human rights situation. As already noted, that same year China was admitted to the World Trade Organization.

A notable diplomatic success was the agreement signed in 1984 with Great Britain to return Hong Kong to Chinese sovereignty in 1997. China in turn guaranteed that for the next fifty years Hong Kong would retain its own laws and institutions. The People's Republic thus acknowledged the economic importance of Hong Kong, which, by the mid-eighties, had developed into a major world financial and trade center with a thriving manufacturing sector. Symbolizing the future, China's Central Bank erected the city's tallest skyscrapers (1982–1990), designed by I.M. Pei (Ieho Ming Pei, 1917–), the Chinese-born American architect who in 1983 had received architecture's highest award, the Pritzker Prize. Much younger, and not nearly as famous, was Yuen Kwok-chung (1964–), whose *Triptych* (Figure 16.3), which was exhibited at the 1994 Hong Kong Contemporary Art Biennial Exhibition, invites the viewer to see the barcode as the true flag of Hong Kong and infer that commercial consumerism (mediated through Hong Kong?) is what links the US and the P.R.C. The Chinese title, "study hard and make progress every day" would make a splendid slogan for a textbook, but here heightens the sardonic effect. Fortuitously, in the exhibition catalog *Triptych* is preceded by a painting titled *Perplexity* and followed by *Coiling Incense Smoke.*

Though *Triptych* represents the money-making spirit of Hong Kong and of would-be Hong Kongs further up the China coast, the city also provided a haven for the likes of the noted philosopher of "New Confucianism," Mou Zongsan (1909–1995), and highly original painters like Irene Chou from Shanghai (see Afterward Figure A.1) and Liu Guosong from Taiwan (see Figure 16.5).

FIGURE 16.3 *Triptych 1994,* Yuen Kwok-chung (1963–). Most people in the People's Republic at this time would probably recognize the American flag as well as their own but had never seen a barcode. That, however, was a familiar symbol in Hong Kong. Acrylic on canvas, 184 × 290 cm.

With the erosion of its old ideological base, the government of the P.R.C. could seek legitimacy from its economic performance—the success of "managed consumerism," as Richard Kraus has termed it. Or it could emphasize "orchestrated nationalism"[12]—orchestrated lest it get out of hand in demonstrations that could interfere with the conduct of foreign policy and might even threaten the established order. During the nineties it pursued both consumerist and nationalist aims. With Hong Kong safely in the fold, the de facto independence of Taiwan remained a major irritant.

While chafing over foreign criticism of its suppression of human rights in Tibet and elsewhere, it was particularly troubled by Taiwan's failure to be persuaded of the benefits of its "one country–two system policy." On the eve of Taiwan's presidential elections in 1996, the P.R.C. fired missiles and conducted naval maneuvers in a show of force, and, as the new century began, the future of P.R.C.-Taiwan relations remained very much in doubt.

Intellectuals and Artists in the Nineties

In the P.R.C. the authorities continued to jail dissidents and did not tolerate political opposition. They allowed people to choose their own jobs but no longer guaranteed them a job. In general, the government gave people more latitude in

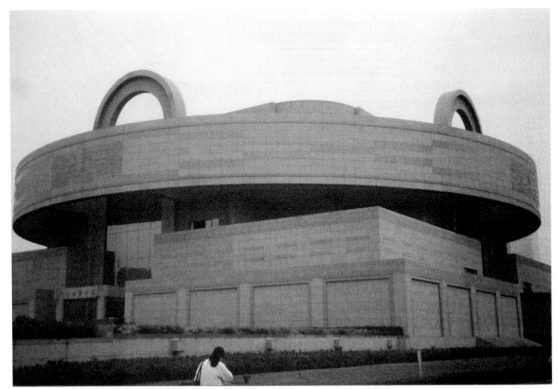

FIGURE 16.4   Shanghai Museum (1996), architect Xing Tonghe. The circular building placed on top of a square recalls the tradition that heaven is round and earth is square, while the arches on the roof resemble the handles on ancient bronzes.

PHOTOGRAPH © LORE SCHIROKAUER.

the conduct of their lives, to enjoy their electric appliances and other new possessions. People were allowed freedom of movement. The arts continued much in the spirit of the eighties, producing a profusion of styles and agendas, frames and shattering of frames, as well as a renewed appreciation of tradition, including Confucianism. An unusually satisfactory marriage of new and old was the Shanghai Museum (Figure 16.4), by the Shanghai architect Xing Tonghe, completed in 1996 to house the city's treasures, including China's foremost collection of bronze vessels from the first dynasties.

Many of those prominent in the eighties remained productive. Wang Meng fought off his critics and advocated cultural pluralism with the market as judge. In 1992 he founded *Green Leaves*, a journal on the environment. Mo Yan published *Wine Republic*. Characterized by David Der-wei Wang as a "Swiftian satire and Kafkaesque fable," it follows a detective sent to a country where people eat children. Wang comments:

In a world where the high and the low, the fragrant and the putrid, mingle, nobody has clean hands; the protagonist is fittingly murdered by being drowned in a manure pit at the end of the novel. Eschatology and scatology turn out to be two readings of the same reality.[13]

In 1995 Chen Kaige directed "Farewell My Concubine" which found a warm reception overseas. The work of some of the most experimental artists was confined to their apartments while the audience of others, like the computer artist Feng Mengbo, was primarily overseas. Feng, a resident of Beijing, explained the thought behind his series of paintings "Taxi! Taxi! —Mao Zedong I–III" as follows:

In 1990, when I was still at the academy, I suddenly realized that the way Mao Zedong waved his hand at the army [of Red Guards] gathered in Tiananmen Square during the Cultural Revolution was very similar to the way people wave to hail a taxi. So I copied the image of Mao waving and put a common yellow taxicab in front of him—the kind you see everywhere in Beijing today.[14]

Mao had been taken off his pedestal and made to hail a cab! Once inside he was likely to encounter a Mao traffic safety charm. To recover from the shock would he have taken a swig of "The East is Red" health drink, thirsting for the days when this had been the anthem of the revolution?

Cui Jian, the rock star, had his ups and downs, but mostly was tolerated by the authorities and allowed to perform at home and abroad. David Fricke, critic for *Rolling Stone* heard him in concert in 1995 and wrote:

But just as he challenges the arthritic authority of his country's leaders, Cui tolerates no laws or limits to his music. The rumble of Chinese barrel drum fattened the surge of angular guitar grooves. Beastie-style beats, fierily Jamaican ska and the roadhouse rattle of early Springsteen collided in such anthemic fireballs as "The Other Shore," "Together we confront the same reality—Together we sing a song loudly."[15]

Listeners will need to judge the results for themselves as postmodern Chinese intellectuals engage "in a new search for a real 'hybridization' or 'hybridity' based on a dialectical synthesis beyond the old dichotomies between the traditional and the modern, the particular and the universal."[16]

One dichotomy that was breaking down was that between the thought and symbolic world of artists and writers living in the People's Republic and those living elsewhere in a Chinese or semi-Chinese world. While critics worried about the hybrid culture, the mixing of elements from different traditions continued to the point that when a joint exhibit was held in New York in 1999, it was often difficult to distinguish the works of those in the P.R.C. from the works of those outside. Mainland exiles in America, Europe, Australia and New Zealand as well as artists and writers from Taiwan contributed to "a China defined not by geopolitical boundariers and ideological closures but by overlapping cultural and shared imaginative resources."[17]

Taiwan

As noted in Chapter 14, Taiwan's first two years under the Guomindang-controlled Republic of China were so oppressive as to provoke the violence of 1947. One result of Guomindang actions was that the Taiwanese elite was decimated. Ironically, this removed not only resistance to the political dominance of the Nationalists but also a potential source of opposition to land redistribution and other economic reforms undertaken during the fifties with American backing, pressure, and advice. As in postwar Japan, the end of landlordism had profound economic and social effects.

During the Japanese years, Taiwan had acquired much of the necessary infrastructure for industrialization, and many of the approximately two million civilian refugees who fled from the mainland also brought training and skills that contributed to the development of light industry and commerce. Capital came in part from the great sums of money the Nationalists brought over with them. Until terminated in 1966, American economic aid also helped, and once the Japanese economy had recovered, Japanese companies invested heavily. The government generally supervised and advanced development, first building up infrastructure and then fostering exports. In 1965 it created special Export Processing Zones where companies enjoyed tax incentives and were free of import taxes as long as they exported whatever they made or assembled.

Culturally, the government saw its mission as that of preserving old Chinese traditions. Taiwan became the home for institutes of higher learning. The use of the local Taiwanese language was suppressed and, as in the P.R.C., instruction was in Mandarin. A museum was built to house the priceless Palace Collection the Nationalists brought with them from the mainland.

At a time when mainland artists were caught in the political storms, artists in Taiwan and elsewhere were free to explore new ways to draw on their tradition in order to create forms of expression suitable for the twentieth century. One of the most gifted of these was Liu Guosong (Liu Kuo-sung, 1932–) who was born in Shandong, educated in Taiwan, established himself as a painter there, taught many years in Hong Kong, and returned to Taiwan before retiring to California.

FIGURE 16.5 *The Metaphysics of Rocks,* Liu Guosong. The artist uses calligraphy, brushwork, and collage. Ink and acrylic with collage on paper, 1968, 68.6 × 67.3 cm.

© LIU KUO-SUNG. USED BY PERMISSION OF THE ARTIST.

As Liu explained, "We are no longer ancient Chinese nor modern Westerners. We do not live in the Song or Yuan society, nor in the modern European or American environment. If it is false for us to copy old Chinese paintings, isn't it the same to copy modern Western painting?"[18] Liu is deeply conversant with both traditions. Chu-tsing Li describes the collage in Liu's *Metaphysics of Rocks* (Figure 16.5) as follows:

> In the lower middle part are two pieces of collage, one large and the other small, both suggesting rock shapes. The paper is in color, but combined with some textures printed with wrinkled paper. Thus there seem to be several kinds of rocks, done with different techniques and brushwork. Yet none of them is realistic enough to resemble real rocks. But each gives us an idea of some quality of rocks, such as jutting up, having interesting textures, or showing watery surfaces.[19]

Liu went on to paint a distinctive series on the sun and moon, continued to experiment with textures and techniques, and paint abstractions that suggested the metaphysics of mountains.

Under the Guomindang, the Republic of China remained ideologically committed to the reunification of China and to Sun Yat-sen's Three Principles of the People. Until ousted from the United Nations in 1971, its claim to speak for China was widely accepted abroad. At home, although the Guomindang was reformed, it remained dictatorial, refusing to share substantive power with the Taiwanese, that is, people of Chinese stock who had settled on the island before 1945. Though the native Taiwanese did win elections to local governments, real control remained in the hands of the central government. Prosperity and repression kept dissent to a minimum. Among those imprisoned on Green Island was Bo Yang (1920–), given ten years for translating an English language comic deemed insulting to Chiang Kai-shek. His acerbic critique of Chinese ways won him a wide readership on the mainland.

When Chiang Kai-shek died in 1975, there was an easy and smooth passing of power to his son Chiang Ching-kuo (in *pinyin,* Jiang Jingguo, 1910–1988). Progress was sufficient for the economy to come through both the oil crisis and the diplomatic defeats of the seventies in good shape. As in Japan, there was a turn to more advanced technology such as computers. In 1980 the state established a science-oriented industrial park and an electronics industry.

By that time Taiwan had attained a level of per capita income second in Asia only to Japan. In many ways, it became a modern country. By 1979 over half the people owned a color television set and 90 percent had refrigerators. During the eighties air-conditioners became common while cars largely captured the road dominated previously by motorbikes.

The normalization of U.S. relations with the P.R.C. meant that relations with Taiwan were formally downgraded. Semi-formal relations were maintained, but the Guomindang's claim to the rulership of all of China was weakened, and those born in Taiwan who coupled demands for democratization with calls for a Republic of Taiwan found their case strengthened. Chiang Kai-shek's response had been repression, but his son alternated between jailing leaders of the opposition and instigating reform. The latter was predominant during his last two years, when martial law was revoked, press restrictions were eased, and the prohibition against opposition parties relaxed.

These reforms allowed the Democratic Progressive Party (D.P.P.) to field candidates in the election of December 1986. Inhabitants of Taiwan were, for the first time in thirty-eight years, allowed to visit relatives on the mainland. The government was confident that they would return with an appreciation for the higher standard of living they enjoyed on Taiwan. In practice, even the post-1945 newcomers came to see themselves as different from mainlanders and as having much in common with their fellow Taiwanese.

When Chiang Ching-kuo died in January 1988, he was succeeded by Lee Teng-hui (Li Denghui, 1923–), a Taiwanese with a Ph.D. in agricultural economics from Cornell, who brought more Taiwanese into the top party and government posts and included fourteen holders of American doctorates in his cabinet. The emergence of a strong middle class, strong advances in education, and continuing affluence provided fertile ground for continued movement in the direction of greater democracy, while the ultimate nature of a Taiwanese identity remained in dispute. The GMD won the election of 1989, but the D.P.P. gained ground. Despite the P.R.C. show of force, Lee was victorious in Taiwan's first direct popular presidential election in 1996. However, he had to face not only D.P.P. opposition but divisiveness within his own party that led to a major defection in 2000. In the election of that year, Chen Shui-Pien (also written Shui-pien, Shui-bien, or Shuibian) (1951–) of the D.P.P., with 39.3 percent of the vote, defeated two rival candidates to become the Republic of China's youngest and first non-GMD president. His vice president, the women's rights advocate Lu Hsiu-lien (Xiulian, Annette Lu, 1944–) was the first woman elected to that high office. Elected on a promise to put an end to widespread corruption, Chen, on assuming office, played down his Taiwanese nationalism and gave priority to domestic house-cleaning. Beijing, which had issued threatening statements before the election and had made it clear that it would not rule out the use of force if Taiwan declared independence, was quieted for the time being; but the example of a party losing an election to an opposition running on an anticorruption platform must have been distasteful, not to say unnerving, to those too deeply implicated in the mainland status quo.

Notes

1. Christopher R. Wren, "Comparing Two Communist Paths to 'Reform,' " *The New York Times,* Sept. 6, 1987, Section 4, p. 2.
2. Geremie R. Barmé, In *The Red: On Contemporary Chinese Culture* (New York: Columbia Univ. Press, 1999), p. 123.
3. Shen Tong, *Almost A Revolution* (Boston: Houghlin Mifflin, 1990), p. 310, as quoted in Andrew E. Jones, *Like A Knife: Ideology in Contemporary Chinese Popular Music* (Ithaca: East Asia Program, Cornell Univ., 1992), p. 95.
4. *The New York Times,* August 16, 2001, p. A13.
5. *The New York Times,* November 21, 2002, p. A16.
6. *Xinmin wanbao (New People's Evening News),* Shanghai, May 11, 1994, as quoted by Deborah S. Davis in her introduction to *The Consumer Revolution in Urban China,* ed. Deborah S. Davis (Berkeley: Univ. of California Press, 2000), p. 9.
7. Jean C. Oi, "Two Decades of Rural Reform in China: An Overview and Assessment," in *The China Quarterly* no. 159 (Sept. 1999), p. 627.
8. Richard Baum and Alexei Shevchenko, "The State of the State," in Merle Goldman and Roderick MacFarquhar, eds., *The Paradox of China's Post-Mao Reforms* (Cambridge, Mass.: Harvard University Press, 1999), pp. 345 and 349. The list of labels at the beginning of this paragraph is taken from the same source, where each label is documented.
9. Lionel M. Jensen, "Everyone's a Player, but the Nation's a Loser: Corruption in Contemporary China," in Timothy B. Weston and Lionel M. Jensen, *China Beyond the Headlines* (Latham, Md.: Rowman and Littlefield, 2000), p. 42.
10. Stephen Feuchtwang, "Religious Resistance," in Elizabeth J. Perry and Mark Selden, eds., *Chinese Society: Change, Conflict and Resistance* (London and New York: Routledge, 2000), p. 171.
11. *Eastern Express,* October 5, 1955, p. 39, as quoted in Elizabeth J. Perry, "Crime, Corruption, and Contention" in Goldman and MacFarquhar, p. 323.
12. Richard Kraus, "Public Monuments and Private Pleasures in the Parks of Nanjing: A Tango in the Ruins of the Ming Emperor's Palace," in Deborah S. Davis, ed., *The Consumer Revolution in Urban China,* p. 306.

13. David Der-wei Wang, *Fin-de-siecle Splendor: Repressed Modernities of Late Qing Fiction, 1849–1911* (Stanford: Stanford Univ. Press, 1997), p. 332.

14. Quoted in Geremie R. Barmé, *In the Red: On Contemporary Chinese Culture,* p. 231.

15. David Fricke, "Cui Jian: New York, The Bottom Line, Aug. 31, 1995," *The Rolling Stone,* November 2, 1995.

16. Min Lin with Maria Galikowski, *The Search for Modernity: Chinese Intellectual and Cultural Dis-* course in the Post-Mao Era (New York: St. Martin's Press, 1999), p. 197.

17. David Der-wei Wang, "Chinese Fiction for the Nineties," in David Der-wei Wang and Jeanne Tai, eds., *Running Wild: New Chinese Writers* (New York: Columbia Univ. Press, 1994), p. 238.

18. Quoted in Chu-tsing Li, *Liu Kuo-sung—The Growth of a Modern Chinese Artist* (Taipei: The National Gallery of Art and Museum of History, 1969), p. 32.

19. Ibid., p. 53.

The New Japan

17

Key Dates

1952	Termination of the Occupation
1954	Resignation of Prime Minister Yoshida
1955	Formation of the Liberal Democratic Party (L.D.P.)
1956	Admission of Japan to the United Nations
1960	Demonstrations against Continuation of U.S.–Japan Mutual Security Treaty
1968	Kawataba Awarded Nobel Prize
1971	Floating of the Dollar
1972	Visit of Prime Minister Tanaka to Beijing
1976	Lockheed Scandal
1980	Automobile Production Exceeds that of U.S.
1989	Death of Shōwa Emperor Recruit Scandal
1990	Stock Market Plunge
1991	Begin Decade of Weak Economy
1993	L.D.P. Crisis
1994	Ōe Awarded Nobel Prize

After regaining independence in 1952, Japan went on to achieve such phenomenal economic growth that by the 1970s it had become one of the world's industrial giants. By the 1980s, people in the United States and Britain were turning to Japan for lessons in industrial management. Despite a setback in the last decade of the century, Japan remained an economic power second only to the United States.

Japan's economic growth was part of a broader transformation that affected every aspect of life. The pace of change was steadier than in China, but that did not make it less extensive or profound. The absence of the drastic shifts in direction that punctuated Chinese history enables us to discuss the new Japan in a single chapter—but makes it harder to periodize. We have chosen to break our story at 1989, when a new emperor ascended the throne, primarily because the end of the cold war coincided with the end of the economic exuberance of the eighties.

I. The New Japan, 1952–1989

The Economy

Government and Politics

The Seventies and Eighties

The Economy

In Japan as elsewhere, economic and political history are deeply intertwined. As we have seen, the Japanese economy was greatly stimulated by the Korean War. Thereafter Japan continued to profit from access to foreign raw materials, technology, and markets, including those of the United States. Because of popular sentiment, constitutional constraints, and the country's reliance on the American "nuclear umbrella," Japan was freed from the burden of supporting a large and costly military establishment, releasing funds and energies for economic development. At the same time, business benefited from a pro-business political system.

Politically, the period began with Yoshida in power and his Liberal Party in control of the Diet. He remained in office until 1954, when he was forced to resign in the wake of a scandal involving the shipping industry. In the elections of 1955 the Democratic Party, a rival conservative party, won a plurality but not the majority required to govern. It therefore entered into negotiations with the Liberal Party that led to the formation of the Liberal Democratic Party (L.D.P.) which dominated Japanese politics until 1993.

By 1953, economic production had practically returned to pre-war levels, although the volume of trade was still only half of what it had been previously. After 1954, the economic surge continued, transforming recovery into growth at an average of 10 percent a year from 1955 to 1974 (including over 11 percent during the 1960s). During the fifties, with government support, great strides were made in heavy industry—despite the fact that Japan lacks raw materials and is poor in energy resources. By building manufacturing plants in port cities, which provided the advantage of low-cost ocean transport, and through the sophisticated application of modern technologies, Japan was able to become the world's leading shipbuilder and the third largest producer of iron and steel (after the United States and the Soviet Union). By 1974 its steel production reached 89 percent of that of the United States. There were investments in chemicals, textiles, and consumer products. The washing machine, vacuum cleaner, and refrigerator of the fifties were soon joined by the television set and the air-conditioner, with the video recorder, microwave, and computer following in the eighties. Car production reached 10 million in 1966, dubbed "year one of the My-Car Era" by the media. Cameras and watches, and even pianos—it is difficult to think of a major consumer technology in which Japan failed to excel.

Some of these products were built by new companies, such as Sony or Honda, founded by entrepreneurs who took advantage of the opportunities offered by postwar economic dislocation to build up new enterprises from scratch. Other ambitious men (in what remained a man's world) reorganized or rejuvenated older companies, often importing technology by buying rights to foreign patents. In the dominant position in the economy, however, familiar old names reappeared, including Mitsui, the world's oldest major firm, as well as Mitsubishi, Sumitomo, and others.

The names were old, but they now designated a new kind of enterprise grouping consisting of affiliated companies *(keiretsu)* rather than the family-centered *zaibatsu* of the prewar period. Each group included a bank, very likely an insurance company, a real estate firm, and a cluster of companies engaged in every conceivable line of business, where its main competitor was most frequently a member of a rival group. The activities of the various member firms of each group were coordinated in periodic meetings of their presidents in presidents' clubs. Interlocking directorships, mutual stock holdings, and internal financing further held the organizations together, although more loosely than in the old *zaibatsu*. The *keiretsu* grew in size and strength until in the mid-seventies a study by Japan's Fair Trade Commission found that the six major groupings, composed of a total of 175 core companies, held 21.9 percent of all the capital in Japan and had a controlling interest in another 3,095 corporations that held 26.1 percent of the nation's capital. To this must be added their substantial investments in other companies that they influenced without controlling.

Among the member firms of these enterprise groupings, the most spectacular were trading companies *(shōsha)* that conducted their business not only at home but all over the world: exporting and importing, transporting and storing, financing and organizing a host of multifarious projects—an airport in Kenya, a large commercial farm on Sumatra, a petrochemical industry for Iran, or copper mining in Zaire, linked by communications networks that, for a time, were unparalleled. Furthermore, Mitsui, Mitsubishi, and the others built their own research organizations, analyzing information, charting future trends, and drawing up plans to provide for future project recommendations. Their experts engaged in city planning, energy research, and research into the world's oceans.

Japanese companies provided varied services and facilities for their employees, including company dormitories for the unmarried. There were company athletic teams and a host of recreational activities, such as organized outings to mountain retreats. These were intended to foster not only the health and well-being of the employees but also to strengthen feelings of group solidarity and identification with the sponsoring firm, which used them to convey an image of paternalistic solicitude. At Toyota, Japan's leading automobile manufacturer, white-collar men received an entire year of training, including a month in a company camp. Recruitment patterns that centered on certain universities, encouraging ties between men entering a company in the same year, an emphasis on longevity in promotions, the practice of extensive consultation, and a strong preference for decision by consensus all helped foster management solidarity.

For the most part, Japanese companies, especially the large modern concerns, retained the loyalty of their employees, who were made to feel that what was best for the company was also best for Japan. This business ideology gained credence from management's practice of plowing earnings back into the firm so that it could continue to grow and hopefully surpass its rivals. At the same time the efficacy of persuasion should not be exaggerated, for company extras increasingly became matters not of paternalism but of contractual rights subject to collective bargaining, like fringe benefits in other countries. However, management was able to get workers to agree to moderate wage increases and fringe benefits. The threat of foreign competition was also used effectively, and for many years Japanese companies enjoyed a lower labor bill and more labor peace than many of their competitors in Europe and America. The quest for economic growth gave Japan a sense of national purpose even as it promised an improved standard of living for the people.

Japan's concentration on economic development was epitomized in the income-doubling policy of Ikeda Hayato (1899–1965, prime minister 1960–1964), that provided for the doubling of per capita production in ten years. The government fostered growth by establishing a political climate favorable to economic expansion, by investing in infrastructure, by adopting appropriate fiscal and monetary policies, and by setting production targets, assigning priorities, and generally orchestrating the economy. It sponsored the bullet train, which in 1964 reduced what had been a major overnight journey between Kyoto and Tokyo to a trip of 3 hours and 10 minutes. The government built roads and dams, and financed the reclamation of coastal lands.

While the Construction Ministry controlled the bulk of infrastructure spending, the Finance Ministry and the Ministry of International Trade and Industry (MITI) coordinated economic growth. The importance of the MITI reflected the crucial role of foreign trade in Japan's economy and the determination of the government to oversee the country's economic as well as political relations with other countries. By deploying foreign exchange allocations, manipulating quotas, and establishing barriers protecting native capital from foreign competition, the government channeled the flow of investment funds. It could also extend or deny tax privileges. It thus had at its disposal a variety of weapons to bring recalcitrant firms into line if persuasion and/or pressures failed. Generally, it preferred to rely on discussion and to act as much as possible on the basis of a shared government–business consensus. Businesses competed with each other within a more tightly defined arena than in most other capitalist nations.

Consensus was possible not only because of the shared aims and interests of government and business but also because of ties between government and the business community. Often these ties were personal, for the men at the top in the private sector and those heading the influential and prestigious government ministries tended to share similar backgrounds (both included a high proportion of Tokyo University graduates). Some of the ties were ideological, since Japan was ruled during these years by conservatives. And some of the ties were financial, for elections were costly and business constituted a major source of funds for conservative politicians.

Government and Politics

After 1955 the L.D.P. was opposed by the two Socialist parties (the Japan Socialist Party and the Democratic Socialist Party), by the Clean Government Party (formed in 1964, it first ran candidates for the lower house in 1967), by the Communist Party, and by independent politicians. This opposition was too divided to constitute a serious alternative to conservative rule, but it was sufficient to prevent the L.D.P. from gaining the two-thirds majority in the Diet needed for revising the constitution. Some conservatives, concerned about Japan's security, favored the revocation of Article IX so as to enable Japan to acquire its own military power. In view of a dangerous world and in response to American urgings, the Self-Defense Forces were expanded to include well-equipped naval and air arms, and the defense budget continued to increase. However, Japan continued to forego offensive weapons or capabilities, and total defense expenditures remained limited to 1 percent of gross national product until 1987.

About a quarter of L.D.P. Diet members were former bureaucrats, as were Prime Minister Ikeda, his immediate predecessor, Kishi Nobosuke (1957–1960), and his successor, Satō Eisaku (1964–1972). Subsequently, only Nakasone Yasuhiro (1982–1987) occupied that position for more than two years. Throughout the period, the well-educated, capable, and prestigious higher bureaucracy wielded great influence on the making as well as execution of policy.

Dominating the internal dynamics of the L.D.P., and thus determining the composition of Japan's government, was the interplay of political factions. After 1972 all prime ministers came from five factions—formal, recognized political groupings built around a leader, usually a potential prime minister. From his faction a member derived political and financial support in his election campaigns and backing in his attempts to gain high government or party office. In return, he owed his faction leader political support, especially during the complex maneuvering that determined the party presidency and the prime ministership. What counted was skill in assembling political combinations and seniority, not popular appeal.

The L.D.P.'s origin as an association of independently based politicians helps to account for the strength of the factions. Another factor was a system of multi-member election districts in which there were frequently more conservative candidates than could reasonably expect to win election. Thus, in a five-member district, there might be four L.D.P. candidates with only three likely to win. In such cases, they would be backed by rival factions within the L.D.P.

The power of the factions set limits on the prime minister's authority and weakened the party at the grass-roots level, where each politician cultivated his (or in rare cases her) own local support organization composed of various groups within his constituency. The politician maintained his following by supporting various community activities and offering personal assistance to constituents. He kept his political machine oiled by maintaining a "pipeline to the center," so that he could take credit for obtaining public works and other special-interest legislation. In seeking to fulfill these expectations, politicians depended on the political clout of their faction and a purse kept full by friendly interests. Although the most successful politicians were solidly entrenched, there were enough shifts in political fortunes on both the local and the national levels to provide for political interest. More importantly, the system retained the flexibility to adjust policies to changing circumstances.

For the opposition parties of the left, these were years of frustration. The two Socialist parties were closely associated with labor, each linked to one of the labor confederations. They depended on organized labor for votes, and labor leaders figured prominently in their leadership. Many of their Diet members also came from a labor background. Ideologically, the Socialists ran the gamut from Maoist radicals calling for revolution to moderate reformists. During the fifties the Communist party was very weak, but it picked up strength in the late sixties after adopting pragmatic policies. However, even had they been able to unite, the three leftist parties lacked the strength to topple the L.D.P. regime.

Domestically, the opposition parties viewed with special alarm L.D.P. measures that looked suspiciously like a retreat from Occupation reforms and a return to the past—for example, measures to recentralize the police and education functions and to give Tokyo greater control over local government. Socialist fears were fortified by the prominence in the conservative leadership of men who had held cabinet offices in the thirties and had been purged from politics by the Occupation authorities. The left was adamantly opposed to government moves to recreate a military establishment, and did what it could to block or at least delay the expansion of the Self-Defense Forces.

The Left also objected to the government's pro-American foreign policy, protested against the continued presence of American bases, and against American nuclear weapons and tests. Unrestrained by expectations of forming a government themselves, they engaged in bitter struggles, including boycotts of the Diet and physical disruption, prompting police intervention. The L.D.P. for its part did not refrain from using its majority to ram legislation through the Diet with little regard for the niceties of parliamentary procedure. This is what Minister Kishi did in 1960 to gain renewal of the Security Treaty with the United States, first signed in 1952 along with the peace treaty. The renewal of this treaty prompted demonstrations sufficiently strong to prompt the cancellation of President Dwight Eisenhower's planned visit to Japan.

Political animosity now reached its greatest intensity. Opponents felt that instead of providing for Japanese security, the treaty endangered Japan, threatening to involve it in American wars. The specter of nuclear war was particularly terrifying to a people who had experienced Hiroshima and Nagasaki. The Socialists mustered impressive support for their opposition to the renegotiated treaty. Union workers, housewives, students, professors, and members of diverse organizations took to the streets in mass demonstrations in which millions of people participated. There was also a one-day general strike. All this did not block ratification or enactment of the treaty, but Kishi did resign.

After the 1960 confrontation, politics simmered down to less violent exchanges as the success of Japan's economic development became apparent. Ikeda's ten-year plan to double per capital GNP was actually achieved in only seven years. Although there were student protests against the Vietnam war, the Security Treaty was renewed in 1970 with little trouble.

In 1964 the political scene was complicated by the appearance of the Clean Government Party, formed by the Sōka Gakkai (Value Creation Society), a religious sect. As implied by its name, the party program opposed corruption, but it was vague on other issues. After obtaining 10.9 percent of the vote in the 1969 election, it declined to 8.5 percent in 1972, but remained a presence for the rest of the century. The L.D.P. aroused little enthusiasm and was particularly weak in the cities. Before 1967 its candidates had received over half of the vote, but in the election of that year it declined to 48.8 percent, and continued slowly downward until it bottomed in 1976 at 41.8 percent. Even then it remained by far the largest vote getter, and also benefited from an electoral system that favored rural areas.

The Seventies and Eighties

In the seventies, Japanese resilience was tested by a series of short-term economic and political shocks. The first came in 1971, when the United States, Japan's largest trading partner, placed a 10 percent surcharge on imports and abandoned a fixed rate of exchange. Instead, it was left to the international monetary market to determine the value of the yen, with the result that it rose, making Japanese goods more expensive overseas but also making imports cheaper. Both these American actions were aimed at reducing, if not eliminating, a mounting U.S. trade-and-payment deficit with Japan, but they proved ineffective, and the problem persisted.

A political blow followed these economic acts when, still in the same year, Washington announced the impending visit of President Nixon to China, an act on which Japan was not consulted and which undercut Prime Minister Satō, who, primarily to please Washington, had been following the unpopular policy of maintaining the fiction that the Nationalist regime on Taiwan was the government of China. In 1972, after Tanaka Kakuei (prime minister, 1972–1974), became the first Japanese prime minister to visit Beijing, Japan recognized the P.R.C.

The next shock came in 1973 when the Arab oil boycott reminded Japan of its dependence on imported energy, and was followed by a quadrupling of the price of this vital import. As a result, during 1974–1976 Japan suffered a severe recession. However, the system demonstrated remarkable resilience. An outstanding example was the rescue of the Japanese automaker Mazda, saved from collapse through the cooperation of government-backed financial interests, management, workers, dealers, suppliers, and the local community. This "lesson in managing interdependence" led two American experts to conclude, "Relatively low interest rates, MITI bureaucrats, trade barriers, and the like are, no doubt, important factors in a comparative history of economic growth, but only managers and workers build cars and other products. And their capacity to pull together in a crisis is a crucial measure of a society's strength."[1]

In the later seventies and eighties Japan's emphasis on high technology led to a decrease in dependence on imported raw materials. By 1984 Japan had reduced its use of imported raw material per unit of manufacture to 60 percent less than it had been twenty years earlier. This change also positioned Japan to compete with the emerging economies of such neighbors as Korea and Taiwan. Encouragement was given electronics, telecommunications, biochemicals, and machine tools. In these ways the economy continued to sustain a population that by 1985 had reached 121 million, up from 65 million in 1930 and about four times the number of inhabitants of Japan at the time of the Meiji Restoration.

As elsewhere, the move away from "smoke-stack industries" hurt the labor movement by reducing the number of its members. Furthermore, the great majority of people considered themselves middle-class. Growth of GNP declined to the level of other fully developed countries, but Japan's trade imbalance, especially with the United States, posed a continuing problem. Expectations to the contrary, it was not solved by the rising value of the yen, which did, however, facilitate Japanese investment in the United States.

One business response to new conditions was the transformation of Japanese companies into multinationals. Increasingly, Japanese concerns, in addition to trading in world markets, became involved in manufacturing overseas. These operations were generally successful on the factory floor, but it proved more difficult to internationalize management or "localize" the "transplants." In many cases, Japanese companies were resented for reserving the best jobs for those at home, for building factories far from the troubled, job-hungry cities, for favoring their *keiretsu* partners, and generally taking advantage of opportunities abroad denied to foreign companies at home.

In politics as in economics, the system proved vulnerable but resilient. Early in 1976, the Lockheed scandal ("Japan's Watergate") shook the political world, as it was revealed that millions of dollars of the American company's funds had been used to corrupt the highest Japanese government officials. Although prosecutors lacked the independence and tools to be truly effective, they were able to indict the former prime minister Tanaka Kakuei, who was found guilty in a 1983 decision upheld in 1987.

Predictions that the L.D.P. would decline to the point of losing its ability to form a government proved false. It reached a low of 41.8 percent of the popular vote in 1976, but made a strong comeback in 1980. In 1986 it won 49.6 percent of the vote, entitling it to 300 seats, the highest number of the party's history. Not only the party but its internal factional structure remained essentially the same. Despite the Lockheed scandal, Tanaka continued to control his faction until he suffered a stroke in 1985.

The leading political figure in the eighties was Nakasone Yasuhiro (1918–), who, as prime minister during 1982–1987, brought an unusually vigorous style of leadership and national assertiveness into the office. Prosperity, self-confidence, and American pressure combined to induce the government in 1986 to exceed the previous 1 percent of GNP cap in the military budget for the next year. Though the increase was modest, it had symbolic significance. At the same time the Socialist Party dropped its long-standing opposition to the Self-Defense Forces based on Article IX of the constitution. It now held that the Self-Defense Forces were "unconstitutional but legal." Ten years earlier the Supreme Court had ruled that the constitutionality of the forces was for the legislature to decide, and had also left it up to the legislature to rectify an electoral system that was unconstitutional in discriminating against urban voters.

Nakasone cooperated with the United States to reduce the trade surplus by emphasizing domestic spending, cooperating on monetary policy, and trying to open Japanese markets to more imported goods. The last of these, however, was difficult in face of powerful, deeply entrenched domestic interests and business patterns. Farmers and construction companies were just two examples of major domestic constituencies on which many L.D.P. leaders had long depended. For the rest of the eighties, the trade imbalance was more acute than ever. Japan developed expertise in industrial ceramics, robotics, and biotechnology.

The yen remained strong, propelled by a hot economy that sent the stock market soaring and raised land prices to astronomical levels. Japan became a major exporter of capital—building factories and buying foreign debt, prestigious hotels, and trophy real estate such as New York's Rockefeller Center, acquired by a Mitsui affiliate in 1989. Nevertheless, the balance of payments remained in Japan's favor.

In keeping with a general trend in the capitalist world, Japan divested itself of the government railway in 1987 and also sold its shares in the National Telegraph and Telephone Company and in Japan Air Lines. By that time Nakasone had been succeeded by Takeshita Noboru (1924–), who headed the Tanaka faction after 1985, but lasted less than two full years (Nov. 1987–June 1989). He was forced to resign under a cloud arising out of revelations that the head of the Recruit group of companies had attempted to buy influence by giving large amounts in shares and money to leading politicians and bureaucrats. The next prime minister, who lied about giving hush money to a mistress, lasted two months. His successor, too, was a weak leader. The L.D.P.-dominated system was coming unglued, and now the financial bubble burst. Between January and October 1990 the stock market plunged 48 percent, and in 1991 recession set in.

II. Society, Thought, and the Arts

Social Change and Quality of Life

Film

Intellectual Life and Literature

The Visual Arts

Social Change and Quality of Life

Economic growth brought unprecedented affluence. The very physiognomy of the Japanese people changed as an improved diet produced a new generation taller and healthier than their parents. By 1990 the Japanese people had the world's highest rate of life expectancy, and this was still the case in 2000 when it reached 74.5 years.

People now ate more fish and meat. Dairy products became daily staples, and wheat consumption rose steadily. Japan became a nation of coffee as well as tea drinkers. During the seventies the arch of McDonald's hamburgers spread from Tokyo's Ginza to the provinces, where it was soon joined by the figure of Colonel Sanders inviting passers-by to partake of Kentucky Fried Chicken, while Mr. Donut and Dairy Queen did their part to propagate fast-food culture American-style.

Changes in dress were equally dramatic. In the eighties blue jeans became the universal dress of the young, and pants were worn in public by women of all ages as a matter of course. Conversely, the kimono was reserved for special occasions, but wealthy sophisticates now could prance about in the latest fashions by Japan's world renowned designers.

Consumerism reigned as old crafts declined, and traditional elegance gave way to modern practicality—except that the modern was not always practical, for during the eighties so many realized their dream of owning an automobile that the roads were choked and the savvy driver had to learn how to "diagnose traffic paralysis."[2] Fortunately, public transportation within and between cities was excellent, although in Tokyo's rush hour ("crush hour" would be more appropriate) "pushers" had to cram the people quickly into the overflowing subways.

There was a shift of population from the country into cities. Nevertheless, since mechanization reduced the need for farm labor, agricultural production increased. Thanks to the L.D.P., the government purchased rice at several times the international price. The prewar gulf between urban wealth and rural poverty disappeared, and the spread of television accelerated the process, begun by radio, of diminishing the cultural gap. However, despite the omnipresence of the television set, the Japanese remained the world's most avid consumers of newspapers, magazines, and comic books.

Public transportation, communication, and security were excellent early on, but the environment suffered. Japan's industrial zone, running along the Pacific coast from Tokyo to northern Kyushu, developed into a "polluters' paradise":

> Polluted air choked urban residents with respiratory difficulties, which were fatal in some areas. Water pollution wiped out coastal fishing along the industrial belt. In the cities exhaust from automobiles mixed with pollutants from smokestacks and produced toxic photochemical smog during the day.[3]

Only after Tokyo became enshrouded in a semiperpetual screen of smog did the government take action. In Mie prefecture asthma was linked to pollution, and in Toyama a river caused cadmium poisoning. Most notorious was the "Minamata Disease" (1953) caused by people eating fish contaminated by methyl mercury discharged by a fertilizer plant in Kyushu. Thanks to obstruction by the company and government connivance, the victims had to wait until 1968 for official acknowledgment that mercury was the cause. In 1973 a group of Minamata plaintiffs prevailed in court and won the largest tort award in Japanese history. In 1978 a National Institute for Minamata Disease was established. The name "Minamata" still conjures up both the deadly threat of environmental pollution and people's determination to fight back.

Government measures taken in the seventies did ameliorate the problem, but the quality of air and water remained a matter of concern, and excessive dam construction boded ill for the future of Japan's rivers. Visual pollution was all too apparent as Japan's industrial area became one of the ugliest to be found anywhere. While the Japanese people continued to cherish nature in miniature, lovingly tending tiny gardens on the most unlikely bits of land, Japan's business and political leaders, in their rush to modernize, sacrificed much of the natural beauty that had once been Japan's cherished heritage.

In the eighties, preserving the environment was widely accepted as a public good, so much so that in 1990 the Ministry of Construction sponsored an International Flower and Greenery Exposition even as it was planning an airport that would kill the last healthy coral reef in Okinawa. By the end of the eighties, environmentalists were expressing concern not only over the situation at home, but were also calling attention to the destruction Japanese companies were inflicting on the tropical forests of Borneo and other lands. If the aims of Japanese environmentalists were similar to those elsewhere, the same was even more true of the power of the forces arrayed against them.

Even before the land boom of the eighties, the escalating price of land and housing in Japan's large cities forced young married couples to live with their in-laws because they could not afford separate establishments, or to crowd into tiny apartments in drab and monotonous buildings made of reinforced concrete. Raising a family in such confined quarters was no easy task. Although the small apartments reduced women's household chores, releasing time for other activities, the residents of such buildings were slow to develop a sense of community, since they regarded these quarters as temporary, marking a stage of their lives and careers soon to be surmounted.

The absence of grandparents in the new housing was but one of the factors making for discontinuity between the generations. Such discontinuity was not unique to Japan; in other countries too, rapid changes during the postwar years created a "generation gap." However, in Japan the gap was particularly severe. Not only did the younger people grow up in a society that had suddenly become very different from that of their parents, but a whole generation of wartime leaders had been thoroughly discredited and the old values blamed for leading the nation to catastrophe. Included were many of the values that had strengthened the cohesiveness of Japanese society.

New lifestyles and values appeared in the factories as young workers preferred to spend their leisure time manipulating pachinko (vertical pinball) machines, playing video games, or listening to rock music rather than going on company outings. They valued skill more than length of service, and tended to regard the factory not as a second home but merely as a place to work. The number of hours they would have to spend there was also decreasing, and a survey conducted in 1990 revealed that workers were more interested in obtaining more leisure than in higher pay.

Those fortunate enough to survive a brutal entrance examination system gained admission to universities oriented largely to research and graduate work. Ostensibly paternalistic, the universities demonstrated their supposed concern for the youngest members of the academic community by virtually guaranteeing graduation to all matriculants. Neglected after having worked so hard for university entrance, the students expressed their discontent in radical political activities. Their dissatisfaction helped fuel widespread demonstrations and disruptions in the later sixties, directed against both national and university policies. In this again, Japanese young people were, of course, not alone, and, as elsewhere, the pendulum swung back to greater conservatism in the seventies and eighties.

The general loosening of traditional patterns and values presented contemporary Japanese with a wide range of choices but within what remained, by and large, a closely knit society. For example, young people increasingly insisted on making their own selection of a spouse, and they were now always consulted before a marriage was arranged by their parents. Nevertheless, even in love marriages, most young people still asked their employer or teacher to serve as official matchmaker. A surprisingly large number continued to leave the initiative to their parents. Under the postwar legal system, wives as well as husbands could now initiate divorce proceedings; the divorce rate grew but remained low.

Women now had more options. Many remained content with their traditional roles, which gave them a predominant influence over their children and firmly established the home as their field of authority. Although submissive to their husbands in public, most wives controlled the family budget, ran the household, and often treated their husbands as they would an older, somewhat difficult, and rather special child. They accepted their exclusion from much of their husbands' social lives, which the husbands spent largely in the company of their fellow workers. Such couples, like their Tokugawa predecessors, led separate social lives. These wives did not share in their husband's nightlife.

However, as time went on, an increasing number of women chose a career and either a companionate marriage or life as a single. They made progress in the professions and, more slowly, in business, where they often had to choose between temporary employment followed by marriage or the more regular male-oriented career path. The passage of the Equal Opportunity Act in 1985, making sex discrimination illegal, reflected a new consciousness, but the law lacked teeth.

As in all periods of social change, there were some who suffered because change was too rapid and others for whom it was too slow. Among the former were old people, bewildered and distressed by the whirl about them. One of the strengths of the old society had been the dignity and security afforded to the aged, but now cramped quarters and new ideas ate away at old values and threatened traditional comforts. These were people who found that the social rules had changed just when their turn came to reap the rewards the system offered those who played by the rules. While the erosion of respect for the aged diminished the traditional attractions of longevity, forced retirement at an early age (usually fifty-five) and the devaluation of savings because of continual inflation deprived the old of a sense of economic security. Most families did manage to take care of the elderly one way or another. Most old people were not shunted off into nursing homes or set up in special retirement communities, but the social arrangements made for the elderly by their children were often grudging and poisoned by resentment.

At the other end of the spectrum were those who felt that change was too slow. They felt stifled rather than supported by a social system that still expected the individual to be subordinate to the group, whether it be family or company. They also balked at conforming to a social hierarchy that had lost much of its theoretical support. The discontented were a disparate group. They included career women frustrated by roadblocks and ceilings, those constrained to maintain and live with parents, and people seeking to fill the vacuum left by the passing of the old values with something more solid than consumerism and the race to elevate the economic standing of their country. Their discontent was frequently shared by students and by radicals impatient for a more egalitarian society. Some of the young men without prospects for university study joined motorcycle gangs. However, most worked out a modus vivendi for themselves, and many of the young gradually came to terms with society.

The great majority of the population, however, neither mourned the passing of the old nor were impatient for the arrival of the new. Appreciative of the increase in material wealth, they were nevertheless unsure of the future. Many turned to religion, maintaining home altars, visiting temples and shrine, going on pilgrimages. Shrines and temples had always offered prayers and amulets protecting against disease, assurance of safe childbirth, and the like. Adjusting to new conditions, many now offered traffic-safety charms while a temple in Tokyo added air safety. Shrines and temples offering examination success were popular with young people. The elderly were serviced by temples offering prayers and amulets to quiet their fears of senility. This had excellent prospects of becoming a growth industry, for, as a byproduct of longevity, Japan counted half a million senile people by 1994, and the average age of the population was on the rise.

New religious sects arose seeking to satisfy the spiritual hunger and alleviate the mental malaise brought on by loss of community. As they moved from traditional village to modern city, people sought "a religious frame of meaning relevant to contemporary life."[4] Attracting the largest membership was Sōka Gakkai, the sponsor of the Clean Government party. Doctrinally based on Nichiren Buddhism, it denounced all other faiths, and insisted that its members proselytize relentlessly and go on a pilgrimage to the head temple at the foot of Mt. Fuji, where an average of 10,000 people a day came to pay their homage. By passing a series of examinations, the faithful could rise in an academic-like hierarchy of ranks. For the devoted members, the sect provided not only spiritual community but a sense of personal worth and of belonging to a large, integrated, purposeful group. Others found it more difficult to find new certainties, however, for the world offered a bewildering range of choices.

Film

If, as is often said, film was the characteristic art form of the twentieth century, then the worldwide acclaim accorded Japanese films is but one more indication of Japan's full participation in that century's culture. By no means were all Japanese films masterpieces: Japanese companies were second to none in turning out ephemeral entertainments—samurai movies that were the artistic equivalents of American westerns, unbearably sentimental tear-jerkers, horror and monster films, and, in the seventies and eighties, a wave of erotica with little artistic or social value but plenty of sexual action. Such films, reflecting social stereotypes and people's daydreams, are of considerable interest to psychologists and social scientists, but it is important to remember that the stereotypes they contain—the self-sacrificing but self-centered mother, the wife finding herself, daughters in various degrees of revolt—are never simple mirror images of society. The more ambitious and truly fine films reflected the times and the society, but rose above them. The major films were the creations of fine actors, sensitive cameramen, and, above all, great directors who were able to use the medium to create their own personal styles, conveying their own personal visions. If they had anything in common, it was a superb visual sense employed to create an atmosphere. Some may be said to have used the camera to paint their vision on the screen.

Exercising classic restraint in his insistence on a strict economy of means (empty spaces, simple objects, minimal plot) and avoiding anything superficial or artificially clever was Ozu Yasujiō (1903–1963), whose traditionalism also extended to his subject matter, for he was the filmmaker par excellence of the Japanese family. Other directors, like their Chinese counterparts, were highly critical of their country's traditions and values. For example, in *Harakiri* (*Seppuku*, 1962), directed by Kobayashi Masaki, the hero sets out to avenge his son, who had been forced to commit an unimaginably painful *seppuku* (ritual suicide) using a sword with a bamboo blade, but in the end the whole system is revealed to be founded on hypocrisy. Or there is *Night Drum* (*Yoru no Tsuzumi*, also known as *The Adulteress*, 1958), directed by Imai Tadashi, in which a samurai kills the wife he loves. By doing what society demands, he deprives his own life of meaning. Such vivid and moving historical films were among the triumphs of the postwar cinema, a part of a continuing and sometimes bitter dialogue with a still-living past.

An outstanding director was Kurosawa Akira (1910–1998). His world-famous *Rashomon* (1950) suggests the relativity of all truth through a demonstration of the power of human subjectivity and self-interest. *Ikiru* (1952) takes the viewer through a Faust-like quest for meaning in life. The main character, a petty bureaucrat dying of cancer, in the end finds fulfillment in one meaningful social act: surmounting endless red tape and bureaucratic obstructionism, he gets a small park built. Kurosawa's mastery of large scenes with vast casts as well as his versatility and creative vigor was apparent in *Ran* (1985), an imaginative metamorphosis of King Lear into sixteenth-century Japan. Like his earlier *Seven Samurai* (1954), it is one of those rare films in which powerful and sensitive acting, beautiful visual composition and realistic detail, story line and structure, friction and harmony, violence and stillness blend into a major artistic statement.

In the 1980s Japanese studios increasingly churned out films of violence and pornography. Refreshing exceptions were films of Itami Juzo (Ikeuchi Yoshihiro, 1933–1997) who poked fun at the Japanese way of burial in *The Funeral* (1984), noodlemania in *Tampopo* (1986), and tax collection methods in *A Taxing Woman* I and II (1987, 1988). His satire on the Japanese mob, *Minbo no Onna—The Gentle Art of Extortion* (1994), provoked the Yakuza (organized crime) to a physical attack on his person. Itami survived this, but later committed suicide, leaving a note explaining this act as proving the untruth of rumors that he was having an affair with a much younger woman.

Intellectual Life and Literature

After the war Japan rejoined the international intellectual community, participated in scientific and scholarly meetings at home and abroad, and increasingly contributed to specialized disciplines in important ways. Many scholars became conversant with a foreign language, usually English, and all had access to a broad and steady stream of translations.

Writings addressing broader human or philosophical issues, published in journals of opinion and in books, have attracted less attention abroad than have the works of the filmmaker or novelist. One reason, no doubt, is the language barrier. Another may be that much was derivative. Also, many Japanese intellectuals, like their American counterparts, applied their energies to studying their own society and to addressing their own countrymen. Notably fascinating but problematical has been the literature of exceptionalism (*Nihonjinron*) that burgeoned in the seventies and continued thereafter to fuel a sense of self-confidence and assertiveness. This literature, which focused on Japanese uniqueness, included the highly respected and stimulating work of such scholars as the psychiatrist Doi Takeo and the sociologist Nakane Chie. Lesser scholars, however, expounded on and frequently took pride in the uniqueness of just about every aspect of Japanese behavior, institutions and climatic and racial characteristics. Increasing cosmopolitanism did not prevent the persistence of insularity.

What it meant to be Japanese was also one of the themes explored in postwar fiction. After the war older novelists published manuscripts they could not release during the war, while new writers sounded new themes. An outstanding example of the former is the long novel by Tanizaki translated as *The Makioka Sisters*.

In 1947 Kawabata published the last installment of *Snow Country*. Previous segments of the novel had been published in various journals over the course of the preceding twelve years, as though each part were a stanza in a *renga* (linked verse) rather than a building block for a novel. In this and later works Kawabata explored "the ceaseless attempt of his male heroes to free themselves from their alienation and egotism to achieve a kind of monastic state of grace by a purifying contact with a pure, virginal girl."[5]

Kawabata's novels sacrifice structure and plot for the sake of naturalness and poetry. *A Thousand Cranes* (1948) and *The Sound of the Mountain* (1951) followed, each imbued with the author's visual sensibility and with his concern for beauty and sadness, inseparable as ever in Japanese literature, and evoking what one critic termed a "vibrant silence." The essential Japaneseness of Kawabata's method and vision was clearly demonstrated in his Nobel Prize acceptance speech (1968). Translated as *Japan, the Beautiful, and Myself*, it is an evocation of the Japanese tradition, a string of poems and images held together by a perception of beauty and truth.

Japan's literary classics were written by women, but most of the eminent writers during the Tokugawa period and in the first years of Meiji were men. Women writers reappeared toward the turn of the century, but really came into their own after the war. As Donald Keene pointed out, "At no time since the Heian period had women figured so prominently in the literary world." Appropriately, one of the most distinguished among them, Enchi Fumiko (1905–1986), translated *The Tale of Genji* into modern Japanese (1972–1973). She also wrote realistic novels such as *Waiting Years* (1957) and the subtle and imaginative *Masks* (1958).

A brilliant and versatile but uneven writer was Mishima Yukio (1925–1970), who, in a series of well-constructed novels, developed his ideas on such themes as the nature of beauty and the relationships between art and life, warrior and poet. One of his most compelling novels is *The Temple of the Golden Pavilion* (1956). Based on an actual act of arson in postwar Kyoto, it includes powerful psychological and philosophical explorations. A dramatist and critic as well as novelist, Mishima was prolific, self-contradictory, and even self-parodying. He tried to mold his life and his body as he did his art. Wishing to be both athlete and artist, he took up body building and developed a strong torso, but on spindly legs. Seeking to achieve a unity of knowledge and action, as in the philosophy of Wang Yangming, whom he admired, Mishima's culminating act was a dramatic public *seppuku* committed in 1970 after the completion of his final work, a tetrology entitled *The Sea of Fertility*. He was joined in death by a member of his small, private rightwing army. Mishima exhorted the Self-Defense Force to rise up before performing his ritual suicide at their Headquarters. Regarded by the public as irrelevant and bizarre, Mishima intended this act to be a fulfillment of his life's work.

A productive writer who was well-known abroad was Endō Shūsaku (1923–1996), who, in a series of brilliant novels, grappled with the tensions between his Catholic faith and his Japanese heritage. Just as Endō contributed to modern Christian as well as Japanese literature, Abe Kobō (1924–1993) earned an international reputation as an existentialist. He is perhaps best known for his novel *Woman in the Dunes* (1962), subsequently made into a film. In this work as well as later novels such as *Face of Another* (1964), *The Boxman* (1973), and *The Ark Sakura* (1984), and in such plays as *Friends* (1967), Abe explored themes and predicaments besetting the contemporary human condition, including the search for identity.

The search for identity and roots also infuses the work of Ōe Kenzaburō (1935–), two of whose novels, *A Personal Matter* (1964) and *The Silent Cry* (1967), were widely read in Japanese and in translation. Insight into psychological complexities of modern people—including the sources of violence, a concern for social morality, and a strong personal symbolism—and his grappling with basic problems of existence in the second half of the twentieth century mark him as a major writer who speaks to the central problems of his age.

Working a different vein was Inoue Yasushi (1907–1991), many of whose novels were set in China, including his last, *Confucius* (1989), in which the sage, seen through the eyes of a disciple, is treated with great respect. Less well-known abroad is Maruya Saiichi (1925–), an entertaining writer, serious but funny, whose *Singular Rebellion* (1972) provides a delightful, comic window into the times.

The Visual Arts

Like filmmakers and novelists, Japanese painters, potters, and architects won international recognition. As earlier, some artists found their inspiration in, and took their cues from, the latest trends, so that Japan had its practitioners of abstract expressionism, action painting, pop art, and the various other international art movements, which, at their best, represented the search for a style appropriate to a bewildering age and, at their worst, degenerated into fads.

More traditional was the work of artists who strove to create beauty without attempting to convey a symbolic message. Japanese potters, innovators as well as traditionalists, continued to blend shapes, textures, and colors to create works worthy of the tradition.

An old genre in new form was the woodcut. Unlike the earlier *ukiyo-e* artists, their twentieth-century successors took responsibility for the entire process of print making. They did their own cutting and printing, although they might have students assist them in the more routine aspects of the process. Among the finest was Munakata Shikō (1903–1975), also a gifted painter, whose style was influenced by traditional Japanese folk art, but who also developed new techniques. One was to apply color on the back of the print and let it seep through the paper to create gentle, diffused coloring. This helped Munakata create a general decorative effect, as in his rendition of the clothing in *Lady in Chinese Costume* (Figure 17.1). In subject matter his work ranges from the religious to the sensuous and the whimsical (for example, a nude with the artist's eyeglasses resting on her belly). In tone his art is positive—there is no echo here of the agony of the century. There are strong hints of Persia and India, but in the vigor of his lines, his gentle eroticism, and the decorative qualities of his art, Munakata resembles Matisse, while his coloring is reminiscent of Chagall.

Perhaps no art is as revealing of society as architecture. Although many opportunities were missed in the rush of postwar reconstruction, and Japan's industrial centers are among the ugliest cities in the world, there were also buildings of great distinction. The achievements of Tange Kenzo (1913–), designer of the Hall Dedicated to

FIGURE 17.1   Japanese woodblock (c. 1945). Woodcut, 21 × 15 inches.

Peace at Hiroshima, were recognized internationally when he received the Pritzker Prize in 1987. The Swimming Pool and Sports Center he designed for the 1964 Tokyo Olympics won wide acclaim. Thirty years later he designed the Tokyo City Hall Complex (1995). His buildings can also be seen in Singapore, Europe, North Africa, the Middle East, and Minnesota (The Arts Complex in Minneapolis, 1970–1974). In addition to designing superb buildings, Tange involved himself deeply in urban planning.

One of Tange's most creative students was Isozaki Arata (1931–). Postmodernist in seeking a "shifting, revolving, flickering style" rather than a "lucid, coherent institutional style" for his Tsukuba Science Center, Isozaki is also an internationalist who could write, "the Katsura Palace, the Parthenon, the Capitoline piazza, and so on all live in a time and place equidistant from us. Anything occurring in the history of architecture even the history of the world—is open to quotation."[6] Such quotation yields new and complex meaning. But often Isozaki does not quote, and some of his most successful buildings employ solid geometric forms, as in his Museum of Contemporary Art in Los Angeles. Illustrated here (see Figure 17.2) is the tower for his arts center in Mito, which, although located in a place once famous for historiography, does not refer to anything except itself.

The diversity of modern Japanese architecture is far too great for any single building possibly to be representative, but architecture can, among other things, be fun. The example of Japanese "pop architecture" in Figure 17.3 was built to house an exhibit on coffee for an exposition celebrating the completion of an artificial island in Kobe. Later, it was turned into a permanent coffee museum and given a more dignified but conventional exterior. Perhaps the cup ranneth over and the joke wore off —humor may be as ephemeral as beauty. Still, it is a splendid museum, housing exhibits on the history, the preparation, and the consumption of coffee and also providing facilities for study and a "training room" for coffee makers. It is a striking reminder that Japan, which had perfected the tea ceremony, now became a world leader in coffee appreciation, famed

FIGURE 17.2   Art Tower Mito in Mito Ibaragi. 1986–1990. 100 m. high. A postmodernist, architect Isozaki Arata often includes historical references in his buildings, but he also delights in the play of space and forms.

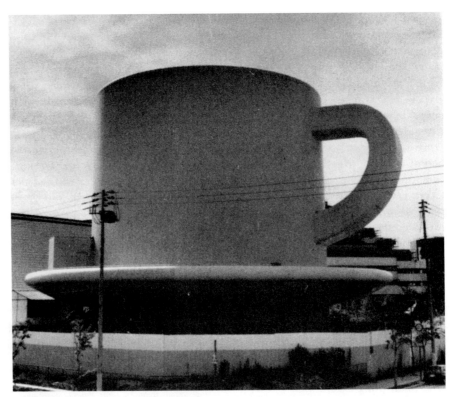

FIGURE 17.3   Coffee Pavilion, Port-pia Exposition, Kobe 1981. Takenaka Construction Firm. Height 25 m. Diameter, c. 22 m. Built to house a coffee exhibit, this "pop" architecture later became a permanent coffee museum and took on a more dignified but conventional exterior.

Photograph © Lore Schirokauer.

for its many and varied coffee houses serving the choicest South American beans. A serious beverage befitting hard workers and diligent students, coffee had found a home in Japan.

III. The Nineties, 1989–2001

The death of the emperor in January 1989 had little immediate political effect. Most Japanese were happy with the personality of the new, more accessible emperor, the first to have married a commoner. However, the performance of Shinto funeral and enthronement rites as official ceremonies troubled those committed to a secular state. And the focus on the monarchy drew renewed attention to the past role of the throne in leading Japan into the dark valley of authoritarianism and war. The tendency of high government officials to minimize wartime atrocities, government reluctance to compensate Korean "comfort women" forced into sexual slavery during the war, claims that the Pacific War had been righteous, and the widespread view of the Japanese exclusively as history's innocent victims combined to disturb people, at home and abroad, who knew otherwise.

For progressives, Japan had paid far too high a price for development. They saw the system as "a kind of state capitalism brokered by the elites that held the masses in thrall and precluded the emergence of a genuine democratic polity . . . a capitalism brokered by conservative elites in order to achieve nationalist goals."[7] A strong voice for a more positive appraisal was that of Murakami Yasusuke (1931–1993), professor of economics at Tokyo University and author of *An Anti-classical Political-Economic Analysis* (1992). Murakami blamed Japanese imperialism on the West and historical circumstances, and emphasized the positive achievements of Japanese-style developmentalism. A nuanced thinker, he was not uncritical, and sharply warned against Japanese particularism, but, convinced that there was more than one road to success, he maintained that Japan, with its "capacity to nurture a community of cultural systems,"[8] had achieved a viable way that could serve as a model for late developing nations and enable Japan to be a leader in the post–Cold War world.

The message that there is more than one road to development was a timely one for a world in which only one super-power remained and triumphalism was in the air, but during the nineties it seemed increasingly less likely that Japan would serve as an economic, let alone political, exemplar. Essentially, the country managed to muddle through the decade, but did not shine.

As already noted, recession set in in earnest in 1991. That same year Japan contributed $13 billion to the war effort in the Persian Gulf, but did not send troops. Two years later, however, despite Article IX of the Constitution, it sent a token non-combatant force to support United Nations peacekeeping in Cambodia. Yet talk of Japanese membership in an expanded Security Council remained talk, and a new, more prominent international role eluded the nation with the world's second-largest economy. If the Persian Gulf War again highlighted Japan's dependence on foreign oil, the conference on global warming held in Kyoto in 1997 was a reminder that we all live on the same planet.

During the 1990s the economy sputtered along, each small spurt followed by a stall, so that it neither advanced into sustained recovery nor sank into the depths of depression. The excesses of spending abroad were liquidated—Rockefeller Center went bankrupt in 1995. Japan was not as badly hit by the "Asian Crisis" of 1998 as Korea, but nevertheless suffered serious losses. At the end of the decade there was an uptick, but all too soon it was clear that the banking system remained unsound and that Japan had not yet found a way back to economic health. Reflecting an expectation that the economic malaise would continue, the stock market in the summer of 2001 declined to a seventeen-year low.

Where earlier the Japanese economic system had been widely admired, the pressures now were toward opening its markets to American-style entrepreneurs and foreign companies and goods. By the end of the decade the *keiretsu* were dissolving as banks sold stocks and companies became more dependent on equity financing. American financial institutions became a major presence. Among the companies taken over by international firms based elsewhere was Mazda, the erstwhile survivor of the oil shock, which now became a Ford subsidiary. Movement toward more efficient marketing and even discounting accelerated. In 2000 the outlook for telemarketing and e-commerce was promising.

A number of factors kept the economy afloat. A vital one was Japan's sheer wealth. This enabled the government to finance very substantial deficit spending on public works, to underwrite housing projects and small business loans, and generally to prime the economy. In 1994 it completed the scintillating Kansai Airport. Designed by the Italian architect Renzo Piano (Pritzker, 1999), it was built offshore in eighteen meters of water on soft foundations that kept subsiding, running the cost up to the enormous figure of roughly 5 trillion yen with no end yet in sight. In addition to stimulating the economy with construction money, this project gave easy international access to the Osaka area.

There were numerous smaller projects nourishing the politically and economically important construction industry. In 1995 these included 400 dams either under construction or planned. By that time postwar Japan had already built 1000 dams, many of which were already clogged by over a billion tons of silt. Writing in 1996, Gavan MacCormack described the situation as "an ecological nightmare to which Japan is only beginning to wake."[9] Economic recovery remained Japan's top priority.

Another way the government sought to stimulate the economy was by lowering interest rates, which at one point reached zero. Even so, the yen did not sink precipitously. The balance of payments with the United States remained in Japan's favor, although by 2000 China had replaced Japan as the country with the largest U.S. trade deficit.

An element of strength was Japan's continued technological excellence. People everywhere eagerly bought Japanese cars, laptop computers, and electronics. Robotics not only led to triumphs in manufacturing but also gave birth to toys which delighted children throughout the world. It is too early to know whether robotic cats and dogs will also eventually catch on. Somewhere between a tool and a toy were the cellular e-mail telephones ubiquitous among Japanese teenagers who found a space of their own in cyberspace.

Companies cut back but tried to limit layoffs. People did not prosper, but most continued to work. The authorities worried less about present or future unemployment than about the aging of the population and a declining birthrate that reached 1.34 per thousand in 1999. An increase to 1.35 in 2000 was thought to be temporary, a product of a belief that this was an especially propitious year ("the millennial factor"). Further decline was expected as women sought more fulfilling roles than that of the traditional mother. At home, as abroad, the spending boom was over. While there was an increase in poverty, most people were able to maintain a satisfactory lifestyle.

People had little faith in government, but there was not a sense of urgency sufficiently strong to stir up an effective public demand for a radical change in political direction or leadership. That all was not well with government was dramatically revealed by its failure to prepare for or deal adequately with the earthquake that shook the Kobe area in 1995, officially designated not earthquake-prone. Over 6000 people died, and the heart of one of Japan's most modern and international cities was destroyed along with a brand new highway, revealing shoddy construction made possible by corruption. Government failure to assure adequate standards was matched by the slowness and inadequacy of its response. In contrast, organized crime stepped in to provide help and relief. The government was effective in suppressing the apocalyptic Aun Shinrikyō sect after it used sarin in a 1995 Tokyo subway attack, but, faced with a nuclear mishap in 1999, the government's response was again slow and inept.

On the political stage the L.D.P. finally came apart in 1993 when there was a major factional exodus, but the first non-L.D.P. prime minister, Hosokawa Morihito, lasted less than a year (August 1993–April 1994) before he too was undone by involvement in yet another scandal. In 1989, under the leadership of Doi Takako (1928–), the first woman to become a major force in Japanese politics, it looked as if the Socialists might grow into a viable second party, but this did not happen. Instead, badly divided and compromised by ill-advised political alliances, they declined. Though the women's vote was important, and two women served in the cabinet for a short time, at century's end over 95 percent of the Diet members were men. With men also in control of the bureaucracy, government and politics remained male domains.

Coalition governments between 1993 and 1996 were hampered by internal rivalry and conflict. One thing that was accomplished in 1994 was a major change in the electoral system, abolishing multi-member districts and providing for a total of 500 seats, 300 from small single-member districts and 200 filled by proportional representation. In 1996 the first election under the new law was held, with the result that a weakened and divided L.D.P. regained power.

Prime Minister Hashimoto Ryutarō (1996–1998) was succeeded by Obuchi Keizo (1937–2000), who died very suddenly and unexpectedly in May, 2000. His successor, Mori Yoshirō (1937–), lost no time causing widespread consternation by calling Japan "a divine nation with the emperor at its core," saying out loud what more circumspect rightist politicians kept to themselves. New elections were held in June with the result that the opposition gained strength, but Mori managed to remain in office until April 2001, when he was succeeded by Koizumi Junichirō (1942–) who owed his position to a landslide victory in provincial party elections rather than through the usual political horse trading by faction leaders.

Koizumi, an unconventional politician noted for an outspoken and frank manner, with an easy sense of humor and something of a bad-boy image, came in with a broad but vague program of financial reforms, which he warned would cause short-term economic pain for the sake of long-term recovery. He also called for constitutional change to legalize the military, and pleased nationalists by visiting the Yasukuni Shrine paying homage to Japan's fallen soldiers, including those condemned as war criminals. Koizumi took a bold step in appointing an outspoken woman as Japan's first female foreign minister. She was Tanaka Makiko (1944–), the eldest daughter of former prime minister Tanaka Kakuei. In July Koizumi, Japan's most popular prime minister since World War II, was able to lead the L.D.P. to an electoral victory. This was a personal triumph, but whether he could follow through and actually remake the banking system, halt public works projects, and get the L.D.P. to change its ways remained very much to be seen. Many were disillusioned after he gave in to Foreign Ministry pressure and forced Tanaka out of the cabinet at the end of January 2002. In other respects too, including economic policies, his administration showed little appetite for the kind of bold innovation once associated with Koizumi's name.

An ardent critic of Establishment thinking was Ōe Kenzaburō, who in 1994 became only the second Japanese, or for that matter East Asian, to receive the Nobel Prize for literature. In conscious contrast to Kawabata, he entitled his acceptance speech, "Japan, the Ambiguous and Myself," and not long after shocked the public by refusing the Imperial Order of Culture. In 1995 he completed his trilogy *The Burning Green Tree* (*Moegaru midori no ki*, 1992–1995). Like Mishima's tetrology, it ends with a death, but, to quote Susan Napier:

> Unlike Mishima whose dead protagonists leave the living with only a feeling of betrayal and emptiness, or Abe whose characters survive in misery, and above all unlike Murakami whose protagonists commit a sort of suicide to the outside wold, Ōe gives us a vision of the outside world revitalized by the sacrifice of a body.[10]

As we have seen, Mishima and Abe belonged to the recent past, but Murakami Haruki (1949–), a prominent writer of the eighties and nineties, represented a generational shift that Ōe deplored. He said of it:

> In contrast to much postwar writing which fictionalized the actual experience of writers and readers, who, as twenty- and thirty-year-olds, had known war, Murakami and Yoshimoto convey the experience of a youth politically uninvolved or disaffected content to exist within a late adolescent or postadolescent subculture.[11]

Yoshimoto is Yoshimoto Banana (Yochimoto Mahoko, 1964–) who had adopted "banana" as her pen-name. Both writers are easy to read and prolific. Both were attuned to the market, enjoyed sensational sales, and were found lacking in gravitas by their elders. Bananas are, after all, delicious but not taken all that seriously. Both were steeped in popular culture, probably read too many comic books, and have been taken to represent a postmodern commodification of literature. Especially Yoshimoto Banana, beginning with *Kitchen* (1987), is treated as much as a cultural as a literary phenomenon. Her novels often depict alternate lifestyles in deadpan, commonplace language. They signal the disintegration of the traditional family, but are bright and cheerful. Murakami, who once ran a jazz bar, wrote long novels filled with the music of his youth, interesting situations, and characters not given to reflection. Pico Iyer had this to say about *The Wind-up Bird* (*Nejimaki-dori kuronikuru*, 1994–1995):

It does not require much reflection that almost every image in the book's 600 pages—a dry well, a haunted house, a faceless man, a dead-end street—stands in some way for a hollowed out Japan, whose motto might be, "I don't think, therefore I am." Again and again, characters say, "I was like a walking corpse" or "I was now in a vacant house" or "I felt as if I had turned into a bowl of cold porridge." Murakami's storytelling ease and the pellucid, uncluttered backdrop he lays down allow moments to flare up memorably. Yet the overall effect of his grand but somewhat abstract novel is to give us X ray after X ray into the benumbed soul of a wannabe Prozac Nation.[12]

In the nineties, the director Kurosawa, then in his eighties, drew on his earlier films to produce works new in content and technique. An example of the latter, discussed by Stephen Prince, is his use of axial cutting, while the dreams in *Dreams* (1990) represent an old theme given new meaning. Once he had seen dreams as being in tension with social commitment, but now Kurosawa cherished them as "the fruit of pure and human desire," and went on to say "A human is a genius while dreaming."[13] Be that as it may, it takes a great artist to convey a dream to others. One who was able to do so was Miyazaki Hayao (1941–), who, in a series of works, raised film animation to new heights. His *Princess Mononoke* (1997) won widespread popular and critical acclaim. Similarly, *Spirited Away* (2001) broke all box-office records in Japan.

Japanese architects too continued to dream. One who did so with great imagination was Ando Tadao (1941–; Pritzker, 1995), a self-taught master who, early in his career, built a lovely, small Christian church in Osaka. Among his most notable subsequent works were an underground temple entered though stairs in a lotus pond (1991) and, on Naoshima, an island in the Inland Sea, a museum/hotel for contemporary art (1995). The art, mostly non-Japanese, is not confined to the inside, but continues outdoors, and includes an enormous pumpkin and a Chinese stone garden. In 1997 I. M. Pei completed his masterpiece, the Miho Museum at Shigaraki. Like Ando's temple and museum/hotel, it is mostly underground, and it too blends in with and makes the most of the natural beauty of the landscape.

As earlier, Japanese artists participated in all the international styles and movements of the day. Some of them spent considerable time overseas. Performance and installations remained popular, conveying the sense that art, like all things, was not forever. A sculptor obsessed with time was Miyajima Tatsuo (1957–), whose *Running Time* (1994) consisted of battery-powered "U-cars," each with a colored, single-number LED (light emitting diode) counter on its roof and with sensors front and back so that the cars changed direction as they randomly bumped each other. The effect has been likened to "glowing numerical fireflies," while the artist himself explained that the "u" refers to the "uncertainty principle," as in the physics of Heisenberg.[14]

Running Time, like the writings of Banana Yoshimoto and Murakami Haruki, is a work in a modern idiom with it own aesthetic appeal. It says something in a new way without reference to what others in the long tradition have said on the subject. Like traditional works of art, it leaves interpretation to the viewer, but, unlike them, it does not demand the cultivation of connoisseurship to unlock the message.

Notes

1. Richard Pascale and Thomas P. Roblen, "The Mazda Turnaround," *The Journal of Japanese Studies 9*, no. 2 (Dec. 1983), p. 263.

2. David Plath, "My-Car-isma: Motorizing the Showa Self," in Carol Gluck and Stephen R. Graubard, eds., *Showa: The Japan of Hirohito* (New York: W.W. Norton, 1992), p. 239.

3. Koji Taira, "Dialectics of Economic Growth, National Power, and Distributive Struggles," in Andrew Gordon, ed., *Postwar Japan as History* (Berkeley: Univ. of California Press), p. 171.

4. Ian Reader, *Religion in Contemporary Japan* (Honolulu: Univ. of Hawaii Press, 1991), p. 233, apropos Agonshu.

5. Roy Starrs, *Soundings in Time: The Fictive Art of Kawabata Yasunari* (London: Curzon Press, 1998), p. 218.

6. Isozaki Arata in Masao Miyoshi and H. D. Harootunian, eds., *Postmodernism and Japan* (Durham: Duke Univ. Press, 1989), pp. 57 and 59.

7. Kenneth B. Pyle, "The World Historical Significance of Japan" in Kozo Yamamura, ed., *A Vision of a New Liberalism? Critical Essays on Murakami's Anticlassical Analysis* (Stanford: Stanford Univ. Press, 1997), pp. 233 and 237.

8. Ibid., p. 127.

9. Gavan McCormack, *The Emptiness of Japanese Affluence* (Armonk, N.Y.: M.E. Sharpe, 1996), p. 46.

10. Susan J. Napier, "Ōe Kenzaburō and the Search for the Sublime at the End of the Twentieth Century," in Stephen Snyder and Philip Gabriel, eds., *Ōe and Beyond: Fiction in Contemporary Japan* (Honolulu: Univ. of Hawaii Press, 1999), pp. 32–33.

11. Quoted by Snyder and Gabriel on page 2 of their introduction.

12. Pico Iyer in *Time*, vol. 150, no. 8 (Nov. 3, 1997) available at www.time/magazine/1997/dom/971103/abook.tales_of_the_html.

13. Kurosawa as quoted in Stephen Prince, *The Warrior's Camera: The Cinema of Akira Kurosawa*, revised and enlarged edition (Princeton: Princeton Univ. Press, 1999), p. 303.

14. Exhibition catalog. *Tatsuo Miyajima (1957) BIG TIME*, organized by Michael Auping, Fort Worth: Modern Art Museum of Fort Worth and Hayward Gallery London (June 19–August 17, 1997), pp. 25–26.

18

The Two Koreas and Vietnam

When we last discussed Korea and Vietnam, both were divided between northern and southern systems. During the next half-century, the two Korean regimes failed to make peace, but the cease-fire that had ended the fighting in 1953 held, and the people were spared further warfare. In contrast, Vietnam achieved unification in 1975, but only after bitter and prolonged fighting and untold suffering. In both cases military concerns and military men played a major role in shaping new, post-colonial policies and societies.

I. Korea

Aftermath of the Korean War in the Republic of Korea (South Korea)

Military Rule and Economic Development in the Republic of Korea

The Republic of Korea since 1988

The Democratic People's Republic of Korea (North Korea) under Kim Il-sung

The Problem of North-South Relations

Aftermath of the Korean War in the Republic of Korea (South Korea)

The years after the cease-fire at P'anmunjŏm were bleak for the people of the Republic of Korea. Throughout the south, the fighting had forced families to flee their homes and villages and seek food and shelter in miserable refugee camps. Returning home and restoring life to some semblance of normalcy was extremely difficult. There was little food to buy, prices were high, and the shattered economy offered little employment to help people recover. Massive amounts of overseas assistance from the United Nations and South Korea's wartime allies succeeded only in keeping the population from starving.

Under Japanese colonialism, the southern part of Korea had been the peninsula's food-producing region. After the division of the country in 1945, the south had struggled to diversify and industrialize in order to develop a better-balanced regional economy. The Korean War ended that effort, however, and left the Republic of Korea abjectly dependent on foreign aid, not only for basic manufactured goods such as clothing, but also for food and other raw materials.

The long road back from devastation was marked in small increments: an increase in electrical power generation, the building of a chemical fertilizer plant, the opening of a textile factory, more coal for cooking and home heating, construction of a cement plant, and the opening of an oil refinery. In the countryside, a network of government-organized extension agencies provided training and credit to farmers. These efforts were the building blocks for the new national economy, but they were overshadowed always by the overwhelming problem of Korea's national division, the need to maintain a large standing army, and the question of whether war would break out again and destroy everything. It was a bitter time for the Korean people, and it took enormous courage and determination for the country to survive.

The Korean War era greatly affected Korea's artists and writers. Liberation itself, so full of hope in the beginning, led immediately to a struggle to redefine Korean identity in terms of north and south, suddenly re-politicizing the arts in terms of the Cold War. On top of recriminations about collaboration with the Japanese—in a famous case, the novelist Yi Kwangsu was accused of collaboration—Korean intellectuals also had to deal with the nation's own alienation, producing, in the words of Marshall Pihl, "a literature [that] was little better than a deformity incapable of expressing the wholeness of the Korean experience."[1] The Korean War era itself was full of human drama, and did eventually lead to a rich output of novels and stories by writers such as Hwang Sunwŏn, Kim Tongni, and Cho Chongnae among others.[2]

President Syngman Rhee, who remained in office as President of the Republic of Korea until 1960, retained much personal prestige. His administration's record, however, was disappointing, and his ruling Liberal Party was notoriously corrupt. Rhee exploited popular emotions to rally support, inveighing against an array of demons that included not only the North Korean Communists but also the Japanese. He told his people that the Communists were poised to invade at any moment and that the people must support his regime as the best hope of deterring a new war. He told them that the Japanese were out to colonize Korea again and that Koreans should not accept Japanese aid or allow Japanese investment to help them rebuild. On occasion he also criticized the United States for interfering in Korea's internal affairs and trying to take advantage of the Korean people, though his government was a major beneficiary of all types of American aid, political, economic, and military. As a result, the Republic of Korea was a very isolated nation, enjoying significant relationships only with the United States and its anti-Communist clients, notably the Republic of China on Taiwan and the Republic of Vietnam based in Saigon.

Rhee was president for twelve years, being reelected in 1952 and 1956. These two elections were somewhat irregular; however, his third attempt at reelection in 1960 was so blatantly corrupt that the people rose up in protest. After demonstrations swept South Korea in March and April 1960, Rhee was forced to resign, and eventually moved to Hawaii, where he spent the rest of his life in exile.

Between the summer of 1960 and May of 1961, the Republic of Korea was governed by a democratically elected government under a new, parliamentary-type constitution. Prime Minister Chang Myŏn (John M. Chang) wrestled with the country's ongoing economic and political problems while trying to maintain democratic freedoms of assembly, expression, and association. His time in power was short—less than a year, during which he was unable to get the economy under control, and many of his countrymen feared that the country was in danger of being torn apart by dissident factions. It was for these reasons, and ostensibly to restore a sense of social discipline and national direction, that elements of the R.O.K. Army struck in a coup d'état on May 16, 1961, overthrew the Chang government and constitution, and began ruling under martial law.

Military Rule and Economic Development in the Republic of Korea

In a way, it was predictable that the South Korean military would rise to power in a coup. The army was the best-organized and disciplined element in the country, and it was heavily armed. In 1961 the R.O.K. Army was one of the largest in the world. The United States, having created, trained, and equipped the South Koreans to hold the line on the "frontier of freedom," found itself in no position to roll back the coup and insist that Korea's democratic experiment continue. Instead, it reluctantly accepted the Korean officers' claim that conditions required the establishment of a firm central authority in Seoul and a reorganization of the South Korean system as a bootstrap effort to achieve modernization through intensive labor.

Korea remained under direct military control for two years. The coup leader, Major General Park Chung-hee (Pak Chŏnghŭi, 1917–1979), presided over a tight circle of military men whose power derived from their personal networks. They started out as a group of alumni from the same class of the Korean Military Academy. As they created their new state structure, they invented new institutions and assumed new, civilian-style positions. One of the coup planners, Lieutenant Colonel Kim Chŏngp'il (Kim Jongpil, 1926–) became head of the Korean Central Intelligence Agency (KCIA), a type of secret police that monitored not only national security but also the economy, political activities of individuals, the press, the universities, and religious and labor leaders. Kim Chŏngp'il also founded a new political party through which the army leaders, after "retirement," ran for civilian office in 1963, winning elections that gave them a majority in the National Assembly and installed General Park as President of the Republic of Korea.

With his men ensconced in control of the army, administration, economy, and National Assembly, General Park single-mindedly pursued the goal of economic betterment for the people of Korea. His methods remain a topic of controversy in South Korea. Though his leadership was strict, he was seen as personally honest. He took the country and its low-wage workers on a forced march. Progress was made, but the price was high. Yet there is a rough consensus that conditions in 1961 required assertive leadership and that the Army was in a logical position to "save the nation."

As president, General Park supervised a central Economic Planning Board that laid out a series of five-year plans providing for the consolidation of Korea's economic infrastructure, and setting ambitious production targets. The results were remarkable. From the beginning, the five-year production targets were met ahead of schedule and were followed by ever more ambitious goals. By the end of the 1960s there were noticeable improvements in the supplies of food and energy, and in areas such as public health and education.

Using his political clout to "normalize" relations with Japan, Park obtained a package of loans and aid that helped jump-start the industrialization process. He contributed two Army divisions to the U.S.-led effort to defend the Republic of Vietnam, with Washington paying Seoul in dollars for all the costs of the deployment, thus providing the R.O.K. with a valuable flow of foreign exchange. The United States also granted preferential status to Korean companies that bid on construction projects such as runways and port facilities in the Republic of Vietnam. Their participation in Vietnam enabled South Koreans to feel that they had "repaid" the United States for saving them from their own near-takeover by the North Korean Communists in the early 1950s. It also made them feel that they were on the verge of becoming an industrial trading nation in their own right.

One of President Park's signature programs was the Saemaŭl ("New Community") Movement that was aimed at boosting productivity and raising living standards in the countryside. The Saemaŭl Movement helped farmers get credit, fertilizer and pesticides, and brought electricity, safe water, better roads and communications, more schools, better health, and birth control to South Korea's villages. Korea's rural areas underwent significant changes as living standards rose—and also as many of the young people growing up on farms were lured to the cities, where life seemed to be getting better even more rapidly. In a single generation, the population of South Korea went from 80 percent rural to 80 percent urban, and the nation was unified as never before by the power of common experience and mass communication.

Despite dramatic progress, there continued to be disparities in the way the burdens and benefits were distributed. Farm people continued to do backbreaking work that was only partly alleviated by mechanization. Factory workers powered production in the R.O.K., but they labored in wretched conditions with few safeguards from injury or illness. The Park government kept tight control over labor, and forbade strikes. Labor organizers who tried to teach workers how to band together for better working conditions often ended up in jail. Low wages and scant workers' benefits were keys to the country's economic growth, achieved on the backs of its workers. It is not an exaggeration to say that an entire generation of South Koreans sacrificed themselves to create the relative prosperity that their children now enjoy.

Big business, on the other hand, got considerable support from the Park government as it tried to emulate imperial Japan in the creation of favored conglomerates called *chaebŏl* (the Korean equivalent of the Japanese term *zaibatsu*). The government intervened to guarantee financing for these clusters of companies, some of whose names are now famous around the world. The Samsung *chaebŏl*, for example, started as a textile manufacturer and branched out into light electronics, household appliances, cameras and computers. Components of the Hyundai *chaebŏl* included construction, shipbuilding, automobiles, department stores, and tourism. Government favoritism nurtured the *chaebŏl*, which, in turn, created jobs, exported Korean goods to earn hard currency, and occasionally returned the favor by supporting government candidates financially. As products from South Korea won market share overseas, the *chaebŏl* came to control a large part of the national economy.

Development of the *chaebŏl* conglomerates concentrated enormous wealth in the hands of relatively few large capitalists, and by the 1970s there were irresistible demands from workers for a better share of the nation's new prosperity. In 1979, amid a wave of labor unrest, President Park Chung-hee was assassinated by one of his own deputies. Within months a new military strongman emerged. He was General Chun Doo-hwan (Chŏn Tuhwan, 1931–), who used his partisans in the army to seize control, first of the military, and then of the nation itself. In the process, he crushed a popular uprising against him in the southwestern city of Kwangju in May, 1980, a disastrous move that cost the lives of hundreds of civilians. Though Chun manipulated the factions of his followers and the nation's laws to seize the presidency, and was able to rule from 1980 until 1988, the Kwangju massacre made him one of the most hated figures in the history of the Republic. Because of the way he came to power, he was not regarded as a legitimate president, and was able to remain in power mainly through threats and use of police power.

The city of Seoul won the bid for the 1988 Summer Olympics, and despite Chun Doo-hwan's dubious presidency, South Koreans worked hard to set the stage for grand international show. Korea enjoyed a surge in construction; the *chaebŏl* boomed; and despite concerns over possible interference by the North, the 1988 summer games were a great success. In 1987, however, virtually on the eve of the games, General Chun provoked a political crisis by naming an army cohort as his hand-picked successor for president. The nominee was General Roh Tae-woo (No Tae'u, 1932–), a figure associated with Chun's virtual coup of 1979–1980, and the campuses and streets of Korea erupted in popular protests. This time Chun was unable to crush the opposition and was forced to allow a popular election. Ironically, General Roh won the presidency when the opposition fractured into competing camps. By 1988, however, it was clear that the people of South Korea had forced a change in the direction of democracy. Roh's five years as president were marked by increasing liberalization, a much freer press, and startling new overtures toward China and the Soviet Union. Opening relations with the communist countries helped promote South Korea as a worldwide economic power. There was change at home and abroad.

The Republic of Korea since 1988

South Koreans see the 1988 Summer Olympics as their international debut, the celebration of their emergence from poverty to prosperity and from dictatorship to democracy. Staging the successful Olympics is connected to the Democracy Movement of 1987 in which the people rose up and demanded the right to elect their own leaders and to enjoy expanded freedom to think, associate, travel, and worship. Belief in their own achievements and increased national confidence convinced them that they did not need to organize everything around the fearful memory of the Korean War. The growth of civil society, the high level of education, the success in the world markets, and recognition and respect from other countries created the atmosphere for a new era in national life.

If the transition from military dictatorship to democracy was at the heart of this national mood, the individual who symbolized it was Kim Dae-jung (Kim Taejung, 1925–), a longtime opposition leader from southwestern Korea. Kim Dae-jung had made a career of challenging dictatorship, even daring to challenge President Park Chung-hee as he ran for reelection in 1971. When Kim nearly won that election, Park launched a campaign of persecution against him, variously imprisoning him, putting him under house arrest, kidnapping him, and more than once trying to kill him. When Kim publicly opposed the emerging strongman Chun Doo-hwan in 1980, Chun had him sentenced to death. It took an international outcry to get the sentence lifted.

By the early 1990s, the 44 million citizens of the Republic of Korea were enjoying a standard of living undreamed of as recently as the 1970s. Full employment and universal literacy, together with strong community values, pride, and purpose seemed to be paying off. Amid continual fear of renewed war with the North, traffic jams, industrial pollution, and labor unrest, the people in general nevertheless found that they had time for vacations, reading, and television watching, and money for luxury goods. Many ordinary Koreans became wealthy overnight by selling suburban farmland that was in sudden demand for housing in the country's booming urban areas. These profits fueled investments and consumption, paid for college educations, private cars, and even relocation to such places as Los Angeles and New York. People sported fine clothes, cell phones, and jewelry. Seoul came to offer fine dining, several prime arts centers, a world-class film industry, and stores selling everything from books and CDs to imported foods and heavy appliances. Between 1993 and 1997, under Kim Young-sam (Kim Yŏngsam, 1927–), the first civilian president since 1963, the dream of modernization seemed at last to have come true.

However, beneath the surface there was much instability. In the name of "globalization" the R.O.K. government had permitted money to flow too freely between Korea and foreign financial institutions. The Korean conglomerates in particular had taken on too much debt to finance expansion into areas that proved too risky, and the debts suddenly turned bad in 1997. Unable to repay short-term loans, several of South Korea's biggest *chaebŏl* suddenly found themselves facing bankruptcy. When the Korean government was unable to save them, the country's banking system proved short of funds to pay its international obligations. Only days before the presidential election of 1997, citizens of the R.O.K. were obliged to watch in humiliation as the outgoing Kim Young-sam administration was reduced to begging for billions of dollars in emergency loans from the International Monetary Fund (IMF). A hurried IMF bailout amounting to $57 billion—the largest ever arranged by the Fund—temporarily enabled the R.O.K. to survive the crisis. In return for the bailout, the IMF demanded control of South Korea's financial system and the institution of strict austerity measures. Massive layoffs created disturbances across the economic spectrum, and ordinary Koreans paid a high psychological and social price for their government's mismanagement.

The leader who inherited this situation was Kim Dae-jung, elected president in December 1997. When he took office in February 1998, he was forced to start by asking the people to accept unemployment, the closure of badly-run banks and businesses, and a sell-off of distressed components of the big Korean conglomerates. The strong medicine took effect within a year of the crash, and by the year 2001 the R.O.K economy was far along the road to recovery. Though there were many signs of lingering trouble, most Koreans had jobs again and much of the underlying instability had been eliminated. President Kim Dae-jung deserved part of the credit for this, but once again it was the Korean people themselves who proved they had the discipline to meet the crisis with their own hard work and determination.

The Democratic People's Republic of Korea (North Korea) under Kim Il-sung

Kim Il-sung's decision to reunite the country by military force in 1950 turned out to have been a massive mistake. The southern population did not rise up as expected to welcome his army, and he miscalculated the intentions of the United States and United Nations. When the tide of battle turned after the Inch'ŏn Landing and the D.P.R.K. itself was in danger of being overrun by United Nations forces, Kim Il-sung had to accept intervention by the People's Republic of China. The second and third years of the war brought a rain of bombs from the U.S. Air Force as it tried to force the Communist side to surrender or agree to a cease-fire. Though the bombing was of questionable political value, it did succeed in pulverizing most of the D.P.R.K.'s industrial plants and reducing the quality of life in the north to mere subsistence. By the end of the war the citizens of the D.P.R.K., though still tough and determined, were completely unable to provide for themselves.

North Korea's physical recovery was enhanced by postwar aid from China, the Soviet Union, and the socialist countries in Europe. In P'yŏngyang there were recriminations. When challenged or criticized, Kim Il-sung responded by purging rivals and instigating a reign of terror. He blamed the wartime disaster on bad advice, noting that Pak Hŏnyŏng, the leading southern Communist, had assured him that the people of the south were poised for revolt and waiting for their chance to rise up and welcome the North Korean army. When this proved wrong, Kim accused Pak of secretly working for the Americans, and had him executed as a spy. In this atmosphere, which came to resemble that of the Soviet Union under Stalin, personal loyalty to the "Great Leader" became the foremost criterion for success and survival in the D.P.R.K. Thus Kim Il-sung was able to escape judgment for the disasters that he had brought upon his people.

One feature of Kim Il-sung's rule was the invention of the North Korean political philosophy known as *juch'e*, which means "self reliance." One purpose of the "juch'e idea" was to inspire the people to work hard to achieve true national independence from foreign aid and control. Another was to establish North Korea as neutral in the ideological disputes that were developing among the socialist countries. True self-reliance was, in fact, beyond North Korea's capabilities. When the communist superpowers phased out foreign aid, North Korea continued to depend on a system of barter trading in which Korean raw materials such as lumber and minerals were traded to the Soviet Union, for example, for oil. North Korea also exchanged labor for imports, by sending workers to help clear timberland in Siberia. In the 1960s and 1970s, this combination of reconstruction at home, aid from abroad, and barter trading enabled North Korea to outdistance the south in restoring the economy. Though North Korean workers enjoyed little freedom of expression or movement, having to work wherever they were assigned for pay that was extremely low by world standards, the state provided their housing, education, health care, and other necessities of life.

After the Korean War, though North Korea recovered more rapidly than the south, owing to massive socialist-bloc aid and a centrally controlled economy, its growth slowed and performance began to lag behind that of the south. It developed economic imbalances and commodity shortages owing in part to poor management and to the isolation that was imposed upon it by the international community, led by the United States. For decade after decade, American diplomatic pressure effectively prevented North Korea from taking advantage of the planning and funding resources that were available to the Republic of Korea as well as other developing economies around the world. As a result, the D.P.R.K. was almost entirely reliant on the socialist community for vital assistance with energy, manufacturing goods, and basic technical training. One result was that the D.P.R.K. developed along lines favored by the Soviet Union, with emphasis on central direction and heavy industry such as railroads, steel, and chemicals, at the expense of consumer goods manufacturing. The D.P.R.K.'s enormous military establishment also drained resources from the state budget. This meant that daily living standards for ordinary people did not rise as they did in the south, where consumer goods were a much higher priority. By the 1980s, when South Korea became one of the trading powers of the Pacific Rim, making money by exporting textiles, electronics, automobiles, and other consumer items, North Korea remained preoccupied with food sufficiency and the export of raw materials to pay for whatever consumer goods it could afford to buy.

North Korea's foreign relations were similarly lopsided, as the D.P.R.K. remained isolated from the mainstream of world organizations and excessively reliant on support from the socialist community. As a state with an avowedly Marxist-Leninist political philosophy, the D.P.R.K. claimed to be committed to world revolution. It was fundamentally hostile to Western-style democracy and capitalism, and its steady output of invective against the United States, Japan, the R.O.K., and the West in general, while not damaging, won few new friends.

Occasionally the D.P.R.K. took action in ways that aggravated its isolation. For example, in 1968 a team of D.P.R.K. agents almost succeeded in assassinating President Park Chung-Hee in Seoul. The D.P.R.K. captured a U.S. Navy intelligence ship that was accused of violating North Korea's territorial waters, letting nearly a year pass before releasing the crew. In 1969 the D.P.R.K. shot down an American intelligence plane. In 1983 D.P.R.K. agents planted a bomb that killed many members of the South Korean cabinet during a visit to Rangoon, Burma (Myanmar) and just missed killing President Chun Doo-hwan himself. In 1987 they planted a bomb on a South Korean airliner that blew up over the Andaman Sea, killing more than 200 passengers and crew. These and other "revolutionary" actions succeeded in getting the D.P.R.K. labeled a "terrorist state," and eroded the willingness of governments around the world to do legitimate business with it. North Korea also engaged in a lively arms export trade, selling guns and missiles to countries such as Iran and Libya. On the one hand the D.P.R.K., after decades of economic pressure and sanctions from the West, had little besides weapons worth exporting. On the other hand, weapons sales to adversaries of the

Western democracies did little to encourage the lifting of sanctions or to repair the Kim regime's reputation for state-sponsored terrorism.

When the socialist community collapsed in Eastern Europe and the Soviet Union also fell, North Korea was forced to pay for many of the things that it had formerly traded for raw materials and labor. When the Russian Federation started demanding cash for the oil it had been bartering to North Korea, and China followed suit, North Korea suffered an immediate energy shortage that brought its national economy to a standstill. The lack of fuel for transportation affected production at all levels and led to many system breakdowns. With North Korea's history of state terrorism, the world was not sympathetic to its plight. There was a dramatic contraction of the national economy and severe hardships for the people of North Korea in the mid-1990s. This was further aggravated by weather disasters that ruined crops and caused famines in certain parts of the country, and hundreds of thousands of vulnerable people, mainly older citizens and children, perished.

Kim Il-sung, commonly referred to by northerners as their "Great Leader," was President of the Democratic People's Republic of Korea, the head of its ruling Korean Workers Party, and commander-in-chief of its armed forces from 1948 until his death in July 1994. The people of North Korea, by all accounts, are a patriotic population who believe that they owe everything to their late leader. They revere his memory and they respect his son and successor, Kim Jong-il (1942–). However, Kim Il-sung used the people's respect to construct a remarkable personality cult. Statues of Kim Il-sung, some fifty or sixty feet high, were erected all over the country during his lifetime. The people were told to wear Kim Il-sung buttons on their clothes to indicate their loyalty and to welcome him warmly when he came to visit factories and farms to give them "on-the-spot guidance." The country's top university bears his name, as do many other institutions. North Korean history books assign him a major role in defeating Japan in the Second World War. Various Kim family members and in-laws have occupied many key positions in the regime. Early in his career, his son Kim Jong-il became known as the ruling party's "party center" and the country's "Dear Leader," titles that identified him as the likeliest candidate to succeed the "Great Leader" himself.

Outsiders sometimes have trouble fathoming North Korean political culture, rejecting the legitimacy of the Kim personality cult and dismissing North Korea as a country ruled by irrational people who cannot comprehend modern civilization or even what is in their own best interests. The United States Government has variously labeled North Korea a "terrorist state," a "rogue state," and a "state of concern." For many years, Westerners have been assessing North Korea and predicting a collapse that has never come. The mysterious survival and resilience of North Korea baffles people who think in Western terms and judge by Western standards. However, history as the North Koreans have experienced it can offer us some clues about their motivations and political culture.

The Democratic People's Republic of Korea has been isolated from the non-Communist world virtually from its birth in 1948. Very few North Koreans have been outside their country. Few have studied foreign languages or met foreigners other than Chinese and Russians. The entire system has been locked down under tight information control. North Koreans read few foreign books and see virtually no foreign films or newspapers. They have not enjoyed the music that has helped shape the modern age. Instead, the popular culture of the D.P.R.K. has been inward-looking, drawing lessons from North Korea's own experience. One lesson is xenophobic: foreigners are a threat. Another is pride in surviving the Korean War and a determination to avenge the national damage caused by perceived Western (that is, American) imperialism. Another is a hatred of Japan arising from the colonial past.

When it comes to formative influences from Korea's history, the D.P.R.K. remembers the hereditary monarchy of the Chosŏn dynasty, the system that preceded Japanese colonialism, and the elite Confucian bureaucracy that supported it. Despite resentment of Japanese colonialism, the North Korean system also draws lessons from imperial Japan. For example, in World War II, Japan used the term *kokutai* ("national body," or "national polity") to speak of Japan and its people as an organic whole headed by the Emperor. The second syllable of the Korean word *juch'e* is the same as the "tai" of the Japanese word *kokutai*, carrying something of the same emotional meaning that attaches to unquestioning loyalty and belonging.

These particular "lessons of history" have created a unique worldview in the D.P.R.K., one that can only be understood by making the effort to imagine what the people there see as their own national interests. They help explain features of the North Korean system: its extreme emphasis on group loyalty, its ultranationalism and fierce determination to claim independence, its resentment of the West, and even its acceptance of a dynastic succession in the passage of power.

When Kim Il-sung died, his country was already in deep trouble. Since the fall of communism in Europe and the end of the Soviet Union, much of the D.P.R.K.'s support system had vanished. The D.P.R.K.'s barter system had ended, and the Kim regime was having to pay for imports of vital commodities such as fuel oil. A rudimentary nuclear power industry had become an international threat, and the D.P.R.K. was under intense pressure to shut it down. The economy that once had outrun its southern rival had started to contract, and famine seemed to stalk the land.

Kim Jong-il succeeded his father during this perilous time. In 1994 he was little-known in the outside world. Those who claimed to know him said that he was a spoiled playboy with few skills of his own, and many outsiders predicted that he would be unable to survive whatever power struggles were bound to ensue. In the south, there was talk about going north to take over the wreckage of the Communist regime. Some former refugees talked of going back to reclaim their lost property. And yet, despite the severe economic crisis and a desperate shortage of basic needs, Kim Jong-il's regime took hold and managed to survive. In 1998, after showing due reluctance in good Confucian style, the younger Kim accepted his father's title of "Great Leader," and became general secretary of the ruling political party. He left the post of president vacant in memory of his father, however, as if to suggest that the late President Kim Il-sung will always occupy the position in spirit.

The Problem of North-South Relations

The problem of national reunification had been at the top of the agenda for both Koreas since the armistice in 1953. Since the two systems are incompatible, it is hard to see how they might be reunited without the extinction of one or the other. With huge armies on either side of the border mutually ruling out a military solution, it has been necessary to seek common ground in pursuit of national reunification. To be sure, powerful interests on both sides are heavily invested in the status quo, chief among them the military establishments whose very existence is premised on a continuing military stalemate. However, in the 1990s there were small steps toward relations between the two regimes that raised hopes for some degree of contact and reconciliation.

The two Koreas have floated many reunification proposals over the years. Most of these have seemed to be propaganda initiatives, advanced in terms that were designed to be rejected by the other side. Each claims to be the "legitimate" or "legal" government of the Korean people. The D.P.R.K. points out that the United States (more properly the United Nations Command) signed the armistice document for the U.N. side, and that it is the United States, and not its puppet the R.O.K., that should handle the business of changes in the armistice leading to reunification. The United States insists that the two Koreas talk to each other; that is, that the R.O.K. and D.P.R.K. should deal with each other as equals. Thus, even the beginning of a conversation between the two has meant a concession by the northern side.

The multiple disasters in the D.P.R.K. during the 1990s have softened the northern position somewhat. Another change has been the R.O.K.'s active pursuit of better relations with communist countries since 1988, including the former socialist countries of Eastern Europe and the Soviet Union, and today the People's Republic of China and Socialist Republic of Vietnam. From 1993 through 1997, the Kim Young-sam administration in South Korea pursued a hard line against the north, for example, greatly offending the D.P.R.K. by its ostentatious lack of mourning for the death of the "Great Leader" in 1994. The Kim Dae-jung administration, however, has pursued a much softer "Sunshine Policy" toward North Korea, tolerating insults and steadily promoting trade and "confidence-building" measures of many kinds. As a result, southern companies have built factories in the D.P.R.K. and created a steady flow of goods between the two sides, creating stakes in peaceful interaction. Many southerners have visited the north, and not a few are at work on projects there. Indeed, the most astonishing product of the Sunshine Policy was the visit, in June 2000, of President Kim Dae-jung to P'yŏngyang to shake hands and talk with Chairman Kim Jong-il. The event was heavy with symbolism and promises of change. It capped a process of conciliation for which Kim Dae-jung was awarded the Nobel Peace Prize later in the year. And although the unification process reverted to its normal glacial pace, the people of South Korea, and presumably some citizens of the D.P.R.K., had a welcome chance to see each other as countrymen.

II. Vietnam

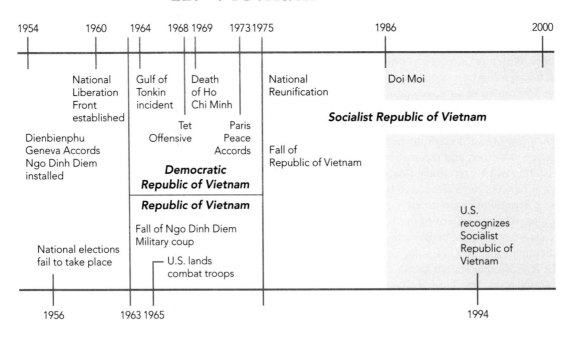

The Regime of Ngo Dinh Diem

The Fall of Diem and American Escalation, 1963–1968

Maintaining a Society at War: South Vietnam

Maintaining a Society at War: The D.R.V.

The Vietnam War: The Final Phase

The Socialist Republic of Vietnam:
The First Decade, 1976–1986

Doi Moi, 1986–Present

The failure to hold elections in 1956 left Vietnam divided, with governments in the north and south fighting each other, striving to establish their legitimacy, achieve economic and military strength, and to form their people into a strong state capable of dominating the entire country. Prolonging and deepening the conflict between them was the intrusion of foreign powers, particularly the United States.

The Regime of Ngo Dinh Diem

In the 1950s, the government of Ngo Dinh Diem in Saigon made many attempts to win support from the people of southern Vietnam. However, Diem lacked a natural constituency. His political base, such as it was, consisted of support from refugee Catholics from the north, landlords of the Mekong Delta, and government officials whose salaries he paid. His second, and perhaps more important prop, came from American officials who saw him as Vietnam's best alternative to the Communist Ho Chi Minh, and who were determined to ensure his success. Diem was little-known in his country's farming communities and small towns. In those areas, popular discontent was fanned by the arrival of his appointees to rule and tax the peasants—police and civil administrators more interested in pleasing their superiors in Saigon and lining their own pockets than in serving the interests of the local people.

Under Ngo Dinh Diem, the government of the Republic of Vietnam faced many urgent problems. Millions of peasants did not own their own farms. As late as 1960, 15 percent of the people owned 75 percent of the land, but Diem consistently postponed doing anything about a long-promised land reform program. Consequently, there was rising discontent among landless peasants and great disappointment in the central government, which felt entitled to tax them, draft their sons into the army, and harass suspected political opponents, but felt no equivalent obligation to improve their living conditions and public services.

Revolutionary elements took full advantage of the unhappiness in the South Vietnamese countryside. As Diem grew more suspicious of his own people and employed ever more repressive police measures, some of his opponents used terrorism to spread their own influence among the peasants. One tactic was to kill some of the most unpopular Saigon appointees—proving that no one was safe from revolutionary reprisals, and winning favor among the most disaffected. Vietnamese Communists justified their use of violence as the only path open to them now that the Republic of Vietnam was excluding them from the legitimate political process.

Anti-government strikes grew numerous in the late 1950s when an atmosphere of national emergency settled over the Saigon government. Though the Republic of Vietnam had an elected legislature, Diem dominated it like a king rather than an elected chief executive. Because of the "emergency," he devoted much of the American aid that was meant for development to security purposes. The emergency was also the reason for arresting his critics, often holding them without warrant or trial. Seeking to surround himself with people of unquestionable loyalty, he turned to family members—brothers and their in-laws—to serve in the most sensitive positions. His brother Ngo Dinh Nhu was put in charge of the security forces and given effective police power over the entire population. His brother Ngo Dinh Can was in charge of all government appointments and contracts. Both men quickly acquired reputations for extreme corruption. A fourth brother, Ngo Dinh Thuc, was the Catholic archbishop of Hue and leader of the church in Vietnam.

At the Third National Congress of the Vietnam Workers Party in Hanoi, in September 1960, the members set an agenda that placed national unification on a par with socialist development in the north. The "masses" were identified as the best means to this end, and party leaders said they hoped to bring about the collapse of the Diem regime without provoking large-scale intervention by the United States. To mobilize the masses in the south, the party conceived a "National Front for the Liberation of South Vietnam" (known as the National Liberation Front, or "NLF"), designed to rally all of the political factions that opposed the Diem government. The NLF was born on December 20, 1960, on a rubber plantation in the south near the Cambodian border, and it came to represent a coalition of leftist political factions in the south as well as the guerrilla fighters who sapped the strength of the Saigon regime through organized acts of military resistance.[3]

In the early 1960s, the government of the Republic of Vietnam was thrown on the defensive, even in the capital, by the rise of opposition among Buddhist groups angry about religious discrimination. The government hired Catholic officials while the Army's officer corps was almost entirely comprised of Catholics, with Buddhists relegated to the ranks. Ngo Dinh Nhu, meanwhile, had begun a program of counter-terror against the National Liberation Front, arresting and torturing suspected Communists to extract information, and intimidating villagers in a campaign to end their cooperation with NLF agents. He employed special forces, who were in effect his own private army, to attack not only NLF members but other political opponents, including Buddhists. When Buddhists staged a protest demonstration in Saigon in May 1963, the Army of the Republic of Vietnam (ARVN) opened fire on them, killing nine and wounding fourteen. The public erupted in a furor that was greatly aggravated by the deaths of several monks who set themselves on fire in public suicides. Ngo Dinh Nhu's wife was once heard referring to these as "Buddhist barbecues."

The Fall of Diem and American Escalation, *1963–1968*

The United States, meanwhile, increasingly came to see South Vietnam as a test case in the Cold War, a small country under assault by Communist forces backed by foreign powers seeking to extend Communist control over all of Southeast Asia. The "domino theory" held that if the Republic of Vietnam fell to Communism, Cambodia, Laos, and the rest of Southeast Asia would be ripe for conquest, and that the line would have to be drawn somewhere, sometime, before the entire Pacific Rim came under the sway of Moscow and Beijing. American leaders reasoned that it would be better to take a stand in southern Vietnam while "counterinsurgency" could still be effective, than to fight a larger and more difficult war somewhere else. There had been successful "counterinsurgency" campaigns against leftist rebels in the Philippines and Malaya, and the Kennedy Administration was confident that with the right advice, training and development, the Saigon government could overcome the Communist effort to disrupt the South Vietnamese countryside. Accordingly, in 1962 the Kennedy Administration dispatched more than 11,000 military advisors and combat support personnel to guide the R.V.N.'s counterinsurgency campaign. However, even this level of American support was unlikely to be helpful if the Saigon government remained corrupt, ineffective, and unpopular.

In the summer of 1963, the United States began getting signals from ARVN sources that planning was underway for a military coup against Ngo Dinh Diem. The Kennedy Administration, while nominally committed to supporting constitutional governments in allied countries, was sufficiently frustrated with Diem to listen to the coup plotters and to give what amounted to a green light for action. In November, the Americans stood aside while Army generals deposed the Ngo brothers and overthrew their government, killing President Ngo Dinh Diem and his brother Ngo Dinh Nhu in the process. Though shocked at the murders, the American administration quickly gave its support to the generals who headed the new regime.

President John F. Kennedy himself was assassinated in Dallas later in the same month, November 1963. At the time of his death, his top foreign policy officials were engaged in a top-to-bottom review of American policy in Southeast Asia, and contemplating changes that ranged from abandonment of the Saigon government to the introduction of U.S. ground forces in an all-out military campaign. Kennedy's death interrupted the review, and for the ensuing year the American advisors remained in Vietnam trying to organize the ARVN's counterinsurgency campaign. Meanwhile, Kennedy's successor, Lyndon B. Johnson, ran for election in 1964 on an implied promise to keep the United States out of war.

In August 1964, a U.S. naval destroyer, engaged in intelligence and sabotage operations in the Gulf of Tonkin off the coast of the Democratic Republic of Vietnam, was attacked by D.R.V. torpedo boats. A second attack, later proven not to have happened, was reported the following night. Concerned about protection of U.S. forces in the area, President Johnson had Congress pass a resolution, known as the Gulf of Tonkin Resolution, that gave him the authority for whatever was necessary, including military action, to protect American personnel in the region and to shield the nations in the region from Communist attack. Most of the congressmen and senators who voted for the Gulf of Tonkin Resolution did not realize that it was, in effect, a declaration of war, and that Johnson eventually would use it as the legal basis for sending more than half a million soldiers to Southeast Asia. Johnson and his successor, Richard Nixon, eventually carried the war to Laos and Cambodia, bombing all three countries and vastly expanding the war, so that it engulfed the societies of the entire region.

An essential element of the war was the D.R.V.'s slow but steady supply of men and matériel to support and reinforce the NLF against the Saigon government and the Americans.[4] After 1964, units of the People's Army of Vietnam (PAVN) from the north also traveled to the south to fight the ARVN and Americans. The NLF appealed for support in the provinces of South Vietnam by promising land reform. It also continued to threaten supporters of the R.V.N. and families of

ARVN soldiers, drawing support away from the R.V.N. government. The NLF demanded a role in South Vietnamese politics and a withdrawal of foreign (meaning U.S.) forces. Their northern support came via the "Ho Chi Minh Trail," a system of roads and trails leading southward through the jungles and inland mountains. Much of the Ho Chi Minh Trail passed through the nominally neutral territory of Laos and Cambodia. Much of it was obscured by foliage and invisible from the air. Much of the movement took place at night for protection from American bombing. Branches of the trail led to the Mekong River delta, just a few miles west of Saigon, where they deposited significant military power virtually on the doorstep of the R.V.N. government. The military objective then was to hurt the Saigon government and American forces so badly that the U.S. would eventually withdraw, leaving the R.V.N. to face the Communist insurgency without outside help.

The effectiveness of the Ho Chi Minh trail prompted America's campaign to defoliate the jungle and, eventually, President Nixon's decision to send bombers and ground forces into Laos and Cambodia to interfere with the supply lines through neutral territory. These decisions were fateful, for American intervention was the catalyst that led to revolutionary change in Cambodia and eventually the rise of the murderous Khmer Rouge. And in Laos, so many American bombs fell on the countryside that the beleaguered Laotians coined the term "ironing" to describe the planting of metal in their fields. The death toll among noncombatants in both countries, collateral victims of the Vietnam war, ran to hundreds of thousands of innocent people. Deaths in Cambodia resulting from the political upheavals related to the war ran in the millions.

In Vietnam, the United States struggled to stabilize the Saigon government. The 1963 coup against Diem was only the first in a series of military uprisings. It took two years to find a combination of generals who could create a semblance of stability. Though the successive military leaders who presided over the R.V.N. between 1965 and 1975 sometimes surprised observers with flashes of competence, the NLF succeeded in convincing many Vietnamese that they were merely agents of the United States.

From 1965 until 1968, the U.S. Military Assistance Command in Vietnam (MACV) claimed that combined U.S. and R.V.N. forces, temporarily augmented by units from other "allied" countries such as Australia and the Republic of Korea, were making steady progress against the "Viet Cong," as American and Saigon officials typically referred to the NLF and their allies in the field. Indeed, considering the imbalance in firepower, the NLF and PAVN seemed badly overmatched. The United States flew fighter-bombers from carrier decks in the Tonkin Gulf wherever it wished, hitting targets in either part of Vietnam at will (see Figure 18.1). B-52s from U.S. Air Force bases on Guam and in Thailand dropped more bombs on Indochina than were used in all of Europe and the Pacific during World War II. American, R.V.N., and allied ground forces, equipped and financed by U.S. taxpayers, were well supplied with weapons, ammunition, vehicles, air support, food, and medicine. Americans built ports and landing fields to handle the equipment, and American bases grew into small cities. Americans even tried to alter the environment in Vietnam by sending special planes to spray defoliants on the jungles.

The poison, known as "Agent Orange," was meant to remove the natural protection over the Ho Chi Minh Trail and expose the men and trucks beneath to American bombing, but it also caused much additional damage, including genetic defects among Vietnamese and Americans who came in contact with it.

Americans who remembered American victories in World War II had difficulty grasping the reality in Southeast Asia, that lightly armed Vietnamese peasants could get the better of the gigantic military force that Washington sent to Vietnam. Yet the war was not decided by money or numbers. Early in the war at Ap Bac, for example, 2,500 ARVN soldiers, with their American advisors, helicopters, weapons, and vehicles, were defeated by 200 NLF resisters who inflicted heavy casualties on them and destroyed five of their aircraft.[5] Ho Chi Minh explained such events by claiming that the Vietnamese were fighting a patriotic war on their own soil against a foreign—that is, colonial—power, and he argued that the United States had merely replaced France in what was a protracted war of national liberation. Where Americans tended to see the war in terms of days and months, Ho saw it in terms of years and decades. From his perspective, the defeat of the United States—like the defeat of the colonial idea everywhere—was certain in the long run. He never wavered in his belief that the Vietnamese cause was just, that foreign intervention in his country was wrong, and

FIGURE 18.1   The Pont Doumer, renamed Long Bien Bridge, after U.S. bombing. See Figure 12.1 for an artist's view of the bridge during French colonization.

FROM HANOI, *BIOGRAPHY OF A CITY*, BY WILLIAM S. LOGAN. COURTESY UNIVERSITY OF NEW SOUTH WALES PRESS, SYDNEY. QUOTED FROM *JOURNAL D'UN DIPLOMATE FRANÇAIS, 1966–1969*, BY FRANÇOIS DE QUIRRELLE (PARIS: TALLENDIER, 1992), P. 132.

that eventually a combination of Vietnamese nationalism and American fatigue would lead to an American withdrawal and the reunification of Vietnam by his own forces. In this, of course, he was eventually proven correct.

In January 1968, during the lunar new year holiday called "Tet," a combination of NLF and PAVN units attacked all across the south in an all-out effort to overrun U.S. and ARVN military positions. The Ho Chi Minh trail and other NLF supply routes had made it possible to position the attackers at key points throughout the country, and on January 31 they struck, it seemed, everywhere at once. The streets of Saigon rang with gunfire and the rumble of heavy vehicles as NLF guerrillas actually entered the American Embassy compound and briefly occupied the very heart of the U.S. presence in their country. U.S. and ARVN defenders struck back, and within a week most of their success had been negated. In military terms, the defense of South Vietnam during the "Tet Offensive" was a success. However, in psychological terms, Tet was a defeat for the United States. MACV officials had been telling the American public that the "Viet Cong" were nearly vanquished and that they could "see the light at the end of the tunnel." The fact that they were caught by surprise humiliated them, and in the United States there were severe repercussions. President Johnson devoted himself to finding a way to negotiate an end to the war, and finally bowed out of the 1968 election, in part because he dreaded being humiliated by the voters at the polls. After the public relations fiasco of Tet, the American people turned against the military effort in Vietnam, and there was a dramatic rise in public protests and antiwar activity, including resistance to the draft. There was a review of America's Vietnam policy, and later in 1968, when MACV asked for enough additional soldiers to bring the total to three quarters of a million, Washington refused. By this time, there were 543,000 American soldiers in Indochina, battles were raging and bombs were dropping all over Vietnam, half a million Vietnamese people were being made homeless every year, and 130,000 Vietnamese civilians were being killed or wounded every month.[6] Frustration with the war and incredulity at the U.S. Government's inability to get the better of the NLF and Ho Chi Minh were major factors in the election of the Republican Richard Nixon as president in 1968.

Maintaining a Society at War: South Vietnam

Traditional Vietnamese society was based on family and harmony in the community. At the local level, villagers were largely autonomous, and managed their own affairs. Village leaders, though not elected in the modern sense, emerged and asserted themselves by virtue of age, accomplishments, and public respect. In part at least, local communities were governed by consent.

Colonialism weakened this consent through taxation, realignment of property, patterns of labor recruitment, conscription, and institutional intrusions such as the colonial police. Resentment over colonial rule generated modern nationalism in Vietnam. However, it was not until the introduction of the mechanized power of the Diem regime in the 1950s that the countryside experienced revolutionary disruption. Some of the disruption was the byproduct of establishing representative democracy in Vietnam. Indeed, Diem convened several sessions of his national parliament while he was president, and recruited a high level of voter participation in every election. But the purpose was not to increase local influence in national affairs. Rather, it was the opposite, to impose Saigon's power on districts in the countryside, to install strangers from the government bureaucracy (invested with armed authority) in their midst, and to take away the power of people to decide local matters for themselves.[7]

Vietnamese society, however, has never been easy to organize by any central authority. The French were never able to control the secret societies such as the Binh Xuyen crime syndicate that developed partly as a response to colonialism. Other groups that opposed French rule were criminalized because of their ideas. Anti-French religious organizations, such as the Cao Dai and Hoa Hao, developed and had to survive in the twilight of the underworld. After the demise of French rule, the R.V.N. government and U.S. military authorities likewise found them troublesome. Indeed, some of America's earliest fiascoes in Vietnam were attempts to buy the backing of the Cao Dai and Hoa Hao sects and the Binh Xuyen syndicate for the Diem regime in the mid-1950s.[8]

The National Liberation Front co-opted many from these strata of southern Vietnamese society as it organized itself, in effect, as a secret society. The people of Vietnam were familiar with this shadowy form of organization. Even their use of terror tactics was familiar, and when NLF guerrillas appeared at night and took control of a village, the peasants knew better than to report them to the ARVN the next day. Having to live under NLF control by night and Saigon's control by day certainly made the countryside unsafe. One answer was to remove villagers into "strategic hamlets"—concentration camps where they slept at night surrounded by fences and South Vietnamese troops. But the villagers hated leaving their houses exposed overnight, and the program was very unpopular. Instead of winning the "hearts and minds" of the people, the R.V.N. only succeeded in alienating them further.

If NLF strength came partly from secrecy and terror, it also derived from a positive message of patriotism and independence. Young people across the country were susceptible to the nationalist appeal, aimed at ridding the country of what looked like foreign occupation. American forces were known for their disrespectful behavior in Vietnam, and often acted like conquerers rather than allies. The rhetoric of democracy was not as effective as the anger generated by the numerous racist epithets that were used to refer to Vietnamese people. Educated Vietnamese resented the lordly demeanor of American enlisted men spending money on cheap entertainment in the camp towns that sprang up around U.S. bases.

In the 1960s, life in the Republic of Vietnam was completely militarized. Military priorities dominated everything. The foreign presence pumped money into the economy and created many thousands of jobs, even though those who made their living from the war could see that the American presence was making the violence incalculably worse. The war disrupted education and the lives of young men drafted for army service. The farming economy was disrupted by the fighting and damage to the supply system. Human rights went by the boards as the government spied on citizens and rounded up suspected NLF agents, holding them without trial, sometimes in the infamous "tiger cages."

It is all the more remarkable, therefore, that after the fall of Ngo Dinh Diem in 1963 and the escalation of the war by the United States, intellectuals in the R.V.N. actually acquired more freedom to write and express themselves via literature and journalism. Some of the writing supported the NLF and appealed for freedom from American domination. Novels, stories, and poems became an important outlet for the anger that rose from racial and sexual friction with the Americans and the vast disparities in power that came with the war. Writers looked for ways to express feelings about the moral ruin of Vietnam, of the damage to families and the nation. One group expressed itself through romanticism; another through existentialism.[9] On the NLF side, the writing was more overtly political, following socialist realism to inspire and rally people in the patriotic cause of independence, even when the words were romantic. In the poem "You Have Got Into University," by Giang Nam, a resistance fighter imagines a reunion with his sister who is a student:[10]

> Tomorrow, when the motherland is unified,
> Tomorrow, you will come back and give me lessons,
> And we shall not have to write on the wall with coal any more
> Or dread the horror of the police searches.
> You will say to me "Come on, big brother, courage!"
> And I shall smile, remembering the moonlight,
> And our motherland, that gave you wings
> And the honor of marching with those up at the front.
> I shall need to keep a long sleepless night
> To tell you about the South, and its struggle and agony:
> "In those days, little sister, I had
> But one school on earth—the Revolution!"

Maintaining a Society at War: The D.R.V.

After the French left Indochina in 1954, the Hanoi-based regime of the Democratic Republic of Vietnam under Ho Chi Minh embarked on a revolutionary program designed to make North Vietnam a socialist state. In advance of this transformation, as many as 800,000 northerners fled to the south, migrating with whatever they could carry, in order to escape what turned out to be a violent purge of class enemies. In keeping with Marxist theory, the government carried out a thorough land reform that wrested property from big owners and redistributed it to the landless. The Vietnamese land reform resembled the reorganization of the rural economy in Communist China, involving the identification, trial, and sometimes execution of newly defined criminals. Though the government later expressed regret for the excesses of its overzealous agents, it cost an estimated 50,000 lives.[11]

The government spared the lives of many educated and propertied people because it needed their skills. These were a middle echelon of specialists who staffed the medical care system, mass education system, and mass organizations such as neighborhood committees. Though deprived of their wealth, these useful citizens duly submitted to rule by the Workers' Party (the Lao Dong Party, previously the Indochinese Communist Party). The Communist cadres who bossed them were headed by veterans of the longstanding resistance against France, including legendary independence fighters such as Vo Nguyen Giap, Pham Van Dong, and Ho Chi Minh himself, who presided over state and party. Ho became the center of a personality cult, but did not exercise anywhere near the kind of control wielded by Kim Il-sung in Korea. After some vacillation the Party decided not to follow the Chinese lead but adopted Stalinist policies much like those of North Korea, and increasingly sided with the Soviet Union in its dispute with China. The lead in this was taken by Le Duan (1908–1986), a member of the Party since its foundation who, when the country was divided in 1954, was put in charge of organizing the Communist underground in the south. Le Duan was First Secretary at the time of Ho's death in 1969, and remained in power for the rest of his life.

The population in general appears to have accepted the regime, although it does not appear to have embraced socialism with enthusiasm. As workers, they had little time for politics; when the war in the South started affecting their lives in the late 1950s, they did their duty and continued working in small jobs as farmers, laborers, miners, and tradespeople. Above all, North Vietnam was a very poor country with a primitive agricultural economy faced with the urgent task of social and economic modernization.

Ho Chi Minh and the Lao Dong Party determined first to fight for reunification with the south and expulsion of the foreign forces that were beginning to control the Saigon government. Thus they opted to continue what they called their "war of national liberation" before trying to modernize their state. For them, the decade from 1965 to 1975 became a time of total mobilization in the struggle to support the NLF in the south and, increasingly, to survive continual bombing by American warplanes.

American leaders imagined that their bombing might cripple the D.R.V. economy and compel the Hanoi government to capitulate or at least abandon the effort in the south. They assumed that the D.R.V. had enough of an industrial economy to be reduced by blowing up ports, railroads, and factories. It was hard for them to grasp the fact that the poverty and simplicity of North Vietnam's mostly agricultural economy created a kind of resilience that helped it withstand attacks from high altitude B-52s and carrier-launched fighter-bombers. The Soviet Union aided Hanoi with anti-aircraft guns and surface-to-air missiles (SAMs) that took a heavy toll on American planes and pilots. After the U.S. started bombing North Vietnam in 1965, the D.R.V. began collecting downed pilots as prisoners of war. The numbers of killed and missing, as well as the POWs who eventually were returned, became a major issue in U.S.-Vietnamese relations for a generation after the end of the war. It is ironic to note that the supply situation in North Vietnam actually improved during the American bombing because of increased foreign aid from the socialist countries. Trucks that were destroyed on the Ho Chi Minh trail, for example, were readily replaced with newer trucks from abroad.

The Hanoi government claimed that popular morale in North Vietnam remained high throughout the war, but this is belied by postwar accounts of a general war-weariness that descended after several years of bombing, creating pressure for progress or at least a settlement. This pressure was not the kind envisioned by the Americans, however. It did not propose accepting the legitimacy of the foreign presence in Vietnam or a continued role for the United States, and it did not envision Vietnam as anything other than a socialist state ruled by the Workers Party. It was rather a profound impatience with the length of the struggle and a lack of triumph or satisfaction when things went well in the south. Thus the Tet offensive, which was a political, if not military, victory for the NLF and Hanoi, was recognized as having been extremely costly and by no means an occasion for celebration in the north. The damage wore at North Vietnam's infrastructure, degrading transportation and energy facilities and preventing the kind of economic and social development that might otherwise have been achieved.

Hanoi accepted aid from Communist allies, but it should be noted that the Soviets and Chinese Communists were bitter rivals at the time, and that the Chinese sometimes blocked the shipment of Soviet aid by rail through their territory. Most Soviet aid came by ship and was delivered in the port of Haiphong, creating a tempting bombing target for the Americans, who, nonetheless, could not afford to bomb Soviet ships. Trade with North Vietnam also came from other Western countries, such as France and Britain, who greatly annoyed the United States by failing to honor America's requests for a boycott of the Vietnamese market.

The Vietnam War: The Final Phase

When Richard Nixon became President of the United States in 1969, he implemented a policy of "Vietnamization," by which U.S. troops were to be withdrawn from Vietnam by stages and R.V.N. Vietnamese forces were to take over more of the fighting, supported by American money and matériel. Nixon thus hoped to reduce the number of American battle casualties and calm the outrage at home over what was, by then, seen as a failed military adventure. Nixon, however, was determined not to lose the war, and demanded "peace with honor." To effect this, he pursued negotiations with the D.R.V. at a long-running conference in Paris. The negotiations faltered over many points: the participation of the NLF, the legitimacy of the R.V.N. government, whether negotiations could proceed while the United States was bombing the D.R.V., and when to release U.S. prisoners from D.R.V. detention. Even the shape of the conference table had to be negotiated (it was round).

The key element of Nixon's pursuit of "peace with honor" was that the United States must not appear to have been defeated in Vietnam. Early on in the negotiations it seemed that the Nixon Administration was also determined to guarantee the survival of the Republic of Vietnam as well. To force his point on the opposing side, he ordered dramatically increased bombing in neighboring Laos and Cambodia, aimed at increasing the costs of using the Ho Chi Minh Trail. In May of 1970 he sent American forces on an invasion into Cambodia to attack NLF sanctuaries that were dangerously close to Saigon. This attack had a military purpose, but it was a political disaster. In the United States, university campuses erupted with protests against the widening of the war, and at Kent State University in Ohio, the National Guard fired on the protesters, killing four and injuring several others. The sight of uniformed guardsmen firing on American students galvanized opposition to the war and made it necessary, first and foremost, to find a way out.

The Paris negotiations continued in earnest through the middle of 1972. Meanwhile, the Nixon Administration was torn between "hawks," who thought that Hanoi might still be forced to pull out of the south, and "doves," who thought the U.S. should settle for the best deal it could get and pull out. The effect of American actions in Southeast Asia are still debated, for it was only after an intensive campaign of carpet bombing by B-52s that Hanoi finally agreed, in January 1973, to a settlement with the U.S. whereby American prisoners would be returned and U.S. troops would be withdrawn from the south. The belief lingers that Hanoi was "forced" to settle. However, it settled largely on its own terms. The American negotiator, Henry Kissinger, later said that he had wanted a "decent interval" between the American pullout and what was even then seen as an inevitable final attack by Hanoi to overrun the south. Kissinger and Nixon did not want it to appear that the American pullout had triggered the collapse of the Saigon government and the "bloodbath" that was expected to follow when the Communists punished the losers.

The deal held for two years. In March 1975, after Kissinger's "decent interval," North Vietnam renewed the attack on the south with a major campaign that lasted only a few weeks. Saigon fell on April 30, with the last American personnel and helicopters departing in a disorderly crush along with crowds of refugees who feared Communist reprisals. The Americans evacuated many Vietnamese who were tainted by collaboration, but left many more behind.

The Socialist Republic of Vietnam: The First Decade, 1976–1986

Victorious at last, the leaders of the Vietnamese Communist Party (previously the Workers' Party) and the new Socialist Republic of Vietnam faced a major task of reconstruction. In the north, industrial and transportation facilities had been much damaged by repeated bombing. In the south, the war left innumerable villages in ruins, vast areas stripped of foliage by napalm and chemicals, millions of homeless people, and an estimated 3.5 million landmines, which, for the next quarter of a century, caused some two thousand casualties a year.

On top of all this, the government faced the challenge of forging the 24 million people of the north and the 22 million of the south into a single Socialist nation-state. This entailed first of all extending socialism to the south. Many southern soldiers, officials, religious practitioners, and intellectuals were sent to "reeducation camps," and trusted party members, often northerners, were placed in positions of authority. In December 1976 the Fourth Party Congress convened under the leadership of Le Duan and declared that socialism could be substantially achieved in ten years. The unified national government, now calling itself the Socialist Republic of Vietnam, took action accordingly. In 1978 it announced the nationalization of industry and commerce, launching "the second battle of Saigon," aimed at the destruction of the city's traders and shopkeepers. These were mostly ethnic Chinese who operated small enterprises in Cholon, the bustling Chinese quarter of Saigon, which by then had been renamed Ho Chi Minh City. Many of these people were forced into other occupations and/or relocated to "New Economic Zones" in the underdeveloped parts of the country. Thousands of others fled the country, risking their lives in small boats moving through treacherous, pirate-infested waters to find refuge in Hong Kong or Thailand.

Meanwhile, collectivization of agriculture was also extended to the south, at least on paper. However, it ran into resistance, and proceeded unevenly and with very mixed results. Rising prices and bad weather disrupted farm life for several years and frustrated efforts at reorganization. By 1979 it was clear that the economic program was not working. In that year Vietnam, following the Chinese example, partially relaxed economic controls by allowing for a contract system under which farmers could sell their rice on the open market once they had fulfilled their state quota. Collectivization never took off in the south: by 1985 official sources reported that no more than 25 percent of farming households had joined any kind of collective organization.

Victory brought no reduction in military expenses and no peace. As it consolidated its control in the south, the government of the Socialist Republic of Vietnam became concerned about Chinese ambitions in Cambodia and the influence of the People's Republic of China over the new Khmer Rouge government there. After a series of border clashes with Chinese-backed forces of Pol Pot's Khmer Rouge regime, Vietnamese troops seized the initiative and invaded Cambodia, attempting to set up a satellite regime. The P.R.C. responded in February 1979 by sending an army across the border into northern Vietnam. This military excursion lasted only seventeen days, but the threat of renewed invasion forced the Vietnamese military to maintain two large armies at opposite ends of their country. This was in addition to a force of 40,000 that was kept in Laos.

The need to spend as much as forty percent of its national budget on military matters severely restricted the Vietnamese government's ability to advance a reform agenda. Thus, during the first decade of unified Vietnam, the party and government remained under the stern control of Le Duan in a state of neither war nor peace. However, Le Duan's death in 1986 opened up possibilities for change.

Doi Moi, 1986–Present

At its Sixth National Congress in December 1986, the Vietnamese Communist Party adopted a policy of economic liberalization under the slogan "Doi Moi," literally "renovation," a term that was sufficiently elastic to cover a wide range of policies. Generally, it meant a reduction of the state's role in the economy in favor of the free market, less government control over agriculture, commerce, and industry, and greater openness to foreign trade and investment.

At the same time there was a shift in foreign policy. In 1989 Vietnamese forces were withdrawn from Cambodia and Laos, paving the way for better relations with China. In 1991, after a conference between the two countries' foreign ministers, tensions eased with the P.R.C., but Vietnam remained apprehensive about Chinese expansionism. Robert Templer aptly characterizes the relationship with China as a "guarded friendship" once again.[12] An area of particular concern were the tiny groups of islands known as the Paracels and Spratleys, located in what the Chinese call the "South China Sea" but Vietnamese insist is the "East Sea." Only thirty-three of these islands lie permanently out of water, but it is the possibility of oil beneath them that prompted not only China and Vietnam but also Taiwan, Malaysia, the Philippines, and Brunei to advance claims of sovereignty.

In 1994 the United States lifted its trade embargo and in the following year extended diplomatic recognition. Also in 1995, Vietnam gained security and diplomatic leverage by joining the Association of Southeast Asian Nations (ASEAN). There was also an economic side to this, as Vietnam joined the ASEAN Free Trade Area, formed economic ties with ASEAN countries, and received investments from Singapore, Malaysia and other ASEAN members.

Vietnam's economic policy under Doi Moi resembled that of China, except that the state sector remained more important and state regulation continued to be pervasive. As in China, the government sought political stability as well as economic growth, and countenanced no political opposition. Especially after the 1989 Tiananmen uprising in Beijing, the Vietnamese government kept a close eye on the press. However, the discrediting of Marxism–Leninism in Europe and the collapse of the Soviet Union, along with the obvious success of business ventures in China, eroded the credibility of Communism in Vietnam and increased the importance of the government's economic and political performance as the basis for its legitimacy.

With this erosion of ideology on top of the social damage resulting from the war, corruption spread on all levels, from the lowest inspector to high officials specifically charged with the fight against crime. Corruption aggravated inefficiency and no doubt retarded economic growth. Nevertheless, the economy in Vietnam grew impressively. The country survived the end of foreign aid that came with the dissolution of the Soviet Union, and was able to reorient its trade away from dependence on the former socialist bloc. The most dramatic and highly symbolic achievement was that Vietnam no longer had to import rice, but began exporting it, instead. The gross domestic product increased steadily during the 1990s. During the five years prior to the Asian fiscal crisis of 1997–1998, it grew over 8 percent a year.

However, the economy had begun to slow down even before the Asian Economic Crisis, in what has been called the first of four "typhoons" of 1997–1998. The second "typhoon" was rural unrest in Thai Binh province in the north. High taxes and transportation costs had left many peasants impoverished. The third "typhoon" was literally a typhoon, the worst in half a century. Finally, Vietnam was hit by the Asian financial crisis. With its national economy less integrated into the global system than states such as Thailand and the Republic of Korea, Vietnam suffered comparatively less. Nevertheless, it experienced a major decline in foreign investment and trade with its Southeast Asian neighbors, who accounted for 60 percent of its foreign trade and provided 70 percent of its foreign investment.

Government during these years was not dominated by any single individual. Policy decisions were reached by forging agreement among the Party's factions, with leaders disinclined to rock the boat. They preferred to maintain social and political stability rather than risk the consequences of taking drastic action to reform "the favoritism for 6,000 inefficient and debt-ridden state enterprises and a weak and corrupted financial and banking system" that Carlyle A. Thayer has termed the "root causes" of Vietnam's troubles.[13] The government continued to promote state enterprises, even as the private sector grew at a much faster rate.

As in many developing countries, rapid modernization is not without consequences for other aspects of life, such as the environment. Plans to build a highway along the path of the Ho Chi Minh trail represent the government's commitment to large-scale development without much attention to the environmental impact, reminiscent of Japanese dam building and the Three Gorges Dam project in China.

Doi Moi in Vietnam has been compared to Perestroika ("restructuring") in the former Soviet Union, the movement launched by Mikhail Gorbachev the same year that led to *glasnost*, or "openness." In Vietnam there has been a similar, though less extensive and certainly less consequential, relaxation of control over artistic and intellectual life. A varied and vigorous literature replaced Soviet- and Chinese-style "social realism," as writers took the pulse of the times. Ho Anh Thai (1960–), who in 1988 published a story about a hypocritical official who watches so much pornography that he gradually turns into a goat, went on to be accepted as a member of the Hanoi Writers' Association. However, the portrayal of party hypocrisy and ruthless careerism presented by Duong Thu Hung (1947–) in *Paradise of the Blind*, also published in 1988, was more than the political establishment could tolerate. Though Duong Thu Hung was part of a troupe that once traveled in the war zones to "sing louder than the bombs," her works were banned, and she was made to serve seven months in prison. Since her 1991 imprisonment she has lived in Hanoi, but can only publish her work overseas. Her *Memories of a Pure Spring* presents a devastating contrast between wartime idealism and postwar cynicism. One of its themes is a harrowing glimpse of Vietnamese prison life.

Bao Ninh (1952–) expresses his own gritty comprehension of Vietnam's recent history in *The Sorrow of War* (1990). War, with all its brutal violence and futility, is just something that happens and that one endures in order to survive. The main character does not lose his humanity, but he also does not find his way back to a fulfilling life. There is little to choose here between victory and defeat. Though the work lacks the hopeful vision sought by the Party, Bao Ninh has nonetheless won several prestigious literary awards within Vietnam.

Under circumstances that discourage direct political commentary, writers sometimes resort to historical allegories to make their points. Such is the work of the writer most adored for his command of the language, Nguyen Huy Thiep (1950–), who has used historical settings with contemporary meaning that include controversial treatments of Gia Long, founder of the Nguyen Dynasty, and of Nguyen Du, author of *The Tale of Kieu*. Thiep's impoverished, ineffectual Nguyen Du suggests the general marginalization of artists and intellectuals by the modern political process, as well as the Vietnamese hate-love relationship with China. In his portrait of Gia Long, politicians come off as cruel, duplicitous, anti-intellectual, hypocritical, self-absorbed, and egomaniacal. Their pathological fear of social change prevents them from undertaking the reforms necessary to improve society.

There has also been a flowering of art in such a variety of styles that it is impossible to single out one artist or work as representative. Nguyen Tun Nghiem (1922–) was trained in Western techniques but developed a style very much his own. While his "A Buffalo Calf Given in Land Reform," painted in 1968, reflects what was politically correct at the time, he preferred to draw on Vietnamese myths and tradition. It is therefore fitting that he is presented here by his charming and delicate rendering of Vietnam's most beloved classic (see Figure 18.2). Pham Cam Thuong (1957–) belongs to different generation, but he too is grounded in the tradition that has provided him subject matter for four books as well as for his art (see Figure 18.3). *Metamorphosis* is Buddhist and Vietnamese but may also suggest a metaphor for the human condition at the turn of the century.

Vietnam never had a Cultural Revolution, but its party and government shared the Marxist aversion to religion, suppressed sects they felt to be subversive, and severely limited those that had too large a following to be crushed. The government also discouraged household altars and other aspects of Vietnamese popular religion. However, with the relaxation of controls and a decline in the official Marxist faith, traditional religion has revived and boomed. Traditional tombs have reappeared in the Mekong delta and elsewhere, while the hills on the way to the Catholic cathedral at Pham Diem, south of Hanoi, are dotted with crosses. Although still suffering from government hostility, Cao Dai is back. Throughout Vietnam, the myriad deities in the various kinds of temples do not lack for offerings of incense and fruit.

At the turn of the twenty-first century, Vietnam remains an ostensibly Marxist state that continues to resemble the Chinese state more than it does its Southeast Asian neighbors. This looks very much like the traditional relationship in modern form. Similarly, its

FIGURE 18.2 *Story of Kieu* (1972), Nguyen Tu Nghiem. Gouache on paper, 11.5 × 8 inches.

FIGURE 18.2   *Metamorphosis 2000,* Pham Cam Thuong. Woodblock print, 21 × 27.5 cm.
© PHAM CAM THUONG. USED BY PERMISSION OF JUDITH HUGHES DAY, FINE CONTEMPORARY VIETNAMESE ART.

apprehensions concerning China have not disappeared, but appear muted into a kind of "background hum."[14]

And finally, after years of war and more years of regrets and hostile memories, relations with the United States continued to improve. President Bill Clinton was warmly welcomed when he visited in 2000, although his hosts were unreceptive to his concerns for human rights. This may suggest the formation of yet another "guarded friendship," but in 2001 Congress passed and President George W. Bush signed an agreement negotiated by the Clinton Administration to normalize trade relations between the two countries.

Notes

1. Marshall R. Pihl, "Contemporary Literature in a Divided Land," in Donald N. Clark, ed., *Korea Briefing 1993* (Boulder: Westview Press, 1993), p. 83.

2. For an introduction to literature of this period, see Marshall R. Pihl and Bruce and Ju-Chan Fulton, eds., *Land of Exile: Contemporary Korean Fiction* (Armonk, N.Y.: M. E. Sharpe, 1993).

3. William J. Duiker, *Ho Chi Minh: A Life* (New York: Hyperion Books, 2000), pp. 524–25.

4. The American argument that the South Vietnamese insurgency was actually camouflage for a North Vietnamese invasion was presented in a "white paper": U.S. Department of State, *Aggression from the North: The Record of North Vietnam's Campaign to Conquer South Vietnam, Far*

Eastern Series 130, publication 7839 (Washington, D.C.: U.S. Government Printing Office, 1965).

5. This episode is recounted by Neil Sheehan in *A Bright Shining Lie: John Paul Van and America in Vietnam* (Vintage Books, 1988), pp. 212–65.

6. Thomas D. Boettcher, *Vietnam: The Valor and the Sorrow* (Boston: Little, Brown and Co., 1985), p. 341.

7. Allan E. Goodman, *Politics in War: The Bases of Political Community in South Vietnam* (Cambridge, Mass.: Harvard University Press, 1973), pp. 1–30.

8. George C. Herring, *America's Longest War: The United States and Vietnam, 1950–1975* (New York: John Wiley and Sons, 1979), pp. 51–54.

9. Maurice M. Durand and Nguyen Tran Huan, *An Introduction to Vietnamese Literature,* trans. by D. M. Hawke (New York: Columbia University Press, 1985), pp. 137–43.

10. Durand and Huan, p. 173.

11. U.S. Library of Congress, *Vietnam: A Country Study,* ed. Ronald J. Cima (Washington, D.C.: U.S. Government Printing Office, 1989), p. 105.

12. Robert Templer, *Shadows and Wind: A View of Modern Vietnam* (New York: Penguin Books, 1998), p. 298.

13. Carlyle A. Thayer, "Vietnam, the Asian Financial Crisis and Doi Moi," in *Harvard Asian Quarterly,* Oct 5, 2001. http//www.fas.Harvard.edu/ ~asiactr/haq/20000/001a003.htm.

14. Templer, p. 301, referring to tensions over the Paracels and Spratleys.

Afterword:
East Asia in the Era
of Globalization

All around the globe the modern era saw the growth in power of the nation-state to a degree unprecedented by any institution in human history even as economic links were formed that became the precursor of contemporary globalization. At the start of the twenty-first century, in East Asia as elsewhere, the state's role in managing national economies was diminishing in the face of a global economic and financial system grown beyond the power of even the strongest state to control. Nevertheless, the nation-state remained the dominant military and political institution, and nationalism remained prevalent. Both globalization and nationalism held promise of a brighter future, but both also entailed dangers. It remains very much to be seen whether sovereign states can solve global problems while focused on local issues and while national rivalries continue to generate international dangers.

Nationalist Tensions

Though the two Koreas are often referred to as rivals, their positions on the peninsula are not equal. South Korea has many advantages: twice the population, thirty times the national productivity, incalculably more personal income, and ties throughout the world. North Korea is a small state that relies on its own will and discipline and considerable luck in recent years in turning misfortune to its advantage. Both sides are intensely nationalistic and they accuse each other of subservience to foreign powers. They remember the ordeal of the Korean War and they blame each other for it. They despise each other's rulers and mistrust each other's institutions. It is highly unlikely that they will suddenly drop their differences and embrace each other as members of the same family. Yet underneath all the rhetoric of division, there remains a common language and a deep-seated bond that shows whenever Korean delegations meet to talk about their hesitant next steps toward reconciliation. The election of South Korean president Kim Dae-jung in 1997 created an opportunity to shift the goal a bit, from reunification (which is unlikely) to reintegration, under which each side can keep its national myths and structures, but in which communication is freer and common stakes are developing. It is reasonable to hope that this process will continue, and that it can become the basis for healing the conflicts that divide the 70 million Korean people.

Despite differences in scale and relative size, the commonalities and disparities between Taiwan and the People's Republic are similar in that the two sides reject each other's political and economic systems and tell different versions of China's modern story. One side—Taiwan—has achieved much greater wealth than the other. Like Hong Kong, Taiwan is an element of "Greater China," with a standard of living dramatically higher than that of the P.R.C. itself. There is every sign that the flow of knowledge, goods, and people between Taiwan and the mainland will continue to accelerate, creating common ground and stakes in a peaceful reintegration of the Chinese nation.

Though economic reintegration of China is taking place, political reintegration remains a very difficult problem. The P.R.C. insists that it wants peaceful reunification with Taiwan—but on its own terms. Meanwhile, it is willing to wait for changes to occur that will permit political reintegration, whatever those changes might be. However, it will *not* permit overt secession and the establishment of an independent republic on Taiwan that rejects the principle of Taiwan's belonging to "one China." The P.R.C. has made it clear that in that circumstance, it would intervene militarily to enforce Taiwan's "belonging" to China.

Under this threat from the mainland, the Republic of China on Taiwan continues to proceed cautiously in asserting its intention to move toward independence, even though its president, Chen Shui-Pien, was elected on an independence platform. Other countries, meanwhile, remain nervous about the potential for conflict between the two governments. The United States, which has committed itself to defend Taiwan from encroachment or invasion from the mainland, sometimes aggravates tensions in the Taiwan Straits by selling weapons to Taiwan and making careless references to Taiwan as a "country." Both things raise hackles in Beijing and remind the P.R.C. that the United States is a main reason why what the P.R.C. sees as a purely domestic issue remains unsolved after more than fifty years.

Economic Globalization

Global economic integration, a continuous, long-term trend in modern history, continues apace along with an almost universal pursuit of economic growth, even at the expense of other values. Thus economic globalization progresses far more rapidly than global efforts at protecting the environment, for example.

Given the prominence of Japan and the Japanese model of economic development, adopted by the Park Chung-hee government in South Korea in the 1960s, and influential throughout the region, East Asia serves as something of a laboratory for the policy of promoting globalization by encouraging the freest possible flow of capital and goods across international boundaries, unhindered by government regulation. Consequently, East Asia has also displayed some of globalization's greatest contradictions. As a theory, globalization rests on the proposition that free trade enriches everyone and creates stakes for the peaceful resolution of conflicts, and is therefore a good antidote to war. Globalization is the realization of what was envisioned at the end of World War II in the "Bretton Woods System" that created the World Bank, the International Monetary Fund (IMF), and the system of free trade promotion that evolved into the World Trade Organization (WTO) of the 1990s.

In theory, globalization is supposed to promote the flow of investment capital from rich countries to poor ones, creating employment and prosperity among less advantaged peoples as they work to supply the part of the world that consumes most of the products they make. In this way, poor people work to raise their living standards, profits flow to the people that supply the capital, living standards converge, and everyone gets what they need. Unexpected events and distortions in this picture are to be dealt with by infusions of emergency capital (debt) from the International Monetary Fund.

This theory has worked fairly well in East Asia. Certainly Taiwan and South Korea are shining examples of the rational application of capital and know-how to the problem of developing economies that are very short of resources other than their people. Vietnam after 1986 and the P.R.C. after 1980 are also examples of how parts of this theory—the trade elements of it at least—can be applied to boost national income and living standards. However, the theory has not proved stable or consistent. The economic crisis in South Korea in 1997–1998 was the result of too much foreign capital flowing into Korea in the form of foreign bank loans, without sufficient precautions or regulation. The "globalization explanation" was that corruption and "crony capitalism" had diverted much of the money, creating speculation, excessive levels of debt, and corruption of the system. The IMF bailed

Korea out—with emergency loans that had to be paid back. Korea, fortunately, was able to do so, and had righted itself by 2001. The blame went to Korean banks and industries and the Korean government itself, for interrupting the "pure" forces of the market.

The Korean case, however, raised questions about whether the IMF had not actually functioned primarily to guarantee the bad loans, forcing the Koreans to pay them back—in effect punishing the borrowers for reckless borrowing—while protecting the lenders from the consequences of their reckless lending. In the end, ordinary citizens in Korea lost their jobs, Korean companies of all sizes and types were forced to close, and Koreans lost a proportion of their savings through the devaluation of their currency. For them, globalization was definitely a mixed blessing, and it is little wonder that Koreans refer to their economic collapse as the "IMF crisis."

The worldwide critique of globalization uses such cases as examples of who actually wins and who actually loses in a system that is advertised as being good for everyone. Reformers point to unmanageable debt, stagnant real wages, massive unemployment, and the misallocation of resources as primary consequences of globalization. These in turn fuel the illiteracy, starvation, uncontrolled migration, trafficking in humans, and even slavery, crime, epidemics, and terrorism that afflict much of the world. These facts of life should not be regarded as solely the circumstances of the "less fortunate," but rather must be seen as coming back to haunt the richer countries of Europe, North America, and East Asia if they remain indifferent to them. The appalling events of September 11, 2001, in New York and Washington should have made that plain.

The experiences of the various nations of East Asia raise interesting questions about whether the neo-liberal theories of globalization are viable in the world as it is, or whether they were created for an imaginary world that does not, and will not ever, exist. Many believe that universal theories such as globalization as advanced by the United States and the West in general lack categories that can account for the variations that exist in the world.

For example, when the Japanese stock market collapsed in 1991 and put an end to the country's much-touted economic "bubble," it was widely assumed that Japan would weather the crisis and recover. However, with the Japanese recession now entering its second decade with no end in sight, the Nikkei stock index still sinking, and the Tokyo suburbs full of vacant office towers since the 1980s, there are doubts that Japan, rich and globalized as it already is, can ever realize the promise of globalization for its own people over the long term. The Japanese social and political system was designed to provide lifetime employment, support small shopkeepers and family farms, and to preserve big businesses and banks even if they deserve to sink into bankruptcy. Providing full employment, fostering families, protecting the environment, and preserving communities are values of the Japanese social system, but not of the market. Neither is the "crony capitalism" that connects Japan's bureaucracy, big businesses, financial institutions, and political parties. Japan's economic difficulties can be traced to the fact that it refuses to sacrifice these values in favor of the requirements of the global market. It seems reasonable to think that all countries retain their own values in similar ways and cannot be expected to be responsive only to global market forces.

At the other end of the spectrum, Vietnam, since 1986, has been opening its market and creating entrepreneurial opportunities for its citizens. Burdened by the legacy of post-colonial wars, corruption, and the failures of socialist economics, Vietnam also has to contend with a very young population for which education resources are stretched to their limits. Vietnam has created a stock market, opened its doors to foreign business investment, constructed industrial parks and special economic zones where foreign businesses can take advantage of low-paid Vietnamese labor, and ventured into the world of international finance by borrowing. The results are dramatic and highly visible in the small vehicle traffic, hustle of shopkeepers and peddlers, the small businesses, repair shops, and restaurants that flourish everywhere.

Joining the global economic system has meant greater prosperity, but has also brought increased dependence on forces beyond Vietnam's borders, risking vulnerability to external fluctuations in demand for Vietnam's new products. For example, in the year 2000, Vietnam signed a new trade agreement with the United States. Certain Vietnamese companies sought foreign loans to build catfish farms on the expectation that refrigerated freight airplanes could whisk frozen Vietnamese catfish to stores in the United States. However, American catfish growers, fearing competition from Vietnam, succeeded in getting the U.S. government to increase tariffs on imported catfish. Suddenly the Vietnamese faced a danger that the globalized catfish market was about to dry up, leaving behind only the globalized debt.

Cultural Globalization

Parallel to economic globalization, one can speak of cultural globalization, both in terms of a youth culture with shared taste in music and dress, and of a global "trans-cultural" avant-garde of literary and visual artists, in which East Asia is well represented. If these people have found inadequate representation in our text, we make amends herewith by including an illustration from one of the earliest of their number, Irene Chou (Zhou Luyun, 1924–), who left Shanghai for Hong Kong in 1949, but now resides in Australia. In an eloquent style very much her own, she addresses issues that transcend our globe and time (see Figure A.1). Among the younger generation we could cite Ha Jin (1956–), winner of the 1999 National Book Award, who once served in the People's Liberation Army, but owes his reputation to novels written in English, and Gao Xingjian (1940–), China's first Nobel Prize winner (2000), who moved to Paris in 1989, where Myung-whun Chung (b. Seoul 1953) was in his first year as conductor of the Opera. Chung was just one of the outstanding East Asians to contribute to musical life far from home. His older sister, Kyung-wha Chung, is an internationally renowned violinist. Similarly, Nam June Paik, an American born in Korea in 1932, won fame with his neon constructions, including a show rendering "postmodern life in cyberspace."[1] In that sense, his reach, like that of Irene Chou, may even be said to extend beyond our globe.

The globalization of thought and art often encounters resistance. Neither Ha Jin nor Gao Xingjian can be published in China, and East Asian countries are hardly alone in their suspicion of the outside world. Everywhere today change is valued as capable of producing a better society and a better life, but agreement of what would be better for one's people remains elusive. For example, in China and Vietnam people can now change jobs and are free to travel, but tolerance for dissent remains limited. However, the internet and the rise of cheap and easy global communications have implications for political change that worry many of the conservative regimes in East Asia. The P.R.C. learned this in 1989, when fax machines and satellite television completely undermined its ability to control the flow of news about the Democracy Movement. Today, internet access is unknown to ordinary people in North Korea, where the regime depends for its survival on complete control of information. In Vietnam, however, internet cafés abound. Though the government tries to filter what comes in via the World Wide Web, email can put any Vietnamese in instant touch with relatives overseas and other sources of information. This facilitates the free flow of ideas, information about business opportunities, and, no doubt, critical thoughts about the shortcomings of the Vietnamese system as it exists. In Vietnam, as elsewhere, the libertarian environment of the internet may serve to be the most authentic and revolutionary globalizing force of all.

FIGURE A.1 *Coda,* Irene Chou. Working in an individual yet global sensibility that speaks to many cultures, Chou may yet be surprised to find her painting as coda to our book.

© Irene Chou. Used by permission of artist and Mandy Lee, iPreciation Gallery. (http://www.ipreciation.com)

Cinema, one of the earliest genres of global influence, remained a major avenue of influence across national boundaries. Film not only told stories but represented whole peoples and ways of life. Hollywood images of American life are notorious for their portrayal of the United States as a sun-drenched suburb and, concurrently, as a nation of violent cities. The coexistence of these two images in the minds of people all over the world are proof of the vast abilities of cinema to further, or distort, understanding. The television age has simply extended this power into the homes of even the most remote communities around the globe.

The influence of cinema, however, was by no means all one way. Kurosawa Akira, Chen Kaige, and Zhang Yimou have already been cited in earlier chapters of our text. To them we should add South Korea's Im Kwŏn-taek (b. 1936), active since the early 1960s in Korea and then in Asian film festivals, a director who created such internationally acclaimed films in the 1990s and 2000s as *Sŏp'yonje* ("The Western Style") and *Ch'unhyang* ("Fragrance of Spring"). *Ch'unhyang*, which won worldwide praise for its cinematography and acting, is Korea's most famous morality play, in which the faithful bride Ch'unhyang, who suffers terribly for her fidelity while her husband is away serving in the government in Seoul, is ultimately vindicated when he returns home as a powerful official.

Other examples of transnational influence within East Asia and between the region and the rest of the world are legion. East Asians have become passionately involved in international sports, whether it be in hosting the Olympics or the competition for the World Cup in football (soccer). In the other direction, East Asian martial arts have won a devoted following in the West.

Religion is another vast field of intense and varied interaction, as seen in the appeal of messages directed at all people by such global religions as Buddhism, Christianity, and Islam, and also in the return of many people to their local, traditional beliefs and gods. This return to local creeds and loyalties is itself a global phenomenon. As in other areas of endeavor, attempts to work out a viable balance between the local and the global remain crucial as the twenty-first century gets under way.

Note

1. Ann Elliott Sherman at http://www.metroactive.
   com/papers/metro/02.29.96/paik9609.html.

Suggestions for Further Study

The Web site of the Association for Asian Studies (www.aasianst.org) maintains a list of the numerous Web sites dealing with East Asia. It also publishes the *Annual Bibliography of Asian Studies* online in many libraries. We have also posted our suggestions on individual topics and periods on our book page at the Wadsworth Web site (www.moderneastasia.wadsworth.com), and we limit our suggestions here to broad surveys that can help readers begin further research. We also suggest that the works we have quoted in our text merit reading in toto.

General

To place East Asian history in a global perspective, see the succinct history of the modern world by China specialist Robert B. Marks, *The Origins of the Modern World: A Global and Ecological Narrative* (Lanham, Md.: Rowman and Littlefield, 2002). Michael Sullivan, *The Meeting of Eastern and Western Art: From the Sixteenth Century to the Present Day* (London: Thames and Hudson, 1973, 1989) is informative and perceptive on Chinese and Japanese art. *Asian Religions in Practice: An Introduction,* edited by Donald S. Lopez Jr. (Princeton, N.J.: Princeton University Press, 1999) does not discuss Korea or Vietnam, but does deal extensively with East Asian Buddhism. Wm. Theodore de Bary, *East Asian Civilizations: A Dialogue in Five Stages* (Cambridge: Harvard University Press, 1988) is a broad and brief interpretative survey. A different perspective is provided by Gilbert Rozman, *The East Asian Region: Confucian Heritage and Its Modern Adaptation* (Princeton, N.J.: Princeton University Press, 1991).

China

Keith Schoppa, *The Columbia Guide of Modern Chinese History* (New York: Columbia University Press, 2000) is the best place to begin further study of topics in Modern Chinese History. The various volumes of the *Cambridge History of China,* edited or coedited by John K. Fairbank, are a major resource. Joseph S. M. Lao and

Howard Goldblatt, *The Columbia Anthology of Modern Chinese Literature* (New York: Columbia University Press, 1995) includes fiction, poetry and essays. Murray A. Rubinstein, *Taiwan: A New History* (Armonk, N.Y.: M. E. Sharpe, 1999) covers the entire history of the island.

Korea

For a general introduction to Korea see Donald N. Clark, *Culture and Customs of Korea* (Westport, Conn.: Greenwood Press, 2000), and Donald S. Macdonald and Donald N. Clark., *The Koreans: Contemporary Politics and Society*, 3rd ed. (Boulder, Col.: Westview Press, 1996). For detailed treatment of the two separate societies, see Andrea Matles Savada and William R. Shaw, *South Korea: A Country Study*, 4th ed., Department of the Army Pamphlet DA Pam 550-41 (Washington, D.C.: U.S. Government Printing Office, 1992), and Andrea Savada, *North Korea: A Country Study*, 4th ed., Department of the Army Pamphlet DA Pam 550-81 (Washington, D.C.: U.S. Government Printing Office, 1994).

Among histories of Korea, the best overall survey remains Carter J. Eckert, et al., *Korea Old and New: A History* (Seoul: Ilchokak Publishers for the Korea Institute, Harvard University, 1990), supplemented by the documentary collection by Peter H. Lee, Yongho Ch'oe, and Wm. Theodore de Bary entitled *Sources of Korean Tradition*, 2 vols. (New York: Columbia University Press, 1996–2000). For the modern history of Korea, a useful survey is Bruce Cumings, *Korea's Place in the Sun* (New York: W. W. Norton, 1997). For the history of North Korea, nothing surpasses Dae-sook Suh, *Kim Il-sung: The North Korean Leader* (New York: Columbia University Press, 1989), though it is necessary to supplement it with more recent information. Suggestions include Kongdan Oh and Ralph Hassig, eds., *Korea Briefing 2000–2001: First Steps Toward Reconciliation and Reunification* (Armonk, N.Y.: M. E. Sharpe, 2002).

Japan

Gary D. Allinson, *The Columbia Guide to Modern Japanese History* (New York: Columbia University Press, 1999) includes a resource guide. Helen Hardacre, *The Postwar Development of Japanese Studies in the United States* (Leiden: Brill, 1998) provides assessments, complete with bibliography, of the current state of American Japanese studies on history, foreign relations, art, religion, literature, anthropology, political analysis and law that prove excellent points of departure for further study. *The Cambridge History of Japan* is a major resource. Hitomi Tonomura et al., *Women and Class in Japanese History* (Ann Arbor: Center for Japanese Studies, University of Michigan, 1999) includes essays covering all periods of Japanese history.

Vietnam

Vietnam is included in the *Cambridge History of Southeast Asia* (New York: Cambridge University Press, 1992). Reliable reference works include William Duiker, *Historical Dictionary of Vietnam*, 2nd ed. (Lanham, Md.: Scarecrow Press, 1998), and Mark W. McLeod and Nguyen Thi Dieu, *Culture and Customs of Vietnam* (Westport, Conn.: Greenwood Press, 2001). For additional bibliography see David G. Marr, *World Bibliographical Series*, vol. 147, *Vietnam* (Oxford, U.K.: Clio Press, 1993). William J. Duiker, *Ho Chi Minh* (New York: Hyperion, 2000) is now the standard work on the life of the Vietnamese independence leader as well as a useful survey of modern Vietnamese history. The Vietnam War is much documented in the United States, mostly from an American point of view. A standard survey is Stanley Karnow, *Vietnam: A History*, 2nd revised and updated ed. (New York: Penguin Putnam, 1997), whose original edition (1984) served as a companion volume to the thirteen-part Public Broadcasting Service documentary entitled "Vietnam: A Television History."

Index